MW01632238

Life and Mortality in Ugaritic

EXPLORATIONS IN ANCIENT NEAR EASTERN CIVILIZATIONS

Series Editors

1. *Of Courtiers and Kings: The Biblical Daniel Narratives and Ancient Story-Collections*, by Tawny L. Holm
2. *The Sacrificial Economy: Assessors, Contractors, and Thieves in the Management of Sacrificial Sheep at the Eanna Temple of Uruk (ca. 625–520 B.C.)*, by Michael Kozuh
3. *Children in the Ancient Near Eastern Household*, by Kristine Henriksen Garroway
4. *Fishers of Fish and Fishers of Men: Fishing Imagery in the Hebrew Bible and in the Ancient Near East*, by Tyler R. Yoder
5. *Child Sacrifice in Ancient Israel*, by Heath D. Dewrell
6. *The Dragon, the Mountain, and the Nations: An Old Testament Myth, Its Origins, and Its Afterlives*, by Robert D. Miller II
7. *Life and Mortality in Ugaritic: A Lexical and Literary Study*, by Matthew McAffee

Life and Mortality in Ugaritic

A Lexical and Literary Study

MATTHEW McAFFEE

EISENBRAUNS | University Park, Pennsylvania

Library of Congress Cataloging-in-Publication Data

Names: McAffee, Matthew, author.
Title: Life and mortality in Ugaritic : a lexical and literary study / by Matthew McAffee.
Other titles: Explorations in ancient Near Eastern civilizations.
Description: University Park, Pennsylvania : Eisenbrauns, [2019] | Series: Explorations in ancient Near Eastern civilizations | Includes bibliographical references and index.
Summary: "Identifies and analyzes the Ugaritic terms most commonly used to talk about life and mortality in order to construct a more representative framework of the ancient perspective on these topics"—Provided by publisher.
Identifiers: LCCN 2019005497 | ISBN 9781575066639 (cloth : alk. paper)
Subjects: LCSH: Ugaritic language—Lexicology. | Life—Terminology. | Death—Terminology.
Classification: LCC PJ4150 .M33 2019 | DDC 492/.67014—dc23
LC record available at https://lccn.loc.gov/2019005497

Printed in the United States of America
Published by The Pennsylvania State University Press,
University Park, PA 16802-1003

Eisenbrauns is an imprint of The Pennsylvania State University Press.

The Pennsylvania State University Press is a member of the Association of University Presses.

It is the policy of The Pennsylvania State University Press to use acid-free paper. Publications on uncoated stock satisfy the minimum requirements of American National Standard for Information Sciences—Permanence of Paper for Printed Library Material, ANSI Z39.48-1992.

CONTENTS

ACKNOWLEDGMENTS

This book is the result of a long journey that began several years ago during my first graduate courses in Ugaritic under Professor Dennis Pardee at the University of Chicago. That initiation into the world of Ugaritic studies has informed the direction of my research endeavors ever since. This project constitutes a significant revision of my University of Chicago dissertation entitled, "Life and Mortality in Ugaritic: A Literary, Lexical, and Comparative Analysis." I am indebted to Professor Pardee for his steady guidance and seasoned expertise during the course of its completion. His influence upon my own approach to the study of Ugaritic cannot be overstated. I must also thank Professors David Schloen and Theo van den Hout for their advisory role as members of my dissertation committee.

I am also grateful to Jim Eisenbraun for his willingness to consider this project for publication and his recommending it to editors Grant Frame, Brent Strawn, and Nick Veldhuis for consideration in the series Exploration in Ancient Near Eastern Civilizations. I would especially like to thank the blind reviewer for the perceptive comments and recommendations, which I have aimed to incorporate into the final version of the book.

One of the major factors in making this book see the light of day is the support I have received from my home institution, Welch College. The administration has been enthusiastically supportive of my work and has made special allowances for me in bringing this project to completion. A special note of thanks is due to my research assistants, Zachary Vickery and Billy Champion, who have worked tirelessly tracking down sources and editing manuscripts.

Finally, and most importantly, I must express my deepest gratitude to my family: my four children, Abigail, Lydia, Samuel, and Marianne, and my wife,

Anna. I dedicate this book to Anna for her unwavering love and commitment, and for her willingness to listen to tedious arguments about dead languages!

I commit this work to Christ the Lord and pray that it might somehow bring glory and honor to his name.

Matthew McAffee
Welch College, Gallatin, TN
Spring 2018

ABBREVIATIONS

< >	missing text
<< >>	erased text
[ ]	restoration
⸢ ⸣	partial restoration
′	corresponding parallel cola
(!)	problematic reading
{ }	consonantal form
/ /	vocalized form
√	root
*	hypothetical form
1	first person
2	second person
3	third person
AB	Anchor Bible
AbB	*Altbabylonische Briefe in Umschrift und Übersetzung*. Edited by F. R. Kraus. Leiden: Brill, 1964–.
ABD	*Anchor Bible Dictionary*. Edited by David Noel Freedman. 6 vols. New York: Doubleday, 1992.
AcBib	Academia Biblica
AcOr	*Acta Orientalia*
AfO	*Archiv für Orientforschungen*
AfOB	Archiv für Orientforschungen: Beiheft
AHw	*Akkadisches Handwörterbuch*. Wolfram von Soden. 3 vols. Wiesbaden, 1965–1981.
AJBA	*Australian Journal of Biblical Archaeology*

ALASP	Abhandlungen zur Literatur Alt-Syren-Palästinas und Mesopotamiens
AMD	Ancient Magic and Divination
ANEM	Ancient Near East Monographs
ANET	*Ancient Near Eastern Texts Relating to the Old Testament.* Edited by James B. Pritchard. 3d ed. Princeton: Princeton University Press, 1969.
AnOr	Analecta orientalia
AOAT	Alter Orient und Altes Testament
AS	Assyriological Studies
AuOr	*Aula orientalis*
AuOrSup	Aula Orientalis Supplement
AUSS	*Andrews University Seminary Studies*
BA	*Biblical Archaeologist*
BAH	Bibliothèque archéologique et historique
BAR	*Biblical Archaeology Review*
BASOR	*Bulletin of the American Schools of Oriental Research*
BASORSup	Bulletin of the American Schools of Oriental Research Supplements
BDB	Brown, Francis, S. R. Driver, and Charles A. Briggs. *A Hebrew and English Lexicon of the Old Testament*
Bib	*Biblica*
BibOr	Biblica et orientalia
BibSem	The Biblical Seminar
BKAT	Biblischer Kommentar, Altes Testament
BM	British Museum
BMECCJ	Bulletin of the Middle Eastern Culture Center in Japan
BO	*Bibliotheca orientalis*
BR	*Biblical Research*
BSac	*Bibliotheca Sacra*
BSOAS	*Bulletin of the School of Oriental and African Studies*
BZAW	Beihefte zur Zeitschrift für die alttestamentliche Wissenchaft
c	common
C	causative stem
CAD	*The Assyrian Dictionary of the Oriental Institute of the University of Chicago*. Chicago: The Oriental Institute of the University of Chicago, 1956–2010.
CAL	The Comprehensive Aramaic Lexicon. Online: http://cal1.cn.huc.edu/.

CAT	*The Cuneiform Alphabetic Texts from Ugarit, Ras Ibn Hani, and Other Places*. Manfried Dietrich, Oswald Loretz, and Joaquín Sanmartín. ALASP 8. Münster: Ugarit-Verlag, 1995.
CBET	Contributions to Biblical Exegesis and Theology
CBQ	*Catholic Biblical Quarterly*
CC	Continental Commentaries
CIS	*Corpus Inscriptionum Semiticarum*. Paris, 1881–.
const.	construct
COS	*The Context of Scripture*. Edited by William W. Hallo and K. Lawson Younger Jr. 3 vols. Leiden: Brill, 1977–2002.
CRAI	*Comptes rendus des séances de l'Académie des Inscriptions et Belles-Lettres*
CT	*Cuneiform Texts from the Babylonian Tablets in the British Museum*
CTA	*Corpus des tablettes en cunéiformes alphabétiques découvertes à Ras Shamra-Ugarit de 1929 à 1939*. Edited by Andrée Herdner. MRS 10. Paris: Geuthner, 1963.
CTH	*Catologue des Textes Hittites*. Emmanuel Laroche. Paris: Klincksieck, 1971.
DBSup	*Supplément au Dictionnaire de la Bible*. Edited by Louis Pirot and André Rovert. Paris: Letouzey & Ané, 1928–.
D	doubled stem
DDD	*Dictionary of Deities and Demons in the Bible*. Edited by Karl van der Toorn, Bob Becking, and Pieter W. van der Horst. Leiden: Brill, 1999.
DJD	Discoveries in the Judaean Desert
DJPA	*Dictionary of Jewish Palestinian Aramaic of the Byzantine Period*. Michael Sokoloff. Ramat-Gan: Bar-Ilan University Press, 1990.
DN	divine name
DNWSI	*Dictionary of North-West Semitic Inscriptions*. Jacob Hoftijzer and Karel Jongeling. 2 vols. Leiden: Brill, 1995.
du.	dual
DUL	*A Dictionary of the Ugaritic Language in the Alphabetic Tradition*. Gregorio del Olmo Lete and Joaquín Sanmartín. Translated and edited by Wilfred G. E. Watson. HdO 67. Leiden: Brill, 2003.
f	feminine
FAT	Forschungen zum Alten Testament
fem.	feminine

G	ground stem
GKC	*Gesenius' Hebrew Grammar*. Edited by Emil Kautzsch. Translated by Arther E. Cowley. 2nd ed. Oxford: Clarendon, 1910.
GUOST	*Glasgow University Oriental Society: Transactions*
HALOT	*The Hebrew and Aramaic Lexicon of the Old Testament*. Ludwig Koehler, Walter Baumgartner, and Johann J. Stamm. Translated and edited under the supervision of Mervyn E. J. Richardson. 4 vols. Leiden: Brill, 1994–1999.
HdO	Handbuch der Orientalistik
HSM	Harvard Semitic Monographs
HSS	Harvard Semitic Series
HTR	*Harvard Theological Review*
HUCA	*Hebrew Union College Annual*
ICC	International Critical Commentary
IEJ	*Israel Exploration Journal*
Int	*Interpretation*
JANER	*Journal of Ancient Near Eastern Religions*
JANESCU	*Journal of the Ancient Near Eastern Society of Columbia University*
JAOS	*Journal of the American Oriental Society*
Jastrow	Jastrow, Marcus. *A Dictionary of the Targumim, the Talmud Babli and Yerushalmi, and the Midrashic Literature*. 2nd ed. New York: Putnam, 1903.
JBL	*Journal of Biblical Literature*
JCS	*Journal of Cuneiform Studies*
JNES	*Journal of Near Eastern Studies*
JNSL	*Journal of Northwest Semitic Languages*
Joüon	Joüon, Paul. *A Grammar of Biblical Hebrew*. Translated and revised by T. Muraoka. SubBi 27. Rome: Pontifical Biblical Institute, 2006.
JPOS	*Journal of the Palestine Oriental Society*
JQR	*Jewish Quarterly Review*
JRAS	*Journal of the Royal Asiatic Society of Great Britain and Ireland*
JSOT	*Journal for the Study of the Old Testament*
JSOTSup	Journal for the Study of the Old Testament Supplement Series
JSS	*Journal of Semitic Studies*
KAI	*Kanaanäische und aramäische Inschriften*. Herbert Donner and Wolfgang Röllig. 2nd ed. Wiesbaben, 1966–1969.

KBo	*Keilschrifttexte aus Boghazköi*. Leipzig, 1916–1923; Berlin: Gebr. Mann, 1954–.
KTU	*Die keilalphabetischen Texte aus Ugarit*. Manfried Dietrich, Oswald Loretz, and Joaquín Sanmartín. AOAT 24. Neukirchen-Vluyn: Neukirchener Verlag, 1976.
KUB	*Keilschrifturkunden aus Boghazköi*. Berlin: Akademie, 1921–.
Lane	Lane, Edward W. *An Arabic-English Lexicon*. 8 vols. London: Williams & Norgate, 1863. Repr., Beruit: Librairie du Liban, 1968.
LAPO	Litteratures anciennes du Proche-Orient
LBA	Late Bronze Age
Leš	*Lešonenu*
LHBOTS	Library of Hebrew Bible/Old Testament Studies
LSAWS	Linguistic Studies in Ancient West Semitic
m	masculine
MRS	Mission de Ras Shamra
MThSt	Marburger theologische Studien
NEA	*Near Eastern Archaeology*
NMES	Near and Middle Eastern Series
OIMP	Oriental Institute Museum Publications
OLA	Orientalia Lovaniensia Analecta
OLZ	*Orientalistische Literaturzeitung*
Or	*Orientalia* (NS)
OrAnt	*Oriens Antiquus*
OTS	Old Testament Studies
p	plural
Payne Smith	*Thesaurus syriacus*. Edited by R. Payne Smith et al. Oxford: Clarendon, 1879–1901.
PC	prefixed conjugation
PEQ	*Palestine Exploration Quarterly*
pers. comm.	personal communication
PIBA	*Proceedings of the Irish Biblical Association*
PN	proper name
POS	Pretoria Oriental Series 6
PRU	*Le Palais Royal d'Ugarit*
QuSem	Quaderni di semitistica
RB	*Revue biblique*
RBS	Resources for Bible Study

REJ	*Revue des études juives*
RGRW	Religions in the Graeco-Roman World
RHPR	*Revue d'histoire et de philosophie religieuses*
RHR	*Revue d'histoire des religions*
RlA	*Reallexikon der Assyriologie*. Edited by Erich Ebeling et al. Berlin: de Gruyter, 1928–.
RSEHA	*Revue sémitique d'épigraphie d'historie ancienne*
RSO	Ras Shamra Ougarit
s	singular
SAHL	Studies in the Archaeology and History of the Levant
SAOC	Studies in Ancient Oriental Civilizations
SBL	Society of Biblical Literature
SBLDS	Society of Biblical Literature Dissertation Series
SC	suffixed conjugation
SCS	Septuagint and Cognate Studies
SEL	*Studi epigrafici e linguistici sul Vicino Oriente antico*
Sem	*Semitica*
SemCl	*Semitica et Classica*
sg.	singular
SHANE	Studies in the History of the Ancient Near East
SHR	Studies in the History of Religions
Siphrut	Siphrut: Literature and Theology of the Hebrew Scriptures.
SJOT	*Scandinavian Journal of the Old Testament.*
SL	*A Syriac Lexicon: A Translation from the Latin, Correction, Expansion and Update of C. Brockelmann's* Lexicon Syriacum. Michael Sokoloff.Winona Lake, IN: Eisenbrauns; Piscataway, NJ: Gorgias, 2009.
SMEA	*Studi Micenei ed Egeo-Anatolici*
SMSR	*Studi e materiali di storia delle religioni*
StMed	Studia Mediterranea
StOr	Studia Orientalia
StSem	Studi Semitici
SubBi	Subsidia Biblica
suff.	suffix
TDOT	*Theological Dictionary of the Old Testament*. Edited by G. Johannes Botterweck and Helmer Ringgren. Translated by John T. Willis et al. 15 vols. Grand Rapids: Eerdmans, 1974–2006.
TJ	*Trinity Journal*

TUAT	*Texte aus der Umwelt des Alten Testaments*. Edited by Otto Kaiser. Gütersloh: Mohn, 1984–.
UBL	Ugaritisch-biblische Literatur
UF	*Ugarit-Forschungen*
Ugaritica	*Ugartica*. Edited by Claude F.-A. Schaeffer, et al. Paris: Geuthner, 1939–1978.
UNHAII	Uitgaven Nederlands Historisch-Archaeologisch Instituut et Istanbul
VT	*Vetus Testamentum*
VTSup	Supplements to Vetus Testamentum
WAW	Writings from the Ancient World
WVDOG	Wissenschaftliche Veröffentlichungen der deutschen Orient-Gesellschaft
ZA	*Zeitschrift für Assyriologie*
ZAW	*Zeitschrift für die alttestamentliche Wissenschaft*
ZDMG	*Zeitschrift der deutschen morgenländischen Gesellschaft*

Introduction

The discovery of the Ugaritic corpus from the late thirteenth–early twelfth centuries BC has offered scholars a treasure trove of textual and archaeological data elucidating a Semitic culture of the northwestern corner of the Levant at the time. The variegated nature of these texts provides a wide array of genres, ranging from the ritual to the mythological, from epistolary to economic, and more. Scholars in the field of Ugaritic studies have probed these texts with the goal of illuminating the religion and culture of the inhabitants of this fascinating Late Bronze Age country.

Lexicography is an important tool in our attempt to understand the values and ideas of different cultures from different times. The problem in dealing with dead languages such as Ugaritic is that it is often difficult to avoid investing a given word with the assumed semantic values of our own translation equivalents. Perhaps I could illustrate this problem with our basic assumptions about Ugaritic *ḥyh* "to live," and *mt* "to die." For the modern interpreter, "to die" seems simple enough to define, being the opposite of living and the termination of one's state of existence. However, when faced with the mythological world of the Ugaritic pantheon, it would appear that these terms have quite different semantic values. For the gods, at least, dying seems not to be a definitive termination, but instead reflects a limited span of incapacitation. On the other hand, the goddess ʿAnatu offers ʾAqhatu the prospect of ongoing "life" (*ḥym // blmt*), a type of existence compared to the life that the god Baʿlu enjoys.[1] One might

1. Of course, some scholars have raised doubts about the viability of this proposition, but most accept that the proposition is a genuine offer. It remains unknown what would have happened if

counter that when it comes to the mythological world, anything goes, but at the same time it is important to keep in mind that these texts have been written by mortal humans in the language most familiar to them, and therefore must be reflective of their own ways of thinking about life and death, at least in some measure. Understood in this way, mythology not only expresses ideas related to an otherworldly realm but also projects the shared beliefs and values of its own cultural setting.

Jan Assmann distinguishes between three horizons of afterlife conceptions in the ancient world: (1) death as an otherworld reality where the dead go to prolong their life, (2) death as a reality in this life in that the dead live on through progeny, and (3) death as the Elysian conception in which a person is saved from death. Assmann categorizes Christianity and Greek Gnosticism according to the first type, Mesopotamia and Israel according to the second, and Egypt as embodying all three.[2] Assmann does not consider Ugarit in this schema, but I assume the Ugaritic materials would fall in line with Mesopotamia and Israel according to his taxonomy. While such broad categorizations are useful organizationally, we cannot press them as hard and fast boundaries. Indeed, Israel shared many beliefs about the afterlife that were common among Mesopotamian cultures as well, but not always. Ugarit is a much closer geographical and cultural parallel to Israel and exhibits certain features that are distinct from the East Semitic views of death and the netherworld. Christopher B. Hays, for instance, notes the following three distinctions: (1) Ugaritians developed unique terminology to describe death and afterlife, (2) the Mesopotamian fear of the dead largely contrasts the Ugaritic portrayal of the divinized dead and their divine power, and (3) Ugaritic tombs are uniquely located within the household complex.[3] Furthermore, as I will argue more fully in chapter 5, Ugaritic royal ideology reflects aspects of the afterlife that blur the lines between Assmann's second and third categories, envisioning death as both otherworldly and future progeny. In short, at Ugarit life and death, as evidenced by the terms used to describe them, are inexorably linked together.

Recent psychological studies have reflected on the perceived relationship between life and death exhibited in modern cultures, thus demonstrating a universal tendency in human thought about personal mortality. Robert Jay Lifton

---

he had accepted this offer. Nonetheless, the point of the story is not that he accepted and died anyhow, but that he refused the offer, declaring it to be fraudulent.

2. Jan Assmann, *Death and Salvation in Ancient Egypt* (Ithaca, NY: Cornell University Press, 2005), 10–11.

3. Christopher B. Hays, *Death in the Iron Age II and in First Isaiah*, FAT 79 (Tübingen: Mohr Siebeck, 2011), 132.

believes that "man does not create culture out of his need to deny death . . . but rather as his way of living out his unique awareness that he both dies and continues."[4] Similarly, Havi Carel argues that "death is not merely an external endpoint about which we can say nothing, but a structuring force that shapes life ontologically and influences our understanding of it every living moment."[5] She continues, "Every form of life is finite, and every human life is accompanied by an awareness of this fact. Every human project, expectation and action takes place within this framework."[6] Carel attempts to combine the philosophy of Heidegger with the psychoanalysis of Freud in her treatment of life and death, describing both thinkers as viewing death "as a metaphysical force rather than a material event," explaining that "death must be understood as a defining limitation generating metaphysical constraints on life."[7]

Human language provides a major link between the ancient and modern worlds as individuals of all times grapple with the reality of personal mortality. From the ancient perspective, text is at the forefront of the exchange. There are many interpretive challenges to overcoming the barrier that impedes one's ability to understand the world beyond these texts, to be sure. Nonetheless, I am optimistic in being able to come to a moderate level of cognizance regarding the worldview these ancient texts represent. The barriers erected by cultural distance are one reason why lexicography is of crucial importance, and it is also why such care has to be applied to the process of ascertaining word meanings from their own literary environs.

Lexicography and Method

My approach to lexicography follows the comparative philological tradition, described by some scholars as applied linguistics more so than theoretical linguistics. Michael O'Connor explains, "Linguistics has its theoretical and applied sides. At least notionally, theoretical linguistics presents a substructure of assumptions and arguments to undergird its every move, while applied linguistics is more oriented to language-based tasks."[8] In this vein of thought,

4. Robert Jay Liften, *The Broken Connection: On Death and the Continuity of Life* (New York: Simon & Schuster, 1979), 6.

5. Havi Carel, *Life and Death in Freud and Heidegger* (Amsterdam: Rodopi, 2006), xiii.

6. Carel, *Life and Death*, xiii–xiv.

7. Carel, *Life and Death*, 116.

8. Michael O'Connor, "Semitic Lexicography: European Dictionaries of Biblical Hebrew in the Twentieth Century," in *Israel Oriental Studies XX: Semitic Linguistics; The State of the Art at the Turn of the Twenty-First Century*, ed. Shlomo Izre'el (Winona Lake, IN: Eisenbrauns, 2002), 174.

Mark S. Smith stresses the "indigenous information about words" in an effort to engage the ancients' use of the language and "their specific linguistic and cultural contexts." He continues, "Lexicography includes the ancients' operating assumptions. How did they think about words?" Smith cites the ancient Levantine tradition of lexical lists as an "indigenous" example of the practice. These lists might identify a given word in Sumerian, for instance, and cite parallel words from other languages such as Akkadian, Hurrian, and Ugaritic.[9]

Unfortunately, not every ancient word appears in a lexical list. The situation at hand thus necessitates multiple levels of analyzing the texts in which words occur before modern interpreters can interpret their meaning properly. Smith identifies the following three contextual levels in determining word meanings: (1) the form and sound of the word itself, (2) the syntactical phrasing of the word, whether in prose or poetic verse, and (3) the word's place in a series of clauses or a colon of poetry.[10] These levels are useful guides in applying philological analysis to the task of discerning lexical meaning for ancient texts. In my estimation, levels (2) and (3) are the primary "indigenous" means of controlling the lexicographical task. Especially useful for this task are poetic word pairs, which provide unique insight for interpreters standing outside a given linguistic/cultural context, enabling them to perceive how the ancient poet regarded a given word as an appropriate parallel for another. In such cases, the poets were not simply producing bland synonyms of equal semantic value; rather, they were skillfully producing word associations whereby one term allows us to ascertain the "semantic nuance" of another.[11] In chapter 2, I devote more attention to the nature of poetic pairs and their importance for this lexical study of life and death in Ugaritic.

Smith also stresses the importance of the external context in determining the meaning of words—the world outside the text involving the "cultural associations and sensibility that a given word brings to the text for its author and audience."[12] Etymology inevitably arises in this discussion, specifically its contribution (if any) to the task of lexicography. It is necessary for interpreters to maintain an appropriate distinction between semantics and etymology, since etymological equivalents are routinely not the same semantically, as Moshe Held correctly maintained.[13] Held illustrated this point with the Semitic root *mḫṣ*, "to strike,"

9. Mark S. Smith, "Words and Their Worlds," in *Biblical Lexicography: Hebrew and Greek: Semantics—Exegesis—Translation*, ed. Eberhard Bons, Jan Joosten, and Regine Hunziker-Rodewald, BZAW 443 (Berlin: de Gruyter, 2015), 4–5.

10. Smith, "Words and Their Worlds," 7.

11. Smith, "Words and Their Worlds," 6.

12. Smith, "Words and Their Worlds," 8–9.

13. Moshe Held, "*mḫṣ* / **mḫš* in Ugaritic and Other Semitic Languages," *JAOS* 79 (1959): 169; Chaim Cohen, "The 'Held Method' for Comparative Semitic Philology," *JANESCU* 19 (1989):

whose semantic meaning is the same in all the Semitic languages attesting it, except Arabic. In Arabic the etymological equivalent to *mḫṣ* is *maḫaḍa* meaning "to churn (milk by shaking)."[14] A few decades ago James Barr rightly criticized the most egregious offenders of the etymologizing method that had become fashionable in biblical lexicography, cautioning, "there is no such question about the meaning of words, as distinct from texts. Words can only be intelligibly interpreted by what they meant at the time of their use, with the language system used by the speaker or writer."[15] In other words, the only legitimate way to understand the meaning of words is to identity individual uses synchronically, before giving attention to their diachronic developments in a given language or their relation to cognates in other languages (in this case, the Semitic languages). The way we come to understand the meaning of a given word is to analyze it in a particular literary context, which serves the main purpose of this book.

Such a corrective, however, should not swing the pendulum too far in the opposite direction by abandoning the comparative element of lexicography altogether, since it does have an important role, even if secondary. As John F. Healey urges, "comparative lexicographers should exercise due caution and good method rather than cease to function completely!"[16] Healey's method of control when considering comparative lexical data is to prefer proximity over the remote. Etymological connections with corresponding terms in closely related languages are more significant than distant connections. The success of this formulation depends upon an evaluative measure of proximity, for which Healey devises four areas of measurement: linguistic, chronological, geographical, and historical.[17] The problem for Ugaritic is that in certain instances a given root may only otherwise occur in a remote linguistic setting (e.g., a cognate from Modern South Arabian or Arabic), which at the least requires caution in determining its meaning in Ugaritic.[18] Lexicographers stand on firmer ground when a Ugaritic

---

10–11. This principle was the first of five Held devised regarding Semitic (particularly, Ugaritic) lexicography: (1) "special stress on disclosing the meaning of words by means of the inductive method rather than the use of the etymological one," (2) "clear-cut distinction between archaic language of the epics and the language of ritual and economic texts," (3) "emphasis on poetic usage and parallelism," (4) "strict attention to the principle of interdialectical distribution," and (5) "classification of each word under its appropriate category as a means of establishing the lexical relationship between Ugaritic and the other Semitic languages."

14. Held, "*mḫṣ* / **mḫš* in Ugaritic," 171; Cohen, "The 'Held Method,'" 11.

15. James Barr, *The Semantics of Biblical Language* (Oxford: Oxford University Press, 1961), 139–40.

16. John F. Healey, "Ugaritic Lexicography and Other Semitic Languages," *UF* 20 (1988): 61.

17. Healey, "Ugaritic Lexicography," 61–62.

18. For Modern South Arabian Healey ("Ugaritic Lexicography," 63) is referencing Gary A. Rendsburg, "Modern South Arabian as a Source for Ugaritic Etymologies," *JAOS* 107 (1987):

hapax legomenon occurs in one of the Canaanite dialects, which, as Josef Tropper argues, lie in closest proximity to the Ugaritic language.[19] Nonetheless, even here one must maintain that the results of such etymological analysis remain somewhat tentative until further uses of the term emerge in newly discovered texts.

Johannes C. de Moor offers a useful guide for Ugaritic lexicographers as they make their way through the limited textual materials before them. He outlines his general method as follows: (1) establish the correct reading of the text, (2) give primary attention to the literary context of words, (3) analyze syllabic spellings of words when possible, (4) utilize comparative philology when necessary, and (5) identify the semantic range of a given word.[20] I will offer brief remarks on the merits of this methodological framework for Ugaritic lexicography.

Smith's three-level method of lexicographical analysis maintains much-needed control in formulating word meaning, but additional factors warrant consideration for Ugaritic. The poor physical condition of many Ugaritic tablets often make it difficult to determine readings at crucial junctures in the text. This factor is certainly not unique to Ugaritic, but it factors prominently when a word occurs in the context of a disputed reading. Textual variants in Biblical Hebrew manuscripts and scholarly reconstructions pose similar problems for Hebrew lexicography, as Barr aptly noted in his 1973 essay, cautioning that the possibility of "reconstructed texts have to be kept in view at every point by the lexicographer."[21]

In that same publication, de Moor identified challenges unique to Ugaritic lexicography. As a matter of first importance, he emphasized the need for establishing textual readings by carefully examining hand copies and the best editions available, citing Herdner as the authoritative edition of the time. He warned, "One can never rely on transliteration alone; hand copies and possible duplicates should always be consulted."[22] Since de Moor's remarks in 1973 Ugaritologists

623–28, with whom I interact later in this book. For Arabic, see, e.g., Josef Tropper and Hani Hayajneh, "El, der scharfsinnige und verständige Gott: Ugaritisch *lṭpn il d pid* im Lichte der arabischen Lexeme *laṭīf* und *fuʾād*," *Or* 72 (2003): 159–82, also noted later in this book.

19. Josef Tropper, "Is the Ugaritic Language a Canaanite Dialect?" in *Ugarit and the Bible: Proceedings of the International Symposium on Ugarit and the Bible, Manchester, September 1992*, ed. George J. Brook, Adrian H. W. Curtis, and John F. Healey, UBL 11 (Münster: Ugarit-Verlag, 1994), 351. Tropper further specifies that the lexical evidence suggests that Phoenician is a closer proximate to Ugaritic than Hebrew. See also Healey's description of Hebrew, Phoenician, Arabic, Akkadian, South Arabian, Ethiopic, and Aramaic regarding their lexical relationship to Ugaritic ("Ugaritic Lexicography," 63–68).

20. Johannes C. de Moor, "Ugaritic Lexicography," in *Studies on Semitic Lexicography*, ed. Pelio Franzaroli, QuadSem 2 (Firenze: Istituto di linguistica e di lingue orientali, Università di Firenze, 1973), 79–101 (also referenced in Wilfred G. E. Watson, "Ugaritic Lexical Studies in Perspective," *SEL* 12 [1995]: 219, but without mentioning de Moor's fifth methodological principle).

21. James Barr, "Hebrew Lexicography," in Franzaroli, *Studies on Semitic Lexicography*, 104–5.

22. Johannes de Moor, "Ugaritic Lexicography," 79–81.

have achieved considerable advances in the epigraphic study of Ugaritic tablets. Exemplary in this regard is the French series Ras Shamra Ougarit and its publication of many previously unpublished texts, replete with hand copies, transcriptions, epigraphic notes, and philological commentary.[23] Additionally, scores of epigraphic studies on individual texts or portions of texts published in research journals and monograph series provide further guidance in the maze of disputed readings, not to mention the high-resolution photographs published in Inscriptifact under the auspices of the University of Southern California West Semitic Research project. I have attempted to engage with such materials in my own lexical analysis of life and mortality where pertinent, especially when the context of a given passage is partially broken and for which scholars have proposed different readings.

In addition to textual analysis, de Moor's point (3)—analyze syllabic spellings of words when possible—is especially pertinent for Ugaritic lexicography, since the existence of a syllabic spelling yields important morphological data about a given word that informs our understanding of its meaning.[24] I have given due attention to syllabic spellings when available, especially in my treatment of the roots *ḥwy* and *hyy* in chapter 1 and my analysis of proper names throughout the book.

In light of these methodological considerations, I have organized this book as primarily a lexical study. Doing so provides a certain level of control in formulating the views and ideas held by the ancients about death and life. The investigation of this subject must therefore begin with an identification of the most commonly used terms, from which one can then formulate a more theoretical understanding of the ancient perspective. This classical approach to the study of word meaning, as described and defended above, does not intend to discredit or even disparage other methods of investigation, such as those with a more topical/thematic or even theoretical bent, but rather means to stress the need for greater control in formulating the contours of ancient thought. The first layer of understanding must come from particular words and their contextual meaning. Or, to put it differently, the first step is to identify the lexical building blocks which represent the ancient perspective on a given topic—here, the concepts (or semantic ranges) of life and death—from which we can construct a somewhat representative framework.

23. Most recently, see Pierre Bordreuil and Dennis Pardee, with Robert Hawley, *Une bibliothèque au sud de la ville ***: Textes 1994–2002 en cunéiforme alphabétique de la maison d'Ourtenou*, RSO 18 (Paris: Maison de l'Orient et de la Méditerranée, 2012).

24. De Moor, "Ugaritic Lexicography," 84.

The following study is therefore organized according to two main objectives: lexical and literary. For the reasons I have just outlined, my focus is mainly lexical in nature and thus occupies the first four chapters of the book. In the remainder of this introduction I will orient the reader to the study by sketching a lexical overview of the semantics of life and mortality reflected in Ugaritic. The majority of scholarly work in this area has tended to prefer a more conceptual or theoretical treatment, identifying topics such as death, death/mortuary/funerary cult, afterlife, and so on. To be clear, these studies are not guilty of surface-level analysis, having enriched our understanding of ancient Ugaritic thought in many important ways. My modest intention here is to complement the already existent body of literature on this topic, and perhaps even to advance the discussion considerably by providing a more focused lexical analysis of the Ugaritic terms involved.

I should also observe that scholars have mostly been interested in matters relating to death, death cult, or one's netherworld existence, with lesser attention to the concept of life, at least explicitly. It is clear that these two realities—life and death—are interwoven, if not inseparable, in human experience; therefore, it should come as no surprise to see that same integration in these ancient texts having been produced out of and in response to that experience. I encounter this reality foremost in my examination of the root for life, *ḥyy* "to live," and the term *npš* "neck, vitality," both of which are best understood from the backdrop of one's mortality. We cannot adequately grasp the significance of *mt* "to die" without first having wrestled with the concept of life. I have therefore given ample attention to both of these semantic notions by identifying and analyzing their respective terms.

A Lexical Analysis of Life and Mortality in Ugaritic

I turn now to survey the semantic inventory of these two concepts as reflected in the Ugaritic corpus of texts. The two main Ugaritic roots that concern matters of life and mortality are *ḥyy/ḥwy* and *mwt*, that is, the roots expressing life and death. In addition to these terms, there are several poetic words and phrases which allow for an expanded assessment of the semantics of life and death. Closely related to these roots and important for this investigation are the body-part terms *npš* "throat, life, soul," *kbd* "liver," and *lb* "heart," as well as the terms with which they appear in parallel in poetic diction. Also important for life and mortality at Ugarit are the inhabitants of the underworld. Môtu, the personified god of death, is of great importance for this analysis because of his place in the

Ugaritic pantheon and because of the unseemly divine figures associated with him. Another important apsect of death at Ugaritic occurs in the *rpủm*, in whose ranks kings, heroes, and perhaps others are gathered at death. Broadly speaking, these terms provide the parameters of the discussion, and I will at this point briefly survey the lexical characteristics that derve attention.

ḥyy/ḥwy

David Marcus conducted a morphological study on the roots *ḥyy* and *ḥwy* to map out their distribution throughout the Ugaritic textual corpus and to show that each one marks a distinct function. Marcus argues that the distribution of these roots demonstrate that *ḥyy* is used exclusively for the G stem, while *ḥwy* is reserved for the derived stems, namely, the D and the Št.[25] Gregorio del Olmo Lete and Joaquín Sanmartín follow this viewpoint in their arrangement of these roots, listing all G stem forms with medial {y} and all D and Št stem forms with medial {w}.[26] In terms of literary genre, the verbal forms of these roots are most widely attested in the mythological texts with fewer instances elsewhere.

The basic sense of the G stem (*ḥyy*) is "to live, be alive." In the Kirta Epic, for instance, the 3ms PC occurs with the negative particle in parallel with *tmnt*: *krt špḥ lṭpn wqdš ủ ỉlm tmnt špḥ lṭpn l yḥ* "Kirta is the offspring of the knowing and holy one. Do gods die? Would the offspring of the knowing one not live?" (KTU 1.16 I:21–23). Here, the negated G stem PC form is used to express the opposite of living: not continuing to live, or ceasing to be alive.

The D stem (*ḥwy*), on the other hand, provides the factitive of the G stem, namely, "to make/keep alive." The various nuances of the D stem are more difficult to ascertain contextually.[27] In some passages it seems to denote a continuation of the state of being alive, as in the oft-cited ʾAqhatu Epic where ʿAnatu offers the hero immortality in exchange for his bow: *ảp ảnk ảḥwy ảqht* [*ǵ*]*zr* "Moreover, I will keep the hero ʾAqhatu alive" (KTU 1.17 VI:32). The action expressed by this D stem PC form refers to the *ḥym* "life"//*blmt* "not dying" offered above in line 27 of this text. Yet the D stem can also denote the sense of restoration or renewal as it does in one of the letters where the writer describes making repairs to a house: *w ảnk ḥrš lqḥt w ḥwt hbt* "And as for me, I have hired an artisan and have restored the house" (KTU 2.70:15).

25. David Marcus, "The Verb 'to Live' in Ugaritic," *JSS* 17 (1972): 76–82.

26. *DUL*, 379.

27. Note that *DUL* (379) lists the meaning of the D stem as follows: "to give (back) life/revive, leave alive, resuscitate."

As we turn our attention to the noun forms associated with this root, a number of points need to be made. First, it appears that the distinction between the roots *ḥyy* "to live" and *ḥwy* "to make live" holds true for the derivational nouns. The form *ḥy* (medial {y}) functions as the noun meaning "life" (forms: *ḥy, ḥym, ḥ* in the absolute case) as in the following example from the ʾAqhatu myth: *ỉrš ḥym wảtnk blmt wảšlḥk* "Ask for life and I will give (it) to you, immortality and I will grant (it) to you" (KTU 1.17 VI:27–28).[28] Similarly, the adjective *ḥy* indicates the state of being alive: *wtnḫ bỉrty npš k ḥy bʿl ảlỉyn k ỉṯ zbl bʿl ảrṣ* "My *npš* can rest in my chest because the valiant Baʿlu is alive; the Prince, lord of the earth, exists" (KTU 1.6 III:19–21).[29]

On the other hand, one might argue that those derivational nouns with medial {w} are more reflective of the D stem *ḥwy* "to make live." For example, some scholars suggest that the form *ḥwy* refers to a storehouse[30] where equipment for chariots is stored: *wṯlṯ ṣmdm wḥrṣ ảpnt bd rb ḥršm d šṣả ḥwyh* "And three pairs (as one lot) of wheels in the hands of the chief of the craftsmen who delivered (it) to the storehouse" (KTU 4.145:8–10).[31] It is possible that the etymology of this term stems from the fact that the storehouse preserves the life of the chariot equipment by sheltering it from the elements. Unfortunately, so far this is the only occurrence of *ḥwy* with this particular nuance.[32]

With these considerations in mind, I provide a comprehensive analysis of these two roots (*ḥyy* and *ḥwy*) in chapter 1 in an attempt to sort out their semantics. I consider the viability of Marcus's theory regarding the G stem/D stem divide, ultimately finding it viable. Particularly pertinent to the D stem *ḥwy* is Baʿlu's so-called revivification depicted in the ʾAqhatu Epic (KTU 1.17 VI:26–30). I survey the literature regarding the nature of revivification in Ugaritic and offer my own assessment of its meaning in light of my broader semantic analysis of the roots *ḥyy* and *ḥwy*.

npš

From within the broader Northwest Semitic context, scholars have appealed to the Ugaritic evidence to explain that the concrete sense of *npš* must have

28. See RS 94.2284:12: *ḥ npšk wḥ n*[. . .] "By the life of your *npš* and the life of [my] *n*[*pš*]." For a discussion of this text, see the *editio princeps* in Bordreuil, Pardee, and Hawley, *Une bibliothèque au sud de la ville ****, 180–86. See also Pierre Bordreuil and Dennis Pardee, *A Manual of Ugaritic*, LSAWS 3 (Winona Lake, IN: Eisenbrauns, 2009), 250–52.

29. Note that *ḥy* is parallel with *ỉṯ*, the particle of existence.

30. *DUL*, 380.

31. *ḥwy* + adverbial {h}.

32. Cf. *ḥwy* in KTU 1.17 VI:30 and 1.176:17 (broken context).

been "neck" or "throat."[33] Del Olmo Lete and Sanmartín adduce five additional derivational meanings for this body part word in Ugaritic: (2) appetite, desire; (3) breath, force, soul; (4) soul, spirit, life; (5) people (collective and individual); and (6) (piece of) offal.[34] As for del Olmo Lete and Sanmartín's sixth meaning, "(piece of) offal," it would occur exclusively in the ritual texts. Accordingly, the sense of *npš* in these instances would refer to the internal organs of an animal essential for life. They cite the following text as evidence for this meaning: *npš l ỉlỉb* "a (piece) of offal to DN" (KTU 1.119:14).[35] Yet, this suggestion is not the only (or perhaps even the best) interpretation for the meaning of *npš* here. Pardee, for example, renders all similar occurrences in the ritual texts as "neck," which is especially convincing in those cases where it appears with *ảp*, "nose," as in *ả⌜p⌝ w ⌜np⌝ š l ʿnth*, "a snout and a neck for ʿAnatu" (KTU 1.43:12–13 = RS 1.005:12–13).[36] In all such contexts, the term in concert with *ảp* designates the portion of the animal offered to the said deity.[37] In this book I provide a comprehensive analysis of *npš* throughout the ritual texts, arguing that "(a part of the) neck" is indeed its concrete meaning.

The concrete sense of "(a part of the) neck" for Ugaritic *npš* finds support outside the ritual corpus as well, as in the following well-known mythological text: *l yrt b npš bn ỉlm mt b mhmrt ydd ỉl ǵzr tbʿ*, "Indeed, go down into the throat of the god Môtu; depart into the pit of the beloved divine hero" (KTU 1.5 I:6–7/RS 2.[002] + 3.[565] I:6–7).[38] Here, *npš* is parallel with *mhmrt*, possibly meaning "pit," from the verbal root *hmr* "to pour out" as attested in Arabic.[39] Biblical Hebrew attests the noun *mahmôrâ* in Ps 140:11, which from context also appears

33. See, e.g., *DNWSI*, 746–48, where Jacob Hoftijzer and Karel Jongeling suggest that in Northwest Semitic the concrete sense of "throat, breath" would have naturally developed into the more abstract meaning "life."

34. See *DUL*, 636–37.

35. One should note here that, according to the photographs of this text, only the first letter of the divine name is legible (see photographs in Bordreuil and Pardee, *Manual of Ugaritic*, plate 14).

36. Dennis Pardee, *Ritual and Cult at Ugarit*, ed. Theodore J. Lewis, WAW 10 (Atlanta: Society of Biblical Literature, 2002), 71. See also Pardee, *Les textes rituels*, RSO 12 (Paris: Éditions Recherche sur les Civilisations, 2000), 243–47 for his interaction with the secondary literature on the interpretive options for *ảp* and *npš* in the Ugaritic ritual texts. This interpretation has a long history, e.g., Johannes C. de Moor ("Studies in the New Alphabetic Texts from Ras Shamra II," *UF* 2 [1970]: 321), "throat"; Paolo Xella (*I testi rituali di Ugarit I*, StSem 54 [Rome: Consiglio Nazionale delle Ricerche, 1981], 32), "lung"; Patrick Miller (review of *Le culte à Ugarit: D'apres les textes de la pratique en cunéiformes alphabetiques*, by J. M. de Tarragon, *JBL* 101 [1982]: 595), "throat," to name a few.

37. Cf. also RS 1.005:15; RS 1.009:38; RIH 77/2B:3; RIH 77/10B:2, 9; RIH 78/4:8, 9, as listed in Pardee, *Textes rituels*, 1186–87.

38. The regular description of the Death god's *npš* "throat" in the Baʿlu myth is rather ironic in light of its derived meaning "life force."

39. Lane, 2900.

to indicate some kind of a pit.[40] Marvin Pope concluded that *mhmrt* and *npš* both "refer to Mot's gullet as the avenue of Baal's descent into the netherworld."[41] Thus, *npš* referring to a part of the body may designate either the external "neck," reflected in the ritual text cited above, or the internal "throat," as in the text just mentioned. As Pardee has already noted, the latter internally focused meaning includes two passageways: the one via the esophagus to the stomach, and the other via the trachea to the lungs.[42] From this explanation, one can make sense of the secondary meanings having to do with matters of the appetite and desire on the one hand, and those dealing with the breath as the symbol of life on the other. I treat all such instances of *npš* = "throat" in chapter 2 and query the viability of reconstructing a separate meaning "appetite," which I think is lacking in Ugaritic.

The holistic conceptualization usually espoused in modern Semitic scholarship for *npš* (especially among Hebrew Bible specialists) encounters a bit of trouble if the root sense of this word was historically either "neck/throat" or "(a part of the) neck."[43] Essentially, it would have originally designated a particular body part, even if we grant that it eventually came to symbolize the person's life as a whole. A more nuanced explanation, however, might suggest that this symbolism arose from the fact that the ancients understood that part of the body (i.e., the throat located within the neck) to be the place where breath (and, perhaps, food) passes. It is also possible to conclude from this observation—namely, that *npš* originally indicated a particular part of the body—that it later came to represent a component of one's existence in the immaterial sense. I consider these options more fully in chapter 2.

mwt

In Ugaritic *m-t* is the root expressing death. Ugaritic *m-t* (presumably the hollow root < *m-w-t) occurs only in the G stem, unlike Biblical Hebrew which also attests the C stem "to cause to die" (active and passive).[44] Also unlike Biblical

40. BDB, 243.

41. Marvin H. Pope, "A Little Soul-Searching," *Maarav* 1 (1978): 28.

42. Pardee, *Textes rituels*, 245.

43. Denied by Miriam Seligson, *The Meaning of* נפש מת *in the Old Testament*, StOr16/2 (Helsinki: Societas Orientalis Fennica, 1951), 46–69.

44. Cf. Hebrew and Aramaic *mwt* (BDB, 559; *HALOT*, 562; *DNWSI*, 605). No consensus exists regarding the historical nature of this root, with some scholars arguing for a biconsonantal root with medial long vowel and others reconstructing a triconsonantal root with medial {w/y}. See ch. 3 (§3.2). For the C stem, see BDB, 560; *HALOT*, 562–63. Note also the attested polel and polal stems.

Hebrew, the Ugaritic verb can refer to the death of mortals or the death of divine beings. For example, the hero ʾAqhatu declares that he must die the death of all mortals in response to ʿAnatu's offer of immortality: *mt kl ảmt wản mtm ảmt* "The death of all I will die; I myself will surely die" (KTU 1.17 VI:38). Yet the mighty Baʿlu also dies following his confrontation with Môtu: *mǵny lbʿl npl lảrṣ mt ảliyn bʿl ḫlq zbl bʿl ảrṣ* "We arrived at Baʿlu fallen to the earth. The valiant Baʿlu is dead; the Prince, lord of the earth, has perished" (KTU 1.5 VI:8–10). The surrounding parallels utilized for describing *m-t* here—*npl lảrṣ* "fallen to the earth"//*mt* "he is dead"//*ḫlq* "he has perished"—are likewise important indicators of Ugaritic conceptions of death. I analyze these parallel expressions extensively in chapter 3.

As I mentioned for the roots *ḥyy* and *ḥwy* above, *m-t* is not limited to the literal sense of dying alone. In the same way that *ḥwy* can describe much-needed repairs to a dilapidated house, so *m-t* occurs once with reference to a fleet of ships off the coast of Tyre: *ảnykn dt likt mṣrm hndt b ṣr mtt* "Your ships which you sent to Egypt, these are dead (in the water) off Tyre" (KTU 2.38:10–13). Scholars have suggested that the description "dead ships" in this context may imply the ships had run aground and were thus immobilized.[45] More simply, however, in light of the fact that this root often occurs parallel to *ḫlq*, it may actually mean that the ships had been incapacitated by the storm mentioned in the next line. In other words, the destructive winds left the ships stranded and immobilized off the coast of Tyre. At any rate, this particular occurrence of *m-t* is insightful regarding the Ugaritic view of death because it allowed them to apply the same language to damaged ships. Again, I provide an extensive assessment of these possibilities in my treatment of this Ugaritic letter in chapter 3 (§3.2.4).

There are two more forms derived from this root, one being identified by del Olmo Lete and Sanmartín as the noun *mt* for a particular "dead person," and the other being the noun *mt* (/môtu/ < /*mawtu/) meaning "death" in the abstract.[46] The first of these two forms might just as well be a substantivized verbal adjective (/mîtu/) meaning, "dead (person)."[47] This form appears in the myth of ʾIlu's banquet as a means of comparing his drunken stupor to that of a

45. The meaning, "run aground" listed in *DUL*, 596 (with a question mark) seems unlikely since the ships end up in Acco. Jacob Hoftijzer ("Une lettre du roi de Iyr," *UF* 11 [1979]: 386) simply states that although the ships had been in an accident, it was not a total loss since the entire crew is still present.

46. *DUL*, 569–70.

47. Josef Tropper (*Ugartische Grammatik*, AOAT 273 [Münster: Ugarit-Verlag, 2012], 649) reconstructs /mâtu/ < /*mawātu/, but the Hebrew form is *mēt* (BDB, 559; *HALOT*, 562). On the problem of the historical development of this form in Hebrew, see Joshua Blau, *Phonology and Morphology of Biblical Hebrew*, LSAWS 2 (Winona Lake, IN: Eisenbrauns, 2010), 253.

dead man: *ql il km mt il k yrdm arṣ* "ʾIlu fell down like a dead man, ʾIlu was like those going down to the earth" (KTU 1.114:21–22).[48] This form also conveys the sense of "mortal," which is derived from the meaning of the G participle, "one who dies," or more loosely, "one (capable of) dying." This usage appears in the Kirta Epic when his mortality comes into question: *ảp ảb i k mtm tmtn* "Indeed, O father, would you die like mortals?" (KTU 1.16 I:3–4).

The abstract notion of death is a well-attested meaning for *mt*, not least in the familiar text from the ʾAqhatu myth already cited above: *mt kl ảmt* "The death of all I will die" (KTU 1.17 VI:38). One of the more interesting features of this form is its usage as the name of divinized Death. This phenomenon distinguishes Ugaritic from its Northwest Semitic counterparts where the Death god is largely absent.[49] The majority of contexts containing the divine name "Death" occur in the Baʿlu cycle, specifically the contest between Môtu and Baʿlu. Note, for instance, the following example: *mt ʿz bʿl ʿz . . . mt ql bʿl ql* "Môtu was strong; Baʿlu was strong . . . Môtu fell; Baʿlu fell" (KTU 1.6 VI:20–22). This particular deity is not limited to the mythological corpus, however, as many scholars find a reference to Môtu in one of the letters: *w yd ilm p k mtm ʿz mi* "the hand of the gods is here, for Death is exceedingly strong" (KTU 2.10 [=RS 4.475]:11–12).[50] If this interpretation is correct (and I think it is), we have a reference to divinized Death outside the mythological context that associates him with a severe plague being experienced in a real-world setting. I will say more about this feature in chapter 3 (§3.3.2).

One of the major problems related to the noun forms derived from this root is their potential confusion with *mt* (/mutu/), "man."[51] There are a few passages where scholars differ in their interpretation of *mt*: /mutu/ "man" or /môtu/ "death?" For example, in one of the extispicy texts one finds the reading *hm mt yʿl bnš* (KTU 1.127:29), which del Olmo Lete and Sanmartín translate, "if death attacks someone," but which Pardee reads, "if the man (= warrior) attacks, the

48. Note also the parallel expression for a dead man: *yrdm arṣ* "those going down to the earth."

49. Scholars have noted, however, the occasional personification of death in Biblical Hebrew poetry (note especially Hab 2:5; cf. Isa 5:14; Prov 1:12; 27:20; 30:15–16; Ps 141:7), leading John Healey ("Mot," *DDD* 1122–32) to surmise the possibility of "mythological overtones" in these cases, which were later read in a demythologized way. See also Theodore Lewis, "Mot," *ABD* 4:922–24; Heinz-Josef Fabry, "מוֹת," *TDOT* 8:205–206. This same potential also existed for Hebrew *šᵉʾôl*.

50. For a treatment of this text, see Dennis Pardee, "As Strong as Death," in *Love and Death in the Ancient Near East: Essays in Honor of Marvin H. Pope*, ed. John Marks and Robert Good (Guilford, CT: Four Quarters Publishing Company, 1987), 65–69. Marvin H. Pope (*Song of Songs*, AB 7C [Garden City, NY: Doubleday, 1977], 688) also takes this to be a reference to Môtu, though his translation differs slightly from that of Pardee. See also *DUL*, 598.

51. Cf. Akkadian *mutu* (*CAD* 10.2:314–16).

(male) personnel (of the city) will. . . ."[52] A comprehensive study of this root requires careful examination of each and every potential ambiguity in light of immediate contexts and more distant parallel expressions or themes.[53]

rpủm

The final lexical investigation of this book addresses the distribution of the term *rpủ(m)*, the plural form traditionally interpreted as "shades (of the dead)," which would identify these individuals as denizens of the underworld. I treat this word and its poetic parallels in chapter 4. Of major interest to discussions about the *rpủm* is their association with the royal funerary context at Ugarit, where they are often identified as the "divinized and immortalized royal ancestors."[54] As Healey reminds us, a proper understanding of Ugaritic kingship plays a central role in formulating a comprehensive view of Ugaritic immortality.[55] There are two parit-icularly important *rpủm* texts, a royal funerary ritual (KTU 1.161 [=RS 34.126]) and the King List (KTU 1.113 [=RS 24.257]), that have spurred on a great deal of interest and controversy, offering further clarity in our understanding of the Ugaritic *rpủm*. The main item of contention in the King List has been the word *il* prefixed to a given king's name, leading many scholars to assume some form of royal divinization, even if low-grade in nature.[56] This factor led Healey to conclude that "the kind of immortality available to kings was not available to ordinary men ... immortality was thought of as reserved to the gods."[57] But in reality we have come full circle again, for the Ugaritic mythological texts pull back the curtain on a pantheon of gods who can and do die (e.g., Baʿlu, Yammu, and Môtu), even though that state is apparently never final.

Another aspect emerging in one's assessment of the *rpủm* is the existence (or lack) of a death cult at Ugarit. Josef Tropper has been a strong advocate for the existence of ancestor worship in the Ugaritic texts, taking the phrase *ỉlỉb*, for

52. *DUL*, 597. *COS* 1:293. Pardee bases his reading of /mutu/ here on the description of ʿz "the strong man" attacking the gate // *qrd* "the warrior" attacking the walls in KTU 119:26–27.

53. On this problem, see Manfried Dietrich and Oswald Loretz, "*mt* 'Môt, Tob' und *mt* "Kieger, Held' im Ugaritischen," *UF* 22 (1990): 57–65.

54. John F. Healey, "The Ugaritic Dead: Some Live Issues," *UF* 18 (1986): 28.

55. Healey references the significance of earlier work on the *rpủm* like that of Dermot J. Ryan, "Rpum and Rephaim: A Study in the Relationship Between the rpum of Ugarit and the Rephaim of the Old Testament" (M.A. thesis, National University of Ireland, 1954). See ch. 4 for a fuller bibliography of studies on the *rpủm*.

56. See discussion of Theodore J. Lewis, *The Cults of the Dead in Ancient Israel and Ugarit*, HSS 39 (Atlanta: Scholars Press, 1989) below.

57. Healey, " Ugaritic Dead," 28.

example, as evidence for the divinization of royal ancestors (*göttlicher Vater*).[58] He marshals the *marziḥu* as another indicator of an ancestor cult, describing it as a feasting event in which the participants invoke the favor of the *rpủm* (KTU 1.20–22). He finds a similar motif in KTU 1.161, which not only commemorates the departed king, but also invokes the blessings of the *rpủm* for the royal family.[59] The attempt to interpret the *marziḥu* as a ritualistic society for venerating the dead, however, has been justly questioned. Pardee contends that even though the *marziḥu* was often devoted to a particular deity, the textual data confirm that it was nothing more than a social group whose primary interest was the consumption of wine.[60] I revisit this question more extensively in chapter 4.

Theodore J. Lewis in his published dissertation entitled, *Cults of the Dead in Ancient Israel and Ugarit*, approaches the ritual of the dead synchronically, analyzing the ancient Ugaritic and biblical texts that purportedly attest a formal death cult, which would also offer valuable information concerning their views of the afterlife. In his study, Lewis adopts the nomenclature "cult of the dead" as a description of "those acts directed toward the deceased functioning either to placate the dead or to secure favors from them for the present life."[61] This approach assumes that the ancient world perceived the dead (e.g., the *rpủm*) as having the potential to bestow favor on the living, or held to the more sinister belief that the dead were capable of inflicting harm against the living in certain circumstances. Lewis limited his investigation to the second millennium BC context of Ugarit and tried to prove that a formal death cult existed as precedence for vestiges of such a cult in the Hebrew Bible.

More specifically, Lewis devoted his primary attention to KTU 1.161 (=RS 34.126), calling it a mortuary ritual text instituted for the following purposes: to provide essentials for the deceased in their departure to the underworld (e.g., libations and offerings), and to secure favors and blessings for those who are still living.[62] The Ugaritic King List (KTU 1.113 [=RS 24.257]) and the formula

58. Josef Tropper, *Nekromantie: Totenbefragung im Alten Orient und im Alten Testament*, AOAT 223 (Kevelaer: Butzon & Bercker; Neukirchen-Vluyn: Neukirchener Verlag, 1989), 126.

59. Tropper, *Nekromantie*, 159.

60. Dennis Pardee, "*Marziḥu*, *Kispu*, and the Ugaritic Funerary Cult," in *Ugarit, Religion and Culture: Proceedings of the International Colloquium on Ugarit, Religion and Culture, Edinburgh, July 1994; Essays Presented in Honour of John C. L. Gibson*, ed. Nicolas Wyatt, Wilfred G. E. Watson and Jeffrey B. Loyd, UBL 12 (Münster: Ugarit-Verlag, 1996), 278–79.

61. Lewis, *Cults of the Dead*, 2.

62. Lewis, *Cults of the Dead*, 31. Cf. Pardee ("*Marziḥu, Kispu*, and the Ugaritic Funerary Cult," 274) who contends that this text is the only ritual text dealing with the funerary rituals for the dead, but at the same time denies that it is mortuary. Pardee (273) adopts the following distinction in terminology for funerary ritual at Ugarit: "funerary cult" in the sense of funeral rituals performed by the living, and "mortuary cult" for the cult of those who have already passed into

il + royal name are also important for Lewis. He interprets the preceding *il* as an indicator of a low-grade divination, but one that did not necessarily include any notion of immortality. In other words, the departed kings were not deified in the literal sense, but "became an *ilu*," or perhaps "became a *rp'*."[63] They "entered into the revered company of the *rp'm* and continued to exist in the underworld"; they were not cut off from the land of the living and could be beseeched for favors.[64] More problematic is Lewis's interpretation of KTU 1.17 I:25–34 (=RS 2.[004]), known as the Duties of an Ideal Son from the ʾAqhatu myth. Lewis rightly noted that this text concerns the duties of a son toward his father, "especially while still living," pointing out that the matters outlined therein are not exclusively funerary in nature.[65] However, the establishment of divine ancestor worship is hard to maintain for *nṣb skn ỉlibh*, translated by Lewis, "One who sets up the stela of his divine ancestor." Many scholars have questioned this meaning for *ỉlibh*, instead opting for a more straightforward rendering, "god of his father," that is, the patron deity of the family clan.[66] It is rather curious that Lewis would find evidence for ancestor worship in *ỉlibh*, while denying the better case for, at the least, a funerary context in lines 28–29.[67] Finally, Lewis tones down the interpretation of the *marziḥu* as primarily organized for ancestor worship, noting its identification as a sort of drinking club, but still maintains a loose death cult association that must have developed after-the-fact.[68]

Some scholars have expressed serious doubts about the existence of this sort of death cult in the Levant during the second millennium BC. Brian B. Schmidt has offered one of the more extensive criticisms of the typical death cult interpretation for these texts. He broadened the discussion to include evidence from

---

the underworld. According to this terminology, Pardee does not accept that KTU 1.161 addresses the "mortuary cult" of the deceased.

63. Lewis, *Cults of the Dead*, 49. Cf. the usage of *ʾĕlōhîm* with reference to the deceased Samuel in 1 Samuel 28:13.

64. Lewis, *Cults of the Dead*, 50.

65. Lewis, *Cults of the Dead*, 69.

66. E.g., Pardee, "*Marziḥu, Kispu*, and the Ugaritic Funerary Cult," 283 n. 17; Brian B. Schmidt, *Israel's Beneficent Dead: Ancestor Cult and Necromancy in Ancient Israelite Religion and Tradition* (Winona Lake, IN: Eisenbrauns, 1996), 59.

67. Though Pardee ("*Marziḥu, Kispu*, and the Ugaritic Funerary Cult," 238 n. 17) denies the ancestor cult interpretation for *ỉlibh*, he is open to this possibility for lines 28 and 29: *lảrṣ mšṣủ qṭrh lʿpr ḏmr ảṭrh*, "Who causes his incense to go out with regard to the ground; who guards his resting place with regard to the dust." Lewis's case for interpreting *qṭrh* as "his life" is not entirely convincing (*Cults of the Dead*, 54, 60–5). The appeal to KTU 1.18 IV 24 (=RS 3.340) will not work here, since *qṭr* in that instance is modified by *km*, indicating that *qṭr*, presumably "smoke" or "incense," illustrates the exiting of life, i.e., his life goes out . . . like incense/smoke by way of his nose." For more on this text, see ch. 1 (§1.2.2.2).

68. Lewis, *The Cults of the Dead*, 94.

late third to early second millennium materials at Ebla and Mari, as well as the late second millennium corpus from Ugarit before moving on in his final analysis to the Hebrew Bible.[69] Whereas earlier Ugaritic scholars saw death cult everywhere, Schmidt sees no evidence for death cult anywhere.

First off, Schmidt judiciously rejects the plausibility of taking *ỉlib* as having anything to do with deified ancestors or their worship, instead building his case for the translation, "the gods of the fathers."[70] With regard to the duties of the faithful son (KTU 1.17 I:26b–33), he interprets the expression taken by Lewis to be a reference to ancestor worship as a charge to venerate the patron deity: *nṣb skn ỉlibh*, "One who sets up the stelae of his father's gods."[71]

Further, Schmidt thinks there is no textual basis for the view that the formulaic *ỉl* + royal name refers to a dead, deified king. Following Mario Liverani, he takes the repeated *ỉl* + royal name not as a reference to the deified king, but as a reference "to those dedicated to the personal god of the former kings who might have been a major god of the pantheon."[72] This interpretation appears to be a bit forced. One might reasonably argue for it in the case of the rather nonspecific *ỉlib* "god of such-and-such father." Yet here, its repetition with each of the specified names of known Ugaritic kings is harder to explain in that it would be the unspecified god of the specified king. I will return to this problem again in chapter 5.

Returning to the *rpủm*, Schmidt's unwillingness to admit that this term ever refers to deified, departed kings leads him to suggest that they represented the lingering memory of legendary war heroes. In the fiercest of battles, the dead of this band of living warriors rapidly increased, which "led to the *rpủm* concept taking on a specifically postmortem dimension as expressed exclusively in the epithet *rpỉm qdmym* 'the ancient Rephaim' in 1.161."[73] According to his analysis, what had existed as a historical reality, and at the same time mythically heroic, eventually came to be associated with the underworld.[74] As for any notion of ancestor cult in KTU 1.161, Schmidt views this text as a coronation ritual with

69. Schmidt, *Israel's Beneficent Dead.*

70. Schmidt, *Israel's Beneficent Dead,* 58.

71. Schmidt, *Israel's Beneficent Dead,* 59. As one would expect, it is worth noting that Schmidt denies any mortuary connection with the *marziḥu* (62–66).

72. Mario Liverani, "La royauté syrienne de l'âge de bronze récent" in *Le palais et la royauté,* ed. Paul Garelli RAI 19. (Paris: Geuthner, 1974), 329–56; rejected by Dennis Pardee, *Les textes paramythologiques de la 24e campagne (1961),* RSO 4 (Paris: Editions Recherche sur les Civilisations, 1988), 173 n. 25. Quotation from Schmidt, *Israel's Beneficent Dead,* 69.

73. Schmidt, *Israel's Beneficent Dead,* 91.

74. Schmidt, *Israel's Beneficent Dead.* Cf. this view with that of Conrad L'Heureux, *Rank Among the Canaanite Gods: El, Ba'al, and the Repha'im,* HSM 21 (Missoula, MT: Scholars Press, 1979), 201–23.

elemental mourning rites for the deceased king Niqmaddu, father of the newly appointed king ʾAmmurapiʾ, who publically recited his name in commemoration. The weakened dead below (i.e., the *rpủm*) receive and deliver Niqmaddu's throne to the netherworld, perhaps as escorts, but not as objects of veneration in any sort of death cult ritual.[75]

I consider these theories more extensively in chapter 4, but do so from within the constraints of my lexical analysis of *rpủm*. There I collect every instance of this term in the extant Ugaritic texts and analyze their contexts in detail. A major corpus of interest in this investigation is provided by the so-called *rpủm* texts (KTU 1.20–22), which I discuss at length (§4.3.4). I also consider the relationship (if any) of the *rpủm* to *rpủ mlk ʿlm* "Rāpiʾu, King of Eternity" mentioned in KTU 1.108:1, providing my own interpretation and discussion of this text. I believe the etymological connection between them is compelling. The funerary ritual text KTU 1.161 concludes my discussion of the *rpủm* as I assess its contributions for or against a royal cult of the dead at Ugarit.

A Literary Analysis of Life and Mortality in Ugaritic

Many uncertainties persist in the study of life and death at Ugarit even though the well-known mythological texts dealing with these issues have been analyzed rather extensively. For example, as mentioned above, ʿAnatu's offer of immortality to ʾAqhatu has been discussed at length in the literature, yet, when it is analyzed in light of what we know from the Kirta Epic, two competing viewpoints on what it means for a god to die emerge. In the case of ʾAqhatu, he is promised the opportunity to count years with Baʿlu, an immortality that allows continual renewal (*k yḥwy*) (KTU 1.17 VI:27, 30). Although Baʿlu passes through death experientially (descending into the throat of Môtu), it is not final because he is somehow able to revive to life again. Or in the case of Yammu, despite the fact that Baʿlu kills and dismembers him, he reappears in the following scenes. As for Kirta, son of ʾIlu, however, the prospects of experiencing death seem irreconcilable with his title "son of ʾIlu," as those closest to him lament: "Do gods die? Does the offspring of the gracious one not live?" (KTU 1.16 I:22–23). Could it be that the Ugaritic view of life and mortality is not uniform? Or, does Kirta's status as a royal figure suggest that we are dealing with a social hierarchy in matters of life and death?

75. L'Heureux, *Rank Among the Canaanite Gods*, 120. See also p. 109, and his interpretation of *dbḥ* in KTU 1.161:1 as "sacred celebration," a translation that seems to be a bit pressed. Even the examples cited for this interpretation hardly deny a cultic context.

The royal context is certainly a crucial vantage point for reconstructing the ancient Ugaritic understanding of life and death. In fact, some scholars even propose that the events in the life and times of the gods is a projection of Ugaritic royal ideology, or at the least, closely connected to it conceptually. This consideration raises larger questions about the interpretation of Ugaritic mythology itself, and how these poetic narratives functioned in their ancient context.

But all such investigations need an interpretive anchor, which is what lexicography potentially does for this study. Analyzing the use of terms from a particular semantic range not only helps us to define individual words more precisely, but also forces us to consider the meaning of other terms in those same contexts that inform our understanding of the conceptual framework they produce in the literature. This feature of lexical study raises my analysis to the higher literary level of texts, moving attention from the minutia of lexical terms and contexts to the complex ideas they convey. Thinking along these lines leads us to the literary study of life and death and thus compels us to consider several overarching horizons or themes of investigation: mythology and the language of correspondence, life and revivification, the anatomy of life, the life and death of physical objects, the intersection of mythology and burial, and the royal dead. From these thematic horizons, outlined in chapter 5, I synthesize the results of my lexical study of life and mortality in Ugaritic.

A Cultural and Comparative Analysis of Life and Mortality

Two final items warrant attention in this introduction. The first concerns the relevance of archaeology to this book. Although the argument of my study is largely textual, archaeological evidence factors significantly in my treatment of mythology and death ritual in chapter 5 (§5.6). The archaeological investigation of burial structures at Ugarit offers a perspective that is external from the textual record, but nonetheless dovetails with it. My foray into the archaeology of Ugaritic burial practices answers Smith's call to give attention to the outside world of the text, even though etymology is his primary interest in that discussion.[76] I am interested in showing that Ugaritic burial structures demonstrate that the ancients interpreted death in terms of the living. Moreover, the mythological depiction of death, burial, and revivification in the realm of the gods and the concerted effort to overcome the mortality of members of the royal household both correspond with the funerary material remains uncovered among the

76. Smith, "Words and Their Worlds," 8–9.

inhabitants of Ugarit's general population. This evidence provides an important means of linking together the upper and lower levels of society into a common thread of beliefs about the dead and their relationship with the living.

The second and final consideration addresses the available comparative evidence from the Northwest Semitic funerary inscriptions of the first millennium BC. These inscriptions offer a context closely related to the Ugaritic materials, both in time and location. They show further developments in certain ideas latent at Ugarit. One of these developments involves the term *nbš* (= *npš*) "soul." The recently discovered Katumuwa inscription from the ancient Sam'alian kingdom of Zincirli has been the center of much discussion among scholars. Front and center is the idea of a disembodied *npš*, apparently indicated in the expression "my *nbš* in the stele." Many scholars have insisted that we understand this idea from the Hittite perspective where souls leave the body to embark upon their journey to the underworld. But the Ugaritic notion that the *npš* exits the body at death may in fact offer a nearer parallel, though admittedly in a latent form. Because of current interest in these texts I have included an appendix at the end of the book where I discuss how my study on the Ugaritic outlook informs one's understanding of the corresponding first millennium BC funerary context. Furthermore, my treatment will also require brief comment on the Hittite viewpoint, since the Anatolian context has been of chief concern for interpreters of the Sam'alian cultural and religious contexts, particularly regarding the nature of one's soul postmortem.

CHAPTER 1

An Analysis of Words for "Life" in Ugaritic

1.1. Introduction

The first matter of importance in establishing the Ugaritic perspective on life is to conduct a thorough analysis of its lexical inventory by which this concept was expressed throughout the literature. The lexemes that demand the concentration of my investigation at the outset are the roots *ḥwy/ḥyy*, meaning "to live." My analysis does not end here, however, for a number of other important terms associated with the concept of life are attested. Some of these additional terms appear throughout the mythological and epic literature in parallel with *ḥwy/ḥyy* (e.g., *blmt*, "not dying," *iṯ* [particle of existence]) and thus provide important clarification for our understanding of the meaning of the primary Ugaritic roots. It is only natural to treat these parallels in this first chapter on the roots *ḥwy/ḥyy*, and so, my remarks about them will be interspersed throughout the analysis of these roots. More broadly speaking, however, there are other words that also served an important place in the Ugaritians' concept of life deserving considerable attention in this book, words such as *npš* "neck, life" (//*brlt*), *lb* "heart," *kbd* "liver, innards, mind," to name a few. I address these and others like them in chapter 2 in light of my analysis of *ḥwy/ḥyy* in this chapter.

1.2. The Roots *ḥwy/ḥyy*

As mentioned in the introduction above, Marcus's morphological study of the roots *ḥwy* and *ḥyy* mapped out their distribution throughout the Ugaritic corpus and showed that each has a distinct function. Marcus argued that *ḥyy* is used exclusively for the G stem, while *ḥwy* is reserved for the derived stems, namely, the D and the Št.[1] Del Olmo Lete and Sanmartín, editors of the standard dictionary for Ugaritic studies, also follow this viewpoint and conveniently arrange these roots as follows: all G stem forms with medial {y} and all D and Št stem forms with medial {w}.[2] The distribution of these roots appears likewise to correspond with literary genre: the verbal forms are most widely attested in the mythological and epic texts with fewer instances elsewhere. Marcus's observations appear to offer a valid assessment of the available data regarding the attestations in Ugaritic—I have found nothing to disprove his hypothesis in this study. But before I move on to my own treatment of this root, it is important to establish the basic argument of this proposal as well as an assessment of its viability from the Ugaritic texts themselves.

There are three principal reasons cited in favor of this argument for a distinction between the roots with medial {y} and {w}. First, we should note those cases where the medial {y} forms occur as verbal forms. Marcus cites *ḥyt* in KTU 1.3 V:31, interpreting it as a second-person masculine singular of the G stem: *tḥmk il ḥkm ḥkmt/k ʿm ʿlm ḥyt ḥẓt,* thus translating, "Your decree, O El, is extremely wise, forever may you live and prosper."[3] Below, I will argue that *ḥyt* is better read as a nominal form, but one could nonetheless suggest a different verbal form where medial {y} is present: *ḥytn w šlmtn* "I am alive and well."[4] A number of apocopated forms of this root occur throughout the epic texts, which unfortunately do not help us because of their loss of what would have been medial {y}.

This consideration leads to a second line of evidence for the theory in question, and that is the attestation of this root in proper names. Marcus cites *yḥšr* in alphabetic script (KTU 4.243:11), which also appears in the Akkadian syllabic script as ia-ḫé-šar. [5] He normalizes the name as *yaḥêšar,* the first element being a G stem jussive, and all together means "May the prince live." The syllabic rendering of this name reads ia-ḫé, likely the realization of the diphthong /ay/, since a medial {w} would have yielded something more like ia-hu.[6] A similar

1. Marcus, "The Verb 'to Live' in Ugaritic," 76–82.

2. *DUL*, 379.

3. Marcus, "The Verb 'to Live' in Ugaritic," 76.

4. On this text see Dennis Pardee, "New Readings in the Letters of ʿzn bn byy," in *Vorträge Gehalten Auf Der 28. Rencontre Assyriologique Internationale in Wien, 6.–10. Juli 1981*, AfOB 19 (Horn: Berger, 1982): 39–53; Pardee, *COS* 3:108–9. According to this interpretation, *ḥytn* is a 1cs of the G stem with enclitic {n}. See the discussion on this text below.

5. *PRU* 3:86 (text 15.119:4).

6. Marcus, "The Verb 'to Live' in Ugaritic," 78.

distinction exists in the Phoenician proper name consisting of the root *ḥyy* + *mlk*.[7] On the one hand, the proper name *yḥmlk* might represent a G stem vocalized as /yeḥîmilk/ "May Milk live," while *yḥwmlk* would seem to distinguish an underlying D stem: /yeḥawwimilk/ "May Milk make alive."[8] The problem with the Phoenician evidence, however, is that outside proper names this distinction is not apparent in that all forms attest medial {w}.[9] Furthermore, in Punic a verbal form with medial {w} appears to be in the G stem: *ḥwʾ* ⸢*š*⸣[ʿ]⸢*nt*⸣ *šmn šš* "He lived/was alive sixty-eight years" (KAI 128.3).

Finally, I mention the evidence from the polyglot vocabularies where two distinct Ugaritic forms, one with medial {y} and another with medial {w}, correspondingly interpret two different Akkadian terms.[10] The Akkadian word *balāṭu*, according to *CAD*'s meaning 3, "to be alive," is rendered syllabically in Ugaritic as [ḫ]é-y[a]-[m]a.[11] A few lines below, Akkadian *eṭēru*, meaning 3 in the *CAD*, "to save a person," is represented in the Ugaritic column with the syllabic form ḫu-wV-ú.[12] These data are significant in that they exhibit the {y/w} interchange in connection with two distinct Akkadian lexemes. That being said, we must exercise caution in thinking of a one-to-one equivalency, since the meaning of

7. Marcus, "The Verb 'to Live' in Ugaritic," 79.

8. For the G stem, see KAI 4.1. Marcus also cites the Hebrew PN *yeḥîʾal* (Ezra 8:9; 10:2, 21, 26) as a parallel ("The Verb 'to Live' in Ugaritic," 78), but in Hebrew we should keep in mind that the {y/w} distinction is not operative, since all verbal stems of this type are medial {y} (see *HALOT*, 309–10; BDB, 310–11). For the D stem, see KAI 10.1.

9. See *DNWSI* 354–55. Of course, this could be because all attested Phoenician forms are in the D stem.

10. Marcus, "The Verb 'to Live' in Ugaritic," 81. See also John Huehnergard, *Ugaritic Vocabulary in Syllabic Transcription*, revised ed., HSS 32 (Winona Lake, IN: Eisenbrauns, 2008), 123–24.

11. *CAD* 2:52. *Ugaritica* 5, 137 I:20″. Cf. ḫé-ya-ma (*Ugaritica* 5, 131:6′). Marcus also cites the Canaanite gloss ḫa-ya-ma in the Amarna letters (EA 245:6), also appearing in association with Akkadian *balāṭu*. In syllabic Ugaritic, the value /yV/ can be registered by either the IA or PI signs (Huehnergard, *Ugaritic Vocabulary*, 237). Furthermore, the vowel quality is ambiguous, being either /ia/, /ie/, /ii/, or /iu/ (see René Labat, *Manuel d'épigraphie akkadienne: signes, syllabaire, idéogrammes*, 6th ed. [Paris: Geuthner, 1995], 101).

12. *CAD* 4:401. Transcribed in *Ugaritica* 5, 137 II:17′ as ḫu-wa-u, leading some scholars to normalize the form */ḥuwwāyu/ (e.g., Daniel Sivan, *Grammatical Analysis of the Northwest Semitic Vocables in Akkadian Texts of the 15th–13th C.B.C. from Canaan and Syria*, AOAT 214 (Kevelaer: Butzon & Bercker; Neukirchen-Vluyn: Neukirchener Verlag, 1984], 179 n. 1). Huehnergard (*Ugaritic Vocabulary*, 290 n. 107) simply renders the cuneiform as ḫu-PI-ú, noting that final {y} is unlikely for this form due to the fact that the Ú sign is not used elsewhere in syllabic Ugaritic for /yu/, but rather represents either a long vowel when following a Cu sign (e.g., ša-du-ú = /šadû/, alphabetic *šdw*) or the presence of gutturals {ʾ}, {h}, or {ʿ} (236 n. 106). The values registered by the PI sign are ambiguous in Akkadian, indicating either /wa/, /wi/, /we/, or /wu/ (see Labat, *Manuel d'épigraphie akkadienne*, 177; cf. Rykle Borger, *Mesopotamisches Zeichenlexikon*, AOAT 305 [Münster: Ugarit-Verlag, 2010], 165). Huehnergard notes that in Ugaritic Akkadian, only the values /wa/ and /wu/ are attested (*Ugaritic Vocabulary*, 235). In light of these considerations, it seems more plausible to normalize the signs ḫu-PI-ú as /ḥuwwû/ in Ugaritic.

Akkadian *balāṭu* is not limited in the G stem to being alive or well but can also denote a recovery from illness.[13] Or in the case of *eṭēru*, its fundamental sense is "to take something away (from somebody)," and only secondarily means "to save a person."[14] Essentially, we are dealing with "rough" equivalencies. What is important to gather from this polyglot vocabulary is the mere fact that two distinct Akkadian words correspond to Ugaritic *ḥwy* and *ḥyy*.

When taken together, I find these three arguments compelling in favor of Marcus's theory concerning the middle radical of this root. Therefore, the assumption that ḥ-y-y = the G stem while ḥ-w-y = the D or Št stems is maintained throughout this chapter. In what follows, I will try to establish the G stem from those forms where medial {y} shows up, followed by an assessment of potential apocopated forms. It reasonably follows, then, that those verbal forms where medial {w} is present must of necessity be D stems since the doubled {w} remains in all forms, hypothetically even in jussive forms.[15]

Before turning our attention to the attested forms themselves, I need to comment further on the matter of apocopation. In particular for the G stem, all PC forms apocopate the medial {y}, thus making their lexical identification more difficult. In Ugaritic, the medial {y} is retained in SC forms with a consonantal pronominal element, which allows for the G/D stem distinction just outlined, evidenced in the 1cs form *ḥytn* "I am alive" (KTU 5.10:2; 5.11:3), versus the 1cs in *ḥwt hbt* "I have restored this house" (KTU 2.70:15).[16] The absence of {y} in all PC forms, however, is more difficult to explain. In certain cases, one might argue that the apocopated form is markedly jussive, as, for example, in the clause *npš tḥ pǵ[t]* "As for (her) *npš*, may PǴT live" (KTU 1.19 IV:36). Unfortunately, this will not work for KTU 1.16 I:23: *špḥ lṭpn l yḥ* "Would the offspring of the knowing one not live?" where a jussive interpretation does not appear to make sense.

Josef Tropper hypothesizes the historical development of this form as follows: /yaḥyiy/ > /yaḥyî/ > /yaḥî/.[17] This historical reconstruction encounters problems, especially considering the Hebrew evidence for the G stem of this root where both long and short forms are attested: /yiḥye^{h}/ for the indicative, and /y^{e}ḥī^{y}/ for the jussive.[18] In the long form, the retention of the final vowel

13. *CAD* 2:52.

14. *CAD* 4:401.

15. There appear to be no D stem jussives for this root so far attested in Ugaritic.

16. See the discussion of these texts to follow.

17. Josef Tropper, *Ugaritische Grammatik*, 2nd ed., AOAT 273 (Münster: Ugarit-Verlag, 2012), 660.

18. See BDB, 311. The Hebrew evidence is important for its status as the most fully vocalized language attested among the Canaanite dialects. For a fuller treatment on Ugaritic as a Canaanite language, see Tropper, "Is the Ugaritic Language a Canaanite Dialect?"

(*sĕgōl* {h}) preserves the medial {y}, while the loss of the final vowel in the jussive form results in its loss since the final {y} in /y^{e}ḥī^{y}/ is a *mater* for the long /i/ vowel. According to Tropper's reconstruction, the final {y} is lost as a result of the contraction of /iy/, resulting in the change /yaḥyî/ > /yaḥî/. The short forms in proto-Hebrew and Arabic, however, evince a final short vowel and not the hypothetically long vowel in Tropper's contracted /î/.[19] The Hebrew evidence for III-*h* roots indicates the shortened forms that dropped the final short vowel of the indicative resulted in apocopation (e.g., the nominal forms: /qatiyu/ > /qatiy/ > /qati/) rather than the contraction of /iy/ > /î/. The fact that we have no evidence for a final long vowel for the shortened III-*h* forms in Hebrew most likely indicates that it was historically short: *yiben* < /*yibn/ < /*yibna/ < /*yibnay/.[20]

Returning to the Ugaritic situation, if we are to consider seriously this comparative evidence, it would seem to necessitate an alternative reconstruction for ḥ-y-y. In light of these considerations, Pardee has proposed that the shortened forms for this root in Ugaritic developed along these lines: /*yaḥyiy/ > /*yaḥyi/ > /*yaḥy/ > /yaḥî/.[21] I find this reconstruction to be a more satisfying accounting of the comparative data.

This brings us full circle to the lingering question involving the function of such long and short forms attested for the Ugaritic III-*y*/*w* roots. Is there evidence in Ugaritic for a marked distinction in usage for these forms (e.g., indicative vs. jussive)? Ugaritic only attests the shortened PC form for this root, and one of these is clearly not a jussive (KTU 1.16 I:23, cited above). Admittedly, we are only dealing with one of many other roots that need to be considered in formulating a comprehensive view of the verbal system (far beyond the scope of this discussion), but this particular datum raises problems for Tropper's contention that the III-*y*/*w* roots offer proof of a functional modal system in Ugaritic.[22] More broadly, Tropper builds his case upon the attested verbal forms found in

19. Hebrew: /yapt/ < /*yapti/; or with anaptyctic vowel: /yáʿaś/ < /*yaʿs/ < /*yaʿśi/ (for more examples, see Blau, *Phonology and Morphology of Biblical Hebrew*, 251; Bordreuil and Pardee, *Manual of Ugaritic*, 55–56). Arabic: jussives /yarmi/ and /yalqa/ (see Wheeler M. Thackston, *An Introduction to Koranic and Classical Arabic* [Bethesda, MD: Ibex, 2000], 119; W. Wright, *Arabic Grammar*, 3rd ed. [Mineola, NY: Dover, 2005], 1:90). This observation is also noted in Dennis Pardee, review of *Ugaritische Grammatik*, by Josef Tropper, *AfO* 50 (2003/2004): 318–19 (http://orientalistik.univie.ac.at/fileadmin/documents/Rezension_Tropper_AOAT273.pdf). See the same argument in Ebbe Egede Knudsen, "An Analysis of Amorite," *JCS* 34 (1982): 9.

20. See BDB, 124.

21. Pardee, review of *Ugaritische Grammatik*, 319. In Hebrew, the final long vowel is written with {y} *mater lectionis*.

22. Tropper, *Ugaritische Grammatik*, 2nd ed., 653–58.

the poetic texts rather than those in Ugaritic prose, another factor that obfuscates the situation.[23]

That some modal system was operative in Proto-Semitic seems fairly clear, wherein a /YQTLu/ form would have functioned as an indicative while a /YQTLØ/ marked a jussive or perfective/preterite (cf. Heb. *waw* consecutive), but whether or not such a system was functional in Ugaritic poetic texts is hard to determine. Edward L. Greenstein has analyzed all /YQTL/ forms in Ugaritic narrative verse in search of a solution to this problem.[24] He concludes that the evidence for the III-*y*/*w* roots does not allow us to reconstruct a markedly distinct verbal system beyond that of the shortened jussive with Ø-ending versus the indicative with *-u* ending, instead suggesting that many forms with or without final *y*/*w* are selected for stylistic, not grammatical reasons.[25] This observation from Greenstein is not only helpful for understanding III-weak roots in general, it also is particularly pertinent to ḥ-y-y—it offers one of several possible explanations for apocopated versus unapocopated forms of the root. Sometimes there is a lexical factor, for which he cites the fact that most /YQTL/ forms of the verb *bky* "to weep" appear unapocopated, while most /YQTL/ forms of *ḥdy* "to see" are apocopated.[26] This assessment works for the PC forms of *ḥyy*, all of which appear apocopated in narrative contexts and are thus not jussives (KTU 1.16 I).[27] Therefore, one might conclude that apocopation in the G stem PC forms of *ḥyy* is a key feature of this particular root—all such forms apocopate irrespective of usage, but perhaps in different forms reflecting the original short and long forms. One problem with this simple formation, however, is that the form in question appears in direct speech: *špḥ lṭpn l yḥ* "Would the offspring of the knowing one not live?" (KTU 1.16 I:23). A different solution would be to identify the form as a contracted long form: not /yaḥ/ but /yaḥû/ < /yaḥyiyu/.[28]

23. See Bordreuil and Pardee's criticisms of this approach in *Manual of Ugaritic*, 45.

24. Edward L. Greenstein, "Forms and Functions of the Finite Verb in Ugaritic Narrative Verse," in *Biblical Hebrew in Its Northwest Semitic Setting: Typology and Historical Perspectives*, ed. Steven E. Fassberg and Avi Hurvitz (Winona Lake, IN: Eisenbrauns, 2006), 75–102.

25. Greenstein, "Forms and Functions of the Finite Verb," 86.

26. Greenstein, "Forms and Functions of the Finite Verb," 85.

27. See the list of forms cited in Greenstein, "Forms and Functions of the Finite Verb," 86, where he also mentions *l yḥ* "he will not live" as cited here.

28. See Dennis Pardee, review of *Biblical Hebrew in Its Northwest Semitic Setting*, by Steven Fassberg and Avi Hurvitz, *JNES* 71 (2012): 169–70, citing Ugaritic {ṯlủ}, which shows a contracted form of III-*y* /YQTLû/ and not Greenstein's "yabkī" or "yabki." Pardee concludes: "Thus one may envision a system containing two /YQTLu/ forms, without and with contraction (/yabkiyu/ and /yabkû/), alongside the /YQTLØ/ form (/yabki/) of which the only remaining function would be that of the jussive."

While this is true for the G stem, the situation for the D stem is somewhat different. This is because of the D stem's characteristic doubling of the middle radical {w}, which theoretically would always preserve it. Thus in the PC of this root, medial {w} forms are attested with or without a final {y}. As I have already mentioned, Greenstein makes a strong case against the view that the absence or presence of apocopation marks function (e.g., long vs. short indicative forms). To put it more exactly, Greenstein argues that most of the time apocopation is phonologically conditioned in Ugaritic—it is not marking a morphologically distinct form with a distinct function (except for the jussive).[29] For example, he points out that the addition of a prefixed {w} to III-*y* verbs seems to result in the loss of final {y}.[30] With regard to the evidence from the root *ʿny*, he concludes that the "short form of YQTL *ʿny* in its formulaic function should not, therefore, be adduced as evidence of a *yaqtul* preterite in Ugaritic."[31]

This assessment works for the broader picture of Ugaritic III-*y* verbs, and for the most part I think it is correct. However, the D stem ḥ-w-y offers a more varied distribution than this and is worth presenting here in light of Greenstein's overall proposal. The following attestations from ʾAqhatu deserve attention:

k bʿl ***kyḥwy***	"like Baʿlu **when he is revived**" (KTU 1.17 VI:30)
ảp ảnk ***ảḥwy*** *ảqht [ǵ]zr*	"Even **I** myself **will make** the hero ʾAqhatu **live**" (KTU 1.17 VI:32)
ảp mprh ảnk ***lảḥwy***	"Even **I** myself will **not let** the soldier **live**" (KTU 1.18 IV:27)
ʿl qṣʿth hwt ***lảḥw***	"On account of his arrows **I did not let** that one **live**" (KTU 1.19 I:16)

Out of these three occurrences, only the last one is apocopated. It is important to see that Greenstein's phonological argument does not provide a satisfactory accounting of these forms—two of the three prefixed verbs are not apocopated (*kyḥwy* and *lảḥwy*) while the other is (*lảḥw*). Or, we might compare the non-prefixed verb in the clause *ảp ảnk ảḥwy*, which remains unapocopated with the

29. Greenstein, "Forms and Functions of the Finite Verb," 84–85; contra Tropper, *Ugaritische Grammatik*, 2nd ed., 653–58.

30. Greenstein makes his case by analyzing the Ugaritic verb *ʿny* "to answer, reply," showing that of the twelve legible attestations of the YQTL form of this root in the ʾAqhatu Epic all are without final {y}. Yet, in every instance the form is preceded by {w}. Similarly, in the Baal cycle there are nineteen apocopated forms and all are with prefixed {w} (see Greenstein, "Forms and Functions of the Finite Verb," 83 for references).

31. Greenstein, "Forms and Functions of the Finite Verb," 84.

addition of the negative particle, *ảp mprh ảnk lảḥwy*. What we do find, however, is that the apocopated form is used to express completed action, or the fact that ʿAnatu had in fact killed the hero. On the other hand, the unapocopated forms express ʿAnatu's announcement of what she is about to do.

This isolated example of what looks like a morphosyntactical distinction requires caution, however, since the broader body of evidence for III-*y* roots cited in Greenstein's study points in a different direction, at least during the time period of the Ugaritic texts that have come down to us. Nonetheless, these examples may provide vestiges of an earlier stage of the language when the /YQTLu/ = imperfective and /YQTLØ/ = perfective distinction was operative. I would therefore qualify Greenstein's assessment that the apocopated and unapocopated III-*y* forms are always used in free variation with the acknowledgment that in this particular instance, the vestigial morphosyntax appears intact.[32]

1.2.1. The G Stem

The basic function of the G stem (ḥ-y-y) is to express the state of being alive. The only form where medial {y} appears so far in Ugaritic is in the SC form *ḥytn* from KTU 5.10 and 5.11:

KTU 5.10:1–2

(1) *ʿzn bn byy l ảḫth ʿṯ!y*	ʿZN, son of BYY, to his sister ʿṮTY.
(2) ***ḥytn*** *w šlmtn*	**I am alive** and well.
(3) *rgm l ủmy šlm bʿlkm*	Say to my mother: Your lord is well.

KTU 5.11

(1) *ʿzn bn byy* ?[. . .]	ʿZN son of BYY . . .
(2) *bʿl yšủl šlmk*	The master asks (concerning) your well-being.
(3) ***ḥytn*** *l p špš*	**I am alive** (and well). At the command of ŠPŠ
(4) *yṯbtn bbt trtn*	I am dwelling at the house TRTN.

These two letters are difficult to make out interpretively. Their elusive nature becomes clear when one attempts to analyze the two attestations of the root *ḥyy*, which scholars have interpreted in a number of ways. Some scholars have analyzed *ḥytn* as two words: *ḥy tn*, the first word being a masculine noun of this root functioning as the direct object of the imperative *tn* (< *ytn*): "give life."[33]

32. Bordreuil and Pardee refer to "archaisms" (*Manual of Ugaritic*, 49).
33. *CAT* transcribes accordingly: *ḥy tn w šlm tn* (5.10:2); *ḥy tn l p špš* (5.11:4).

As an introduction to the letter, it would serve as some form of greeting, perhaps meaning, "give (a report of) life," but this kind of greeting does not appear elsewhere in the Ugaritic epistolary materials. This interpretation would naturally read the second expression similarly: "give (a report of) well-being," though once again, it is not the typical Ugaritic greeting for a letter.[34] André Caquot, on the other hand, reads these forms as verbal nouns with a first-person pronominal suffix "our life."[35] The problem for this interpretation is twofold: (1) the parallel *šlmt* + 1cp suffix in KTU 5.10 would be the only attestation of such a verbal noun for this root, and (2) the parallel *yṯbt* + 1cp suffix in KTU 5.11 would likewise be without parallel.

Pardee has conducted an extensive study of these two texts wherein he proposes the reading *ḥytn* as I have adopted here.[36] As for KTU 5.10:2, he suggests that on the basis of the distribution of *-tn* forms in these two letters the form in question must be verbal. These *-tn* forms are as follows:

ḥytn w šlmtn	(KTU 5.10:2)
štntn	(KTU 5.10:4)
ḥytn	(KTU 5.11:3)
yṯbtn	(KTU 5.11:4)

He notes that *yṯbtn* provides the strongest evidence for the 1cs SC interpretation, since the context would not allow a second-person form. According to this analysis, the historical base of *ḥytn* is /qataltu/ + n(a): /*ḥayiytu/ > /ḥayîtu/ or /ḥayyātu/ (on analogy of Heb. *sabbôtî*),[37] and as Pardee points out, *ḥytn* should have stronger force than the standard *ḥyt*.[38] Due to the problems already noted for earlier interpretations of this form, I have adopted Pardee's analysis.

34. More commonly, letter greetings begin with the sender's wish that all be well with the recipient, usually with the PC of *šlm* (e.g., *yšlm lk* "May it be well with you" [KTU 2.38:4]), followed by a statement of well-being from the sender, as well as a request for the recipient to return word of his well-being (e.g., *hnny ʿmn šlm ṯmny ʿmk mnm šlm rgm ṯṯb* "Here with me it is well; there with you, whatever is well return word" [KTU 2.38:6–9]). For a list of the formulaic greetings in the epistolary materials, see Dennis Pardee, "Epigraphic and Philological Notes," *UF* 19 (1987): 210–11; and the fuller treatment in Pardee, "Une formule épistolaire en ougaritique et accadien," in *Semitic and Assyriological Studies Presented to Pelio Fronzaroli by Pupils and Colleagues*, ed. Paolo Marrassini (Wiesbaden: Harrassowitz, 2003), 446–75.

35. André Caquot, "Correspondance de ʾUzzin fils de Bayaya (RS 17.63 et 17.117)," *Ugaritica* 7:390–91, 393. Cf. *DUL*, 381, which analyzes *ḥyt* as a feminine noun corresponding to the masculine noun *ḥy*.

36. Pardee, "New Readings," 39–53.

37. But, at least in Hebrew, *ḥyy* does not show the normal geminate pattern.

38. Pardee, "New Readings," 41.

The importance of this example is that it offers a form in which the medial {y} of the root *ḥyy* is preserved, and thus distinguishes it from the root *ḥwy*.

The G stem SC is also attested three times in the Baʿlu cycle (KTU 1.6 III:2, 8, 20), each referring to the storm god's own revivification following his reported death after having been defeated by the god Môtu, announced repeatedly, *bʿl mt* "Baʿlu is dead!" (KTU 1.5 VI:9, 23; 1.6 I:6, 41). The form *ḥy* in KTU 1.6 III must therefore be interpreted in contrast to these pronouncements of Baʿlu's death. As for the context of these forms, the first occurs in the protasis of a conditional clause, the second in the corresponding apodosis, and the third in the subsequent narrated fulfillment of the condition. ʾIlu sets forth the condition whereby he might confirm that Baʿlu is alive—in a dream it will rain, thus verifying, albeit indirectly, the storm god's existence.

(2) *w hm* ***ḥy*** *ỉ[lỉyn bʿl]*	If the mighty Baʿlu **is alive**,
(3) *w hm ỉṯ zbl bʿ[l ỉrṣ]*[39]	if the Prince, lor[d of the earth], exists,
(4) *b ḥlm lṭpn ỉl d pỉd*	in a dream of the knowing one, the kindly god,
(5) *b ḏrt bny bnwt*	in a vision of the creator of creatures,
(6) *šmm šmn tmṭrn*	the heavens will rain oil,
(7) *nḫlm tlk nbtm*	the torrents will flow with honey,
(8) *w ỉdʿ k* ***ḥy*** *ỉlỉyn bʿl*	then I will know that mighty Baʿlu **is alive**,
(9) *k ỉṯ zbl bʿl ỉrṣ*	that the Prince, lord of the earth, exists.

Lines 10–13 are a repeat of lines 4–7 as the narrative recounts the actualization of ʾIlu's stated condition. Lines 14–21 express ʾIlu's delight in verifying by vision that Baʿlu is alive:

(14) *šmḫ lṭpn ỉl d pỉd*	The knowing one, the kindly god, is rejoicing,
(15) *pʿnh l hdm yṯpd*	his feet he rests on the footstool,
(16) *w yprq lṣb w yṣḥq*	he unfurrows his brow and laughs,
(17) *yšủ gh w yṣḥ*	he lifts up his voice and cries out:
(18) *ỉṯbn ỉnk w ỉnḫn*	I myself will return and rest,
(19) *w tnḫ b ỉrty npš*	my *npš* will rest in my chest,
(20) *k* ***ḥy*** *ỉlỉyn bʿl*	for mighty Baʿlu **is alive**,
(21) *k ỉṯ zbl bʿl ỉrṣ*	the Prince, lord of the earth, exists.

An important feature of these attestations of *ḥy* is the appearance of the parallel *ỉṯ*. The nature of the form *ỉṯ* appears to be a particle denoting existence

39. Lines 2–3 reconstructed from lines 8–9.

(cf. Hebrew *yēš*, Phoenician *yš*, Aramaic *ʾyty*, Arabic *laysa* "not to be," Akkadian *išû* "to have").[40] Followed by the preposition *l* with a pronominal suffix this form indicates possession (lit.: X is to Y).[41] Given the fact that {ḥy} occurs in parallel with the quasiverb *iṯ*, I have analyzed it as a G stem 3ms SC, and thus yields another datum in support of the suggestion that the G stem root was *ḥyy* and not *ḥwy*.[42]

From the content of ʾIlu's dream, I conclude that it is not the personal appearance of Baʿlu that verifies his existence; rather, it is the effects of his personhood as demonstrated in the rainfall that indicates that Baʿlu is no longer dead.[43] The parallel *ḥy* "he is alive" // *iṯ* "he exists" does not mean that *iṯ* is simply a synonym for *ḥy* in Ugaritic, but instead functions as a qualifier for what ʾIlu means in expressing that Baʿlu is alive. That these terms do not always mean the same thing is evident from the ʾAqhatu cycle where *iṯ* describes the remains of the hero, whether or not they "exist" inside the falcons that had devoured him. Baʿlu frantically goes about to see if any fat or bones of ʾAqhatu remained inside the stomach of the falcons: *hm iṯ šmt hm iṯ ʿẓm* "if there be fat, if there be bones" (KTU 1.19 III:4, 19, 33, 39). His search leads him to find some of the *šmt* "fat" and *ʿẓm* "bones" of the hero, mind you the dead hero, which he later gives a proper burial. Returning to the Baʿlu cycle, the context of these three attestations of *ḥy* (KTU 1.6 III:2, 8, 20) suggests that being *ḥy* "alive" is equated with the existence

40. Hebrew: BDB, 441; *HALOT*, 443; Phoenician: *DNWSI*, 472; Aramaic: *DNWSI*, 50; Arabic: Lane, 2684; Akkadian: *CAD* 7:289. Note that Tropper has taken things a step further, arguing that *iṯ* is essentially a finite verb from the root ʾ-ṯ-y "to be" (*Ugaritische Grammatik*, 2nd ed., 819–20). In his review of Tropper's grammar Pardee has criticized this particular assessment, e.g., noting the instance in KTU 1.19 where *iṯ* is modified by a feminine noun, yet without the expected feminine *-t* suffix: *hm iṯ šmt hm iṯ ʿẓm* "if there be fat, if there be bone" (KTU 1.19 III:4) (review *of Ugaritische Grammatik*, 231).

41. E.g., KTU 1.3 III:21; 2.70:29.

42. Admittedly, one could also analyze *ḥy* as an adjectival form given the fact that its parallel *iṯ* is not a finite verb. In the contrasting reports of Baʿlu's death, however, one finds *mt*—also potentially the 3ms of the G SC or an adjective—parallel with the verbal form *ḫlq* "to perish" (KTU 1.5 VI:9–10), which suggests that *mt* should be taken as a verbal form rather than the adjective (see my discussion in ch. 3 [§3.2.1.2]).

43. This observation lends further support for the so-called "seasonal pattern" motif that has been suggested by some scholars to stand behind these narratives. (The so-called "seasonal pattern" has recently been expressed by Bordreuil and Pardee in their *Manual of Ugaritic*, 16–17. Wyatt has been a persistent critic of this standard viewpoint, calling it "entirely farfetched" [Nicolas Wyatt, "The Religious Role of the King in Ugarit," in *Ugarit at Seventy-Five*, ed. K. Lawson Younger Jr. (Winona Lake, IN: Eisenbrauns, 2007), 43].) In this passage, the sole means of ʾIlu determining that Baʿlu is indeed alive is to observe the return of rainfall. What is noticeably absent from these narratives (though one should be cautious in drawing firm conclusions due to the damaged portions of the Baʿlu cycle) is any mention of Baʿlu personally presenting himself to ʾIlu in the event of his return to life. His personal presence is only felt indirectly through the effects of nature.

of behavior associated with one's personality, in this instance, the character of Baʿlu as the personal storm god. As the example from the ʾAqhatu Legend shows, *ḥy* is more than the "existence" of mere flesh and bone. To put it another way, being alive is shown through the existence of personal activity.

Moving along to the PC of this stem, there are two attestations in the mythological texts, the first being KTU 1.16 of the Kirta Epic. The appearance of the 3ms PC of the G stem here occurs with the negative particle and is parallel with the root m-t "do die." There are two instances of this construction in this text, the first being KTU 1.16 I:23:

(20) *i̇ km yrgm bn i̇l*	O thus he is called a son of ʾIlu;
(21) *krt šph̩ ltpn*[44]	Kirta is the offspring of the knowing and holy one.
(22) *wqdš*	
u̇ i̇lm tmtn	Do gods die?
(23) *šph̩ ltpn* ***l yh̩***	Would the offspring of the knowing one **not live**?[45]

These two questions appear again in 1.16 II:43–44 word-for-word. In these two instances, the negated G PC form is used to express the opposite of living: not continuing to live, or ceasing to be alive.

The form *yḥ* occurs in KTU 1.12, but it has typically not been identified with the root *ḥyy* in the scholarly discussion of this text. The main focus of the text is on recounting the conflict between Baʿlu and the devourers. Scholars have noted its affinities to the theogony in KTU 1.23 based upon the similarity between the devourers of 1.12 and the gluttonous goodly gods born to the two wives of ʾIlu in 1.23.[46] The first column of 1.12 begins with a description of the voracious appetite of the devourers and then commences to introduce Baʿlu on the hunt for them. Column II is badly broken, but toward the end presents Baʿlu as fallen (*npl* [II:53]) after his conflict with the devourers. The second column will be of importance for my lexical analysis of death later in the book (i.e., the expression *npl* "to fall"), but for now, I should note the occurrence of *yḥ* in line 35. The broader context is given below:

44. On the meaning of this word, see Tropper and Hayajneh, "El, der scharfsinnige und verständige Gott," 156–82. This interpretation appears preferable to the earlier rendering "benevolent" (see *DUL*, 507).

45. On the interpretation of the apocopated forms of this root, see the earlier discussion in this chapter (§1.2).

46. See Nicolas Wyatt, *Myths of Power: A Study of Royal Myth and Ideology in Ugaritic and Biblical Tradition*, UBL 13 (Münster: Ugarit-Verlag, 1996), 220–31; Wyatt, *Religious Texts from Ugarit: The Words of Ilimilku and His Colleagues* (Sheffield Academic Press, 1998), 162.

(28) *ỉl ypʿr* (29) *šmthm*	ʾIlu proclaims their names.
(30) *bhm qrnm* (31) *km ṯrm*	On them are horns like oxen,
w gbṯt (32) *km ỉbrm*	and humps like bulls.
(33) *w bhm* [[*b*]]*pn bʿl*[47]	And the face of Baʿlu was on them.
(34) *bʿl ytlk w yṣd*	Baʿlu walks about and hunts;
(35) ***yḫ*** *pảt mlbr*[48]	**He approaches** the edge of the desert.
(36) [[*n*]]*wn*[49] *ymǵy ảlkm*	And look, he comes to the devourers,
(37) *w ymẓả ʿq*[[*m*]]*qm*	and he encounters the destroyers.
(38) *bʿl ḥmdm yḥmdm*	Baʿlu indeed desires (them);
(39) *bn dgn yhrrm*	the son of Dagan becomes inflamed about (them).
(40) *bʿl ngṯhm b pʿnh*	Baʿlu approaches them on foot,
(41) *w ỉl hd b ḫrẓʿh*[50]	and the god Haddu on (his) paw[?].

47. The meaning of the expression *bhm pn bʿl* has been understood in different ways. Wyatt (*Religious Texts*, 164) understands the *b* preposition to indicate interest, i.e., that "Baal shows an interest in them." In a similar fashion, though with a different interpretive outcome, André Caquot, Maurice Sznycer, and Andrée Herdner (*Textes ougaritiques Tome I: Mythes et légendes*, LAPO 7 [Paris: Cerf, 1974], 341 n. o) think the expression means that Baʿlu was advancing "against" the devourers. Conversely, Johannes C. de Moor has argued that it somehow refers to the devourers' facial resemblance to Baʿlu, i.e., they literally had a face like his and were therefore hybrid creatures, "bulls with an anthropoid face" (*An Anthology of Religious Texts from Ugarit*, Religious Texts Semitic Studies Series 6 [Leiden: Brill, 1987], 131). H. L. Ginsberg ("Baʿlu and his Brethren," *JPOS* 16 [1936]: 144) interpreted the text similarly, "and upon them shall be the face of Baʿlu," though the textual grounds for a quasivolitive translation are unfounded. Cf. Gregorio del Olmo Lete, *Mitos y leyendas de Canaan*, Feuntes de la Ciencia Bíblica 1 (Madrid: Ediciones Cristianidad, 1981), 482. I am inclined to follow the latter suggestions on contextual grounds, since the preceding lines describe the devourers' bull-like features that would naturally lead to the comparison with Baʿlu to follow. Furthermore, it would result in two parallel statements introduced by *bhm*.

48. Scribal error for *mdbr*.

49. Possibly conjunction *w* + the presentative particle *hn* with apocopated {h}. On this particle, see Wilfred G. E. Watson, "Comments on Ugaritic *wn*," *AuOr* 12 (1994): 229–32, with references. For earlier references, see Dennis Pardee, "Ugaritic Bibliography," *AfO* 34 (1987): 394

50. Uncertain etymology. The major difficulty involves the fourth letter {ẓ}, etymologically *ṣ*, *d*, or *ẓ* (Pardee, "Ugaritic Bibliography," 388). *DUL*, 409; cf. Syriac *karsūʿō* "joint" (*SL*, 656), Arabic *kursūʿ* "the prominent extremity of the ulna, next to the little finger at the wrist" (Lane, 2999), and Akkadian *kursinnu* "lower leg (of animals or humans)" (*CAD* 8:566). Caquot and Sznycer (*Textes Ougaritiques* 1, 343 n. w) cite Arabic *ḫarîd* "serrated tooth of a lion." The problem with these etymologies, however, is that the semantics of the cited forms do not correspond well with the meaning of *ḫrẓʿ* in its context here, parallel to *pʿn* "foot." Wyatt (following de Moor, *Anthology of Religious Texts*, 131) renders it "on tip-toe" (*Religious Texts*, 164), but does so solely on the basis of context without recourse to etymology. The sense of the passage would lead us in this direction, but with unknown etymological bases.

The interpretive problem for my interests in this chapter concerns the meaning of the form *yḥ* in line 35. It has been suggested that the root underlying this form must be that of w-ḥ-y, proposed by Theodor Gaster for *twtḥ* in KTU 1.3 III:20, presumably a Gt stem.[51] He appeals to the Arabic root w-h-y and its connotation of "hasten," or "walk quickly," for which Umberto Cassuto notes further confirmation in its parallel *tlsmn* (KTU 1.3 III:19) from the root l-s-m meaning "to run, hurry."[52] The form is attested elsewhere in the mythological texts, all of which are in the Gt stem.[53] This interpretation seems to be the one favored by many interpreters without comment.[54] An alternative to this view is to suggest that the root for *yḥ* in KTU 1.12 is n-ḥ-y meaning "to proceed (toward)."[55] For this etymology scholars have appealed to the Arabic root *naḥā*, "to move toward," or "to purpose" or "intend" something, as well as the Hebrew verb *nḥh*, "to lead, guide."[56]

These suggestions are not without problems. As it relates to the suggested root w-ḥ-y, the fact that all other forms thus far attested at Ugarit are in the Gt stem with this meaning may constitute a negative argument, but, admittedly, not necessarily a strong one. The Ugaritic evidence for the second proposed etymology (√n-ḥ-y) is scantier, the only other suggested attestation being in KTU 1.19 I:18: *prʿ qẓ yḥ*, rendered by del Olmo Lete and Sanmartín, "the firstfruit(s) of the summer (fruit) will shrivel" (apparently with uncertainty).[57] Virolleaud read the form more cautiously, reconstructing *y*[*bl*(?)],presumably from the root y-b-l meaning "to bear, carry."[58] According to his own collation of the text, however,

51. Theodor H. Gaster, "Ugaritic Mythology," *JNES* 7 (1948): 189.

52. Umberto Cassuto, האלה ענת (Jerusalem: Bialik Institute, 1951); English edition: *The Goddess Anath: Canaanite Epics of the Patriarchal Age*, trans. Israel Abrahams (Jerusalem: Magnes, 1971), 126–27. See also *DUL*, 504.

53. Cf. KTU 1.1 III:11, 1.3 IV:56; reconstructed for 1.1 II:2, 23.

54. E.g., de Moor, *Anthology of Religious Texts*, 131.

55. See Tropper, *Ugaritische Grammatik*, 2nd ed., 661, "to turn around, go away" ("sich wenden zu, weggehen"; cf. 144, 626). Cf. Wyatt, *Religious Texts*, 164: "and he came to the edge of the desert"; del Olmo Lete, *Mitos y leyendas de Canaan*, 482 (citing the root *n/yḥy*, thus apparently undecided and simply translates: "headed toward" ["se dirigió hacia"]).

56. For Arabic: Lane, 3029. The idea of a purposeful move toward the edge of the desert would work semantically if we take the previous statement concerning Baʿlu's face being on the devourers in line 33 (*w bhm pn bʿl*) to mean that Baʿlu intentionally set out to hunt them. However, as noted earlier, this interpretation would ignore the parallelism of the physical descriptions of these divine entities: *bhm qrnm // bhm pn bʿl*. For Hebrew: BDB, 634.

57. Reading according to *CAT*, but in *KTU* Dietrich, Loretz, and Sanmartín read *yḥ**. *DUL*, 629.

58. Charles Virolleud, *La légende phénicienne de Danel publiée d'après les tablette de Ras-Shamra, avec une introduction à l'étude de la civilisation d'Ugarit*, BAH 21, MRS 2 (Paris: Geuthner, 1936), 125. This reading is favored by Herdner in a footnote (*CTA* 19 I:18 n. 6), but in her transcription

Pardee contends that {ḥ} here is unlikely: the sign after {y} begins with two vertical wedges, rendering either of the above readings unlikely.[59] At any rate, the evidence for the root n-ḥ-y at Ugarit is meager at best. In terms of semantics, the Arabic evidence offers an appropriate correspondence for the context of KTU 1.12, "to move toward," though there seems to be an additional nuance of intention or purpose that would not be as suitable to the context here. The Hebrew evidence for the semantics of the root is not helpful for the proposed meaning of Ugaritic n-ḥ-y, since the notion of leading or guiding would be nonsensical contextually. Admittedly, the Arabic evidence for *naḥā* renders interpreting the form as such in 1.12 at least plausible, but not conclusive.

The root ḥ-y-y is attested in Ugaritic, as in the case of the G stem SC form *ḥytn* in KTU 5.10:2 and 5.11:3 noted above.[60] Morphologically speaking, it is tempting to interpret *yḥ* here in KTU 1.12 as another form of the root ḥ-y-y, which would avoid the morphological, etymological, and semantic problems of the aforementioned suggestions. From the narrative context, however, it is difficult—if not impossible—to defend. For this reason, I have interpreted *yḥ* as being derived from the root *nḥy* on the basis of Arabic *naḥā* "to move towards, approach," thus excluding *yḥ* as an attestation of *ḥyy*.

There are a few additional occurrences of the G stem worth mentioning briefly before moving on to the D stem. The first two appear in conjunction with *npš*:

KTU 1.17 I:36–37

[*mt h*]*rnmy npš* ***yḥ*** *dnỉl*	As for (his) *npš*, **may** DNỈL, man of HRNMY **live**;
[*mt rp*]*ỉ brlt ǵzr*	As for (his) *brlt*, may the hero, man of RPỈ (live).

KTU 1.19 IV:36

npš ***tḥ*** *pǵ*[*t*]	As for (her) *npš*, **may** PǴT **live**.

I consider these two passages in the following chapter where I analyze the terms *npš* and *brlt* in detail. Suffice it to say here that the form in each of these cases appears to be a jussive expressing the desire for the addressee's life to continue. The G stem PC also occurs in KTU 1.82:34: *w tḥ ṭbt*, possibly, "may you live in

she simply reads *y*[--]. In the photograph provided in *CTA* (Pl. XXIX) it is difficult to make out anything beyond the {y}. *DUL*, 948–49.

59. Pers. comm.

60. Cf. the following PC forms: KTU 1.16:23; 1.17 I:36; 2.7:9; 6.30:1.

good health."[61] Unfortunately, this portion of the tablet is too broken to make sense of the context. Finally, the G stem appears on a brief ivory inscription, probably another jussive expressing a wish for the continued existence of the honoree, this time in contrast to the G stem PC of the root m-t. The inscription in its entirety is as follows (KTU 6.30):

yḥ w l ymt **May he live** and not die.[62]

1.2.2. The D Stem

Following the analysis of Marcus, the morphological feature of the D stem that differentiates it from the G is its spelling with medial {w}.[63] This feature of the Ugaritic distribution of this root distinguishes it from its Northwest Semitic cognates where the evidence is mixed without semantic distinction.[64] As for the meaning of the D stem in Ugaritic, it expresses the factitive of the G stem, namely, "to bring about a living state." The various nuances of the D stem are more difficult to ascertain contextually, however.[65] In some passages, scholars have suggested it denotes a continuation of the state of being alive (i.e., "to keep alive"), while in others it seems to denote the sense of restoration or renewal (i.e., "to return to life"). In the following discussion, I aim mainly to analyze the various contexts wherein the D stem occurs in an attempt to refine further our understanding of the factitive meaning of ḥ-w-y in Ugaritic.

In turning attention to these instances of the D stem *ḥwy*, I first examine one of the more exegetically exercised texts from the Ugaritic epic literature. The story of ʾAqhatu is a favorite in the scholarly literature for its interest in matters of immortality, specifically as it relates to ʿAnatu's offer of a Baʿlu-kind of existence

61. Following Gregorio del Olmo Lete, "KTU 1.82: Another Miscellaneous Incantation/Anti-Witchcraft Text against Snakebite in Ugaritic," *AuOr* 29 (2011): 248.

62. Reedited by Dennis Pardee in J. Gachet and Dennis Pardee, "Les ivoires du Palais Royal (fouille 1955)," in *Études ougaritiques I: Travaux 1985–1995*, ed. Margerite Yon and Daniel Arnaud, RSO 14 (Paris: Éditions Recherche sur les Civilisations, 2001), 202–3 (with less certainty as to reading).

63. Marcus, "The Verb 'to Live' in Ugaritic," 76–82.

64. Cf. Biblical Hebrew: medial {y} in all attested stems (G, D, and C) (*HALOT*, 309–10; BDB, 310–11); Phoenician/Punic: medial {w} in attested stems (D and C) (*DNWSI*, 354–55) (though Marcus ["The Verb 'to Live' in Ugaritic," 79] appeals to the proper name *yḥmlk* [/yḥîmilk/] as evidence for medial {y} in the G); Imperial Aramaic: medial {y} in all attested stems (G and C) (*DNWSI*, 355); Syriac: medial {y} in all attested stems (G, D/tD, and C) (Payne Smith, 139; *SL*, 446–47).

65. Note that *DUL* (379) lists the meaning of the D stem as follows: "to give (back) life/revive, leave alive, resuscitate."

to the hero ʾAqhatu. However, the initial stage of my investigation shall remain lexical, leaving literary matters to be taken up at a later point in the book. With this in mind, the D stem (*ḥwy*) appears in each of the three tablets of the ʾAqhatu story: KTU 1.17 VI:30, 32; 1.18 IV:13, 27; and 1.19 I:16. I deal with these passages successively, each with its own transcription, translation, and discussion of the broader context of the attested forms. Following my discussion of these verses from ʾAqhatu, I will then mention a few other passages where this root also appears in the D stem.

1.2.2.1. KTU 1.17 VI:16–38

(16) [*tšủ gh*] *w tṣḥ*	[She lifts up her voice] and cries:
šmʿ mʿ (17) [*l ảqht ǵzr*	"Listen, O valiant ʾAqhatu.
ỉ]*rš ksp w ảtnkʾ*	Ask for silver and I will give (it to) you,
(18) [*ḫrṣ wảš*]*lḥk*	[gold and I will gr]ant (it to) you.
w tn qštk ⸢*l*⸣[66] (19) [*ʿnt*	But give your bow to [ʿAnatu;
tq]*ḥ*[67][*q*]*ṣʿtk ybmt lỉmm*	let] the sister-in-law of Liʾmu [ta]ke your arrows."
(20) *w yʿn ảqht ǵzr*	And the valiant ʾAqhatu replies:
ảdr ṯqbm (21) *b lbnn*	"The strongest[68] are the ash trees in Lebanon,

66. *CTA* reads (?)[*l*]. *CAT* reads *ʿm* without any indication of reconstruction, but according to the photographs in *CTA* the tablet appears damaged at the end of the line. The reading *ʿm* offered by *CAT* is not the typical way the verb *ytn* marks an indirect object, which is almost always introduced with the *l* preposition. Note the following example from tablet 19 of the ʾAqhatu story recounting the context here: *ảp qšth l ttn ly* "Also, his bow he did not give to me" (KTU 1.19 I:16) (for additional references, see Richard Whitaker, *A Concordance of the Ugaritic Literature* [Cambridge: Harvard University Press, 1972], 323–25). The combination *ytn* + *ʿm*, on the other hand, is reserved for the special idiom *ytn pnm ʿm* X "he set the face toward X," as in the e.g., *l ytn pn ʿm bn ỉl mt* "Indeed, they set their faces toward the son of ʾIlu, Môtu" (KTU 1.5 II:14) (for additional references, see Whitaker, *Concordance*, 324–25). For this reason, the reading of *CTA* seems preferable, perhaps reconstructing a word divider preceding the *l*.

67. Favoring *CTA* since the markings in the photograph appear to resemble the lower wedge of a {ḥ}. *CAT* conversely reads [*btlt*] *ʿn*[*t*], but I am unable to make out any trace of an {n} here (see *CTA*, pl. XXVII).

68. The most common interpretation of these lines is to take *ảdr* as the *qātil* adjective, functioning here as a superlative: "the mightiest of X" (Caquot and Sznycer, *Textes ougaritiques 1*, 431; del Olmo Lete, *Mitos y leyendas*, 377; Wyatt, *Religious Texts*, 272). Tropper (*Ugaritische Grammatik*, 2nd ed., 313) follows the standard interpretation, but simply notes that in the fourth cola the syntax varies. Pardee (*COS* 1:346) interprets *ảdr* here and in the following occurrences as a 1cs verb of the root n-d-r "to vow": "I'll vow ash-wood from Lebanon." The problem with this usual interpretation appears in the last line of the series, *ảdr b ǵl ỉl qnm* (line 23), where the construct phrase would be split by *b ǵl ỉl*. In this case, neither can *ảdr* simply function as an attributive adjective for *qnm* due to the absence of a final {m} on *ảdr*, which has led some to emend the text (e.g., *DUL* [318]: *ảdr* <*qnm*> *b ǵl ỉl* {*qnm*}). De Moor (*Anthology of Religious Texts*, 237) also sees the problem with interpreting these as constructs and takes *ảdr* as a G stem SC from the root *ʾdr* "to be great,

ảdr gdm b rủmm	the strongest are the sinews of wild bulls,
(22) *ảdr qrnt b yʿlm*	strongest are the horns of the mountain-goats,
mtnm (23) *b ʿqbt ṯr*	the tendons from the hocks of bulls,
ảdr b ǵl ỉl qnm	the strongest are the reeds in ǴL ỈL.
(24) *tn l kṯr w ḫss*	Give (these) to Kôṯar-wa-Ḫasīsu.
ybʿl qšt l ʿnt	Let him make a bow for ʿAnatu,
(25) *qṣʿt l ybmt lỉmm*	arrows for the sister-in-law of Liʾmu."
w tʿn btlt (26) *ʿnt*	And the girl ʿAnatu replies:
ỉrš ḥym l ảqht ǵzr	"Request life, O valiant ʾAqhatu.
(27) *ỉrš ḥym w ảtnk*	Request life and I will give (it to) you;
bl mt (28) *w ảšlḥk*	not dying and I will grant (it to) you.
***a**šsprk ʿm bʿl* (29) *šnt*	I will make you count years with Baʿlu;
ʿm bn ỉl tspr yrḫm	with the son of ʾIlu you will count months,
(30) *k bʿl k **yḥwy***	like Baʿlu when **he is revived**.
yʿšr ḥwy[69]	They prepare a feast; he is revived.
yʿš(31)*r w yšqynh*	They prepare a feast and give him drink.
ybd[70] *w yšr ʿlh* (32) *nʿm*[*n*[71]	The goodly one improvises and sings on his behalf,

excellent": "The ash trees from the Lebanon are excellent." Though this proposal is tempting, the fact that a G stem for de Moor's root *ʾdr* occurs nowhere else in Ugaritic (not even in Hebrew! [see BDB, 12; *HALOT*, 16]) makes this suggestion unsustainable. The appeal of Pardee's proposal is that it avoids emendation, but Wyatt's (*Religious Texts*, 272 n. 104) criticism that this interpretation would strangely necessitate ʾAqhatu supplying these materials seems plausible contextually, but not insurmountable. As Wyatt also points out, the same problem persists for Giovanni Garbini's ("Il verbo adr in Ugaritico," *OrAnt* 29 [1990]: 57–62) appeal to Phoenician *ʾzr* "to cut" and Fred Renfroe's (*Arabic-Ugaritic Lexical Studies*, ALASP 5 [Münster: Ugarit-Verlag, 1992], 35 n. 21) appeal to Aramaic *dry* "to carry, bring," since in these proposals ʾAqhatu would again provide the materials (both cited favorably in Watson, "Ugaritic Lexical Studies," 220). In light of these considerations, I have opted to interpret *ảdr* as a predicate adjective: "mighty are the ash trees . . . mighty are the sinews . . . , etc." According to my interpretation, ʾAqhatu is pointing out the unique strength of these materials as a means of convincing ʿAnatu that they could be fashioned into a formidable weapon, thus deflecting her attention from his coveted bow. This interpretation seems to pose the least amount of difficulty etymologically, syntactically, and contextually.

69. Note the switch to the SC, which would appear to emphasize the single act of being revived as a whole. This contrasts the surrounding PC forms describing the feasting and drinking in progress.

70. Possibly a final weak root b-d-y, "to improvise (a song)" (so Caquot and Sznycer, *Textes ougaritiques* 1, 432). Cf. Hebrew *bdʾ* "to devise, invent (in a negative sense)" (BDB, 94; *HALOT*, 109); Syriac, *bdy* "to invent, speak falsely, invent" (Payne-Smith, 35; *SL*, 119); Arabic *badaʾa* "to begin" (Lane, 163), *badaha* "to come upon suddenly" (Lane, 169). Others suggest a geminate root b-d-d meaning "to talk idly," which in this context might indicate "chanting" (so del Olmo Lete, *Mitos y leyendas*, 378; Pardee, *COS* 1:347; Wyatt, *Religious Texts*, 273). Cf. Hebrew *bad* (< *bdd* II) "idle talk" (BDB, 95; *HALOT*, 109); Syriac *bdd* "to be confounded, disordered" (*SL*, 118).

71. Cf. KTU1.3 I:9–19.

w] *ʿnynn*[72]	[and I] answer him.
*ảp ảnk **ảḥwy*** (33) *ảqht* [*ǵ*]*zr*	**I** myself can also **revive** the [va]liant ʾAqhatu."
w yʿn ảqht ǵzr	And the valiant ʾAqhatu replied:
(34) *ảl tšrgn y btltm*	"Do not entangle me, girl,
dm l ǵzr (35) *šrgk ḫḫm*[73] *mt*	for your entanglings are a snare to a valiant man.
ủḫryt mh yqḥ	As for the last destiny, what can one receive?
(36) *mh yqḥ mt ảṯryt*	What can a man receive hereafter?
spsg[74] *ysk* (37) [*l*] *riš*	They will pour *spsg* [on] (my) head,
ḥrṣ[75] *l ẓr qdady*	*ḥrṣ* on the top of my cranium.
(38) [*ảp*]*mt kl amt*	I [also] will die the death of all;
w ản mtm ảmt	and I myself must certainly die."

This passage constitutes the heart of the story as the goddess ʿAnatu attempts to obtain through coercion and bartering the desirable bow crafted by

72. Pardee, in examining the tablet more closely, believes that the available space in the break is too small for a three-letter restoration (as *CAT*: nʿm[n . w y]ʿnynn; and *CTA*: nʿm[n . wt]ʿnynn), opting for the restoration of the word divider plus one sign after the {n}: [n. w]ʿnynn (*COS* 1:103), with the second form parsed as a 1cs PC. There is fairly broad agreement that the sequence /ʾ/ . . . /ʿ/ would have gone to /ʿ/ in Ugaritic (see David T. Tsumura, "Vowel *sandhi* in Ugaritic," in *Near Eastern Studies Dedicated to H. I. H. Prince Takahito Mikasa on the Occasion of His Seventy-Fifth Birthday*, ed. Masao Mori, Hideo Ogawa, and Mamoru Yoshikawa, BMECCJ 5 (Wiesbaden: Harrassowitz, 1991], 428–31 and Tropper, *Ugaritische Grammatik*, 2nd ed., 157).

73. The three principal interpretations of this word are: (1) "briar, bramble, hook" (cf. Hebrew *ḥôªḥ*); (2) "pit, hole" (cf. Arabic *ḫawḫat* "hole" [Caquot and Sznycer, *Textes ougaritiques 1*, 220 n. g (also appealing to Hebrew *ḥôªḥ* in 1 Sam. 13:6)]); and (3) "mud, mire, filth" (cf. Akkadian *ḫaḫû/ḫuḫû* [*CAD* 6:30–31, 225]).

74. A consensus on this Ugaritic term has not yet been reached. The latest proposal is that of Erich Neu ("Hethitisch zapzagi-," *UF* 27 [1995]: 395–402) who appeals to Hittite /zapzagi-/ for it being a precious mineral or stone. Pardee (*COS* 1:347 n. 46) points out that this term also occurs in an administrative text (*PRU* II, 106:8) with other words for semiprecious stones. This might lend further credibility to Neu's proposal. H. L. Ginsberg ("The North-Canaanite Myth of Anath and Aqhat, II" *BASOR* 98 [1945]: 22 n. 55) suggested the translation "glaze" and connected this term with the problematic occurrence of *ksp sygym* in Prov 26:23 (offering the emendation: *k-spsyg* "like glaze"). He argued that the pouring of such a glaze on the head might be a metaphor of old age, citing the sprinkling of hair in Hos 9:7 as a parallel (21 n. 56). William F. Albright ("The 'Natural' Force of Moses in the Light of Ugaritic," *BASOR* 92 [1944]: 33 n. 19) cited the Mesopotamian practice of pouring hot asphalt over the heads of criminals. Others have appealed to the Neolithic funerary practice of plastering the skulls of deceased ancestors (Caquot and Sznycer, *Textes ougaritiques 1*, 432–33 n. b; defended valiantly by Baruch Margalit, *The Ugaritic Poem of AQHT*, BZAW 182 [Berlin: de Gruyter, 1989], 307–10, 316–19), a view that has drawn significant criticism.

75. "White stuff" (Pardee, *COS* 1:347); "gold" (i.e., *ḫrṣ*, thus Wyatt, *Religious Texts*, 274). To some degree, our understanding of this term will depend on the interpretation of the problematic parallel *spsg*. If we take *spsg* as a kind of precious mineral, then *ḥrṣ* as a kind of precious material would work better. On the whole, however, the reading of *spsg* . . . *ḥrṣ* remains uncertain.

Kôṯar-wa-Ḫasīsu for the hero ʾAqhatu.[76] In terms of a broad overview of the story's content, the first three extant tablets recount Dānîʾilu's desire for a son, Baʿlu's intercession to ʾIlu on behalf of Dānîʾilu, ʾIlu's blessing Dānîʾilu with a son (ʾAqhatu), and Kôṯar-wa-Ḫasīsu's gift of a bow to Dānîʾilu for his son ʾAqhatu. Because of the broken nature of these tablets, important developments of the story remain unknown. One of these lacunae occurs in the lines leading up to this exchange between ʿAnatu and ʾAqhatu concerning his coveted bow, leaving the circumstances in which she sees the bow (line 10) not entirely clear.[77]

The 3ms PC of the D stem *yḥwy* occurs in line 30. In this context, ʿAnatu has just asked ʾAqhatu to give her his bow, evoking him to respond by listing a series of mighty materials from which she might construct her own bow. This leads ʿAnatu to make her offer more tantalizing, urging ʾAqhatu to ask her for *ḥym* "life" (see discussion below), which she would be able to grant in exchange for his bow. The D stem in this passage provides a means of explaining the kind of *ḥym* ʾAqhatu could enjoy if he were willing to assent to her wishes.

Does this form indicate a kind of revivification (i.e., a return from the dead) or does it involve a continually sustainable life? The expression *bl mt* (negative particle + G infinitive or common noun of √m-t = "not dying") in line 27, parallel with *ḥym*, would suggest that it is the preservation of life. For instance, Mark S. Smith explains that the parallel "life"//"nondeath" appears "to suggest the continuation of human life, and not life after death or immortality."[78] However, when one considers that the kind of "not dying" in view is defined by the experience of Baʿlu, who dies but does not remain dead, the sense of *yḥwy* must involve a continuation through revivification.[79] The factitive nuance for this stative root (i.e., "to be alive" or "in [the state of] existence") indicates an action that produces, reestablishes, or maintains the state of being alive, (i.e., "to make alive").[80]

Another issue that deserves attention here is the grammatical voice of this form. Many translators interpret *yḥwy* as an intransitive, thus rendering *k yḥwy*

76. Pardee (*COS* 1:343) calls this episode "the kernel of the story."

77. Most scholars agree that from the standard words for eating and drinking identified in the first fifteen lines of this column, ʿAnatu may have spied the bow at a feast (e.g., Caquot and Sznycer, *Textes ougaritiques 1*, 429–31; de Moor, *Anthology of Religious Texts*, 235–36; Pardee, *COS* 1:346; Wyatt, *Religious Texts*, 270 n. 90).

78. Mark S. Smith, *Poetic Heroes: Literary Commemorations of Warriors and Warrior Culture in the Early Biblical World* (Grand Rapids: Eerdmans, 2014), 109.

79. Note that in Biblical Hebrew, the D stem of *ḥyy* can denote both preservation (e.g., Gen 12:12 "let live") and revivification (e.g., 2 Kgs 8:1 "restore life"), but never at the same time.

80. On the meaning of the factitive in Biblical Hebrew, see Bruce K. Waltke and Michael O'Connor, *An Introduction to Biblical Hebrew Syntax* (Winona Lake, IN: Eisenbrauns, 1990), 396–404.

as roughly: "when he revives."[81] Others prefer to read it transitively, even without an explicit object, and believe that Baʿlu has the power to revive others—*k yḥwy*: "when he revives (X)."[82] Neither of these interpretations is entirely satisfactory, however. On the one hand, to take the form as an intransitive would in reality amount to some sort of reflexive due to the fact that the action would affect the subject. This interpretation is highly problematic for the D stem. If one compares the D of *ḥyh* in Biblical Hebrew, for example, all forms are accompanied by an explicit object, which only makes sense for *ḥyh*: a stative intransitive in the G stem "to be alive" is transitivized in the D stem: "to make X alive."[83] Of course, the passive stem, unattested for this root in Biblical Hebrew, could not take an object, and would thus be intransitive.[84]

The best way to explain the Ugaritic evidence might simply be to argue that the forms of *ḥwy* with an object suggest the active voice, while those without objects must instead denote a passive form.[85] For the passage I am investigating here, this makes good sense of the context. In lines 32–33, the active of the D stem occurs when ʿAnatu declares her power to revive the hero ʾAqhatu: *ảp ảnk ảḥwy ảqht [ǵ]zr* "I myself can even revive the valiant ʾAqhatu." Her promise of granting him the ability to count years, *k bʿl k yḥwy* "like Baʿlu when he is revived," would then most naturally read as a passive. Would this interpretation suggest that ʿAnatu somehow claims responsibility in Baʿlu's revivification?

This issue arises when one attempts to identify the meaning of the form *ḥwy* toward the end of line 30. Josef Tropper interprets it as a G participle /ḥāwiy-/.[86]

81. Pardee, *COS* 1:347: "when he comes (back) to life"; Tropper, *Ugaritische Grammatik*, 2nd ed., 550: "by granting (eternal) life" ("indem/wie er [ewiges] Leben gewährt"). Cf. the proposal of Wyatt (*Religious Texts*, 273) in taking the first *k* as comparative and the second as an emphatic: "Like Baal he shall live indeed," which seems less plausible to me.

82. Caquot and Sznycer, *Textes ougaritiques 1*, 433: "When Baʿal gives life" ("Quand Baʿal donne la vie"); de Moor, *Anthology of Religious Texts*, 238: "Just as when Baʿlu brings to life"; Klass Spronk, *Beatific Afterlife in Ancient Israel and the Ancient Near East*, AOAT 219 (Kevelaer: Butzon & Bercker; Neukirchen-Vluyn: Neukirchener Verlag, 1986), 151, 155: "when he brings to life."

83. Again, see the discussion in Waltke and O'Connor, *Biblical Hebrew Syntax*, 400–401. See also Stuart A. Ryder, *The D-Stem in Western Semitic*, Janua Linguarum 131 (Hague: Mouton, 1974), 92–93.

84. In Postbiblical Hebrew, the niphal, not the pual, is used for the passive of *ḥyh* in the sense of being resurrected from the dead (Jastrow, 454).

85. On the passive voice in Ugaritic, see Bordreuil and Pardee, *Manual of Ugaritic*, 47; and more specifically on the D passive, Tropper, *Ugaritische Grammatik*, 2nd ed., 567–70.

86. Tropper, *Ugaritische Grammatik*, 2nd ed., 666. Cf. also Meindert Dijkstra and Johannes C. de Moor, "Problematic Passages in the Legend of Aqhâtu," *UF* 7 (1975): 187, who read the form as a G participle, but translate "the reviving one prepares a feast." According to their interpretation, *ḥwy* refers to the one preparing a feast in a ritual associated with Baʿlu's resurrection. This kind of meaning for a G participle is untenable, as we would instead expect, "the living one." De Moor has apparently moved away from this earlier interpretation, as his translation in *Anthology of Religious Texts* would suggest: "(when) he [Baʿlu] has brought to life" (238).

Karel van der Toorn, on the other hand, follows an earlier suggestion that the text is corrupt due to dittography.[87] Nicolas Wyatt apparently interprets the form as an adjective ("Alive, he shall be feasted"), and similarly Pardee translates, "they give a feast to the living one."[88] Without immediately resorting to the scribal error argument put forth by van der Toorn, the G participle interpretation poses difficulty if we are to follow Marcus's theory that the medial {w} root was reserved for the D stem.[89] This consideration led André Caquot and Maurice Sznycer to interpret this form as a 3ms PC of the D stem: "he makes live."[90] As I have just considered above, the absence of a named object makes this proposal difficult, and therefore might suggest another D passive: "they gave a feast; he is revived. They gave a feast and gave him drink." Accordingly, ʿAnatu's words provide a further explanation of Baʿlu's revivification: unnamed participants prepare a feast, after which he is revived. The next clause explains the event more specifically: they prepare a feast and give Baʿlu drink, to which ʿAnatu claims to respond (line 32).[91] The issue here is not Baʿlu's ability to give life, but his ability to come back to life, which is exactly what ʿAnatu claims to be able to offer the hero ʾAqhatu. Van der Toorn is probably right in critiquing Klaas Spronk's desire to translate *k bʿl k yḥwy* "Just as Baal when he brings to life," but van der Toorn's desire to lessen its connection with the following clause introduced by *ảp* seems unnecessary, and even unwarranted contextually.[92] Rather, ʿAnatu appears to be claiming responsibility for Baʿlu's revivification and therefore offers ʾAqhatu the same prospect in exchange for his bow. After all, in the Baal cycle it is ʿAnatu who finds Baʿlu's body and has it brought to ṢPN for burial, which would seemingly corroborate with her claims of responsibility here.[93]

The last attestation of the D stem *ḥwy* in this passage shows up in the clause spanning lines 32–33: *ảp ảnk ảḥwy ảqht* [*ǵ*]*zr* "I myself can even revive the [va]liant ʾAqhatu." I have already considered this form briefly in my discussion

87. First proposed by Theodor H. Gaster, "The Story of Aqhat i," *SMSR* 12 (1936): 147 n. 2; followed by Karel van der Toorn, "Funerary Rituals and Beatific Afterlife in the Ugaritic Texts and in the Bible," *BO* 48 (1991): 46; and apparently del Olmo Lete, *Mitos y leyendas*, 377, representing this form as empty brackets in his translation. This view was rejected earlier by Caquot and Sznycer, *Textes ougaritiques 1*, 432 n. w.

88. Wyatt, *Religious Texts*, 273. Pardee, *COS* 1:347.

89. Marcus, "The Verb 'to Live' in Ugaritic," 78.

90. "Il fait vivre"; Caquot and Sznycer, *Textes ougaritiques 1*, 432.

91. I.e., if we maintain the reconstruction offered above instead of the usually proposed {y} of the 3ms (see note 72). There is contextual support for this reconstruction, however, in the clause immediately following: *ảp ảnk ảḥwy ảqht* [*ǵ*]*zr* "I myself can even revive the valiant ʾAqhatu." In other words, in much the same way that she answers the feast-givers in the revivification of Baʿlu, so too will she grant this kind of revival to ʾAqhatu.

92. Van der Toorn, "Funerary Rituals," 46. Spronk, *Beatific Afterlife*, 151, 155.

93. See KTU 1.6 I:15–16.

of the form *ḥwy* in line 30, but I should also qualify that it is the active voice of the D stem in light of the expressed object *ảqht* [*ǵ*]*zr*. The factitive meaning of the stative root *ḥwy* in this case would seem to denote the preservation of a living state. The comparison with Baʿlu's revivification emphasizes his continued existence through revivification, which ʿAnatu promises to do for ʾAqhatu: As Baʿlu continues to live on through revivification, so too will I preserve your life.

1.2.2.2. KTU 1.18 IV:12–27

(12) *šmʿ l btlt ʿnt*	"Listen, girl ʿAnatu.
ảt ʿ[*l qšth*] (13) *tmḫṣh*	You yourself must strike him f[or his bow];
qṣʿth hwt l ***t***⌜***ḥ***⌝[***wy***][94]	(for) his arrows **you** must not **let** that one **l**[**ive**].[95]
(14) *nʿmn ǵzr št ṯrm*[96]	The goodly warrior prepares a meal,
w[. . .] (15) *ỉštir b ḏdm*[97]	and [. . .] remains in tents,
w nʿrs[98][. . .]	and settles down [. . .]"

94. *CTA*: lt[ḥwy]; *KTU*: ltḥ*[wy]; *CAT*: ltḥ[wy]. According to InscriptiFact's color photographs of this tablet, the left-most portion of the horizontal wedge of the {ḥ} is visible.

95. Cf. Deut 20:16: *lōʾ tᵉḥayyê kōl-nᵉšāmâ* "you shall not let anything that breathes live" (lit.: "you shall not let any breath live").

96. Taking *ṯrm* from the Ugaritic root ṯ-r-m meaning "to cut" > "to eat" (*DUL*, 931) (so Caquot and Sznycer, *Textes ougaritiques 1*, 438; Pardee, *COS* 1:349 n. 69; Wyatt, *Religious Texts*, 283 n. 147). The occurrence of *l lḥm* // *l ṯrm* in line 19 strengthens the case for its existence here. Others opt for the interpretation "bulls" (< *ṯr* "bull") (e.g., del Olmo Lete, *Mitos y leyendas*, 384: "The goodly priest has prepared bulls" ["El Prócer Apuesto ha preparado toros"]). Furthermore, there is a difference of opinion concerning the subject of this action, Caquot and Sznycer understanding YṬPN to be a verb expressing the instruction for ʿAnatu to prepare a meal: "Prepare a meal" ("Apprête un repas")" taking *nʿmn ǵzr* with the preceding clause (*Textes ougaritiques 1*, 438; cf. Margalit, *Ugaritic Poem of AQHT*, 155, who takes *nʿmn ǵzr* with the preceding line, but still has ʾAqhatu preparing the feast). It seems to make better sense syntactically, however, to take *nʿmn ǵzr* as the subject of *št*, perhaps depicting ʾAqhatu feasting after a successful hunt (de Moor, *Anthology of Religious Texts*, 245; Pardee *COS* 1:349; Wyatt, *Religious Texts*, 283; David P. Wright, *Ritual in Narrative: The Dynamics of Feasting, Mourning, and Retaliation Rites in the Ugaritic Tale of Aqhat* [Winona Lake, IN: Eisenbrauns, 2001], 128)

97. Following Pardee (*COS* 1:245 n. 29, 349) and Richard J. Clifford (*The Cosmic Mountain in Canaan and the Old Testament*, HSM 4 [Cambridge: Harvard University Press, 1972], 51–53, 124–25).

98. Several suggestions have been made concerning the interpretation of this term. Earlier interpretations connected this form with Akkadian *erēšu* B "to plant" (see *CAD* 4:285–89) (e.g., G. R. Driver, *Canaanite Myths and Legends*, 1st ed., OTS 3 [Edinburgh: T&T Clark, 1956], 57, 141). Caquot and Sznycer (*Textes ougaritiques 1*, 438) render, "and we will make cakes" ("et nous ferons des gâteaux"; presumably from Postbiblical Hebrew *ʿrs* "to knead dough" [see Jastrow, 1120]). Others take the form to be a 1cs PC from the root ʿ-r-s, based upon Arabic *ʿarasa* "to prepare a wedding feast" (see Lane, 1998) (Dijkstra and de Moor, "Problematic Passages," 195; de Moor, *Anthology of Religious Texts*, 245), or simply, "to rejoice" (see *DUL*, 184; cf. del Olmo Lete, *Mitos y leyendas*, 384; Wyatt, *Religious Texts*, 284). Pardee (*COS* 1:349 n. 69) also appeals to Arabic *ʿarasa*, but singles out Lane's meaning # 1: "to bind," in Arabic, in the sense of binding the neck of a camel

(16) *w tʿn btlt ʿnt*	And girl ʿAnatu replies:
ṯb[99] *yṭp w*[. . .] *lk*	"Return, YṬP<N> and [. . .] you.
(17) *ảštk km nšr b ḥb*[*šy*]	I will set you like a hawk in [my] belt,
(18) *km diy b tʿrty*	like a bird in my quiver.
ảqht [*km yṯb*] (19) *l lḥm*	ʾAqhatu, [as he sits] to eat,
w bn dnil l ṯrm	the son of Dānîʾilu to feast,
[*ʿlh*] (20) *nšrm trḫpn*	[over him] hawks will hover,
ybṣr [*ḥbl d*](21)*iym*	the [flock of b]irds will keep watch.
bn nšrm ảrḫp ản[*k*]	Among the hawks, I myself will hover,
ʿl (22) *ảqht ʿdbk*	over ʾAqhatu positioning you.
hlmn ṯnm qdqd	Hit him twice on the head;
(23) *ṯlṯid ʿl ủdn*	three times over the ear.
špk km šiy[100] (24) *dm*	Pour out (his) blood like a *šiy*,
km šḫṭ l brkh	(his blood) on his knees like one slaughtering.
tṣỉ km (25) *rḥ npšh*	Let his *npš* go out like wind,
km iṯl brlth[101]	like spittle his *brlt*,
km (26) *qṭr b ảph*	like smoke from his nostrils.
ủ ảp mprh[102] *ảnk*	But then, **I** myself **will not allow** the soldier **to**
(27) ***l ảḥwy***	**live on**."

"to settle down" for the night (Lane, 1998). Jacob Hoftijzer also makes this etymological connection and translates: "[he] has made a halt" ("A Note on G 1083³: *ʾištʾir* and Related Matters," *UF* 3 [1971]: 363). The form itself would likely be an N-stem SC: "he settles down." This interpretation, though not conclusive, would make sense in the immediate context of *ištir b ḏdm* "remains in tents."

99. The precise meaning of *ṯb* is not entirely clear. On the one hand, the form could be from √y-ṯ-b meaning "to sit, dwell," and would suggest that ʿAnatu is telling YṬPN to sit down and listen to her plan for the demise of ʾAqhatu (thus Caquot and Sznycer, *Textes ougaritiques 1*, 438; Margalit, *Ugaritic Poem of AQHT*, 155; Pardee, *COS* 1:349). On the other hand, from a strictly formal analysis, we could be dealing with the hollow root ṯ-w-b, "to return," which might offer the sense of "pay attention" (del Olmo Lete, *Mitos y leyendas*, 384; Wright, *Ritual in Narrative*, 128; Wyatt, *Religious Texts*, 284). De Moor (*Anthology of Religious Texts*, 245) translates the expression quite literally: "Return, Yattupa, and [I shall return] to you." I find the contextual sense of the second option more difficult and have opted for interpreting the form to be from y-ṯ-b.

100. This word remains uncertain. Wilfred G. E. Watson appeals to the Akkadian cognate *šâʾu* "to fly" (though with metathesis; see *AHw* 3:1205) and interprets it as referring to a certain bird of prey ("Two Similes in *Aqht*," *UF* 23 [1991]: 360). Pardee cites the same root in Arabic, which means "to draw up mud from the bottom of a well," reading a participle here: "one emptying (a bucket)" (*COS* 1:350 n. 74). Others have understood this term to mean "murderer, assassin" on the basis of Arabic *sāʾa* "to hack," or more commonly "to revile" (see Lane, 1284) (Caquot and Sznycer, *Textes ougaritiques 1*, 438; de Moor, *Anthology of Religious Texts*, 245; del Olmo Lete, *Mitos y leyendas*, 384; *DUL*, 798; Wyatt, *Religious Texts*, 285). Though the majority of scholars adopt this last option, the semantics of the Arabic root do not exactly suggest "murderer" or "assassin."

101. A full study of this term is given in ch. 2 (§2.3).

102. Perhaps another scribal error to be read {mhrh} on the basis of its occurrence in line 38 (suggested by Pardee, *COS* 1:350 n. 75), being explained as the omission of one additional

The last few lines of ʿAnatu's speech to YṬPN have attracted the attention of interpreters interested in this predictive description of ʾAqhatu's sudden end. For my purposes here, I am primarily concerned with the two appearances of the root ḥ-w-y in the D stem. I will hold my comments on the significance of lines 24–26 for the next chapter where I probe the meaning of *npš* and its parallel *brlt*, and hopefully enhance our understanding of the Ugaritic view of life.

At first glance, the interpretation of this root in lines 13 and 27 appears to be straightforward, yet there seems to be a slightly different nuance for the D stem in this text than its counterparts in KTU 1.17. I must caution, however, that the first proposed attestation is reconstructed, the main discrepancy having to do with how much of the {ḥ} is still visible. Thankfully, the parallel in KTU 1.19 I:16 makes the reconstruction *l t*⸢*ḥ*⸣[*wy*] fairly certain.

The broader context of these forms presents ʿAnatu and YṬPN devising a plan to kill ʾAqhatu so that the goddess might acquire his coveted bow. In line 13, YṬPN advises ʿAnatu to strike the warrior with a fatal blow in order to seize his bow, adding: *qṣʿth hwt l t*⸢*ḥ*⸣[*wy*]. It becomes immediately clear in the translations that interpreters are reading this D stem in a permissive sense, i.e., "you must not *permit* that one to live on." As ʿAnatu sets forth her plan to put an end to the valiant warrior, she describes the smiting of his head, the pouring out of his blood, and the resulting exit of his *npš*, concluding: *ủ ảp mhrh ảnk l ảḥwy*, again usually translated something to the effect, "And so, I myself will not allow the soldier to live on" (line 27).[103] The connection between these uses of *ḥwy* and those from KTU 1.17 becomes clearer when one translates them as straightforward factitives: "I myself will not make the soldier live on." In other words, in light of the D stem in KTU 1.18 and the revivification of Baʿlu, ʿAnatu will kill ʾAqhatu. Death is certainly the fate of every man according to the hero himself (KTU 1.17 VI:38), but the offer of continual ("eternal"?) life through renewal is not only out of the question, the life he now lives is about to be cut short.[104]

horizontal wedge (Pardee's own collation of the text confirms the reading *mprh* [pers. comm.]). The literal meaning of *mhrh*, then, would be the abstract + 3ms suffix: "his soldier-status."

103. E.g., line 13: Caquot and Sznycer: "you will not let [live]" ("tu ne laisse [eras pas vivre]"; *Textes ougaritiques I*, 438); Pardee: "you will not [let] him [live]" (*COS* 1:349); Tropper: "you will/should let live" ("du wirst/sollst am Leben lassen"; *Ugaritische Grammatik*, 2nd ed., 195); Wyatt: "should not let him live" (*Religious Texts*, 283). Interestingly, del Olmo Lete translates the form to mean revivify, but in the positive: "that I will quicken him (from) prostration" ("que yo le vivificaré [de] su postración"; *Mitos y leyendas*, 384).

104. Margalit's perception on this point is worth noting briefly here, though I disagree with the direction of his interpretation. One might assume that he senses a problem in translating this form as "let live" as he remarks: "It ought to be clear from the context that the verb √*ḥwy* . . . cannot be analyzed as (G) 'to live' or (D) 'resurrect; bring back to life.'" Concerning line 27, he continues,

From the context of these forms, the meanings of these factitives must be viewed in light of ʿAnatu's promise to grant the hero a Baʿlu-kind of existence. Here, there are two possible outcomes for ʾAqhatu: (1) give up his bow in exchange for the promise of perpetual life through revivification like Baʿlu; or (2) keep his bow, forfeit the goddesses' offer, and suffer a premature death. In the latter sense, the goddess ʿAnatu does more than retract her gift; she brings about the opposite state for the hero—death. In this sense *l yḥwy* = *mt*.

The end of KTU 1.18 column IV recounts the actualization of ʿAnatu's premeditated murder of the hero (lines 29–42). Another form of the root *ḥwy* has been reconstructed at the end of line 41:

(40) *ảbn*[105] *ảnk*	I myself would have (re)built
w ʿl q[*štk mḫṣtk*][106]	But on account of [your bow I struck you]
(41) *qṣʿtk ảt **l ḥ***[***wt***...]	(for) your arrows, **you have not been permitted to l**[**ive**...]

Because of the damaged nature of the right side of this tablet, the interpretation of these lines remains provisionary. However, the appearance of {ḥ} just before the break in line 41 makes the reconstruction of some form of *ḥwy* all but certain, especially from the parallel statement to follow in KTU 1.19 I:15–16. The precise morphology of this root is the main concern here. The personal pronoun *ảt* and the negative *l* naturally lead to the conclusion that it is a SC verbal form, while the parallel expression in the following column would suggest the D stem.[107]

"The idea of resurrecting the victim whose murder she had so meticulously planned could never have crossed Anat's mind, certainly not at this stage of the plan" (*Ugaritic Poem of AQHT*, 335 n. 3). Positing a √*ḥwy* II meaning, "to dispossess," on the basis of an Arabic cognate, however, is unconvincing and unnecessary. Furthermore, his insistence on reading {l} as an asseverative is equally without basis, since the negative particle works perfectly fine contextually, not to mention the fact that Margalit's proposal requires emendation. Wright (*Ritual in Narrative*, 128 n. 6) agrees with Margalit that it should not be interpreted to mean "you shall bring (him) back to life."

105. Taking the form to be from the root b-n-y "to build" (Cyrus Gordon, *Ugaritic Literature: A Comprehensive Translation of the Poetic and Prose Texts* [Rome: Pontifical Biblical Institute, 1949], 93: "I shall repair"). Although Caquot and Sznycer follow this reading in *Textes ougaritiques 1* (440), André Caquot in a subsequent publication cautions against it and instead suggests the middle-weak root b-y-n "to understand" ("Une nouvelle interprétation de KTU 1.19 I 1–19," *SEL* 2 [1985]: 94; followed by Wyatt, *Religious Texts*, 287 n. 163).

106. Reconstructed on the basis of KTU 1.19 I:15–16.

107. Following Cyrus H. Gordon, *Ugaritic Textbook: Grammar, Texts in Transliteration, Cuneiform Selections, Glossary, Indices*, AnOr 38 (Rome: Pontifical Biblical Institute, 1965), 249 (followed by *CTA*); contra the reconstruction of *CAT*: ḥ[ytk] (cf. *KTU*: ḥ*[ ]). The problems with this reconstruction are twofold: (1) the fact that this form is preceded by *ảt* makes a 2ms suffix highly unlikely.

Keeping in mind the tentative nature of my remarks on these lines in light of the poor condition of the tablet, the interpretation I offer here meshes well with the broader context of the passage. Due to the repeated *w ʿl . . . qṣtk* we can reasonably assume some sort of restatement of the same formula found in lines 12–13 above, only this time it is in the mouth of ʿAnatu after the murder of ʾAqhatu. In essence, the form of *ḥwy* expresses ʿAnatu's "I told you so," even though some of the details from her speech remain unknown. Taking *ảbn* from the root b-n-y "to build," instead of the hollow root b-y-n "to understand," works well in light of the broader context: "I would have rebuilt you like Baʿlu, just as I promised, but on account of your bow and for your arrows you have not been permitted to live."[108] The irony of the whole affair is that ʾAqhatu did not simply reject the perpetual life ʿAnatu offered him; he chose death instead.

On another level, I must comment briefly on the motif of talking to a dead person. Why is ʿAnatu addressing the dead hero here? On the one hand this feature might simply function in the narrative rhetorically, almost as though she is speaking from a guilty conscience. Yet her words in KTU 1.19 I:12–17 (see below) are better understood in this way, where she laments her deeds against ʾAqhatu by referencing him in the third person. In this passage (KTU 1.18 IV:40–41), however, she addresses him directly in the second person: "on account of your arrows." It is possible that such a motif suggests that being "dead" from the Ugaritic worldview does not necessarily mean the termination of one's personal existence. Perhaps this example correlates with the tendency of people in the modern world to speak to their dead loved ones as though they are listening, presumably from one's belief in the perpetual existence of the departed somewhere. This idea is not so far removed from Ugarit, where Yammu and Baʿlu both die, but are able to reappear.[109] Perhaps this "reappearance" (or "revivification") is what ʾAqhatu believes to be the privilege of the gods, while a mere shadowy existence beyond the grave awaits all mortals.[110]

This would require interpreting the verbal form as a 1cs and taking the independent pronoun as a fronted object (problematic syntactically), while making the pronominal suffix resumptive. This reconstruction presents a rather complicated syntax. (2) Since the parallel rendition in KTU 1.19 I:15–16 attests the D stem *ảḥw*, I would be more inclined to see the same here.

108. Note also that for this interpretation, *ḥwt* would have to be a D passive. Note also the irony of these words, as if ʿAnatu places the blame squarely on the shoulders of ʾAqhatu for his own demise: "If you would only have given to me your bow, this would never have happened."

109. Cf. ʿAnatu's dismemberment of Môtu in KTU 1.6 II:31–35, though in this case the verb *mt* is not used to describe Môtu's resultant state.

110. I consider the term *rpủm* in ch. 4.

1.2.2.3. KTU 1.19 I:12–17a

Finally for the ʾAqhatu story, the D stem of *ḥwy* shows up again in KTU 1.19 at the beginning of the first column. A number of difficulties arise in the interpretation of the surrounding context of this particular attestation, but for the purposes of this discussion I will simply provide its immediate context (lines 12–17a):

(12) *ảqht yʿn k mr* <<*k mr*[?]>>[111]	ʾAqhatu was brought low like a bitter one,
(13) *k ảpʿ il b gdrt*	like a terrible viper in a wall,
klb l (14) *ḫṭh imḫṣh*	(as) a dog to its stake I struck him.
kd ʿl qšth (15) *imḫṣh*	For on account of his bow I struck him,
ʿl qṣʿth hwt (16) ***l ảḥw***	on account of his arrows, I **did not allow** that one **to live on.**
ảp qšth l ttn (17) *ly*	But his bow was not given to me.
[...]	[...]

The last few signs of line 17 are broken, leaving their interpretation uncertain. For the third and final time we find yet another version of the familiar refrain "for his bow . . . for his arrows," which already appeared in KTU 1.18 IV:12–13 and 40–41. Again, these words are spoken by the goddess ʿAnatu, only this time they follow what appears to be the loss of ʾAqhatu's bow that she killed to obtain (note especially lines 16–17a).[112] This 1cs PC of the D stem *ḥwy* in the negative, then, expresses the fact that the goddess did not revive ʾAqhatu; instead, she killed him and allowed him to remain dead.

1.2.2.4. KTU 1.24:10

Another PC form of the D stem occurs in a mythological text depicting the divine wedding of Nikkal and Ib. The first letter of the form has to be reconstructed (likely a prefixed {y}), but the remaining letters are clear: *-ḥwyn*. The context of this form is as follows:

(7) *hl ǵlmt tld b*⌜-⌝[-?]	Look, may the young woman bear [...]
[-? -]⌜-⌝[--] (8) *ʿnhả*[113] *l ydh*	[ ] for his hand,
t⌜*z*⌝*d*[*n*---]⌜-⌝(9)*pt l bšrh*	[ ]for his flesh.

111. Dittography.

112. See the remarks of Pardee, *COS* 1:350 n. 80; cf. Wyatt, *Religious Texts*, 287 n. 165.

113. Most scholars agree that *ʿnhả* is a scribal error for *ʿnhn* (< *ʿn* + 3fs suff. + enclitic *n*), which would have resulted from the omission of one additional horizontal wedge.

*dm⌜r⌝[---]**ḥ**(10)**wyn***	??? [?]**make live**,
⌜w⌝ mtrḫ⌜t⌝[--]⌜-⌝h[114]	and a woman given in marriage [...][115]

Although the broken nature of this text renders its interpretation at various junctures uncertain, most scholars interpret *-ḥwyn* to be some form of the verb *ḥyy* "to live."[116] Caquot and Sznycer reconstruct a prefixed {t} with the divine couple as subject: "[Let them] vivify all his flesh with the blood [...]."[117] Wyatt, on the other hand, following *CAT*'s reconstruction *ảb[h y]ḥwyn* for lines 9–10, reads *ảbh* as the subject of *yḥwyn*: "Her father gave her life."[118] It is important to note that Wyatt's rendering of this verbal form, "gave her life," apparently intends to capture the idea that the factitive meaning of the D stem in this case focuses on one's entrance into life, while Johannes C. de Moor's translation "let live" is less specific.[119] Pardee's recent epigraphic study of this text, however, has rendered many of the earlier conclusions regarding these lines most unlikely. The context immediately preceding *-ḥwyn* is unfortunately completely lost, and thus impedes a sure analysis of its form and context. The most that can be said is that a young woman's bearing a child is mentioned in line 7 and that a woman is said to have been given in marriage in line 10. It therefore remains uncertain as to whether the D stem *-ḥwyn* denotes the renewal of a living state (if it is somehow related

114. Adrianus van Selms, *Marriage and Family Life in Ugaritic Literature*, POS 1 (London: Luzac, 1954), 17 n. 13, proposed the following reconstruction for this passage:

lydh tzd[n wt]
pt lbšrh dmy [y]ḥ
wyn kmtrḫ[t bbt]h

Note also *CAT*:

(7) hl ǵlmt . tld bn [xxx]
(8) ʿnhả . l ydh tzdn š
(9) pt l bšrh . dm ảb[h . y]ḥ
(10) wyn . k mtrḫt . b[hkl]h

115. I follow Dennis Pardee's recent collation of this text in, "Un chant nuptial ougaritique (RS 5.194 [CTA 24]): Nouvelle étude épigraphique suivie de remarques philologiques et littéraires," *SemCl* 3 (2010): 17, 20, 25. See also Wyatt, *Religious Texts*, 336–47.

116. Margalit, however, offers a markedly different reconstruction and interpretation here: dm t(!)q*[ḥ qm]ḥ wyn "Then she to[ok flo]ur and wine" ("Alliteration in Ugaritic Poetry: Its Role in Composition and Analysis," *UF* 11 [1979]: 556).

117. "[Qu'elles] vivifient toute sa chair avec le sang [...]"; Caquot and Sznycer, *Textes ougaritiques 1*, 392, reading the break before the form of *ḥyy* as *ả[dm]* and analyzing the preceding signs *ptlbšrh* as *kl bšrh* (i.e., combining the signs for {p} and {t} to read a {k}). Herdner also transcribes an {ả} before the break, but offers no reconstruction for what follows.

118. Wyatt, *Religious Texts*, 338.

119. "For [her] fa[ther will] let her live" (de Moor, *Anthology of Religious Texts*, 143).

to being given in marriage) or the initial entrance into a living state (if it is rather related to the birth mentioned in line 7).

1.2.2.5. KTU 1.82:6

KTU 1.82, an elusive incantation text directed against demonic forces, provides two more examples of the D stem *ḥwy*. It is a difficult text to interpret, largely stemming from the tablet's condition, but also partly due to its subject matter; therefore, scholars note the tentative nature of our understanding of it. To date, there are three major studies of KTU 1.82, the first appearing in *Ugarit Forschungen* by de Moor and Spronk,the second by Caquot in the Loretz Festschrift, and the third being found in del Olmo Lete's article entitled, "KTU 1.82: Another Miscellaneous Incantation/Anti-Witchcraft Text against Snakebite in Ugaritic" in *Aula Orientalis*.[120] Most recently, Adam Miglio has published a focused analysis of the first seven lines of this incantation.[121] As these studies have noted, the text appears to be a collection of incantations against evil spirits of various kinds, though for del Olmo Lete, instead of seeing them as a disconnected collection, he argues for a common thread: they all concern the bite of a snake and are comparable to KTU 1.100 and 1.107.[122]

My interest in this text has to do with the context and meaning of the form *ḥw* in line 6 and that of *ảḥw* in line 19.[123] First of all, *ḥw* is somehow associated with the goddess Šapšu, the psychopomp of the underworld perceived to have significant powers therein. More specifically, this text emphasizes the *ql špš*, "the voice of Šapšu," after which the form *ḥw* either denotes an appeal to *ql špš*, or perhaps the utterance of *ql špš*. Also, it is interesting to observe the mention of the

120. Johannes C. de Moor and Klaas Spronk, "More on Demons in Ugarit (KTU 1.84)," *UF* 16 (1984): 237–50, accompanied by the authors' personal hand copy of the tablet. See also de Moor, *Anthology of Religious Texts*, 174–81. André Caquot, "Un recueil ougaritique de formules magiques," *SEL* 5 (1988): 31–43; see also Caquot, in, *Textes ougaritiques 2: Textes religieux et rituels, correspondance*, ed. André Caquot, Jean-Michel de Tarragon, and Jesús-Luis Cunchillos, LAPO 14 (Paris: Cerf, 1989), 61–70. Del Olmo Lete, "KTU 1.82," 245–65. Cf. del Olmo Lete, *Canaanite Religion According to the Liturgical Texts of Ugarit*, 2nd ed., trans. by Wilfred G. E. Watson, AOAT 408 (Münster: Ugarit-Verlag, 2014), 320–26. The first edition of this title appeared as *Canaanite Religion According to the Liturgical Texts of Ugarit*, trans. Wilfred G. E. Watson (Bethesda, MD: CDL, 1999), 373–78, translated from the earlier Spanish title, *La religión cananea: según la liturgia de Ugarit. estudio textual*, AuOrSup 3 (Barcelona: AUSA, 1992).

121. Adam E. Miglio "A Study of the Serpent Incantation KTU 1.82:1–7 and Its Contributions to Ugaritic Mythology and Religions," *JANER* 13 (2013): 30–48.

122. Del Olmo Lete, *Canaanite Religion*, 2nd ed., 320–21.

123. Note that instead of *ḥw* in line 6, Caquot followed the *editio princeps'* reading *ḥr*, translating *špš ḥr*: "Shapash, be ardent" ("Shapash, sois ardente"), and taking *ql* with what precedes ("Recueil ougaritiques," 35–36; Caquot, *Textes ougaritiques* 2, 65 n. 177).

deity Môtu in line 5, against whom this incantation is directed.[124] Additionally, the repeated references to Baʿlu throughout this incantation (lines 1, 2, 6, etc.) suggest that an allusion to the infamous contest between Baʿlu and Môtu in KTU 1.5–1.6 is operative here, where the goddess Šapšu also plays a significant role in that divine duel. This allusion to the Baʿlu cycle and the storm god's contest with Môtu is not only significant for the role that Šapšu plays there, but also for the reference in that text to her *ql* "voice." As Baʿlu and Môtu clash in battle, Šapšu scolds Môtu for his part in the scuffle, whom the narrative afterwards describes: *yrủ bn ỉlm <m>t ṯtʿ ydd ỉl ǵzr yʿr mt b qlh* "Môtu, son of ʾIlu, fears, the beloved hero of ʾIlu, is frightened; Môtu is aroused at her voice" (KTU 1.6 VI:30–32).[125] In other words, according to the Baʿlu cycle, it is the voice of Šapšu that holds sway over Môtu and thus offers sufficient rationale for its invocation in this incantation as a magical formula for the reversal of his deadly powers.

Returning to the interpretation of *ql špš ḥw* (line 6), de Moor and Spronk translate, "Voice of Shapshu, bring to life!"[126] Similarly, del Olmo Lete renders it, "the cry to/of *Šapšu*: 'save life'!"[127] In both renditions, the form *ḥw* is analyzed as an active imperative of the D stem, "give life," but as I have already noted above, the absence of an explicit object makes this interpretation difficult. This factor leads me to suggest a passive form: "be enlivened" or "be made alive." As a passive expression, it could indicate an appeal to the voice of Šapšu: "Voice of Šapšu, come alive/be enlivened," in the sense that the magical powers of her voice are being invoked to reverse the effects of Môtu in the deadly snakebite. Or, perhaps another way of understanding this phrase might be to take the imperative *ḥw* as the content of *ql špš*, in other words, the direct speech of the goddess: "The utterance of Šapšu: be enlivened," suggesting that she speaks a word of healing to the victim and thus wards off Môtu's powers. Still further, one could also take

124. De Moor and Spronk translate *tǵrm lmt brtk* as, "You are pledging your covenant to Death" ("More on Demons," 240). Del Olmo Lete earlier emended *brtk* to *brqk*: "Unite your rays (against) *Môtu*" (*Canaanite Religion*, 1st ed., 374 n. 140), but has since reverted back to *brtk*, translating: "If your forecast commits (you) to death/*Môtu*" (*Canaanite Religion*, 2nd ed., 321 n. 151). In defense of this interpretation he appeals to Akkadian *bārûtu* "work, lore of the diviner" (*CAD* 2:331–32), thus taking *brtk* as a reference to the divinatory act.

125. Note *DUL*'s translation of *yʿr mt b qlh*: "DN became agitated in his fall" (178). I find this interpretation of *qlh* less likely contextually, since this narrative expression immediately follows Šapšu's outcry to Môtu (lines 22–29) and not his fall mentioned a few lines earlier (line 21).

126. De Moor and Spronk, "More on Demons," 240.

127. Del Olmo Lete, "KTU 1.82," 247; del Olmo Lete, *Canaanite Religion*, 2nd ed., 323; cf. his earlier translation: "a cry to/from Šapšu: give back life!" (*Canaanite Religion*, 1st ed., 374), which changes the nuance of *ḥw* from "return life" to "preserve life." Cf. Miglio: "I will raise (my) voice! 'O Šapšu, give life!'" ("Study of the Serpent Incantation," 33).

ql špš as a reference to the power invoked in the incantation: "By the voice of Šapšu, be enlivened."

In adopting one of these passive interpretations of *ḥw*, it is important to understand that the meaning of the D stem factitive suggests preservation, or more exactly deliverance from the deadly effects of the poisonous snakebite. In other words, it denotes the restoration of health to someone on the precipice of dying.[128] Therefore, any interpretation suggesting the notion of "revived" (presumably from death) life would not make sense since the addressee is still alive and in need of deliverance from death. For this reason, the nuance of del Olmo Lete's translation "save life" is probably the most accurate contextually, though I would rather suggest a passive form of the imperative: "by the voice of Šapšu, be saved/delivered."

The appearance of *ảḥw* in line 19 poses more difficulty in preventing a lucid interpretation because of its broken context, the first portion of the line being entirely lost. I can only speculate as to whether the lost portion contained an object or some sort of adverbial. Therefore, depending on what once existed in the broken line, *ảḥw* could either mean, "I will save X" if there was an object (the ritual performer speaking, or perhaps the goddess Šapšu from line 6), or "I will be saved" in the absence of an explicated object (the victim speaking). Beyond these considerations, the exact meaning of this particular attestation of the root *ḥwy* in the D stem is unknown.

1.2.2.6. KTU 2.70:15

Before moving on to the substantive forms of this root, I shall consider a particularly intriguing occurrence of the D stem, leaving aside for the moment the mythological and epic literature, and moving on to the Ugaritic epistolary corpus. This move is an important step in establishing a proper awareness of a word's meaning because it takes us closer to the *Sitz im Leben* of everyday life at Ugarit.[129] Such an observation does not belittle the important place enjoyed by the Ugaritic mythological and epic literature in our analysis of these terms, nor does it suggest that these designated genres are somehow mutually exclusive (i.e., in the sense that we moderns are prone to dichotomize the "sacred" and the

128. Cf. the similar usage for the piel of *ḥyh* in the Hebrew Psalter (e.g., Ps 71:20).

129. One could make a similar case for the incantation text KTU 1.82 discussed in the previous section of this chapter in light of its utilitarian purposes. These divisions are not hard and fast, however, since the incantations themselves are not only replete with appeals for divine intervention, but they also offer an ancient exhibit on their understanding of the intersection of the supernatural and the natural. I likewise detect a similar awareness in del Olmo Lete's chapter heading in *Canaanite Religion*, 2nd ed., where his treatment of KTU 1.82 and other related texts appears: "The Religion of Everyday Life" (273–338).

"secular"); it simply adds another crucial component to the lexical inventory of life and death from a slightly different angle.[130]

KTU 2.70 (= RS 29.093) records the correspondence of two nonroyal servants to their overlord, one of the two being female (as indicated by *ảmtk* "your maidservant" in line 12).[131] The form *ḥwy* occurs toward the beginning of the main body of the letter:

(11) *hlny bn ʿyn*	Here, Bin-ʿAyāna
(12) *yštảl ʿm ảmtk*	keeps making demands on/of your maidservant.
(13) *w lảk lh w kḥdnn*	Send a message to him and bring it to an end.[132]
(14) *w ảnk ḥrš*	As for me, an artisan
(15) *lqḥt w* ***ḥwt***	I have taken/hired. **I have repaired**
(16) *hbt*[133] *w lm ṯb*	this house. Why has
(17) *bn ʿyn*	Bin-ʿAyāna returned
(18) *w lqḥ ṯqlm*	and taken two shekels
(19) *ksp bd ảmtk*	of silver from the hand of your maidservant?

In this context, the speaker applies this 1cs D stem SC form to an inanimate object, namely, "this house." One might assume from the contents of this letter that the servant speaking here refers to a dilapidated structure needing repair, which, as the letter states, required the skill of the artisan (*ḥrš*) hired in line 14. Thus, the literal meaning of *ḥwt hbt* is, "I revived/restored this house," interpreting it as an active factitive. Without overinterpreting this passage, suffice it to say that the appropriateness of using *ḥwy* to express renewed "life" for humans and deities is also suitable for inanimate objects.[134] As I will show later in my analysis of the Ugaritic semantics for death, this same potential existed for *mt* "to die," being conceived of as the negative counterpart for *ḥyy*, and equally applicable to inanimate entities.[135]

130. The same will be true for our study of the root m-t "to die" to follow, where we will examine its usage in the letters as well.

131. For analysis of this text, see André Herdner, "Lettre de deux serviteurs à leur maître," *Ugaritica* 7:75–78; Pardee *COS* 3:110–11; Bordreuil and Pardee, *Manual of Ugaritic*, 240–41.

132. Literally: "and hide it."

133. Analyzing the form as the deictic particle *hn* + *bt* > *hbt*, likely analogical to the later development of the Hebrew definite article (see Meindert Dijkstra, "Ugaritic Prose," in *Handbook of Ugaritic Studies*, ed. Wilfred G. E. Watson and Nicolas Wyatt, HdO 39 [Leiden: Brill, 1999], 159; Pardee, *COS* 3:110 n. 183; Tropper, *Ugaritische Grammatik*, 2nd ed., 233–34).

134. Cf. a similar application of this root in the inscription of the Phoenician king Yeḥamilk: *hʾt ḥwy kl mplt hbtm* "He [Yeḥamilk] restored all the ruins of the temples" (*KAI* 4.2).

135. The example I will explore is KTU 2.38:10–13, where *mt* refers to ships, i.e., "dead ships" (see the full discussion of this text in ch. 3 [§3.2.4]).

1.2.3. Substantive Forms

I now draw our attention to the substantive forms derived from this root as they appear throughout the Ugaritic textual corpus. I will begin my treatment of substantives with an analysis of the nominal forms, followed by an analysis of attested adjectival forms.

1.2.3.1. Nominal Forms

Ugaritic attests both masculine and feminine nominal forms for this root. I shall begin by examining the masculine forms before moving on to the feminine.

1.2.3.1.1. Masculine Nouns

The masculine noun meaning "life" attests the following forms: once as *ḥ* in the oath formula (sg.), *ḥym* (pl.), *ḥy* (pl. const.), *ḥyk* (pl. + 2ms suff.). The plural construct form *ḥy*, as well as the one singular form *ḥ*, both occur in the Ugaritic letters in association with the noun *npš*:

KTU 2.23:15–19

(15) *w ản* [...]*b*	And I myself...
(16) *ảrš* [...]*š*	make a request for...
(17) *mlk r*[*b bʿl*]*y p l*	the gre[at] king, my [master], and for
(18) ***ḥy*** *np*[*š ả*]*rš*	**the life** of [his] *np*[*š* I] make a request
(19) *l pn bʿ*[*l*]*ṣpn bʿly*	to the face of Baʿ[lu] ṢPN, my lord.

RS 94.2284:12–15[136]

(12) ***ḥ*** *npšk w* ***ḥ*** *n*[*pš*]	By **the life** of your *npš* and **the life** of [my] *n*[*pš*],
(13) *hm ỉṯ d ytn* ⌜*l*⌝ [...]	there was nothing given to me![137]
(14) *w mrṣ lby* [...] (15) *mỉd*	And my heart is very ill (or: sad).

These occurrences are comparable with the G stem forms also associated with *npš* cited earlier from KTU 1.17 I:36 and 1.19 IV:36. As was the case there, I simply mention these forms here for the sake of completion, but I will analyze them

136. For a hand copy and transcription of this text, see Bordreuil and Pardee, *Manual of Ugaritic*, 134, 250. For a color photograph of the tablet, see the accompanying CD-ROM. And now, see the *editio princeps* in Bordreuil, Pardee, and Hawley, *Une bibliothèque au sud de la ville ****, 180–86.

137. Literally: "If there was anything given to me!" This is the one example of an oath formula in Ugaritic that is comparable to that of Biblical Hebrew (1 Sam 1:26; 17:55; 20:3; 25:26; 2 Sam 11:11; 14:19; 2 Kgs 2:2, 4, 6; 4:30) (Pardee, *COS* 3:113 n.205).

more fully in my treatment of the Ugaritic noun *npš* in the following chapter. Nonetheless, I raise Pardee's observation that *ḥ* and *npšk* in RS 94.2284:12 are written without word dividers: ḥnpšk . w ḥn[pšy] (construct chain, the first element consisting of a single element), unlike the expression in KTU 2.23:18 where the two are separated by a word divider: ḥy . np[š].[138] Perhaps the fact that it is an oath formula in RS 94.2284 has contributed to this development, thus blurring the historical distinction between these two lexemes. At any rate, there is an important morphological/phonological difference: {ḥ} = /ḥê/ < /ḥayy∅/ (absolute case), whereas {ḥy} is probably the plural construct form.

The suffixed plural nominal form *ḥyk* appears in the Baʿlu cycle (KTU 1.4 III:9), but unfortunately, the first nine lines of this column are too fragmentary for a sensible translation. It is worth noting that in this particular line, *ḥyk* "your life" is associated with *rḥ* "wind, spirit": [...]*ḥyk w rḥ d*.

There are two particularly important occurrences of the plural suffixed form *ḥyk* in the Kirta Epic. These instances appear at the crucial moment when it is realized that Kirta might die and mourning ensues, first from the mouth of Kirta's son ʾIluḥaʾu and then subsequently from his sister Ṯitmanatu.

KTU 1.16 I:14

ảp (10) *krt bnm ỉl*	Also, Kirta is a son of ʾIlu,
špḥ (11) *lṭpn w qdš*	offspring of the knowing and holy one.
ʿl (12) *ảbh yʿrṣ*	To his father he enters.
ybky (13) *yšnn*	He weeps, he gnashes his teeth,
ytn gh (14) *bky*	he raises his voice with weeping.
b ***ḥyk*** *ảbn ả!šmḫ*[139]	In **your life**, our father, we rejoice,
(15) *bl mtk ngln*	(in) your not dying we find joy.
k klb (16) *b btk nʿtq*[140]	Like a dog in your house we pass/grow old,
k ỉnr[141] (17) *ảp ḫštk*	like a hound also (in) your court.
ảp ảb k mtm[142] (18) *tmtn*	Also, father, like mortals will you die?

138. Pardee, *COS* 3:113 n. 205.

139. Scribal error for *nšmḫ* in light of the 1cs suffix on the preceding noun (*ảbn*), as well as the verbs to follow (*ngln, nʿtq*). Furthermore, the parallel expression in KTU 1.16 II:37 reads *nšmḫ*.

140. Cf. Hebrew *ʿtq* "move forward (spatially)" (BDB, 801); Syriac *ʿtq* "grow old" (Payne Smith, 431; *SL*, 1148), Arabic *ʿtq* "grow old, wear out" (of nonhumans) (Lane, 1946–47). Also, see the discussion in Dennis Pardee, "A Note on the Root *ʿtq* in CTA 16 I 2,5 (UT 125, KRT II)," *UF* 5 (1973): 229–30; Joaquín Sanmartín, "RIŠ ARGMN in den ug. Ritualen," *UF* 10 (1978): 455–56.

141. For a discussion of this term with references, see Pardee, "Note on the Root *ʿtq*," 230. Based on the parallel *klb*, I interpret this word as another noun for dog.

142. Taking *mtm* as /mutīma/ "men" rather than /mītīma/ "those who die."

ủ ḫštk l ntn[143] (19) *ʿtq*	Or indeed your court be given to passing/growing old,
bd ảṯt ảb ṣrry[144]	in the hand of women, father ṢRRY?

The second occurrence of *ḥyk* in KTU 1.16 II:36 is virtually identical to the text transcribed above, the only difference being that it is construed as coming from the mouth of ʾIluḥaʾu's sister Ṭitmanatu upon hearing the news of Kirta's worsening condition and inevitable death.

One of the significant contributions of these two passages for our understanding of this noun is the parallel immediately following in the next line: *bl mtk* "your not dying" (line 15). This expression also occurs once in the ʾAqhatu Epic (KTU 1.17 VI:27) opposite the plural noun *ḥym*:

ỉrš ***ḥym*** *l ảqht ǵzr*	Ask for **life**, O valiant ʾAqhatu.
(27) *ỉrš* ***ḥym*** *w ảtnk*	Ask for **life**, and I will give (it) to you;
blmt (28) *w ảšlḥk*	**not dying**, and I will grant (it) to you.

Taken as a whole, *blmt* is a compound form consisting of the negative particle *bl* + a verbal (or common) noun of the root m-t "to die," that is, "not dying."[145] Del Olmo Lete and Sanmartín note a comparison with the preposition *bl* "without" and their *mt* II (/mutu/) "man, mortal," which would mean something to the effect of "without mortality."[146] Though they opt for the usual analysis of negative particle *bl* + *mt* I "not dying," this comparison is intriguing, but nonetheless probably an unlikely option for *blmt*.[147] This point comes into sharper focus upon considering other examples where the root ḥ-y-y occurs in parallel with m-t "to die." For example, I have already noted in my discussion of the G stem forms of ḥ-y-y the following parallel: *tmtn* // *l yḥ* "you will die" // "you will not live" (KTU 1.16 I:22–23 and II:43–44). This combination provides a negative counterpart for *ḥyk* // *blmtk*, namely, a parallel pair denoting death utilizing a negated form of *ḥyy* as opposed to the opposite with negated *mt*.

On strictly lexical grounds, to speak of "afterlife" at Ugarit in the usual sense of "life after death" is a bit of an oxymoron. It would seem that from the perspective

143. SC N stem from the root y-t-n.

144. On this difficult form, see Pardee, "Note on the Root *ʿtq*," 232–33.

145. See Gordon, *Ugaritic Textbook*, §8.74.

146. *DUL*, 223.

147. For one, *mt* II simply means "man" in Ugaritic, and not "mortal." Cf. *mt mrzḥ* in KTU 3.9:13, which simply means "man of the *mrzḥ*" (on this text, see Pardee, *Ritual and Cult at Ugarit*, 218).

of the Ugaritians, at least as it concerns the distribution of their use of the parallels *ḥy // blmt* and *mt // l ḥyy*, life and death are mutually exclusive. For example, the following remark by Spronk would appear to assume something that does not organically arise from the lexical distribution of the Ugaritic roots *ḥwy/hyy*: "It is also believed that Keret, who is called a son of El during his life, could expect some kind of continuation of this state in the afterlife."[148] The point that needs to be stressed here is that the roots *ḥwy/hyy*, whenever they occur in relation to m-t, one or the other of these terms is negated, so that, strictly speaking, the Ugaritians never spoke in terms of an enduring life after death.[149] This does not rule out the possibility of some sort of enduring, shadowy existence beyond the point of death, at least for a certain stratum of society, but I must stress that it is a different kind of existence, one that is never expressed with the root *ḥwy/ḥyy*.

All of the masculine nouns discussed thus far are with medial {y} (except for the absolute form *ḥ*), but there is one possible example in Ugaritic of a masculine noun with medial {w}. The form is *ḥwy* and it occurs in the administrative text KTU 4.145:10 following a record of chariots and their accessories:

(8) *w ṯlṯ ṣmdm w ḥrṣ*	Three pairs (as one lot)
(9) *ảpnt bd rb ḥršm*	of wheels in the hands of the chief of the craftsmen
(10) *d šṣả* ***ḥwyh***	who delivered (it) to **the storehouse**.

The form *ḥwy* with the accompanying directive {h} apparently refers to a storehouse where this equipment for chariots is kept.[150] One could also explain the meaning of this word from the fact that the storehouse preserves the life of the chariot equipment by sheltering it from the elements. Unfortunately, so far this is the only clear occurrence of *ḥwy* with this particular nuance.[151] Nonetheless, I should also compare the usage of the verbal form *ḥwt* in KTU 2.70:15 cited earlier where the D stem describes the repairs made to a dilapidated house. In a similar way, the noun *ḥwy* in KTU 4.145 denotes the place where items are stored in order to prevent the kind of dilapidation caused by the elements that would require their restoration (= the D stem *ḥwy*).

148. Spronk, *Beatific Afterlife*, 154.

149. Note the apt remarks of Pope, who wonders what kind of a "nondeath" would involve a periodic return to real life. He states further: "How this could be called 'non-death' or 'real life' is difficult to grasp if it meant only an annual return to share a ritual meal. If this is what the goddess offered, it was no great bargain. Small wonder that Aqhat spurned it" (Marvin H. Pope, review of *Beatific Afterlife in Ancient Israel and in the Ancient Near East*, by Klaas Spronk, *UF* 19 [1978]: 457).

150. See *DUL*, 380.

151. Cf. *ḥwy* in KTU 1.17 VI:30 and 1.176:17 (broken context).

1.2.3.1.2. Feminine Nouns

There are two attested feminine nouns formed with medial {y} (KTU 1.3 V:31 and 1.10 II:20). As is commonly the case in Ugaritic poetic narration, the contexts for these two cases are identical, the latter being a repetition of the former.

KTU 1.3 V:31

w t[ʿ]*n btlt ʿnt*	Girl ʿAnatu answers:
(30) *tḥmk il ḥkm*	Your word, O ʾIlu, is wise,
ḥkmk (31) *ʿm ʿlm*	your wisdom is forever,
ḥyt *ḥẓt tḥmk*	your word is **a life** of good fortune.
(32) *mkln åliyn bʿl*	Our king is mighty Baʿlu,
ṯpṭn (33) *in d ʿlnh*	Our ruler, there is no one above him.
klnyy qš̌h (34) *nbln*	All of us carry his goblet;
klnyy nbl ksh	All of us carry his cup.

The context of this passage involves ʿAnatu's complaint to ʾIlu on behalf of Baʿlu in the matter of his lack of a palatial dwelling. At this particular point in her speech the goddess flatters ʾIlu with words of praise concerning his great wisdom before her request that Baʿlu be given the palace he deserves.[152] This passage is repeated verbatim in KTU 1.4 IV:41–46, only this time in the mouth of lady ʾAṯiratu who also joins the fray in support of a palace for Baʿlu. I should also note the variant reading *ḥkmt* in KTU 1.4 IV:41 versus *ḥkmk* here in KTU 1.3 V:30.

Marcus, following H. L. Ginsberg, has proposed to read both *ḥyt* and *ḥẓt* as 2ms SC G stems with an optative sense, "forever may you live and prosper," arguing that the noun for "life" in Ugaritic is *ḥym*, not *ḥyt*.[153] De Moor has argued for a similar rendering of *ḥyt ḥẓt tḥmk*, but goes a step further than Marcus by insisting that the preceding *ḥkmk* must also be read as a precative perfect on the basis of the variant *ḥkmt* in KTU 1.4 IV:41.[154] Yet, for de Moor to have his precative perfects, one of these attested forms has to contain a scribal error, since everything else in both passages is identical, serving the literary purposes of the narrator in depicting the swell of support for Baʿlu's residence. Furthermore, the fact that *ḥkmk* occurs in the immediately preceding line in KTU 1.3 V points in the direction of interpreting *ḥkmt* as the variant form. Despite the objections raised by Marcus and de Moor, the conventional reading of *ḥyt* in this passage

152. As interpreted by Pardee (*COS* 1:254) in his heading for this portion of ʿAnatu's discourse.

153. H. L. Ginsberg, "The Epic of Al'iyn-Baal: Tablet II," *Tarbiz* 5 (1933): 385 (Hebrew). Marcus, "The Verb 'to Live' in Ugaritic," 76.

154. Johannes C. de Moor, "Contributions to the Ugaritic Lexicon," *UF* 11 (1972): 643 n. 21, critiquing Marcus's interpretation of *ḥkmk* as a noun to be unsustainable.

has been a feminine noun, an allomorph of the more common noun *ḥy(m)*.[155] Besides, on stylistic grounds, the verbal interpretation does not adequately maintain the poetics of this passage, said to convey a staccato rhythm by Mark Smith and Wayne Pitard and represented as follows:

tḥmk il ḥkm	a b c
ḥkmk ʿm ʿlm	c d
ḥyt ḥẓt tḥmk	d′ (x of y) a[156]

In the mythological text KTU 1.10 II, possibly the depiction of a love scene between Baʿlu and the goddess ʿAnatu, occurs the curious form *ḥwt*:[157]

(15) *w yʿn btlt ʿnt*	He eyes girl ʿAnatu,
(16) *nʿmt bn åḫt bʿl*	beautiful among the sisters of Baʿlu.
(17) *l pnnh ydd w yqm*	To her face he hurries and stands,
(18) *l pʿnh ykrʿ w yql*	at her feet he prostrates and falls down.
(19) *w yšů gh w yṣḥ*	He lifts up his voice and cries out:
(20) ***ḥwt** åḫt wn årk*[158]	"**Life**, O sister, and longevity!"

On strictly formal grounds, this word could very well be another D stem of the SC type, which from context would have to be read as a 2fs, meaning something to the effect of, "You are revived!" This is exactly what de Moor has already proposed in his translation of this text, and admittedly, it is not entirely out of the question morphologically, though I am not sure how it would be understood syntactically.[159] Additionally, the meaning of this interpretation is difficult to rationalize contextually. It is possible that, given her relentless search for Baʿlu

155. E.g., Gordon, *Ugaritic Literature*, 32; Caquot and Sznycer, *Textes ougaritiques 1*, 176; Baruch Margalit, *Matter of Life and Death: A Study of the Baal-Mot Epic (CTA 4–5–6)*, AOAT 206 (Kevelaer: Butzon & Bercker; Neukirchen-Vluyn: Neukirchener Verlag, 1980), 212; del Olmo Lete, *Mitos y leyendas*, 191; Pardee, *COS* 1:254; Wyatt, *Religious Texts*, 87; *DUL*, 381; Mark Smith and Wayne Pitard, *The Ugaritic Baal Cycle, Volume II: Introduction with Text, Translation and Commentary of KTU/CAT 1.3–1.4*, VTSup 114 (Leiden: Brill, 2009), 327; and others.

156. Smith and Pitard, *Ugaritic Baal Cycle 2*, 333.

157. On the interpretive problems associated with this assessment, see Neal H. Walls, *The Goddess Anat in Ugaritic Myth*, SBLDS 135 (Atlanta: Scholars Press, 1992), 131.

158. *CTA* was more cautious in its transcription here, reading: wnår[-] (*CTA* 10 II:20). *CAT* reads the final sign as unbroken: årk.

159. De Moor translates, "May you be revived, my sister," which seems to interpret this SC form as some kind of precative (*Anthology of Religious Texts*, 113). Cf. Caquot and Sznycer: "Greetings, my sister! May (your days) be prolonged" ("Salut, ma soeur! Que [tes jours] se prolongent" (*Textes ougaritiques 1*, 284).

intimated in the preceding lines, ʿAnatu is utterly exhausted and that these first words of greeting from the storm god urge her to be refreshed from her exertion. This conclusion requires caution, however, since the second half of column ii is entirely lost, but even so, it would still not make sense of *nảrk*, that is, if it is to be read as an N stem participle, "be long."

Another possibility for *ḥwt* is to read it as a feminine noun.[160] This option is attractive because in the context of Baʿlu's words of greeting to ʿAnatu, essentially the first words exchanged between the two of them in this text, ʿAnatu returns with a word of response beginning in line 31, which, unfortunately for us, breaks apart in the following lines. However, her greeting there may offer insight for interpreting Baʿlu's initial greeting, in that she replies: [. . .]? *bʿlm d ỉph*[. . .]*hd d ʿnn n*[. . .] "Baʿlu, the one of/who . . . Haddu, the one of/who. . . ."[161] The exact meaning of these lines remains uncertain due to their broken portions; however, it is reasonable to conclude contextually that in her reply ʿAnatu calls Baʿlu by name, followed by an epithet of some kind (as indicated by the relative *d*) reflective of his role as storm god. If this much is true, then perhaps Baʿlu greets her in a similar manner in line 20, slightly awkward words if he were to greet her with a SC form: "You are revived." Interpreting *ḥwt* as a feminine noun would make better sense contextually as a greeting comparable to the expression *šlm*, "Well-being (to you)!," only in this instance, the greeting is specific to ʿAnatu's quality as a goddess who claims the ability to grant life (e.g., KTU 1.17 VI:27–28).[162]

Also pertinent to one's interpretation of *ḥwt* are the last five signs of the line: *wnảrk*. Traditionally, scholars have analyzed these signs as the conjuctive {w} followed by an N stem participle of the stative root *ʾrk* "to be long."[163] One problem with this suggestion—though not insurmountable—is that the N stem for

160. Cf. the Hebrew feminine abstract noun *ḥayyût*, attested in 2 Sam 20:3.

161. John Gibson appeals to Akkadian *upû*, "mist, cloud," (*Canaanite Myths and Legends*, 2nd ed. [New York: T&T Clark, 2004], 140, listed in glossary), followed by Walls (*Goddess Anat*, 131) and Wyatt (*Religious Texts*, 158). Accordingly, *ʿnn* in the following line is interpreted as "cloud" (cf. Heb. *ʿānān*), thus Wyatt: "O Baal of the mist, [Divine] Hadd of the clouds" (*Religious Texts*, 158). Caquot and Sznycer, on the other hand, simply leave this portion blank in their translation (*Textes ougaritiques 1*, 285). Del Olmo Lete reads these lines quite differently, taking *ỉph* from *phy* "to see, espy" and *ʿnn* from *ʿn* "to eye, see": "[Look] *Baʿlu*, what I've seen, divine *Haddu* what they saw" ("[Mira], *Baʿlu*, lo que he visto, [dios] *Haddu*, lo que vieron"; (*Mitos y leyendas*, 470). The problem with this interpretation is the required shift in person from *ỉph* (1cs) to *ʿnn* (3ms/p?, unless it is the /ʾ/ . . . /ʿ/ > /ʿ/ change, in which case *ʿnn* could be a 1cs [see n. 84 above]). As broken as the text is, these lines would naturally suggest synonymous parallelism: Baʿlu who X . . . Haddu who X.

162. Cf. Wyatt's translation: "Life, sister, and longevity be yours!" (*Religious Texts*, 157). Cf. also the feminine abstract noun attested in Hebrew *ḥayyût* (Exod 1:19).

163. Gordon, *Ugaritic Textbook*, 366; Caquot and Sznycer, *Textes ougaritiques 1*, 284 n. n; del Olmo Lete, *Mitos y leyendas*, 469; Wyatt, *Religious Texts*, 157 n. 6. Herdner interpreted it as a perfect form: "that (your days) are prolonged" ("que [tes jours] soient prolongés"; *CTA*, 50 n. 4).

this root appears to be nonexistent in Hebrew.[164] De Moor has offered a different suggestion, analyzing *nảrk* as a 1cs G stem of the hollow root *ʾwr* "to shine" with a second-person pronominal suffix.[165] However, this interpretation is more difficult contextually—why would Baʿlu use a plural cohortative with reference to himself, since the second-person pronominal suffix would have to refer to ʿAnatu? Del Olmo Lete and Sanmartín have divided these signs differently, analyzing the first two as the particle *wn* (< *w* + *hn*) "and look/behold," and the remaining three as an imperative from *ʾrk* "be long."[166] Perhaps more simply, the particle *wn* could be the conjunctive /wa/ + enclitic {-n}, avoiding the more complicated reconstruction *w* + *hn* > *wn*. Therefore, in light of analyzing *ḥwt* as a noun form introducing Baʿlu's greeting and interpreting *ảrk* as another noun, I render this line: "Life, O sister, and longevity!"[167]

The most common feminine noun is *ḥwt*, meaning "land," and it occurs approximately thirty-five times throughout the Ugaritic corpus.[168] The identification of this meaning is not only detected from the contexts of its uses, but is verified from its appearance in syllabic form in a polyglot vocabulary list. There, it appears in the vocalized form [ḫ]u-wa-tu$_4$ alongside Hurrian [u]-mi-in$_4$-n[i] meaning "land, country."[169] In a legal text one also finds the syllabic form ḫu-wa-⌜ti⌝ in the phrase ša-i-na A.ŠÀ^{meš} ḫu-wa-⌜ti⌝, which John Huehnergard renders, "fields of the land/country."[170] According to the syllabically attested forms, I vocalize the feminine form *ḥwt* in these contexts as /ḥuwwatu/.[171]

The distribution of these forms varies. Once *ḥwt* appears in the Baʿlu cycle in the "land of X" formulation: *k ḥwt ymản* "as (in) the land of YMẢN" (KTU 1.4 I:42).[172] In the letters it occurs with reference to other cities, such as Ugarit: *b ḥwt ủgrt* "in the land of Ugarit."[173] Elsewhere throughout the letters *ḥwt* more

164. Biblical Hebrew only attests the G and C stems for this root (see BDB, 73; *HALOT*, 88).

165. "Let us shine upon you" (de Moor, *Anthology of Religious Texts*, 113).

166. *DUL*, 102.

167. Cf. Biblical Hebrew *ʾōrek* "length" (BDB, 73).

168. KTU 1.4 I:42; 1.103+:1, 4, 5, 16, 37, 41, 45, 50, 51, 53, 56; 1.140:6; 2.18:4; 2.33:9; 2.36:4 (?); 2.36:16, 17, 18 [broken context], 19 [broken context]; 2.39:20; 2.42:10; 2.47:2, 9 [broken context], 13; 2.49:10; 2.73:6; 2.76:10; 2.81:3, 7; 2.81:18; 3.3:4; 3.8:10; 4.779:12; 6.26:3.

169. *Ugaritica* 5, 137 II:10′. Huehnergard reconstructs this line as follows: (Sum.) G[Ú] = (Akk.) [mātu] = (Hur.) [u]-mi-in$_4$ = (Ugar.) [ḫ]u-wa-tu$_4$ (*Ugaritic Vocabulary*, 123).

170. See François Thureau-Dangin, "Trois contrats de Ras-Shamra," *Syria* 18 (1937): 251 (RS 8.213:5).

171. With Huehnergard, *Ugaritic Vocabulary*, 123.

172. See Andrée Herdner, review of *Ugaritic-Hebrew Philology*, by Mitchell Dahood," *Syria* 46 (1969): 132.

173. KTU 2.36:16 (reconstructed in line 19: ḥ]wtm . ủgr[t); 2.81:18. Cf. also b . ḥw[t] nǵṯ "land of NǴṮ (KTU 2.36:17); bʿl . kl . ḥwt [mṣr]m "lord of all the land of [Egyp]t" (KTU 2.81:3–4).

generally denotes "land/country." For example, in a letter from the king of Hatti addressed to the Ugaritic King ʿAmmurāpiʾ, the Hittite king writes:

(17) *w lḥt ảkl ky*	Now as for the tablet regarding the food that
(18) *lỉkt ʿm špš*	you sent to the Sun,
(19) *bʿlk ky ảkl*	your lord, that there is no food
(20) *b ḥwtk ỉnn*	in your land:
(21) *špšn tủbd*	the Sun himself is perishing.

This form occurs eleven times in the birth omen text KTU 1.103+ dealing with malformed animal fetuses. For each of the cases in which *ḥwt* occurs, it also states in what way the malformation will affect the land. For example, the opening line warns that when ewes of the sheep give birth: *ảbn mảdtn tqln b ḥwt* "if it is stone, many will fall in the land" (KTU 1.103+:1).[174]

This particular application of the root *ḥwy* at Ugarit undoubtedly reflects the ancients' dependence upon the agricultural produce from the land for survival. It was the land that provided the opportunity for agriculture, the main source of sustenance for society, and in this sense the land preserves or maintains its life and livelihood. But more specifically, as the distribution of this term suggests, the usage of *ḥwt* is confined to a particular land, whether it be the land of Ugarit or some other specified locale, or the land of a particular referent in the letters (or even the birth omen text). In other words, the usage of *ḥwt* seems to reflect one's tie to a geographical region/town where life is lived and preserved. This notion seems to be shared in common with Biblical Hebrew *ḥawwâ*, also apparently meaning "town, village," as well as the later Punic word *ḥwt* meaning the same.[175] One might also compare the Arabic word *ḥiwā*, which can denote an enclosed area or "circle of tents."[176]

1.2.3.2. Adjectival Forms

The adjective *ḥy* occurs in the Ugaritic letter KTU 2.82:17 where it stands in contrast with the root m-t "to die."[177] This letter addressed to the queen, who is apparently the sender's mother (*ủmy* "my mother"), gives a battle report

174. Cf. KTU 1.103+:4, 5, 16, 37, 41, 45, 50, 51, 53, 56.

175. For Hebrew, see Num 32:41: *wᵉyāʾîr ben-mᵉnaššê hālak wayyilkōd ʾet-ḥawwōtêhem wayyiqrâ ʾethen ḥawwōt yāʾîr* "Jair, son of Manasseh, went and captured their towns/villages and called them 'Towns of Jair.'" Cf. Deut 3:14; Josh 13:30; Judg 10:4; 1 Kgs 4:13; 1 Chr 2:23 (see *HALOT*, 296; BDB, 295). For Punic, see KAI 161.9 (see *DNWSI*, 353).

176. Lane, 679.

177. Cf. the G SC form *ḥy* in the Baʿlu cycle (KTU 1.6 III:2, 8, 20), also in contrast with m-t.

verifying that another individual by the name ʿAbdimilku is still *ḥy* "alive," but that if he should die, the sender would continue to fight:[178]

(8) *ảnk ṯṯ ymm* (9) *kl lḥmt*	Now as for me, for six days I have done nothing but fight.
(10) *w hm ỉnm* (11) *ʿbdmlk*	If ʿAbdimilku is no longer
(12) *npl***ṭ** ***ḥ***[***y***] (13) *w l*⌜*b*⌝[179] [. . .]	saved **al**[**ive**$^?$] and the heart of . . .

(lines 13–15 broken)

(17) *ỉkmy* ***ḥy*** (18) *ʿbdmlk*	However that may be,[180] ʿAbdimilku **is** (still) **alive**.
hm (19) *ymt*	If he dies,
(20) *w ỉlḥmn* (21) *ảnk*	I myself will fight (on).

Earlier in this letter, the sender makes mention of the queen having sent an individual named ʿKY and that ʿAbdimilku had been saved: *ỉd likt ʿky nplṭ ʿbdmlk šʿtq* "When you sent ʿKY, ʿAbdimilku the *šʿtq* was saved" (lines 3–5). It is curious to note the possibility of reading *ḥy* in line 12 as well, as the sender surmises that if ʿAbdimilku were not saved while still alive, then presumably, his heart would be downcast.[181] Of course, this interpretation remains provisional, since the text is partially reconstructed (*ḥ*[*y*]). Given this caveat, what would it mean to be saved alive? Perhaps it would refer to the more desirable outcome of rescuing ʿAbdimilku and thus preserving his life rather than rescuing the remains of someone who has already died. One might compare this expression, *nplṭ ḥy* "to deliver alive," to the D stem imperative from KTU 1.82:6: *ql špš ḥw* "(by) the voice of Šapšu, be delivered." They are two possible ways of expressing the preservation of one's state of existence, and thus deliverance from death. The sender of KTU 2.82 offers hope for the recipient, since ʿAbdimilku is still alive at the time of writing this letter, though he is prepared to continue fighting whether

178. Pardee identifies him as a royal son and not necessarily the reigning king, since in no instance does the king address the queen mother in this way, i.e., *ảdny* "my lady" (*COS* 3:93 n. 34).

179. According to Pierre Bordreuil and André Caquot, "Les textes en cunéiformes alphabétiques découverts en 1978 a Ibn Hani," *Syria* 57 (1980): 259. *CAT* simply transcribes *l*x[xxx]x.

180. Pardee, *COS* 3:93. Cf. Bordeuil and Caquot, "Textes en cunéiformes alphabétiques," 360: "since"; followed by *DUL*, 45.

181. This reconstruction is strengthened by the fact that *ḥy* does occur in line 17 in contrast to what is stated in line 12. That his heart is downcast is suggested by Pardee, in contrast to his heart being uplifted as noted in line 7 (*COS* 3:93 n. 36).

ʿAbdimilku is dead or alive. Structurally, these two conditional clauses exhibit synonymous parallelism:

A	Protasis	*w hm ỉnm ʿbdmlk nplṭ ḥ[y]*
	Apodasis	*w l⌜b⌝ . . .*
B	*ỉkmỷ ḥy ʿbdmlk*	
A′	Protasis	*hm ymt*
	Apodasis	*w ỉlḥmn ảnk*

From this analysis, not being rescued alive basically means that the author feared that ʿAbdimilku would die from wounds received in battle, though this had not yet occurred when the letter was incised.

1.3. Summary

This chapter has set forth a detailed analysis of the roots *ḥwy/ḥyy* and all their permutations as attested in Ugaritic. At this juncture in the discussion I will offer a brief summary of my lexical analysis of the Ugaritic conception of life from the vantage point of this root.

First, according to the distribution and usage of all *ḥyy* and *ḥwy* forms in Ugaritic, the proposal of Marcus that medial {y} = the G stem and medial {w} = the D stem seems to hold true. No form thus far attested in the Ugaritic materials substantially challenges this viewpoint. This conclusion corroborates with my analysis of the comparative evidence supporting Marcus's proposal treated earlier in this chapter.

Second, the G stem of this root indicates one's state of being or existence. This meaning is also reflected in the adjectival forms which occur parallel to *iṯ* (KTU 1.6 III:2–3; 8–9; 20–21), the Ugaritic particle of existence.

Furthermore, the G stem verbal forms (e.g., KTU 1.16 I:22–23; 1.16 II:43–44; 6.30), as well as the attested noun forms (KTU 1.16 I:14; 1.17 VI:27), express a state that is the opposite of the root m-t "to die." According to the distribution and usage of this root, ḥ-y/w-y and m-t are mutually exclusive. In all of the above cases where these two roots occur in relation to each other, the one is conceived of as being the opposite of the other. Therefore, it is important to stress that in Ugaritic m-t "to die" means the end of *ḥwy/ḥyy*. Any suggestion of a continued "existence" postmortem must involve something other than "life" in the strictest sense.

The D stem forms of *ḥwy*, however, indicate one of two possible meanings: (1) a renewed state of being (i.e., a return to life), or more commonly (2) the preservation of that state of being (i.e., to make someone/thing live on). The idea of revivification arises from the usage and context of *ḥwy* in the ʾAqhatu Epic, where the hero is promised the prospects of a life comparable to that of Baʿlu when he is revived (KTU 1.17 VI:30). This is not entirely unrelated to the nuance of preservation, but instead suggests a special kind of preservation via revivification. And if one takes the rejection speech of ʾAqhatu at face value, this ability belongs exclusively to the gods. Preservation, on the other hand, shows up in a number of contexts related to human life and once for an inanimate object. Depending on one's interpretation of KTU 1.24:10, the D stem may refer to the initiation of life, that is, if the form in question refers to the young woman giving birth. One might appeal to the goddess Šapšu to stop the deadly venom of a snakebite, thus saving a life sliding toward death (KTU 1.82:6). In the negative, not allowing one's life to be preserved essentially means to kill someone, which is what ʿAnatu threatens to do to ʾAqhatu and then confesses to have done (KTU 1.18 IV:26–27; 1.19 I:15–16). This example adds an additional nuance to the notion of making someone live on—it is preservation by permission, or in the negative, death by the termination of one's ability to live on. This is different from saving a life in danger of dying, as in the case of saving someone having been poisoned by a snake (KTU 1.82:6). The same case can be made in light of its application to a dilapidated (i.e., dying) house in a Ugaritic letter, meaning that it had been repaired by the craftsmen to the extent that it has once again been made "alive," or perhaps made "useable/functionary" (KTU 2.70:15–16) and will not be destroyed (i.e., will not "die").

The above meanings of the D stem *ḥwy* fall along a temporal continuum, with the focus placed upon one of three perspectives: (1) initiation of life, (2) continuation of life, and (3) renewal of life. I outline these three perspectives as follows:

I. Initiation of life (KTU 1.24:10?)
II. Continuation of life
    a. Preservation through intervention = Reversal of sliding toward death (e.g., remedy for snakebite; restoring dilapidated house)
    b. Preservation hindered through the act of killing (e.g., ʿAnatu and ʾAqhatu)
III. Renewal of life—(e.g., revivification of Baʿlu promised to ʾAqhatu)

CHAPTER 2

NPŠ and Other Terms for Body Parts Especially Associated with the Concept of Life

2.1. Introduction

Having dealt with the roots most basically expressive of the concept of life, I now proceed to the study of terms associated with living beings, humans and animals, which in turn are also projected onto divine beings.

2.1.1. Defining Methodology

The nature of these materials necessitates an arrangement different from that of the previous chapter, in which I analyzed the verbal roots *ḥwy/ḥyy*, their verbal stems and related substantives, throughout the corpus of Ugaritic texts. The words discussed in this chapter are primarily substantives; therefore, I have arranged my treatment of these words into two semantic groups based upon their poetic parallels, as well as other pertinent words from context. This arrangement is crucial for understanding these terms according to their native contexts. Admittedly, these ancient associations are not always readily apparent to the modern way of thinking, reinforcing the realization that the ancient perspective is not our own. These poetic parallels provide a helpful guide in my attempt to analyze and define each word individually in establishing semantic limitations from the ancient context for my lexical study.

I will treat the remaining selected Ugaritic words for life with the following two-fold arrangement: (1) body parts *npš* "neck, throat," parallel *brlt*, and associated terms *rḥ*, *iṯl*, and *qṭr*, and (2) body parts *kbd* "liver, insides," *lb* "heart" (regular parallel for *kbd*), and *ảp* "nose." The first group is the largest, with *npš* drawing the focus of this chapter due to its widespread attestation throughout mythological, epic, epistolary, and ritual texts. The second most important terms are *kbd* and *lb*, the latter most often functioning as the former's poetic parallel; both are attested in mythological and ritual contexts. The term *ảp* "nose" is also mentioned in light of its occurrence in the ritual texts and its well-known association with anger, which I discuss in my treatment of the idiom *b qṣrt npš* "in the shortness of *npš*" (// *ảp*).

As a preliminary observation, one discovers a particular commonality between these two groups in that both involve a development in meaning from the concrete to the abstract. As I will argue below, the concrete meaning of *npš* as understood from its usage in the ritual texts is "neck," from which apparently has developed the more abstract connotation, "person" or "individual." In mythological and epic texts one finds that from the concrete "neck/throat" arises the abstract meaning "vitality" or "life force." Similarly, the word *kbd* denotes the liver of animals, either for sacrifice or extispicy, but elsewhere seems to mean more figuratively "innards." As "innards," I will demonstrate that when *kdb* and *lb* occur as a poetic pair, they refer to one's emotional experience, while *lb* independently refers to conative processes. I explore these features more fully in my treatment of these words throughout this chapter as I attempt to reconstruct the Ugaritic understanding of life, building upon my treatment of the roots *ḥwy*/*ḥyy* in chapter 1. Before doing so, however, I need to make a few introductory remarks regarding the nature of poetic parallelism as it relates to the poetic narrative contexts of these words.

2.1.2. Semantic Parallelism

Scholarly attention to poetic parallelism has advanced significantly in the past few decades, especially in the wake of the discovery and decipherment of the Ugaritic tablets. Earlier treatments of poetic parallelism in the Bible owe much to Robert Lowth's three-fold categorization of synonymous, antithetic, and synthetic parallelism.[1] Recent efforts, however, have moved beyond these limited

1. Robert Lowth, *Lectures on the Sacred Poetry of the Hebrews*, trans. George Gregory (Boston: Buckingham, 1815), 259–73. See also the discussions in Dennis Pardee, *Ugaritic and Hebrew Poetic Parallelism: A Trial Cut (ʿnt and Proverbs 2)*, VTSup 39 (Leiden: Brill, 1988), 170–75, followed by Joel M. LeMon, "The Power of Parallelism in KTU2 1.119: Another 'Trial Cut,'" *UF* 37 (2005): 375–94; Adele Berlin, *The Dynamics of Biblical Parallelism*, rev. and expanded ed. (Grand Rapids: Eerdmans, 2008), 64–72. See also Michael O'Connor, *Hebrew Verse Structure* (Winona Lake, IN: Eisenbrauns, 1980), 88–137; Stanislav Segert, "Parallelism in Ugaritic Poetry," *JAOS* 103 (1983): 295–306; Wilfred G. E. Watson, *Classical Heberw Poetry: A Guide to Its Techniques*, JSOTSup 26 (Sheffield: Sheffield Academic, 1984), 114–59; Brent A. Strawn, "A Woman at Prayer (Psalm 131,

designations in search of a more precise taxonomy of parallel types. Adele Berlin in her study of biblical parallelism identifies four aspects of language, from which she illustrates their respective parallel types: grammatical, lexical, semantic, and phonological.[2] Berlin distinguishes lexical from semantic parallelism by limiting semantic to the relationship between poetic lines of verse, while lexical parallelism more specifically deals with the pairing of individual words.[3] Pardee outlines four types—repetitive (i.e., repetition of the same root), semantic, grammatical, and phonetic—and identifies several neglected aspects in the study of poetic parallelism: parallelism of minor elements, positional parallelism, phonetic parallelism, length compensation, and the overall distribution of parallelism.[4]

For the purposes of this study, I am interested in understanding the nature of semantic parallelism—lexical for Berlin—as a basis for our interpretations of poetic word pairs expressing various nuances of life in Ugaritic.[5] I am concerned with a particular type of pairing wherein a word from one line of verse is in parallel with a different word in a second line of verse with the intent of expressing a similar line of thought. Berlin's appeal to the linguistic theory of word association leads her to explain lexical parallels as arising from a "complex psycholinguistic process" more so than on a semantic basis, which would suggest the "sameness of meaning" for two words in parallel. Yet even Berlin concedes that she does not mean to say that a semantic component is altogether absent, insofar as two parallel terms share a similar semantic field.[6] Such a caveat is inescapable in the face of the data provided by the topic of this book, where Ugaritic poets chose a word as an appropriate correspondent to another—even though one must recognize the parallel is not exactly the same but may instead add nuance to the concept in view. This acknowledgment corresponds to David J. A. Clines' "parallelism of greater precision," which he explains is observable from the fact that the second half of a parallelistic couplet regularly exhibits more precision than the first.[7] Similarly, Stephen Geller has attempted to categorize

2b) and Arguments 'from Parallelism,'" *ZAW* 124 (2012): 423–26; F. W. Dobbs-Allsopp, *On Biblical Poetry* (Oxford University Press, 2015), 68–70, 143–49, 269–76.

2. Berlin, *Dynamics of Biblical Parallelism*, 127–41.

3. Berlin, *Dynamics of Biblical Parallelism*, 64–65.

4. Pardee, *Ugaritic and Hebrew Poetic Parallelism*, 169–91.

5. I agree with Strawn's caution that "parallelism is not mechanistic and cannot be appealed to simplistically" ("Woman at Prayer," 425). Rather, one needs to examine carefully the semantic relationship between two lexemes, as well as the immediate and broader contexts in which the parallel occurs.

6. Berlin, *Dynamics of Biblical Parallelism*, 80.

7. David J. A. Clines, "The Parallelism of Greater Precision: Notes from Isaiah 40 for a Theory of Hebrew Poetry," in *Directions in Biblical Poetry*, ed. Elain R. Follis, JSOTSup 40 (Sheffield: JSOT Press, 1987), 47–70.

a number of these so-called semantic relationships (synonym, list, antonym, merism, identity, and metaphor), moving beyond the overly simplistic categories devised by Lowth (synonymous, antithetic, and synthetic) and devoting a more invested interest in grammatical parallelism.[8]

The word associations attested in the poetic narrative texts from Ugarit show a two-fold importance for my analysis of terms having to do with life: (1) they provide indicators of lexically synonymous items which aid our own understanding of these ancient concepts, and (2) they offer a means for understanding the cultural perceptions of the poet in his associations of individual words. These two observations intricately relate to one another by the simple fact that the lexical meaning of a word and the associations that that word elicits are two sides of the same coin, so to speak. While not denying the legitimacy of lexical considerations, word association theorists emphasize the perceptions of speakers and the cultural climates giving rise to various semantic combinations.[9] This generality is a useful perspective to keep in mind as we continue our lexical investigation of life at Ugaritic and our collection of word pairs from the poetic texts. At the same time, however, it is also important to remember that the word association espoused by modern linguistic theory yields an environment altogether foreign to the ancient one in which Ugaritic poetry would have been composed.[10] There can be no doubt that psycholinguistics does indeed offer many helpful insights for the modern interpreter who is far removed from the ancient world. I would only caution, however, that it is the general idea of word association as a transcultural phenomenon that is useful here in identifying individual word pairs as a means of understanding the unique cultural conceptualizations of the native speaker. Looking for the added nuance of a paired word forces the reader to ask

8. Stephen Geller, *Parallelism in Early Biblical Poetry*, HSM 20 (Missoula, MT: Scholars Press, 1979), 31–42. See also Pardee's assessment of Geller in *Ugaritic and Hebrew Poetic Parallelism*, 171 and n. 15.

9. E.g., Lorand B. Szalay and James Deese, *Subjective Meaning and Culture: An Assessment through Word Associations* (Hillsdale, NJ: Erlbaum, 1978), viii–ix.

10. In particular, word association as a theory proper involves the analysis of pairs derived from the "free associations" produced by individuals in the laboratory. Participants are given a word stimulant to which they verbalize whatever word comes to mind in response to it. The kinds of associations can vary considerably depending on the length of time allowed for a respondent. For example, Herbert H. Clark notes that when respondents are given more time they generally produce richer and more complex types of analogies, while shorter response time tends toward superficiality and less sophisticated associations ("Word Associations and Linguistic Theory," in *New Horizons in Linguistics*, ed. John Lyons [Harmondsworth: Penguin, 1970] 272–73). In Ugaritic poetry, at least, we are dealing not so much with free associations given in rapid response (unless we argue for the oral composition theory, which Berlin goes to great lengths to discount [*Dynamics of Biblical Parallelism*, 66]), but with lexical associations developed in the more controlled environment of composed verse.

more probing questions about the meaning of its counterpart that would allow for the analogy. Or, in other cases, lexically obscure (at least to the modern reader) words paired with more broadly attested ones help to define them.[11] Applying the study of word pairs elicited according to "free association" in the laboratory to similar verbal formations in Ugaritic poetry (or biblical for that matter) is more complex and difficult to determine.[12]

2.2. Life and Body Parts: *npš* = "Neck" and "Throat"

The first semantic group of body parts is centered on the widespread occurrence of the noun *npš* throughout the Ugaritic textual corpus. Because of the number of times this word appears in Ugaritic, I treat it first. The poetic mythological texts provide a useful environment for examining rough semantic equivalencies from the perspective of Ugaritic conceptualizations, keeping us from being held hostage by modern assessments about what is or is not an appropriate synonym for a given word. In Ugaritic, *npš* regularly occurs in poetic parallel with *brlt* and once with *gngn*. Also attested is the expression *qṣr npš* "shortness of *npš*," in one context parallel with *ảlmnt*, and, in a ritual text, with *ảp* and *qṯt*. I shall begin my study of this semantic group by investigating *npš* as it occurs in the predominantly prose ritual texts, after which I will examine its usage and meanings elsewhere.

2.2.1. *npš* = Neck

The Ugaritic ritual texts contain several occurrences of the word *npš* where it refers to a particular part of an animal being offered to a named deity. It appears that this usage is limited to the ritual texts in its identification of the animal body

11. E.g., the less common *brlt* in parallel with the more widely attested *npš*. See my analysis of these two words below.

12. Berlin attempts to do so in her treatment of biblical parallelism, citing the studies of Clark ("Word Associations," 271–86) and James Deese (*The Structure of Associations in Language and Thought* [Baltimore: Johns Hopkins University Press, 1965]). She argues that when we apply their observations about English word associations to Hebrew word pairs they exhibit remarkable similarities. Therefore, Berlin concludes: "In this way Hebrew word pairs—all Hebrew word pairs—can be understood as the product of normal linguistic association" (*Dynamics of Biblical Parallelism*, 68). My only contention is that the processes that produce the pairs analyzed in these studies are not necessarily analogical to those of the ancient poets and therefore cannot be assumed without qualification. Part of the issue here relates to Berlin's unwillingness to acknowledge possible influence from a literary school or tradition in the poet's craft, viewing such pairs as the product of internal psychological processes alone. As Pardee has pointed out, however, it is likely a mixture of both (*Ugaritic and Hebrew Poetic Parallelism*, 173). See also the judicious assessment in Dobbs-Allsopp, *On Biblical Poetry*, 272–76.

part and does not occur elsewhere in Ugaritic, except for the related meaning "throat," well-attested in the mythological texts as discussed below. The Ugaritic ritual texts yield several offering lists wherein *npš* is specified alongside other listed items such as: *ảp* "a nose," *kbd* "a liver," *š* "a ram," *gdlt* "a cow," *dqt* "sheep, ewes," *ʿṣr* "a bird," *ksp* "silver," and *ḫrṣ* "gold." I offer the following examples:

KTU 1.88 (RS 18.107):

št[13] *b* ***npš*** *ỉšt w l tỉkl w l tš*[*t*]	Set(?) fire to **the neck**, and indeed you will eat and dri[nk]. (broken context)

KTU 1.90:3 (RS 19.013):

(1) *ỉd yph mlk* (2) *r*⸢*š*⸣*p ḥgb*	Then the king must look at RŠP ḤGB:
ảp (3) *w* [-] ⸢***n***⸣***pš*** *ksp* (4) *w*	a nose, **a neck**, a shekel of silver, and a
[-] *ḫrṣ*	shekel of gold.

KTU 1.105/RS 24.249:23':

ʿṣr l ṣpn (25') ***npš*** *w š l ršp bbt*	A bird for ṢPN, **a neck** and a ram for RŠP BBT.

KTU 1.106:19 (RS 24.250+):

b ṯmn gn	On the eighth of Gannu:
(19) [***n***]***pš*** *w ảrbʿ* (20) *ʿšrh dqt*	**a neck**, fourteen ewes,
(21) *w šbʿ gdlt*	seven cows,
w k(22)*l šbšlt dg gnh*	and all the fish stew at the garden.

KTU 1.109:12 (RS 24.253):

w b bt bʿl ủgrt	In the temple of Baʿlu of Ugarit:
(12) *kkdm*[14] *w* ***npš***	*kkdm* and **a neck**.

KTU 1.119:14, 15 (RS 24.266):

(13) ⸢*ủ*⸣ *ủrm ủ šnpt l ydbḥ*	A fire sacrifice and a *špnt* offering the king
(14) *mlk bt ỉl*	must sacrifice in the house of ʾIlu:
npš *l ỉ*⸢-⸣[. . .] (15) ***npš*** *l bʿ*⸢*l*⸣ [. . .]	**a neck** for ʾI[. . .], **a neck** for Baʿlu [. . .]

13. *DUL*: *št b npš ỉšt* (119); *KTU*: *šḥ *b npš ỉšt*; *CAT*: *šṯ/ʿ b npš ỉšt*.

14. Possibly: *kbdm* (suggested in *CAT*), but Pardee simply transliterates KKDM (*Ritual and Cult at Ugarit*, 31) in light of the fact that the second letter of this word in the corresponding section from KTU 1.46 (RS 1.009) also reads {k} and not {b}.

KTU 1.164:4 (RIH 77/2B+):

(3) [*ỉ*]⌜*d*⌝ *ydbḥ mlk l ỉlỉb* (4) *b db*	[Th]en the king must sacrifice to ỈlỈB in DB:
ảp w ***npš*** *ksp* (5) *w ḫrṣ*	a nose, **a neck**, silver, and gold.

KTU 1.168:2, 9 (RIH 77/10B+):

(8) *ỉd* ⌜*y*⌝*ph mlk ʿnt* (9) *sl*⌜*z*⌝	Then the king must look at ʿAnatu SLZ:
ảp w ***npš*** *ksp*(10) [*w*] *ḫrṣ*	a nose, **a neck**, silver, and gold.

KTU 1.43:12:

ṯql ḫrṣ (11) *l špš w yrḫ*	A shekel of gold for ŠPŠ and YRḪ;
l gṯr (12) *ṯql ksp ṭb ả*⌜*p*⌝ *w* ***n***⌜***pš***⌝	for GṮR a shekel of good silver, a nose, and **a neck**;
(13) *l ʿnt*⌜*h*⌝[15] *ṯql ḫrṣ*	for ʿAnatu a shekel of gold.

From these examples we can reasonably conclude that *npš* refers to a particular portion of the animal offered as a sacrifice to the deity named in the ritual. The exact identification of the part of the animal specified by *npš*, however, has attracted diverse opinions.

Wolf Gottlieb takes *npš* to mean "lungs" or "chest," similar to the interpretation of Paolo Xella for the expression *ảp w npš* in the ritual texts.[16] Gottlieb, appealing to the Biblical Hebrew evidence, makes his case in light of the fact that the Bible nowhere else attests a word for "lungs," an argument criticized extensively by Pardee.[17] The meaning "lung(s)" has made its way into several

15. The interpretation of the final {h} in this form has troubled scholars, many suggesting that it is a 3ms pronominal suffix, "his ʿAnatu," identifying her as the consort of GṮR (see Manfried Dietrich and Oswald Loretz, "Baal *rpu* in KTU 1.108; 1.113 und nach 1.17 VI 25–33," *UF* 12 [1980]: 175; Spronk, *Beatific Afterlife*, 183; de Moor, *Anthology of Religious Texts*, 170; del Olmo Lete, *Religión cananea*, 193 n. 109). Other scholars have proposed that it could be an adverbial {h} instead, which might lend support for reading the final {m} of *ʿntm* in line 18 also as an adverbial (for a fuller discussion and bibliography, see Pardee, *Textes rituels*, 247–48; Dennis Pardee, review of *'Jahwe und seine Aschera': Anthropomorphes Kultbild in Mesopotamien, Ugarit und Israel; Das biblische Bilderverboot*, by Manfried Dietrich and Oswald Loretz, *JAOS* 115 [1995]: 301–3).

16. Wolf Gottlieb, "The Term 'Nepeš' in the Bible: A Reappraisal," *GUOST* 25 (1973–74): 72; Xella, *Testi rituali di Ugarit I*, 32.

17. Gottlieb reasons, "The fact is that while the other important parts of the organism like the heart, liver, gall, kidneys, bowels, stomach, and intestines are more or less frequently mentioned in the Bible, both as physical organs and in their abstract metaphorical applications, no single mention is made in the whole Bible of a large, important vital organ—the lungs, the essential existence of which could not have escaped primitive man" ("Term 'Nepeš' in the Bible," 72). Pardee, *Textes rituels*, 244–45.

translations of the Ugaritic rituals, but most often without comment.[18] Del Olmo Lete renders all such occurrences of *npš* in the rituals as "entrails" of the animal, which apparently would refer to the internal organs essential for life.[19] These suggestions certainly move the discussion beyond the older tendency among biblical scholars to translate the Hebrew cognate rather monolithically as "life, soul."[20] The Ugaritic ritual context, which often pairs *npš* with *ảp* "nose, snout" (i.e., *ảp w npš* in the above examples), at the least requires that it refers to some part of the animal, rather than the animal as a whole.[21]

Perhaps a better suggestion for the part of the animal referenced in *npš* is "neck," extensively discussed in Pardee's *Les textes rituels*. This interpretation advances the well-attested view that the concrete sense of *npš* is "throat."[22] Ample evidence exists in the mythological texts that *npš* must mean "throat," as in the oft-cited example involving Baʿlu's decent into the "throat" of Môtu in KTU 1.5 I:6–7:

*l yrt b **npš** bn ỉlm mt*	Indeed, go down into **the throat** of the god Môtu,
b mhmrt ydd ỉl ǵzr	into the pit of the beloved divine hero.[23]

I will return to other similar contexts for *npš* later in this chapter, but as it pertains to those of the ritual texts they require a nuanced explanation as to what is meant by offering a "throat" in sacrifice. If the ritual texts indicate a "throat"-offering, Pardee surmises that in the case of *ảp w npš* the "throat" would have been cut

18. E.g., de Tarragon: "lung" ("poumon"; *Textes ougaritiques* 2, 162); Wyatt: "lung" (*Religious Texts from Ugarit*, 2nd ed., BibSem 53 [London: Sheffield Academic, 2002], 358).

19. Spanish "asadura"; del Olmo Lete, *Religión cananea*, 191 (which, by the way, he qualifies as having nothing to do with *npš* = person [193 n. 112]); del Olmo Lete, "Anatomía cultual en Ugarit: Ofrenda de vísceras en el culto ugarítico," *AuOr* 7 (1989): 123; cf. *DUL* meaning 6: "(piece of) offal" (636–37).

20. Though not entirely absent from the Ugaritic literature either. Cf. Gordon, *Ugaritic Literature*, 114: "body-and-soul offering" (translating *ảp w npš* in KTU 1.43:15); Edward L. Greenstein, "Another Attestation of Initial h > ʾ in West Semitic," *JANESCU* 5 (1973): 158 n. 14: "live prey" (in KTU 1.105:25′, arguing for this translation in light of the fact that *npš* normally means "life" or "living thing").

21. As suggested by de Moor, "Studies in the New Alphabetic Texts from Ras Shamra II," 321. He states that "it may be assumed that *npš* means 'throat.' Because *npš* stands next to *š* here [RS 24.249:11], it can be inferred that *ảp*, *npš* and *kkdm* were taken from oxen." See also del Olmo Lete, *La religión cananea*, 32.

22. De Moor, "Studies in the New Alphabetic Texts from Ras Shamra II," 321; Pope, "Little Soul-Searching," 26; Miller, review of *Le culte à Ugarit*," 595; van Selms, *Marriage and Family Life*, 129 n. 2 (but "breath" or "incense" in the ritual texts). Seligson denied this concrete meaning for *npš* in *The Meaning of* נפש מת *in the Old Testament*, 46–69.

23. See Pope, "Little Soul-Searching," 28.

out of the animal at the same time the snout was removed, both of which were offered as edibles for the gods. These edible animal parts offered to the gods were symbolically representative of the animal's life, which, by the way, provides one possible explanation (but not the only one) for the derived meaning "life."[24] On the other hand, the Akkadian cognate *napištu* attests both the internal meaning "throat" and the external "neck," which leads Pardee to suggest that this double-significance could be operative for Ugaritic *npš* as well.[25] If the *npš* of ritual texts indeed indicates "neck," one might propose that the flesh from the neck of the animal (also reserved for certain priests), together with its snout, was offered to the deity.[26]

In looking at the texts themselves, the "neck" interpretation certainly seems plausible, if not the most satisfactory. For example, in KTU 1.88, despite its broken context, the mention of setting fire to the *npš* followed by eating and drinking makes the most sense if it is taken as a reference to burning the meat of the animal's neck. Furthermore, its association with other identifiable parts of the animal—the *ảp* "nose" or even *kbd* "liver"—makes "neck" a simpler option over "throat."[27] Again, the flesh from the neck of an animal (whether *š* "ram" or unspecified) as something reserved for the priests would suggest a choice portion and thus an appropriate offering alongside *ksp* "silver" and *ḫrṣ* "gold."[28]

Another commendable aspect of the interpretation *npš* = "neck" is that it provides the fullest explanation for the derived meanings extant in Ugaritic.[29] The two known passageways of the neck allow for derivational meanings in one of two directions: (1) the passageway via the esophagus to the stomach and (2) the passageway via the trachea to the lungs.[30] The neck contains the esophagus—its entrance is the throat—through which food passes into the stomach. Yet, the neck also contains the windpipe or trachea which enables the passage

24. Pardee, *Textes rituels*, 246. Pardee also appeals to the Greek parallel of presenting various edible parts of the sacrificial animal as an offering to the gods (*Textes para-mythologiques*, 36–38).

25. *CAD* 11:303–4. Note, however, that *CAD* only offers the translation "neck" for humans; one or two of the examples listed for animals could arguably be translated "neck."

26. Pardee, *Textes rituels*, 246.

27. As in KTU 1.46:1: *npš ṯʿ w* ⌜*ṯ*⌝[*n*] ⌜*k*⌝*bdm* "a neck as a *ṯʿ*-offering and two livers." Or, consider also KTU 1.109:12 if one were to adopt the emendation *kkdm* > *kbdm*: *kbdm w npš* "a liver? and a neck."

28. For the argument that it was reserved for the priests, see Pardee, *Textes rituels*, 246. Note also that Akkadian *tikku* "neck" can denote a cut of meat (*CAD* 18:401). The choice portion designation may have been defined ideologically rather than in terms of butcher's cuts.

29. This meaning has also been suggested as a possible meaning in Biblical Hebrew (e.g., *ʿad nepeš* "up to the neck" in Jonah 2:6).

30. Pardee, *Textes rituels*, 245.

of air essential for life. Two abstractions may arise from the body's air conduit: (1) the breath which flows through the trachea and (2) the movement associated with breathing. This second notion involving the movement of breathing could provide the basis for *npš* as vitality or life force. As I will show in my analysis of these usages shortly, *npš* in such cases seems to emphasize the thing that produces life and that can wane or expire altogether. Finally, the move toward "life" more generally (as well as the related meaning "person" or "individual") involves both aspects of the main derivations from "neck." Both the esophagus and the body's main airway are essential for life: cutting off either passageway results in the termination of life.

2.2.2. *npš* = Throat

In addition to the Ugaritic ritual usage of *npš* meaning "neck," the mythological texts are replete with contexts requiring the translation "throat." By way of comparison, the biblical tradition offers a few examples for which scholars have noted the appropriateness of the rendering "throat." The most common citation is Isa 5:14:

lākēn hirḥîbâ šᵉʾôl ***napšāh***	Therefore, Sheol has enlarged **its throat**,
ûpāᵃrâ pîhā liblî-ḥōq	and opened its mouth without measure.

The imagery of a personified Sheol opening wide its throat resembles that of Môtu in Ugaritic mythology. Similar imagery also appears in Hab 2:5, only this time Sheol appears in parallel with Death:

ʾᵃšer hirḥîb kišʾōl ***napšô***	in that he enlarges **his throat** like Sheol,
wᵉhûʾ kammāwet wᵉlōʾ yiśbāʿ	and he is like Death: he is not satisfied.

Both of these examples from Biblical Hebrew bring to mind the mythology of Môtu as he is described in Ugaritic, to which I now turn our attention.

2.2.2.1. The Baʿlu Cycle

The mythological Baʿlu cycle elucidates our knowledge of *npš* in Ugaritic, thrusting the reader to the fore of the conflict between the death god Môtu and the storm god Baʿlu. In these texts, the death god's *npš* functions as the passageway of the dead, even the defeated Baʿlu, the irony of it all being highlighted by this word's usual association with matters of life, not death. In all such contexts, *npš* is Môtu's gullet characterized by an insatiable appetite for dead corpses.

KTU 1.5 I:7:

ảnk ỉspỉ ủṭm[31]	I myself am devoured by double ʾ*uṭu*-measures,
(6) *ḏrqm ảmtm*[32]	(as) dung I die.
l yrt	Indeed, you must descend;
l yrt (7) *b* ***npš*** *bn ỉlm mt*	Indeed, you must descend into **the throat** of Môtu, son of ʾIlu,
b mh(8)*mrt ydd ỉl ǵzr*	into the well/pit of the beloved hero of ʾIlu.

The context of this utterance from Môtu comes toward the end of his reply to the bombastic taunts of Baʿlu having taken up residence in his newly constructed palace. The last column of KTU 1.4 breaks off, so the earlier part of the speech has to be reconstructed from 1.5 I:12–27 where the messengers repeat Môtu's address to Baʿlu.[33] Here, *npš* is parallel with *mhmrt*, which possibly means "pit," from the verbal root *hmr* "to pour out" attested in Arabic.[34] Biblical Hebrew attests the noun *mahmôrâ* in Ps 140:11, which from context also appears to indicate a pit of some sort.[35] In commenting on KTU 1.5 Pope concludes that *mhmrt* and *npš* both "refer to Mot's gullet as the avenue of Baal's descent into the netherworld."[36]

Immediately following KTU 1.5 I:8, the narrative depicts the messengers setting out to deliver Môtu's message to Baʿlu (lines 9–11). The message takes us

31. The meaning of this word has been variously understood. Caquot and Sznyzer translate the word as "moaning" ("gémissant"; *Textes ougaritiques 1*, 241; cf. Pardee, *COS* 1:265: "with groans"). For this meaning, Arabic *ʾṯṯ* "to utter a sound, noise, cry" (Lane, 66) provides an etymological parallel that works here. Del Olmo Lete: "pieces" ("pedazos"; *Mitos y leyendas de Canaan*, 213; cf. *DUL*, 123, and de Moor, *Anthology of Religious Texts*, 70: "span"). This interpretation is based upon Akkadian *ūṭu* "span, half cubit" (*AHw* 3:1447). Wyatt renders it "elbows" or "hands" (*Religious Texts*, 116 n. 9). Adrianus van Selms ("A Systematic Approach to CTA 5,I,1–8," *UF* 7 [1975]: 482) is undecided, proposing either "nose, nostril" (cf. KTU 1.2 I:13 [broken context]), a possible error for *dṭ*, or "forearms" (cf. Jewish Aramaic *ảṭmā* "flank, thigh") (cf. Mark S. Smith, *The Ugaritic Baal Cycle Introduction with Text, Translation and Commentary of KTU 1.1–1.2*, VTSup 55 [Leiden: Brill, 1994], 284). For my rendering "double ʾ*uṭu*-measures," I appeal to the attestation of *ủṭ* as a measure in the economic text RS 94.2401 (see Bordreuil, Pardee, and Hawley, *Une bibliothèque au sud de la ville* ***, 117–18, no. 50). This interpretation is also made more appealing in light of *klảt ydy* "double handfuls" in KTU 1.5 I:19–20 (cited below).

32. This line is interpreted a couple of ways. Pardee takes *ảmtm* as the 1cs PC of *mt* "to die," taking the verb as a passive relating to Môtu "As dung I am dying" (*COS* 1:265 n. 213; cf. Caquot and Sznycer, *Textes ougaritiques 1*, 241; del Olmo Lete, *Mitos y leyendas*, 213). According to this view, Môtu is agonizing over Baʿlu's taunts. Others relate *ảmtm* to Hebrew *ʾammâ* "forearm" and take the preceding verb as an active referring to Môtu: "I will devour (you) from hand to forearms," i.e., limb-by-limb (de Moor, *Anthology of Religious Texts*, 70; Wyatt, *Religious Texts*, 116).

33. See Pardee, *COS* 1:264 n. 201.

34. Lane, 2900.

35. BDB, 243.

36. Pope, "Little Soul-Searching," 28.

through the end of column I where the text breaks off just prior to the passage corresponding to KTU 1.5 I:5–8 cited above.

KTU 1.5 I:12–20:[37]

tḥm bn ỉlm (13) *mt*	Message of Môtu, son of ʾIlu,
hwt ydd bn ỉl (14) *ǵzr*[38]	word of the beloved warrior of ʾIlu:
p ***npš***[39] ***npš*** *lbỉm* (15) *thw*	And **my throat** is **the throat** of a lion of the steppe,
hm[40] *brlt ảnḫr* (16) *b ym*	or the gullet of *ảnḫr*[41] in the sea;
hm brky[42] *tkšd* (17) *rủmm*	or it searches for the pool (like) wild bulls,
ʿn k ḏd ảylt	(for) a spring like the herd of hinds;
(18) *hm ỉmt ỉmt* ***npš*** *blt*[43]	or truly, truly **my throat** swallows heaps (of
(19) *ḥmr*	things).[44]
p ỉmt b klảt (20) *ydy ỉlḥm*	And truly with double handfuls[45] I devour:
hm šbʿ (21) *ydty b ṣʿ*	look, seven are my portions in a plate;
hm ks ymsk (22) *nhr kl*	look, (into) a cup they mix a whole river.
ṣḥn bʿl ʿm (23) *ảḫy*	Invite me, O Baʿlu, with my brothers,
qrản hd ʿm ảryy	call me, O Haddu, with my fellows,
(24) *w lḥmm ʿm ảḫy lḥm*	and eat bread with my brothers,
(25) *w štm ʿm ảḫy yn*	and drink wine with my brothers.
(26) *p nšt bʿl* [*ṭ*]*ʿn ỉṭʿnk*[46]	And you have forgotten, O Baʿlu, I can certainly pierce you through . . .[47]

37. Cf. the parallel text in KTU 1.133:1–11, considered to be a scribal exercise.

38. Pardee notes that the formula is written erroneously with the addition of *bn* from the previous formula (*bn ỉlm mt*), and thus we should read here: *ydd ỉl ǵzr* "beloved warrior of ʾIlu" (*COS* 1:265 n. 216).

39. np{.}š (see transcription in *CAT*).

40. Interpreting the conditional particle *hm* "if" in these lines is difficult, occurring five times in just seven lines. Wyatt (*Religious Texts*, 116–17 n. 11) emends two of these, but only in the footnotes accompanying his translation (due to the parallels in KTU 1.133): *lbỉm thw . hm* > *lbỉm thwm* "lion of the deep" (lines 14–15); *ỉlḥm . hm* > *ỉlḥmhm* "I devour them" (line 20). As for the first emendation, in addition to the fact that the parallel is identical in KTU 1.133, is the presence of a *mater* in *thwm*, which would be unusual for Ugaritic. As for the second emendation, the presence of *hm* at the beginning of the parallel line would most naturally indicate one should expect it in line 20 as well.

41. Some kind of marine animal (*DUL*, 79), here compared to the ferocious appetite of a lion.

42. Cf. Biblical Hebrew *bᵉrēkâ* "pool, pond" (e.g., 2 Kgs 18:17; Isa 7:3). Note that the final {y} of *brky* in this text cannot be the construct plural since *matres* are largely absent from Ugaritic.

43. Note that the expression *npš blt* "my throat swallows" is parallel with *ỉlḥm* "I devour."

44. Cf. Biblical Hebrew *ḥōmer*: "heap of frogs" (Exod 8:10); "heap of waters" (Hab 3:15).

45. Following Pardee, *COS* 1:265.

46. Cf. Biblical Hebrew *ṭʿn* "to pierce through" (*HALOT*, 377–78).

47. The text breaks from here to the end of the column.

The word *npš* occurs three times in this passage, each in reference to the insatiable appetite of the death god Môtu. This text allows us to fill in the details of Môtu's speech in response to Baʿlu's taunts, since it is presumably the repeated version delivered by his messengers. One of the difficulties of interpreting this passage has to do with two syntactical matters: (1) the message being introduced by the conjunction *p*, and (2) the five occurrences of the particle *hm*. The conjunction *p* most usually indicates a continuation of thought with what precedes, which makes it all the more strange as the particle introducing Môtu's message: "And my throat is the throat of a lion of the steppe."[48] Baʿlu's bombastic speech in KTU 1.4 VII: 45–52 that precipitated this entire exchange, however, might offer a helpful link, be it a single word. There, Baʿlu disparages the boasts of Môtu uttered from his *npš*:

(45) *dll ảl ỉlảk l bn* (46) *ỉlm mt*	Should I not send a messenger to Môtu son of ʾIlu,
ʿdd l ydd (47) *ỉl ǵzr*	a herald to the beloved warrior of ʾIlu?
yqrả mt (48) *b* ***npšh***	Môtu calls out in **his throat**,
ystrn[49] *ydd* (49) *b gngnh*	the beloved one tells it within himself:
ảḥdy d ym(50)*lk ʿl ỉlm*	I am the only one who rules over the gods,
l[50] *ymrủ* (51) *ỉlm w nšm*	who fattens gods and men,
d yšb(52)[ʿ] *hmlt ảrṣ*	who satisfies the multitude of the earth.

Upon taking up residence in his newly constructed house, Baʿlu attempts to shore up his reign by challenging the rule of his rival Môtu, which leads to a series of correspondences between the two of them. Unfortunately for us, the first message Baʿlu sent is entirely lost from KTU 1.4 column VIII. What we do have, however, is the first word of Môtu "and my throat," as well as this statement from Baʿlu concerning Môtu calling out in his throat, which immediately precedes Baʿlu's sending of the first message. In light of these two factors, it is entirely possible that something similar to Baʿlu's remark in KTU 1.4 VII:47–48

48. Tropper, *Ugaritische Grammatik*, 2nd ed., 788 (§83.12) (see also the remarks of Pardee in *Textes para-mythologiques*, 159). *DUL* (656) lists meaning 2 as "asseverative," but one of the two examples comes from this text (and the parallel in KTU 1.133:16). The other example comes from the letter KTU 2.26:7 (RS 26.264), but even there the conjunction *p* may be taken in light of what was just mentioned: *iky ảškn ʿṣm l bt dml p ảnk ảtn ʿṣm lk* "How shall I prepare the timbers for the house of DML? *Then* I myself will give the timbers to you."

49. Possibly Gt stem of *srr*, cognate with Arabic *srr* "to tell" (Lane, 1337), as suggested by Pardee (*COS* 1:263 n.193).

50. Likely {d} with the three bottom vertical wedges omitted (l vs. D).

was included in his first correspondence with Môtu. We cannot say for sure, but the nature of the conjunction *p* would suggest that Môtu directly takes up a point already raised by Baʿlu—the throat of Môtu.[51]

Returning to KTU 1.5 I, the five instances of the particle *hm* and their interpretation deserve further comment. Most scholars analyze this particle as the conditional particle, which also functions as a coordinating disjunctive conjunction.[52] According to this analysis, scholars usually indicate its occurrence in this text by the translation "or."[53] Other scholars render *hm* simply as "and," leaving *p* and *hm* indistinguishable in the translation.[54] De Moor translates the particle rather woodenly as a series of conditional clauses.[55] In the instances not emended, Wyatt explains *hm* as marking comparison: "as ... so" and thus another usage of the conditional particle *hm*.[56] Whatever is to be done in interpreting these particles, the usage of the first three does not readily conform to that of the last two, which upon closer scrutiny in some way illustrate the intensity of Môtu's devouring appetite: he eats seven portions in a single setting; an entire river is mixed into his cup.[57] For this reason, I suggest following Tropper's alternative analysis for these two forms in lines 20 and 21, taking *hm* as an expansion of the presentative particle *hn*: *hn* + enclitic *m* > *hm*.[58]

Some scholars interpret *npš* in KTU 1.5 I:15 as "appetite," emphasizing the abstract conception of Death's hunger, which compels him to fill his mouth

51. Note that *p* occurs three times in this address (lines 14, 19, and 26). The first *p* introduces Môtu's address, possibly as a connection to something mentioned in the address of Baʿlu, while the second and third serve to tie major sections of the address together by connecting what precedes with what follows. For a different interpretation of *p* in this text, see Richard J. Clifford, "Mot Invites Baal to a Feast: Observations on a Difficult Ugaritic Text (CTA 5.i = KTU 1.5.I)," in *"Working with No Data": Semitic and Egyptian Studies Presented to Thomas O. Lambdin*, ed. David M. Golomb (Winona Lake, IN: Eisenbrauns, 1987), 58–59.

52. Tropper, *Ugaritische Grammatik*, 2nd ed., 793; cf. Biblical Hebrew *ʾim*.

53. Caquot and Sznycer, *Textes ougaritiques 1*, 242; del Olmo Lete, *Mitos y leyendas*, 214 (the first three instances in lines 15–18); Tropper, *Ugaritische Grammatik*, 2nd ed., 794.

54. Pardee, *COS* 1:265; del Olmo Lete, *Mitos y leyendas*, 215 (the last two instances in lines 20 and 21).

55. De Moor, *Anthology of Religious Texts*, 70–71.

56. Wyatt, *Religious Texts*, 117 n. 12.

57. Interpreting them disjunctively here does not make sense: "And truly with double handfuls I devour, or seven are my portions in a plate, or (into a cup) they mix a whole river." Simply rendering them as conditionals might work here ("And truly with double handfuls I devour, if seven are my portions in a plate, if [into] a cup they mix a whole river"), but it does not make sense of the first two, which appear to connect a series of parallel, disjunctive statements.

58. Tropper, *Ugaritische Grammatik*, 2nd ed., 794. As I have already noted, del Olmo Lete renders these two forms distinctly in his translation, though his interpretation is different from what is being proposed here (*Mitos y leyendas*, 214–15).

with whatever he can find.[59] Yet within this same context, *npš* a few lines earlier (line 7) necessarily refers to Môtu's throat (//*mhmrt* "watery pit") as the avenue of descent to the underworld and not his appetite. One might expect such a change in meaning in a few short lines from the concrete "throat" to the abstract "appetite" to be clearer contextually. It is possible that "appetite" offers a more sensible subject for the verb *kšd* in line 16, which refers back to *npš* in line 14: *brky tkšd rủmm* "it searches for the pool (like) wild bulls." On the other hand, the "throat" of Môtu actively seeking out its prey could constitute a metonymic device: Môtu is defined by this one feature of his anatomy regularly emphasized in these texts—his throat. It is also compelling to allow the clearer example of *npš* from line 7 to inform our choice of translation in lines 14 and 18. There it is without question referring to his throat as the passageway of the dead. Furthermore, the specifics of Môtu's claims regarding his *npš* involve concrete entities: his *npš* devours heaps (lines 18–19); he eats double handfuls (lines 19–20). At this point in the discussion it is enough to say that "appetite" is certainly possible for *npš* in lines 14 and 18, but is not required.

In the aftermath of this conflict that resulted in Baʿlu's death, the Baʿlu myth yields another example of *npš* in KTU 1.6 II, lines 17 and 18.[60] The goddess ʿAnatu, after having buried the corpse of Baʿlu and having informed ʾIlu of his death, goes after Môtu for revenge. I introduce this text at the point where Môtu replies to ʿAnatu's shout: *ảt mt tn ảḫy* "You, Môtu, give up my brother!"

59. E.g., del Olmo Lete, *Mitos y leyendas*, 214; de Moor, *Anthology of Religious Texts*, 70; Wyatt, *Religious Texts*, 116; *DUL*, 637.

60. It also occurs earlier in KTU 1.5 V:4 where it could possibly be rendered "throat," or even "neck," but the first few lines of this column are too broken to permit a sensible translation. As it stands, the text reads:

(4) [ ]k . **npš** . ʿgl	[ ] **the throat** of the bullock
(5) [ ]nk . ảšt.n . b ḫrt	[ ] I myself will place him in the hole
(6) ỉlm . ảrṣ . . .	of the gods of the earth.

Although Wyatt translates *npš* as "appetite" here, he does entertain the possibility of construing it as "lung," possibly, "offered as a sacrifice of redemption for a first-born?" (*Religious Texts*, 123 n. 39). In light of my discussion above (§2.2.1. *npš* = "neck"), I would suggest instead, "neck of a bullock," which would also necessitate a ritual context. Nonetheless, we cannot be sure of its meaning without having more of the preceding text preserved.

"The gods of the earth": possibly, "the gods of the underworld." The word *ḫrt* here has been related to Ugaritic *ḫr* "nostrils" (KTU 1.103:6) and Hebrew *ḥōr* "hole" (√*ḥrr*), particularly in 1 Samuel 14:11 where it refers to holes in the ground where the Israelites hid from the Philistines (Pardee, *COS* 1:267 n. 226). This leads Pardee to suggest that in this context, *ḫrt* would refer to hole, not in the sense of a grave dug, but with reference to caves, caverns, or crevices leading down into the earth.

KTU 1.6 II:13–19:

(13) *w ʿn bn ỉlm mt mh*	And Môtu, son of ʾIlu answered:
mh (14) *tảršn l btlt ʿnt*	What are you asking, Girl ʿAnatu?
(15) *ản ỉtlk w ảṣd*	I went along and hunted,
kl (16) *ǵr l kbd ảrṣ*	every mountain to the heart of the earth,
kl gbʿ (17) *l kbd šdm*	every hill to the heart of the fields.
npš *ḫsrt* (18) *bn nšm*	**My throat** lacked sons of men,
npš *hmlt* (19) *ảrṣ*	**my throat** (lacked) multitudes of the earth.
mǵt l nʿmy ảrṣ (20) *dbr*[61]	I arrived at the pleasant land, the pasture,
ysmt šd šḫlmmt[62]	the beautiful field at the realm of death.
(21) *ngš ảnk ảlỉyn bʿl*	I encountered Mighty Baʿlu,
(22) *ʿdbnn ảnk <k> ỉmr b py*	I set him like a lamb in my mouth,
(23) *k llỉ b ṯbrn q<n>y*	he was ground up like a kid in the crushing
<n>ḫt hw	of my jaws.[63]

In what follows, ʿAnatu seizes Môtu, splits him open, burns him with fire, grinds him up, and scatters his remains in the field. I will return to this text in chapter 3 where I treat words for death (§3.2.1.2), but for now I will consider this context in relation to *npš*. Those scholars who favor interpreting *npš* as "appetite" elsewhere in the mythological texts are less inclined to do so here.[64] In keeping with what we have seen thus far in the Baʿlu cycle, the throat of Môtu imagery seems most likely. He places Baʿlu in his mouth and crushes him to bits, which then provides what was lacking for his throat.

Before moving on to the Ugaritic epic texts, I should cite an additional text from the Baʿlu cycle, only this time from the earlier contest between the sea god Yammu and Baʿlu. The meaning of this passage is somewhat obscure, but it is nonetheless important because it has been cited as yet another example of *npš* as "throat" outside the Baʿlu/Môtu conflicts.

61. Cf. Biblical Hebrew *dōber* "pasture" (BDB, 184); Syriac *dabrōʾ* "field, land" (Payne Smith, 83).

62. On the meaning and significance of this word, see my treatment of the root *mt* "to die" in ch. 3 (§3.2.1.2).

63. Cf. KTU 1.4 VIII:17–20.

64. Wyatt maintains consistency and translates "appetite" (*Religious Texts*, 134). Oddly enough, del Olmo Lete interprets each instance differently: "vitality" ("vigor") in line 17 and "breath" ("aliento") in line 18 (*Mito y leyendas*, 227). I find this interpretation the least convincing contextually. The majority seem to favor "throat" (see Caquot and Sznycer, *Textes ougaritiques 1*, 259; de Moor, *Anthology of Religious Texts*, 87; Pardee, *COS* 1:270 n. 255).

KTU 1.2 III:20

(20) *lb?m*[65] *t/ảrd b np*[?]*ny trḥṣn kṯrm*[66]	X goes down my [?]; they will be washed like bulls(?)

Sorting through the numerous difficulties in the interpretation of this line is beyond my purposes here, so I will not belabor the point.[67] The context of this passage involves ʿAṯtaru's reply to Sapšu, and perhaps Yammu, concerning ʾIlu's commanding Kôṯaru-wa-Ḫasīsu to construct a house for Yammu, with ʿAṯtaru apparently disputing the legitimacy of Yammu's claim to kingship.[68] Smith has suggested that KTU 1.5 I:14—*p npš npš lbỉm* "and my throat is the throat of a lion"—may elucidate the meaning of the difficult expression here, if indeed we are to read *lbủm* in 1.2 III:20. This consideration leads Smith to interpret this line: *lbủm ảrd bn*[*p*]*šny* "(like) a lion I will descend with my appetite."[69] The fundamental problem of this text, however, is that the reading *np*[*š*]*ny* can no longer be sustained. According to Pardee's collation of this text, the disputed sign is not {š}, but perhaps {q}—he notes that the right portion of the sign is preserved and looks nothing like {š}.[70] This reading would therefore render all such discussions on *npš* in this text a moot point.

65. *CTA*: lb-m . (t/ả)rd . bn[p]šny . trḥṣn . kṯrm; *KTU*: lb*d*m . ảrd . bn š*(?)nq . trḥṣn . k*ṯrm; *CAT*: lbdm . ảrd . b npšny . trḥṣn . kṯrm. Pardee (*COS* 1:248 n. 52) notes that the initial sign could be *lbủm* "lions," *lbdm* "alone," or *lbbm* "hearts," none of which makes much sense contextually. Smith reads *lbủm*, noting that *CTA*'s emendation to *lbdm* on contextual grounds is unnecessary since there is no evidence of a second or third head of a horizontal wedge for this sign (*Baal Cycle 1*, 217). He reads the entire line: *lbủm ảrd bn*[*p*]*šny*, translating, "(like) a lion I will descend with my appetite" (254). If we read *trd*, it would be a third person verb, "X goes down," while *ảrd* would be first person, "I go down," which seems to make least sense of the two. *DUL* (638) takes *npšn* with the *-ān* suffix, interpreting it as the "place of souls," which seems unlikely. Caquot and Sznycer: "*Only* I will go down; in my throat they will be crushed" ("*Seul* je descendrai; dans ma gorge seront broyés"; *Textes ougaritiques 1*, 124–25), reading the first sign as *lbbm* "heart" (+ enclitic *m*), first person *ảrd* "I descend," *npšny* as "my throat," and *trḥṣn* from Akkadian *raḫāṣu* "to crush." They read *kṯrm* with what follows as a reference to Kôṯaru. Del Olmo Lete: "In loneliness I will descend to my cupboard (?) that servants wash" ("En solitario descenderé a mi 'almario'(?) que lavarán hábiles [craidos]"; *Mito y leyendas*, 168). The meaning of this term therefore remains unclear.

66. The reference to "washing" (*rḥṣ*) is rather strange and has been variously understood (see Smith, *Baal Cycle 1*, 217, 253–56). However, one does find an interesting parallel in the Kirta Epic when the healer cures King Kirta's illness: *w ṯṯb trḥṣ nn b dʿt npšh l lḥm tptḥ brlth l ṯrm* "She sits down, washes him with regard to his sweat; she opens his throat for eating, his gullet for feeding" (KTU 1.16 VI:10–12). Still, this does not solve anything in interpreting the passage here.

67. See the extensive discussions in Smith, *Baal Cycle 1*, 217, 253–56.

68. Pardee, *COS* 1:248 n. 51.

69. Smith, *Baal Cycle 1*, 254.

70. Pardee (pers. comm.).

2.2.2.2. The Epic Texts

Toward the end of the Epic of Kirta there is another occurrence of *npš* which suggests the interpretion "throat." The tablet KTU 1.16 on the whole deals with the sickness of King Kirta and the prospects of his eventual death, though at the point where *npš* appears he is unexpectedly healed of the deathly illness. Leading up to this healing, ʾIlu, after having failed to find a god willing to heal Kirta, fashions a goddess for this specific task:

ȧnk (26) *i̇ḥtrš*[71] *w ȧškn*	I myself will craft and establish;
(27) *ȧškn ydt* [*m*]*rṣ*	I will establish a female expeller of the sickness,
gršt (28) *zbln*	a female ejector of the illness." (KTU 1.16 V:25–28)

The text breaks for the rest of this column, but when the narrative resumes in column VI, ʾIlu announces:

(1) [*m*]*t dm ḫt*	O [Mô]tu, be shattered,
šʿtqt[72] *dt*[73]	O Šaʿtiqatu be powerful.
(2) *li̇*[74]	

The detail of her work in expelling this sickness is presented a few lines below:

(10) *w ṯṯb trḫṣ nn*[75] *b dʿt*	She sits down, washes him with regard to his sweat,
(11) ***npšh*** *l lḥm tptḥ*	she opens **his throat** (for) eating,
(12) *brlth l ṯrm*[76]	his gullet for feeding.
(13) *mt dm ḫt*	Môtu is shattered,
šʿtqt (14) *dm lȧn*[77]	Šaʿtiqatu is powerful. (KTU 1.16 VI:10–14)

71. Cf. Kôtaru-wa-Ḫasīsu who is described as the *ḥrš yd* "the hand crafter" (KTU 1.17 V:19).

72. This name is a Š nominal form from the root *ʿtq* "to pass," which in the N stem is used to speak of aging, growing old (*DUL*, 191). She is appropriately named for her role in causing the sickness to pass from Kirta.

73. Probably an error for {dm}.

74. Taking this form as a 3fs G imperative from the root *lʾy* "to be powerful, prevail."

75. Note that the suffix is separated from the verbal form by a word divider: trḫṣ . nn.

76. The root *ṯrm* means "to cut, carve," which in this instance would indicate "feeding oneself" (see *DUL*, 931).

77. Defining the form of *lȧn* is difficult. Since Šaʿtiqatu is markedly feminine, one would expect the verbal form to be feminine as well: *lȧt*. Furthermore, it makes sense contextually to interpret the form *li̇* in line 2 as a feminine imperative as Šaʿtiqatu is commanded to act, which would warrant another verbal form in line 14 depicting her adherence to ʾIlu's command. It also works well with the parallel verbal form *ḫt* (lines 1 and 13). One option is to take {lȧn} as a scribal error for {lȧtn} by omission of the single vertical wedge of the {t} that would have preceded the {n}, thus

The lady healer is said "to open" the throat/gullet of Kirta so that he might be able to eat and regain the nourishment necessary for his life to continue. In so doing, Death is shattered. As we observed in the Baʿlu cycle, Death is ironically associated with *npš*, only this time it is the *npš* of Kirta in view and not that of Môtu. The mythological texts personify Death as a gaping throat devouring the dead—his throat is the passage way of the dead. The Kirta story deptícts Môtu apparently restricting Kirta's throat with the inevitable result of passage into his, and so ʾIlu sends Šaʿtiqatu the healer to shatter Death's power and thus conquer the terminal illness inflicted upon Kirta.

The meaning "throat" seems to be unavoidable in this passage.[78] What would it mean to open one's appetite, as some commentators have interpreted the expression?[79] Besides, the verb *ptḥ* in Ugaritic appears only to take concrete nouns as objects and not abstracts, which would offer another strike against it meaning "appetite."[80] This lexical consideration, as well as the overall context just outlined, once again favors interpreting *npš* as "throat" in this text from the Kirta Epic.

The Epic of ʾAqhatu also offers a few examples of *npš* resembling the same context wherein the meaning "throat" is the most appropriate translation.

KTU 1.17 V:16–31

(16) *šmʿ mṯt dtny*	Listen, Damsal Danātay:
ʿbd (17) *imr b pḫd*[81]	Prepare a lamb from the flock
l ***npš*** *kṯr* (18) *w ḫss*	for **the throat** of Kôṯaru-wa-Ḫasīsu,[82]

interpreting *lảtn* as a 3fs G SC with enclitic {n}. This emendation would yield a rather rare form, however, which is not ideal methodologically. A second option, therefore, would be to take *lản* as a noun being used adverbially. The main problem with this option is that it does not provide the expected parallel for the verbal form *ḫt*, though it does avoid the undesirability of emending the text to a rarely occurring verbal form. Taking *lản* as an adverbial accusative means that it would fill the predicate slot of the parallel line, which would constitute a verbless clause, rendered literally, "Šaʿtiqatu is with power," meaning that Šaʿtiqatu acts with the power that results in the defeat of Môtu. I should also remark that the particle *dm* in both clauses would function asseveratively: Môtu is indeed shattered // Šaʿtiqatu is indeed with power.

78. Caquot and Sznycer, *Textes ougaritiques 1*, 570; de Moor, *Anthology of Religious Texts*, 221; Pardee, *COS* 1:342 n. 95.

79. E.g., del Olmo Lete, *Mitos y leyendas*, 320; Wyatt, *Religious Texts*, 238.

80. E.g., opening a window (KTU 1.4 VII:25), opening a jar of wine (KTU 1.15 IV:16), opening a house (KTU 1.100:71–72). The same can be said for Biblical Hebrew (see the more extensive list of concrete objects in BDB, 834–35). The only abstract object listed for *ptḥ* in *DUL* is this passage, which should instead be interpreted concretely as "throat," and not "appetite" (686).

81. Akkadian *puḫādu* "lamb, young male sheep" (*CAD* 12:476–80).

82. This double deity also appears in the Baʿlu cycle as the one responsible for crafting Baʿlu's weapons for his battle against Yammu (KTU 1.2 IV:7–15, 18–23). Also, in KTU 1.2 III:7–9 ʾIlu instructs him to construct a house for Yammu.

l brlt hyn d (19) *ḥrš yd*	for the gullet of HYN who is the handcrafter.
šlḥm ššqy (20) *ỉlm*	Give the gods food and drink,[83]
sảd kbd hmt	support (and) honor them,
bʿl (21) *ḥkpt ỉl klh*	lords of ḤKPT,[84] gods of it all.
tšmʿ (22) *mṯt dnty*	Damsel Danātay listened;
tʿbd ỉmr (23) *b pḫd*	she prepared a lamb from the flock
l ***npš*** *kṯr w ḫss*	for **the throat** of Kôṯaru-wa-Ḫasīsu,
(24) *l brlt hyn d ḥrš* (25) *ydm*	for the gullet of HYN who is the handcrafter.
ảḫr ymǵy kṯr (26) *w ḫss*	Then Kôṯaru-wa-Ḫasīsu arrive,
bd dnỉl ytnn (27) *qšt*	into the hand of Dānîʾilu they give the bow,
l brkh yʿdb (28) *qṣʿt*	on his knees they place the arrows.
ảpnk mṯt dnty (29) *tšlḥm tššqy ỉlm*	Then the Damsal Danātay gives the gods food and drink;
(30) *tsảd tkbd hmt*	she supports (and) honors them,
bʿl[85] (31) *ḥkpt ỉl klh*	lords of ḤKPT, gods of it all.
tbʿ kṯr (32) *l ảhlh*	Kôṯaru goes off to his tent,
hyn tbʿ l mš(33)*knth*	HYN goes off to his residence.

Columns III and IV immediately preceding this passage are completely lost, but the broader context involves the promise and arrival of Dānîʾilu's son, ʾAqhatu. The particular situation of this text concerns the arrival of Kôṯaru-wa-Ḫasīsu to present the infamous bow—infamous because of its being coveted by ʿAnatu—to ʾAqhatu as promised earlier in lines 2–3.[86] As Kôṯaru-wa-Ḫasīsu arrives, Dānîʾilu instructs his wife to prepare a lamb for the gods, which he states is for the *npš* of Kôṯaru-wa-Ḫasīsu and the *brlt* of HYN the handcrafter. Again, appetite is certainly a possible meaning in this context, though "throat" might make better sense with the poetic parallel *brlt*.

83. Literally: "make eat, make drink the gods."

84. I.e., Memphis: ḥ(w)t-kʾ-ptḥ "the house of the ka of (the deity) Ptaḥ" (Pardee, *COS* 1:244 n. 19). See also William F. Albright, "Recent Progress in North-Canaanite Research," *BASOR* 70 (1938): 22; Dijkstra and de Moor, "Problematic Passages," 182; Baruch Margalit, "Lexicographical Notes on the Aqht Epic (Part 1: KTU 1.17–18)," *UF* 15 (1983): 81. See *DUL*, 358–59 for additional references.

85. Erasure of {ḥ} following *bʿl*.

86. The identity of the one making the promise in these lines is apparently lost in the missing columns (see the discussion in Pardee, *COS* 1:345 n. 24).

2.2.2.3. *npš* = Appetite?

The poetic narrative texts at Ugaritic regularly employ the word *npš* to signify the throat of deities (Môtu, Kôṯaru-wa-Ḫasīsu), men (Kirta), and even animals (*npš* of Môtu compared with *npš* of a lion). In some cases, it is possible to perceive the abstract notion of "appetite," but in none of these instances does the context favor this translation over "throat" (KTU 1.5 I:15; 1.17 V:23).[87] On the other hand, it is more often true that *npš* requires the interpreter to read "throat": descent into the throat of Môtu (KTU 1.4 VII:48; 1.5 I:7) and the healer goddess opening the throat of Kirta (KTU 1.16 VI:11). It seems reasonable to conclude that the contexts which indubitably convey "throat" should take precedent over those that may or may not allude to "appetite," leading us to side with Pope's assessment that "throat" is the primary connotation in all such instances.[88] I find the evidence for "appetite" as a separate category of usage for *npš* to be somewhat lacking in Ugaritic.

2.2.3. *npš* = Vitality

I now must consider yet another important signification for *npš* in Ugaritic, and that is "vitality" or "life force." This semantic development leads to *npš* functioning as an abstract noun. Upon analyzing *npš* in these contexts I find three major features for this usage: (1) *npš* as something "alive" (*ḥy*), (2) *npš* as something that remains or "rests" within an individual, and (3) *npš* as something that can exit an individual.

87. I am not assuming here a rigid one-to-one correspondence for a given lexical item, but rather I am trying to find the best translation value in English that adequately represents the Ugaritic literary context. For more on translation theory in general, see Susan Bassnett's brief essay, "Translation Theory," in *The Johns Hopkins Guide to Literary Theory and Criticism*, ed., Michael Groden, Martin Kreiswirth, and Imre Szeman, 2nd ed. (Baltimore: Johns Hopkins Universtiy Press, 2005), 909–13, and Edith Grossman's book-length treatment, *Why Translation Matters*, Why X Matters (New Haven: Yale University Press, 2010). She emphasizes the need to find "comparable, not identical, characteristics, vagaries, quirks, and stylistic peculiarities in the second language," since following a "pattern of word-for-word transcription" leads to less than satisfactory results (10). For more on translation technique from an ancient literary perspective, see Emanuel Tov, "The Nature and Study of the Translation Technique of the LXX in the Past and Present," in *VI Congress of the Internation Organization for Septuagint and Cognate Studies, Jerusalem 1986*, ed. Claude E. Cox, SCS 23; Atlanta: Scholars Press, 1987), 337–59; Anneli Aejmelaeus, "Translation Technique and the Intention of the Translator," in *VII Congress of the International Organization for Septuagint and Cognate Studies, Leuven 1989*, ed. Claude E. Cox, SCS 31 (Atlanta: Scholars Press, 1991), 23–36; Aejmelaeus, "What We Talk about When We Talk about Translation Technique," in *On the Trail of the Septuagint Translators: Collected Essays*, CBET 50 (Leuven: Peeters, 2007), 205–22.

88. Pope, "Little Soul Searching," 28.

2.2.3.1. Living *npš*

The first few examples I wish to address are those where *npš* is accompanied by some form of the root *ḥyy* and is thus qualified as being "alive." This feature shows up twice in the ʾAqhatu Epic and once in two Ugaritic letters. I have already treated the root *ḥyy* in the preceding chapter and established that the G stem of *ḥyy*, along with the adjective *ḥy*, indicate one's state of being or existence. The fact that "living" or "alive" sometimes modifies *npš* tells us that these may be used as complementary terms, each with its own lexical significance. The scholarly tendency to translate *npš* as "life" (especially within biblical scholarship) does not exactly reflect its usage in Ugaritic. *npš* can refer to individuals or persons, as I will discuss in the final category of usage to follow, but I should clarify in light of its association with *ḥyy* in these texts that it does not denote an "individual" in the sense of a "living being," but rather an individual in the sense of one in whom the *npš* element exists.[89]

npš occurs in contexts dealing with the living at three points in the ʾAqhatu Epic: once in ʾIlu's pronouncement of blessing upon Dānîʾilu securing the successful birth of a son, and twice in Dānîʾilu's pronouncement of blessing upon his daughter Pūġatu securing the successful destruction of ʾAqhatu's murderer.

KTU 1.17 I:36

(34) [*ks*] *yiḫd il* <*byd*	[A cup] ʾIlu takes <in (his) hand,
krpn bm ymn	a goblet in (his) right hand;
brkm ybrk>[90] *ʿabdh*	he indeed blesses> his servant,
ybrk (35) [*dni*]*l mt rpi*	he blesses [Dānîʾi]lu, man of RPỦ,
ymr[91] *ġzr* (36) [*mt h*]*rnmy*	he pronounces blessing on the warrior, [H]RNMY [man].

89. This same association occurs in the biblical tradition, specifically in Gen 2:7: God formed man with dust from the ground (*ʿāpār min-hāʾadāmâ*), breathed into his nostrils the breath of life (*nišmat ḥayyîm*), and he became a living *nepeš* (*nepeš ḥayyîm*, lit. "*nepeš* of life") (cf. 1 Sam 1:26; 2 Sam 11:11). Interestingly, live animals are also referred to as *nepeš ḥayyîm* (Gen 1:20, 21, 24, 30; 2:19; 9:10, 12, 15, 16; Lev 11:10, 46; Ezek 47:9; Job 12:10). Cf. also the polar opposition expressed in the biblical phrase *nepeš mēt* "*nepeš* of a dead person" (Lev. 21:11; Num. 6:6; 19:13; 23:10).

90. Restored from the parallel blessing formula in KTU 1.15 II:16–20. See Jared J. Jackson and Harold H. P. Dressler, "El and the Cup of Blessing," *JAOS* 95 (1975): 99–101; Dijkstra and de Moor, "Problematic Passages," 177; and Dennis Pardee, "An Emendation in the Ugaritic Aqht Text," *JNES* 36 (1977): 53–56.

91. Uncertain etymology, but regularly parallel to *brk* in Ugaritic. The common translation "strong" ("bitter" > "bitterly strong" > "generally strong") has been shown to be problematic. For an extensive discussion of the etymology and general problems in interpreting this word in Ugaritic, see Dennis Pardee, "The Semitic Root *mrr* and the Etymology of Ugaritic *mr(r)* // *brk*," *UF* 10 (1978): 249–88.

***npš** yḥ dnỉl* (37) [*mt rp*]*ỉ*	**As for (his) vitality**, may Dānîʾilu, man of RPỦ live,
brlt ǵzr mt hrnmy	as for (his) life force, may the warrior, HRNMY man (live).
(38) [. . .]*ḥ*[92] *hw mḫ*[93]	[. . .] may he be successful.

Immediately following this pronouncement of blessing came the specifics of what it entails, which unfortunately were set out in what is now broken text. Despite the physical condition of the tablet, the content of the blessing is rather clear: the promise of a son for Dānîʾilu (lines 38–43), as well as an outline of the duties he will perform (line 38 through to the end of the broken column).[94] The second passage containing this usage is in KTU 1.19:IV lines 36 and 39, where Pūǵatu seeks the favor of her father in avenging the death of ʾAqhatu:

(28) *w tʿn pǵt ṯkmt mym*	Pūǵatu, she who shoulders water, answered:
(29) *qrym ảb dbḥ l ỉlm*	My father offered a sacrifice to the gods,
(30) *šʿly dǵṯh*[95] *b šmym*	he made his[96] *dǵṯ*-sacrifice ascend to the heavens,
(31) *dǵṯ hrnmy b kbkbm*	the *dǵṯ*-sacrifice of HRNMY to the stars.
(32) *l tbrkn ảlk brktm*	Indeed, may you bless me that I might go in a blessed state,
(33) *tmrn ảlk nmrrt*	pronounce a blessing that I might go in a favorable state,

92. The beginning of this line cannot be reasonably reconstructed and remains uncertain, though several suggestions have been made: *CTA*: ả[-]ḫ . hy . mḫ; *KTU*: [ ]ḫ*/ṭ* . hw . mḫ; *CAT*: [XXXX]ḫ/ṭ . hw . mḫ; Dijkstra and de Moor: [ảr]ḫ . hw . mḫ "May his way be successful" ("Problematic Passages," 178).

93. Possible cognates for this word are as follows: Hebrew *mēḥ* "fatling," *mōḥ* "bone-marrow" (*HALOT*, 567; cf. *DNSWI*, 610); Syriac *mawḥōʾ* "brain, marrow" (Payne Smith, 257) denotes "marrow, fatness"; Akkadian *muḫḫu* "skull, top of head, upper part" (*CAD* 10:172–75; *AHw* 2:667). The idea involved in this expression would be that of prosperity, abundance, or success, which fits the context of ʾIlu blessing Dānîʾilu with the prospect of having a son.

94. This material parallels Baʿlu's intercession to ʾIlu on behalf of Dānîʾilu earlier in this column in KTU 1.17 I:23–34, which provides the likely reconstruction of the end of this column.

95. The meaning and etymology of this term remains uncertain. Harry A. Hoffner has proposed that it is one of a few Anatolian loanwords in Ugaritic, perhaps meaning "smoke offering" ("An Anatolian Cult Term in Ugaritic," *JNES* 23 [1964]: 66–68). For a bibliography on its interpretation, see *DUL*, 268.

96. Wyatt thinks the 3ms pronominal suffix "his" cannot be right "when Pughat is speaking directly to Danel, since she is not addressing him in the third person" (*Religious Texts*, 309 n. 262). But the previous two verbal forms (*qrym* and *šʿly*) could very well be interpreted as 3ms SC forms, making Wyatt's objection to the suffixed {h} unconvincing, not to mention the fact that its parallel line is also naturally read in third person: *dǵṯ hrnmy* "the *dǵṯ* of the Harnamite."

(34) *imḫṣ mḫṣ åhy*	that I might strike the one who struck my brother,
åkl m(35)kly [ʿ]l ůmty	that I might bring an end to the one who brought an end upon my clan.
w yʿn dn(36)il mt rpi	Dānîʾilu, man of RPŮ, answered:
npš *tḥ pǵ[t]*	**As for vitality**, may Pūǵa[tu] live,
(37) *ṯkmt mym*	she who shoulders water,
ḥspt l šʿr (38) *ṭl*	who gathers dew for wheat,
ydʿt hlk kbkbm[97] [...]	who knows the goings of the stars.
(39) ***npš*** *hy mḫ*	**As for vitality**, may she be successful:
tmḫṣ mḫṣ [åḫh]	may she strike the one who struck [her brother],
(40) *tkl mkly ʿl ůmt* [..]	may she bring an end to the one who brought an end upon [her] clan.

In both of these passages, *npš* occurs in association with the PC verb of the root *ḥyy* "to live" and has been understood differently by scholars. Caquot and Sznycer interpret the statement directed to Dānîʾilu as ʾIlu's encouragement to renew his life/spirit (*recouvre la vie/l'esprit*) in light of his despondency over not having progeny.[98] Admittedly, they are offering a more idiomatic interpretation of their literal translation "may the *npš* of Danel live," but one might query the legitimacy of "renewal" or "recovery" contextually. In what way is the *npš* of Dānîʾilu urged to "live," or, "exist" as I have defined the G stem of this root in chapter 1?[99] The notion of reviving is also apparent in del Olmo Lete's interpretation, but he translates *npš* as "force" or "vitality."[100] He does much the same in Dānîʾilu's pronouncement of blessing on Pūǵayu in 1.19 IV:36, taking it as his wish for her to cheer up, to change her mood.[101]

Meindert Dijkstra and Johannes C. de Moor take a much different approach, arguing that since the subject of the verbal form *yḥ* can only be Dānîʾilu, *npš*

97. So *KTU* and *CTA*. *CAT*: kbkm.

98. Caquot and Sznycer, *Textes ougaritiques 1*, 423. Note, however, their literal translation, "may the *npš* of Danel live" ("que la *npš* de Danel vive"), which is not entirely feasible since *npš* is not actually in construct with *dnil*, being separated by the verbal form *yḥ* (423 n. x).

99. Caquot and Sznycer translate this expression similarly in KTU 1.19 IV:36: "Long live [Pughat]" ("Que vive [Pughat]"; *Textes ougaritiques 1*, 456).

100. "En (su) vigor reviva Daniilu el Rapaí" (del Olmo Lete, *Mitos y leyendas*, 371). Interestingly, he translates the parallel word *brlt* as "appetite" ("apetito").

101. "In (your) mood revive, Puǵatu" ("En (su) ánimo reviva, Puǵatu"; del Olmo Lete, *Mitos y leyendas*, 398).

must function as an oath formula: "By my life!"[102] Blane Conklin, in his study on oath formulas, documents what he calls the "(By) the Life of X" formula as it occurs in Biblical Hebrew, nine of which yield the combination *ḥy* + *npš* as in the following two examples:

1 Samuel 17:55
ḥê-napšᵉkā hammelek im-yādātî
(By) the life of your soul, O king, [I swear that,] if I know, [may I be cursed].

1 Samuel 20:3
wᵉʾûlām ḥay-yhwh wᵉḥê napšekā kî kᵉpeśaʿ bênî ûbên hammāwet
However, (by) the life of YHWH and (by) the life of your soul, [I swear] that there is but one step between me and death.[103]

The form of the oath formula in these two examples—*ḥê* (sg. const. noun) + *napšekā*—is quite different from the constructions found in the ʾAqhatu tablets—*npš* + PC G stem verbal form.[104] In fact, *npš* is only an ancillary element of the formula qualifying *ḥê* "life of," which is the obligatory component of the "(By) the life of X" type oath. None of Conklin's examples cited for this specific oath attests *npš* as the governing element followed by a verbal form of the root *ḥyy*.[105] Furthermore, Dijkstra and de Moor's syntactical reasoning for interpreting an oath in the ʾAqhatu blessing pronouncements—since Dānîʾilu is the subject of *yḥ*, *npš* must be an oath—provides insufficient basis for seeing an oath formula there.

102. Dijkstra and de Moor, "Problematic Passages," 178, citing comparable idioms from Arabic, Hebrew, and Akkadian (followed by de Moor, *Anthology of Religious Texts*, 229, 263: "(By) my soul"; Margalit, *Ugaritic Poem of AQHT*, 145: "By-my-soul (I swear)"; Wyatt, *Religious Texts*, 261: "By my life!" ; Wright, *Ritual in Narrative*, 204: "By my life"). I should note here that Wyatt, who follows the oath formula interpretation for KTU 1.17 I:36, does not do so for KTU 1.19 IV:36: "Let your spirit flourish, Pughat" (*Religious Texts*, 309), which is somewhat inconsistent.

103. Blane Conklin, *Oath Formulas in Biblical Hebrew*, LSAWS 5 (Winona Lake, IN: Eisenbrauns, 2011), 27, 28. See also 1 Sam 25:26; 2 Sam 11:11; 2 Kgs 2:2, 4, 6; 4:30.

104. On the problem of *ḥê* vs. *hay* in the oath formula, see Conklin, *Oath Formulas*, 24–26.

105. For a list of references for Biblical Hebrew, see Conklin, *Oath Formulas*, 27–29. For references outside Biblical Hebrew for the "Life of X" oath, see Conklin, *Oath Formulas*, 29 (2 Hebrew inscriptions), 79–84 (Ugaritic, Aramaic, and Akkadian). Note the one example he cites from Akkadian with *napšata* as the primary element, followed by the verb of swearing, *tamû* (80). In terms of the Hebrew evidence, Dijkstra and de Moor's mention of Isa 26:9 ("Problematic Passages," 178 n. 71) is not included in Conklin's analysis for the obvious reason that is does not fit the formal criteria of the "Life of X" oath.

That is not to say that an oath involving *ḥy npš* is not attested in Ugaritic, since RS 94.2284 offers just such an example:

(12) *ḥ* ***npšk*** *w ḥ n*[*pšy*]	By the life **of your *npš*** and the life of [my] *n*[*pš*],
(13) *hm iṯ d ytn* ⌜*l*⌝ [...]	there was nothing given to me!
(14) *w mrṣ lby* [...] (15) *mỉd*	And my heart is very ill (or: sad).[106]

There can be no doubt that such oath formulas are amply attested in the Northwest Semitic languages (especially Biblical Hebrew), but this factor does not explain the meaning of the oath itself; we are still faced with the problem of explaining how *npš* serves as an appropriate modifier of one's life.

Having found the above suggestions less than satisfactory, I suggest taking *npš* as an example of *casus pendens*:[107] "As for (his) *npš*, may Dānîʾilu live."[108] As such the statement means to say something about Dānîʾilu (or Pūǵatu to follow) living with regard to *npš*. In my analysis of *npš* thus far, I have noted several instances in which Môtu is defined by his *npš*, or throat, which must signify metonymically one of the main forces governing his existence. In relating this feature to the story of ʾAqhatu, it is important to observe the parallel contexts of these two blessings: ʾIlu's blessing of Dānîʾilu and Dānîʾilu's blessing of Pūǵatu. In both cases the blessing is specifically defined: for Dānîʾilu it means successfully issuing forth progeny; for Pūǵatu it indicates success in avenging the death of her brother ʾAqhatu. One also finds that the word *npš* introduces the utterance of the blessing and therefore must have interpretive significance for what follows. The blessing is predicated on the pronouncer's wish for the recipient's increase in vitality or life forces that would enable him or her to acquire its materialization—the birth of a son to Dānîʾilu; Pūǵatu's defeat of ʾAqhatu's assassin. From this perspective, one might say that these two characters are to live in a way that is governed by *npš*, much like Môtu was driven by his own throat, the primary mythological symbol of his existence.

One final example will conclude my discussion of *npš* + *ḥy*, only this time it comes from a partial Ugaritic letter addressed to the king of Egypt.[109] Significant portions of KTU 2.23 (=RS 16.078) are broken, making interpretation more difficult, but generally speaking the first portion of the letter appears to address

106. On this text, see Bordreuil and Pardee, *Manual of Ugaritic*, 250–52; Bordreuil, Pardee, and Hawley, *Une bibliothèque au sud de la ville ****, no. 67.

107. See Tropper, *Ugaritische Grammatik*, 2nd ed., 882–84. For Hebrew syntax, see GKC, §143.

108. Cf. Pardee's literal translation: "As to (his) throat, may Dānîʾilu live" (*COS* 1:344 n. 13), and more idiomatically: "May Dānîʾilu, [the man] of Rapaʾu, live indeed" (*COS* 1:344).

109. See Pardee, *COS* 3:99 n. 87.

previous correspondence between the kings of Ugarit and Egypt (lines 1–2: *w k rgm špš mlk rb bʿly* "And according to the word of the Sun, great king, my lord"), while the second section records the Ugaritic king's petition on behalf of the king of Egypt:

(15) *w ỉn* [...]*b*	And I myself...
(16) *ỉrš* [...]*š*	make a request for...
(17) *mlk r*[*b bʿl*]*y p l*	the gre[at] king, my [master], and for
(18) *ḥy* ***np***[***šh*** *ỉ*]*rš*	the life of [his] ***np***[*š* I] make a request
(19) *l pn bʿ*[*l*]*ṣpn bʿly*	before Baʿ[lu] ṢPN, my lord.
(20) *w ủrk ym bʿly*	that the days of my lord might be long
(21) *l pn ỉmn w l pn*	before ʾAmon and before
(22) *ỉl mṣrm dt tǵrn*	the gods of Egypt, that they might guard
(23) ***npš*** *špš mlk*	**the *npš*** of the Sun, great king,
(24) *rb bʿly*	my lord.[110]

The first few lines contain gaps, but we may assume an initial request as indicated by *ỉrš* at the beginning of line 16 and the conjunction *p* at the end of line 17 signaling a new (but related) request in the following section. The reconstruction *ḥy np*[*šh ỉ*]*rš* in line 18 is highly plausible in light of the combination of consonants *ḥy np*[?] and the reoccurrence of *npš* in line 23, which to some degree explicates the divine agency of the request beginning in line 18 (i.e., he petitions ʾAmon and the Egyptian gods for the Sun's *npš*, those deities responsible for guarding the king's *npš*).

The meaning of *npš* here finds ample elucidation from the content of the request being made before Baʿlu ṢPN and the Egyptian pantheon: *w ủrk ym bʿly l pn ỉmn w l pn ỉl mṣrm* "That the days of my lord might be long before ʾAmon and before the gods of Egypt." The petition does not concern "life" in general, since the king of Egypt is certainly not in any mortal danger, but it is a particular kind of life: the long and prosperous life of kings. Though it differs slightly from the contexts just examined from the ʾAqhatu Epic, the basic idea is much the same, that is, the vitality or abundance of life. As the blessing pronouncements of ʾIlu and Dānîʾilu enacted a certain *npš* element enabling particular successes—for Dānîʾilu success in acquiring progeny; for Pūǵatu success in avenging ʾAqhatu—the petition recorded in this letter also invokes that same *npš* element for the long and prosperous reign of Šapšu, king of Egypt.

110. The central portion of the reverse of the tablet is entirely lost and thus unreadable. The end of line 32 and the beginning of line 33 read:]pšm mlk[, which *CAT* reconstructs: n]pšm mlk[, but the context is destroyed.

2.2.3.2. Resting *npš*

The meaning and significance of the resting *npš* motif takes us back to the Baʿlu cycle for a moment, where the story of Baʿlu's conflict with Môtu comes to a full crescendo as the storm god descends into the watery pit of Death's throat. During the period between Baʿlu's death and his reappearance later in the story, the gods mourn his passing, particularly with a strong interest in the mourning of ʿAnatu and ʾIlu. It is when Baʿlu comes back to life, so-to-speak, that we find reference to the *npš* of ʾIlu resting within his chest after having dreamed that the storm god was alive:

KTU 1.6 III:19

(14) *šmḫ lṭpn ỉl d pỉd*	The knowing one, the kindly god, is rejoicing,
(15) *pʿnh l hdm yṯpd*	his feet he rests at the footstool,
(16) *w yprq lṣb w yṣḥq*	he unfurrows his brow and laughs,
(17) *yšủ gh w yṣḥ*	he lifts up his voice and cries out:
(18) *ảṯbn ảnk w ảnḫn*	I myself can rest again,
(19) *w tnḫ b ỉrty* ***npš***	**my *npš*** will rest in my chest,
(20) *k ḥy ảlỉyn bʿl*	for mighty Baʿlu is alive,
(21) *k ỉṯ zbl bʿl ảrṣ*	the Prince, lord of the earth, exists.

The obvious question arising here is this: In what way might the *npš* be said to rest in one's chest? It is commonplace to render *npš* here as "soul," but this is a fairly loose translation and does not advance our understanding of *npš* in Ugaritic beyond the stereotypical.[111] Some scholars suggest "heart" or "insides," which from context would refer to ʾIlu's anxious or trembling insides calming to a peaceful state once he learns of Baʿlu being alive.[112] The main idea of the middle-weak root *n-ḫ* in Biblical Hebrew is to settle down, used vividly in Genesis 8:4 of the ark's coming to rest upon the mountains of Ararat.[113] Akkadian *nâḫu* means "to be still," or in certain contexts similar to this one from the Baʿlu story it refers to the calming of one's heart.[114]

111. E.g., del Olmo Lete, *Mitos y leyendas*, 229; de Moor, *Anthology of Religious Texts*, 91; Wyatt, *Religious Texts*, 137; *DUL*, 637; Tropper, *Ugaritische Grammatik*, 2nd ed., 285.

112. E.g., Caquot and Sznycer, *Textes ougaritiques 1*, 262; Pardee, *COS* 1:271: "my innermost being can get some rest," or literally: "and my gullet can rest in my chest" (n. 261).

113. For additional references, see *HALOT*, 679. Note also those uses where the initial entrance into "resting" is in view (e.g., Exod 10:14; Num 11:25; Josh 3:13), or those which emphasize exit from "resting" (= waiting) (e.g., 1 Sam 25:9; Hab 3:16).

114. Most often with *libbu* as subject (*CAD* 11:144–46).

There are two ways one could interpret *npš* in KTU 1.6 III:19. First, in a brief note Wyatt surmises that since this term can denote "throat" and since bodily organs often reflect emotional states, "Perhaps El has been suffering from breathlessness and palpitations."[115] According to these considerations, resting *npš* would indicate ʾIlu's repose from heavy breathing induced by his sorrow over Baʿlu's death. Or, in keeping with the notion of "life force" or "vitality," resting *npš* could suggest the subduing of that vital element within ʾIlu which has been driving him to mourn the loss of Baʿlu with a restless anxiety. If the former interpretation were adopted, which would be *npš* in the concrete sense, this example would naturally fall under the category designated "*npš* = throat" above. However, I have opted for the abstract interpretation of *npš* in this passage meaning "life force/vitality"—thus, subduing the vital element producing mourning—while at the same time acknowledging the plausibility of the previous suggestion.

2.2.3.3. Exiting *npš*

Finally, I give attention to the third expression of *npš* as vital force, in this case indicating its exit from the body at death. Twice in the ʾAqhatu Epic *npš* functions as the subject of the verb *yṣʾ* "to go out."[116] The setting of these occurrences takes us to the occasion of ʿAnatu's assassination of the hero ʾAqhatu, planned and executed after his refusal to trade his bow in exchange for an immortality like that of Baʿlu.[117] These particular usages complement the categories just treated in the previous two sections: to live with regard to *npš*, a *npš* that rests, and now a *npš* that goes out or exits. The first two examples come from the narration of ʿAnatu's consultation with YṬPN who has just urged her not to allow this ungrateful hero—ungrateful with respect to her offer of immortality, never mind the bow—to live on, so she enlists YṬPN to carry out the execution.

KTU 1.18 IV:16–27[118]	
ṯb yṭp w[. . .] *lk*	"Return, YṬP<N> and [. . .] you.
(17) *ảštk km nšr b ḥb*[*šy*]	I will set you like a hawk in [my] belt,
(18) *km diy b tʿrty*	like a bird in my quiver.
ảqht [*km yṯb*] (19) *l lḥm*	ʾAqhatu, [as he sits] to eat,
w bn dnil l ṯrm	the son of Dānîʾilu to feast,
[*ʿlh*] (20) *nšrm trḫpn*	[over him] hawks will hover,

115. Wyatt, *Religious Texts*, 137 n. 89; cf. Pardee's "my gullet can rest in my chest" (*COS* 1:271 n. 261).

116. Also reconstructed in KTU 1.19 II:43.

117. On the nature of this offer, see ch. 1 (§1.2.2.1).

118. See the notes for lines 16–27 of this text in ch. 1 (§1.2.2.2).

ybṣr [*ḥbl d*](21)*ʾym*	the [flock of b]irds will keep watch.
bn nšrm ảrḫp ản[*k*]	Among the hawks, I myself will hover,
ʿl (22) *ảqht ʿdbk*	over ʾAqhatu positioning you.
hlmn ṯnm qdqd	Hit him twice on the head;
(23) *ṯlṯỉd ʿl ủdn*	three times over the ear.
špk km šỉy (24) *dm*	Pour out (his) blood like a *šỉy*,
km šḫṭ l brkh	(his blood) on his knees like a slaughterer.
tṣỉ km (25) *rḥ* ***npšh***	Let his ***npš*** go out like wind,
km ỉṯl brlth	like spittle his *brlt*,
km (26) *qṭr b ảph*	like smoke from his nostrils.
ủ ảp mprh ảnk (27) *l ảḥwy*	And then, I myself will not allow the soldier to live on."

In typical Ugaritic poetic narrative fashion, the next few lines depict YṬPN perpetrating the crime:

KTU 1.18 IV:33–37[119]

hlmn ṯmn[*qdqd*]	He struck him twice [on the head],
(34) *ṯlṯỉd ʿl ủdn*	Three times above the ear,
š[*pk km*] (35) *šỉy dmh*	he po[ured out] his blood [like] a *šỉy*
km šḫ[*ṭ l brkh*]	[on the knee] like a slaugh[terer].
(36) *yṣảt km rḥ* ***npš***[***h***	[His] ***npš*** went out like a wind,
km ỉṯl] (37) *brlth*	his *brlt* [like spittle],
km qṭr b[*ảp* . . .]	like smoke from [(his) nostrils . . .]

ʿAnatu apparently expresses sorrow at what she has done in what follows in the text, which soon breaks off toward the end of the column.

It is true that we are discussing terms associated with life, but as this text makes it painstakingly clear, its collision with the reality of death is inevitable.[120] In this case, the *npš* "goes out" of ʿAqhatu as a result of being struck repeatedly, and in the end fatally, by YṬPN the assassin. The text before us in no short order depicts the death of the hero by describing in detail his life force departing from him, which is the fulfillment of YṬPN's earlier suggestion to end his life (partially reconstructed): *qṣʿth hwt l t*⌜*ḥ*⌝[*wy*] "(for) his arrows you must not let that one l[ive] on" (KTU 1.18 IV:13). The operative feature of *npš* in this narration is its function as the subject of the verb *yṣʾ* "to go out," a phenomenon familiar to Biblical Hebrew,

119. The same phraseology appears in KTU 1.19 II:39, 44 where the text is badly broken, apparently containing the report of the two lads (*ġlmm*) concerning ʾAqhatu's death.

120. See my remarks on the intersection of life and death in the Introduction.

which attests a parallel expression as in the case of Genesis's depiction of Rachel's death: *wayyᵉhî bᵉṣēʾt napšâ kî mētâ* "When her *nepeš* went out, she died" (Gen 35:18).

2.2.3.3.1. *Exiting* npš *and* rḥ *"wind"*

Another important observation regarding the exit of *npš* arises from its comparability to the movement of *rḥ* "wind": *tṣỉ km rḥ npšh* "his *npš* will go out like a wind." As the evidence currently stands, this word is only meagerly attested in Ugaritic and is thus not a prominent component of the repository of life terms in the language, therefore making it distinct from Biblical Hebrew where *rûᵃḥ* signals a significant aspect of Hebrew anthropology alongside *nepeš*.[121] The best example for understanding the basic meaning of *rḥ* in Ugaritic comes from the Baʿlu cycle in Môtu's reply to the storm god's banquet invitation in KTU 1.5 V:7. The text is broken in the first few lines, becoming legible at line 5:[122]

ảštn[123] *b ḫrt* (6) *ỉlm ảrṣ*[124]	I will place him in the hole of the gods of the earth.
w ảt qḥ (7) *ʿrptk rḥk*	And as for you, take your clouds, your wind,

121. See the excellent treatment of Biblical Hebrew *rûaḥ* in Richard C. Steiner, *Disembodied Souls: The Nefesh in Israel and Kindred Spirits in the Ancient Near East, with an Appendix on the Katumuwa Inscription*, ANEM 11 (Atlanta: SBL Press, 2015), 81–92. He argues that recent attempts to limit its meaning to "breath, wind" rather than "spirit" are unwarranted, since in many biblical contexts "breath" does not make sense. Scholars have tended to attribute the "spirit" meaning for *rwḥ* to Persian or Greek influence, which Steiner denies. He explains the relationship between Hebrew *nepeš* "soul" and *rûaḥ* "spirit" as follows: "There are grounds to conjecture that the נפש consisted of two components: (1) the נפש הבשר, a bodily component located in the blood, and (2) the רוח, a spiritual component bestowed by God" (83).

122. Incidentally, *npš* appear in line 4, but it is difficult to make out its meaning there. What we can say, however, is that it appears in the first of two parallel lines:

(4) [ ]k . **npš** . ʿgl	[ ] the ***npš***, the bullock
(5) [ ]nk . ảšt.n . b ḫrt	[ ] I will place him in the hole
(6) ỉlm . arṣ . . .	of the gods of the earth . . .

Given the broken state of this text, the syntax of *npš ʿgl* is uncertain (*npš* of the bullock?). From what we do have here, it is safe to say that the parallel for *npš ʿgl* must be the 3ms verbal suffix in *ảštn* "I will place him."

123. The preceding word *CAT* reconstructs as b]nk (*KTU*: [ ]XXn*k), perhaps a reference to the son Baʿlu is about to father (Wyatt, *Religious Texts*, 123 n. 40), but we are not entirely sure. One could also reconstruct the 1cs pronoun *ʾnk*, but again it is mere speculation.

124. I.e., "the gods of the underworld." The word *ḫrt* here has been related to Ugaritic *ḫr* "nostrils" (KTU 1.103:6) and Hebrew *ḥōr* "hole" (√*ḥrr*), particular in 1 Sam 14:11 where it refers to holes in the ground in which the Israelites hid from the Philistines (Pardee, *COS* 1:267 n. 226). This leads Pardee to suggest that in this context, *ḫrt* would refer to a hole, not in the sense of a grave dug (as Cyrus H. Gordon, "Ugaritic ḫrt/ḫirîtu 'Cemetery'," *Syria* 33 [1956]: 102–3; followed by Caquot and Sznycer, *Textes ougaritiques 1*, 247 n. e; and de Moor, *Anthology of Religious Texts*, 77 n. 368), but with

mdlk[125] (8) *mṭrtk*	your *mdl*, your rain,
ʿmk šbʿt (9) *ǵlmk*	with you seven of your lads,
ṯmn ḫnzrk	eight of your officials,
(10) *ʿmk pdry bt ảr*	with you PDRY, daughter of ẢR,
(11) *ʿmk ṭly*[126] *bt rb*	with you ṬLY, daughter of RB.

This text clearly associates *rḥ* with other weather related terms, all of which Môtu instructs Baʿlu to take with him in his descent to the underworld. The context of the term itself, alongside *ʿrpt* "clouds" and *mṭrt* "rain," supports its interpretation as the weather element "wind."

Three underlying forms are realized as *rḥ* in Ugaritic, however: *rḥ* I: "wind"; *rḥ* II: "aroma"; and *rḥ* III: "millstone."[127] It is difficult to determine whether *rḥ* = "wind" comes from the root r-w-ḥ (> /rūḥu/) or r-y-ḥ (> /rīḥu/).[128] In Biblical Hebrew the middle-{w} root (*rûaḥ*) is reserved for the meaning "wind, spirit," while the middle-{y} root produces words of scent (*rêaḥ* "scent, odor" and √*ryḥ* "to smell"), as does Syriac (*rūḥō* "wind, spirit" and *rīḥō* "smell, odor").[129] Old Aramaic also shows medial {w} for the noun "wind, spirit" (*rwh*) as does Syriac, but the evidence is mixed for Arabic, attesting both *rawḥu* and *rīḥu* for "wind, spirit."[130] In light of the evidence from these Semitic languages, I posit that the medial-{w} root (*/rūḥu/) would most likely have been the origin of the word for "wind" with the medial-{y} root (*/rīḥu/) providing the word for "scent, aroma."[131] The etymological evidence for *rḥ* III "millstone," witnessed consistently in Hebrew, Syriac, and Arabic as derived from a III-weak root r-ḥ-y, suggests the same for Ugaritic, attested once as *rḥm*.[132]

Once the *rḥ* forms in Ugaritic are sorted out, only three instances remain denoting "wind."[133] It is important to emphasize at this juncture that, unlike

---

reference to caves, caverns, or crevices leading down into the earth. Wyatt renders it similarly "in a hole of the earth-gods" (*Religious Texts*, 123; cf. del Olmo Lete, *Mitos y leyenda*, 220).

125. Uncertain etymology: "thunderbolt" (Johannes C. de Moor, "Der mdl Baals im Ugaritischen," *ZAW* 78 [1966]: 69–71); "lightning" (Robert M. Good, "Some Ugaritic Terms Relating to Draught and Riding Animals," *UF* 16 [1984]: 80–81). For a fuller bibliography, see *DUL*, 527.

126. Incorrectly written as {tṭly}.

127. According to *DUL*, 736.

128. See Tropper, *Ugaritische Grammatik*, 2nd ed., 123.

129. For Hebrew, see BDB, 924–26; *HALOT*, 1197–1201, 1226–27. For Syriac, see Payne Smith, 533–34, 539.

130. For Old Aramaic, see *DNWSI*, 1066. For Arabic, see Lane, 1180–81.

131. KTU 1.3 II: 2–3: *kpr šbʿ bnt rḥ gdm w ảnhbm* "henna for seven daughters, scent of coriander and *ảnhbm*."

132. Hebrew: *rēḥayim* (du.) (*HALOT*, 1216); Syriac: *raḥyō* (Payne Smith, 537); Arabic: *raḥā* (Lane, 1057). KTU 1.6 II: 34: *b rḥm tṭḥnn* "with millstones she ground him."

133. In addition to KTU 1.5 V:7 and 1.18 IV lines 25 and 26 cited above, see KTU 1.4 II:8; 1.79:6; 1.166:22; 1.172:26; 5.22:14 (broken or uncertain contexts).

Hebrew, there is no evidence in Ugaritic for *rḥ* meaning "spirit," not even in the death of ʾAqhatu, because "wind" is the natural element being compared to the abstract *npš* element departing from the hero of the story. Some scholars believe this text simply compares one's breath exhaling from the mouth or nostrils to the rushing wind, which would require that *npš* mean "breath" here.[134] Thus far I have not found evidence for such an interpretation of *npš*, the closest candidate being KTU 1.6 III:9 if it is taken to convey the movement of ʾIlu's throat as he breathes heavily, but even there it would refer to the actual breathing apparatus (i.e., the throat or windpipe) and not the breath itself. Of course it could denote breathing in the abstract, but this interpretation would require yet a third semantic development (i.e., throat > movement of throat > the act of breathing). The imagery of wind might better reflect the fact that although it remains unseen to the human eye, it nonetheless produces demonstrable effects.[135] In other words, the vital force that animates a living person exits the individual at death, and the manner of its departure somehow resembles the movement of the wind.

2.2.3.3.2. *Exiting* npš *and* iṯl *"spittle"*

A second comparison with the exiting *npš* occurs in the next line: *km iṯl brlth* "(let) his *brlt* (exit) like spittle." I will revisit the problematic term *brlt* once I have exhausted all remaining contexts for *npš* and attempt a more detailed look at its meaning in Ugaritic, but at this point will make the following observation: every occurrence of *brlt* in the texts examined thus far in which the word *brlt* is attested, all of which are in parallel with *npš*, seems to refer to the throat.[136] But KTU 1.18 column IV will not permit such a meaning, since it would be nonsensical to speak of one's "throat" exiting the body. I have already argued above that the occurrences of *npš* in these texts suggest a more abstract notion, which is equally required of *brlt* here in light of its appearance in poetic parallelism with *npš*.

As far as *iṯl* is concerned, besides its appearance in the ʾAqhatu Epic, one clear example appears in KTU 1.1 II:9, but the broken nature of that text prohibits reconstructing a sensible context.[137] Its only clear context is here in the ʾAqhatu Epic, which allows at least a couple of observations. Given that *brlt* has so far only appeared in parallel to *npš* = "throat," one can safely say that *iṯl* must have something to do with the throat. The next thing to note is that the preceding parallel, *rḥ* "wind," indicates the movement of some natural element.

134. Del Olmo Lete, *Mitos y leyenda*, 385; Wyatt, *Religious Texts*, 286.

135. Cf. the New Testament imagery for Greek *pneuma* in John 3:8.

136. KTU 1.5 I:14–15; 1.17 V:17–18, 23–24 (see the discussions on these texts above).

137. *CAT* reconstructs *npšh* before it ([np]š[h]. w iṯl), but the only visible sign is {š}.

The only other recourse for understanding *iṯl* besides these observations from the present passage is etymology, and even then options are limited. De Moor has cited Hittite *iššalli-* for interpreting Ugaritic *iṯl* as "spittle, saliva," citing Hans Ehelolf, who clarified that the actual nuance of the Hittite refers to that (liquid) which comes out of the mouth.[138] Wilfred G. E. Watson has also marshaled evidence for the spittle interpretation of *iṯl* in Ugaritic in several publications.[139] The appeal to Akkadian *ušultu* "vein, blood vessel" has limited potential semantically in that the context would require something more along the lines of "blood," not blood "vein" or "vessel"—how exactly would a blood vein exit?[140] Del Olmo Lete, following earlier suggestions, takes this line to mean that his spirit (goes out) like a vapor based upon its parallel with *rḥ* without suggesting an etymology.[141] Baruch Margalit has gone in an entirely different direction, rejecting de Moor's Hittite etymology and analyzing *iṯl* as a derivative of the root ʾ-ṯ (Arabic: "to be luxuriant") + a morpheme *-l*, which he argues denotes potentiality. He ends up interpreting the form to indicate a plant not yet in full bloom.[142] This etymology appears less likely than earlier appeals to the cognates in Arabic (*ʾaṯl*) and Hebrew (*ʾēšel*) for the tamarisk tree, but a further problem for either of these proposals is that the imagery of a fading/withering *iṯl*-flower will not work for the governing verb of motion, *yṣʾ* "to go out."[143] In the end, the Hittite etymology proposed by de Moor for spittle appears to pose the fewest problems, leading us to conclude with Wyatt's insightful comment that saliva, along with other bodily fluids, thus contains "elements of the vitality of the individual" tragically wasted in the murder of ʾAqhatu.[144]

138. Johannes C. de Moor, "Frustula Ugaritica," *JNES* 24 (1964): 364. See also Heinz Kronasser, *Etymologie der hethitischen Sprache* (Wiesbaden: Harrassowitz, 1962), 1:42, 212, 262. See also Dijkstra and de Moor, "Problematic Passages," 196. Hans Ehelolf, "Heth. *milit* = 'Honig,'" *OLZ* 36 (1933): 6 n. 3.

139. Wilfred G. E. Watson, "Sul termine ugaritico iṯl," *SEL* 4 (1987): 57–65; Watson, "Spitting Imagery Again," *UF* 19 (1987): 411–12; Watson, "Sundry Ugaritic Notes," *UF* 22 (1990): 422.

140. *CAD* 20:329.

141. "like an exhale his spirit" ("como una exhalación su espíritu"; del Olmo Lete, *Mitos y leyendas*, 385, cf. 523). See Gordon, *Ugaritic Textbook*, 369 (§19.421): "breath, gust"; H. L. Ginsberg, "Ugaritic Myths and Epics," in *Religions of the Ancient Near East: Sumero-Akkadian Religious Texts and Ugaritic Epics*, ed. Isaac Mendelssohn (New York: Liberal Arts Press, 1955), 271: "like a vapour."

142. Margalit, *Ugaritic Poem of AQHT*, 342–43.

143. For the etymology, see, e.g., Henri Cazelles, "Ugarit: La légende d'Aqhat," *Annuaire de l'École Pratique des Hautes Études* 87 (1978–79): 219–20, cited by Margalit. This verb of movement denotes exit or emergence from something, so that "fading" would be a most inappropriate connotation. Furthermore, Biblical Hebrew attests this same root in reference to plants, but as we might expect, it depicts the plant at its beginning stage "coming out" or "emerging" from the ground, not its final stage of withering away (see Deut 14:22; 1 Kgs 5:13; Isa 11:1).

144. Wyatt, *Religious Texts*, 285 n. 155.

2.2.3.3.3. *Exiting* npš *and* qṭr *"smoke, incense"*

A third and final comparison for the exiting *npš* is made here with *qṭr* "smoke, incense" and, oddly enough, is qualified by the phrase *b ủph* "in his nose." The noun *qṭr* occurs only a few times in Ugaritic, but in each instance it is associated with the verb *yṣ*ʾ "to go out":[145]

KTU 1.17 I:27:

l ủrṣ mšṣủ qṭrh	who makes his *qṭr* go out with regard to the earth;
(28) *l ʿpr ḏmr ủṯrh*	who guards his resting place with regard to the dust.

KTU 1.18 IV:26 (restated in line 37):

tṣỉ km (25) *rḥ npšh* . . .	His *npš* goes out like wind . . .
km (26) *qṭr b ủph*	like *qṭr* from his nose

KTU 1.169:3:

w tṣủ lpn ql ṯʿy	May they go out before the voice of the cult official,
(3) *k qṭr ủrbtm*[146]	like smoke (from) a window,
k bṯn ʿmdm[147]	like a serpent (from) a column,
(4) *k yʿlm ẓrh*[148]	like wild goats to a summit,
k lbỉm skh	like lions to a den.

The first two examples come from the ʾAqhatu Epic, the first one in KTU 1.17 being the subject of much discussion as it falls within the so-called duties of an ideal son.[149] This text has been noted for its importance in interpreting KTU 1.18 IV:26 and 37, not only for the obvious reason that it is from the same narrative, but also for its likely association with the funerary cult. I say more about this text in my lexical treatment of death at Ugarit in the following chapters, but I should note here that although the funerary context of KTU 1.17 I:27–28 is plausible, it does not exactly correspond to the exiting *npš/brlt* of KTU 1.18 IV. For

145. Note that such is not the case for Biblical Hebrew, where, e.g., the noun *qᵉṭōret* "incense" never occurs with the verb *yṣ*ʾ, but is attested with several different verbs: *bw*ʾ "come," *lqḥ* "take," *ntn*, "place, set," *ʿlh* "send up" (C stem), *qṭr* "offer incense" (D stem), *qrb* "offer" (C stem), *śym* "put, place," *śmḥ* "rejoice" (D stem) (see references in *HALOT*, 1096).

146. Pardee reads: ủr<.>btm (*Ritual and Cult*, 160). This expression apparently designates the place where light enters the house, i.e., "window."

147. Cf. Hebrew *ʿammûd* "tent pole, pillar" (*HALOT*, 843); Addadian *imdu* "stanchion, support" (*CAD* 7:109–10).

148. Note the directional {h} attached to these two words: *ẓrh* (lit. "to the back side"); *skh* ("to the shelter").

149. For discussion and bibliography on this text, see Lewis, *Cults of the Dead*, 53–71; Schmidt, *Israel's Beneficent Dead*, 59–62.

example, Lewis's appeal to *qṭr* in KTU 1.18 IV for interpreting *qṭrh* in KTU 1.17 I as "his life" does not hold up, since in the former the *npš*/*brlt* of ʾAqhatu is said to exit *km qṭr* "like smoke."[150] In other words, the imagery that is depicted in the funerary context of KTU 1.17, "smoke going out from the ground," provides the analogy for ʾAqhatu's exiting *npš*/*brlt* in KTU 1.18 IV.

What is important in both of these cases is that *qṭr* "goes out"; in KTU 1.17 I it is made to go out *l ảrṣ*. Wyatt's proposal to translate the preposition *l* here with "into" does not make sense of the natural imagery of "smoke, incense," which goes up, not down.[151] Furthermore, the sense of "entrance into" is not possible for the verb *yṣʾ* in that it always denotes "exit from."[152] Therefore, the meaning of the *l* preposition in *l ảrṣ mšṣủ qṭrh* must mean, "to make his smoke come out (vertically) with respect to the ground," or more simply, "to ascend from the ground," as most translators prefer.[153]

Not only does KTU 1.17 I explain the imagery invoked in the exit of ʾAqhatu's *npš*/*brlt* in KTU 1.18 IV, but it also does the same for its appearance in the incantation text KTU 1.169. The situation being addressed in this text has been much disputed, but there seems to be general agreement for interpreting it as an incantation exorcising some kind of demonic infliction or illness.[154] The importance of this text for the present discussion, however, is limited to its mention of exiting *qṭr*, which appears in a four-member series of comparisons depicting the exit of the affliction from the body.[155] The last two comparisons are distinguished from

150. Lewis, *Cults of the Dead*, 54, 60–65.

151. Wyatt, *Religious Texts*, 256 n. 30.

152. It can depict "departure toward" something, as in KTU 1.169:4, but this is not the same as "entrance into" something.

153. E.g., Caquot and Sznycer, *Textes ougaritiques 1*, 344; del Olmo Lete, *Mitos y leyendas*, 369; de Moor, *Anthology of Religious Texts*, 228; Pardee, *COS* 1:344. Hebrew attests a similar usage for the verb *yṣʾ* with regard to a *migdāl*: *hammigdāl hayyôṣēʾ* "the projecting tower" (Neh 3:25, 26, 27), obviously a reference to the stature of the tower projecting outward/upward from the ground. It is also possible that *l ảrṣ* in KTU 1.17 I:27 is meant to be interpreted metaphysically, as in "with regard to the underworld," since the parallel *l ʿpr* could also be taken in this way: "with regard to the dust (= underworld)" (see my discussion in ch. 5 [§5.6]).

154. See Yitzhak Avishur, "The Ghost-Expelling Incantation from Ugarit (Ras Ibn Hani 78/20)," *UF* 13 (1981): 13–25; F. Saracino, "Ras Ibn Hani 78/20 and Some Old Testament Connections," *VT* 32 (1982): 338–41; Manfried Dietrich and Oswald Loretz, "Ugaritische Rituale und Beschwörungen," *TUAT* 2:333–36; de Moor, *Anthology of Religious Texts*, 183–86; Caquot, *Textes ougaritiques 2*, 53–60; Daniel Fleming, "The Voice of the Ugaritic Incantation Priest (RIH 78/20)," *UF* 23 (1991): 141–54; Wilfred G. E. Watson, "Imagery in a Ugaritic Incantation," *UF* 24 (1992): 367–68; Dennis Pardee, "Poetry in Ugaritic Ritual Texts," in *Verse in Ancient Near Eastern Prose*, ed. Johannes C. de Moor and Wilfred G. E. Watson, AOAT 42 (Kevelaer: Butzon & Bercker; Neukirchen-Vluyn: Neukirchener, 1993), 211–13; Pardee, *Textes rituels*, 875–93; Pardee, *Ritual and Cult*, 159–61; Wyatt, *Religious Texts*, 442–49; del Olmo Lete, *Canaanite Religion*, 2nd ed., 384–86.

155. There is a difference of opinion as to what is exiting here. Many scholars have read this as the exit of the tormenter/demon, which would read *tṣủ* as a 2ms form: "May you exit" (e.g., del

the first two by the suffix {h} denoting direction, "going out toward something," a factor that leads most commentators to see the first pair as emphasizing going out from something: incense goes out from a window and serpents go out from a column, while wild goats depart to the summit and lions depart to their den.

The point of this extended discussion of *qṭr* in its attested contexts is simply to show the way in which the *npš* of Dānîʾilu is being depicted in the ʾAqhatu Epic: the human element that somehow exits the individual when he dies. According to Ugaritic phraseology for *qṭr*, it is something that goes out or away from the ground and this no doubt explains what is meant by *b ảp* "from the nose" in KTU 1.18 IV:26—the *npš* goes out from the nostrils as smoke goes out from a window (cf. KTU 1.169=RIH 70/20:3).

2.2.3.4. *npš* = Vitality Summary

This particular category of usage for *npš* in Ugaritic demarcates a significant development for our understanding of this term. Along with its association with the root *ḥyy* "to live" and its ability to "rest" within someone, this last motif of "exiting" *npš* signals a semantic shift away from the more commonly attested concrete meanings "neck" and "throat," though I must stress that it is not a mutation, but rather a natural devlopment. As I noted earlier, the mythology of Môtu and his insatiable *npš* "throat," which one might perceive to be the driving force of Death's existence simply from the regularity of its association with him in the mythological texts, may provide sufficient basis in Ugaritic thought for the development from throat to vital force.

This raises other questions, one of the more controversial being the degree to which Ugaritians envisioned a disembodied *npš*, or whether they simply envisioned the exit of one's *npš* as the point of life's termination. The ongoing scholarly conversation regarding the identity and existence of the mysterious Rapaʾūma (*rpủm*) would certainly figure into this question, but these matters will have to await further sorting out later in this book (ch. 4). For now, suffice

Olmo Lete, *Canaanite Religion*, 2nd ed., 408; Wyatt, *Religious Texts*, 444). Saracino interprets it as a 3mp form "may they go out" referring back to *dbbm* in line 1, the so-called "demon flies" ("Ras Ibn Hani 78/20," 339). Pardee also takes it as a 3mp: "Those who cause the pain of your penis, so that they go away at the voice of the *ṯʿy*-official" ("Ceux qui provoquent la douleur de ta verge, de sorte qu'ils s'en vont à la voix de l'officiant-*ṯʿy*"; *Textes rituels*, 876, 877, 881–82; see also Pardee, *Ritual and Cult*, 160). The typical reading of {tgẖṭk} as a 2ms PC form of the root *gẖṭ* would be a *hapax legomenon*, which, although not entirely impossible, is unknown in Semitic. Biblical Hebrew does attest *tûgâ* meaning "grief" (*HALOT*, 1695) and thus provides an etymological basis while the proposed root *gẖṭ* does not (suggested by Oswald Loretz and Paolo Xella, "Beschwörung und Krankenheilung in RIH 78/20," in *Materiali Lessicali ed Epigrafici* [Rome: Consiglia Nazionale delle Ricerche, 1982], 1:37, 39–40; Xella, *La terra di Baal [Ugarit e la sua civiltà]*, Biblioteca di Archeologia (Rome: Curio, 1984], 115; followed by Fleming, "Voice of the Ugaritic Incantation Priest," 145).

it to say that as far as Ugaritic is concerned, the word is not used to describe the state of being after death.

2.2.4. *npš* = Attitude/Disposition

In two literary contexts *npš* suggests the aspect of attitude or one's disposition: one epic (KTU 1.16 VI:34, 47), the other ritual (KTU 1.40:22, 31, 39). In each case the construct phrase *qṣr npš* "shortness of *npš*" occurs. This usage provides yet another abstraction of the term, though not entirely distinct from the meaning "vital force." For instance, it is useful to think of *qṣr npš* as an application of "*npš* = vitality" to a particular type of vitality: a vitality that is somehow shortened.

Robert Haak has conducted a helpful comparative study of this Ugaritic expression in search of a solution for interpreting *qṣr npš* and *qṣr rwḥ* in particularly difficult contexts throughout the Hebrew Bible.[156] For Ugaritic, Haak concludes that *qṣr npš* must allow for two connotations based upon the distinguishable contexts of KTU 1.16 VI:34, 47 and 1.40:22, 31, 39. The tendency for scholars to translate *qṣr npš* negatively as "impatience" inevitably arises from the fact that the ritual setting of KTU 1.40 concerns expiation of sin against another person in the community, signaling that the action in view must be something negative.[157] But this standard rendition will not work for KTU 1.16 VI where the context of the expression suggests something along the lines of "lowliness" or even "weakness" rather than "impatience." This factor has led Haak to conclude that *qṣr npš* possesses two connotations, impatience or weakness, depending on the literary environment of the occurrence.[158] Haak does not explore the potential impetus that produced these two seemingly exclusive connotations, however, but it might become clearer with a consideration of possible connections to the abstract notion of vitality treated above. Before doing so, I will provide a brief rendition of the expression in its two known environments.

KTU 1.16 VI:34:

(32) *šqlt b ǵlt ydk*	You have made your hands fall in slackness:
(33) *l tdn dn ảlmnt*	You do not decide the decision of the widow;

156. Robert D. Haak, "A Study and New Interpretation of QṢR NPŠ," *JBL* 101 (1982): 161–67.

157. For the translation "impatience," see André Caquot, "Un sacrifice expiatoire à Ras Shamra," *RHPR* 42 (1962): 201–11; Wyatt, *Religious Texts*, 344–47; Pardee, *Ritual and Cult*, 81–83. Note, however, del Olmo Lete's translation: "faintheartedness/impatience" (*Canaanite Religion*, 1st ed., 147–49). For a discussion on the ritual setting, see del Olmo Lete, *Canaanite Religion*, 2nd ed., 115–16; Pardee, *Ritual and Cult*, 77–79.

158. Haak, "Study and New Interpretation of QṢR NPŠ," 162–63, 166–67.

(34) *l tṯpṭ ṯpṭ* ***qṣr npš***	You do not judge the judgment of **those short of *npš*.**

(repeated verbatim in KTU 1.16 VI:44–47)

At this point in the Kirta Epic, Kirta's son YṢB levels an accusation against his father who has just recovered from what was thought to be mortal illness, charging that he has grown slack in his rule and attention to kingdom matters, and challenging him to give up the kingship so that YṢB might rule in his stead. As the charge is stated, namely, that Kirta has allowed his control of the kingdom to grow slack, YṢB specifically identifies his father's shortcoming as the failure to administer justice for the *ảlmnt* "widow." The following line functions as the parallel expression of the former, making *qṣr npš* "short of *npš*" parallel to *ảlmnt* "widow" and thus suggesting that *qṣr npš* has to do with the humble or weakened status characteristic of widowhood (or similar states).[159]

KTU 1.40: 22, 31, 39:[160])

(22) *ủ tḫṭin*	Whether you sin:
b ảpkn	in your anger,
ủ b ⸢***q***⸣***ṣrt npš***[***kn***	in **the shortness of** [**your**] ***npš*,**
ủ b qṭt] (23) *tqṭṭn*	[or in the outrage] you have committed.
ủ ⸢*šn*⸣ *ypkm*	Whether your beauty change:
(31) *ủ b ảpkm*	in your anger,
ủ b ***q***[***ṣ***]⸢***r***⸣***t npškm***	in **the sh**[**or**]**tness of your *npš*,**
ủ b qṭt tqṭṭ	or in the outrage you have committed.
(39) *l*[!161] *šn ypkn*	Whether your beauty change:
b ảp⸢*k*⸣[*n*	in yo[ur] anger,
ủ b ***q***]⸢***ṣ***⸣***rt npškn***	[in **the sh**]**ortness of your *npš*,**
ủ b q⸢*ṭt*⸣ (40) *tqṭṭn*	or in the outrage you have committed.

The first portion of the ritual cited here (lines 22–23) contains a series of three prepositional phrases outlining the manner of a person's sin (*ủ tḫṭin*), after which the appropriate sacrifice for expiation (*ṯʿ*-sacrifice of a ram) is specified (lines 23–25). The second two selections (lines 30–32; 39–40) list the same three prepositional modifiers, this time describing the way in which a person has altered his

159. Similarly noted by Haak, "Study and New Interpretation of QṢR NPŠ," 162.

160. Following the collation of Pardee, *Ritual and Cult*, 80. Note that the text from lines 22–23 has been reconstructed for lines 14–15 (see *CAT*; del Olmo Lete, *Canaanite Religion*, 2nd ed., 118–19).

161. Read *ủ* based upon lines 22 and 31.

or her beauty (*ủ šn ypkm*), both sections being followed by the required sacrifice (*ṯʿ*-sacrifices of a donkey).

These formulas are part of a larger six-part structure (or three pairs of paragraphs), the first now missing, in which the word *npy* occurs right after each paragraph's stated theme.[162] The identity of *npy* throughout this text and its relation to *yp* has been understood differently by scholars, the simplest explanation being that of Pardee, who sees both terms as derivatives of the root *ypy* "to be beautiful."[163] He interprets them to mean "well-being," not so much in the sense of *šlm*, but "the sum of political, social, and economic unity and prosperity."[164] According to this analysis, the ritual as a whole deals with expiation on three planes: the first entirely missing, the second dealing with sin (*ḫṭʾ*), in sections 3 (missing) and 4 (lines 19, 22, and 23), and the third dealing with the disruption of communal well-being (*šn ypkm*) in sections 5 and 6 (lines 28, 30, 32, 36, 39, and 40).

Regarding the phrase *qṣr npš*, this brief structural and thematic overview of KTU 1.40 shows the potentially negative/sin application of "short of *npš*" in Ugaritic, but how does this factor into its distinct connotation "weakness" in KTU 1.6 VI:34? The governing word in the construct phrase is the adjective *qṣr*, derived from the stative root meaning "to be short."[165] The main idea is limitation or falling under some physical or metaphysical standard of measurement. The only other time this adjective appears in Ugaritic is in KTU 1.103:39 where it refers to the shortened foot of a defective animal at birth: *qṣrt pʿnh*.[166] The contexts of KTU 1.16 and 1.40 suggest that we are dealing with something

162. Pardee, *Ritual and Cult*, 78, 111 n. 112; Del Olmo Lete, *Canaanite Religion*, 2nd ed., 121.

163. Pardee, *Ritual and Cult*, 111 n. 112, interpreting *npy* as the N verbal noun of √*ypy* and *yp* as the noun "beauty" (cf. Heb *yāpê*). Del Olmo Lete (*Canaanite Religion*, 2nd ed., 123), however, takes *npy* as a noun from √*npy* meaning "purification, expiation," citing cognates in Akkadian (*napû*/*nappû* "to sieve") and Aramaic (*nāpâ* "to winnow"), and Arabic (*nafā* "to remove, sweep"), one of the main problems with this etymology being that the semantic steps from "sieve" to "expiation" are not without difficulty. Lauren Shedletsky and Baruch Levine have proposed that it designates "groups, or jurisdictions within Ugarit," citing evidence for *npy* as a garment worn by those in authority, the "semantic bridge" being jurisdictional units under said authorities ("The *mšr* of the Sons and Daughters of Ugarit [KTU2 1.40]," *RB* 106 [1999]: 325–32). Again, this complicated etymology is less desirable than the simpler appeal to √*ypy*, which provides an etymological basis for both *npy* and *yp*, not to mention "the structural cohesion that the two terms *npy* and *yp* . . . lend to the text" (Pardee, *Ritual and Cult*, 111 n. 112).

164. Pardee, *Ritual and Cult*, 111 n. 112; cf. Tropper, *Ugaritische Grammatik*, 2nd ed., 541: "satisfaction" ("Befriedigung").

165. *DUL*, 716–17; for the corresponding Hebrew forms, see *HALOT*, 1126–27.

166. See Manfried Dietrich, Oswald Loretz, and Joaquín Sanmartín, "Der keilalphabetische šumma izbu-Text RS 24.247 +265 +268 +328," *UF* 7 (1975): 135: "shortness of the foot" ("Kürze des Fußes"); Dennis Pardee, "Ugaritic. RS 24.247+," *AfO* 33 (1986): 125 n. 40: "probably denotes the section between the <ankle> and the hoof."

in the abstract—the abstract quality of widowhood or the abstract quality of impatience—and not the concrete, which naturally leads us to consider the abstract meaning "vitality" or "vital force" for *npš* as a means of explaining the semantic development of this idiom.[167] With regard to the notion of "weakness" in KTU 1.16 VI, it would designate the diminishment of one's vitality brought about by the circumstances characteristic of widowhood (or similar states), thus the opposite of the successful life of vitality portrayed in those contexts where *npš* is associated with the root *ḥyy*—"to live with regard to vitality."[168] In the ritual text of KTU 1.40, however, a shortening of one's vital force (or even passion) depicts the inability to maintain emotional control and composure (i.e., "short-tempered").[169] In both of these instances, "diminishment of vitality" offers a lucid means of explaining the commonality in the application of this one idiom to two contexts: (1) diminishment of vitality induced by widowhood, and (2) diminishment of vitality as lack of vital control of emotions.

2.2.5. *npš* = Person/Individual

The last identifiable category for *npš* in this chapter is "person" or "individual." Surprisingly, this usage does not occur in the any of the familiar Ugaritic passages treated above (e.g., Baʿlu cycle, the Kirta and ʾAqhatu Epics, ritual texts, etc.) but instead shows up in a few administrative lists and once in a letter. I begin my discussion of this usage by introducing the letter KTU 2.38 recording a message from the king of Tyre addressed to the king of Ugarit.

KTU 2.38:20

(10) *ảnykn dt* (11) *likt mṣrm*	Your ships that you sent to Egypt,
(12) *hndt b ṣr* (13) *mtt*	these are wrecked[170] off Tyre
by (14) *gšm ảdr* (15) *nškḥ*	where they[171] found themselves in a bad storm.

167. One could consider a development from the concrete meaning "throat" for KTU 1.16 VI (i.e., weakness induced from a constricted throat), but this would not work as well for "impatience" in KTU 1.40.

168. KTU 1.17 I:36; 1.19 I:36; 1.19 IV: 36, 39; 2.23:18. Note especially that in the ʾAqhatu story "to live with regard to *npš*" has to do with some particular successful outcome: the birth of a son for Dānîʾilu (KTU 1.19 I:36), the revenge of ʾAqhatu's death for Pūġatu (KTU 1.19 IV:36, 39).

169. Understanding *qṣr npš* in KTU 1.40 as "shortness of passion" or "loss of temper" suggests that these three conditions indicate a progression in intensity: anger (internal), loss of temper (outburst of anger), and base acts of outrage.

170. Literally: "dead." I will provide a full treatment of this phrase in my analysis of the root m-t "to die" in ch. 3.

171. Taking the form as an N stem 3mp SC, the subject being the individuals running the ship.

w (16) *rb tmtt*[172] (17) *lqḥ*	The master of "death" took
kl ḏrʿ (18) *bd*[*nh*]*m*	all the grain from their possession.
w ảnk (19) *k*[*l*] *ḏrʿ*[*h*]*m*	As for me, all their grain,
(20) [*k*]*l* ***npš*** (21) *w ảklhm*	every **individual**, and their food
bd (22) *r*[*b*] *tmtt lqḥt*	I took from the hand of the master of "death"
(23) *w ṯṯb ảnk lhm*	and returned (it) to them.

This letter addresses the Tyrian king's recovery of a fleet of Ugaritic ships that were heading for Egypt but were caught in a storm just off the city of Tyre, aptly described as being "dead (in the water)."[173] The word *npš* appears in the list of items that the king of Tyre recovered from the salvage master who had apparently collected them from a wrecked fleet: the grain in their possession, every *npš*, and their food. It is interesting to point out here that the text records a list of recovered items, since all other instances of *npš* = individual occur in administrative lists, which I provide in brief here:

KTU 4.91:13

ʿšrm kkr (12) *brr*	twenty talents of tin;
(13) *ʿšrm* ***npš***	twenty **individuals/persons**;
(14) *ʿšrm zt mm*	twenty (units of) olives in water[174];
(15) *ảrbm* (16) *šmn mr*	forty (units of) oil (perfumed with) myrrh.

KTU 4.102:29[175]

(29) [. . . ʿ]*šrm npš b bt t*[. . .]	[. . . t]wenty, (each) *npš* in the house of T[. . .]

KTU 4.228 (7×)

The first portion of each of the eight lines in this list is broken, with *npš* clearly legible at the end of the first seven lines and the signs {ḥd} visible at the end of line 8 (probably *ảḥd*). I can make out the signs {rbʿ} just before *npš* in line 3, probably indicating cardinal number [*ả*]*rbʿ* "four," but everything else is mostly lost.

172. Pardee: "salvage master" (*COS* 3:94 n. 44). See also the study of Hoftijzer, "Letter du roi de Tyr," 383–88.

173. On this expression, see ch. 3 (§3.2.4).

174. See RS 94.2479:19 (Bordreuil, Pardee, and Hawley, *Bibliothèque au sud de la ville* ***, 65, 66).

175. Census list (according to *CAT*). The use of *npš* here is a tally of individuals in the house of so-and-so. It comes at the end of the census list.

KTU 4.338:1[176]

(1) *spr* ***npš*** *d*	The accounting of (the group of) **individuals** when
(2) *ʿrb*[177] *bt mlk*	they entered the royal house,
(3) *w b spr l št*	but had not been placed in the record:

(4) *yrmʿl*	3[178]	YRMʿL:	3
(5) *ṣry*	2	ṢRY:	2
(6) *iršy*	3	ỈRŠY:	3
(7) *yʿḏrd*	3	YʿḎRD:	3
(8) *ảyảḫ*	2	ẢYẢḪ:	2
(9) *bn ảylt*	1	Son of ẢYLT:	1

This list provides an accounting of persons having entered the royal household without having been officially listed in the royal record. Lines 4–9 tabulate the personal names of individuals, one name for each line followed by a number between one and three, perhaps representing the number of individuals accompanying the person named.

As I have already mentioned, the particular meaning "individual" appears to be limited to lists, at least as the corpus of Ugaritic texts currently stands. The context of such lists involves concrete items, either counted (KTU 4.91:13; 4.102:29; 4.228; 4.338:1) or listed as a whole (KTU 2.38:20). By way of comparison, I might add that *npš* also occurs quite regularly amid other listed items for sacrifice in the ritual texts (e.g., a nose, a liver, goats, rams, fourteen ewes) where, I have argued, *npš* means "neck" (see discussion above). As for the meaning "individual," it most likely derived from the vital element of the person, and thus *npš* in these cases would represent one in whom the vital element for life exists.

2.3. Life and Body Parts: *brlt* as a Parallel of *npš*

The term *brlt* is a most elusive lexeme for Ugaritologists and has long been the subject of etymological study in light of its limited usage in Ugaritic, but, as the

176. For a discussion of lines 10–18, see Manfried Dietrich and Oswald Loretz, "Schiffshandel und Schiffsmiete zwischen Byblos und Ugarit (KTU 1.17 I 1)," *UF* 22 (1990): 89–96.

177. This verb must be plural, since a singular would require a feminine verbal form in light of the fact that *npš* is a feminine noun. I take the singular form *npš* as a collective referring to the group of individuals being accounted for in this tally, while the plural verb /ʿarabū/ expresses the real-world plurality.

178. Numbers are indicated by counting vertical wedges. For a photograph of the tablet, see *Ugaritica* 4:62 fig. 46.

matter currently stands, a consensus has not been reached. Before considering such proposals, I will summarize its occurrences, as limited as they are, in light of my own conclusions regarding the meaning and usage of *npš* outlined in this chapter. Unfortunately, *brlt* never occurs independent of *npš*, which, if it did, might offer welcomed semantic clarity. Nonetheless, so long as the current situation remains, the main avenue for probing its meaning is to adduce what we can from its relation to *npš* in context. Secondarily, I will survey proposed etymologies for *brlt* from the literature and assess their merits.[179]

2.3.1. *brlt* Usage in Ugaritic

I have organized the usages of *npš* // *brlt* into two categories as a result of my discussion above: "throat" and "vital force."[180] The more common of the two is "throat" in light of its wider distribution, appearing in the Baʿlu cycle (KTU 1.5 I:15), the Kirta Epic (KTU 1.16 VI: 12), and the ʾAqhatu Epic (KTU 1.17 V:18, 24); the meaning "vital force" is restricted to the ʾAqhatu story, once in ʾIlu's pronouncement of blessing to Dānîʾilu and four times in the repeated refrains describing ʾAqhatu's exiting *npš* // *brlt* (KTU 1.18 IV:25, 37; 1.19 II:39, 44).

Throat:

KTU 1.5 I:15

p npš npš lbỉm (15) *thw*	And my throat is the throat of a lion of the steppe,
hm ***brlt*** *ảnḫr* (16) *b ym*	or **the gullet** of *ảnḫr* in the sea;
hm brky tkšd (17) *rủmm*	or it searches for the pool of wild bulls,
ʿn k d̲d ảylt	(for) a spring like the herd of hinds;

KTU 1.16 VI:12

(10) *w t̲tb trḫṣ nn b dʿt*	She sits down, washes him with regard to his sweat,
(11) *npšh l lḥm tptḥ*	she opens his throat (for) eating,
(12) ***brlth*** *l t̲rm*	his **gullet** for feeding.

KTU 1.17 V:18[181]

ʿbd (17) *ỉmr b pḫd*	Prepare a lamb from the flock
l npš kt̲r (18) *w ḫss*	for the throat of Kôt̲aru-wa-Ḫasīsu,
l ***brlt*** *hyn d* (19) *ḥrš yd*	for **the gullet** of HYN who is the hand crafter.

179. For a defense of my approach to lexicography, see the Introduction.

180. Alfredo Criscuolo also lists "appetite, desire" as a range of meaning for *brlt* ("Metafore anatomiche: ugaritico *brlt*," *SEL* 24 [2007]: 29), which I question for *npš*, as outlined earlier in this chapter.

181. Refrain repeated in KTU 1.17 V:24.

Vital Force:

KTU 1.17 I:37

npš yḥ dnil (37) [*mt rp*]*i*	As for (his) vitality, may Dānîʾilu, man of RPỦ live,
brlt *ǵzr mt hrnmy*	as for (his) **vital force**, may the warrior, HRNMY man (live).

KTU 1.18 IV:25[182]

tṣi km (25) *rḥ npšh*	Let his vitality go out like wind,
km iṯl ***brlth***	like spittle his **vital force**,
km (26) *qṭr b àph*	like smoke in his nostrils.

I begin with a few observations concerning the distribution of *brlt* with regard to *npš* throughout these texts. First, when *npš* occurs in a line followed by a poetic parallel, *brlt* is not always used.[183] For example, in KTU 1.4 VII:48 the parallel for *npš* is *gngn*, which appears to be another word for throat.[184]

yqrȧ mt (48) *b* ***npšh***	Môtu calls out in **his throat**,
ystrn ydd (49) *b* ***gngnh***	the beloved one tells it in **his insides**.

The word *mhmrt* "well, pit" functions as its parallel in KTU 1.5 I:7:

l yrt (7) *b* ***npš*** *bn ilm mt*	Indeed, you must descend into **the throat** of Môtu, son of ʾIlu,
b ***mh***(8)***mrt*** *ydd il ǵzr*	into **the well/pit** of the beloved hero of ʾIlu.

182. Refrain repeated in KTU 1.18 IV:37; 1.19 II:39, 44.

183. Note that the comment of Rendsburg, which seems to assume *brlt* = *npš*, "This vocable appears consistently as the parallel member of *npš*, so its meaning is well established" ("Modern South Arabian," 626), is not entirely accurate since it is not necessarily *the* parallel member of *npš*. The sensitivity of B. Cutler and J. Macdonald is preferable: "It is obvious that the meaning of *brlt* must be sought in terms of its textual parallelism to *npš* and that any literal cognate suggested must be within, or at least close to, the semantic range of *npš*" ("An Akkadian Cognate to Ugaritic *brlt*," *UF* 5 [1973]: 68).

184. See also KTU 1.16 VI:26: *ȧp yṣb yṯb b hkl w ywsrnn ggnh*: "YṢB also returned to the palace and his throat instructed him." Pardee: "apparently another word for 'throat' (< 'tube')" (*COS* 1:342 n. 97). The etymological suggestions for this term are diverse. Pope suggests the Arabic cognate *janan/janjan/jinjin* meaning "heart, breast, chest" (Lane, 463) ("Little Soul Searching," 26; see also *DUL*, 303). Renfroe appeals to Biblical Hebrew *gargᵉgōt* (BDB, 176) and *gārôn* (BDB, 173), both of which mean "neck." He also cites Akkadian *gaggurītu* (< *gangurītu*) (*CAD* 5:9), which refers to the neck of an animal, and suggests that the Hebrew form exhibits assimilated *n* > *r* (*Arabic-Ugaritic Lexical Studies*, 105). I find this second proposal to be the most satisfactory for the usage of *gngn* in Ugaritic. See the useful summary of the etymological proposals for *gngn* in Smith and Pitard, *Ugaritic Baal Cycle* 2, 690.

In KTU 1.5 I:18 the verbal expression *npš blt* "my throat swallows" is paralleled with a single first person verb: *ilḥm* "I devour":

(18) *hm imt imt* ***npš blt*** (19) *ḥmr*	or truly, truly **my throat swallows** heaps (of things).
p imt b klát (20) *ydy* ***ilḥm***	And truly with double handfuls **I devour**.

Finally, once *npš* is in parallel with itself in KTU 1.6 II:17–18:

npš *ḫsrt* (18) *bn nšm*	**My throat** lacked sons of men,
npš *hmlt* (19) *árṣ*	**my throat** (lacked) multitudes of the earth.

These examples are important because they demonstrate that *brlt* is not an exact synonym for *npš* even though the two terms share significant semantic overlap.

Second, it might be helpful to define the type of parallelism for the poetic lines in which the lexical pair *npš* // *brlt* occurs. In most cases, the first line is restated in the second via semantic and grammatical parallelism (KTU 1.16 VI:12; 1.17 I:37; 1.17 V:18, 24; 1.18 IV: 25, 37; 1.19 II:29, 44), or what has been traditionally called "synonymous" parallelism.[185] Yet in one instance (KTU 1.5 I:15) the second line mirrors the first in its wording (i.e., grammatical parallelism) but introduces a new item for comparison:

p npš ***npš lbim*** (15) *thw*	And my throat is **the throat of a lion** of the steppe,
hm ***brlt ánḫr*** (16) *b ym*	or **the gullet of** ***ánḫr*** in the sea;

The same kind of parallel structure appears in the ʾAqhatu Epic with regard to the exit of the hero's *npš* // *brlt*:

tṣi km (25) ***rḥ npšh***	Let his **vitality** go out like **wind**,
km ***iṯl brlth***	his **vital force** like **spittle**

A final point concerning the distribution of *brlt* in Ugaritic is that it always appears as the second member of the parallel pair.[186] One might charge that

185. See the discussion on parallelism above (§2.1.2).

186. Moshe Held identified fixed pairs of synonymns in Ugaritic and Hebrew, designating them as A-words and B-words. According to Held, the A-word is the more common term, while the B-word is less common and is mostly restricted to its poetic function as the second member of a given poetic pair (Held, "Studies in Ugaritic Lexicography and Poetic Style" [Ph.D. diss., Johns

this observation is simply stating the obvious, but at the same time it is not altogether irrelevant. We should consider Ugaritic poetic parallelism more broadly on this point, especially due to the limited nature of *brlt* as characteristically one (among others) poetic pair for *npš*. In fact, its usage is limited to poetry alone, unlike *npš* with its wider attestation in all the Ugaritic literary genres. Though this issue does not necessarily advance our understanding of the semantics of *brlt* per se, it is worth mentioning the existence of the so-called pair inventory, or stock phrases purportedly available to or traditionally known by Ugaritic poets.[187] It could be that the only reason *brlt* has come down to us in the first place is because of its traditional use in poetry as an oft-used pair for *npš*, but is not utilized in other contexts.

2.3.2. *brlt* Etymology

Pope has provided a helpful survey of the etymological suggestions up until the point of his publication (1981).[188] The most common language of interest to scholars in devising an etymology for *brlt* has been Akkadian, yielding several purported cognates. William F. Albright cited Akkadian *billurtu* meaning "cross," which he argued developed semantically to "individual" analogical to Hebrew *tāw*, a mark of possession resembling a cross that came to symbolize one's identity.[189] Considering a more complicated phonological development, de Moor has been drawn to Akkadian *balāṭu* "life," arguing for dissimilation of *ll* > *rl* and assimilation of *ṭt* > *tt*, both of which are attested sound changes in Semitic.[190] B. Cutler and J. Macdonald have put forth Akkadian *mîriltu/mêriltu*, an older byform of *mîrištu/mêrištu*, as an etymological candidate for *brlt* meaning "wish, desire, request," meanings that they claim "happily fit the Ugaritic contexts."[191] More recently Gary Rendsburg has shifted attention to Modern South Arabian,

Hopkins University, 1957], 6–8, 18; Held, "Additional Pairs of Words in Synonymous Parallelism in Biblical Hebrew and in Ugaritic," *Leš* 18 [1953]: 144–60; see also Robert Boling, "'Synonymous' Parallelism in the Psalms," *JSS* 5 [1960]: 221–55). For other studies on the significance of stock parallel pairs in Ugaritic and Hebrew, see H. L. Ginsberg, "The Rebellion and Death of Baʿlu," *Or* 5 (1936): 171–72; H. L. Ginsberg and B. Maisler, "Semitised Ḫurrians in Syria and Palestine," *JPOS* 14 (1934): 248–49 n. 15; Umberto Cassuto, "ספרות מקראית וספרות כנענית," *Tarbiz* 14 (1943): 1–10; Cassuto, *Goddess Anath*, 25–32. For a more recent discussion and bibliography, see Berlin, *Dynamics of Biblical Parallelism*, 65–72.

187. Denied by Berlin, *Dynamics of Biblical Parallelism*, 66.

188. Marvin H. Pope, "An Arabic Cognate for Ugaritic *brlt*?," *UF* 13 (1981): 305–6. See also the discussion in Cutler and Macdonald, "Akkadian Cognate," 67–70.

189. William F. Albright, "Are the Ephod and Teraphim Mentioned in Ugaritic Literature?," *BASOR* 83 (1941): 41–42 n. 24.

190. De Moor, "Frustula Ugaritica," 364 n. 77.

191. Cutler and Macdonald, "Akkadian Cognate," 68–70.

mentioning both *ʾăberēt/ʾăberét* "desire to weep" and *ʿabrɛt* "lump in the throat, desire to weep."[192] Rendsburg admits the complicated phonology required for his proposal (√*brt* + expanded *l* > *brlt*; loss of preformative {ʾ} or {ʿ}) but at the same time points out similarly complicated developments in other languages. Finally, I note Alfredo Criscuolo who has entertained the possibility that *brlt* is a loan word from Hurrian *wur-* "desire," requiring the phonetic changes *w* > *b*, which he points out is well-attested for Hurrian loans, and the dissimilation of *r* > *l*.[193]

In considering these proposed etymologies, I find Pope's appeal to Arabic *burâʾil* and *burʾûla-t* most intriguing due to its close semantic resemblance to Ugaritic *brlt*. He notes the Arabic lexicographers' explanation of the term as designating "the neck feathers of the rooster" and its denominatives denoting "the act of puffing up the neck feathers."[194] As Pope aptly observes, the appeal of this etymology is that the meaning of the Arabic term is associated with the neck, though one might object that it actually denotes the neck feathers and not the neck itself. Another semantic problem for this proposal is that nowhere in Ugaritic does *brlt* mean "neck," only "throat" and by extension "vital force." For this reason, Rendsburg's Old South Arabian suggestion is tempting, since "lump in the throat" is at least closer to "throat," notwithstanding the phonological challenges it faces. The other etymologies listed above run into the problem of semantics, mainly because they focus on words whose meanings more closely correspond to the lexical range of *npš* (e.g., individual, life), not *brlt* (throat, vital force). The proposal of Cutler and Macdonald based upon Akkadian *mîriltu/mêriltu* "wish, desire, request" errs not only in its failure to relate semantically to Ugaritic *brlt*, which never means "wish" or "desire," but also in the faulty assumption of this meaning for *npš*, a suggestion I have already questioned above.

2.3.3. *brlt* Summary

The etymological question unfortunately remains unresolved. The two most favorable options having been offered thus far are those of Pope and Rendsburg, even though they are not without difficulties. Returning to Ugaritic usage, the above overview suggests that its meaning is limited to that of "throat" and by extension "vital force," though this secondary meaning is found in only one literary context. Since "throat" is more widely attested, I propose that this meaning must have been the basic sense for *brlt*. Unlike *npš*, the meaning "neck" is not

192. Rendsburg, "Modern South Arabian," 626.

193. Criscuolo, "Metafore anatomiche," 29–31.

194. Pope, "Arabic Cognate," 306. The phonetic problem of the glottal stop in the Arabic form, Pope argues, could be explained as "a late, secondary development that would not find representation in the Ugaritic form."

attested for *brlt* and is therefore more limited in its semantic development. Due to the fact that *brlt* is restricted to the role of being the secondary member of the *npš*/*brlt* poetic pair, it must have been the least common of the two terms as a word for "throat" in Ugaritic. As I already noted for *npš* above, this term apparently underwent the same semantic development from "throat" to "vital force," as attested in the ʾAqhatu Epic.

2.4. Life and Other Body Parts: *kbd*, *lb*, and *ảp*

The second most common word group illustrating this relationship between life in the abstract and particular body parts is *kbd* "liver" and *lb* "heart." I intend to summarize the lexical data as a means of providing context for what I have already demonstrated for *npš*; I will hold off discussing the broader significance of this feature until chapter 5 where I provide a more comprehensive literary synthesis of life and death at Ugarit. Much like *npš*, several Ugaritic body part words take on metaphysical meaning expressive of various aspects of one's life experience. The term *npš* apparently designated the neck of an animal in the ritual context on the one hand, or the throat of deities, humans, and animals in the mythological and epic texts on the other. That particular body part was then applied to a corresponding aspect of life experience—the throat represents the animating force of a living being. There are similar examples throughout Ugaritic for *kbd*, *lb*, and *ảp*, which I summarize in the following sections.

2.4.1. *kbd* and *lb*

Next to *npš*, the two most prominent examples of body parts used to designate certain life aspects are *kbd* and *lb*. In the mythological and epic texts these two terms regularly occur as a parallel pair. Most often *kbd* occurs parallel to *lb*, but it also appears alongside *ṯd* "breast, chest" (2×) and *ỉrt* "chest" (1×, but following *lb*). As for *lb*, when it occurs in a poetic pair it is always with *kbd*, but there are two instances where *lb* is found in a list of various external body parts (e.g., *ǵr* "skin," *lḥ* "cheek," *dqn* "chin," *ḏrʿ* "arm").[195] The importance of these words for this study is the fact that they are used to denote vital components of an individual life. Both *kbd* and *lb* find a wide variety of usages, both of which appear to be rooted in Ugaritic ritual—admittedly, *kbd* is by far the more common item found in the offering lists, but *lb* does occur once in the offering list of KTU 1.39:8. This ritual context suggests that the term refers to animal parts, but in other genres

195. KTU 1.5 VI:14–22; 1.6 I:3–5.

their referents become more diverse, including deities, humans, more animals, and even the earth. The appropriateness of one term serving such a variety of functions finds precedent in my analysis of *npš* above, where its cultic reference to the neck of an animal offered in sacrifice to a given deity stands alongside its application to the throat of deities and humans in the attested mythologies and epics.

2.4.1.1. *kbd* and *lb* in Ritual

In the ritual texts *kbd* denotes the liver of an animal presented as an offering to a particular deity. The evidence for this meaning of *kbd* comes from its appearance in texts inscribed on liver models utilized for divination at Ugarit, as for example in KTU 1.143 (=RS 24.326):

(1) *kbd dt ypt*	The liver (model) of YPT
(2) *bn ykn*ʿ	son of YKNʿ
(3) *k ypt*ḥ *yr*⌜*ḫ*⌝ *hnd*	when this month began.[196]

One also encounters this term in offering lists where the liver is mentioned with other animal parts such as the neck (*npš*), as well as whole animals like a bull (*ỉlp*) or ram (*š*):

KTU 1.46:

(1) [ ]*ṯ slḫ npš ṯ*ʿ *w* ⌜*ṯ*⌝[*n*] ⌜*k*⌝*bdm*[197]	[ ]Ṯ SLḪ, a neck as a *ṯ*ʿ-offering and two livers.

KTU 1.109:

(8) *w kbd w š l šlm* ⌜*k*⌝*bd*	A liver and a ram for ŠLM, a liver,
(9) *ảlp w š l b*ʿ*l ṣpn*	a bull, and a ram for BʿL ṢPN.

The data for *lb* are more limited in the ritual materials, only occurring in the formulaic expression *ủrm lb* attested three times, as here in KTU 1.39 (=RS 1.001):

(7) ʿ*nt š*	For ʿAnatu a ram;
ršp š	for RŠP a ram;
dr ỉl w p[*ḫ*]*r b*ʿ*l* (8) *gdlt*	for the circle of ʾIlu and the gathering of Baʿlu a cow;

196. On these liver models, see Pardee, *Ritual and Cult*, 127–29.
197. Following the collation of Pardee, *Ritual and Cult*, 127.

šlm gdlt	for ŠLM a cow;
w b ủrm ⌜*l*⌝*b* (9) *rmṣt ỉlhm bʿlm*	and in the flame a heart as a roast-offering for ỈLHM and BʿLM.[198]

Here, *lb* is described as being roasted by fire, wherein the heart of the animal was removed, roasted in the flames, and consumed by the official conducting the sacrifice during the ritual.[199] Also in the ritual texts is an instance where *lb* denotes the internal mind or thoughts of the king as he carries out the ritual: *k lbh yr*[*gm*] *ml*⌜*k*⌝ "according to his heart the king will speak" (KTU 1.41:52–53). This example reflects its usage in the noncultic texts where it most often designates the internal psyche of an individual deity or human being. In this case the king speaks freely according to what is apparently on his mind during the ritual event.

2.4.1.2. *kbd* Outside Ritual

I now turn our attention to the mythological and epic texts where *kbd* is widely used to mean "the insides" of deities, humans, and animals, as well as the inner recesses of the earth. The fact that *kbd* can indicate the insides of an animal in these texts provides a substantial connection with what is known from the ritual setting and the offering of a liver to the gods. The liver within the animal is generalized to mean "the insides." This usage takes place in Baʿlu's search for the remains of the slain ʾAqhatu as he splits open the innards of the hawks in KTU 1.19 III:

(7) *b ph rgm l yṣả*[200]	Scarcely had the word left his mouth,
b špth hwt	(scarcely had) it (left) his lips,
(8) *knp nšrm bʿl yṯbr*	Baʿlu breaks the wings of the hawks.
(9) *bʿl ṯbr dỉy hmt*	Baʿlu broke their pinions.
tǵ!*ln*[201] (10) *tḥt pʿnh*	They fell under his feet,
ybqʿ kbdthm w[*yḥd*]	He splits open their innards and [gazes.]
(11) *ỉn šmt ỉn ʿẓm*	There is neither fat nor bone.

This meaning is comparable to those cases where *kdb* refers to the inner recesses of the earth. One example will suffice from the Baʿlu cycle, which describes ʿAnatu's searching high and low for the remains of Baʿlu in KTU 1.5 VI:[202]

198. Cf. also KTU 1.87 (=RS 18.056):19 and reconstructed for KTU 1.41 (=RS 1.003):17–18.
199. For a defense of this interpretation, see Pardee, *Textes rituels*, 56–59.
200. Erasure of unknown sign following the first letter of this word.
201. Probably {tqln}.
202. See also KTU 1.1 II:20; 1.3 III:16, 17; 1.3 IV:10 (2×), 24, 25, 30, 31; 1.6 II:17, 18; 1.7:28.

(26) *ʿnt ttlk w tṣd*	ʿAnatu goes and searches
kl ǵr (27) *l kbd árṣ*	every mountain to the *kbd* of the earth,
kl gbʿ (28) *l kbd šdm*	every hill to the *kbd* of the field.

These references could be rendered, "to the innermost parts of the earth" or "to the recesses of the earth" as a way of communicating the extensiveness of ʿAnatu's search.

The reference to the insides of an animal and the recesses of the earth is extended to include the inner part of deities as well. The closest example of *kbd* as the "depths" of a deity occurs when it is said that Baʿlu will descend into the *kbd* of Môtu (KTU 1.5 II):

yʿrb (4) *bʿl b kbdh*	Baʿlu will enter into his *kbd*,
ph yrd (5) *k ḥrr zt*	(into) his mouth like a roasted olive,
ybl árṣ w pr (6) *ʿṣm*	(as) the produce of the earth and the fruit of trees.

In other words, Baʿlu will enter into the deepest recesses of Môtu where all the dead must go.[203] But *kbd* can also designate the inner emotional experience of an individual god or human. For example, in a rather disturbing manner, the violent ʿAnatu is presented as experiencing tremendous enjoyment from within (*kbd* and *lb*) as she slaughters her victims in KTU 1.3 II:

(23) *mid tmtḫṣn w tʿn*	She strikes in abundance and looks,
(24) *tḫtṣb w tḥdy*	she fights and gazes.
ʿnt (25) *tǵdd*[204] *kbdh b ṣḥq*	As for ʿAnatu, her *kbd* swells with laughter,
ymlù (26) *lbh b šmḫt*	her *lb* is filled with rejoicing,
kbd ʿnt (27) *tšyt*	the *kbd* of ʿAnatu (is filled with) triumph.
k brkm tǵll b dm (28) *ḏmr*	Up to the knees she wades in the blood of a warrior,
ḥlqm[205] *b mmʿ mhrm*	to the neck in the gore of fighters.

Though in broken context, the ʾAqhatu Epic also attests a similar usage of *kbd* in parallel with *irt* "chest," referring to the human character of Pūǵatu and her

203. Pardee comments that this metaphor for death involves "entering into the body of Môtu, god of death, where it expresses the end point after entry" (*COS*,1:244 n.15). In one sense, the next line's imagery of entering the mouth of Môtu "like a roasted olive" almost suggests the stomach here.

204. Written with an erased {d} following the first sign of the word.

205. "neck" on the basis of Arabic *ḥalq* (Cyrus H. Gordon, *Ugaritic Handbook: Revised Grammar, Paradigms, Texts in Transliteration, Comprehensive Glossary*, AnOr 25 [Rome: Pontifical Biblical Institute, 1948], 397, more recently defended by Rendsburg, "Modern South Arabian," 628).

determined revenge in the death of her brother: [*ả*](18)*ḫd d iṯ b kbdk tšt d*[*iṯ b*] (19) *irtk* "[S]ieze that which is in your *kbd*, set that which[is in] your chest" (KTU 1.18 I). This usage of *kbd* resembles the tendency of *lb* to refer to forethought or the determination to carry out some action.

2.4.1.3. *lb* Outside Ritual

The lexeme *lb* is distinct from *kdb* in its common association with one's inner mental capacity. It is true that *lb* shares a certain level of semantic overlap with *kbd* in its potential to refer to the depths of the earth or the internal emotional experiences of individuals, but at the same time its typical usage connotes mental activity more so than emotional.[206] This aspect is not limited to deities and humans, but can be said of animals too, illustrated in the following depiction of a female animal in search of her young—here compared to ʿAnatu in her desperation to find Baʿlu (KTU 1.6 II):

w r[*ḥm*[207] *ʿnt*] (6) *tngṯh*	The m[aid ʿAnatu] goes searching for him,
k lb ảr[*ḫ*] (7) *l ʿglh*	like the *lb* of a cow for her calf,
k lb ṯả[*t*] (8) *l imrh*	like the *lb* of a ewe for her lamb,
km lb ʿn[*t*] (9) *ảṯr bʿl*	so is the *lb* of ʿAnatu after Baʿlu.

206. The depths of the earth are possibly referred to in KTU 1.15 V:15: *w b lb tqb*[*rn*] "and in the heart you must bury him," but this reference to *lb* could otherwise signify emotional preparation for the prospects of Kirta's burial (as suggested by Wyatt, *Religious Texts*, 217 n. 181). One must keep in mind, however, that the fragmentary nature of the tablet renders all such readings far from certain. The internal emotional experiences of individuals are referred to in KTU 1.3 II:26 (// *kbd*) cited above. See also KTU 1.19 IV:34–35 (// *kdb*). Note that the situation here is almost the opposite of what we find in Hebrew, where *lēb* commonly conveys both emotional distress (e.g., Ps 13:3) and joy (e.g., Pss 4:8; 13:6; 16:9) in addition to conative processes (see additional references in *HALOT*, 513–15). Hebrew *kābēd*, however, seems to be restricted to the physical "liver," with only one certain example in which it is used to communicate emotions (Lam 2:11) (see references in *HALOT*, 456). See the helpful summary in Smith and Pitard, *Ugaritic Baal Cycle 2*, 164–74, as well as the discussions of Terence Collins, "The Physiology of Tears in the Old Testament: Part 1," *CBQ* 33 (1971): 18–38 and Collins, "The Physiology of Tears in the Old Testament: Part 2," *CBQ* 33 (1972): 185–97; Gary Anderson, *A Time to Mourn, A Time to Dance: The Expression of Grief and Joy in Israelite Religion* (University Park: Pennsylvania State University Press, 1991). More recently, David A. Bosworth has tied weeping to attachment theory, arguing that weeping is not simply an individual activity involving the release of bad emotions but rather signifies attachment to another individual as a plea for solace and relationship. For more on this motif in the Bible, see Bosworth, "Weeping in the Psalms," *VT* 62 (2013): 36–46; Bosworth, "The Tears of God in the Book of Jeremiah," *Bib* 94 (2013): 24–46; Bosworth, "Daughter Zion and Weeping in Lamentations 1–2," *JSOT* 382 (2013): 217–37; Bosworth, "Weeping in Recognition Scenes in Genesis and the Odyssey," *CBQ* 77 (2015): 619–39.

207. Restored from line 27. The word *rḥm* "womb" serves by metonymy for "girl, damsel, maid" (*DUL*, 737).

On the one hand, one might understand this passage to denote the frantic search of ʿAnatu for Baʿlu as an emotionally charged pursuit, yet on the other hand the point may simply be that she set her mind/determined to find him. This is comparable to the mind of a heifer that is singly consumed with finding her calf. It is a single-mindedness or determined focus that is in view here. This nuance is also attested twice in the Ugaritic letters where *lb* occurs as the object of the verbal root *št*, literally meaning "to focus one's mind on something," or "to set one's focus on something," which from context seems to indicate worry. This usage occurs in the following example from KTU 2.38 where the king of Tyre advises the king of Ugarit not to worry about his lost ships because he has taken care of them:

(24) *w ảnyk ṯt*	Your ships are mooring
(25) *by ʿky ʿryt*	at Acco, stripped.
(26) *w ảḫy mhk*	Now my brother should not
(27) *b lbh ảl yšt*	worry about anything (lit. set anything in his heart).[208]

Returning to the literary texts, *lb* refers to the predetermined plan (or will?) of the gods in the event of ʾAqhatu's death in KTU 1.19 I:

k ḥrṣ ảbn (10) *ph*	As the stones of his mouth tore,
tỉḫd šnth	his teeth seized;
w ảkl b qmm[209] (11) *tšt*	they placed food in his *qmm*;
ḥrṣ k lb[210] *ỉlnm*[211]	he tore according to the plan of the gods.

Though the interpretation of the last line of this passage has been disputed among scholars, the reading adopted here is certainly plausible in light of the

208. Cf. KTU 2.30:22–24.

209. Pardee (*COS* 1:351 n. 86) interprets *qmm* as "devouring (maw)" on the basis of the Arabic root *qmm* meaning "to devour" (cited in *DUL*, 703 from Albert de Biberstein-Kazimirski, *Dictionnaire Arabe-Français* [Paris: Maisonneuve, 1860], 808).

210. There is a discrepancy as to whether the text reads *ḥrṣ k lb ỉlnm* "he tore according to the wish of the gods," or *ḥrṣ klb ỉlnm* "the hound of the gods tore" (see Caquot and Sznycer, *Textes ougaritiques 1*, 442; del Olmo Lete, *Mitos y leyendas*, 387). The former seems best in the absence of any "hound of the gods" mentioned elsewhere in Ugaritic (see Pardee, *COS* 1:351 n. 87).

211. Wyatt takes this form to be the tree word, "terebinth" (*Religious Texts*, 291). He argues against Margalit who takes the form as a reference to chthonic deities (*Ugaritic Poem of Aqhat*, 157), since all such occurrences exhibit consonantal {y}: *ỉlny*(*m*) (see *DUL*, 60). He suggests Pardee's proposal is similar to Margalit's, but it appears that Pardee simply takes the form as plural "gods" (*COS* 1:351), which is not the same as "chthonics." The problem with Wyatt's proposed "terebinth" is that this word occurs with {ả} elsewhere in Ugaritic (e.g., KTU 1.12 I:20).

fact the *lb* usually indicates mental processes, which in this case would specify the plans of the gods subsequently carried out by the actor in these lines.[212]

One final comment concerns the usage of *lb* in a context suggesting a reference to the external portion of the body rather than the internal. Most commentators interpret *lb* in KTU 1.5 VI:21 and 1.6 I:5 as "chest":[213]

(3) *thdy lḥm w dqn*	She lacerates cheek and chin,
t[ṯ]l[ṯ] (4) *qn ḏrʿh*	she p[l]ow[s] her upper arm;
tḥrṯ km gn (5) *ảp lb*	she tills also (her) *lb* like a garden,
k ʿmq tṯlṯ bmt	she plows (her) back like a valley (KTU 1.6 I).

This apparent reference to the chest is readily explained by the fact that it is the chest cavity as the locale of the heart, knowledge that no doubt arises from the ancient familiarity with the insides of animals from ritual settings. As I have already mentioned, *lb* is one of the animal parts listed in such ritual contexts.

2.4.1.4. *kbd* and *lb* Summary

Next to *npš*, the liver (*kbd*) and the heart (*lb*) are the two most prominently mentioned body parts that take on metaphorical meanings related to life as experienced at Ugarit. Examining the distribution of these two words leads to several observations. First, *kbd* is the more common item in ritual with a number of "livers" being listed in the ritual texts, while *lb* as an animal "heart" occurs only once. Outside the ritual context, *kbd* commonly denotes the "insides" of deities, humans, animals, and the earth. However, when *kbd* appears in parallel with *lb*, the pairing usually indicates emotions such as rejoicing (e.g., KTU 1.12 I:13; 1.19 I:24), but can also indicate conative processes (e.g., KTU 1.18 I:17). Finally, when *lb* stands on its own, it seems to indicate conative processes and not so much emotional experience (e.g., KTU 1.6 II:25, 26; 1.17 VI:41; 1.19 I:11).

2.4.2. *ảp* "Nose"

My survey would stand incomplete without mentioning the familiar term *ảp* "nose," which occurs regularly throughout the ritual materials, always with *npš*.[214] The appearance of *ảp* with *npš* in these cases indicates the prescribed offering of

212. The subject of these verbs remains uncertain due to the break at the beginning of the tablet.

213. E.g., Caquot and Sznycer, *Textes ougaritiques 1*, 253; del Olmo Lete, *Mitos y leyendas*, 223; de Moor, *Anthology of Religious Texts*, 82; Pardee, *COS* 1:268; Wyatt, *Religious Texts*, 129.

214. For references, see §2.2.1 above.

the animal's snout and neck for the designated deity. The metaphorical meaning of *ảp* as "anger" is well-understood by scholars in light of its wide-spread attestation in the Hebrew Bible, but this usage is established for Ugaritic as well. For example, in the ritual text KTU 1.40:22 (cited above) *ảp* shows up alongside *qṣr npš* "shortness of *npš*" in a list of sins committed (*ḫṭ'*), which I render again here:

(22) *ủ tḫṭin*	Whether you sin:
b ảpkn	in your anger,
ủ b ⌜*q*⌝*ṣrt npš*[*kn*	in the shortness of [your] *npš*,
ủ b qṭt] (23) *tqṭṭn*	[or in the outrage] you have committed.[215]

In this three-fold list one detects a progression in intensity: from anger to angry outbursts to base acts committed in rage. The importance of *ảp* for my interests here, however, is that it yields yet another datum illustrating the connection between body parts and life, in this case consisting of the nose as metonymy for anger.

2.5. Summary

In this chapter I have surveyed the meaning and usage of the term *npš* throughout the known Ugaritic corpus and have arrived at four main connotations: (1) neck, (2) throat, (3), vitality/life force, and (4) individual, person. The first two can be said to denote the governing bases for all other usages, the first one being limited to the context of ritual, while the second finds expression throughout the ʾIlimilku literature, including both mythic and epic stories. Within this same literary context we find that *npš* also indicates vitality or life force, which leads me to suggest that it is a semantic development from "throat," perhaps even stemming from the unusual but persistent portrayal of Môtu as defined by his own insatiable throat—might we say, the driving force of his unhappy existence. The final use outlined in this chapter is relegated to administrative lists alone, where individuals/persons are indicated by this same term, which must have meant human persons in whom the vital element exists.

It is often assumed that *npš* can denote "appetite" or "desire," but this usage is not clearly detected in Ugaritic. This observation does not deny related nuances in other languages where the development from "throat" > "appetite" must have occurred (e.g., Hebrew); I am simply suggesting its appearance in what we know from the Ugaritic texts is not entirely clear.

215. See also KTU 1.40:31, 39 cited in §2.2.4 above, as well as KTU 1.2 I:35, 43, 1.6 V:21.

I have also shown one particular application of *npš* as "life force" in the expression *qṣr npš*, which I define as indicating a shortening of one's vitality, and thus it is a subset of *npš* = vitality. This particular Ugaritic idiom is applied in two separate contexts, both of which can be explained as expressing "diminishment of vitality": (1) diminishment of vitality induced by widowhood, and (2) diminishment of vitality as the lack of one's vital control of emotions.

The *npš* element defined as "vitality" or "life force" occurs in contexts with the root *ḥyy* "to live," in which cases I have determined *npš* to signify that vital element within persons enabling their success. This particular significance is illustrated by three examples: (1) Dānîʾilu's success in acquiring progeny (KTU 1.17 I:36), (2) Pūǵatu's success in avenging the valiant ʾAqhatu's death (KTU 1.19 IV:36, 39), and (3) the success of the king of Egypt's long and prosperous reign (KTU 2.23:18, 23).

One of the more interesting features of *npš* in Ugaritic is its apparent exit as it is depicted with regard to one's death. This particular usage is found exclusively in the poetic narration of ʾAqhatu's death—his vital force (*npš*) leaves the dying hero in a way comparable to the movement of wind (*rḥ*), the secretion of spittle (*iṯl*) from the mouth, or the smoke of incense (*qṭr*) rising from the ground. The imagery of this expression appears to represent the departure of one's life force/vitality from the body, which results in the body's lack of animation. This meaning anticipates the more fully developed notion of "disembodied souls" attested in Northwest Semitic inscriptions and the Hebrew Bible. Richard C. Steiner's monograph treatment of this motif convincingly establishes its usage in numerous Biblical Hebrew contexts. Steiner appeals to the expression "exit of *npš*" found in Ugarit and the Bible as evidence that Northwest Semitic cultures believed the *npš* departed from the body at death.[216] He cites JoAnn Scurlock's reference to this same concept in Mesopotamian sources, again showing its widespread acceptance in the broader cultural context. As she explains, the *zaqīqu* and *eṭemmu* souls "were believed to depart from the body at death and both souls eventually found their way to the Netherworld, where they were supposed to receive a continuous set of funerary offerings from the living."[217] I will say more about this expression in the Appendix of this book where I consider its relevance in evaluating the interesting reference to Katumuwa's *nbš* inhabiting his funerary monument. My point at this juncture is simply to emphasize that

216. Steiner, *Disembodied Souls*, 20, 71–72.

217. JoAnn Scurlock, "Soul Emplacements in Ancient Mesopotamian Funerary Rituals," in *Magic and Divination in the Ancient World*, ed. Leda Ciraolo and Jonathan Seidel, AMD 2 (Leiden: Brill, 2002), 1.

the understanding of *nbš* in the Katumuwa inscription corresponds with what is already known from the Ugaritic and biblical perspectives.

It is also important to remark on the relationship between body parts and Ugaritic conceptions about life. The appropriation of body parts as expressions for corresponding aspects of life demonstrate a strong linkage between human/animal anatomy and metaphorical meaning. This phenomenon of applying metaphorical meaning to certain human body parts may or may not have been established from the ritual context, where familiarity with the internal anatomy of the sacrificial animals would have allowed for making analogies between animal and human life.[218] As such, it is rather remarkable that the ritual killing of animals and the body parts examined in the lifeless corpse would result in expressions denoting the subtle nuances of human existence. This particular facet of Ugaritic lexicography poses a somewhat paradoxical intersection of perceptions drawn from life and death.

One final observation concerns the distributive meaning of *npš* in Ugaritic, particularly the limitation of certain usages to certain genres. For example, all instances of *npš* = "neck" occur in the ritual texts, while "throat" is exclusive to the literature of ʾIlimilku (e.g., the Baʿlu myth and the Epics of Kirta and ʾAqhatu). Most times "vitality, life force" is limited to the ʾIlimiliku literature with a couple examples showing up in the letters. Interestingly, the application of *npš* = "vitality" in the idiom *qṣr npš* bridges ritual and epic in its occurrence in both genres.

218. Smith and Pitard make a similar point for the situation in the Hebrew Bible (*Ugaritic Baal Cycle 2*, 167).

CHAPTER 3

An Analysis of Words for "Death" in Ugaritic

3.1. Introduction

In the previous two chapters of this book I have focused on the semantics of life as it is witnessed in the textual corpus extant at Ugarit, having examined the roots *ḥyy*/*ḥwy* in chapter 1 and the noun *npš* and words with which it appears in parallel (along with *kbd* // *lb*) in chapter 2. I now take up matters associated with death. It is not as though this topic has not already been broached in what I have covered thus far, since many of the same passages dealing with life inevitably have to deal with corresponding concerns about death and dying. Perhaps this observation comes into sharpest focus when considering the Ugaritians' interest in the *npš* "throat" of the death god Môtu, both the gateway through which all the dead enter the underworld (including the gods!) and at the same time the body part associated with the vital force of one's life.

In this chapter I organize my treatment of "death" first of all according to the distribution of the verbal root *mt* meaning "to dię," and second according to its corresponding adjectival and noun forms. In dealing with the noun for "death" in Ugaritic one is immediately faced with its well-developed personification in the death god Môtu, mainly in the mythological texts with a few possible references elsewhere, which I examine in the third section of this chapter. Finally, it is necessary to consider possible confusion between the forms *mt* as /môtu/ "death" and *mt* as /mutu/ "man" in that they are orthographically identical despite their underlying morphological distinction. In a few cases it is difficult to determine which form makes the best sense contextually, necessitating a closer examination of the available data for these two words in Ugaritic.

Death is a prominent topic within the Ugaritic poetic narratives, which leaves us with a number of parallel pairs that are helpful in determining the finer nuances of how the ancient poets perceived the act of dying. Taken together, the verbal and substantival forms of this root have produced an array of parallels outnumbering those attested either for the roots *ḥyy/hwy* or for *npš*. I will comment on the following list of parallels in my lexical analysis of m-w-t in this chapter: *npl ảrṣ* "to fall to the earth"; *yrd ảrṣ* "to go down to the earth"; *spʾ* "to be devoured"; *ḫlq* "to be destroyed"; *yṣʾ npš* "exiting *npš*"; *l yḥ* "not to live"; *ỉlm/ỉlnym* "gods."

3.2. The Root m-w-t

The root for dying in Ugaritic is the hollow root *m-w-t, and as the evidence currently stands, this verb only occurs in the G stem. Hollow roots do not show D-stem forms in Ugaritic; this stem being replaced by the L-stem (cf. Hebrew *polel*), consisting of a lengthened vowel following the first radical and reduplication of the final radical, which would have presumably yielded **mtt* (*/mātita/).[1] It is generally agreed that this root exhibits stative /qatil/ SC forms and /yaqtul-/ PC forms.[2] In Ugaritic, the stative /qatil/ form (/mīta/) is used in contexts describing the state of the dead, usually in reports of someone's death: "PN is dead."[3] In one instance it is used of Baʿlu when Môtu warns him that he is going to die, explaining the signs that will verify to the gods at that time that "you are dead" (mītata).[4] In one of the letters the SC form is used to describe the state of a fleet of ships: "your ships . . . are dead" (ʾanayyukana mītat).[5] The PC /yaqtul-/ forms most often describe the act of dying that will occur at some point in the future.[6] The 1cs form occurs in Môtu's speech to Baʿlu as he explains what happens when the storm god strikes Lôtan: "(as) dung I die" (ḏariqūma ʾamūtuma).[7] This text seems to refer to an ongoing experience that Môtu has when Baʿlu strikes this sea creature, which is defined in the previous line as being "devoured with moans." In this regard the /yaqtul-/ describes the process of dying, or the type of action that brings about the state of being dead. Therefore,

1. Orthographically, the consonantal combination {mtt} is attested in Ugaritic (KTU 1.5 V:17), but from context it is properly analyzed as a 2ms G SC: /mītata/, "you are dead."

2. Hebrew SC *mēt* and PC *yāmût* (see BDB, 559; *HALOT*, 562).

3. KTU 1.2 IV:32, 34; 1.5 VI:9, 23; 1.6 I:6, 41; 1.19 II:42.

4. KTU 1.5 V:17.

5. KTU 2.38:13.

6. KTU 1.14 I:16; 1.16 I:3, 17, 22; 1.16 II:40, 43; 1.17 V:38.

7. KTU 1.5 I:6.

the morphosemantics of this root indicate the following perspectives on death reflective of real-life experience: (1) the process of dying, (2) the inevitable event of dying in the future, and (3) the resultant state of being dead.[8]

3.2.1. *mwt* in the Baʿlu Cycle

As might be expected, the verb for dying occurs several times in the Baʿlu cycle, first in mighty Baʿlu's contest with Yammu, followed by his extended conflict with the death god Môtu. I provide a more extended discussion of death's personification in my analysis of this root's substantival forms in section 3.3 of this chapter. This factor raises obvious theological questions concerning Ugaritic beliefs about the pantheon and the nature of the divine, which I touch on in chapter 5. For now, I will introduce the occurrences of this root and comment on their respective meanings.

3.2.1.1. Baʿlu and Yammu

The first example comes from the struggle between Baʿlu and Yammu with the resulting death of the sea god Yammu. The narrative description of their conflict consists of two movements/rounds (KTU 1.2 IV:11–18; 18–27), introduced by a speech from the craftsman deity Kôṯaru-wa-Ḫasīsu in favor of Baʿlu, urging him to smite his enemy and to take up his eternal kingship (KTU 1.2 IV:7–10). Each of the two movements begins with Kôṯaru's construction of a doubly-named mace, the weapon for Baʿlu against Yammu, followed by an address to the double mace as to what it will do in Baʿlu's hand, and concluded by a description of the skirmish with regard to the mace attacking Yammu. The declaration of Yammu's death appears after the second movement in KTU 1.2 IV:34:

w yrtqṣ ṣmd bd bʿl	The mace leaps in the hand of Baʿlu,
(24) ⌜*km*⌝ *nšr b ủṣbʿth*	like a bird in his fingers,
ylm qdqd zbl (25) ⌜*ym*⌝	it strikes Prince Yammu on the head,
bn ʿnm ṯpṭ nhr	Ruler Naharu between the eyes.
yprsḥ[9] *ym*	Yammu topples,
yql (26) *l ảrṣ*[10]	he falls to the ground;

8. On the morphosemantics of Biblical Hebrew *mwt*, see Dennis Pardee, review of *Dies Leben ist der Tod*, by Markus Grimm, *JNES* 62 (2003): 130–31.

9. Taking the form as an N stem PC quadraliteral root *prsḥ* "to topple, fall and grovel" (cf. *DUL*, 682, analyzing a G stem "to collapse"). The principal etymology for this quadraliteral comes from Akkadian *napalsuḫu/naparsuḫu* "to fall to the ground, squat, grovel," and "to make prostrate" in the Š stem (*CAD* 11:271–72; *AHw* 2:733).

10. Cf. the expression *npl l ảrṣ* "to fall to the earth" as a parallel expression for dying.

tnġṣn pnth[11]	his joints collapse,
w ydlp[12] *tmnh*	his body slumps.
(27) *yqṯ*[13] *bʿl w yšt*[14] *ym*	Baʿlu drags and dismembers Yammu,
ykly ṯpṭ nhr	he finishes off Ruler Naharu.
(28) *b šm tgʿrm ʿṯtrt*	By name, ʿAṯtartu reproaches (him):
bṯ[15] *l ảliyn* ⸢*b*⸣[*ʿl*]	Scatter (him), O Mighty Baʿlu,
(29) *bṯ l rkb ʿrpt*	scatter (him), O Cloud Rider,
k šbyn zb[*l ym*	for Prin[ce Yammu] is our captive,
k] (30) *šbyn ṯpṭ nhr*	[for] Ruler Naharu is our captive.
w yṣả b[...]	Then X went out ...
(31) *ybṯ nn*[16] *ảliyn bʿl*	Mighty Baʿlu scattered him,

11. Julian Obermann connected this word to the Hebrew architectural term *pinnâ* "corner," here used figuratively as "hips" or "joints" ("How Baal Destroyed a Rival: A Mythological Incantation Scene," *JAOS* 67 [1947]: 204 n. 26; cf. Moshe Held, "Studies in Comparative Semitic Lexicography," in *Studies in Honor of Benno Landsberger*, ed. Hans G. Güterbock and Thorkild Jacobsen, AS 16 [Chicago: Oriental Institute of the University of Chicago, 1965], 405; H. L. Ginsberg, *ANET*, 131).

12. Cf. Hebrew *dlp* in Eccl 10:18 of a collapsed house (Smith, *Baal Cycle 1*, 350).

13. Cf. Arabic *qaṯṯa* "to scatter" (Lane, 2487; as suggested by Obermann, "How Baal Destroyed a Rival," 205).

14. Probably a G stem from √*štt* meaning "to scatter, dismember." Cf. Arabic *šatta* "to separate, chop up into pieces" (Lane, 1501; proposed by Obermann, "How Baal Destroyed a Rival," 205; followed by Caquot and Sznycer, *Textes ougaritiques 1*, 138 n. a). Adrianus van Selms cites a biblical parallel from Ps 49:15, *kaṣṣōn lišʾōl šattū*, which he translates: "like sheep they are dragged to the netherworld" ("Yammu's Dethronement by Baal: An Attempt to Reconstruct Texts UT 129, 137, and 68," *UF* 2 [1970]: 266). Other proposed roots range from *nšt* "to dry up," (James A. Montgomery, "Ras Shamra Notes IV: The Conflict of Baal and the Waters," *JAOS* 55 [1935]: 276), to *šyt* "to put, place" (Johannes C. de Moor, *The Seasonal Pattern in the Ugaritic Myth of Baʿlu According to the Version of Ilumilku*, AOAT 16 (Kevelaer: Butzon & Bercker; Neukirchen-Vluyn: Neukirchener Verlag, 1971], 138–39), to *šty* "to drink" (Frank M. Cross, *Canaanite Myth and Hebrew Epic: Essays in the History of the Religion of Israel* [Cambridge: Harvard University Press, 1975], 115) (see the discussion in Smith, *Baal Cycle 1*, 352–54). The meaning of the Arabic cognate seems to make the best sense contextually.

15. Analyzing a G stem from √*bṯṯ* "to scatter, fly in all direction," appealing to Arabic "water flying around in all directions" (Lane, 151; see also Obermann, "How Baal Destroyed a Rival," 206; John Gray, *The Legacy of Canaan: The Ras Shamra Texts and Their Relevance to the Old Testament*, 2nd ed., VTSup 5 [Leiden: Brill, 1965], 29 n. 1). The earlier suggestion to interpret this form as arising from a root cognate with Hebrew *bwš* "to be ashamed, put to shame" (Driver, *Canaanite Myths and Legends*, 13) is taken up by J. W. Olley, who argues for a forensic meaning here: ʾAṯtartu is shaming Baʿlu, considering what he did to Yammu as wrong ("A Forensic Connotation of *bôš*," *VT* 26 [1976]: 233–34; cf. de Moor, *Anthology of Religious Texts*, 41). The semantics of "scatter" work perfectly well in the context, whereas the notion of shame is more difficult. Line 31 would seem to militate against reading *bwš* in light of the suffix: ybṯ.nn (de Moor's proposed dative suffix seems highly unlikely [*Seasonal Pattern*, 139]). It is also compelling to note that the scattering imagery accords with ʿAnatu's treatment of Môtu in KTU 1.2 II:30–35, as Caquot and Sznycer have already observed (*Textes ougaritiques 1*, 139 n. b).

16. Note that the pronominal suffix is separated from the verbal form by a word divider: ybṯ . nn.

w[...]	[...]
(32) *ym l mt*	Yammu is indeed dead,
bʿl yml[*k*...]	may Baʿlu reig[n...]
...	...
(34) *yʿn ym l mt* [ ]	answers: Yammu is indeed dead [...]

In one sense this passage describes the kinds of battle wounds that ultimately lead to one's death: being struck on the head and between the eyes with a mace. These two actions constitute mortal injuries in contrast to round one in KTU 1.2 IV:11–18 where Baʿlu strikes Yammu on the shoulders and in the chest, after which he recovers for another round.[17] Once the mortal blows have been executed, the narrative provides several clauses depicting Yammu's death: (1) "Yammu topples," (2) "he falls to the ground," (3) "his joints collapse," and (4) "his body slumps." The Akkadian cognate *napalsuḫu/naparsuḫu* often denotes the act of prostration—falling to the ground in obeisance—but it can also refer in general to objects toppling over, as in one case of a chariot breaking and tipping over onto someone.[18] In this context, the verb suggests the initial toppling of Yammu immediately following his fatal blow to the head.

This toppling leads to his outright fall to the ground, ironically resembling the same description of Baʿlu following his skirmish with Môtu in KTU 1.5 VI:8–9 (but with *npl*).[19] The specificity of this idiom is highlighted by the fact that in the final conflict between Baʿlu and Môtu at the end of the cycle, ironically, where neither one of them die, both are described as falling, but not to the ground.[20] As for the context of KTU 1.2 IV, one should be cautious about reading too much of a "netherworld" imagery here, though such a reading is rather plausible in the case of KTU 1.5 VI where Baʿlu falls to the ground at the entrance to Môtu's realm. At any rate, the act of falling to the ground in death as expressed here,

17. Smith outlines the difficulties associated with the interpretation of *ktp* and *bn ydm* in lines 14, 16 of this text (*Baal Cycle 1*, 345–47). Interpretaters of *ktp* have traditionally appealed to Biblical Hebrew *kātēp* "shoulder" (*HALOT*, 505–6) and Syriac *katpāʾ* "shoulder, shoulder-blade" (Payne Smith, 231). As Smith notes, however, the Akkadian cognate *katappātu* "sternum or parts of the ribs" (*CAD* 8:303) poses problems for this etymology. Smith proposes that "the general quality of the parallel term *qdqd*, 'crown,' used for the second weapon suggests that *ktp*, though attested elsewhere in the sense of shoulder, may refer to a part of the body more general than 'shoulder,' perhaps 'torso'" (*Baal Cycle 1*, 346).

18. For this text, see Ernst F. Weidner, "Assyrische Beschreibungen der Kriegs-Reliefs Aššurbânaplis," *AfO* 8 (1932–1933): 178, line 21 (cited in *CAD* 11:271).

19. *mǵny l bʿl npl l ảrṣ mt ảliyn bʿl* "We arrived at (the place where) Baʿlu had fallen to the earth; Mighty Baʿlu was dead."

20. *mt ʿz bʿl ʿz ymṣḫn k lsmm mt ql bʿl ql* "Môtu is strong; Baʿlu is strong. They trample each other like running (animals). Môtu falls; Baʿlu falls" (KTU 1.6 VI:20–22).

coupled with its occurrence in KTU 1.5 VI:8–9 of Baʿlu at Death's gates, anticipates the stronger nomenclature of "descending to the underworld" (*yrd ảrṣ*) attested elsewhere in the Ugaritic literary texts.[21]

Whereas the first two expressions, "toppling" and "falling," offer an ingressive perspective on the act of dying, the latter two demonstrate its consummate effect—a lifeless corpse. In this way, the joints of Yammu give way, no longer supporting the body, and it slumps to a motionless heap. In chapter 2 I discussed the exiting *npš* motif at length, one that occurs in the ʾAqhatu Epic in parallel with the verb *mt*, albeit in a broken context (KTU 1.19 II:32–34).[22] There I noted that *npš* signifies the exit of one's vitality or life force. Though that language is not used here, it may represent the same phenomenon, that is, death as the exit of one's life force, illustrated in this text by the slumping, lifeless corpse of Yammu after having been fatally struck by Baʿlu.

Immediately following Yammu's collapse, Baʿlu goes about dismembering his lifeless body. The narrative allusions to ʿAnatu's comparable treatment of Môtu have been duly noted by scholars, yet the purported agricultural imagery (i.e., sowing seed) for that passage does not appear to be operative here.[23] One might argue for an *ad sensum* correlation between these two passages, since the semantics of "scattering" are not exactly the same (*drʿ* is an agricultural term while *bṯ* is not).[24] In fact, assuming for the sake of argument that KTU 1.5 VI does invoke agricultural imagery (withholding judgment on this question until my analysis of the text below), its allusion is to the sowing of seed when crops are planted.

Twice one finds the emphatic announcement of Yammu's death—*ym l mt* "Yammu is indeed dead (lines 32, 34)—following the extended description of his fatal fall to the ground and Baʿlu's mutilation of his corpse. Incidentally, discussions on the ordering of the tablets at this juncture in the Baʿlu cycle raise another interesting problem: Does Yammu's death pronouncement signal his *terminus ad quem* or not? Misgivings about the traditional arrangement of the columns (I–II, III, and IV) assigned to KTU tablet 1.2 (*CTA* 2) have been around as early as their initial publication.[25] The physical condition of these tablets with

21. Cf. KTU 1.5 VI:25; 1.114:22.

22. The reconstruction of the exiting *npš* motif in the passage is fairly certain due to its recurrence in other contexts (e.g., KTU 1.18 IV:24–26). For an analysis of this motif, see ch. 2 (§2.2.2.3).

23. Caquot and Sznycer, *Textes ougaritiques 1*, 139 n. b; Smith, *Baal Cycle 1*, 357; Pardee, *COS* 1:249 n. 63.

24. Note, however, that *kly* does occur in both texts (KTU 1.2 IV:27 and 1.6 II:36).

25. For a history of interpretation on this question, see Smith, *Baal Cycle 1*, 20–23. Note, however, Pardee's criticism of Smith for his lack of epigraphic considerations on the matter (review of *The Ugaritic Baal Cycle, Vol. 1*, by Mark Smith, *JNES* 57 [1998]: 46–48). See comments concerning

their badly broken columns has rendered the issue of their ordering all the more problematic.

Scholars have mainly focused on the placement of fragmentary column III, which has traditionally been placed between columns I–II and IV. Smith offers a helpful survey of the placement issue, arguing largely on literary (and some epigraphic) grounds that "it would be prudent to position '1.2 III' before 1.2 I."[26] His literary argument comes from a survey of "figures and events" found in similar narratives from Greek and Egyptian traditions, which no doubt were influenced by "a West Semitic story involving Astarte, Baal, and Yamm."[27]

Devoting more focused attention to epigraphic considerations, Pardee has also argued for a reversal of the assumed orientation for KTU 1.2, but yielding the significant result that column IV preceeds columns I–II.[28] As Pardee has noted concerning the interpretive significance of such an adjustment, "the ordering of events in the cycle of stories about *Baʿlu* in terms of the new orientation of this tablet [IV] will require some time."[29] As to the question raised above—is this death pronouncement the end of Yammu?—the reversal of columns I–II with column IV answers in the negative: following his death and mutilation at the hands of Baʿlu (end of what was column IV), Yammu suddenly reemerges to send a delegation to ʾIlu requesting that Baʿlu be handed over (beginning of what was column I). The delegated message is then transformed from instigation to retaliation. The likelihood of this reading is strengthened by the similar chain of events that unfold following ʿAnatu's slaughter of Môtu: he returns from ʿAnatu's mutilation demanding, at the least, substitutionary retribution, whereby Baʿlu must hand over one of his brothers for the death god to devour (KTU 1.6 V:7–23). So, in the world of mythology at least, a deity's death is not construed as his final end. The deaths of Baʿlu and Môtu will prove the same.

Charles Virolleaud's reservations about their ordering in Pardee, *The Ugaritic Texts and the Origins of the West Semitic Literary Composition*, The Schweich Lectures of the British Academy, 2007 (Oxford: Oxford University Press, 2012), 71 n. 62.

26. Smith, *Baal Cycle 1*, 25.

27. Smith, *Baal Cycle 1*, 25.

28. Pardee, *Ugaritic Texts*, 69–72. The contribution of his argument is largely epigraphic in nature, identifying that typically the flatter side of a given tablet constitutes its obverse. The rounded surface of the tablet would naturally flatten as the edges of the soft clay would sag as the scribe wrote on the reverse. What was originally thought to be the reverse of KTU 1.2 (columns I–II) turns out to have a flattened surface, indicating that it is more likely the tablet's obverse. See also Pardee, "RS 3.367, Colonne 'IV': Étude épigraphique suivie de quelques remarques philologiques," in *"He Unfurrowed His Brow and Laughed": Essays in Honor of Professor Nicolas Wyatt*, ed. Wilfred G. E. Watson, AOAT 299 (Münster: Ugarit-Verlag, 2007), 227–28; Pardee, review *of The Ugaritic Baal Cycle*, 47.

29. Pardee, *Ugaritic Texts*, 71.

3.2.1.2. Baʿlu and Môtu

Several occurrences of the G stem (PC and SC) of the root *mwt* occur in the Baʿlu-Môtu cycle (KTU 1.5–1.6) and all of them refer to the death of Baʿlu following his battle with Môtu. The first occurrence is located in Môtu's message in response to Baʿlu's hubristic taunts following his acquisition of a palace, taunts that escalate to a full-blown fight between them leading to Baʿlu's own death. Môtu's message carries with it a level of despondency as he seemingly loathes the tragedy of his own state of affairs as the god of death. The first part of the message is lost from the break at the end of column VIII of KTU tablet 1.4, but may be restored provisionally from its recitation at the beginning of KTU 1.5 column I (lines 14ff.). The verbal root *mwt* occurs at the beginning of KTU 1.5 column I:

(1) *k tmḫṣ ltn*[30] *bṯn brḥ*	When you strike Lôtan, the fleeing serpent,
(2) *tkly bṯn ʿqltn*	(when) you finish off the winding serpent,
(3) *šlyṭ*[31] *d šbʿt rả šm*	the coiling (serpent) with seven heads,
(4) *tṯkḥ*[32] *ttrp šmm*	the heavens wither (and) waste away,
k rs[33] (5) *ỉpdk*	like the *rs* of your garment,
ảnk ỉspỉ ủṭm[34]	I myself am devoured with moans,
(6) *ḏrqm ảmtm*	(as) dung I die.
l yrt (7) *b npš bn ỉlm mt*	Indeed, you must descend into the throat of Môtu, son of ʾIlu,
b mh(8)*mrt ydd ỉl ǵzr*	into the pit of the beloved hero of ʾIlu.

The first few lines of this passage recall the exploits of Baʿlu against Lôtan, here described as the fleeing serpent, the winding and coiling serpent with seven

30. On the connections with biblical Leviathan, see André Caquot, "Le Léviathan de Job 40,25–41,26," *RB* 99 (1992): 40–69, and recently, Eric Ortlund, "The Identity of Leviathan and the Meaning of the Book of Job," *TJ* 34 (2013): 17–30.

31. Gray (*Legacy of Canaan*, 30–31 n. 3) proposes a Š stem from √*lwṭ*, which means "to wrap (up)" in Hebrew (*HALOT*, 523), here taken in the sense of a coiling serpent. See also Wilfred G. E. Watson, "Ugaritic and Mesopotamian Literary Texts," *UF* 9 (1977): 274–75, who mentions a possible √*šlṭ*, cognate with Akkadian *šalāṭu* "to slit," referring to the monster's neck splitting into seven heads, but he also cautions that evidence for this root is weak. Contextually, the previous two references to the serpent's manner of movement ("fleeing" and "winding") make Gray's proposal all the more viable. For other references, see *DUL*, 822.

32. Cf. Hebrew *škḥ*, perhaps meaning "to wither, waste away" (*HALOT*, 1490–91), for which Marvin Pope explains the following semantic development: "to be/grow hot" > "to wilt, wither away" (review of *The Legacy of Canaan*, by John Gray, *JSS* 11 [1966]: 240).

33. Uncertain etymology.

34. For lines 5–8 see the discussion in ch. 1 (§1.2.2.1).

heads.[35] The fate of this sea creature, often connected to the biblical Leviathan of Job 40 and 41, is somehow tied to that of the death god: when Baʿlu strikes Lôtan and finishes him off, Môtu thus dies. Môtu is essentially warning Baʿlu that he too must die—he must descend into the throat of Death. The throat (*npš*) of Môtu is envisioned here and elsewhere as the gateway of the dead, even one that Baʿlu is not exempt from entering. In fact, the brunt of Môtu's complaint concerns his terrifying throat, if we may reconstruct what leads up to this passage from its recounted delivery to Baʿlu at the beginning of KTU 1.5 I (as rendered earlier in ch. 2 [§2.2.2.1]):

p npš npš lbỉm (15) *thw*	And my throat is the throat of a lion of the steppe,
hm brlt ảnḫr (16) *b ym*	or the gullet of *ảnḫr* in the sea;
hm brky tkšd (17) *rủmm*	or it searches for the pool (like) wild bulls,
ʿn k ḏd ảylt	(for) a spring like the herd of hinds;
(18) *hm ỉmt ỉmt npš blt* (19) *ḥmr*	or truly, truly my throat swallows heaps (of things).
p ỉmt b klảt (20) *ydy ỉlḥm*	And truly with double handfuls I devour:
hm šbʿ (21) *ydty b ṣʿ*	look, seven are my portions in a plate;
hm ks ymsk (22) *nhr kl*	look, (into) a cup they mix a whole river.
ṣḥn bʿl ʿm (23) *ảḫy*	Invite me, O Baʿlu, with my brothers,
qrản hd ʿm ảryy	call me, O Haddu, with my fellows,
(24) *w lḥmm ʿm ảḫy lḥm*	and eat bread with my brothers,
(25) *w štm ʿm ảḫy yn*	and drink wine with my brothers.
(26) *p nšt bʿl [ṭ]ʿn ỉṭʿnk*	And you have forgotten, O Baʿlu, I can certainly pierce you through . . .[36]

According to the logical progression of Môtu's speech, his *npš* is insatiable like that of a lion or terrifying water creature, and it seeks out things to fill it by the handfuls. It is this *npš* that the dead, including Baʿlu, must enter.[37]

35. See Bernard F. Batto's discussion of the seven-headed chaos monster (and possibly the seven-headed serpent-monster) depicted in Mesopotamian combat myths in *In the Beginning: Essays on Creation Motifs in the Ancient Near East and the Bible*, Siphrut 9 (Winona Lake, IN: Eisenbrauns, 2013), 31–33.

36. The text breaks from here to the end of the column.

37. In this same context, the impending death of Baʿlu is described as entrance into the liver (*kbd*) of Môtu like a roasted olive descending into one's mouth (KTU 1.5 II:2–6):

(2) [*špt l ả*]*rṣ špt l šmm*	[(one) lip to the e]arth, (one) lip to the heavens,
(3) [*yšt*]*lšn l kbkbm*	[he sets] (his) tongue to the stars.

The presentation of death in these texts warrants three comments. First is the fact that the death god to some degree experiences death, provided my reading of *ảmtm* in line 6 is correct: each time Baʿlu smites the mighty sea creature Lôtan, so Môtu suffers the pains of death.[38] Here, *ảmtm* "I die" functions as the second member of the parallel pair with *ỉspỉ* "I am devoured." In keeping with the dominant imagery that is Môtu's throat, death is a matter of being devoured or even swallowed as the throat of a lion swallows its prey. Again, at least according to the scenario envisioned for the gods, death is not final. The situation before us is comparable to Môtu's being "devoured" by ʿAnatu in KTU 1.6 II:9–37, which seems to assume his death even though the root *mwt* never occurs there, after which Môtu complains again of his mistreatment (KTU 1.6 V:11–23). Second, the inevitable death of Baʿlu is expressed in terms of descending into the throat of Death: *l yrt b npš bn ỉlm mt*: "Indeed, you must descend into the throat of Môtu, son of ʾIlu" (KTU 1.5 I:6–7). Furthermore, Death's throat into which Baʿlu must descend is called a pit, perhaps a watery pit as the Arabic root *hmr* "to pour" suggests.[39] Finally, there is a close association between death and water in this passage. The throat of Môtu is like the gullet (*brlt*) of the *ảnḫr* creature in the midst of the sea (*b ym*): it searches for a pool of water (*brk*) like wild bulls, and they mix in the cup a whole river (*nhr*) to quench its thirst. It is into this watery pit (*mhmr*) that Baʿlu must descend in death. These associations may arise from the fact that Lôtan, associated in this text with Môtu who suffers when the seven-headed serpent is struck, is apparently associated elsewhere with the sea god Yammu (KTU 1.3 III:37–42).[40]

---

yʿrb (4) *bʿl b kbdh*	Baʿlu will enter into his insides,
ph yrd (5) *k ḫrr zt*	he will descend into his mouth like a roasted olive,
ybl ảrṣ w pr(6) *ʿṣm*	(as) the produce of the earth and (as) the fruit of (its) trees.

In this context, the reference is to the liver of Môtu. Pardee points out that this is a metaphor for death: "entering into the body of Môtu, god of death, where it expresses the end point after entry" (*COS* 1:244 n.15). In one sense, the next line's imagery of entering the mouth of Môtu "like a roasted olive" seems to suggest the stomach here.

38. Note the similar conclusion drawn by Pardee (*COS* 1:264 n. 210).

39. Lane, 2900.

40. Note especially the description in KTU 1.3 III:41–42, which mirrors that of Lôtan in KTU 1.5 I:1–3: *mḫšt bṯn ʿqltn šlyṭ d šbʿt rảšm* "I [ʿAnatu] struck the winding serpent, the coiling (serpent) with seven heads." On the possible connections between the reptilian and watery enemies of Baʿlu, see Pardee, *COS* 1:252 n. 92. Elizabeth Williams-Forte identifies this creature with Môtu on iconographic and textual grounds ("The Snake and the Tree in the Iconography and Texts of Syria During the Bronze Age," in *Ancient Seals and the Bible*, ed. Leonard Gorelick and Elizabeth Williams-Forte, Occasional Papers on the Near East 2/1 [Malibu, CA: Undena, 1983], 34–38), a claim that has been countered by W. G. Lambert ("Trees, Snakes and Gods in Syria and Anatolia," *BSOAS* 48 [1985]: 444). Williams-Forte objects to the earlier tendency to equate Lôtan with Yammu in light of their close associations in the Baʿlu cycle (e.g., Theodore H. Gaster, *Thespis:*

In summarizing death in this passage, one finds a three-fold parallelism of death imagery, the root *mwt* occurring in the center line:

ảnk ỉspỉ ủṭm	I am devoured with moans,
ḏrqm ảmtm	(as) dung I die;
l yrt b npš bn ỉlm mt	You must descend into the throat of Môtu, son of ʾIlu

In KTU 1.5 V:5–17, Môtu apparently invites Baʿlu to his realm where the storm god "will be counted among those who go down into the earth" (lines 15–16). The first portion of this column is missing approximately twenty-five lines, with fifteen or so lost from the previous column IV, rendering the immediate context lost. From the descriptions of weather elements associated with the storm god Baʿlu and the addressee's impending descent to the underworld, I presume that Môtu is speaking to Baʿlu in keeping with the broader context of the narrative:

ảštn b ḫrt (6) *ỉlm ảrṣ*[41]	I will place him in the hole of the gods of the earth.
w ảt qḥ (7) *ʿrptk rḥk*	As for you, take your clouds, your wind,
mdlk[42] (8) *mṭrtk*	your watering devices, your rain,
ʿmk šbʿt (9) *ǵlmk*	with you your seven lads,
ṯmn ḫnzrk	your eight officials,
(10) *ʿmk pdry bt ảr*	with you PDRY, daughter of ẢR,
(11) *ʿmk ṭly bt rb*	with you ṬLY, daughter of RB,
ỉdk (12) *pnk ảl ttn*	then set out indeed
tk ǵr (13) *knkny*[43]	for the mountain of my *knkn*,

Ritual, Myth, and Drama in the Ancient Near East [New York: Schuman, 1950], 137–200; Avrid S. Kapelrud, *Baal in the Ras Shamra Texts* [Copenhagen: Gad, 1950], 101–3), yet her alternative to equate the serpent creature with Môtu seems to swing too far in the other direction. From the textual evidence (i.e., KTU 1.3 III:41–42; and 1.5 I:1–3), the most that can be said is that a close association between these two deities indeed exists. The fact that Môtu suffers harm when Baʿlu strikes the serpent Lôtan does not necessitate their being one and the same, however.

41. I.e., the gods of the underworld. The word *ḫrt* here has been related to Ugaritic *ḫr* "nostrils" (KTU 1.103:6) and Hebrew *ḥōr* "hole" (√*ḥrr*), particularly in 1 Sam 14:11 where it refers to holes in the ground in which the Israelites hid themselves from the Philistines (Pardee, *COS* 1:267 n. 226). This leads Pardee to suggest that in this context, *ḫrt* would refer to hole, not in the sense of a grave dug, but with reference to caves, caverns, or crevices leading down into the earth. Cf. Caquot and Sznycer: "dans le cimetière divin, la terre" (*Textes ougaritiques 1*, 247).

42. Taking the form as a D stem participle of √*dly*, a root attested in Hebrew meaning "to draw (water)" (BDB, 194).

43. Wyatt interprets *knkn* as "tunnel" and entertains the possibility of identifying this form with *gngn* in KTU 1.91:22, translating "the mountain of my gullet" (*Religious Texts*, 124 n. 43).

šả ǵr ʿl ydm	raise the mountain upon your hand,
(14) *ḫlb l ẓr rḥtm*	the promontory to the back of (your) palms.
w rd (15) *b tḫpṯt ảrṣ*[44]	Descend into the baseness of the earth,
tspr b y(16)*rdm ảrṣ*	you must be counted among those going down to the earth,
w tdʿ ỉlm (17) *k mtt*	and the gods will know that you are dead.

This text finds an earlier parallel in KTU 1.4 VIII:1–24 when Baʿlu sends his messengers to deliver his hubristic taunt to Môtu's realm. What is ironic about this connection is that Baʿlu's warnings to the messengers, which concern the dangers associated with Môtu and his realm, anticipate his own inevitable demise.

Two statements are of note in this passage for its designation of a place associated with Baʿlu's death mentioned in line 17. The first one comes at the beginning of Môtu's address as he declares that he will place Baʿlu in the "hole of the gods of the earth" (*b ḫrt ỉlm ảrṣ*), presumably the region of the underworld. Reference to *ỉlm ảrṣ* has led scholars to assume this passage is dealing with chthonic deities, or even more specifically, deified ancestors.[45] The identity of the Ugaritic *rpủm* is not without controversy among Ugaritic scholars, but I should note here that in the opening lines of KTU 1.20 I one finds the equations [*rp*]⌜ủ⌝*m* // *ỉlnym* // *mt mtm*, "Rapaʾūma" // "gods" // "men of the dead," which at the very least supports the notion that the ancients believed these departed kings had obtained some level of deified status.[46] Furthermore, the Ugaritic King List (KTU 1.113) corroborates this assessment, where the names of kings are preceded by the designation, *ỉl* "god, divine."[47] In KTU 1.161, a ritual text dealing with the funer-

Caquot and Sznycer conjecture the meaning "grave" (*Textes ougaritiques 1*, 248 n. i). Pardee appeals to Arabic *knn* "to cover, cover up, hide," translating *ǵr knkny* as "the mountains of my covert" (*COS* 1:267 n. 229). The earlier interpretation of Claude F.-A. Schaeffer as "libation tube" (*The Cuneiform Texts of Ras Shamra-Ugarit*, The Schweich Lectures [London: British Academy, 1939], 46–56) is no longer tenable in light of Wayne Pitard's recent analysis of the archaeological data ("The 'Libation' Installations of the Tombs at Ugarit," *BA* 57 [1994]: 20–37; see also Pardee, "Ugaritic Funerary Cult," 280).

44. Alternatively *bt ḫpṯt* "house of baseness." Cf. Biblical Hebrew *bêt ʿôlāmô* "house of eternity" (Eccl 12:5), *bātê hannepeš* "houses of the *nepeš*" (Isa 3:20), and the Zincirli inscription of KTMW *wšmt wth bsyr/d ʿlmy*, "and I set it in the chamber(?) of my eternity (=my eternal [burial] chamber)" (following Dennis Pardee, "A New Aramaic Inscription from Zincirli," *BASOR* 356 [2009]: 53, 60–61). The absence of a word divider, however, makes the division *b tḫpṯt* "into baseness" more plausible.

45. E.g., de Moor, *Anthology of Religious Texts*, 77 n. 368; Pardee, *COS* 1:267 n. 226.

46. I treat this text more fully in ch. 4.

47. On this text, see Pardee, *Ritual and Cult at Ugarit*, 195–204; and the detailed discussion in Pardee, *Textes paramythologiques*, 165–78.

ary rites for the dead, the *rpủm* are associated with *ảrṣ* "the underworld" in the construct phrase *rpỉ ảrṣ* (line 9, reconstructed in line 2: *rpi ả*[*rṣ*]).[48]

The second place designation in this text (KTU 1.5 V) appears in lines 14–15: *rd bt ḫpṯt ảrṣ* "descend into (the house of) servitude/abjection of the earth."[49] Earlier scholarship read *bt ḫpṯt* differently, instead taking the initial {b} as the *b* preposition, followed by a *t*- preformative feminine noun *tḫpṯt* meaning "filth, corruption," which Gaster rendered, "in the corruption of the netherworld."[50] Adrianus van Selms argued for this reading partly because of the absence of a word divider following the {t}, but he departed from Gaster by interpreting its lexical meaning in light of the root *ḫpṯ* "to be free," suggesting that *tḫpṯt* refers to a piece of land given for military service, "free from taxes," in which the deceased would have been buried.[51] Subsequent scholarship has tended to read the expression in question as two separate words (i.e., *bt ḫpṯt*), as does Gray who renders it in keeping with the previously proposed etymology from Arabic *ḫabaṯa* "filth": "house of corruption."[52] G. R. Driver, however, cites 2 Kgs 15:5 where the *bêt ḥopšît* refers to a house of quarantine for lepers, a view that has attracted a growing consensus among scholars.[53] Still, others have maintained the etymology derived from *ḫpṯ* "to be base/low" with van Selms, or more exactly, "fugitive, runaway," like de Moor's interpretation "house of freedom" as a euphemism for the netherworld.[54] Similarly, Oswald Loretz has identified *ḫpṯt* in KTU 1.4 VIII:7 and 1.5 V:15 as the *ḫupšu*-class of escapees mentioned in the Alalakh texts, which in the case of Ugaritic *b tḫpṯt* would indicate "into baseness."[55] In Ugaritic, the root *ḫbṯ* appears to mean "to serve as a *ḫpṯ*," for which the noun *ḫupṯu* indicates "a person

48. See also KTU 1.108:23′-24′.

49. This same expression also occurs in KTU 1.4 VIII:7.

50. Theodor H. Gaster, "The Canaanite Epic of Keret," *JQR* 37 (1947): 292. The etymological basis for this proposal is Arabic *ḫabaṯa* "filth, corruption" (see Lane, 693), as proposed by Pierre Grelot, "*Ḥofšī* (Ps. LXXXVIII 6)," *VT* 14 (1964): 256–63.

51. Cf. Biblical Hebrew *ḥpš* (*HALOT*, 341–42). Van Selms, *Marriage and Family Life*, 131–32.

52. Gray, *Legacy of Canaan*, 2nd ed., 55 n. 5, 59.

53. G. R. Driver, *Canaanite Myths and Legends*, 2nd ed., ed. John C. L. Gibson (Edinburgh: T&T Clark, 1978), 66 n. 8. For those adopting this view, see, e.g., Caquot and Sznycer: "in the house of underground confinement" ("dans la demeure de réclusion souteraine"; *Textes ougaritiques 1*, 220 n. c, 248); del Olmo Lete: "the abode of seclusion of the 'earth'" ("a la morada de reclusión de la 'tierra'"; *Mitos y leyendas de Canaan*, 211, 220); Pardee: "place of seclusion" (*COS* 1:263, 267).

54. *DUL*, 401. DeMoor, *Anthology of Religious Texts*, 66 n. 304, though citing 2 Kgs 15:5.

55. Oswald Loretz, "Die hebräischen Termini *ḥpšj* 'freigelassen, Freigelassener' und *ḥpšh* 'Freilassung,'" *UF* 9 (1977): 165; and Manfried Dietrich and Oswald Loretz, "Philologische und inhatliche Probleme in Scrheiben KTU 2.17," *UF* 14 (1982): 84. Note, however, that Loretz renders the phrase *bt ḫpṯt* and translates it "house of release" ("Haus der Freilassung"), qualifying that it is not so much a place of freedom, but rather that it emphasizes a lowly existence ("whereabouts of a lower kind" ["Aufenthaltsort niederer Art"]) ("Hebräischen Termini *ḥpšj*," 165).

of a socially inferior status."[56] Finally, I should mention the quite different suggestion offered by Nicholas Tromp.[57] He cites Biblical Hebrew *ḥōpeš* and its occurrences in Ps 88:6 and Ezek 27:20, which in the latter text Gesenius translated as "horse blanket/cover" (*Reitdecken*), leading Tromp to translate it in Ps 88:6 as "to cover," or "couch."[58] This interpretation for Ugaritic *ḫpṯt* in the Baʿlu-Môtu cycle would indicate a place of rest, that is, "the house of the couch of the earth." This last option requires a rather complicated semantic development—fabric > fabric covering a horse > fabric covering a couch > couch—and therefore seems less likely. The biblical parallel from Ps 88:6 is compelling in its association with baseness in the subsequent verse: *šattanî bᵉbôr taḥtiyyôt* "you have placed me in the lowest pit" (Ps 88:7).[59] Returning to Ugaritic, the mention of Môtu placing Baʿlu into the *ḫrt ỉlm ảrṣ* "pit of the gods of the earth" a few lines earlier in KTU 1.5 V:5, assuming the veracity of this interpretation, nicely parallels the imagery of baseness here.[60] Furthermore, Môtu charges Baʿlu to gather his weather entourage in preparation for descent, for these elements will be bound with him in death. The significance of the weather elements and their notable absence during Baʿlu's descent into the *tḫpṯt ảrṣ* makes better sense if the operative death imagery in this passage is baseness.

Considering further these weather elements that accompany Baʿlu in his descent to the underworld brings to mind the corresponding narrative in KTU 1.5 VI:2–9 where ʾIlu ascertains that the storm god is indeed alive. The basis of his conclusion is the return of the weather elements associated with him:

(2) *w hm ḥy ả[lỉyn bʿl]*	If the mighty Baʿlu is alive,
(3) *w hm ỉṯ zbl bʿ[l ảrṣ]*	if the Prince, lor[d of the earth], exists,
(4) *b ḥlm lṭpn ỉl d pỉd*	in a dream of the knowing one, the kindly god,
(5) *b ḏrt bny bnwt*	in a vision of the creator of creatures,
(6) *šmm šmn tmṭrn*	the heavens will rain oil,
(7) *nḫlm tlk nbtm*	the torrents will flow with honey;
(8) *w ỉdʿ k ḥy ảlỉyn bʿl*	then I will know that mighty Baʿlu is alive,
(9) *k ỉṯ zbl bʿl ảrṣ*	that the Prince, lord of the earth, exists.[61]

56. For the verbal form *ḫbṯ*, see RS 96.2039:9; 94.2457:82; 94.2592:5′, 7′, and the discussions in Bordreuil, Pardee, and Hawley, *Bibliothéque au sud de la ville ****, 179, 195, 196–98. See also the noun form *ḫpṯ* in RS 94.2592:12′ (Bordreuil, Pardee, and Hawley, *Bibliothéque au sud de la ville ****, 198).

57. Nicholas Tromp, *Primitive Conceptions of Death and the Nether World in the Old Testament*, BibOr 21 (Rome: Pontifical Biblical Institute, 1969), 159.

58. See Akkadian *ḫib/pšu* "wool of a certain quality" (*CAD* 6:181).

59. E.g., Pss 88:9; 107:10, 16; Lam 3:6–9.

60. Cf. the imagery of death as descent into Môtu's *npš* "throat" // *mhmrt* "watery pit" in KTU 1.5 I:6–8 discussed above.

61. On this passage, see the discussion in ch. 1 (§1.2.3.2).

In the same way ʾIlu determines that the storm god has come back to life—namely, the return of rain—so Môtu declares the means by which the gods shall determine his death: the removal of cloud, wind, and rain from the earth. The literary connection between KTU 1.5 V:16–17 (*w tdʿ ỉlm k mtt* "The gods will know that you are dead") and KTU 1.5 VI:8 (*w ỉdʿ k ḥy ảlỉyn bʿl* "I will know that mighty Baʿlu is alive") is undeniable, adding weight to the view that the divine struggle between life and death depicted in the Baʿlu cycle exhibits some level of phenomenological reflection on weather patterns.[62] From the mythological perspective, cloud, wind, and rain have disappeared because Môtu has confined them with Baʿlu in the underworld; their reappearance must mean that he is alive again.

To summarize the usage of *mwt* in KTU 1.5 V:5–17, three observations are in order. First, this passage envisions death in terms of a location: Môtu places (*št*) Baʿlu there; it is the hole of the gods of the underworld, or the baseness of the earth; Baʿlu takes with him there his weather powers and associates PDRY and ṬLY. Second, the way of entrance to the abode of the dead is downward, as indicated by the root *yrd* in KTU 1.5 V:14 and comparable to one's descent (also *yrd*) into the throat of Môtu in KTU I.5 I:7–8. Third, the dominant death imagery operative in this text seems to be that of baseness for the reasons just outlined above.

The last series of occurrences of the root *mwt* in the Baʿlu cycle falls within the announcements of Baʿlu's death. The first of these comes from the messengers in their report to ʾIlu upon their discovering Baʿlu's dead body outside of Death's realm. The text is from KTU 1.5 column VI:

mǵny (6) *l nʿmy ảrṣ dbr*[63]	We arrived at the pleasant place of the earth, the pasture land,
(7) *l ysmt šd šḥl mmt*[64]	at the beautiful place of the field, the edge of Death's abode;
(8) *mǵny l bʿl npl l ả*(9)*rṣ*	We came to Baʿlu, fallen to the earth.

62. For a discussion of these views, see Smith, *Baal Cycle 1*, 60–75.

63. Cf. Hebrew *dōber* "pasture" (Isa 5:17; Mic 2:12; see *HALOT*, 212); Syriac *dabrōʾ* "field, land, country" (Payne Smith, 83). Other proposals have explained *dbr* as the plague/pestilence term (cf. Hebrew *deber* "plague"; see *HALOT*, 212, and references in *DUL*, 264).

64. This expression has produced several interpretations. Kjell Aartun argues that Ugaritic *šḥl* must be connected to Arabic *sāḥil* meaning "edge, coast, shore; land strip, edge of valley, etc." (see Lane, 1320). He interprets the Ugaritic *šḥl* as "border, side, edge" ("Neue Beiträge zum ugaritischen Lexicon (II)," *UF* 17 [1986]: 31). Earlier, Driver made a similar suggestion, translating *šḥl mmt* "the edge of the strand of death," citing Arabic *sâḥilu mamâtin* "plain of death" (*Canaanite Myths and Legends*, 107 n. 5). René Dussaud simply transliterated it as "a field of *sḥllmmt*" ("un champ de *sḥlmmt*"; "Le sanctuaire et les dieux phéniciens de Ras Shamra," *RHR* 105 [1932]: 280). See also

mt ảliyn bʿl	Mighty Baʿlu was dead,
(10) *ḫlq zbl bʿl ảrṣ*	perished was the Prince, lord of the earth.

This text has spawned a great deal of scholarly speculation concerning the Ugaritic conception of the so-called afterlife. For example, Margalit attempts to build the case for a more pleasant conceptualization of the abode of the dead in Ugaritic thinking, capitalizing on the occurrence of *nʿmy* "lovely" and *ysmt* "delightful" in this passage and rejecting the euphemistic interpretation in favor of the literal sense of a kind of beatific existence in the realm of the dead.[65] Pardee's critique of this interpretation is worth noting here: the locale of this description seems to lie outside the realm of Môtu, therefore rendering both the beatific and euphemistic interpretations somewhat of a moot point.[66] Without solid grounding for this idealistic rendition of death, the effort to suggest that Baʿlu would have received VIP treatment from Môtu in the pleasant fields of *šḫlmmt*, which in actuality end up being outside his abode, is unsustainable.[67]

This leads us to consider the difficult expression *šḫlmmt*. As my rendering of this passage above indicates, I have adopted the Arabic etymology *sāḥil* meaning "shore, coast" for Ugaritic *šḫl*.[68] The previous context wherein Baʿlu secures progeny from a heifer before descending to the underworld makes this option the most convincing, which would otherwise be unexplainable were *šḫlmmt* within Death's realm.[69] The objection of de Moor concerning this interpretation, instead arguing that *šḫl* means "plain" on the basis of the parallel *dbr* "pasture land" for *šd* "field," is not sustained either, since the latter two terms do not necessitate that *šḫl* cannot mean "edge" contextually.[70] On the contrary, the added qualification of *šḫl* in the second line would simply emphasize that

Gray, *Legacy of Canaan*, 2nd ed., 60 n. 4. The form *mmt* appears to be a *m*- preformative noun from the root *mt* meaning "the abode/realm of Death."

65. See, e.g., de Moor, *Seasonal Pattern*, 191, for the euphemistic interpretation. Margalit, *Matter of "Life" and "Death,"* 127–28.

66. Pardee, *COS* 1:267, n. 234. The principal issue concerns the meaning of *šḫl mmt*, which Margalit simply renders together as a PN (*Matter of "Life" and "Death,"* 125). As already noted, in Arabic one finds the word *sāḥilu*, referring to the shore of a sea or great river (Lane, 1270), which would work here in the sense of the shore of Môtu's realm. For a bibliography on this expression, see *DUL*, 812.

67. Margalit, "Death and Dying in the Ugaritic Epics," in *Death in Mesopotamia: Papers Read at the XXVIe Recontre assyriologique international*, ed. Bendt Alster, Mesopotamia 8 (Copenhagen: Akademisk, 1980), 246. Note also the criticisms of Spronk, *Beatific Afterlife*, 204, where he concludes that the realm of the dead was a place to be feared, a place of "darkness, coldness, hunger, thirst, and the god of the dead who devours his victims."

68. See Lane, 1320.

69. As noted by Pardee, *COS* 1:267 n. 234.

70. De Moor, *Seasonal Pattern*, 186.

the locale in view is the edge of the pastureland or field, just before entering the netherworld proper. Other proposals such as that of Ginsberg cite Akkadian *šiliḫtu* and Hebrew *šelaḥ* meaning "channel, stream," from the root *šlḥ* "to pour out," requiring metathesis for the Ugaritic form (*šlḥ* > *šḥl*).[71] This proposal appeals to Job 33:18 and the crossing of the *šelaḥ* "stream/river" of death.[72] In either case, the picture that emerges is one that carries the reader right up to the gates of Death, but leaves him in the region just this side of its borders. As far as the descriptors *nʿmy* "pleasant" and *ysmt* "beautiful" are concerned, the fact that they describe a mountainous region (KTU 1.5 V:12–15), coupled with the fact that *nʿmy* is similarly used of Baʿlu's mountain in KTU 1.3 III:31, suggests that *nʿm* and *ysm* are descriptive of mountainous areas associated with divine beings.[73]

The first actual depiction of the dead Baʿlu occurs at lines 8–9 as the messengers recount having arrived at the place where *bʿl npl l ỉrṣ* "Baʿlu had fallen to the earth." This imagery seems to indicate a fatal fall in conflict, but the long break at the end of column V means that the events leading up to this point in the narrative are unknown. The skirmish escalating between Baʿlu and Môtu toward the end of the cycle but curtailed by Šapšu (KTU 1.6 VI:10–22) offers a ready comparison. It is tempting to think that *ỉrṣ* should mean "underworld" in this context (i.e., fallen to the underworld), but as I already mentioned regarding *šḥl mmt*, the location where Baʿlu's body is found is not the underworld, but its precipice. Perhaps a double entendre is intended here: he has literally fallen to the ground in the conflict, which is taken to be a symbolism of his entrance into Death's realm.

Line 9 offers the second parallel expression for Baʿlu's death: *mt ỉliyn bʿl* "Mighty Baʿlu was dead" // *ḫlq zbl bʿl ỉrṣ* "perished was the Prince, lord of the earth." The verbal root *ḫlq* is widely attested in Ugaritic as a means of describing the complete devastation of agricultural produce (KTU 2.61:11–12), a city (KTU 2.61:11–12), livestock (KTU 1.103+:16), and even land (KTU 1.103+:4). The corresponding adjective shares a similar distribution, but it also occurs in a couple of lists that scholars have interpreted as cataloguing "missing" or "perished" (*ḫlq*) persons (e.g., KTU 4.611:2, 4, 8).[74] In light of its association with the death of Baʿlu in this passage, I wonder if *ḫlq* as a means of identifying persons indicates

71. Ginsberg, "The Epic of Al'iyn-Baal: Tablet II," *Tarbiz* 5 (1933): 380–90 [Heb.]. For *šiliḫtu*, see *CAD* 17, 2:443; for Hebrew *šelaḥ*, see *HALOT*, 1517: "canal" as offshoot, being derived from the root *šlḥ* "to send, shoot." For the metathesis, note Syriac *šāḥlāʾ* "streaming, flowing" (*SL*, 1543), derived from a root *šḥl* "to strain, drip, flow" (*SL*, 1542).

72. See Pope, *Job*, AB 15 (Garden City, NY: Doubleday, 1983), 250; Tromp, *Primitive Conceptions of Death*, 147–48.

73. Pardee, *COS* 1:267 n. 234.

74. *DUL*, 393–94.

they are presumed dead until otherwise found. The interesting connection between this context and the Baʿlu cycle is that the storm god is in some sense depicted as missing (note ʿAnatu's frantic search for Baʿlu in KTU 1.5 VI:25–26), only to be declared as "dead" once found (KTU 1.5 VI:8–10; 1.6 I:6).[75]

The presentation of Baʿlu's death here in KTU 1.5 VI, when taken in comparison to the speech of Môtu in KTU 1.5 V:5–17 as discussed above, raises the possibility of two different perspectives of death in Ugaritic. I have already discussed at length the presentation of death that involves descent into the recesses (*kbd* "liver") of Môtu via his throat (*npš*).[76] At the same time, however, Death declares that he will place Baʿlu in the hole of the gods and that the storm god must descend into the baseness of the earth, which presents a slightly different picture of death. The former is highly mythological in depicting Baʿlu's entrance into Death's mouth, while the latter imagery rather reflects dying from the perspective of the living, perhaps alluding to the proper burial ʿAnatu will provide for his dead body later in the cycle.[77] Despite the fact that Baʿlu is presumed to have already entered into the *npš* of Môtu, the messengers discover his lifeless body in KTU 1.5 V:8–10.

Following the announcement of the lads, ʾIlu descends (*yrd*) from his throne and enters into a time of mourning for Baʿlu, after which he exclaims (KTU 1.5 VI):

(23) *bʿl mt*	Baʿlu is dead,
my lỉm	what (will become) of the people?
bn (24) *dgn*	The son of Dagan (is dead),
my hmlt	what will become of the multitudes?
ảṯr (25) *bʿl ảrd b ảrṣ*	After Baʿlu I will descend into the earth.

Perhaps anticipated by the narrative's depiction of ʾIlu descending to mourn for Baʿlu, ʾIlu declares that he will descend after Baʿlu into the underworld. The same series of events reoccurs in the following narrative, only this time it involves ʿAnatu's discovery of Baʿlu's dead body followed by its burial with the aid of Šapšu in KTU 1.6 I:

75. In KTU 1.5 VI:8–10 a threefold description of Baʿlu as dead occurs (*npl l ảrṣ // mt // ḫlq*), whereas in KTU 1.5 VI:30 and 1.6 I:6 only *npl l ảrṣ* and *mt* appear, separated by ʿAnatu's mourning.

76. For *kbd*, see KTU 1.5 II:3–6 and the discussion in ch. 2 (§2.4.1.2). For *npš*, see KTU 1.5 I:6–8 as discussed above.

77. This point is confirmed by the fact that the verbal expression *tqbrnh* "she buried him" is parallel with *tštnn b ḫrt ỉlm ảrṣ* "she placed him in the hole of the gods of the earth" in KTU 1.6 I:17–18.

(6) *bʿl mt*	Baʿlu is dead,
my lỉm	what (will become) of the people?
bn dgn	The son of Dagan (is dead),
(7) *my hmlt*	what will become of the multitudes?
ảṯr bʿl nrd (8) *b ảrṣ*	After Baʿlu we will descend into the earth.
ʿmh trd nrt (9) *ỉlm špš*	With him Šapšu, luminary of the gods, will descend.
ʿd tšbʿ bk (10) *tšt*	Until she is sated she drinks weeping,
k yn udmʿt	like wine (she drinks) tears.
gm (11) *tṣḥ l nrt ỉlm špš*	She cries aloud to Šapšu, luminary of the gods:
(12) *ʿms mʿ ly ảlỉyn bʿl*	Please, bear for me Mighty Baʿlu.
(13) *tšmʿ nrt ỉlm špš*	Šapšu, luminary of the gods heeds,
(14) *tšu ảlỉyn bʿl*	she lifts mighty Baʿlu
l ktp (15) *ʿnt k tšth*	to the shoulder of ʿAnatu as she lifts him,
tšʿlynh[78] (16) *b ṣrrt ṣpn*[79]	she takes him up to the heights of ṢPN.[80]
tbkynh (17) *w tqbrnh*	She weeps for him and buries him,
tštnn b ḫrt (18) *ỉlm ảrṣ*	she places him in the hole of the gods of the earth.

In Ugaritic the dead go down into the underworld, and presumably the act of mourning depicts a ritual descent of the living after their dead loved ones. In both of these texts, the announcement of Baʿlu's death is followed by ritual mourning, and in the second text the ritual mourning is followed by the burial of Baʿlu's body. KTU 1.6 I:17–18 confirms the above suggestion that placing the deceased in the hole of the gods of the earth (cf. KTU 1.5 V:5–6) serves as a mythological metaphor for burial, since the expression occurs here in parallel with *tqbrnh* "she buried him." Furthermore, it is important to recognize Šapšu's prominence in the funerary ritual, depicted as lifting Baʿlu's body to the shoulders of ʿAnatu and causing her to carry him to the heights of ṢPN for burial.[81]

The poetic narrative depiction of Baʿlu's death and burial in KTU 1.6 I exhibits features common to the poetic funerary ritual of KTU 1.161. This text is thought to articulate the funeral ceremony for the second-to-last known king of Ugarit,

78. Note the use of the Š stem here, literally: "she causes him to go up." The use of the causative suggests that it is Šapšu who is causing ʿAnatu to bear the body of Baʿlu to ṢPN.

79. Written: ṣpʾn.

80. Apparently the residence of Baʿlu according to KTU 1.3 III:29; IV:19, 37–38.

81. On Šapšu as psychopomp, see *špš pgr* "Šapšu of corpses" in KTU 1.39 (RS 1.001):12, 17 and KTU 1.102 (RS 24.246):12 and the discussion in Pardee, *Textes rituels*, 68–70.

Niqmaddu III (line 13).[82] In the opening lines the *rpủm* (lines 2, 4–5, 9) and the assembly of Didānu (lines 3 and 10) are summoned to the ceremony, as well as the former Ugaritic kings ʿAmmiṯtamru and Niqmaddu (likely distinct from the Niqmaddu of line 13).[83] I will return to this text when I consider the role of the *rpủm* in the next chapter, but for now I am interested in lines 19–22 and their depiction of Šapšu commanding the deceased king to descend into the earth, thus granting a useful comparison for KTU 1.6 I:8–18:

ʿln špš tṣ⸢*ḥ*⸣	From above Šapšu cries out:
(20) *ảṯr* [*b*]*ʿlk l ks*⸢*ỉ*⸣	After your lords from the throne,
ảṯr (21) *bʿlk ảrṣ rd*	after your lords descend to the earth,
ảrṣ (22) *rd w špl ʿpr*	to the earth descend and go down into the dust.[84]

The prominence attributed to Šapšu in her commanding the deceased king's descent to the underworld is notably reminiscent of her role in KTU 1.6 I in the burial of Baʿlu—she enables ʿAnatu to carry his body to the heights of ṢPN for burial.[85] Another factor in this passage that correlates with what I have found in the Baʿlu cycle is the association between "descending to the earth" and the ritual of burial—Šapšu commands the deceased kings "to descend to the netherworld" within the liturgy of the funerary ritual.

The final occurrence of the root *mwt* in the Baʿlu cycle appears in KTU 1.6 I:41. The context is that of ʿAnatu informing ʾIlu of Baʿlu's death, after which she calls upon ʾAṯiratu and her sons to gloat over his demise, a statement that must assume their hostility toward the storm god. The text reads:

tšmḫ ht (40) *ảṯrt w bnh*	Let her rejoice, ʾAṯiratu and her sons,
ỉlt w ṣb(41)*rt ảryh*	let the goddess and the clan of her kin (rejoice),
k mt ảlỉyn (42) *bʿl*	for mighty Baʿlu is dead,
k ḫlq zbl bʿl (43) *ảrṣ*	for the Prince, lord of the earth, has perished.

As in KTU 1.5 VI:8–10, the verb *mt* "he is dead" is parallel with *ḫlq* "he perished."

82. Pardee, *Ritual and Cult*, 85–86.

83. Pardee, *Ritual and Cult*, 114 n. 125.

84. For an alternative interpretation of these lines, see del Olmo Lete, *Canaanite Religion*, 2nd ed., 159.

85. Cf. also KTU 1.6 VI: where she is said to rule the *rpủm*:

špš (46) *rpỉm tḥtk*	Šapšu, you rule the RPỦM,
(47) *špš tḥtk ỉlnym*	Šapšu, you rule the deities;
(48) *ʿdk ỉlm*	in your entourage are the gods,
hn mtm	even the dead.

3.2.2. *mwt* in the Kirta Epic

The root for death in Ugaritic occurs a number of times in the Epic of Kirta where the subject of King Kirta's death becomes one of the dominant themes of the story. Its importance is made readily apparent in the opening scene of the epic depicting the tragic loss of Kirta's brothers and wives—the topic of death sets the stage for this epic.

3.2.2.1. The Death of Kirta's Wives

It is in this opening scene where the first attestation of *mwt* (3fs PC) occurs in reference to the death of one of Kirta's wives (KTU 1.14 I):

(10) *krt ḥtkn rš*	As for Kirta, (his) offspring is crushed,
(11) *krt grdš mknt*	As for Kirta, (his) home was a ruin.
(12) *ảṯt ṣdqh l ypq*	His rightful wife he has not obtained,
(13) *mtrḫt yšrh*	his legitimate spouse (he has not obtained).
(14) *ảṯt trḫ w tbʿt*	He marries a wife and she disappears,[86]
(15) *ṯảr ủm tkn lh*	relative of a mother (he marries) who becomes his.
(16) *mṯlṯt*[87] *kṯrm tmt*	A third dies in good health,
(17) *mrbʿt zblnm*	a fourth (dies) in sickness,
(18) *mḫmšt yỉtsp* (19) *ršp*	a fifth Rašap gathers for himself,
mṯdṯt ǵlm (20) *ym*	a sixth the lad(s) of Yammu (gather for themselves),
mšbʿthn b šlḥ (21) *ttpl*	a seventh falls by the sword.

Throughout this listing the seven wives of Kirta die in turn, each death owing to a different cause, providing a variety of parallel expressions for death. I outline the seven threats against Kirta's progeny as follows:

1. He fails to marry a woman deemed his "rightful wife"
2. He marries another woman, but she goes away
3. A third woman dies in good health
4. A fourth woman dies in sickness
5. A fifth woman is gathered to Rašap
6. A sixth woman is gathered to the lad(s) of Yammu
7. A seventh woman falls by the sword

86. Literally: "goes away."
87. The letter {m} is incised over what looks to have been a {t}.

The first case relates to the fact that although there was a socially ideal match, unknown circumstances prevented him from securing the marriage.[88] The second example simply notes that Kirta eventually obtained a wife, but again, for reasons left unstated, she went away.[89] One cannot be sure of the circumstances surrounding the departure of Kirta's second wife, but its mention among the remaining wives who are said to have died may indicate *tbʿt* is a euphemism for death.[90] Still, the passage may speak of her disappearance enigmatically as a means of anticipating the reported deaths of the five additional wives of Kirta.[91] Kirta's third wife dies (*tmt*) in good health, while the fourth dies in sickness. In parallel to the deaths of wives three and four, the narrative provides two mythological expressions for the deaths of wives five and six, which I shall now analyze in light of three considerations: (1) the depiction of death as being gathered, (2) the significance of the god Rašap, and (3) the reference to the lads of Yammu.

3.2.2.1.1. *Death and the Root ʾsp*

The root *ʾsp*, typically rendered "to gather," occurs frequently in Ugaritic in the G (or possibly D), G passive, Gt, and Š stems.[92] A most instructive usage of this root occurs in the ʾAqhatu Epic in an agricultural context for the gathering of the harvest. In this text Dānîʾilu spies something green sprouting forth in the field, parched from drought, and twice states (KTU 1.19 II:17):

88. Others interpret the *l* of the verbal expression *l ypq* in line 12 as an asseverative: "he had indeed obtained" (e.g., William F. Albright, "Was the Patriarch Terah a Canaanite Moon-God?" *BASOR* 71 [1938]: 38; Caquot and Sznycer, *Textes ougaritiques 1*, 504; del Olmo Lete, *Mitos y leyendas*, 289; Wyatt, *Religious Texts*, 180). This interpretation, however, does not make the best sense of the context, since the listing of these seven women is intended to show the destruction of Kirta's household, namely, his inability to acquire lineage. In defense of interpreting the *l* as the negative particle, see Gordon, *Ugaritic Literature*, 67; Gray, *Legacy of Canaan*, 2nd ed., 132; de Moor, *Anthology of Religious Texts*, 192; Pardee, *COS* 1:333.

89. The meaning of *tbʿt* "she departs" has been understood in various ways. Johannes C. de Moor and Klaas Spronk have proposed interpreting the verb to mean "she rebelled" ("Problematic Passages in the Legend of Kirta (I)," *UF* 14 [1982]: 155; followed by de Moor, *Anthology of Religious Texts*, 192), but this meaning for the root *bʿ* "to go" seems unlikely, since one might expect an additional preposition (*b* or *l* + pronominal suffix) explicating this nuance. Gray appeals to the Arabic III-weak root *tby* "to follow" (see Lane, 293–95) and translates, "she gave him issue" (*Legacy of Canaan*, 2nd ed., 133 n. 1). This interpretation, however, encounters the same contextual problem already mentioned for an asseverative reading of *l* in line 12—the passage demonstrates Kirta's failure to acquire issue.

90. Caquot and Sznycer suggest that her going away should be understood as "a result" ("un résultatif"; *Textes ougaritiques 1*, 505 n. i). See also Driver, *Canaanite Myths and Legends*, 29.

91. For this reason I render *tbʿt* above as simply, "she disappears" (cf. Gordon, *Ugaritic Literature*, 67; Pardee, *COS* 1:333; Wyatt, *Religious Texts*, 181).

92. See references in *DUL*, 113–14.

(17) *ủr*[93] *tỉspk yd ảqht* (18) *ǵzr*	O plant, may the hand of the valiant ʾAqhatu gather you,
tštk b qrbm ảsm	may (the hand of ʾAqhatu) put you into the granary.
(repeated in lines 24–25)	

Pardee's caution against reading into this statement that Dānîʾilu expects his son to return from the dead is warranted. Rather, one may reasonably conclude that at this point in the narrative Dānîʾilu must be unaware of ʾAqhatu's death, which only heightens the tragedy of the scene.[94] My main interest in this passage, however, is its utilization of *ʾsp* as an expression for harvesting (the hand gathering the produce), which is then paralleled by a reference to the harvest's storage (the hand placing the produce in storage), so that the poetic pair expresses the harvest event in its totality, from the initial harvesting of the crop to its final storage. In another instance, *ʾsp* occurs in an apotropaic setting, apparently concerning a venomous snake bite. The text is fragmentary, but it is relatively certain that *ʾsp* depicts the invoked gods "gathering" or "removing" the venom. Principal among the invoked divinities is Šapšu, who is twice called upon in this text as the first and last of the gods to be summoned, as here (KTU 1.107):

ỉsp ⌜*šp*⌝*š l hrm ǵrpl*	Gather, O Šapšu,[95] from the mountain the cloud,
ʿl ảrṣ (45) [*ảs*]⌜*p*⌝*t*[96] *ḥmt*	from the earth, [O gath]erer of venom.[97]

The nuance of *ʾsp* here, along with its other attestations in this text, signifies the removal of deadly venom.

These two contexts demonstrate that the Ugaritic root *ʾsp* can denote both collection and removal, which correlates well with its more widely attested cognate in Biblical Hebrew. In a number of instances Hebrew *ʾsp* is used with reference to

93. Cf. Biblical Hebrew *ʾôrâ* "herb" in 2 Kgs 4:39 (see BDB, 21; *HALOT*, 25: "light plant," i.e., sensitive to light).

94. Pardee, *COS* 1:352 n. 101. De Moor, *Anthology of Religious Texts*, 252 n. 191; Wyatt, *Religious Texts*, 299 n. 216.

95. For Šapšu's similar role in other contexts, see KTU 1.82:6; and 1.100.

96. The difficulty of this form is the suffixed {t}, which would preclude the imperative, although such is reasonably assumed for *ỉsp* in the previous line. One could opt for a SC verbal form, "you have gathered" (apparently Wyatt, *Religious Texts*, 394), but the rationale for such a shift is rather elusive. (Del Olmo Lete offers no distinction in his translation of these two forms [*Canaanite Religion*, 2nd ed., 318].) Pardee's participial interpretation provides some explanation of the two distinct forms, even though the rationale for the distinction remains unclear (Pardee, *Ritual and Cult*, 191 n. 57).

97. Note that Rašap is also invoked in this text for "gathering" the venom (line 40).

death, specifically of someone being gathered to his ancestors (or people), thus resembling the imagery of Kirta's fifth and sixth wives. For example, the dead Israelite monarchs are often said to be gathered to their fathers, as it is stated for King Josiah in 2 Kgs 22:20:

> *hinnî ʾōsipkā ʿal-ʾăbōtêkā wᵉneʾᵉsaptā ʾel-qibrōtêkā bᵉšālôm*
>
> Look, I am gathering you to your fathers. You will be gathered to your burial-place in peace.

A similar expression appears in the patriarchal narratives, as for example in the case of Abraham in Gen 25:8:

> *wayyigwaʿ wayyāmot ʾabrāhām bᵉśêbâ ṭôbâ zākēn wᵉśābēaʿ wayyēʾāsep ʾel-ʿammāyw*
>
> Abraham expired and died at a good old age as an old and satisfied man, and he was gathered to his people.[98]

These Hebrew examples appear to present death rather positively in their depiction of one's entrance into the company of the dead (cf. the departed king of KTU 1.161:18–22).

The development of this idiom for dying may arise from the agricultural imagery of gathering the harvest for storage, which has been transferred to the funerary context of gathering the dead in preparation for burial. This expression is also found in Jer 8:2 where judgment against Judah's idolatry is defined in terms of revoking the funerary rite of burial:

> *lōʾ yēʾāsᵉpû wᵉlōʾ yiqqābērû lᵉdōmen ʿal-pᵉnê hāʾᵃdāmâ yihyû*
>
> They will not be gathered and buried. They will become as dung upon the face of the ground.[99]

From this perspective, the agricultural imagery of gathering the harvest for storage, attested both at Ugarit and in the Hebrew Bible, provides the rationale for the idiom that envisions death as a type of gathering. In Ugaritic, the gathering

98. Note that this word is plural: "his peoples." E. A. Speiser suggested that this peculiar usage of the plural in this idiom may stem from its alternation with "fathers," as in Gen 15:15 (*Genesis*, 3rd ed., AB 1 [Garden City, NY: Doubleday, 1985], 187).

99. See also Jer 8:33; 9:21. Cf. Ezek 29:5.

imagery provides another notion for death similar to that of descent into the underworld, which also appears to be connected to burial.[100]

This connection does not mean, however, that the gathering necessarily refers to the act of burial itself. From the biblical evidence Steiner notes that the gathering always takes place before burial, as in the examples cited above—"I am gathering you to your fathers . . . you will be gathered to your burial-place" (2 Kgs 22:20); "you will not be gathered and buried" (Jer 8:2). In some cases the biblical expression utilizes the Hebrew verb *bwʾ* "to come, go," as in Gen 15:15:[101]

w^eʾattâ tābôʾ ʾel-ʾ^abōteykā b^ešālôm

You will go to your fathers in peace.

In other words, these texts refer to two events: (1) metaphysical gathering to one's kin, and (2) physical interment of the body. Steiner concludes that it "implies the existence of a soul or spirit that leaves the body at death, before interment, and continues to exist in disembodied form."[102] As in the Hebrew Bible, Ugaritians apparently understood burial to offer a physical representation of one's metaphysical entrance into the realm of the dead. As for the untimely deaths of King Kirta's fifth and sixth wives, their metaphysical gathering concerns entrance into the company of two unseemly deities: Rašap and Yammu.

3.2.2.1.2. *Rašap*

The Ugaritic divine personage Rašap is one of the principal deities of the underworld, functioning at some level as the Ugaritic counterpart of the Mesopotamian god Nergal.[103] In Ugaritic Rašap is closely associated with Šapšu, as for example in KTU 1.78 where he is said to be her gatekeeper:

(1) *b ṯṯ ym ḥdṯ* (2) *ḥry*	During the sixth days of the new moon of ḤYR,
ʿrbt (3) *špš*	Šapšu entered (i.e., set),
ṯǵrh (4) *ršp*	her gatekeeper being Rašap.[104]

100. As noted for KTU 1.6 I:8–18; 1.161:20–22 (see discussion above).

101. Steiner, *Disembodied Souls*, 95–96.

102. Steiner, *Disembodied Souls*, 97.

103. Rašap is written logographically in Akkadian as dGÌR.UNU.GAL (see *Ugaritica* 5:18.26, and the four column arrangement of this text alongside KTU 1.47 [=RS 1.017]; 1.118 [=RS 24.264+]; and 1.148 [=RS 24.643:1–9] in Pardee, *Ritual and Cult*, 14–15); Nergal is written dMAŠ.MAŠ (see John Huehnergard, *The Akkadian of Ugarit*, HSS 34 [Atlanta: Scholars Press, 1989], 360).

104. Opinions on the interpretation of this short text are divided. Teije de Jong and Wilfred H. van Soldt interpreted this text as a reference to a solar eclipse, but did not justify this interpretation philologically ("Redating an Early Solar Eclipse Recorded [KTU 1.78]: Implications for the

Šapšu is designated as ruling the *rpům*, the dead (*mtm*) being in her entourage (KTU 1.6 VI:45–48) in the conceptualization of her descent into the underworld at sunset and subsequent reemergence at dawn.[105] As such, she functions as the psychopomp of the dead, invoked in the royal funerary ritual to transport Ugarit's recently deceased king to the underworld where he is welcomed as the newest member of the *rpům* (KTU 1.161:18–22). As her gatekeeper, Rašap inevitably enjoys a prominent position among the underworld divines. Rašap also occurs in a number of deity lists, as well as several offering lists, and appeared in several local manifestations.[106]

It is often noted that Rašap was considered to be the malevolent god of pestilence, based largely upon his appearance in the comparative Northwest Semitic context, as well as his equation with the Mesopotamian deity Nergal.[107] Originally known as a warrior god, Nergal eventually comes to be more closely associated with death, which Eduard Lipiński attributes to his reputation for inflicting death upon his victims. In light of his becoming the god of death, Lipiński notes, "Negal became a full-fledged god of the netherworld when his identification with Resheph was already accomplished."[108]

In terms of what we know from Ugarit, scholars have cited his mention at the beginning of the Kirta Epic in the death of the king's fifth wife as Ugaritic evidence for his reputation as the "plague-god."[109] Yet, the imagery of Rašap as

---

Ugaritic Calendar and for the Secular Accelerations of the Earth and Moon," *Ex Orient Lux* 30 [1987–1988]: 65–77; de Jong and van Soldt, "The Earliest Known Solar Eclipse Record Redated," *Nature* 338 [1989]: 238–40; cf. F. R. Stephenson, "The Earliest Known Record of a Solar Eclipse," *Nature* 228 [1970]: 651–52; Christopher B. F. Walker, "Eclipse Seen at Ancient Ugarit," *Nature* 338 [1989]: 204–5). Del Olmo Lete also follows the solar eclipse view, but admits that precise astronomical calculations require more data than are currently available (*Canaanite Religion*, 2nd ed., 295). Also following the lunar eclipse hypothesis is Eduard Lipiński, although he takes a different approach in rendering *ʿrbt špš ṯġrh ršp w bdm tbqrn skn* as "the Sun-goddess entered her gate: Resheph, and the diviners will challenge the governor" (*Resheph: A Syro-Canaanite Deity*, OLA 181 [Leuven: Peeters, 2009], 110). Dennis Pardee and Noel Swerdlow ("Not the Earliest Solar Eclipse," *Nature* 363 [1993]: 406) have disputed this interpretation, instead arguing, largely on philological grounds, "that it refers to a repeated sighting of Mars (= Rašap) at sundown for six days in a row, after which the planet would no longer have been visible at sundown" (Pardee, *Ritual and Cult*, 131).

105. Note the progression of the sun from west to east as a progression through the netherworld in KTU 1.15 V:18–19 (Pardee, *COS* 1:339 n. 61).

106. Deity lists, e.g., KTU 1.47:27; 1.102:10; 1.118:26; 1.123:31. Offering lists, e.g., KTU 1.39:4, 7; 1.79:8; 1.91:11, 15; 1.105:7. Local manifestations, e.g., *ršp idrp* (KTU 1.148:32), *ršp bbt* (KTU 1.105:25′), *ršp gn* (KTU 6.62:2), *ršp ḫgb* (KTU 1.90:2), *ršp mhbn* (KTU 1.105:1′-2′), *ršp mlk* (KTU 1.105:7′-8′). For a full listing of occurrences of local manifestations, see Pardee, *Textes rituels*, 988–89.

107. First identified with Nergal in a third millennium BCE bilingual from Ebla (see discussion and references in Lipiński, *Resheph*, 24–27).

108. Lipiński, *Resheph*, 27.

109. E.g., Paolo Xella, "Resheph," *DDD*, 701; John Day, "New Light on the Mythological Background of the Allusion to Resheph in Habakkuk III 5," *VT* 29 (1979): 353–54.

"the god of pestilence," per se, is not actually expressed, but must be drawn from literary sources outside Ugarit. This acknowledgment is not meant to deny his potential malevolency at Ugarit, however. As other scholars have noted, such a view finds credence in the following expression from the incantation text of KTU 1.82:3: [...] *bˁl ḥẓ ršp* "[...] lord of the arrow, Rašap."[110] The broader context of this text chronicles a list of incantations against venomous snake bites, and in this case it is addressed to Rašap directly. At some level, this incantation assumes a certain malevolent quality for Rašap, which is not surprising given his identification as the gatekeeper of the netherworld.[111] It is also interesting to observe that Môtu is mention by name in line 5, followed by an appeal to *ql špš* "the voice of Šapšu" in line 6 that she would preserve the life of the one having been bitten, again demonstrating the close association between Rašap, Šapšu, and even the death god Môtu.[112] I might also add here Rašap's apparent reputation as a warrior deity (like Nergal) in a royal sacrificial list (KTU 1.91:15), where he is identified as *ršp ṣbỉ*, possibly, "Rašap of the army."[113]

Yet, in spite of these malevolent characteristics, his relative popularity among certain members of Ugaritic society is striking, particularly noticeable among the cult officials bearing his name.[114] Furthermore, the place of Rašap as a member of the pantheon receiving recurring offerings bolsters the claim that this deity possessed a certain beneficent quality at Ugarit, which may accord with Xella's conclusion from the extant comparative evidence concerning the "double character of Reshep: benevolent, on the one hand, dangerous, on the other."[115]

Returning to the death of Kirta's wives, the bereaved king is confronted with the unseemly prospects of his fifth wife having been gathered to Rašap. As a parallel expression for the root *mwt* in line 16, death is perceived in terms of the frightening prospects of being gathered into the realm of the dead where Rašap, the gatekeeper, stands ready to receive the king's departed loved one.

3.2.2.1.3. *The Lad(s) of Yammu*

The sixth wife of Kirta is said to have been gathered (gapped) to *ǵlm ym*, typically rendered, "the lad(s) of Yammu" (KTU 1.14 I:19–20). The exact significance

110. See del Olmo Lete, "KTU 1.82," 246–47.

111. De Moor and Spronk go so far as to say, "The 'arrows' of Rashpu are the plagues and diseases he sends among mankind" ("More on Demons," 239), but I should caution that we are dealing with the deadly venom of snakes, not the more general "plagues" or "diseases."

112. See my discussion of this text in ch. 1 (§1.2.2.5).

113. As argued in Lipiński, *Resheph*, 96–98.

114. As noted by Pardee, *Textes rituels*, 42, citing Xella, "Le dieu Rashap à Ugarit," *Les Annals Archéologiques Arabes Syrienne* 29/30 (1979–1980): 145–62. See also Lipiński, *Resheph*, 81–89.

115. Xella, "Resheph," 701.

of this designation is obscure at best. Our knowledge about the deity Yammu comes from his prominent featuring in the first portion of the Baʿlu cycle where he functions as one of two main antagonists (the other being Môtu) in the poetic narration of the challengers to the rule of Baʿlu, the storm god. Yammu also appears in a number of deity lists and a few times is mentioned as the recipient of offerings.[116] However, no other mention is made of Yammu's purported *ǵlm(m)*, leading scholars in various directions in their analysis of the expression *ǵlm ym*.[117]

Mitchell Dahood equated the phrase *ǵlm ym*, translated, "youth of the sea," with the deity Kôṯaru, citing his various associations with the sea in both Ugaritic (e.g., *bn ym* in KTU 1.4 VII:15–16) and classical parallels.[118] Similarly, F. Charles Fensham appeals to Hebrew *ʿelem* (cf. fem. *ʿalmâ*) and points out that Hebrew *bn* "son" often indicates belonging to a group, leading him to translate, "A sixth part becomes part [i.e., lad] of the sea (or Yam)."[119] Others have suggested that *ǵlm ym* may refer to death by drowning, for which Ginsberg interpreted *ǵlm* as a verbal form meaning "to engulf."[120] Interpreting *ǵlm* as a verbal form is not necessarily a requirement for this interpretation, since "lads of Yammu" could conceivably refer to a mythological rendition of the event of one's drowning.[121] Gaster denied Ginsberg's claim that *ǵlm* must be read as a verbal form and thus argued for yet another interpretation, taking *ym* as the word for "day" and *ǵlm* as denoting "disaster": "a dark day" in parallel with the preceding clause depicting Rašap gathering the fifth wife unto himself (i.e., "a sixth [gathered] on a dark day").[122] However, Gaster's proposal is overly complicated and further obscures the meaning of the second member of the parallel, not to mention the fact that *ǵlm* regularly appears in this epic with reference to Kirta: *nʿmn ǵlm il* "the goodly lad of ʾIlu" (e.g., KTU 1.14 I:40–41). Caquot and Sznycer have similarly critiqued

116. Deity lists, e.g., KTU 1.47:30; 1.102:3; 1.118:29. Offering lists: KTU 1.39:13; 1.46:6.

117. See the summary of views in Manfried Dietrich and Oswald Loretz, "Das Porträt einer Königin in KTU 1.14 I 12–15: Zur ugaritischen Lexikographie (XVIII)," *UF* 12 (1980): 204 n. 66.

118. On the interpretation of the phrase *bn ym*, see de Moore, *Seasonal Pattern*, 160–61. For classical parallels, see Mitchell Dahood, "The Breakup of Stereotyped Phrases: Some New Examples," *JANESCU* 5 (1973): 84.

119. F. Charles Fensham, "Remarks on Certain Difficult Passages in Keret," *JNSL* 1 (1971): 20.

120. For drowning, see Baruch Margalit, "Studia Ugaritica II: Studies in Krt and Aqht," *UF* 8 (1976): 144; Pardee, *COS* 1:333 n. 10 (with ?). Ginsberg cites Hebrew *ʿālam* "to conceal, hide" (see H. L. Ginsberg, *The Legend of King Keret*, BASORSup 2–3 [New Haven: American Schools of Oriental Research, 1946], 34; followed by Wyatt, *Religious Texts*, 181 n. 18; Leila Badre, et al., "Notes ougaritiques I: Keret," *Syria* 53 [1976]: 101–2).

121. Even if the mythology is now "neutral" or "a dead metaphor" for drowning, as Wyatt suggests (*Religious Texts*, 181 n. 18). Cf. Driver: "pages of Yam," which he explains as "the waves of a storm" (*Canaanite Myths and Legends*, 2nd ed., 82 n. 7).

122. Gaster, "Canaanite Epic of Keret," 289–90.

Ginsberg's verbal interpretation, but take the usual meaning of *ǵlm* as the parallel subject of *yitsp* "the pages of the god Yam."[123] This last option appears to be the least problematic of those just mentioned in that it makes reasonable sense of the parallel—a fifth Rašap gathers to himself, a sixth the lads of Yammu (gather in, ultimately for Yammu)—and corresponds to the following occurrences of *ǵlm* for Kirta throughout the epic.

It thus remains for us to consider the significance of Kirta's sixth wife being gathered to the lad(s) of Yammu, presuming acceptance of my interpretation of *ǵlm ym* just outlined. Unlike the so-called "double character" of Rašap, all things Yammu in Ugaritic literature depict this member of the pantheon as one of the main threats to life and stability in his potential overthrow of the storm god's rule. While Baʿlu might be said to represent the source of life in the cosmos, Yammu stands on the other side with Môtu, the second major antagonist of the Baʿlu cycle, representing the threat against all life. Smith explains it well:

> On the one side of the Baal Cycle stands Baal, the source of life in the cosmos, and on the other side are Yamm ("Sea") and Mot ("Death"), the sources of destruction and death in the universe. Yamm embodies the chaos that threatens the life of the world. Mot is Death incarnate. The struggle between Baal and his opponents represents the conflict between life and death.[124]

His "lad(s)" may be envisioned as attendant(s), perhaps representing a similar function to that of Rašap as the gatekeeper of Šapšu, and as such a chief deity of the underworld, yet relegated to a subservient role within Môtu's realm. As it has already been noted by several scholars, "death" in this case may involve the literal dangers of the sea, perhaps by drowning, and thus it is depicted in mythological fashion as being gathered by Yammu's attendants.

The seventh and last manner of dying in this list involves falling by the sword: *b šlḥ ttpl* "falls by the sword."[125] The imagery invoked in this description resembles that of combat, comparable to the fall of Yammu in his combat with Baʿlu where it is stated that he "falls to the ground" (*yql l árṣ*) after having been

123. "Les pages de dieu Yam," Caquot and Sznycer, *Textes ougaritiques 1*, 506–7 n. o. Cf. del Olmo Lete who takes it as a singular form: "the Hero Yammu" ("el Prócer Yammu"; *Mitos y leyendas*, 290).

124. Smith, *Baal Cycle 1*, 59. See also pp. 84–86.

125. See Pardee, *COS* 1:333; Wyatt, *Religious Texts*, 181. The noun /šilḥu/ is derived from the root *šlḥ* meaning "to throw, cast" (see *DUL*, 816) and is cognate with Hebrew *šelaḥ* "missle, weapon" (BDB, 1019).

fatally struck on the head (KTU 1.2 IV:25–26). The text does not indicate why the queen of Ugarit would have suffered death by sword in battle, leading scholars to offer other suggestions. Dietrich and Loretz have proposed interpreting *šlḥ* as the divine name (i.e., Thrower) for a personified river of the underworld.[126] The appeal of this suggestion is that the previous two deaths are also described mythologically as death by divine cause.[127] However, unlike Rašap and Yammu, evidence for a deity Šilḥu in Ugaritic appears to be lacking, therefore rendering the death by sword interpretation more likely. Accordingly, the seven deaths may be arranged to indicate an increase in the level of tragedy associated with each one. If being gathered to the lads of Yammu is a mythological representation of drowning in the sea, this final death may indicate a still more horrendous event—death by sword.

3.2.2.2. The Death of Kirta

Several other G PC forms of the root *mwt* occur in KTU 1.16 column I, only this time it applies to the potential death of the epic's protagonist, King Kirta. This usage is followed by several instances of the verbal noun *mt* (*/mawātu/ > /mātu/) (or possibly common noun). These occurrences of the root for death show up at a crucial point in the Kirta Epic where the narrative zeros in on the royal personage's threat of facing death. I have already analyzed a portion of this passage (KTU 1.16 I:9–19) in my treatment of *ḥyy* "to live" in chapter 1 where the negated verbal noun (or common noun) occurs as a parallel for the plural suffixed noun *ḥyk* "your life."[128] These forms occur in the royal family's mourning over Kirta's immanent death, first in the speech of Kirta's son ʾIluḥaʾu, and second from his sister Ṯitmanatu. The speech of ʾIluḥaʾu begins at KTU 1.16 I:2:

(2) *k klb b btk nʿtq*[129]	Like a dog in your house we pass/grow old,
k ỉnr (3) *ḫštk*	like a hound (in) your court.
ảp ảb ỉ k mtm (4) *tmtn*	Will you also, father, like mortals die?
ủ ḫštk l ntn (5) *ʿtq*	Or indeed, your court be given to passing/ growing old,
bd ảṯt ảb ṣrry	into the hand of women, father ṢRRY?

126. Dietrich and Loretz, "Porträt einer Königin," 204 n. 67. See also de Moor and Spronk, "Problematic Passages," 156; de Moor, *Anthology of Religious Texts*, 192 n. 9; and broader study of Matitiahu Tsevet, "The Canaanite god Šälaḥ," *VT* 4 (1954): 41–49.

127. As noted by Wyatt, *Religious Texts*, 182 n. 20.

128. See the notes for KTU 1.16 I:9–19 in ch. 1 (§1.2.3.1.1).

129. The first part of this speech is missing from the broken portion at the end of KTU 1.15 column VI. This portion can be reconstructed from its repetition in KTU 1.16 I, line 14.

(6) *tbkyk ảb ǵr bʿl*	Will the mountain of Baʿlu weep for you, father,
(7) *ṣpn ḥlm*[130] *qdš*	Ṣapānu, the holy stronghold,
(8) *nny ḥlm ảdr*	Nannaya, the powerful stronghold,
ḥl (9) *rḥb mknpt*	the wide-spread stronghold?
ảp (10) *krt bnm ỉl*	Moreover, Kirta is a son of ʾIlu,
špḥ (11) *lṭpn w qdš*	offspring of the knowing and holy one.
ʿl (12) *ảbh yʿrṣ*	To his father he enters.
ybky (13) *yšnn*	He weeps, he gnashes his teeth,
ytn gh (14) *bky*	he raises his voice with weeping.
b ḥyk ảbn ả[!]*šmḫ*[131]	In your life, our father, we rejoice,
(15) *bl mtk ngln*	(in) your not dying we find joy.
k klb (16) *b btk nʿtq*	Like a dog in your house we pass/grow old,
k ỉnr (17) *ảp ḫštk*	like a hound also (in) your court.
ảp ảb k mtm[132] (18) *tmtn*	Also, father, like mortals will you die?
ủ ḫštk l ntn (19) *ʿtq*	Or indeed your court be given to passing/growing old,
bd ảṯt ảb ṣrry	into the hand of women, father ṢRRY?
(20) *ỉ km yrgm bn ỉl*[133] (21) *krt*	O thus Kirta is called a son of ʾIlu,
špḥ lṭpn (22) *w qdš*	the offspring of the knowing and holy one.
ủ ỉlm tmtn	Do gods die?
(23) *špḥ lṭpn l yḥ*	Would the offspring of the Knowing One not live?

This speech is repeated in the mouth of Ṯitmanatu in KTU 1.16 II:36–60, which breaks off as the condition of the column deteriorates at that portion of the tablet.

The G PC *tmtn* occurs in lines 4 (2ms), 18 (2ms), and 22 (3mp), with the negated verbal noun *mt* (/mātu/) (or common noun) appearing in line 15.[134] The first two PC verbs (2ms, referring to Kirta) are modified by the phrase *k mtm* "like men," thus taking the second member of the phrase as the masculine plural noun /mutīma/ "men" (< /mutu/ "man"), rather than as a derivative of

130. Cf. Biblical Hebrew *ḥayil* "power, force, army" (*HALOT*, 311–12).

131. Scribal error for *nšmḫ* in light of the 1cp suffix on the preceding noun (*ảbn*), as well as the verbs to follow (*ngln, nʿtq*). Furthermore, the parallel expression in KTU 1.16 II:37 reads *nšmḫ*.

132. Taking *mtm* as /mutīma/ "men" rather than /môtīma/ "those who die."

133. On lines 20–22, see the discussion in ch. 1 (§1.2.1).

134. In Ṯitmanatu's speech from the next column (KTU 1.16 II), the G PC appears in lines 40 and 43, and the verbal noun in line 37.

the root *mwt* "to die." An obvious question emerges from this context: Why should one expect Kirta not to die like any other man? The question finds partial explanation in the third instance of the G PC in line 22, where its plural subject is *ilm* "gods": *ủ ilm tmtn* "Do gods die?"

The titles for Kirta as a royal figure throughout this epic emphasize a certain divine status in his association with ʾIlu. For instance, ʾIlu is said to be his father in *ṯr ảbh il* "the bull, his father ʾIlu," and he is correspondingly designated as *bnm il // špḥ lṭpn w qdš* "son of ʾIlu // offspring of the knowing and holy one," or even *ʿbd il* "servant of ʾIlu," while he is also named *nʿmn ǵlm il* "the goodly one of ʾIlu."[135] These associations are further heightened in his exalted position among the *rpủm* as the inevitability of his death from illness draws nigh: *mỉd rm [krt] b tk rpỉ ảr[ṣ] b pḫr qbṣ dtn* "Kirta is greatly exalted in the midst of the *rpủm* of the underworld, among the gathering of the assembly of DTN."[136] The emphasis is more than ʾIlu offering Kirta a place among these semidivine ancestors of the royal throne, but rather is his exaltation among them. Simon Parker thinks the Kirta Epic demonstrates that the older view of divine kingship is meant to be questioned here, since it is ʾIlu who truly proves to be the immortal sovereign superintending the affairs of the mortal king. Concerning the question, "Do gods die?," Parker surmises, "If Kirta is divine, then gods are not immortal. If the gods are immortal, then Kirta cannot be divine."[137] But, as Wyatt has astutely observed, the whole thrust of the narrative would seem to point in the other direction: namely, the divine status of the king.[138] Indeed, the narrative's titular formulae for Kirta throughout this epic leads in such an interpretive direction, especially in light of their close resemblances to those ascribed to Baʿlu, in particular his being the *bn il* in the ʾAqhatu Epic, with its similar interest in the assumed immortality of the gods.[139]

135. *ṯr ảbh il*: KTU 1.14 II:6, 23–24; IV:6. *bnm il*: KTU 1.16 I:10, 20–22; II:48–49 (broken). *ʿbd il*: KTU 1.14 III:49, 51. *nʿmn ǵlm il*: KTU 1.14 I:40; II:7; 1.15 II:15–16 (broken), 20.

136. KTU 1.15 III:13–15; cf. the reconstruction of the same expression a few lines earlier in KTU 1.15 III:2–4 where *krt* and *ảrṣ* are fully preserved: [mỉd . rm .] krt [b tk . rpỉ .] ảrṣ [b pḫr] . qbṣ . dtn.

137. Simon B. Parker, "The Historical Composition of KRT and the Cult of El," *ZAW* 89 (1977): 174; Parker, *The Pre-Biblical Narrative Tradition: Essays on the Ugaritic Poems Keret and Aqhat*, RBS 24 (Atlanta: Scholars Press, 1989), 212–13.

138. Nicolas Wyatt, "Just How 'Divine' Were the Kings of Ugarit?" *AuOr* 17–18 (2000): 135. Or, as Wyatt states elsewhere: "The fact remains, however, that theological language was used of him [the king], in a way that indicates that he was set apart from common humanity and even from the priesthood and the nobility, and he somehow shared in the ontology of the divine realm" ("Religious Role of the King," 69).

139. E.g., *bn il* (KTU 1.17 VI:29). Note that this particular reference concerns the nature of Baʿlu as one who defies death through a renewal of life (for a discussion of this passage, refer to ch. 1 (§1.2.2.1); see also Nicolas Wyatt, "Ilimilku's Ideological Programme: Ugaritic Royal Propaganda, and a Biblical Postscript," *UF* 29 [1997]: 775–96).

Returning to KTU 1.16 I, the threefold occurrence of the root *mwt* appears in a context wherein the narrative grapples with the very nature of the Ugaritic royal office and its representative, Kirta. The negated verbal noun *bl mtk* "your not dying" in line 15 provides the antonym for *ḥyk* "your life" in the previous line. As I already noted in my discussion of the root *ḥyy* in chapter 1, the parallels *ḥy* // *bl mt* and *mt* // *l ḥyy* suggest that living and dying are mutually exclusive categories.[140] Heightening this point is the fact that in this text, where the prospects of death linger heavily, despite its following ʾIlu's blessing and promise of an exalted position among the *rpủm*, death prohibits the continuation of life. Neither would it appear justifiable to simply conclude that a king's so-called immortality is thought to find realization in the promulgation of offspring, since it is the two children of the king who thus mourn his untimely end. In response to Parker's contention that the "traditional doctrine" of royal divinity is somehow being deconstructed by the narrator in exchange for a more "mortal" depiction of kingship, one could suggest that ʾIlu's healing the sick king in some sense maintains the status quo by keeping the otherworldly status of the Ugaritic monarchy intact.[141] Therefore, premature death may be the real issue at stake here, which would threaten the reputation of the royal personage as "son/offspring of ʾIlu." Furthermore, the probable allusion to Baʿlu's ability to renew life in the ʾAqhatu Epic (KTU 1.17 VI:29) may signify that in a similar fashion, Kirta is able to beat the odds of death through the divine intervention of ʾIlu.[142]

3.2.3. *mwt* in the ʾAqhatu Epic

The verbal root *mwt* occurs at two key junctures in the Epic of ʾAqhatu: the first two in the well-known exchange between the hero and the goddess ʿAnatu in her attempt at securing his coveted bow (verbal noun in KTU 1.17 VI:27; 1cs G PC in KTU 1.17 VI:38), and the third in the announcement of his death to his father Dānīʾilu (KTU 1.19 II:42). I have already devoted significant attention to the first context in chapter 1 in my discussion of the root *ḥwy* "to make alive."[143] Therefore, my comments on this text will assume much of what I have already stated in my treatment there.

140. See ch. 1 (§1.2.3.1.1).

141. Parker, *Pre-Biblical Narrative Tradition*, 213.

142. Besides, in the Legend of ʾAqhatu it appears as though ʿAnatu claims some level of responsibility for Baʿlu's ability to renew life in her offering to do the same for ʾAqhatu (as was argued in ch. 1, §1.2.2.1).

143. Ch. 1 (§1.2.2.1).

3.2.3.1. ʾAqhatu and ʿAnatu (KTU 1.17 VI)

The first verbal form of *mwt* in this epic occurs in the hero's stated refusal to give up his bow to ʿAnatu. In this exchange lies an expression of humanity's finiteness and the fact that every person will eventually die, which resembles the similar sentiments spoken by those of Kirta's household mourning the king's approaching death. For the sake of convenience, I provide below the text and translation of this speech as the goddess makes her offer of the Baʿlu-kind of life:[144]

w tʿn btlt (26) *ʿnt*	And the girl ʿAnatu replies:
irš ḥym l ảqht ǵzr	"Request life, O valiant ʾAqhatu.
(27) *irš ḥym w ảtnk*	Request life and I will give (it to) you;
bl mt (28) *w ảšlḥk*	not dying and I will grant (it to) you.
ảšsprk ʿm bʿl (29) *šnt*	I will make you count years with Baʿlu;
ʿm bn il tspr yrḫm	with the son of ʾIlu you will count months,
(30) *k bʿl k yḥwy*	like Baʿlu when he is revived.
yʿšr ḥwy	They prepare a feast; he is revived.
yʿš(31)*r w yšqynh*	They prepare a feast and give him drink.
ybd w yšr ʿlh (32) *nʿm[n*	The goodly one improvises and sings on his behalf,
w]ʿnynn	[and I] answer him.
ảp ảnk ảḥwy (33) *ảqht [ǵ]zr*	I myself can even revive the [va]liant ʾAqhatu."
w yʿn ảqht ǵzr	And the valiant ʾAqhatu replied:
(34) *ảl tšrgn y btltm*	"Do not entangle me, girl,
dm l ǵzr (35) *šrgk ḫḫm*[145] *mt*	for your entanglings are a snare to a valiant man.
ủḫryt mh yqḥ	As for the last destiny, what can one receive?
(36) *mh yqḥ mt ảṯryt*	What can a man receive hereafter?
spsg ysk (37) [*l*] *riš*	They will pour *spsg* [on] (my) head,
ḥrṣ l ẓr qdady	*ḥrṣ* on the top of my cranium.
(38) [*ảp*]*mt kl ảmt*	I [also] will die the death of all;
w ản mtm ảmt	and I myself must certainly die."

144. For a more detailed analysis of this text, see ch. 1 (§1.2.2.1).

145. The three principal interpretations of this word are: (1) "briar, bramble, hook" (cf. Hebrew *ḥô^{a}ḥ*); (2) "pit, hole" (cf. Arabic *ḫawḫat* "hole" [Caquot and Sznycer, *Textes ougaritiques 1*, 220 n. g (also appealing to Hebrew *ḥô^{a}ḥ* in 1 Sam. 13:6)]); and (3) "mud, mire, filth" (cf. Akkadian *ḫaḫû*/*ḫuḫû* [*CAD* 6:30–31, 225]).

In chapter 1, I defined the nature of ʿAnatu's offer of immortality—literally *blmt* "not dying"—as a continuation of existence through revivification. This observation arises from the fact that it is compared to the revivification of Baʿlu and his ability to come back to life after having died, bringing to mind the Môtu-Baʿlu conflict depicted in the Baʿlu cycle, wherein Baʿlu, who was once declared to be dead, is subsequently pronounced "alive."[146]

The verbal forms of line 38 are both 1cs G PC. The first clause is constructed with a cognate accusative: the intransitive verb /ʾamūtu/ + the cognate accusative noun /môtama/ "I die the death."[147] The cognate /môtama/ is further defined by the adjective *kl*: the death of every person." In the second clause, the verbal form is modified by *mtm*, which could be taken in one of two ways. It is morphologically possible to interpret *mtm* as the plural noun /mutîma/ "men," perhaps taking it as a comparative: "I will die (as) men," or even as a singular noun with enclitic {m}: /mutima/ "I will die (as) a man." One problem with this interpretation is that the comparative particle *k* is left off, though such an omission is not without precedent in Ugaritic. The second option is to interpret *mtm* as the infinitive in absolute usage and with enclitic {m}: /mātuma/, and translate with emphasis, "I will surely die." The strength of this second option is that the syntax, with its added focus on the subject as indicated by the use of the 1cs independent pronoun *ản*, suggests that the second clause is meant to emphasize the first, which would naturally utilize the infinitive absolute construction. It follows that *mtm* as "death" would be restated for such an emphasis. This final point might negate any appeal to *k mtm* "like men" in the Kirta Epic where the poetic structure of the surrounding lines is somewhat different (KTU 1.16 I:3–4):

ảp ảb k mtm (18) *tmtn*	Also, father, like mortals will you die?
ủ ḫštk l ntn (19) *ʿtq*	Or indeed your court be given to passing/growing old,
bd ảṯt ảb ṣrry	in the hand of women, father ṢRRY?

The concern of the ʾAqhatu Epic seems to focus on a comparison/contrast between the life of gods and men. ʿAnatu claims to promise the hero a divine type of existence, one that is characterized by preservation via revivification. Yet, in the narrative's portrayal of ʾAqhatu's response, the view of the hero is one that denies such a possibility for humankind. Therefore, I agree with Wyatt's caution

146. See §3.2.1.2 above.
147. On this syntax in Hebrew, see Joüon, §125q.

that even "if there was a general belief in some kind of survival, to which Aqhat might be expected to subscribe, then what Anat offers is something of a different order of magnitude, a species of divine life."[148]

3.2.3.2. The Announcement of ʾAqhatu's Death (KTU 1.19 II)

The second context for dying in the ʾAqhatu Epic is the announcement of the hero's death to his father, Dānîʾilu. The physical condition of the tablet is broken in the lines leading up to this message (lines 32–39) and has therefore rendered the text obscure in its interpretation.[149] I begin my rendering at line 40 with the introduction of the messengers' report:

(40) *tmǵyn*	They arrive.
tšȧ ghm w[*tṣḥ*]	They lift their voice and [say aloud]:
(41) *šmʿ l dnỉl mt* [*rpỉ*]	Listen, O Dānîʾilu, man of RPỦ,
(42) *mt ȧqht ǵzr*	Valiant ʾAqhatu is dead.
[*šṣȧt*] (43) *btlt ʿnt k r*[*ḥ npšh*]	Girl ʿAnatu [caused his *npš* to go out] like wi[nd],
(44) *k*[150] *iṯl brlth*[151]	his *brlt* like spittle.

In chapter 2 I considered the exiting *npš* motif from this passage, but I must add that it is the only time in the ʾAqhatu Epic when it occurs with the root *mwt*, in this case, as the 3ms G SC *mt* (/mīta/).[152] Defining *npš* here as "vitality" or "life force," this occurrence portrays its exit at death. The imagery of death in this text depicts it as an event involving the departure of life signs from the body, utilizing the natural imagery of wind, spittle, and the burning of incense (in KTU 1.18 IV:24–26, 36–37).

In this respect, comparing the death of the hero ʾAqhatu with that of the storm god Baʿlu is instructive, and it is one that the narrative would seem to suggest in ʿAnatu's promise of a Baʿlu-kind of life to ʾAqhatu. The pronouncement of Baʿlu's revivification is accompanied by observable alterations in the weather patterns—in a dream ʾIlu perceives the renewal of rain as evidence that he is

148. Wyatt, *Religious Texts*, 276 n. 116.

149. See the translation and notes for these lines in Wyatt, *Religious Texts*, 300–302; del Olmo Lete, *Mitos y leyendas*, 382; Caquot and Sznycer, *Textes ougaritiques 1*, 448–49.

150. Note the erasure of an {i} before the {k}.

151. *KTU* and *CAT* reconstruct [k qṭr . b ȧph . bh . pʿnm] at the end of line 44 on the basis of the formulaic expression attested earlier in this text (KTU 1.18 IV:24–26, 36–37). This reconstruction would require the last two words of the line continuing on the edge of the tablet. Herdner simply reconstructs [bh . pʿnm] due to the lack of adequate spacing for the full formula, suggesting that perhaps the scribe inadvertently omitted *k qṭr b ȧph* from the usual expression (*CTA* 19 II:93 n. 3).

152. See ch. 2 (§2.2.3.3).

alive (KTU 1.6 III:1–21). This association is also operative in his death, as for instance in Môtu's message to Baʿlu concerning his inevitable descent into his throat, instructing the storm god to gather his characteristic weather elements (i.e., clouds, wind, watering devices, and rain) in preparation for his entrance into the place of seclusion (KTU 1.5 V:5–17). As for ʾAqhatu, his refusal to accept ʿAnatu's offer brings about his untimely death, which is defined as the exit of life's vital energy, and unlike Baʿlu, it is never again to return.

3.2.4. *mwt* in the Letters: Dead Ships

The Ugaritic letters provide an intriguing example of death being applied to inanimate objects. In chapter 1 I observed the similar potential for the D stem root *ḥwy* "to make alive" in its application to repairing a dilapidated house: *ḥwt hbt* "I have repaired this house" (KTU 2.70:15–16). As noted in that discussion, this example is important because it provides a sample usage from a nonliterary context, and thus complements what we have already observed for this term from its wider attestation in the mythology and epic literature of Ugarit.

In KTU 2.38 this root describes a fleet of damaged ships belonging to the king of Ugarit.[153] The letter is written by the king of Tyre who claims to have rescued the ships and informs the Ugaritic king on their whereabouts. For the sake of context, I provide the text in full:

(1) *l mlk ủgrt* (2) *ảḫy rgm*	To the king of Ugarit, my brother, say:
(3) *tḥm mlk ṣr ảḫk*	Message of the king of Tyre, your brother:
(4) *yšlm lk*	May it be well with you.
(5) *ỉlm tǵrk tšlmk*	May the gods guard you and keep you well.
(6) *hnny ʿmn* (7) *šlm*	Here with me it is well.
ṯmny (8) *ʿmk mnm šlm*	There with you, whatever is well
(9) *rgm ṯṯb*	return word.
(10) *ảnykn dt* (11) *lỉkt mṣrm hndt*	Your ships that you sent to Egypt
(12) *b ṣr* (13) *mtt*	are wrecked at Tyre,[154]
by (14) *gšm ảdr* (15) *nškḥ*	where they found themselves in a bad storm.
w (16) *rb tmtt* (17) *lqḥ*	The master of death took

153. For the *edtio princeps*, see Charles Virolleaud, *PRU* 5 (1965): 81–83, no. 59. See also the new edition in Bordreuil and Pardee, *Manual of Ugarit*, 238–39 (with new copy and photograph).

154. Literally: "your (group of) ships that you sent to Egypt are dead."

kl ḏrʿ (18) *bd*[*nh*]*m*	all the grain from their possession.
w ảnk (19) *k*[*l*] *ḏrʿ*[*h*]*m*	As for me, all their grain,
(20) [*k*]*l npš* (21) *w ảklhm*	every individual, and their food
bd (22) *r*[*b*] *tmtt lqḥt*	I took from the hand of the master of death
(23) *w ṯṯb ảnk lhm*	and returned (it) to them.
(24) *w ảnyk ṯt* (25) *by ʿky ʿryt*	Your ships are docked at ʿAcco, stripped.
(26) *w ảḫy mhk* (27) *b lbh ảl yšt*	My brother should not set anything in his heart.

One of the main interpretive issues here involves the meaning of the root *mwt* being applied to the fleet of ships identified and discussed in lines 10–27. One can assume from this letter that the king of Ugarit had dispatched a fleet of ships from Egypt to Ugarit, and the occasion of the letter is their apparent failure to reach their destination, having been caught in a bad storm along the Tyrian Mediterranean coast line.[155]

One of the immediate problems facing interpreters of this text is the morphological identification of *mtt* in line 13. Jesús-Luis Chunchillos appealed to Akkadian *muttatu* "half" and interpreted the clause as a reference to the loss of "half" the Ugaritic fleet in the storm.[156] The syntax for this rendering, however, is admittedly awkward and highly unlikely—if the demonstrative *hndt* (which refers back to *ảnykn* "your ships") were being modified by Cunchillos's proposed *muttatu* (i.e., "half of these"), one might expect it to precede the demonstrative.[157] Other commentators have understood *mtt* to be a 3fs G stative SC verbal form, "it/she is dead," which would take "your ships" as a collective referring to an entire fleet of ships: "your (group of) ships."[158] As for the logical expla-

155. Pardee (*COS* 3:93 n. 39) suggests that since the ships were transporting grain, it is probable they were returning from Egypt and is perhaps reflective of a period of food shortage in the Hittite Empire (as suggested by Ithamar Singer, "A Political History of Ugarit," in Watson and Wyatt, *Handbook of Ugaritic Studies*, 716). Furthermore, since they were loaded with grain, they were certainly headed north—Ugarit did not sell grain to Egypt in LBA (see Singer, "Political History of Ugarit," 715–19; Jack Sasson, "Canaanite Maritime Involvement in the Second Millennium," *JAOS* 86 [1967]: 126–38).

156. For *muttatu*, see *AHw* 2:689–90; *CAD* 10:310. Jesús-Luis Cunchillos, "Correspondance," in *Texts ougartiques II*, 351–52 n. 8: Half of your fleet that you sent to Egypt is in Tyre [on account of] the torrential rain" ("La moitié de ta flotte que tu avais commandée en Égypte, se trouva à Tyr par [à cause d'] une pluie torrentielle.").

157. Note that in Ugaritic when the demonstrative pronoun is used attributively, it always follows the word it modifies (e.g., KTU 2.33:21, 35; 3.2:1, 14), which is also the case in Hebrew (e.g., Gen 7:1: *baddôr hazzê* "in this generation"; Deut 4:6: *haggôy haggādôl hazzê* "this great nation").

158. Virolleaud, *PRU* 5:82; Gordon, *Ugaritic Textbook*, 431; Sasson, "Canaanite Maritime Involvement," 137; Hoftijzer, "Letter de roi de Tyr," 386; Pardee, *COS* 3:94 (and Bordreuil and Pardee, *Manual of Ugaritic*, 238–39).

nation of being "dead in Tyre," several scholars have suggested that it depicts ships having run aground during the storm and were thus immobilized.[159] This viewpoint poses the obvious problem that in line 24 it is stated that the ships are docked at ʿAcco after the removal of their valuable cargo. Jacob Hoftizer is less specific, simply explaining that these ships had been in an accident, but that it was not a total loss since the entire crew is reportedly still present.[160] Pardee has pointed out that "died" in this context does not refer to sinking, but refers to "the stripping away of the rigging of the boats, leaving them at the mercy of the storm."[161] As Hoftijzer has observed regarding Biblical Hebrew *gšm* and its use for winter rains, along with the additional qualifier *ỉdr* for heavy downpour, the power of this storm left the sails of the ships badly damaged and thus destroyed their capacity to navigate the seas.[162] The strong wind and rain left this fleet of ships stranded and immobilized off the coast of Tyre, where they were plundered and moved to dock at ʿAcco. Line 24 describes these ships as *ʿryt* "stripped, bare," plausibly a feminine G verbal adjective from the root *ʿry* meaning "to be bare, naked."[163] This word's antonym *lbš* "to put on clothing" occurs once in Ugaritic for outfitting the rigging of a ship, which suggests that *mtt* may refer to ships with damaged sails and therefore unable to move.[164]

The significance of this occurrence of the root *mwt* is that it provides an important correspondence with the imagery of death as the exiting of one's *npš* or vitality/life force. The exiting *npš* motif from the ʾAqhatu Epic depicts the departure of one's life force or animation from the body at death. In a similar fashion, the fleet of Ugaritic ships in KTU 2.38 are called "dead" because their sails have been destroyed by the winds and rains of a bad storm and are thus left stranded in the water. Like a lifeless corpse from which the *npš* "life force" has departed, these ships are still and immovable off the coast of Tyre where they were discovered by the Tyrian king and subsequently moved to ʿAcco. Therefore, one might say that death in Ugaritic is presented as an inanimate state

159. Sasson, "Canaanite Maritime Involvement,"137; *DUL*, 596 (listing "run aground" under the root *mt* with ?).

160. Hoftijzer, "Letter de roi de Tyr," 386.

161. Pardee, *COS* 3:94 n. 42.

162. Hoftijzer, "Letter de roi de Tyr," 386. See also Philippe Reymond, *L'eau, sa vie, et sa signification dans l'Ancient Testament*, VTSup 7 (Leiden: Brill, 1958), 19–18. Note, however, that Hoftijzer's interpretation is slightly different from the one advanced here, in that he seems to indicate that "dead" means they were in the sea at a time that was unfavorable for navigation ("Lettre du Roi de Tyr," 386).

163. Hebrew *ʿārâ* "to be naked, bare," *ʿerwâ* "nakedness" (BDB, 788); Arabic, *ʿariya* "to be naked, bare" (Lane, 2029–30).

164. *lbš* for rigging is noted by Pardee, *COS* 3:94 n. 47. KTU 4.322 (RS 18.025):16: *lbš ảnyth bʿrm* "the sails of his ship were burned."

characteristic of dead corpses. Its application to a fleet of ships whose sails need to be repaired implies that this state is not always permanent, at least when it is applied to the great deities of mythology. Though it is not attested at Ugaritic, one wonders if the D stem *ḥwy* "to restore life" could be appropriately applied to the restoration of these ships just as it was applied to the reparation of a dilapidated house (KTU 2.70:15–16).

3.3. Substantive Forms

Several substantive forms are attested for this root throughout the Ugaritic corpus of texts, appearing in both mythological and nonmythological contexts. In what follows, I will first discuss the adjectival forms *mt*/*mtm* "dead," and afterward I will consider the noun *mt* "death," as well as the *t*-preformative feminine noun *tmtt* from the letter KTU 2.38 just discussed. In order to treat these substantival forms adequately, however, I must first deal with the possible confusion of *mt* /môtu/ "death" versus *mt* /mutu/ "man," a situation arising from their indistinguishable orthography. I will address such ambiguities as they arise in my analysis of the potential nominal forms of this root.

3.3.1. Adjectival Forms

In terms of Ugaritic orthography, the adjective *mt* "death" is identical to the 3ms G SC *mt* "he died/is dead." By comparison, Biblical Hebrew also correlates these forms morphologically: 3ms G SC *mēt* "he died/is dead" is the same as the G participle *mēt* "one who dies/is dead."[165] For the Ugaritic corpus I have isolated those occurrences of *mt* whose contexts prohibit a finite verbal interpretation and require being read as substantivized verbal adjectives, "dead (person)." Within these contexts, I identify the masculine singular verbal adjective /mītu/, as well as the masculine plural /mītūma/.

The masculine singular form occurs in KTU 1.114 in its depiction of the drunken stupor of the god ʾIlu on his return home from the *marziḥu* or "drinking club" (line 15).[166] As Hays explains, this club "was an association that owned

165. See the forms cited in BDB, 559.

166. For a general overview of the *marziḥu* at Ugarit, see Marvin H. Pope, "A Divine Banquet at Ugarit," in *The Use of the Old Testament in the New and Other Essays: Studies in Honor of William Franklin Stinespring*, ed. James M. Efird (Durham, NC: Duke University Press, 1972), 170–203. See also Pope, *Song of Songs*, 216–29; Michael O'Connor, "Northwest Semitic Designations for Elective Social Affinities," *JANESCU* 18 (1986): 70–76. For a recent summary of the discussion, see Hays, *Death in the Iron Age II*, 115–22.

real estate, including houses (*CAT* 3.9:4), storehouses (3.9:5) and vineyards (4.642:3, RS 18.01:5), all of which could be rented, presumably for banqueting or festivals."[167]

(17) *ỉl hlk l bth*	ʾIlu goes to his house,
yštql[168] (18) *l ḥẓrh*	He falters at his inner chamber,
yʿmsn nn ṯkmn (19) *w šnm*	Ṯukamuna-wa-Šunama carries him.
w ngšnn ḥby[169]	ḤBY meets him,
(20) *bʿl qrnm w ḏnb*	The one with two horns and a tail;
ylšn[170] (21) *b ḫrỉh w ṯnth*	He tramples him over in his feces and urine.

167. Hays, *Death in Iron Age II*, 115–16, citing Patrick D. Miller, "The Mrzḥ Text," in *The Claremont Ras Shamra Tablets*, ed. Loren R. Fisher, AnOr 48 (Rome: Pontifical Biblical Institute, 1971), 37–48.

168. Št PC of √*ql* "to fall."

169. The identity of this creature with two horns and a tail remains inconclusive. Cyrus H. Gordon took this monster as a predecessor to Satan ("ḤBY, Possessor of Horns and Tail," *UF* 18 [1986]: 129–32), which Paolo Xella tempers in suggesting "the transmission of a mythological element from Bronze Age Syria to the OT," but not necessarily the forerunner of the devil. In light of ʾIlu's condition and its comparison to the dead in the underworld, he therefore thinks *ḥby* is a chthonic deity ("Haby," *DDD*, 377). Johannes C. de Moor appeals to Ethiopic *ḥabiʾ* and translates "steward," stating that this purported "house-keeper of Ilu was a faun-like demon" ("Studies in the New Alphabetic Texts from Ras Shamra," *UF* 1 [1969]: 169; de Moor, *Anthology of Religious Texts*, 136 n. 10; followed by Spronk, *Beatific Afterlife*, 199 n. 4). Kevin Cathcart and Wilfred G. E. Watson note three additional etymologies for *ḥby*: Akkadian *ḫabû* "to draw water or wine" (see *CAD* 6:19); Arabic *ḥbw* "to crawl" (see Lane, 507); Akkdian *ḫuppû* "acrobat" (*CAD* 6:240). They also entertain two further possibilities: reading the form in question as *ḥbl*, which appears unlikely in light of the clearly visible {y} (as observed by Wyatt, *Religious Texts*, 411 n. 38); or alternatively *ḥb ḫḫ* "embracer of filth" (Cathcart and Watson, "Weathering a Wake: A Cure for a Carousal; A Revised Translation of Ugaritica V Text 1," *PIBA* 4 [1980]: 39–40). Pardee has advanced an earlier proposal put forth by Mario Liverani ("Review of *Ugaritica* 5, by Jean Nougayrol et al.," *OrAnt* 8 [1969]: 339) that appeals to Egyptian *ḥby*, the bull Apsis, not only described as having horns and tail, but also noted for his role as psychopomp (*Textes paramythologiques*, 60–62; Pardee, *COS* 1:304 n. 14).

170. The identification of this root has been understood in several ways. Pope advanced the Arabic etymology *lšš* in the reduplicated form *lašlaša* "to run to and fro in fear" (defecating)" ("Divine Banquet at Ugarit," 196; followed by Cathcart and Watson, "Weathering a Wake," 41; and Wyatt, *Religious Texts*, 411). The problem with this particular interpretation is that it would require the subject of the verb to be ʾIlu. The context would naturally suggest ḤBY as the subject here, since the explicit mention of ʾIlu in line 21 seems to note a change of actor: ḤBY meets him and does X; (then) ʾIlu falls. De Moor's appeal to √*lšn* "to rebuke, scold" (see references in *DUL*, 505) works better syntactically, but does not make sense of *b ḫrih w ṯnth* "in his feces and urine" (*Anthology of Religious Texts*, 136). (We should also note that de Moor's interpretation requires a cumbersome rearrangement of the poetic lines.) Pardee has proposed a different Arabic etymology from √*wls*, "walk with a quick step with wide strides and the neck stretched forward (as is said of a camel)" ("marcher d'un pas rapide à larges enjambées et le cou tendu en avant [se dit d'une chamelle]") (*Textes paramythologiques*, 63, citing Biberstein-Kazimirski, *Dictionnaire Arab-Français*, 2:992), thus offering the translation, "he bowls him over in his feces and his urine" (*COS* 1:304). I find this suggestion to be the most satisfactory, both for its ability to make sense of the context and its etymological plausibility.

ql il km mt	'Ilu falls like a dead man,
(22) *il k yrdm*[171] *árṣ*	'Ilu is like one descending to the earth.

Scholars have long noted this text's interest in matters of death and dying with its depiction of the drunken 'Ilu in terms of a dead person's descent into the underworld. The identification of 'Ilu's participation in his *marziḥu* in line 15 has led some scholars to define this ancient society as a cult of the dead. For example, Tropper marshals the *marziḥu* as evidence for an ancestor cult, describing it as a feasting event in which the participants invoke the favor of the *rpủm*.[172] Lewis pulls back slightly from this suggestion by recognizing its reputation as a drinking club, but still insists on maintaining a loose death cult association that in his mind must have developed after-the-fact.[173] Similarly, Hays wants to maintain that the cult of the dead was a significant facet of the *marziḥu*, but not necessarily its primary purpose.[174] The attempt to interpret the *marziḥu* as a ritualistic society for venerating the dead, however, remains unfounded. Pardee contends that even though the *marziḥu* was often devoted to a particular deity, the textual data confirm that it was nothing more than a social group whose primary interest was the consumption of wine.[175]

Rather than offering proof for the existence of a *marziḥu* death cult, death imagery is invoked in KTU 1.114 as a means of illustrating the state of drunkenness, which, incidentally, serves us well in analyzing Ugaritic conceptions of death and dying. I have already noted several other occasions in Ugaritic mythology where death involves falling or descending into the netherworld earlier in this chapter.[176] From this vantage point, I suggest viewing the corresponding imagery from the other direction by asking: How is drunkenness an appropriate representation of a dead person? From the context of KTU 1.114, 'Ilu's condition inhibits his locomotive ability, requiring Ṯukamuna-wa-Šunama to carry him along, and results in his toppling to the ground at ḤBY's trampling force. The picture is that of complete incapacitation, so much so that when 'Ilu falls to the ground his appearance is that of a lifeless corpse. Again, this picture brings to mind the dead ships mentioned in KTU 2.38, where "dead" seems to denote their loss of power for navigational movement in the seas. Here, drunkenness offers yet another portrayal of death as a loss of animation or life force.

171. I interpret this form as the masculine plural G participle from √*yrd* "those descending."

172. Tropper, *Nekromanti*, 159.

173. Lewis, *Cults of the Dead*, 2.

174. Hays, *Death in Iron Age II*, 117.

175. O'Connor, "Northwest Semitic Designations," 67–80; see also Pardee, "Ugaritic Funerary Cult," 278–79.

176. See my discussion of death in the Ba'lu cycle above (§§3.2.1.1 and 3.2.1.2).

The plural adjective *mtm* "the dead" occurs in the closing scene of the Baʿlu cycle (KTU 1.6 VI:48). This section has been described as a hymn rendering praise to Šapšu and her associates following her intervention in the final battle between Môtu and Baʿlu. This hymn may depict her nightly journey through the underworld, specifically highlighting her authority over the *rpủm* who were believed to reside there (KTU 1.6 VI):

ảp l tlḥm (44) *lḥm trmmt*[177]	Also, please eat the bread of offering,
l tšt (45) *yn tǵẓyt*	please drink the wine of libation.
špš (46) *rpỉm tḥtk*	Šapšu, you rule the *rpủm*,
(47) *špš tḥtk ỉlnym*	Šapšu, you rule the deities;
(48) *ʿdk ỉlm*	your company is the gods,
hn mtm	indeed, the dead.
(49) *ʿdk kṯrm ḥbrk*	Your company is Kôṯaru, your companion,
(50) *w ḫss dʿtk*	Ḫasīsu, the one you know.
(51) *b ym ảrš w tnn*	In the sea are ẢRŠ and the Dragon;
(52) *kṯr w ḫss yd*[178]	may Kôṯaru-wa-Ḫasīsu expel (them),
(53) *ytr*[179] *kṯr w ḫss*	may Kôṯaru-wa-Ḫasīsu banish (them).

The chief indicator of Šapšu's supremacy over the inhabitants of the underworld finds expression in lines 45–47 where the form *tḥtk* twice occurs. Many commentators have analyzed this form as the preposition *tḥt* with the 2ms suffix, "under you," as a reference to the sun's position above the earth with the inhabitants of the underworld below.[180] As a further development of this interpretation, Caquot brings out a more nuanced rendering for the preposition *tḥt* in his translation, "under your control," thus ascribing a certain governance to Šapšu.[181] Scholars have noted, however, that the oblique form *rpỉm* raises serious objections to the prepositional interpretation of *tḥtk*, since one would expect *rpủm* (nominative) in the verbless clause, "the Rapaʾūma are under you," and not the oblique form *rpỉm*.[182] Rather, the oblique form *rpỉm* most likely indicates that it

177. Cf. Hebrew *t^{e}rûmâ* "contribution, offering" < √*rwm* (BDB, 929).

178. Taking this form as a G stem jussive of √*ydy* "to cast out, expel" (see *DUL*, 958).

179. Taking this form as a G stem jussive of √*ntr* "to escape, banish" (see *DUL*, 652).

180. E.g., Charles Virolleaud, "Fragment Nouveau du poème de Môt et Aleyn-Baal (I AB)," *Syria* 15 (1934): 238; Theodor H. Gaster, "The Combat of ʾAleyân-Baʿal and Mōt: Two Missing Portions," *JRAS* 2 (1936): 232; René Dussaud, *Les découvertes de Ras Shamra (Ugarit) et l'Ancien Testament*, 2nd ed. (Paris: Geuthner, 1941), 187; Caquot and Sznycer, *Textes ougaritiques 1*, 270.

181. "Sous ta dépendance," André Caquot, "La divinité solaire ougaritique," *Syria* 36 (1959): 97.

182. Ginsberg, "Rebellion and Death of Baʿlu," 198 (cf. Ginsberg, *ANET*, 141); de Moor, *Seasonal Pattern*, 241; Pardee, *COS* 1:273 n. 279.

is the object of a verb, for which scholars have proposed the root *ḥtk*, a kinship term likely meaning, "to exercise paternal authority."[183] The noun form from this root occurs in KTU 1.16 II:15 meaning, "progenitor, father," and seems to denote "rule, authority" in KTU 1.108:23.[184]

Šapšu rules over the *rpủm* and the *ỉlnym*. The poetic pairing of these two terms reappears in the Rapa'ūma texts KTU 1.20 I:1–2 and 1.21 II:3–4, 11–12, though the broken nature of these texts warrant caution. As noted above, she is associated with underworld deities in KTU 1.161:19–22, where she commands the deceased kings to descend into the underworld, and earlier in the Baʿlu cycle, it is Šapšu, luminary of the gods (*nrt ỉlm*), who aids ʿAnatu in carrying the corpse of Baʿlu to the heights of Ṣapānu for burial (KTU 1.6 I:14–16).

All of these considerations concerning Šapšu and her prominent role in matters of the dead ought to inform our interpretation of *mtm* in KTU 1.6 VI:43. A few scholars have opted to read *mtm* as /mutūma/ "men," against those who render it as the adjective /mītūma/ "dead ones."[185] Schmidt contends that *mtm* must mean "humans," largely upon structural grounds, arguing for a chiastic arrangement of the text: A: *rpủm* "shades"; B: *ỉlnym* "gods"; B′: *ỉlm* "gods"; A′: *mtm* "men," so that the *rpủm* are associated with *mtm* "men," and the *ỉlnym* with the *ỉlm*.[186] Admittedly, this reading corresponds with Schmidt's proposal to deny that the *rpủm* were conceived to be divinized in any way, which I deny for reasons outlined more fully in the next chapter. Curiously, Wyatt adopts Schmidt's chiastic structure, but interprets its significance differently, suggesting that the arrangement of terms is according to an "inversion of rank": the *rpủm* are higher in rank than mortals, but are lower in rank than the chthonic gods of the underworld. Unlike Schmidt's belabored attempt to show that Šapšu actually did not descend into the underworld, Wyatt points out that during the day she reigns

183. De Moor, "Studies in the New Alphabetic Texts from Ras Shamra I," 179; Pardee, *COS* 1:273 n. 279. Other proposals include: "to divide" (George Barton, "The Second Liturgical Poem from Ras Shamra: A Liturgy for the Festival of the God Alein," *JAOS* 55 [1935]: 51); "to walk quickly" (cf. Arabic *ḥtk* "to hasten") (Gray, *Legacy of Canaan*, 2nd ed., 187; Gordon, *Ugaritic Textbook*, 399); "to care for" (Akkadian *etēku*) (Gordon, *Ugaritic Textbook*, 399; Dietrich and Loretz, "Baal *rpu*," 178); "to fix/establish (by judicial decision)" (Frank Moore Cross, "The Canaanite Cuneiform Tablet from Taanach," *BASOR* 190 [1968]: 45 n. 24); "to judge/preside over" (Lewis, *Cults of the Dead*, 36).

184. See Dietrich and Loretz, "Baal *rpu*," 178; Wyatt, *Religious Texts*, 398 n. 25.

185. As "men": Gray, *Legacy of Canaan*, 2nd ed., 187; del Olmo Lete, *Mitos y leyendas*, 235; Wyatt, *Religious Texts*, 144. As "dead ones": Caquot and Sznycer, *Textes ougaritiques* 1, 270; de Moor, *Seasonal Pattern*, 240; Lewis, *Cults of the Dead*, 36; Pardee, *COS* 1:273; Driver, *Canaanite Myths and Legends*, 2nd ed., 81.

186. Schmidt, *Israel's Beneficent Dead*, 86. Similarly, see L'Heureux, *Rank Among the Canaanite Gods*, 195–99; countered in J. N. Ford, "The 'Living Rephaim' of Ugarit: Quick or Defunct?" *UF* 24 (1992): 93–96.

over gods and mortals above, while she reigns over the *rpủm* and *ỉlnym* during her nightly trek through the underworld.[187] One gets the impression that Wyatt understands the *rpủm* in this text to be mere mortals located in the underworld, as Schmidt argues from the purported chiastic structure; however, elsewhere Wyatt calls them "divinized dead kings," an assessment not shared by Schmidt.[188]

Much of the issue here comes full circle to one's interpretation of *mtm* in line 48. Wyatt's concession on this point is rather telling: while agreeing with del Olmo Lete's translation, "men," the fact that Šapšu journeys through the underworld, he argues, may warrant understanding *mtm* "to include the dead."[189] Contextually, then, one wonders: Why prefer *mtm* "men" over *mtm* "the dead"? Furthermore, Schmidt's chiasm may not actually offer the best poetic analysis given that it does not consider the context of the following lines. Lines 45b–53 divide naturally into a series of three bicola with a concluding tricolon. Analysis of each poetic line reveals two chiasms: one in the first bicola and one in the concluding tricolon:

bicolon 1:	*špš*	*rpỉm*	*tḥtk*
	špš	*tḥtk*	*ỉlnym*
bicolon 2:	*ʿdk*	*ỉlm*	
	hn	*mtm*	
bicolon 3:	*ʿdk*	*kṯrm*	*ḥbrk*
	w	*ḫss*	*dʿtk*
tricolon:	*b ym*	*ảrš*	*wtnn*
	kṯr w ḫss		*yd*
	yṯr		*kṯr w ḫss*

These four groupings are linked together by a series of three repeated words (*špš* // *špš*; *ʿdk* //*ʿdk*; *kṯr w ḫss* // *kṯr w ḫss*), thus tying together bicola 2 and 3. In each of these three major divisions (bicolon 1 // bicola 2 and 3 // tricolon) the recurring theme of the hymn concerns Šapšu's entourage of assorted divinized beings: (1) *rpỉm* // *ỉlnym*; (2) *ỉlm* // *mtm* and *kṯr* // *ḫss*; (3) *kṯr w ḫss* // *kṯr w ḫss*. According to this poetic analysis, *mtm* "men" would be thematically intrusive, while the case for *mtm* "the dead" is much stronger for the following two reasons: (1) it is parallel to *ỉlm*, which suggests "(divinized) dead," and (2) the

187. Wyatt, *Religious Texts*, 144 n. 123.

188. Wyatt, *Religious Texts*, 315 n. 1.

189. Del Olmo Lete, *Mitos y leyendas*, 235. Wyatt, *Religious Texts*, 144 n. 122.

appearance of *rpỉm* (//*ỉlnym*, thus, "dead, divinized kings") in the preceding bicolon.[190] Therefore, I render *mtm* here as "dead ones," or more precisely, "(divinized) dead."

Also relevant to this discussion is the appearance of *mtm* in the Rapaʾūma text KTU 1.20 I:3, which offers a usage corresponding to what I am arguing for KTU 1.6 VI:48. KTU 1.20 I:1–3 reads as follows:

(1) [	*rp*]⌜*ủ*⌝*m tdbḥn*	[the RP]ỦM you shall give a sacrifice/prepare a feast,
(2) [	]⌜*b*⌝*ʿd ỉlnym*	[se]ven (times) the deities,
(3) [	]⌜?⌝*mt mtm*[191]	[ ] the men of the dead,

The sequence {mt mtm} in line 3 is not without difficulty, especially in light of the broken nature of the first portions of lines 1–10 of this tablet, therefore rendering my comments here provisional. One of the fundamental challenges of these lines has to do with the consonantal sequence *mtmtm* in line 3. Various proposals have been made, depending on whether one reads {k} or {w} before it: *k mt mtm* "when men have died," *km tmtm* "so that when you (pl.) die," (⌜*w*⌝) *mt mtm* "men of/among the dead" (i.e., "dead men").[192] At least poetically, the phrase in question is parallel with [*rp*]⌜*ủ*⌝*m* and *ỉlnym* of the preceding two lines. The identical parallel *rpủm* // *ỉlnym* in KTU 1.6 VI:46–48 immediately preceding the poetic pair *ỉlm* // *mtm* should inform our interpretation of KTU 1.20 I:1–3, where *mtmtm* is parallel with both *rpủm* and *ỉlnym*. In this case, there does not

190. For a defense of this interpretation, see ch. 4. A condensed version of this argument also appears in Matthew McAffee, "Rephaim, Whisperers, and the Dead in Isaiah 26:13–19," *JBL* 135 (2016): 79–80.

191. From the photographs provided through Inscriptifact, the first visible sign is chipped in the middle of the sign so that its identity is uncertain. Scholars have suggested {k} or {w}, both of which would seem to fit in the allotted space, but the individual wedges of the sign are not legible from the most recent photographs. Immediately following this illegible sign one can make out a faint {m}, after which there occurs {tmtm}, yielding the sequence *w/k mtmtm*. Wayne Pitard helpfully observes that earlier photographs must be examined regarding the first letter of this sequence, since the tablet has been damaged since its initial discovery ("A New Edition of the 'Rāpiʾūma' Texts: KTU 1.20–22," *BASOR* 285 [1992]: 44). Both the photograph of Virolleaud (*Légende phénicienne de Danel*, plate 17) and that of *CTA* (plate 31) seem to support reading {w} just before the first {m}: ⌜w⌝mt mtm. In a recent epigraphic and literary study of this text, however, Dennis Pardee reads a partially restored {k} ("Nouvelle étude épigraphique et littéraire des textes fragmentaires en langue ougaritique dits 'Les Rephaïm' [*CTA* 20–22]," *Or* 80 [2011]: 39). L'Heureux suggested reading the disputed sign as an {ả} (*ảmtm*), but this proposal has not gained much support (*Rank Among the Canaanite Gods*, 130–31).

192. *k mt mtm*: Caquot and Sznycer, *Textes ougaritiques* 1, 477 n. a; Theodore J. Lewis, "The Rapiuma," in, *Ugaritic Narrative Poetry*, ed. Simon B. Parker, WAW 9 (Atlanta: Scholars Press, 1997), 197: "like the ancient dead." *km tmtm*: Del Olmo Lete, *Mitos y leyendas*, 417. (⌜*w*⌝)*mt mtm*: Wyatt, *Religious Texts*, 315 n. 4; Pitard reads ⌜*w*⌝*mtmtm*, but without translation ("New Edition," 42).

appear to be an exegetical way around reading the sequence *mtmtm* as in one way or another referring to the dead: either *km tmtm* "when you die" or *mt mtm* "men of/among the dead," in which only one of the two forms could be taken as a derivative of /mutu/ "man." This occurrence of *mtm* therefore supports my interpretation of the same form in KTU 1.6 VI:48 and thus offers another example of the masculine plural adjective "dead (persons)," who, in both contexts, are associated with the *rpủm*. I will return to a fuller analysis of the *rpủm* in chapter 4.

Four additional instances of *mtm* are found in the Ugaritic corpus, but given their broken contexts we are unable to secure a lucid interpretation. I list them here for the sake of completion, acknowledging that each of the three forms could be analyzed in one of two ways: (1) masculine plural adjective /mītūma/ "the dead," or (2) masculine singular noun /mutu/ "man" + enclitic {m}.

KTU 1.15 V

(12) [ʿl] krt . tbkn	[Over] Kirta you must weep,
(13) [km .]rgm . ṯrm	[like] the expressions of bulls.
(14) [?]? . mtm . tbkn	... the dead/man you must weep
(15) [?]t . w b lb . tqb[rn]	... and in the heart you must bury (him),
(16) [?]qmṣ . mtm . ủṣbʿ[t]	... the distance of the dead/man with regard to the finger (?)

KTU 1.10 I:10
[ ] . mtm

KTU 4.195:16
ṯt . tg[?] . l . mtm

3.3.2. Nominal Forms

We now move on to consider possible nominal forms of the root *mwt*. Two nominal forms occur throughout the Ugaritic corpus, one being the masculine singular form *mt* "death," with or without enclitic {m}, the other being the *t*-preformative feminine singular form *tmtt* "death." As it relates to the first of these two noun types, the line of distinction between death in the abstract and the personified deity Death/Môtu runs thin, since four of the five cases examined below could allude to both senses at the same time.[193]

193. There are three other occurrences of *mt* identified for this study, but the broken nature of their respective contexts prohibits interpretation (KTU 1.12 II:41; 1.18 I:28; 1.19 I:17).

The first clear instance of the noun *mt* "death" is found alongside a verbal form of the same root *ảmt*) in the ʾAqhatu Epic (KTU 1.17 VI:38) in the midst of the well-known dialogue between the hero and the goddess ʿAnatu as she attempts to acquire his coveted bow. I have dealt with this passage at length already, and thus I offer an abbreviated rendering of it here:

(38) [*ảp*]*mt kl ảmt*	I [also] will die the death of all;
w ản mtm ảmt	and I myself must certainly die."[194]

In response to ʿAnatu's offer of immortality, ʾAqhatu retorts that he is a mere mortal subject to die the death of all men. Here, the "death of all" is placed in contrast with the kind of life Baʿlu enjoys—preservation through revivification. More exactly, *mt kl* refers to the finality of death and the fact that there is no return for mortals once they are dead, unlike Baʿlu who perpetually comes back to life. The hero scoffs at this offer and affirms his own mortality.

Four other attestations of the masculine singular noun *mt* occur in contexts that may evoke the deity Môtu. The first two passages have likewise already been treated above, both of which occur in the Kirta Epic in the midst of the successful healing efforts of Šaʿtiqatu, having been sent by ʾIlu to save the fatally ill King Kirta. The first instance appears in ʾIlu's final pronouncement over Šaʿtiqatu as he sends her out to save Kirta (KTU 1.16 VI:1–2):

(1) [*m*]t *dm ḫt*	O [de]ath, be shattered,
šʿtqt dt (2) *lỉ*	O Šaʿtiqatu, be powerful.

The second comes at the end of her healing ritual (KTU 1.16 VI:13–14):

(10) *w tṯb trḥṣ nn b dʿt*	She sits down, washes him with regard to his sweat,
(11) *npšh l lḥm tptḥ*	she opens his throat (for) eating,
(12) *brlth l ṯrm*	his gullet for feeding.
(13) *mt dm ḫt*	Death is shattered,
šʿtqt (14) *dm lản*	Šaʿtiqatu is powerful.[195]

That these two texts may be intended to evoke the deity Môtu is suggested by the mythological depiction of King Kirta's healing: the goddess Šaʿtiqatu, fashioned and commissioned by ʾIlu, shatters the effects of death over Kirta.[196] Šaʿtiqatu

194. See chs. 1 (§1.2.2.1) and 3 (§3.2.3.1).

195. On these texts, see ch. 2 (§2.2.2.2).

196. For a recent treatment of this text, see Theodore J. Lewis, "The Shaʿtiqatu Narrative from the Ugaritic Story about the Healing of King Kirta," *JANER* 13 (2013): 188–211.

is not a full-fledged deity of the Ugaritic pantheon, however, so her power is displayed in being able to eradicate the sickness of Kirta and stave off his death, rather than the shattering of the death god himself. That is something even Baʿlu cannot do. Moreover the circumstances also evoke Môtu's destructive presence existing behind the scenes, presenting Šaʿtiqatu's miraculous ability at limiting his power over King Kirta.

A third case wherein the noun *mt* seems to evoke the god Môtu appears in KTU 2.10:12. This letter records correspondence concerning the outbreak of a deadly plague among the military forces of the addressees, TRǴDS and KLBY.[197] The form is *mtm*, which I analyze as a masculine singular with enclitic {m}:

(1) *tḥm ỉwrḏr*	Message of ỈWRḎR:
(2) *l plsy*	To PLSY
(3) *rgm*	say:
(4) *yšlm lk*	May it be well with you.
(5) *l trǵds*	Concerning TRǴDS
(6) *w l klby*	and KLBY,
(7) *šmʿt ḫtỉ*	I have heard that they were utterly
(8) *nḫtủ ht*	crushed. Now,
(9) *hm ỉnmm*	if it is not the case that
(10) *nḫtủ w lảk*	they were crushed, send (word)
(11) *ʿmy w yd*	to me. The hand
(12) *ỉlm p k mtm*	of the gods is here, for death/Môtu
(13) *ʿz mỉd*	is exceedingly strong.
(14) *hm nṯkp*	If they have been defeated,
(15) *mʿnk*	your reply
(16) *w mnm*	and whatever
(17) *rgm d tšmʿ*	word that you hear
(18) *ṯmt w št*	there, place
(19) *b spr ʿmy*	in a letter to me.

197. For the *editio princeps,* see Édouard Dhorme, "Deux tablettes de Ras-Shamra de la campagne de 1932," *Syria* 14 (1933): 235–37 and pl. xxv. See also Ginsberg and Maisler, "Semitised Ḫurrians," 243–67; William F. Albright, "Two Letters from Ugarit (Ras Shamrah)," *BASOR* 82 (1941): 43–49; Manfried Dietrich, Oswald Loretz, and Joaquín Sanmartín, "Der Brief RS 4.475 = CTA 53," *UF* 7 (1975): 529–30; W. H. Ph. Römer, "Zur Deutung zweier Briefe aus Ugarit in alphabetischer Keilschrift," in *Übersetzung und Deutung: Studien zu Alten Testament und seiner Umwelt Alexander Reinhard Hulst gewidmet von Freunden und Kollegen* (Nijkerk: Callenboch, 1977), 135–53; Pardee, "As Strong as Death," 65–69; Pardee, *COS* 3:107–8; Eduard Lipiński, "Allusions historiques dans la correspondence ougaritique de Ras Shamra: Lettre de Ewri-Šarri à Plisiya," *UF* 13 (1981): 123–26; Cunchillos, *Textes ougaritiques II,* 275–80.

The importance of this particular example is that it potentially yields a reference to divinized Death outside the mythological context, here associating him with a severe plague being experienced in a real-world setting.

One of the principal issues of interpretation in this passage concerns the meaning of the phrase *w yd ỉlm p*, as well as its relationship to the clause immediately following: *k mtm ʿz mỉd*. Pardee has noted parallels from Akkadian literature where *qātu* "hand" with a given deity often denotes illness/sickness or pestilence/plague. One example will suffice here from EA 35 (BM 29788):

> *šum-ma i-na* KUR-*ia* ŠU-*ti* ^{d}MAŠ-MAŠ EN-*li-ia gab-ba* LU.MEŠ *ša* KUT-*ia i-du-uk*
>
> Indeed, the hand of my lord Nergal is in my land; he has slain all the men of my land.[198]

The same association is found in Exod 9:3 regarding YHWH's plagues against Pharaoh and the Egyptians:

> *hinnê yad-yhwh hôyâ bᵉmiqnᵉkā ʾᵃšer baśśādê bassûsîm baḥᵃōrîm baggᵉmallîm babbāqār ûbaṣṣōʾn deber kābēd mᵉʾōd*
>
> Indeed, the hand of YHWH is on your property that is in the field—on horses, donkeys, camels, large cattle, and small cattle—with a severe plague.

In the biblical text, *yad-yhwh* is further qualified by *deber kābēd mᵉʾōd* "a severe plague." One thing that emerges from these examples and others like them (from Akkadian) is that a singular deity is in view, therefore making the analysis of *ỉlm* as a plural less likely. This would require that *ỉlm* be a singular with enclitic {m} (like *mtm*) and thus refers to a particular god—in this case, Môtu as identified in the next clause.[199]

Interpreters have been divided over whether to take *k* as the comparative, "the hand of the god here is as strong as death," or causal, "the hand of the god

198. See A. Leo Oppenheim, *Letters from Mesopotamia: Official, Business, and Private Letters on Clay Tablets from Two Millennia* (Chicago: University of Chicago Press, 1967), 120. For additional examples, see those cited in Pardee, "As Strong as Death," 67, as well as *CAD* 13:186–87. For more on this idiom, see J. J. M. Roberts, "The Hand of Yahweh," *VT* 21 (1971): 244–51.

199. Similarly Pardee, "As Strong as Death," 68.

is here, for Death is exceedingly strong."[200] One of the main problems with the comparative interpretation is that the adjective *ʿz* "strong" is not markedly feminine, which would be expected were the hand (fem.) of the god being compared with the strength of Death. This grammatical problem renders the causal interpretation much more favorable, "for Death is exceedingly strong," which would mean that ỈWRḎR considered the divine plague to be the workings of none other than Môtu, the god of death. Môtu's association with the plague of this text corroborates with his role in KTU 1.82:5, where he is the subject of an incantation for venomous snake bite and stands in close proximity to Rašap (line 3), who seems to share an equally calamitous reputation.[201] Just as the incantation of KTU 1.82 seeks to reverse/stop the destruction of the gods in the venom of snakes, so the author of this letter attributes death by plague on the battlefield to the strength of the god Môtu.

One further occurrence of the noun *mt* "death" is found in KTU 1.100, a ritual text (with mythological features) that is apparently intended to deal with the problem of horses having been bitten by poisonous snakes. The first major section of this text (lines 1–60) consists of a series of twelve appeals to major deities, each section introduced by a call to Šapšu with each deity apparently being unsuccessful, followed by a special appeal to Ḥôrānu with his subsequent success (lines 61–69), and ends with a concluding ritual (lines 70–79).[202] The mythological aspect of this text is that of a mare interceding with the gods on behalf of her snake-bitten foal. I am interested in the latter part of this text and its reference to *ʿṣ mt* "tree of death":

ydy b ʿṣm ʿrʿr	He casts a tamarisk from among the trees,
(65) *w b šḥt ʿṣ mt*	from among bushes (he casts) the tree of death.
ʿrʿrm ynʿrảh[203]	With the tamarisk he shakes it off,

200. In a comparative sense: Dhorme, "Deux tablettes de Ras-Shamra," 235; Ginsberg and Maisler, "Semitised Hurrians," 243; Pope, *Song of Songs*, 668; Cunchillos, *Textes ougaritiques II*, 279 n. 16. For the causal view, see, e.g., Albright, "Two Letters from Ugarit," 47; Römer, "Zur Deutung zweier Briefe," 150; Pardee, "As Strong as Death," 68 (followed by Ron Hendel, "The Exodus in Biblical Memory," *JBL* 120 [2001]: 612).

201. It is Môtu who is clearly associated with "plague" at Ugarit, more so than Rašap, gatekeeper of the underworld (see above, §3.2.2.1.2).

202. Pardee, *Ritual and Cult*, 172–73. See also Pardee, *Textes paramythologiques*, 193–226 (with bibliography); Michael C. Astour, "Two Ugaritic Serpent Charms," *JNES* 27 (1968): 13–36; Caquot, *Textes ougaritiques 2*, 79–94; Simon B. Parker, "The Mare and Horon" in Parker, *Ugaritic Narrative Poetry*, 219–23; del Olmo Lete, *Canaanite Religion*, 2nd ed., 305–15; Manfried Dietrich and Oswald Loretz, *Studien zu den ugaritischen Texten I: Mythos, und Ritual in KTU 1.12, 1.24, 1.96, 1.100 und 1.114*, AOAT 269 (Münster: Ugarit-Verlag, 2000), 390–92; Wyatt, *Religious Texts*, 378–94.

203. Reading *ynʿrnh*, the {ả} being an error for {n} resulting from the omission of the third horizontal wedge. On this root, cf. Hebrew *nʿr* (II) "to shake off" (*HALOT*, 707).

(66) *ssnm ysynh*[204]	with the date-palm branch he strikes it,
ʿdtm yʿdynh	with the flowing he makes it disappear,
yb(67)*ltm*[205] *yblnh*	with the carrier he carries it.

This portion of the text renders the climactic work of Ḥôrānu in the removal of the snake venom from the ailing horse. The acts of this incantation are depicted utilizing the following verbs of motion: *ydy* "to cast," *nʿr* "to shake off," *nsy* "to drive out," and *ybl* "to carry." The importance of the tamarisk tree (*ʿrʿr*) is evident from its being mentioned first in the preparations for this ritual (lines 64b–65a) and its occurrence at the top of the list of the other three plants employed in the ritual expulsion of the venom.[206] Michael C. Astour identifies Akkdian cognates for three of the four plant names listed here and documents their usage in the Mesopotamian *namburbê* rite, which served to deliver individuals from all manner of evil. These particular plants were apparaently chosen for use in the the ritual for their purported magical and purifying properties.[207] The "tamarisk" is specifically qualified by the the poetic parallel *ʿṣ mt*. For this association, Astour cites the Babylonian deity Nergal, who is often identified in Akkadian sources as the god of the tamarisk.[208] Accordingly, this particular tree is identified as the ritual weapon of choice against death (interpreting *mt* as an objective genitive), rendering yet another correspondence with the snake venom rituals of KTU 1.82 for humans where Môtu is likewise exorcised.

The usage of *mt* in these four texts offers important insights concerning the worldview of Ugarit. They provide evidence for how the Ugaritians perceived the intersection of their own physical world of sickness and disease with the mythological world of the battling gods. In each of these cases, the

204. I analyze this form as a G SC of √*nss* + 3fs suff., noting the Arabic cognate *nassa* "to postpone/delay, push/drive back" (Lane, 2785; cf. Heb. *nss* "to stagger to and fro" [*HALOT*, 703]; Akk. *nussusu* "shake" [*AHw* 2:806]), here with the meaning "drive out, expel" (Astour, "Two Ugaritic Serpent Charms," 25). Other proposed etymologies include: *nsy* "to test, prove" (Manfried Dietrich and Oswald Loretz, "Die Bannung von Schlangengift (KTU 1.100 und KTU 1.107:7b–13a. 19b–20)," *UF* 12 [1980]: 162; Caquot, *Textes ougaritiques* 2, 92 n. 285); *nsy* (II) "to hit, lash (the legs)" (*DUL*, 645, citing Arabic *nasā*); Akkadian *nesû* "to take off" (de Moor, *Anthology of Religious Texts*, 154 n. 29).

205. Most likely an unidentified ancient plant name associated with the root *ybl* "to carry" (Astour, "Two Ugaritic Serpent Charms," 25; Pardee, *COS* 1:298 n. 26).

206. Pardee, *Textes paramythologiques*, 216. The femine suffixes attached to these verbs undoubtedly refer to the feminine noun *ḥmt* "venom," last mentioned in line 60.

207. Astour, "Two Ugaritic Serpent Charms," 23–24.

208. Astour, "Two Ugaritic Serpent Charms," 25 n. 72. Akkadian: *bīnu* (GIŠ.ŠINIG) (*CAD* 2:239). Note also Johannes C. de Moor's suggested link between the tree of death and the tree of life (*ʿēṣ haḥayyîm*) from Gen 2:9 ("East of Eden," *ZAW* 100 [1988]: 105–11).

mythological personification of Death seems to offer some means of coping with the unavoidable frailty of life, human or otherwise.

Finally, we now turn our attention to the single occurrence of *tmtt* in the letter KTU 2.38.[209] This form has been interpreted in one of three ways: (1) *t*-preformative noun related to /mutu/ "man," (2) *t*-preformative noun from the root *mwt* meaning "death," or (3) *t*-preformative noun related to Arabic *matta* "to extend, draw" meaning "port." It occurs twice in this letter as the writer apparently explains to the recipient that he had taken all items from the hand of the *rb tmtt* (lines 20–22) who had initially confiscated them from the wrecked ships (lines 16–17). Virolleaud understood the expression *rb tmtt* to refer to a sort of gang leader, or pirate, noting the Hebrew cognate *tᵉmûtâ*, an abstract noun meaning "death," thus, "chief of death."[210] Gordon took this phrase rather literally as an epithet of "some deity such as Ršp or Mt," translating it "Lord of Death."[211] Dietrich and Loretz (and others) have suggested that *tmtt* is a collective noun derived from *mt* "man" meaning "humankind."[212] According to this interpretation, *tmtt* as a collective refers to a group of men, in this case, the crew of the ship, and *rb tmtt* therefore denotes the crew's captain. Lipiński goes in an entirely differing direction, citing the Arabic verb *matta* meaning "to extend, draw near, approach."[213] He suggests that the noun form *tmtt* is a naval term for "port" or "moorings," and that the *rb tmtt* would then refer to the chief port official.[214] Conversely, Hoftijzer has maintained the *tmtt* < *mt* (= death) etymology, but offers a naval interpretation whereby the *rb tmtt* signifies an official in charge of salvaging wrecked ships.[215]

The earlier view that regarded *rb tmtt* as a divine epithet seems rather intrusive to the setting of this letter, not to mention the fact that for such a meaning one would expect *rb mt*, not *rb tmtt*, since Môtu is never referred to in this way elsewhere. It is also difficult to ascertain the significance of this portion of the letter if *rb tmtt* refered to the captain of the crew. Why would the king of Tyre

209. For text and translation, see §3.3.2.4 above.

210. "Death": BDB, 560. "Chief of death": Virolleaud, *PRU* 5:82.

211. Gordon, *Ugaritic Textbook*, 498; cf. Mitchell Dahood's translation of *bd rb tmtt lqḥt* as "And I snatched X from the hand(s) of the Master of Death (=Mot)" (*Psalms I: 1–50*, AB 16 (Garden City, NY: Doubleday, 1965], 302).

212. "Mannschaft"; Manfried Dietrich and Oswald Loretz, "Zur ugaritischen Lexikographie (I)," *BO* 23 (1966): 132; cf. Manfried Dietrich, Oswald Loretz, and Joaquín Sanmartín, "Zur Ugaritischen Lexicographie [VII]," *UF* 5 (1973): 93; Cunchillos, *Textes ougaritiques II*, 354 n. 17; *DUL*, 872.

213. See Lane, 339.

214. Eduard Lipiński, "Recherches ugaritiques," *Syria* 44 (1967): 282.

215. Hoftijzer, "Lettre du Roi de Tyr," 386, as suggested earlier by Sasson, "Canaanite Maritime Involvement," 282 (but without philological comment).

inform the king of Ugarit that the captain had "taken" the contents of the ships, which were "in their [the ships?] possession"? In whose possession were these contents and why did the king of Tyre need to retrieve them from the captain, only to hand them over to them (crew?) again? Lipiński's analysis is certainly plausible and is preferable to the former, but one wonders if it best accounts for the context. Hoftijzer's interpretation is supported by the fact that these ships are described as being dead in the water: *ảnykn dt likt mṣrm hndt b ṣr mtt* "Your ships that you sent to Egypt are dead (in the water) at Tyre" (lines 10–13). As explained above, the description of these ships as "dead" involved their being stripped (*ʿryt*) of rigging and thus immobilized.[216] It is conceivable to see a connection between the situation involving "dead" ships and the Tyrian official who takes it upon himself to salvage them. If this interpretation of *tmtt* is correct, I propose rendering *rb tmtt* as "chief of (naval) wreckage operations" or the like, or more simply "salvage master."[217] The basis for the letter itself is the Tyrian king's desire to inform the king of Ugarit that he had suspended salvage operations for these particular ships—apparently the rescue of all valuable goods and persons remaining in the ships—and that they were docked in ʿAcco (stripped of rigging) awaiting further orders.

The feminine noun *tmtt* provides another interpretive datum in this analysis of death at ancient Ugarit, only this time it comes from a letter inscribed by one of its closest neighbors. In this particular case, the death of ships is not conceived as their final termination, but instead presents their incapacitation and their rescue carried out by the officer in charge of salvage procedures, the *rb tmtt* "master of death."

3.3.3. The Death God Môtu

Personified Death is one of the hallmark features of the Ugaritic conception of death, not only attested in its mythologies and epics, but also bleeding over into the psyche of the common with his appearance in incantation and epigraphy. Already in this study we have encountered the death god of Ugarit numerous times, especially in treating the lexeme *npš* in chapter 2, not to mention the death (above) and revivification (ch. 1) of Baʿlu. The following list provides every instance of the death god Môtu analyzed in this study.

216. See §3.2.4, above.
217. Pardee, *COS* 3:94 and n. 44.

KTU	Text	Summary
1.3 V:18	Baʿlu Cycle (broken)	ʾIlu's response to ʿAnatu concerning her request for a palace on behalf of Baʿlu
1.4 VII:46, 47	Baʿlu Cycle	Baʿlu determines to send Môtu a message in which he boasts of power and taunts him
1.4 VIII:17, 23, 26, 30	Baʿlu Cycle	Message of Baʿlu to Môtu (delivered by messengers)
1.5 I:7	Baʿlu Cycle	Message of Môtu in response to Baʿlu (spoken by Môtu)
1.5 I:13	Baʿlu Cycle	Message of Môtu in response to Baʿlu (delivered by messengers)
1.5 II:8, 11, 14, 19, 20	Baʿlu Cycle	Message of Baʿlu in response to Môtu (spoken by Baʿlu)
1.5 III:9, 18, 25	Baʿlu Cycle (broken)	"(to) Môtu I cry out" (3×)
1.6 II:9, 12, 13, 25, 31	Baʿlu Cycle	ʿAnatu punishes Môtu for killing Baʿlu
1.6 V:4	Baʿlu Cycle	Uncertain reading[218]
1.6 V:9	Baʿlu Cycle	Môtu castigating Baʿlu after having been destroyed by ʿAnatu
1.6 VI:5, 7, 9	Baʿlu Cycle (broken)	???
1.6 VI: 17, 18, 20, 21, 23, 24, 30, 31	Baʿlu Cycle	Final contest between Baʿlu and Môtu in which Šapšu intervenes
1.16 VI:1, 13	Kirta Epic	death/Môtu shattered in the ritual of Šaʿtiqatu for sick King Kirta
1.82:5	Incantation	Môtu invoked in incantation concerning venomous snake bite
1.133:2, 9	Scribal Exercise	// 1.5 I:12–16
2.10:12	Letter	"The hand of a god is here, for death/Môtu is exceedingly strong"

218. Perhaps: *ṣḥr mt*, following Herdner, who duly notes the uncertainty of this reading (*CTA*, 41 n. 8). *CAT* reads: *ṣǵrm*. The color photographs available at Inscriptifact show that the text is badly damaged at the beginning of lines 4–7 in column V of KTU 1.6.

It is not suprising to see that the bulk of references to the death god occur in the Baʿlu cycle. However, it is also important to recognize that this theology of death was not limited to the realm of mythology. His reach can be seen in the royal courts of the Epic of King Kirta in his life and death struggle to survive, amid battlefield correspondence concerning a deadly plague, and in the world of ritual where the gods are invoked to mitigate his potency channeled through the deadly venom of vipers. From these examples of Death's personification it would appear that the Ugaritians were interpreting the threats against one's life in terms of the mythological—Šaʿtiqatu battles the powers of Môtu over Kirta; Šapšu is invoked against Môtu and the arrows of Rašap; death on the battlefield is the plague of Môtu.

3.3.3.1. Epithets of Môtu

Throughout the mythological texts, the main formulaic title of Môtu is *bn ỉlm mt* "Môtu, son of ʾIlu."[219] Closely related to this epithet is ʾIlu's identification as Môtu's father: *ỉl ảbk* "ʾIlu your father."[220] The second title for the death god is *ydd ỉlm ġzr* "the valiant beloved of ʾIlu," always occurring in parallel with *bn ỉlm mt*.[221]

The primary epithet *bn ỉlm* "son of ʾIlu" places the death god within the pantheon of the Ugaritic high gods under the paternal/chief god ʾIlu. The semantics of the term *bn* are not always limited to the familial context in Ugaritic, nor is this the case in the Semitic languages in general.[222] In addition to filial connotations, one finds this noun referring to members of a particular group or class. For example, *bn nšm* "sons of men" simply denotes the class of human beings, and correspondingly *bn ỉl*(*m*) "son of the god(s)" indicates the divine class.[223] In the ʾAqhatu Epic, ʿAnatu promises to grant the warrior ʾAqhatu a semidivine existence comparable to Baʿlu, who is qualified in the poetic narrative with the parallel *bn ỉl* "son of ʾIlu" (KTU 1.17 VI:29). According to this perspective, *bn ỉlm* refers to Môtu's status as a major deity within the Ugaritic pantheon. Yet, the filial quality of this epithet is not so easily eliminated from the narrative's depiction of the relationship shared between these divine beings. A case in point is Šapšu's address to Môtu from KTU 1.6 VI:26–27: *ỉk ảl yšmʿk ṯr ỉl ảbk* "How indeed can the bull, ʾIlu your father, listen to you?" The fact that this text specifically

219. KTU 1.4 VII:45–46; 1.4 VIII:16, 30; 1.5 I:7, 12–13; 1.5 II:8, 11, 14, 19, 20; 1.6 II:13, 25, 31; 1.6 V:9; 1.6 VI:7, 9, 24, 30; 1.133:1–2, 15.

220. KTU 1.6 VI:27.

221. KTU 1.4 VII:46–47; 1.4 VIII:31–32; 1.5 I:8, 13–14; 1.5 II:9; 1.6 VI:30–31; 1.133:16–17. Cf. the single variation: KTU 1.4 VIII:23–24.

222. For Ugaritic, see the references in *DUL*, 224–27. For other Semitic languages, see *HALOT*, 137–38; *DNWSI*, 168–72; *CAD* 2:238–39, 242–43.

223. For *bn nšm*, see, e.g., KTU 1.6 II:18.

identifies the god 'Ilu as the father of Môtu would seem to indicate a filial tie. It also warrants interpreting the final {m} of Môtu's title as enclitic, and not the plural morpheme—"son of 'Ilu" and not "son of the gods"—since it is the personal name 'Ilu and not the generic word for divinity. This observation corroborates with the similar title for Baʿlu, *bn dgn* "son of Dagan," which is followed by, [*w yʿ*]*n ṯr ỉbh ỉl* "the bull, his father 'Ilu, replied," again signifying the filial nature of the relationship between Baʿlu and 'Ilu.[224]

The second title for Môtu, *ydd ỉlm ǵzr*, contains two noteworthy features. First of all, this epithet describes the death god as *ydd ỉlm* "beloved of 'Ilu." Evidence for taking Ugaritic *ydd* as being derived from a I-*w* root *wdd* is found in the Arabic verb *wadda* meaning "to love."[225] Akkadian also attests *namaddu* (II) "favorite, beloved one" and *mudādu* "beloved one," and in Old Aramaic the substantive *mwddw* is fairly well-attested, as well as *mwdd* at Sam'al meaning "friend."[226] Hebrew shows several derivatives for this same root: *yᵉdīdût* "loved one," *yādîd* "beloved," and *yᵉdîdôt* "love."[227] The Ugaritic form *ydd* in this divine title is likely a *qatīl* adjective, "beloved one." The variation *mdd ỉlm* (KTU 1.4 VIII:23–24) occurs once, but it is without the accompanying *ǵzr* "valiant one" and the usual parallel *bn ỉlm* "son of 'Ilu."[228]

As an expression of affection, *ydd ỉl* makes the best sense if the parallel title *bn ỉlm* is granted its full filial quality. Oddly enough, *ydd ỉl* presents the god of death as the object of 'Ilu's affection. One might also assume from Šapšu's remarks in KTU 1.6 VI:26–27 that 'Ilu manifests a level of empathy for Môtu, "How can the Bull, your father 'Ilu, listen to you?," which implies that 'Ilu does

224. Note that this is the "*bn* of X" title attested for Baʿlu in Ugaritic mythology, not *bn ỉl*(*m*), which is used of Môtu. This may warrant distinguishing the usage of *bn ỉl* in the 'Aqhatu Epic (KTU 1.17 VI:29) from *bn ỉlm* as an appellative for Môtu: *bn ỉl* for Baʿlu in 'Aqhatu Epic = divine being; *bn ỉlm* for Môtu in Baʿlu cycle = son of the deity 'Ilu. King Kirta shares the royal titularly *bnm ỉl* (KTU 1.16 I:10, 20; II:48), granting him semidivine status as a "son of 'Ilu" (see Pardee, *COS* 1:243 n. 13). As with Baʿlu and Môtu, the Kirta Epic calls 'Ilu the father of Kirta (KTU 1.14 I:38–43):

m ảt krt k ybky	Who is Kirta that he would weep,
ydmʿ nʿmn ǵlm ỉl	(that) the goodly one of 'Ilu would shed tears?
mlk ṯr ảbh yảrš	Does he request the kingship of the Bull, his father,
hm drk[*t*] *k ảb ảdm*	or dominion like (that of) the father of humankind?"

Here, it would seem that King Kirta has been granted a special status as 'Ilu's (adopted?) son, apparently distinct from what is experienced by the rest of humanity as expressed in 'Ilu's epithet *ảb ảdm* "father of humankind."

225. Lane, 2931.

226. *namaddu*: *CAD* 11:207. *mudādu*: *CAD* 10:160, analyzed as a West Semitic loanword. For Old Aramaic, see *DNWSI*, 602–3. For Sam'al, see KAI 214.24, 27.

227. *HALOT*, 389–90. Note also *mwdd* in 1QIs[a] 14:31 for MT *bôdēd* (as observed in *HALOT*).

228. Perhaps a D stem passive participle, or a *m*-preformative noun.

in fact listen to the death god at some level, but that his conflict with Baʿlu could potentially jeopardize this relationship. From what is known about Môtu from the texts analyzed in this chapter, it is surprising that the terror inducing death god would enjoy such a favorable status with ʾIlu. This factor has led de Moor to observe that Ugaritic mythology presents Death in somewhat sympathetic terms, almost as a "sad, even tragic figure."[229]

The next observable feature of this second title for Môtu is that he is called a *ǵzr*. The interpretation of this noun is not without difficulty.[230] It is most commonly rendered "warrior" or "hero" as a reference to Môtu's fighting ability. Cassuto points to the Arabic root *ǵzr*, meaning "to be many, great of strength, mighty," and compares the use of the Hebrew expression *ʿzry hmlḥmh* "mighty men of battle" in 1 Chr 12:1.[231] Strictly speaking, the Arabic root *ǵzr* has more to do with "abundance" or "plenty," which has led several scholars to take the Ugaritic term similarly, perhaps as a reference to one's prime of life or youthful vigor.[232] Another approach is to understand *ǵzr* cultically, as Cutler and McDonald advance, citing its purported parallels with other cultic terms, but this proposal is somewhat restrictive and does not allow for the broader range of its usage.[233] Admittedly, its distribution throughout Ugaritic makes *ǵzr* difficult to sort out semantically. For example, although this word refers to the youthful ʾIluḥaʾu and not his father Kirta in KTU 1.16 I:46, it describes both Dānîʾilu and ʾAqhatu in the ʾAqhatu Epic, which would defy its exclusion to the young. Ugaritic also seems to support the warrior imagery associated with this word, as it occurs in KTU 1.3 II:22 alongside other mititary items:

tṯʿr (21) *ksảt l mhr*	She prepares a seat for the fighter,
ṯʿr ṯlḥnt (22) *l ṣbỉm*	prepares a table for the armies,
hdmm l ǵzrm	a footstool for the warriors.

229. Johannes C. de Moor, "Lovable Death in the Ancient Near East," *UF* 22 (1990): 243.

230. For a bibliography of the earlier literature on this word, see Pardee, "Ugaritic Bibliography," 457–58.

231. Cassuto, *Goddess Anath*, 112. See also Cyrus H. Gordon, "North Israelite Influence on Postexilic Hebrew," *IEJ* 5 (1955): 88; Patrick D. Miller, "Ugaritic ǴZR = Hebrew ʿAzr II," *UF* 2 (1970): 159–75.

232. See Lane, 2254–55: "abundance" (e.g., abundance of milk) or "plenty," and not so much "many" as in "strength of number." Ginsberg, "North-Canaanite Myth of Anath and Aqhat, II," 18 n. 38; Eduard Lipiński, "Review of *Computer-aided Analysis of Amorite*, by Ignace J. Gelb," *JSS* 26 (1981): 279

233. B. Cutler and J. Macdonald, "On the Origin of the Ugaritic Text KTU 1.23," *UF* 14 (1982): 35, citing the earlier work of Hans-Peter Müller, "Magisch-mantische Weisheit und die Gestalt Daniels," *UF* 1 (1969): 90–91.

These observations lead Pardee to conclude that *ǵzr* must designate "a young man in full possession of his forces, able to do battle and to father sons," and he translates it as "valiant."[234] Accordingly, I analyze this form in Ugaritic as a verbal adjective: "valiant one."[235] This approach allows for the semantic nuance of *ǵzr*'s usage in Ugaritic.

Returning to Môtu's epithet, Andrew G. Vaughn argues that *ǵzr* should not be taken as a title of the death god, but as a designation for ʾIlu as a warrior god.[236] It is difficult to accept such a proposal in light of the regularity of this epithet as a parallel of *mt bn ỉlm*, which unequivocally refers to Môtu. Additionally, the one time this epithet occurs independent of *mt bn ỉlm*, *ǵzr* is replaced with Môtu by name: *mdd ỉlm mt* (KTU 1.4 VIII:23–24). Furthermore, in light of this term's emphasis on vigorous strength characteristic of the prime of one's life, it would be unusual to see this applied to ʾIlu who is routinely presented as an old and gray-headed man.[237] On the contrary, Môtu's representation as a dangerous adversary rightly to be feared (esp. KTU 1.4 VIII:4–32) and his designation as the son of ʾIlu make it all but certain that this epithet is attributed to Death. His visciousness as a warrior does not eliminate the fact that he is the progeny of ʾIlu, and thus in some sense the object of his love.

3.3.3.2. Môtu's Death as Agricultural Imagery

Interpreters have detected agricultural imagery in the narrative depiction of ʿAnatu's slaughter of the death god in KTU 1.6 II:31–35.[238] I have rendered the pertinent portion from this text as follows:

(26) *ym ymm yʿtqn*	A day, two days pass,
l ymm (27) *l yrḫm*	days (turn) to months.
rḥm ʿnt tngṯh[239]	Damsel ʿAnatu questions him [Môtu],
(28) *k lb ảrḫ l ʿglh*	like the heart of a cow for her calf,

234. Pardee, *COS* 1:340 n. 78.

235. Cf. Biblical Hebrew G active participle *ʿōzrê* in 1 Chr 12:1 (see *HALOT*, 811).

236. Andrew G. Vaughn, "*ỉl ǵzr*—An Explicit Epithet of El as a Hero/Warrior," *UF* 25 (1993): 423–30.

237. Pardee, *COS* 1:243 n. 13.

238. For a bibliography of the earlier literature, see de Moor, *Seasonal Pattern*, 212 n. 1.

239. In Hebrew, the root **ngṯ* is realized as *ngś*, "to spur on" in the G stem and "to press oneself against" in the N stem (*HALOT*, 670). This root is distinguished from *ngš*, meaning "to approach, step toward." In Arabic, this root can also indicate "to press someone for information" (Lane, 2765–66). In this context, the antecedent for this pronominal suffix would be Môtu who is speaking with her in the immediately preceding lines. Pardee translates, "Maid ʿAnatu interrogates him" (*COS* 1:270 n. 253), taking Môtu as the antecedent of the pronominal suffix. The problem with taking Baʿlu as its antecedent, who is mentioned at the end of the following section, is that he is

k lb (29) *ṯảt l ỉmrh*	like the heart of a ewe for her lamb,
km lb (30) *ʿnt ảṯr bʿl*	so is the heart of ʿAnatu after Baʿlu.
tỉḫd (31) *bn ỉlm mt*	She seizes Môtu, son of ʾIlu,
b ḥrb (32) *tbqʿnn*	with a sword she splits him (open),
b ḫṯr tdry(33)*nn*	with a winnowing fork she winnows him,
b ỉšt tšrpnn[240]	with fire she burns him,
(34) *b rḥm tṭḥnn*	with a millstone she grinds him,
b šd (35) *tdrʿ nn*[241]	in the field she scatters him.
šỉrh l tỉkl (36) *ʿṣrm*	The birds devour,
mnth l tkly[242] (37) *npr*[*m*]	his members the fowl finish off;
šỉr l šỉr yṣḥ[243]	flesh cries out to flesh.[244]

The basis for seeing an agricultural metaphor in these lines comes from the five-fold description of ʿAnatu's slaughter of Môtu: splitting with a sword, winnowing with a winnowing-fork, burning him with fire, grinding him with a millstone, and scattering him in the field (lines 31–35). As Virolleaud explained,

> Of these five operations, the first three relate to the harvest itself and to the purification of the grain, through winnowing and fire; the fourth is the reduction of grain to flour, while the fifth represents sowing. Thus Môt is assimilated entirely to the ear, which provides the grain from which bread is made and also the grain from which the new crop will one day emerge. But to give life, it is necessary that Môt die, and it is under the blows of a goddess that he succumbs, and of the most bellicose goddess.[245]

---

presumed dead at this point in the narrative, and therefore suggests that ʿAnatu is interrogating Môtu concerning the death of Baʿlu.

240. On the burning of corn, see John F. Healey, "Burning the Corn: New Light on the Killing of Mōtu," *Or* 52 (1983): 248–51.

241. Word divider between verbal form and suffix: tdrʿ.nn.

242. Erasure of {y} after the final {y} of this form.

243. Most usually taken as the hollow root *ṣwḥ* "to cry out" (e.g., Wyatt, *Religious Texts*, 136). Pardee appeals to Syrian Arabic *nṣḥ* meaning "grow fat," and interprets the text here: "flesh(-eaters) grow fat on flesh" (*COS* 1:270 n. 258). Pardee argues that "flesh crying out to flesh" makes no sense in this context. However, one might consider the reference to Cain's blood crying out from the ground in Gen 4:10, though admittedly the context is slightly different there: it is blood (*dm*), not flesh (*šʾr*) crying out, and it is crying out to YHWH, not to itself.

244. Cf. its parallel in KTU 1.6 V:11–19.

245. "De ces cinq opérations, les trois premières se rapportent à la moisson même et à la purification du grain, par le vannage et par le feu; la quatrième a trait à la réduction du grain en farine, tandis que la cinquième représente les semailles. Ainsi Môt est assimilé tout entier à l'épi, qui fournit le grain dont on fait du pain et aussi le grain d'où sortira, un jour, la nouvelle récolte. Mais, pour donner la vie, il faut que Môt meure, et c'est sous les coups d'une déesse qu'il succombe, et de

Perhaps one the of more enthusiastic advancements of this interpretation has been the work of de Moor in his *Seasonal Pattern,* arguing that "every action of ʿAnatu has to do with the treatment of the grain." He sees the entire process described in this text as a reflection of the seasonal pattern experienced at Ugarit and its expression in ritual.[246] This viewpoint has encountered significant criticism, an extreme example being Paul Watson's effort to dismiss the metaphor altogether. He argues that the detailed account of the slaughter emphasizes the physical masscre of Môtu's body, ending his existence by scattering his remains (*šỉr*) in a field where the birds devour them piece by piece. For Watson, the thrust of the poem places the reader's focus upon the destruction of the physical representation of the said divine being, the result being his complete annihilation.[247] Yet, the apparent slaughter is somewhat of a foil, since Môtu is anything but annihilated, as evidenced by his reemergence after seven years to contend with Baʿlu (KTU 1.6 V:9).

Other scholars have criticized interpreters for pushing this imagery too far, all the while being willing to grant the metaphorical use of certain agricultural terms without their representing a seasonal pattern *in toto*. For example, the persistent fact that the scattered remains of Môtu do not germinate, but rather are consumed by the birds in their entirety, seems to render de Moor's proposal less likely.[248] Also, Môtu's recounting of this event in KTU 1.6 V:11–20 adds: *ʿlk pht drʿ b ym* "On account of you [Baʿlu] I experienced sowing in the sea" (lines 18–20). Pardee observes that such a metaphorical usage for this root (**ḏrʿ*) finds precedent in Judg 9:45 where salt is sown.[249] This point may lend weight to the fact that the narrated destruction of these gods utilizes certain agricultural terms metaphorically, without pressing them into a full-blown seasonal pattern, as Healey proposes: "A hyperbolic account (using grain-related imagery) of ʿAnatu's violence to Mōtu remains the best explanation of the text."[250] The specific agricultural imagery utilized in presenting Môtu's death in the Baʿlu cycle would be that of sowing.

---

la déesse la plus belliqueuse." Charles Virolleaud, "Un poème phénicien de Ras-Shamra: La lutte de Môt, fils des dieux et d'Aleïn, fils de Baal," *Syria* 12 (1931): 211.

246. De Moor, *Seasonal Pattern,* 212–15.

247. Paul L. Watson, "The Death of 'Death' in Ugaritic Texts," *JAOS* 92 (1972): 60–64.

248. Umberto Cassuto, "Baal and Mot in the Ugaritic Texts," *IEJ* 12 (1962): 79; Samuel E. Loewenstamm, "The Killing of Mot in Ugaritic Myth," *Or* 41 (1972): 378–82; Healey, "Burning the Corn," 250–51.

249. Pardee, *COS* 1:272 n. 271.

250. Healey, "Burning the Corn," 251.

3.3.3.3. Môtu and *npš*

I have already noted in chapter 2 that Môtu is regulary associated with the parallel terms *npš* and *brlt* throughout the mythological literature.[251] In each of these cases, *npš* refers to the gaping throat of Môtu as a euphemism for one's entrance into the abode of the dead.[252] This gateway of death awaits all humankind (KTU 1.6 II:17–19), but it is also the necessary passage-way for the dying god Baʿlu (KTU 1.5 I:6–8). At one level, the use of *npš* in this way exposes the view that Môtu's food is humankind—that is, the *npš* of Môtu consumes the *npš* of humans. On another level, the irony of this connection is that one of the major attributes of Death (i.e., his *npš*=throat) in Ugaritic mythology at the same time denotes the vital force of human life.

3.3.3.4. KTU 1.23: Another Attestation of *mt* = Môtu?

One further text requires consideration as a possible reference to the noun *mt* as the god of death. KTU 1.23 attests the compound name *mt w šr*, for which I offer the following context:

(9) *mt w šr yṯb*	MT-wa-ŠR sits down,
bdh ḫṭ ṯkl	the staff of bereavement in his hand,
bdh (10) *ḫṭ ủlmn*	the staff of widowhood in his hand.

The interpretation of the compound name *mt w šr* is difficult here. The earliest most widely accepted view of this name takes it to be a compound appellative for Môtu.[253] More specifically, de Moor believes Môtu's arrival at the feast signals malevolence—he has in hand staffs of bereavement and widowhood.[254] The second element *šr* has also raised questions, some interpreters taking it as the word for "prince, king" in Semitic, while a few scholars appeal to Arabic *šry* with its negative connotations "to grow angry" and "to do evil."[255] Reading *mt* as the

251. KTU 1.4 VII:48; 1.5 I:7, 14, 18; 1.5 V:4; 1.6 II:17, 18; 1.133:2–4 (//1.5 I:12–16).

252. See ch. 2 (§§2.2.2.1 and 2.2.3.4).

253. Charles Virolleaud, "La naissance des dieux gracieux et beaux: Poème phénicien de Ras-Shamra," *Syria* 14 (1933): 133, 138; H. L. Ginsberg, "Birth of the Gracious and Beautiful Gods," *JRAS* 1 (1935): 48; Caquot and Sznycer, *Textes ougaritiques 1*, 370 n. g; David Tsumura, "A Ugaritic God, *mt-w-šr*, and His Two Weapons," *UF* 6 (1974): 407–13; Driver, *Canaanite Myths and Legends*, 2nd ed., 28 n. 1, 123; del Olmo Lete, *Mitos y leyendas*, 441; Lewis, "Birth of the Gracious Gods," in Parker, *Ugaritic Narrative Poetry*, 207.

254. De Moor, *Anthology of Religious Texts*, 120 n. 15.

255. For Semitic "prince, king," see, e.g., Akkadian *šarru* (*CAD* 17:76ff.); Biblical Hebrew *śar* (*HALOT*, 1350–53). For Arabic, see Lane, 1524. Cf. √*sry* "to stink, become foul" attested in Aramaic (*DJPA*, 389a; Jastrow, 1026) and Syriac (Payne Smith, 389). For negative connations, see Driver, *Canaanite Myths and Legends*, 121 n. 121, 148, 161; Tsumura, "Ugaritic God," 409; de Moor, *Anthology*

death god Môtu would naturally require the second element to be negative as well, thus the Arabic cognate. Another possibility is to interpret *mt* as /mutu/ "man," which finds contextual support in the fact that it occurs in lines 40 and 46 of this text, both in reference to ʾIlu. The problem of the staffs persists, however, since they are called bereavement and widowhood, which makes sense for an uninvited guest like Môtu. Pardee translates *mt-w-šr* "Man-Prince" or "Warrior-Prince," noting that his staffs are named bereavement and widowhood "because warriors slay sons and husbands in battle."[256] Wyatt, on the other hand, interprets the first staff as a reference to ʾIlu's sterility and the subsequent "pruning" as a depiction of circumcision, which then allows for fertility. In his words, "A husband who cannot service his wife effectively makes her a widow."[257]

No one solution answers every difficulty in interpreting these lines. On one level, interpreting *mt* as the death god has the immediate appeal of explaining the apparently negative staffs in his hands. Smith has recently defended this interpretation, citing confirmation from an Aramaic incantation bowl that depicts the Angel of Death with a weapon in each hand.[258] The corresponding inscription speaks of the death angel "taking away children and spouse," which he takes as "the best parallel to the picture of Death" here in lines 8–9.[259] The relevance of this Aramaic incantation bowl to KTU 1.23, however, is not a given and it is likewise important for us to interpret the Ugaritic text from its own context. The appearance of *mt* in lines 40 and 46 as /mutu/ "man" favors the same for line 9, though it does not necessarily dictate it. If taken as another reference to

of Religious Texts, 120 n. 15; C. M. Foley, "Are the 'Gracious Gods' *bn šrm*? A Suggested Restoration for KTU 1.23:1–2," *UF* 19 (1987): 71.

256. Pardee, *COS* 1:277 n. 13.

257. Nicolas Wyatt, "The Pruning of the Vine in KTU 1.23," *UF* 24 (1992): 425–27; Wyatt, *Religious Texts*, 327 n. 11; Wyatt, "Circumcision and Circumstance: Male Genital Mutilation in Ancient Israel and Ugarit," *JSOT* 33 (2009): 422. See also Meindert Dijkstra, "Astral Myth of the Birth of Shahar and Shalim (KTU 1.23)," in *"Und Mose schrieb Dieses Lied auf": Studien zum Alten Testament und zum Alten Orient; Festschrift für Oswald Loretz zur Vollendung seines 70. Lebensjahres mit Beiträgen von Freunden, Schülern und Kollegen*, ed. Manfried Dietrich and Ingo Kottsieper, AOAT 250 (Münster: Ugarit Verlag, 1998), 286–87; and earlier Joseph Aistleitner, "Götterzeugung in Ugarit and Dilmun (SS un Ni. 4561)," *AcOr* 3 (1953): 285–311.

258. See James A. Montgomery, *Aramaic Incantation Bowls from Nippur* (Philadelphia: University Museum, 1913), 127–28, no. 3 and pl. 4. This connection was already suggested in Montgomery, "Ras Shamra Notes II," *JAOS* 54 (1934): 63–64.

259. Mark S. Smith, *Rituals and Myths of the Feast of the Goodly Gods of KTU/CAT 1.23: Royal Constructions of Opposition, Intersection, Integration, and Domination*, RBS 51 (Atlanta: Society of Biblical Literature, 2006), 41; citing Tsumura, "Ugaritic God," 32–33; Driver, *Canaanite Myths and Legends*, 2nd ed., 28 n. 1; and Fleming, "Voice of the Ugaritic Incantation Priest," 48–49. See also Hays, *Death in Iron Age II*, 123–24. According to this view, Smith observes that the pruning and felling of lines 8–11 would therefore represent Death's limbs being pruned and himself being felled (*Goodly Gods of KTU/CAT 1.23*, 47).

the god Môtu, it could offer a certain level of correspondence to Môtu's being mentioned in KTU 2.10:11–13: *w yd ỉlm p k mtm ʿz mỉd* "The hand of the god (=plague) is here, for death is exceedingly strong."[260] The staffs of bereavement and widowhood in the hand of *mt w šr* here in KTU 1.23 would correspondingly depict the results of mighty Death's plague. Finally, it is worth observing that *mt w šr* sits/reigns (*yṯb*) with staff (*ḫṭ*) in hand, resembling the imagery of Môtu toward the end of the Baʿlu cycle (KTU 1.6 VI:26–29):

(26) *ỉk ảl yšmʿk ṯr* (27) *ỉl ảbk*	How indeed will the Bull, ʾIlu your Father, listen to you?
l ysʿ ảlt (28) *ṯbtk*	Surely he will remove the support to your seat;
l yhpk ksả mlkk	Surely he will overthrow the throne of your kingship;
(29) *l yṯbr ḫṭ mṯpṭk*	Surely he will destroy the scepter of your rule.

The context is that of Šapšu rebuking Môtu in his retaliation against Baʿlu on account of ʿAnatu's mistreating him—hacking him to pieces and sowing his remains like seed to the wind. Here, his contest with Baʿlu threatens to give ʾIlu reason for unseating Môtu's rightful reign as the god of death. In this light, KTU 1.23:9–10 offers further specificity regarding the scepter of his rule: it is one of bereavement and widowhood.

However, the lexical link between *mt-w-šr* and *mt* in lines 40 and 46 persists in one's attempt to understand the broader interpretation of KTU 1.23. One of the main issues in dealing with this text is the relationship between its first portion (lines 1–29), which in Pardee's estimation "contain indications of liturgical activity," and the remaining largely mythological portion (lines 30–76) relating the birth of Šaḥru-wa-Šalimu, the gracious gods, their banishment to the desert, and the discovery of the gracious gods' discovery of agricultural produce.[261] If we interpret *mt-w-šr* as a reference to Môtu, thus a malevolent intruder at the banquet, then how does that square with the recurrence of *mt* as a descriptor of ʾIlu in the following mythology? Pardee's suggestion that *mt-w-šr* as a "Man/ Warrior-Prince" prefiguring the appearance of the "Man ʾIlu" in the following lines may offer the most cogent interpretation of this term from context thus far, which would eliminate this occurrence of *mt* as a reference to the deity Môtu.[262]

260. See §3.3.2 above. Smith makes a similar connection with KTU 2.10 (*Goodly Gods of KTU/ CAT 1.23*, 42).

261. Pardee, *COS* 1:275.

262. Note similar problems involved in identifying *ảṯrt w rḥm* (line 13) and *rḥmy* (line 16) (Pardee, *COS* 1:276 n. 13, 278 n. 22).

3.4. Summary

The root expressing the concept for death in Ugaritic is widely attested throughout the corpus of mythology, epic, ritual, and letters. The above investigation of the numerous contexts in which it occurs yields a number of different ways the ancient Ugaritians spoke about death.

Death as Place. The Baʿlu Cycle refers to death as going to "the hole of the gods" (KTU 1.5 V:5–6), which appears to function as a metaphor for burial (KTU 1.6 I:17–18). Concerning this "place," elsewhere death descends into "baseness" (KTU 1.5 V:14–15). Similarly, in the Kirta Epic one of King Kirta's wives "disappears," or more literally, "goes (away)," utilizing the root *tbʾ* (KTU 1.14 I:14). The place of death is therefore envisioned as Môtu's abode.

Death as Downward Descent. The direction of death is primarily a downward affair. The dead fall (*npl*) to the earth (KTU 1.2 VI:25–26; 1.5 VI:8–9), descend (*yrd*) into the earth (KTU 1.5 V:15–16; 1.5 VI:25; 1.114:22; 1.161:19–22), fall into the dust of the earth (KTU 1.161:19–22), or even descend into the *npš* "throat" of Môtu (KTU 1.5 I:6–8). All but one of these cases describes the death of the gods (Yammu, Baʿlu) and kings (KTU 1.161), the one exception being the depiction of ʾIlu's drunkenness *km mt* "like a dead man" (KTU 1.114).

Death as Devastation. Death also involves destruction or devastation. The verb *ḫlq* "to be destroyed" in parallel with *mt* in the Baʿlu cycle to describe the death of Baʿlu (KTU 1.5 VI:10; 1.6 I:42–43) illustrates this point. Outside of Ugaritic mythology, *ḫlq* appears alongside individuals in a list, which may suggest "missing" persons presumed to be "dead" (KTU 4.611:2, 4, 8, etc.). Devastation can also be found in the description of Môtu's throat (*npš*), compared to the vicious throat of a lion or a ferocious sea creature (KTU 1.5 I:14–22). Furthermore, the strength of death/Death is evidenced by the outbreak of a deadly plague (*yd ỉlm*) on the battlefield (KTU 2.10:11–13).

Death as Loss of Animation. The loss of animation observable in a lifeless corpse is most notable in the exit of *npš* motif explored in chapter 2 (KTU 1.18 IV:24–26, 36–37; 1.19 II:42–44). Another relevant comparison is the corresponding notion of "dead ships," most likely refering to their loss of rigging and resultant inability to navigate the seas (KTU 2.33:12–13). Such "dead ships" thus fall under the auspices of the *rb tmtt* "master of death," or more exactly, the chief of salvaging operations. Understood in this way, one could also compare the unconsciousness of ʾIlu and his fall to the ground *km mt* "like a dead man" (KTU 1.114:21–22). His body, immobilized and incapacitated by intoxication, resembles the stillness of a dead corpse.

Death as the Termination of Life. As already observed in chapter 1, death is the opposite of life and thus represents its termination. This aspect is seen especially in the Kirta Epic where life equals not dying and dying equals not living (KTU 1.16 I:14–15, 21–23).

Death as Being Gathered. Kirta's fifth and sixth wives were gathered to Rašap and Yammu (KTU 1.14 I:18–19). Rašap's role as gatekeeper of death's realm, as well as his association with pestilence/plague makes this imagery rather terrifying. Furthermore, Yammu's role as the chief foe of the Storm God makes him an equally unpleasant companion in death. This imagery resembles the biblical view of being gathered, but there it is into the company of one's ancestors, rather than the clutches of the Ugaritic gods of chaos and calamity.

The Mythology of Burial and Mourning. In the Baʿlu cycle the mythological presentation of burial is expressly being placed in the hole of the gods, which parallels the physical act of burial (√*bqr*) in KTU 1.6 I:17–18. In the funerary ritual text KTU 1.161 the deceased king is commanded by Šapšu to "descend to the earth" after his lords and to "go down into the dust," depicting the royal burial from a mythological perspective. Mourning ritual adopts this same language as the living also speak of descending to the earth after the dead (KTU 1.5 VI:24–25).

Death Personified. One of the prominent features of death at Ugarit is its well-developed mythology of a personified death god. The mythology of death, however, is not limited to the mythological texts alone, but spills over into the real world with its threats of sickness and disease. In this context Death becomes the object of incantation against venomous snake bite and wreaks havoc on the battlefield where the "hand of the gods" is strong.

CHAPTER 4

The Ugaritic Rapa'ūma

4.1. Introduction

Having analyzed the words for "death" in the previous chapter, I now move on to discuss the category of the dead known as the Rapa'ūma in the Ugaritic texts. I have deemed it necessary to devote a chapter-length discussion to these entities due to their prominence in matters associated with the dead, especially the royal dead. The distribution of the attested forms under examination in this chapter includes several instances in mythological (the Baʿlu cycle) and epic literature (The Kirta and 'Aqhatu Epics), two ritual texts (KTU 1.108 and 1.161), and one incantation for a venomous snake bite (KTU 1.82). The highest concentration of occurrences is found in the collection of texts dubbed the "Rephaim Texts" or Rapa'ūma Texts (KTU 1.20–22), whose broken nature render their interpretation somewhat elusive, while at the same time offering tantalizing details as to the identity of these figures in the understanding of the Ugaritians. Unlike the words discussed in the previous three chapters (i.e., *ḥyy/ḥwy*, *npš*, and *mwt*), the lexeme *rpủm* is thus far not attested in the letters.

I arrange the following analysis according to the distribution of *rpủm* and its parallels throughout the textual corpus. A number of studies have emerged on the subject of the *rpủm*.[1] My particular contribution to this already crowded

1. In addition to the commonly known translations with accompanying commentary on texts mentioning the *rpủm*, see John Gray, "The Rephaîm," *PEQ* 81 (1949): 127–39; Gray, "DTN and RPỦM in Ancient Ugarit," *PEQ* 84 (1952): 39–41; André Caquot, "Les Rephaim ougaritiques," *Syria* 37 (1960): 75–93; Conrad L'Heureux, "El and the Rephaim: New Light from Ugaritica V," (Ph.D. diss., Harvard University, 1972); L'Heureux, "The Ugaritic and Biblical Rephaim," *HTR* 67

discussion is to offer a strictly lexical analysis of *rpùm* everywhere it occurs in Ugaritic. My goal is to navigate the various scholarly theories explaining their meaning by anchoring my own assessment firmly in the Ugaritic textual corpus. My intent is not necessarily to come up with another theory, but to weigh the various interpretive options in the balance of what is contextually plausible, working my way through the lexical data. I shall begin my analysis by discussing the meaning of the root *rp*ʾ from what can be deduced from its single occurrence in KTU 1.114:28 and consider how this root might inform this lexical study of the Rapaʾūma.

4.2. The Root *rp*ʾ

The verbal root *rp*ʾ occurs once in a text depicting ʾIlu's drunken stupor following his drinking bout at the *marziḥu* (KTU 1.114). Sholars identify the precise genre of this text as *historiola,* which consists of a mixture of myth and magic.[2] In this particular case, the primary referent of the text is the mythological depiction of ʾIlu's participation in the *marziḥu* and his subsequent drunkenness expressed in terms of one's descent into the underworld—"ʾIlu falls like a dead person, like those going down into the underworld" (lines 21–22). The myth ends with ʿAnatu-wa-ʿAṯtartu coming to his aid with powers enabling him to awaken from

(1974): 265–74; Johannes C. de Moor, "Rāpiʾūma—Rephaim," *ZAW* 88 (1976): 323–45; Marvin H. Pope, "Notes on the Ugaritic Rephaim," in *Essays on the Ancient Near East in the Memory of Jacob Joel Finkelstein,* ed. Maria de Jong Ellis, Memoirs of the Connecticut Academy of Arts & Sciences 16 (Hamden, CT: Archon, 1977), 163–82; William Horwitz, "The Significance of the Rephaim," *JNSL* 7 (1979): 37–43; Baruch Levine and Jean-Michael de Tarragon, "Dead Kings and Rephaim: The Patrons of the Ugaritic Dynasty," *JAOS* 104 (1984): 649–59; Michael L. Brown, "'I Am the Lord Your Healer': A Philological Study of the Root *Rapa*ʾ in the Hebrew Bible and the Ancient Near East" (Ph.D. diss., New York University, 1985); Healey, "Ugaritic Dead"; Spronk, *Beatific Afterlife,* 161–96; Gregorio del Olmo Lete, "Los nombres 'divinos' de los reyes de Ugarit," *AuOr* 5 (1987): 39–69; Lewis, *Cults of the Dead,* 5–46, 80–89; Tropper, *Nekromantie,* 134–50; Ford, "Living Rephaim," 73–101; Pitard, "New Edition," 33–77; Mark S. Smith, "Rephaim" *ABD* 5:674–76; Hedwige Rouillard-Bonraisin, "Rephaim," *DDD,* 692–700; Schmidt, *Israel's Beneficient Dead,* 71–122; R. Mark Shipp, *Of Dead Kings and Dirges: Myth and Meaning in Isaiah 14:4b-21,* AcBib 11 (Atlanta: Society of Biblical Literature, 2002), 114–20; Peter J. Williams, "Are the Biblical Rephaim and the Ugaritic RPUM Healers?," in *The Old Testament in Its World,* ed. Robert P. Gordon and Johannes C. de Moor, OTS 57 (Leiden: Brill, 2005), 266–75; Matthew J. Suriano, *The Politics of Dead Kings: Dynastic Ancestors in the Book of Kings and Ancient Israel,* FAT 2/48 (Tübingen: Mohr Siebeck, 2010), 148–65; Hays, *Death in the Iron Age II,* 107–15; Pardee, "Nouvelle étude épigraphique," 1–65; Brian R. Doak, *The Last of the Rephaim: Conquest and Cataclysm in the Heroic Ages of Ancient Israel,* Ilex Foundation Series 7 (Boston: Ilex Foundation, 2012); Smith, *Poetic Heroes,* 137–61.

2. Pardee, *Ritual and Cult at Ugarit,* 167, appealing to the study of David Frankfurter, "Narrating Power: The Theory and Practice of the Magical *Historiola* in Ritual Spells," in *Ancient Magic and Ritual Power,* ed. Marvin Meyer and Paul Mirecki, RGRW 129 (Leiden: Brill, 1995), 457–76.

his incapacitation. This mythological narration provides the basis for the magical remedy prescribed for drunkenness at the end of the text. My concern lies with the occurrence of *rpʾ* and its central significance in this text as a means of expressing ʾIlu's resuscitation from his intoxicated state (KTU 1.114):[3]

(17) *ỉl h⌜l⌝k l bth*	ʾIlu goes to his house,
yštql (18) *l ḥẓrh*	He falters at his inner chamber,
yʿmsn nn ṯkmn (19) *w šnm*	Ṯukamuna-wa-Šunama carries him.
w ngšnn ḥby	ḤBY meets him,
(20) *bʿl qrnm w ḏnb*	The one with two horns and a tail;
ylšn (21) *b ḫrỉh w ṯnth*	He tramples him over in his feces and urine.
ql ỉl km mt	ʾIlu falls like a dead man,
(22) *ỉl k yrdm ảrṣ*[4]	ʾIlu is like one descending to the earth.
ʿnt (23) *w ʿṯtrt tṣdn*	ʿAnatu and ʿAṯtartu go on the hunt,
⌜*š---*⌝[. . .] (24) *q*⌜*d*⌝*š*	. . .
bʿ⌜*-*⌝ [. . .]	
Reverse	
(25) [. . .]⌜*n*⌝ *d*[. . .]	. . .
(26) [*ʿṯ*]⌜*t*⌝*rt w ʿn*⌜*t*⌝[. . .]	[ʿAṯ]tartu and ʿAnatu [. . .]
(27) ⌜*w*⌝ *bhm tṯṯb* ⌜*-m*⌝*dh* [. . .]	and in them she returns [. . .]
(28) *km trpả hn nʿr*	when she might heal (him), look, he awakes.

The verbal form *trpả* in this passage appears to express an act of restoration on the part of ʿAnatu whereby she applies a remedy for ʾIlu's drunkenness.[5] We can ascertain this much despite the broken portion of the text immediately preceding these lines. The nature of this remedy must have a certain level of correspondence with the prescription in lines 29–31. The subject of the verb *trpả* is more difficult to determine from context due to the lacuna, but the prefixed {t} and final {ả} would suggest a 3fs subjunctive (ʿAnatu applies the remedy), or perhaps a dual form (ʿAṯtartu and ʿAnatu apply the remedy).[6]

3. Following Pardee, *Textes paramythologiques*, 14; Pardee, *Ritual and Cult*, 169; Bordreuil and Pardee, *Manual of Ugaritic*, 194–97.

4. For discussion on lines 17–22, see ch. 3 (§3.3.1).

5. See *DUL*, 742, where it glosses this root "to heal, apply a remedy," but with a question mark.

6. Singular: Pardee, *Textes paramythologiques*, 67; Pardee, *Ritual and Cult*, 169. Dual: Samuel E. Loewenstamm, "Eine lehrhafte ugaritische Trinkburleske," *UF* 1 (1969): 77; Anson F. Rainey,

Despite its meager attestation in Ugaritic, this verbal root is amply attested in the cognate languages. Biblical Hebrew provides a number of contexts for the root *rp*ʾ (G, N, D, tD stems) involving both physical healing (from sickness, wounds/hurts of individual or nation, repairing an altar) and metaphysical healing (distress or anxiety).[7] The G participle (*rōpēʾ*) often denotes a healer/physician, while the feminine noun *rᵉpūʾâ* indicating "remedy, medicine" and the {m} preformative noun *marpēʾ* meaning "healing" or "health, profit" are also attested.[8] The biblical evidence for this root correlates with the semantics of the roots *ḥyy/ḥwy*. In Prov 4:22 the noun *marpēʾ* occurs in parallel with *ḥayyîm* "life" concerning the words of wisdom:

ḥayyîm hēm lᵉmōṣʾēhem	They are life to those who find them,
ûlkol-bᵉśārô marpēʾ	healing to all his flesh.

Furthermore, the D stem of Hebrew *rp*ʾ is used once to portray the repair of an altar, much like the D stem *ḥwy* attested in Ugaritic for the restoration of a dilapidated house (KTU 2.70:15–16).[9] The Hebrew example comes from 1 Kgs 18:30:

wayyōmer ʾēliyyāhû lᵉkol-hāʿām gᵉšû ʾēlay wayyigšû kol-hāʿām ʾēlāyw wayᵉrappēʾ ʾet-mizbaḥ yhwh hehārûs

Elijah said to all the people, "Come near to me." And all the people came near to him and he repaired the altar of YHWH that had been torn down.

"The Ugaritic Texts in Ugaritica 5," *JAOS* 94 (1974): 187; Johannes C. de Moor, "Henbane and KTU 1.114," *UF* 16 (1984): 356; Wyatt, *Religious Texts*, 412.

7. See references in BDB, 950–51; *HALOT*, 1272–74. However, see also the discussion of this Hebrew root in Brown, "'I Am the Lord Your Healer,'" 1–8, where he criticizes taking "healing" as the fundamental meaning of this root, instead arguing for "restoration" of all kinds (see his discussion of the Hebrew evidence for this root, pp. 37–96, and the cognate languages, pp. 97–160). Cf. also Williams, "Are the Biblical Rephaim," 266–75, who raises additional objections. He querries three assumptions underlying the notion of healing for these entities: (1) the root *rp*ʾ means "heal," (2) the form *rpủm* is an active participle, and (3) the root meaning "heal" implies "save." Williams devotes the majority of his discussion to the vocalization of *rpủm* with regard to the comparative evidence, concluding that eliminating the participial form from the historical development of Hebrew *rᵉpāʾîm* "significantly reduces any evidence for the Ugaritic figures as healers" (274). Despite Brown and William's arguments to the contrary, however, I see no real problem with the longstanding interpretation of the root *rp*ʾ as "to heal," as I will argue further below.

8. *rp*ʾ as healer/physician in. e.g., Gen 50:2; 2 Chr 16:12. The feminine noun is attested as the plural form *rᵉpūʾōt/-ôt* (Ezek 30:21; Jer 30:15; 46:11). *marpēʾas* healing/cure: Jer 8:15; 14:19 (// *šālôm*); as health: Prov 4:22 (// *ḥayyîm*) (see BDB, 951).

9. See ch. 1 (§1.2.2.6).

These Hebrew examples demonstrate a certain level of semantic overlap between the roots *ḥyy/ḥwy* and *rpʾ*.

This root is also attested outside the Hebrew Bible. A Hebrew bulla identifies an individual as a *rpʾ*: [*lṭbšlm*] / *bn zkr* / *hrpʾ* "[belonging to ṬBŠLM], son of Zakkur, the healer," which Yigal Shiloh identifies as the designated profession of the seal's owner.[10] It is also fairly well-attested in Postbiblical Hebrew.[11] In Phoenician the form *mrpʾ* (perhaps a D stem participle) occurs once meaning "healing," not to mention a few more instances in Punic.[12] The verb *rafaʾa* in Arabic can indicate reparation or the mending of torn garments, and therefore resembles the semantics of *rpʾ* in Biblical Hebrew as noted above.[13] The verbal form *yrpwn* occurs in the Egyptian Aramaic text Aḥiqar and has been interpreted as a derivative of this root, but other scholars have questioned this etymology, instead taking it from the root *rpy* "to relax, hang slack."[14] Syriac almost exclusively attests this second root *rpy* "to relax, slacken," with only one possible example (but with question) of *rpʾ* "to heal" as cited by Michael Sokoloff.[15]

The above lexical information introduces the problem of possible confusion between the roots *rpʾ* "to heal" and *rpy* "to grow slack."[16] The evidence for this root in Ugarit is also slim, attested once in KTU 1.5 I:4 describing the heavens as having grown slack whenever Baʿlu strikes Lôtan, the fleeing serpent: *tṯkḥ ttrp šmm* "the heavens wither (and) grow slack." Again, this root is widely attested in Biblical (G, N, D, tD, and C stems) and Postbiblical Hebrew.[17] In light of this potential root confusion, the proposed etymologies for the *rpủm* are as follows: (1) a masculine plural G active participle from *rpʾ* "to heal" (/Rāpiʾūma/) meaning "healers," (2) a masculine plural substantive from *rpʾ* "to heal" (/Rapaʾūma/) meaning "healthy ones," or (3) a masculine plural substantive from *rpy* (/Rapaʾūma/) meaning "slack ones" or "weak ones."[18]

10. See Yigal Shiloh, "A Group of Hebrew Bullae from the City of David," *IEJ* 36 (1986): 29, 32.

11. Jastrow, 1489–90.

12. Phoenician: *CIS* 1:41.3. For Punic, see references in *DNWSI*, 1081.

13. Lane, 1117.

14. The word is listed under *rpʾ* I "to heal" in *DNWSI*, 1081. The root *rpy* was suggested earlier by J. Halévy, "Les nouveaux papyrus d'Éléphantine," *RSEHA* 20 (1912): 68. CAL also takes this form from the same root as a D: "to make lax" (http://cal1.cn.huc.edu/). Note that the context of this form is badly broken, leading Ginsberg to leave this portion untranslated (*ANET*, 429).

15. *SL*, 1483. There is no entry for *rpʾ* "to heal" listed in Payne Smith (see p. 547).

16. E.g., *marpēh* for *marpēʾ* in Jer 8:15.

17. For Biblical Hebrew, see *HALOT*, 1276–77. For Postbiblical Hebrew, see Jastrow, 1490.

18. For interpreting it as a participle, see, e.g., Caquot, "Rephaim ougaritiques," 76–77: "healers" ("guerisseurs"); de Moor, "Rāpiʾūma—Rephaim, 140–41 (though he proposes a deliberate replacement of the root *rpy* for *rpʾ* behind the biblical Rephaim). Note the related suggestion to interpret this root in terms of fertility, specifically as it relates to the *rpủm* as "dispensers of fertility" (Gray, *Legacy of Canaan*, 2nd ed., 146 n. 5; Eduard Lipiński, "Ditanu," in *Studies in Bible and*

Several Amorite personal names show an *a/i* vowel pattern reflective of a participial form, as in ra-bi-u$_2$-um, which Ignace J. Gelb vocalized as *Rāpiʾum*.[19] The participial interpretation of *rpʾm* is appealing, but it is difficult to reconcile with the vocalization attested in the Masoretic tradition of the Hebrew Bible.[20] The Hebrew plural form *rᵉpāʾîm* requires a *qatal* base in the singular, presumably reconstructed as **rāpāʾ*, while the plural participle would have been **rōpᵉʾîm* from a *qātil* base. In an attempt to reconcile evidence from Amorite onomastics with the biblical materials, de Moor has suggested that the more original must have been *Rāpiʾum* "healers" and that it became unsuitable nomenclature for the Rephaim as "powerless spirits," as they came to be known in the Bible (citing Isa 14:10), which then led to its being replaced by the root *rph* "to be feeble," and thus resulting in *rᵉpāʾîm* "feeble ones."[21] However, such an analysis lacks textual support, since it is always *rᵉpāʾîm* in the biblical tradition with no internal evidence for this supposed morphological change, not to mention the required etymological shift that would have occurred.[22] A simpler solution to this problem is to grant the biblical term its morphological force by interpreting it as plural substantive meaning "healthy ones" (intransitively), which would yield the Ugaritic vocalization /Rapaʾūma/.[23] This approach, however, would leave the Amorite evidence unaccounted for, though Pardee offers the *qātil* pattern as a hypothetical vocalization for the deity *rpủ* ("healer"), who seems to be the head of the *rpủm* ("healthy ones") in KTU 1.108 and may in fact be the same deity as *mlk* since both entities are said to reside in ʿAṯtartu.[24] I will return to

the Ancient Near East Presented to Samuel E. Loewenstamm on His Seventieth Birthday, ed. Yitzhak Avishur and Joshua Blau [Jerusalem: Rubinstein, 1978], 1:95; see further discussion in Michael L. Brown, "Was There a West Semitic Asklepios?" *UF* 30 [1998]: 144–46). For interpreting it as a substantive form, see Pardee, *Ritual and Cult*, 286; cf. Robert M. Good, "Supplementary Remarks on the Ugaritic Funerary Text RS 34.126," *BASOR* 239 (1980): 41, who understands "healthy" or "healed" in the sense of "prepared for burial." For taking the root as *rpy*, see, e.g., Hans Wildberger, *Jesaja*, BKAT 10 (Neukirchen-Vluyn, Neukirchener Verlag, 1965–1981), 594; Manfried Dietrich, Oswald Loretz, and Joaquín Sanmartín, "Die ugaritischen Totengeister *rpu(m)* und die biblischen Rephaim," *UF* 8 (1976): 47.

19. Ignace J. Gelb, et al, *Computer-Aided Analysis of Amorite*, AS 21 (Chicago: Oriental Institute of the University of Chicago, 1980), 29, 346. See also Herbert B. Huffmon, *Amorite Personal Names in the Mari Texts: A Structural and Lexical Study* (Baltimore: Johns Hopkins University Press, 1965), 263.

20. For an excellent overview of the problems associated with vocalizing *rpʾm* in the Hebrew Old Testament, see Williams, "Are the Biblical Rephaim," 267–74.

21. De Moor, "Rāpiʾūma—Rephaim," 140–41.

22. For a III-*h* G stem masculine plural particle in Hebrew, we would expect *rōpîm* analogous to *ʿōśîm* (<*ʿśh*) (Gen 24:49).

23. E.g., del Olmo Lete, *Mitos y leyendas de Canaan*, 304; Pardee, *Ritual and Cult*, 204–5 n. 6.

24. Cf. KTU 1.161:2; 1.100:40–41; 1.107:42 (noted in Pardee, *Ritual and Cult*, 204–5 n. 6). See also Pardee, "A New Datum for the Meaning of the Divine Name Milkashtart," in *Ascribe to the*

this question in my analysis of this text below. Alternatively, Frank Moore Cross suggested that the underlying form could have been a *qatil* adjective, meaning "one who is hale."[25] Conrad L'Heureux thinks this proposal is better than the *qātil* hypothesis in advancing a solution for the problem of the Hebrew vocalization *rᵉpāʾîm,* since "the loss of a short *i* vowel is more likely" than the loss of the initially long /a/ vowel.[26] But this argument is hardly convincing when one considers the reduction pattern for *qatil* adjectives in Hebrew, as in the case of *kābēd* "heavy," whose plural form is *kᵉbēdîm.*[27] The most satisfactory accounting of the Hebrew data remains the plural substantive /Rapaʾūma/: Hebrew singular: **rāpāʾ*, producing a plural *rᵉpāʾîm* according to propretonic vowel reduction.

The etymology based upon the root *rpy* "to be slack" for Ugaritic *rpủm* is difficult to reconcile with the textual materials thus far attested from Ugarit. My analysis in this chapter will attempt to demonstrate that the ancient Ugaritians envisioned the *rpủm* possessing certain powers, therefore invoking them for both blessing (e.g., KTU 1.161:31–34) and specific intervention (KTU 1.82:32). If this perspective indeed emerges from the usage of the term *rpủm* in Ugaritic, as I think it does, it is hard to defend the viability of a root meaning "slack" or "feeble" as an etymology for *rpủm.* This observation would accord with the simple fact that Ugaritic *rpủm* and Hebrew *rᵉpāʾîm* consistently attest {ʾ} as the third root consonant, an unusual circumstance were the underlying root III-*yod* instead of III-*aleph.* Lewis is hesitant to interpret the *rpủm* as "healers" or "healthy ones" due to the fact that it is based on etymology alone and that nowhere in the Ugaritic texts are the *rpủm* associated with healing.[28] This criticism is certainly valid, generally speaking, since the actual usage of words provides the primary basis for assessing their meanings. Yet, the fact that we have a root *rpʾ* (*trpả*) attested once in Ugaritic in a context favorable for translating "X heals" (KTU 1.114:28), coupled with the consistent appearance of a third root consonant {ʾ} in these forms, at the least renders the *rpʾ* etymology highly plausible. Furthermore, the mention of the *rpủm* in the context of eradicating venomous snake bite (KTU 1.82), as well as the powers of the divine personage Ditānu—clearly associated with the *rpủm* (see below)—for healing a sick child (KTU 1.124) at least requires qualification in denying any healing associations

Lord: Biblical and Other Studies in Memory of Peter C. Craigie, ed. Lyle Eslinger and Glan Taylor; JSOTSup 67 (Sheffield: JSOT Press, 1988), 55–68.

25. Cross, *Canaanite Myth and Hebrew Epic,* 20.

26. L'Heureux, "Ugaritic and Biblical Rephaim," 269–70.

27. Exod 17:12. Note also the plural construct form *kibdê* (Exod 3:5, 6).

28. Theodore J. Lewis, "Toward a Literary Translation of the Rapiuma Texts," in Wyatt, *Ugarit, Religion and Culture,* 142; similarly, Robert M. Good, "On RS 24.252," *UF* 23 (1991): 160; Brown, "Was There a West Semitic Asklepios?, "133–54. Cf. Suriano, *Politics of Dead Kings,* 151 n. 7.

for the *rpủm*. The reticence of some scholars in associating the *rpủm* with "healing" also overlooks their power for good as expressed in KTU 1.108. For these reasons, I find the root *rpʾ* "to heal" to be the most satisfactory etymology for Ugaritic *rpủm* in its ability to account for its morphology as well as its distribution throughout the textual corpus.

These considerations should also bear upon the feasibility of van der Toorn's interpretation of *rpủm* as an adjective meaning "pure," which he bases upon the polyglot vocabulary text RS 20.149.[29] In column III line 20′, Huehnergard reads the form RAB-⸢Ú⸣ = rap-⸢ú?⸣ occurring alongside Jean Nougayrol's reconstructed Sumerian EL = Akkadian *tēliltu/ebbu*, for which Huehnergard renders /rapʾu/ and translates "purification?" ("holy"??).[30] However, van der Toorn's favoring of this etymology needs to be tempered by the fact that the Sumerian and Akkadian columns are entirely reconstructed, with only two partially visible signs in the Hurrian column: [n]i-ḫi, which Huehnergard reconstructs with much uncertainty.[31] David Clemens rightly concludes that "uncertainties in reconstruction of the text at this point render the hypothesis tenuous."[32] Indeed, this datum is rather tenuous support for overturning the evidence from the Northwest Semitic languages (especially Hebrew) that seems to suggest a connection between the *rpủm* and the root *rpʾ* "to heal."

Before moving on to treat the specific contexts in which *rpủm* occurs, I also need to consider briefly the element *rpủ* occurring in several Ugaritic personal names.[33] My defense of the etymology *rpʾ* "to heal" versus *rpy* "to grow slack" comports with the semantics seemingly required for these names. For instance, the commonly attested royal name *ʿmrpỉ* is instructive, which William F. Albright

29. Van der Toorn, "Funerary Rituals," 57. Edited by Jean Nougayrol in *Ugaritica* 5, no. 130 iii 20′ (pp. 232–35).

30. See Huehnergard, *Ugaritic Vocabulary*, 26–27, 58, 179, 202, 304. Note that Nougayrol read: LUGA[L(?)]?[ ] (*Ugaritica* 5:235).

31. According to Nougayrol, *Ugaritica* 5:234; cf. Huehnergard: ⸢x-x-x-ni⸣-ḫi (*Ugaritic Vocabulary*, 26–27, 179). Huehnergard: [EL? (tēliltu?/ebbu?)] ⸢x-x-x-ni⸣-ḫi rap-⸢ú?⸣ (*Ugaritic Vocabulary*, 26–27, 179). The presentation of Huenergard's transcription suggests a great deal of uncertainty regarding this reading. That the previous word in the polyglot vocabulary list is visible (Ugaritic: ṭu-ú-ru; Hurrian ši-ḫa-la-e) may provide some basis for this reading, but the rest of the listed items in this text appear not to show any semantic associations that would aid us in our reading of the broken line in question. See Nougayrol's introduction to these texts in *Ugaritica* 5:231, where the difficulty of reconstructing the Sa vocabulary fragments at Ugarit is ascribed to the fact that, although they reflect a systematic ordering of lexemes, the lexeme set varies from one text to another.

32. David M. Clemens, *Sources for Ugaritic Ritual and Sacrifice*, AOAT 284 (Münster: Ugarit-Verlag, 2001), 1:868.

33. For a comprehensive listing of Ugaritic proper names with bibliography, see Dennis Pardee, "Ugaritic Personal Names," *AfO* 36/37 (1989/1990): 390–513.

interpreted to mean, "the people is healed (from an epidemic)," taking *rpi* as a verbal form from the root *rp'* "to heal."[34] The syllabic spelling attested for this name in Ugaritic is ^{m}Am-mu-ra-bi (appearing in Akkadian as *ḫammurabi*), which Wilfred H. van Soldt regards to be of West Semitic origins.[35] As he argues, the first element *ʿm* (/ʿammu/) "people, clan" is commonly attested in Amorite, Ugaritic, and Hebrew names, but was altogether foreign to Babylonian scribes. As for the second element, scholars who propose an Akkadian origin for the name suggest that we should read *rabi* (not *rapi*) and interpret it "X is great," claiming as evidence that it is always written with syllabogram BI instead of PI in southern Mesopotamia.[36] But as van Soldt notes, there are in fact a few instances of this name spelled with syllabogram PI in the south, thus negating the claim that it is always with BI.[37] He explains how this situation might have developed: "The reason that a well-known name as Ḫammurabi was written in the South with BI almost without exception can be due to a Babylonian popular etymology which had changed the incomprehensible *-rāpi'* to the common *-rabi*."[38] The consistent spelling of this name with {p} in Ugaritic alphabetic texts seems to confirm its West Semitic origins, and the persistence of the third {'} in the same points toward an etymology from the root *rp'* "to heal."

The element *rpủ* is attested in other Ugaritic names as well, but for some of them it is unclear whether it should be interpreted as a verbal form ("X heals") or the theonym Rāpi'u.[39] For instance, Parker outlines two possibilities for the name *ủbrpủ*: "Rāpi'u is (my) father" or "Abu is (my) healer."[40] Similarly, one finds *ỉlrpỉ*, meaning either "Rāpi'u is (my) god" or "'Ilu is (my) healer."[41] The name

34. *ʿmrpi* occurs in KTU 1.113:20 (with *il*); 1.161:31; 2.39:2; 2.76:2, 11; 2.78:2; 4.707:22; 4.775:19; 5.22:21; 9.530:2. William F. Albright, "Stratigraphic Confirmation of Low Mesopotamian Chronology," *BASOR* 144 (1956): 28–29 n. 10. Cf. Cyrus H. Gordon, "Observations on the Akkadian Tablets from Ugarit," *RA* 50 (1956): 128 (note, however, his interpretation of the element *ʿm* as a divine name: "the god-Amm"); Joshua Blau and Samuel E. Loewenstamm, "Zur Frage der Scriptio plena im Ugaritischen und Verwandtes," *UF* 2 (1970): 24 n. 31.

35. For the syllabic spelling, see *Ugaritica* 5:463, 486. Wilfred H. van Soldt, *Studies in the Akkadian of Ugarit: Dating and Grammar*, AOAT 40 (Kevelaer: Butzon & Bercker; Neukirchen-Vluyn: Neukirchener Verlag, 1991), 316 n. 125; with Gelb, *Computer-aided Analysis of Amorite*, 32, 261f. and Rykle Borger, review of *Hammurabi von Babylon*, by Hartmut Schmökel, *ZA* 56 (1964): 289.

36. Marten Stol, *Studies in Old Babylonian History*, UNHAII 40 (Leiden: Nederlands Historisch-Archaeologisch Instituut te Istanbul, 1976), 32 n. 10.

37. For references, see van Soldt, *Studies in the Akkadian of Ugarit*, 316 n. 125.

38. Van Soldt, *Studies in the Akkadian of Ugarit*, 316 n. 125.

39. See my full discussion of this deity below (§4.3.6.1).

40. *abrpu* occurs in KTU 4.75 VI:4; 4.96:10; 4.214 III:5. Simon B. Parker, "The Ugaritic Deity Rāpi'u," *UF* 4 (1972): 99. The syllabic spellings for this name are attested as follows: *a*-BUR$_5$-*pí-i* (RS 15.139), *a*-BAR-*pa-a* (RS 22.02), and *a*-BAR-*pu-u* (RS 22.02) (see PRU 3; van Soldt, *Studies in the Akkadian of Ugarit*, 18 n. 162).

41. KTU 4.347:7. Parker, "Ugaritic Deity Rāpi'u," 99.

ʿbdrpủ, commonly translated "Servant of Rāpiʾu," is more problematic due to the final {ủ}, which seems to indicate a nominative rather than the genitive required of a construct interpretation of the name.[42] However, the genitival interpretation "servant of Rāpiʾu" finds justification in the syllabic form ᵐÌR-rap-i, which may indicate that *ʿbdrpủ* reflects a reanalysis of the proper name as a single unit (rather than a construct chain) so that the final {ủ} marks the entirety of the PN as a nominative.[43] Finally, the name *rpản* is rendered syllabically as rap-a-na/ra-ap-a-nu.[44] Cyrus Gordon interpreted the final element of this name as the *-ān* suffix, perhaps meaning "healing" or "restoration."[45]

4.3. The *rpủm*

The intent of this chapter is to analyze all occurrences of *rpủm* throughout the Ugaritic texts as a means of understanding ancient conceptions about them. Therefore, my discussion of the *rpủm* will follow the order of their attestations, beginning with mythological and epic texts, and then moving on to their appearance in ritual contexts.

4.3.1. The Baʿlu Cycle

The *rpủm* are not mentioned in the Baʿlu cycle until the very last preserved section in a hymn of praise to Šapšu and her associates, just after her intervention in the final scuffle between Môtu and Baʿlu (KTU 1.6 VI:43–53). The passage states that Šapšu rules the *rpủm* // *ỉlnym*. I have already treated this text in chapter 3, but offer it again here as we consider more specifically the nature of the *rpủm* from within this context:[46]

ủp l tlḥm (44) *lḥm trmmt*	Also, please eat the bread of offering,
l tšt (45) *yn tǵẓyt*	please drink the wine of libation.
špš (46) *rpỉm tḥtk*	Šapšu, you rule the *rpủm*,

42. KTU 4.269:15; 4.609:33. See Parker, "Ugaritic Deity Rāpiʾu," 99.

43. PRU 3:145f. line 8 (see also Huehnergard, *Ugaritic Vocabulary*, 249). Also argued by Gordon, *Ugaritic Textbook*, §8.71.

44. *rpan* occurs in KTU 4.45:7; 4.103:46; 4.116:4; 4.204:6; 4.269:13; 4.281:19; 4.339:26; 4.658:15; 4.753:9;4.787:6. It appears syllabically in *Ugaritica* 5:147 (text 55 [RS 20.178] line 1).

45. Gordon, *Ugaritic Textbook*, §8.58. Anson F. Rainey is tempted to identify this individual with the ᵐRa-ba-na mār(DUMU) Šu-mì-ia-na ("A Front Line Report from Amurru," *UF* 3 [1971]: 136). See also the proper names *rpỉl* (KTU 4.194:12), *rpỉy* (KTU 4.141 II:14), and *rpỉyn* (KTU 4.232 I:8).

46. See the more detailed discussion of this passage in ch. 3 (§3.3.1).

(47) *špš tḥtk ỉlnym*	Šapšu, you rule the deities;
(48) *ʿdk ỉlm*	your company is the gods,
hn mtm	indeed, the dead.
(49) *ʿdk kṯrm ḥbrk*	Your company is Kôṯaru your companion,
(50) *w ḫss dʿtk*	Ḫasīsu, the one you know.
(51) *b ym ảrš w tnn*	In the sea are ẢRŠ and the Dragon;
(52) *kṯr w ḫss yd*	May Kôṯaru-wa-Ḫasīsu expel (them),
(53) *ytr kṯr w ḫss*	may Kôṯaru-wa-Ḫasīsu banish (them).

I shall make several summary observations from my discussion in chapter 3, particularly as it relates to one's interpretation of the *rpủm*. First, I interpret the two occurrences of *tḥtk* in lines 46 and 47 as the 2fs G stem PC of the root *ḥtk*, a kinship term meaning, "to exercise paternal authority," rather than the preposition *tḥt* "under" plus the 2ms pronominal suffix. That it is *rpỉm* and not *rpủm* renders the predicate nominative interpretation necessitated by the preposition *tḥt* highly unlikely—"O Šapšu, the *rpủm* are under you"—instead indicating an oblique form that is most naturally read as the object of the verb *tḥtk*. This factor places Šapšu in a governing role over the *rpủm*, who are also associated with the term *mtm* in line 48. I have already argued at length that *mtm* is best interpreted as the masculine plural adjective /mītūma/ meaning "dead persons" and not /mutūma/ "persons." Part of the reason for this lies in the poetic parallelism of the passage: *rpỉm* // *ỉlnym* // *ỉlm* // *mtm*. Schmidt's chiastic interpretation (A: *rpủm* "shades"; B: *ỉlnym* "gods"; B': *ỉlm* "gods"; A': *mtm* "men") attempts to show that the *rpỉm* are not intended to represent the quasi-deified dead but are instead living kings, thus denying Šapšu's descent into the underworld, since the *rpủm* are identified as men living on the earth below the gods (*ỉlnym* // *ỉlm*) above.[47] However, this chiastic analysis does not in fact reflect the broader and more complex poetic structure of these lines. My analysis identifies a series of three bicola with a concluding tricola, offered here once again:

bicolon 1:	*špš*	*rpỉm*	*tḥtk*
	špš	*tḥtk*	*ỉlnym*
bicolon 2:	*ʿdk*	*ỉlm*	
	hn	*mtm*	
bicolon 3:	*ʿdk*	*kṯrm*	*ḥbrk*
	w	*ḫss*	*dʿtk*

47. Schmidt, *Israel's Beneficent Dead*, 86.

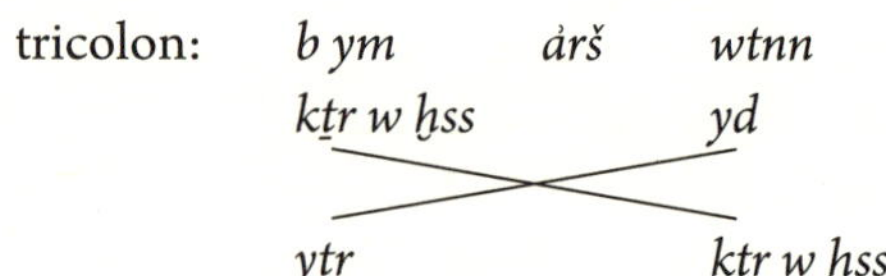

As noted in chapter 3, each of these three sections presents Šapšu's entourage of divine beings: (1) the *rpủm* // divine beings; (2) the gods // the (divinized) dead persons, and (3) Kôṯaru // Ḫasīsu; Kôṯaru-wa-Ḫasīsu // Kôṯaru-wa-Ḫasīsu. Accordingly, two types of divine beings are in view: the greater gods and lesser gods. This hymn therefore expresses the breadth of Šapšu's divine association: she rules over the underworld deities below (*rpủm, mtm*) and she enjoys the companionship of the greater gods of the pantheon (e.g., Kôṯaru-wa-Ḫasīsu).

These observations require further consideration of the nature of the *rpủm* and their subservience to Šapšu. If this text in fact ascribes divinity to the *rpủm*, what kind of divinity is it? The more common term for "gods" is *ỉlm*, but this text also mentions *ỉlnym* as a parallel for *ỉlm*.[48] William Horwitz observed that unlike *ỉlm*, which is a relatively well-known ascription of deity, *ỉlnym* is much more obscure, so much so that its "exact nuance" cannot be determined.[49] The distribution of *ỉlnym* in Ugaritic is mostly limited to matters relating to the *rpủm*, occurring most frequently in the *rpủm* texts KTU 1.20–22, always as a parallel for *rpủm*.[50] But even here, we must caution against assuming too much distinction between *ỉlm* and *ỉlnym* because in one instance *ỉlm* functions as the parallel for what is most likely the *rpủm*, thus indicating a certain amount of semantic overlap between the two.[51] In fact, the same equation is also found in KTU 1.3 VI:34–35 in ʿAnatu's speech prior to her journey to visit Baʿlu at his request:

lk lk ʿnn ỉlm	Come, come, O messengers of the gods,
(33) *ảtm bštm w ản šnt*	You yourself may linger, but I set out,

48. Note that the {y} is most likely not a *mater lectionis* (like Heb. -*īym*), since Ugaritic does not appear to yield evidence for *matres* in its orthography (see Bordreuil and Pardee, *Manual of Ugaritic*, 61; contra Tropper, *Ugaritische Grammatik*, 2nd ed., 51–54 §21.341.2).

49. Horwitz, "Significance of the Rephaim," 38.

50. KTU 1.20 I:2; 1.21 II:4, 12; partially restored in 1.22 II:6, 26.

51. The parallel was observed already by Caquot, "Rephaim ougaritiques," 78. KTU 1.20 II:2:

⸢ả⸣[ṯrh . rpỉm] (2) ndd .	To [this place the *rpủm*]arise,
ảṯrh . ndd . ỉl⸢m⸣	to this place the gods arise.

I will revisit this text in my discussion of the *rpủm* texts below (§4.3.4).

(34) *ủǵr*[52] *l rḥq ỉlm*	(from) ỦǴR to the distant of gods,
ỉnbb[53] (35) *l rḥq ỉlnym*[54]	(from) ỈNBB to the distant of deities.

In this text ʿAnatu declares that she is about to set out "towards Baʿlu in the heights of ṢPN" (lines 37–38), which is presumably a long distance from her own residence in ỦǴR // ỈNBB. The important thing to observe from this example is that *ỉlm* and *ỉlnym* are roughly synonymous in that they are referencing Baʿlu, a distant god.

Phoenician also attests the form *ʾlnm* (const. *ʾln*), often thought of as the functional plural of *ʾlm*, but the evidence is mixed: *ʾln* (const.) is found once in a context clearly indicating a singular (KAI 104.1) and *ʾlm* in many cases seems to represent a plural (KAI 24 I.8).[55] A similar phenomenon occurs in Akkadian with its production of both *ilū* "gods" and *ilānū* "gods."[56] Huehnergard regards the latter form as containing the particularizing suffix *-ān*, which, in the plural, specifies a particular group as a subset of the broader class of the word to which the *-ān* morpheme is attached: *ilū* "gods" vs. *ilānū* "(a particular group) of gods." In other words, the *ilānū* would be a subgroup of divine beings within the broader category of deity. However, Huehnergard also observes that in the later dialects of Akkadian (post-Old Babylonian) the *-ān* forms become the normal plural for *ilum*, and in most cases the original function of the *-ān* suffix has been lost entirely.[57] This situation may offer a parallel for what is happening in Phoenician with its apparent loss of distinction between *ʾlm* and *ʾlnm* forms. At the same time,

52. Wyatt suggests the emendation *lǵr* "to the mountain" (*Religious Texts*, 82 n. 58), but this appears unnecessary in light of the parallel PN (*ỉnbb*, see next note) in the next line.

53. These two terms apparently refer to the location of ʿAnatu's residence (see also KTU 1.13:9 and 1.100:20 where *ỉnbb* seems to indicates a PN).

54. If *ỉlm* and *ʾlnym* are plural nouns, strictly speaking, *rḥq ỉlnym* could not be "most distant 'divine one'" (*DUL*, 60). Rather, the absence of the plural {m} in *rḥq* must indicate a construct phrase: "distant one of the deities." Smith and Pitard render these lines differently: "Ugar is very far, O Gods, Inbab is very far, O Deities" (*Ugaritic Baal Cycle 2*, 279. However, this interpretation would be strange in light of the fact that ʿAnatu is addressing *ʿnn ỉlm* "messengers of the gods," and not the gods themselves. It is therefore more natural to read *l rḥq* as referring to the perceived distance of the region (where Baʿlu dwells) she is about to visit from her own residence in ỦGR // ỈNBB (cf. del Olmo Lete, *Mitos y leyendas*, 187; Pardee, *COS* 1:253).

55. E.g., *bʿl wʾlm* "Baal and the god(s)" (sg. or pl.?) (KAI 26A I.8, II.6, III.11, 16); *bny ʾlm* "sons of the god(s)" (sg. or pl.?) (KAI 26A III.19); *ʾlnm* "gods" (pl. abs.) (KAI 10.10; 14.9, 16, 22; 48.2, 4); *ʾln* "gods of" (pl. const.) (KAI 10.16; 14.18; 19.7; 26A III.5). For additional references, see *DNWSI*, 53, 63.

56. *CAD* 7:91.

57. John Huehnergard, *A Grammar of Akkadian*, 2nd ed., HSM 45 (Winona Lake, IN: Eisenbrauns, 2005), 198. On the *-ān* suffix more generally, see Blau, *Phonology and Morphology of Biblical Hebrew*, 275; Joüon, 240–42 §88M a-f; Waltke and O'Connor, *Introduction to Biblical Hebrew Syntax*, 92.

however, we should exercise caution on this point since it is not a given that the *-ān* suffix in Northwest Semitic shared the same function as it did in Akkadian.

Returning attention to Ugaritic, scholars have been inclined to interpret *ỉlnym* as a by-form of **ỉlnm*, most likely etymologically related to Phoenician *ʾlnm* and Akkadian *ilānū*.[58] Accordingly, the form with {y} would represent some kind of expansion, but the specific function of the morpheme {y} is often left unstated in the literature.[59] I suggest that *ỉlnym* represents *ỉl* + the suffix *-ān* + the gentilic *-īy*/*-iyy* + plural morpheme *ūma*, vocalized as /ʾilānīyūma/ or /ʾilāniyyūma/.[60] The gentilic (or *nisbe*) ending can be attached to nouns as a means of indicating an adjectival quality associated with that noun and is most commonly found with place names indicating a person from location X (e.g., *môʾābî* "Moabite").[61] One might add that in Biblical Hebrew there are a few forms in which the gentilic is attached to nouns already having the *-ān* suffix—e.g., *ʾadmônî* "reddish," *yiddᵉʿônî* "soothsayer."[62] In the case of *ỉlnym*, the exact nuance of the term would refer to a certain type of divine being—in this case, those divine beings who are specifically identified with the Ugaritic royal dynasty. This particular nomenclature falls within the broader category of deity designated by *ỉl(m)* "god(s)," the secondary parallel for *rpủm* (KTU 1.6 VI:48; 1.20 II:2), and therefore qualifies them as a species of the divine class.

4.3.2. The Kirta Epic

We now turn our attention to a single passage from the Kirta Epic in which the *rpủm* are mentioned (KTU 1.15 III:3, 14). I render the broader context of the passage as follows (KTU 1.15 III):

58. See Gordon, *Ugaritic Textbook*, 359; Caquot and Sznycer, *Textes ougaritiques 1*, 442; L'Heureux, "Ugaritic and Biblical Rephaim," 268 n. 14; Baruch Margalit, "Lexicographical Notes on the Aqht Epic (Part II: KTU 1.19)," *UF* 16 (1984): 122; del Olmo Lete, "Nombres 'divinos,'" 63 n. 121; Schmidt, *Israel's Beneficent Dead*, 83 n. 174. Cf. Charles Virolleaud's earlier assessment that *ỉlnym* could be etymologically related to *ʾlwn* "oak tree," or possibly to the divine title Elyon ("Les Rephaim," *Revue des études sémitiques et Babyloniaca* [1940]: 83; noted in Caquot, "Rephaim ougaritiques," 77; Schmidt, *Israel's Beneficent Dead*, 83 n. 174).

59. Note, however, the remarks of Caquot: "*ʾIlnym* is certainly a nominal form derived of *-y* from a substantive *ʾln* surviving in Phoenician with a meaning that can hardly be distinguished from that of *ʾl* 'god'" ("*ilnym* est certainement une forme nominale dérivée en *-y* d'un substantive *ʾln* survivant en phénicien avec une acception qu'on ne peut guère distinguer de celle de *ʾl* 'dieu'") (*Syria* 37 [1960]: 78). See also L'Heureux, "Ugaritic and Biblical Rephaim," 268 n. 14 (noted in Schmidt, *Israel's Beneficent Dead*, 83 n. 174).

60. Blau argues that the gentilic ending must have originally been *-īy* rather than *-iyy* in light of Aramaic *-āy* with a long vowel preceding the {y} (*Phonology and Morphology*, 276; so Tropper, *Ugaritische Grammatik*, 2nd ed., §51.46 h–k).

61. For more examples from Hebrew, see Joüon, 242 §88M g.

62. As noted in Joüon, 242.

(2) [xx *mỉd rm*] *krt*	[Greatly lifted up] is Kirta,
(3) [*b tk rpỉ*] *ảrṣ*	[amidst the *rpủ*] of the earth,
(4) [*b pḫr*] *qbṣ dtn*[63]	[in the gathering] of the assembly of Ditānu.
(5) [*w t*]*qrb wld*	[She will] come near and bear
(6) *bnt*[64] *lk*	daughters for you,
(7) *tld pǵt tp*[xx]*t*	She will bear girl [. . .]
(8) *tld pǵt t*[xxx]*r*	She will bear girl [. . .]
(9) *tld pǵ*[*t* xxx]	She will bear gir[l . . .]
(10) *tld p*[*ǵt* xxx]	She will bear gi[rl . . .]
(11) *tld p*[*ǵt* xxx]	She will bear gi[rl . . .]
(12) *tld p*[*ǵt* xxx]	She will bear gi[rl . . .]
(13) *mỉd rm* [*krt*]	[Kirta] is greatly lifted up
(14) *b tk rpỉ ảr*[*ṣ*]	amidst the *rpủ* of the earth,
(15) *b pḫr qbṣ dtn*	in the gathering of the assembly of Ditānu.

Unfortunately, the physical condition of the tablet at this juncture of the text is rather broken, requiring that the first instance of *rpỉ* be restored in the gap at the beginning of line 3, but the repeated expression in lines 14–15 make this reconstruction relatively certain. The context of this passage deals with ʾIlu's pronouncement of blessing over Kirta, declaring that he will take up a wife and that she would bear him children. The mention of the *rpủm* in this epic text is qualified by two notable features: (1) they are designated by the construct phrase *rpỉ ảrṣ* "Rapaʾūma of the earth/underworld," and (2) the parallel for *rpỉ ảrṣ* is *qbṣ dtn* "gathering of Ditānu." I treat this text by discussing each of these features in turn.

4.3.2.1. *rpỉ ảrṣ* "The Rapaʾūma of the Earth/Underworld"

There has been much discussion over the meaning of this expression in Ugaritic. It occurs elsewhere in the funerary ritual text KTU 1.161:2, 9 in parallel with *qbṣ ddn*, likely the equivalent of *qbṣ dtn* here in the Kirta story. This designation is partially restored in ritual text KTU 1.108, which portrays this company as possessing the powers of Rāpiʾu, king of eternity (lines 23–24). I will comment further on this feature in my treatment of the *rpủm* in the ritual texts below (§4.3.6).

63. On *dtn*, see Pardee, *COS* 1:338 n. 49; Gelb, *Computer-aided Analysis of Amorite*, 17; Gelb, "Two Assyrian King Lists," *JNES* 13 (1956): 222; Huffmon, *Amorite Personal Names*, 184 (see bibliography in *DUL*, 283). On Ditānu as head of the royal dynasty and his status as one of the *rpủm*, see KTU 1.124 (=RS.24.272) (Brown, "Was There a West Semitic Asklepios?," 144; Pardee, *Ritual and Cult*, 170–71).

64. Note that the text reads a word divider before the {t}: bn . t.

Who were the *rpỉ ảrṣ* among whom Kirta is to be exalted? Early interpreters of this text rendered the expression *rpỉ ảrṣ* in different ways. In his initial publication of the Kirta Epic, Charles Virolleaud identified the *rpỉ ảrṣ* as an ancient Canaanite population of giants, citing the Old Testament Rephaim as a parallel.[65] He argued that *rpỉ* in this case is a marker of ethnicity.[66] Similarly, Ginsberg translated this expression "community of the land," interpreting *rpỉ* as a derivative of a root *rpʾ* meaning "to join."[67] He noted that the parallel for *rpủ* here is *qbṣ* "gathering, assembly" and thus understood all forms of *rpủm* as denoting "those gathered." Going in a slightly different direction, but maintaining an earthly interpretation, John Gray rendered *rpỉ ảrṣ* as "the dispensers of the fertility of the earth."[68] This interpretation stems from the fact that Gray believed the *rpủm* were cult functionaries, consisting of the king and his close associates who were designated as *ỉlnym* "divine beings" in view of their cultic responsibilities.[69]

Other proposals have made similar attempts to understand the *rpỉ ảrṣ* as nondivine beings. The appearance of the qualifier *ảrṣ* in this construct phrase led L'Heureux to claim that it designates living persons in this world, or more specifically, "an aristocracy of which the Canaanite kings were a part."[70] L'Heureux did not deny that in some cases the *rpủm* were indeed envisioned as divine beings (e.g., when parallel with *ỉlnym*), therefore arguing that the term *rpủm* has both divine and human referents in the Ugaritic texts.[71] These so-called earthly *rpủm* are put forth as an aristocratic warrior class under the patronage of ʾIlu. Of course, the feasibility of this proposal, at least in part, assumes that *rpủ* in KTU 1.108 is an epithet of ʾIlu, as it was originally suggested by Virolleaud.[72] I will return to this issue in my discussion of *rpủ* in KTU 1.108 below, but for now suffice to say that I find Pardee's criticism of this theory compelling: the god *rpủ* is associated with the *rpủm* in KTU 1.108:21–24, thus limiting his realm to that of underworld.[73] Such an association would be inappropriate for ʾIlu.

65. Charles Virolleaud, "Le marriage du roi Keret (III K): Poème de Ras-Shamra," *Syria* 23 (1942): 150–51; Virolleaud, "Rephaim," 77–83.

66. Virolleaud, "Rephaim," 82.

67. Ginsberg, *Legend of King Keret*, 23, 41; see also *ANET*, 146.

68. Gray, "DTN and RPỦM in Ancient Ugarit," 39.

69. Gray, "Rephaîm," 138.

70. L'Heureux, "Ugaritic and Biblical Rephaim," 271–72. Similarly, see de Moor, "Rāpiʾūma—Rephaim," 324–25; Horwitz, "Significance of the Rephaim," 39.

71. Cf. L'Heureux, *Rank Among the Canaanite Gods*, 201.

72. *Ugaritica* 5:553–55; followed by Samuel E. Loewenstamm, *Comparative Studies in Biblical and Ancient Oriental Literatures*, AOAT 204 (Kevelaer: Butzon & Bercker; Neukirchen-Vluyn: Neukirchener Verlag, 1980), 322.

73. See Pardee, review of *Cults of the Dead in Ancient Israel and Ugarit*, by Theodore J. Lewis, *JNES* 53 (1994): 154. For a fuller discussion of KTU 1.108 (=RS 24.252), see Pardee, *Textes paramythologiques*, 75–118.

Besides, we can just as easily render the term *ảrṣ* as "underworld" in certain contexts, as I noted in chapter 3 for death expressed in terms of one's descent into the *ảrṣ* "underworld."[74] Particularly insightful is Môtu's threat against Baʿlu that he is about to set him *b ḫrt ỉlm ảrṣ* "in the hole of the gods of the underworld" (KTU 1.5 V:5–6). The simplest explanation for the designation *ỉlm ảrṣ* in KTU 1.5 V is that it is a rough equivalent of the *rpỉ ảrṣ* here in KTU 1.15 III.[75] Such an association lends weight to Robert M. Good's proposal to understand it to mean literally "interred," that is, those having been embalmed ("healed") and buried.[76] Nonetheless, other scholars have attempted to advance the nondivine interpretation for the *rpỉ ảrṣ*, perhaps the most extensive support coming frcm the work of Schmidt.[77] Broadly speaking, Schmidt seems to deny the viability of a divine interpretation for *rpủm* at all, and he rests a major portion of his case upon his interpretation of *mtm* in the hymn to Šapšu in KTU 1.6 VI, claiming that this text defies any underworld connection. But, as my analysis of this text shows in the previous chapter, reading *mtm* as "men" is much less convincing than simply interpreting it as "dead persons."[78] This particular datum, where the *rpủm* are associated with *mtm* and *ỉlnym // ỉlm* at the same time, coupled with the construct phrase *rpỉ ảrṣ* attested here, points in two directions: (1) divine being, and (2) dead person.

The simplest resolution to these seemingly contradictory trajectories is to conclude that they are in fact referring to the divinized dead of the Ugaritic royal dynasty, as it has been traditionally suggested. As such, Parker takes the *rpỉ ảrṣ* here in KTU 1.15 III to be the eponymous ancestors of King Kirta, or his deified predecessors, among whom he will be held in high regard through his progeny.[79] For Parker, the blessing of Kirta is related to his being promised a future progeny that will enable him to be held in high regard among the *rpỉ ảrṣ*, that is, his dead ancestors.[80] One might assume that Parker intends to suggest that this exaltation takes place postmortem, though he never states this point explicitly. If Parker were to adopt his alternative rendering of *btk* (line 14) as a

74. Similarly observed by Shipp, *Of Dead Kings and Dirges*, 117.

75. See the discussion of this text in ch. 3 (§3.2.1.2).

76. Good. "Supplementary Remarks," 41; but criticized in Brown, "I Am the Lord Your Healer," 46–47.

77. See especially Schmidt, *Israel's Beneficent Dead*, 80–88. Note, however, Wyatt's assessment that most commentators have rejected the view of L'Heureux regarding the *rpủm* as living persons ("Religious Role of the King," 68).

78. See ch. 3 (§3.3.1).

79. Simon B. Parker, "The Marriage Blessing in Israelite and Ugaritic Literature," *JBL* 95 (1976): 28; Parker, *Pre-Biblical Narrative Tradition*, 90.

80. Contra the charges of Schmidt, *Israel's Beneficent Dead*, 80–81.

comparative "as the *rpủm* of the earth" rather than the usual locative meaning "amidst," then a postmortem exaltation for Kirta would not be required, since his enduring progeny in this life is simply being compared with his royal predecessors.[81] However, a comparative interpretation for *btk* is unnecessary and otherwise unwarranted in this context.[82] More directly, J. N. Ford thinks that Kirta's exaltation amidst the *rpỉ ảrṣ* reflects a promise that the king receives in both this life and the life to come—the progeny of Kirta is the "assurance of an enviable situation in the afterlife."[83] Wyatt describes Kirta's future (postmortem) membership in the *rpủm* as "the outcome of producing a healthy brood of royal offspring," as the broader context of this passage suggests, but notes the irony of Kirta's eventual cursing of his son YṢB, the very son who in part secures the blessing (KTU 1.16 VI:54–58).[84] Interestingly, Wyatt follows Schmidt in interpreting this exaltation as a reference to the funerary rites his son will eventually perform in commemoration of Kirta's death.[85] For Schmidt, the exaltation of Kirta will take place among the "living" *rpủm*, but one would assume that Wyatt sees this commemorative exaltation as being experienced in the underworld realm of the divine *rpủm*. In defense of this interpretation, Schmidt appeals to the funerary ritual KTU 1.161, which he thinks is only a commemorative rite and does not invoke the *rpủm* as deified dead ancestors receiving the recently departed king into their company (see below). One of the lingering problems with both of these approaches, however, concerns the verbal form *rm* in line 13 (reconstructed in line 2), which most likely represents a G stem SC.[86] For a future referent, we would expect the PC, as in the case of *tld* "she will bear," which prophetically announces the births of Kirta's children. The fact that a SC form (denoting perfective aspect) is used here suggests that Kirta's exaltation is already in view. Pardee notes that since KTU 1.108 depicts the *rpủm* as "conduits for divine blessing," it is reasonable to conclude that Kirta's status in KTU 1.15 III does not so much represent a funerary commemoration postmortem, but implies that "he is highly regarded and blessed by them."[87]

81. Parker, "Marriage Blessing," 28.

82. As rightly noted by Schmidt, *Israel's Beneficent Dead*, 80–81 n. 167.

83. Ford, "Living Rephaim," 76.

84. Wyatt, "Religious Role of the King," 68.

85. Wyatt, *Religious Texts*, 210 n. 152; cf. Schmidt, *Israel's Beneficent Dead*, 92, 122.

86. We could also analyze it as a masculine singular G participle, "Kirta who is exalted," which would also refer to Kirta's current situation.

87. See Pardee's treatment of this text in *Textes paramythologiques*, 75–118, and Pardee, *Ritual and Cult*, 192–95; Pardee, *COS* 1:338 n. 49. Similarly, see Lipiński, "Ditanu," 97, who thinks the *rpỉ ảrṣ // qbṣ dtn* are being summoned to bless Kirta with progeny.

4.3.2.2. *qbṣ dtn* "The Assembly of Ditānu"

The second member of the parallel pair I am analyzing here is *qbṣ dtn* "assembly of Ditānu." Rendered in Ugaritic as both *dtn* and *ddn*, this same pairing of *rpủm* with *dt/dn* occurs twice in the funerary ritual text KTU 1.161:[88]

(2) *qrỉtm* ⸢*r*⸣*pỉ ả*[*rṣ* . . .]	You have been called, O *rpủm* of the ea[rth],
(3) *qbỉtm qbṣ d*[*dn* . . .]	You have been summoned, O assembly of D[DN].
(4) *qrả ủlkn r*⸢*p*⸣[*ủ* . . .]	Called is ỦLKN the *rp*[*ủ* . . .]
(5) *qrả trmn rp*[*ủ* . . .]	Called is TRMN the *rp*[*ủ* . . .]
(6) *qrả sdn w rd*[*n* . . .]	Called is SDN and RD[N . . .]
(7) *qrả ṯr ʿllmn*[. . .]	Called is ṮR ʿLLMN [. . .]
(8) *qrủ rpỉm qdmym* [. . .]	They have called the former *rpủm*;
(9) *qrỉtm rpỉ ʾrṣ*	You have been called, O *rpủm* of the earth,
(10) *qbỉtm qbṣ dd*⸢*n*⸣	You have been summoned, O assembly of DDN;
(11) *qrả ʿmṯtm*⸢*r*⸣ *m*⸢*l*⸣*k*	Called is King ʿAmmiṯtamru,
(12) *qrả ủ nqm*⸢*d*⸣ ⸢*mlk*⸣	Called also is King Niqmaddu.

I will revisit this text in more detail below, but I simply observe here that *rpỉ ảrṣ // qbṣ dt/dn* is an established equivalency in Ugaritic, occurring in both poetic epic literature and ritual. In KTU 1.161, the pair function as bookends marking off the former *rpủm* from the more recently deceased Kings ʿAmmiṯtamru and Niqmaddu. Between these bookends, several individual *rpủm* are summoned to the ritual by name, followed by a summary invocation of the *rpỉm qdmym* "former *rpủm*." The fact that these names do not appear in the list of known kings from Ugarit (RS 24.257 and RS 94.2418) suggests that the *rpỉm qdmym* come from ancient mythic times.[89] Lipiński has suggested that the deity Ditānu/Didānu is the eponymous ancestor of the Ugaritic monarchs going back to the earliest Amorite clan of origin, based upon its appearance in two royal names of the first dynasty.[90] This name is attested in Assyrian king lists as di-da-a-an-u and in the Genealogy of the Hammurapi Dynasty (BM 80328), as di-ta-nu, which J. J. Finkelstein observed to be one of the earliest West Semitic tribal

88. The alternation *dtn/ddn* also occurs in the Assyrian King List; see Lipiński, "Ditanu," 92. Text follows Pardee, *Textes rituels,* 817; Pardee, *Ritual and Cult,* 171–72.

89. See Pardee, *Ritual and Cult,* 113 n. 124.

90. Am-mi-Di-ta-na "Headman of Ditanu" and Sa-am-su/si-Di-ta-na "Sun of Ditanu" (Lipiński, "Ditanu," 91–110).

names known in Mesopotamian sources.[91] Lipiński believes that these gathered ones of Ditānu/Didānu should be thought of as "the dead members of this celebrated tribe," observing comparatively that in Hebrew the N stem participle of *ʾsp* similarly denotes being gathered to one's fathers or kin in death.[92] Also taking the *rpỉ ảrṣ* to be "deified predecessors of the king," Parker thinks the *qbṣ dtn* are a more specific designation of that ancestry.[93] As for Kirta in KTU 1.15 III:15, he is presented as being exalted among the dead ancestors of the Ditānu tribe, who are thus summoned to bless Kirta with numerous progeny.[94]

The divine name Ditānu is also attested in KTU 1.124 independent of the formulaic *rpỉ ảrṣ // qbṣ dt/dn* just cited. One of the unique features of this text is the fact that it appears to be couched in terms dealing with the realm of mythology, but written in elevated prose. The content of the text concerns the *ảdn ỉlm* "lord of the gods" and his request for Ditānu to heal a sick child, leading Pardee to wonder if this divine account functions as a "model for similar human cases."[95] For the purposes of this discussion, I present KTU 1.124 as follows:[96]

(1) *k ymǵy ảdn*	When the lord/father of the many
(2) *ỉlm rbm ʿm dtn*	gods reaches Ditānu,
(3) *w yšảl* ⌜*m*⌝*ṯpṭ* ⌜*y*⌝*ld*	and requests a judgment for the child,
(4) *w yʿnynn*[97] ⌜*dtn*⌝	Ditānu answers him:
(5) *tʿny n*⌜*ảd*⌝[98] ⌜*mr*⌝ *q*⌜*ḥ*⌝	you shall reply: a leather bottle of myrrh take
(6) *w št* ⌜*b*⌝ ⌜*bt ḥrn*⌝ *t*⌜*rḥ*⌝	and set in the house of Ḥôrānu, a new
(7) *ḥdṯ m*[*r*] ⌜*q*⌝*ḥ wš*⌜*t*⌝	*trḥ*-bottle of myrrh take and set
(8) *b bt* ⌜*bʿ*⌝*l bnt*[99] *q*⌜*ḥ*⌝[ ]	in the house of Baʿlu, *bnt* take

91. For the Assyrian King List, see Gelb, "Two Assyrian King Lists," 209–30; Gelb, *Computer-aided Analysis of Amorite*, 17. For the Genealogy of the Hammurapi Dynasty, see J. J. Finkelstein, "The Genealogy of the Hammurapi Dynasty," *JCS* 20 (1966): 101.

92. E.g., Num 20:26.

93. Parker, *Pre-Biblical Narrative Tradition*, 90.

94. Lipiński, "Ditanu," 97.

95. Pardee, *Ritual and Cult*, 171.

96. According to Pardee's collation in *Textes paramythologiques*, 180, and Pardee, *Ritual and Text*, 171–72.

97. Written with word divider: w yʿny . nn (here and in line 13).

98. Cf. Hebrew *nōʾd* "skin/leather-bottle" (BDB, 609–10; *HALOT*, 657).

99. The meaning of this word remains uncertain. It is commonly rendered as "tamarisk" on the basis of Akkadian *bīnu* "tamarisk" (*AHw* 1:127; *CAD* 2:239) (see Manfried Dietrich and Oswald Loretz, *Mantik in Ugarit: Keilalphabetische Texte der Opferschau, Omensammlungen, Nekromantie*, ALASP 3 [Münster: Ugarit-Verlag, 1990], 218; Caquot, *Textes ougaritiques* 2, 122 n. 377; Tropper, *Nekromantie*, 151; del Olmo Lete, *Canaanite Religion*, 263; *DUL*, 233). Joaquín Sanmartín defended an earlier suggestion of Manfried Dietrich, Oswald Loretz, and Joaquín Sanmartín ("Bericht über ein Orakel [RS 24.272 = UG. 5, S. 563 NR. 6]," *UF* 7 [1975]: 540–41) to interpret *bnt* as "Figur"

(9) *w št b bt w prʿ[t]*[100]	and set in the house, and it will bring
(10) *hy ḫlh w ymǵ[ ]*	the illness to an end. Your messenger
(11) *mlảkk ʿm dt⌜n⌝*	has reached Ditānu;
(12) *lqḥ mṯpṭ*	he has received a judgment.

---

(13) *w yʿnynn*	Ditānu answers him:
(14) *dtn btn mḥ⌜y⌝*	Wipe (clean) the house:
(15) *l dg w l kl⌜b⌝*	no more fish and no more dog,
(16) *w ảṯr ỉn mr*	and afterward the bitterness will be no more.

One of the first issues related to this text is that of the title *ảdn ỉlm rbm*. Most scholars have understood this to be a reference to ʾIlu.[101] A few scholars have noted, however, the apparent problem in taking *ảdn ỉlm rbm* as a reference to ʾIlu: it would seem to require a greater god consulting a lesser god—in this case ʾIlu consulting Ditānu.[102] Yet, Pardee observes that in Ugaritic prose the word *ảdn* more often designates "father" than it does "lord, master," and therefore suggests that in light of the nonpoetic nature of KTU 1.124 we may well be dealing with the father of the many gods, which could only be ʾIlu in light of his designation *ảb bn ỉl* "father of the sons of ʾIlu" in KTU 1.40:34, 42.[103] At the same time, how-

("Zum Begriff 'Struktur' [*bnt*] im Ugaritischen," *UF* 10 [1978]: 445–46; see also Dietrich and Loretz, "Gebrauch von Götterstatuen in der Mantik von Ugarit [KTU 1.124]," *UF* 12 [1980]: 396; followed by Wyatt, *Religious Texts*, 424 n. 8). Dennis Pardee is uncertain as to the meaning of this word, simply rendering it in transliteration (as I have done here), but observes a possible connection with the Arabic root *bnn* (Lane, 258)and its derived nouns *bunnun* "coffee-berries" and *bannatun* "odor" ("Visiting Ditanu: The Text of RS 24.272," *UF* 15 [1983]: 136).

100. Pardee interprets this form as a 3fs D stem SC of the root *prʿ*, which he defines as "to excel over, bring to culmination" (*Ritual and Cult*, 186 n. 16). This root is etymologically related to the Hebrew noun *peraʿ* meaning "leader, prince" (*HALOT*, 971), and thus the verbal form would suggest gaining mastery over something (see Pardee, "Visiting Ditanu," 137 and Pardee, *Textes paramythologiques*, 188; cf. Dietrich and Loretz, *Mantik in Ugarit*, 211; del Olmo Lete, *Canaanite Religion*, 2nd ed., 263; Wyatt, *Religious Texts*, 424 n. 10). The antecedent of the following feminine pronoun *hy* would naturally be *bnt* from line 8: the *bnt* will bring the illness to an end. (On the correspondence between the verbal forms *wprʿ* and *wymǵ* and Biblical Hebrew *wᵉqatal* and *wayyiqtol* forms, see Pardee, "Visiting Ditanu," 137 and Pardee, *Textes paramythologiques*, 188.)

101. See bibliography in Pardee, "Visiting Ditanu," 132 n. 11; and subsequently, Caquot, *Textes ougaritiques* 2, 121 n. 368. However, Dietrich and Loretz have proposed taking it to be a reference to Baʿlu ("Gebrauch von Götterstatuen," 395–96; followed by Spronk, *Beatific Afterlife*, 193–94).

102. Schmidt, *Israel's Beneficent Dead*, 79; del Olmo Lete, *Canaanite Religion*, 2nd ed., 261; Wyatt, *Religious Texts*, 423 n. 1.

103. Note that in KTU 2.64 (RS 19.102) we read: *l ybnn ảdny rgm tḥm tl[m]yn bnk* "To YBNN, my father, say: Message of T[LM]YN, your son" (lines 1–5). From context, the addressee is called *ảdny*, regarding which the sender identifies himself as *bnk* "your son," demonstrating that *ảdn* in this context indicates a familial rather than a political relationship (cf. Pardee, *COS* 3:94 n. 52). For additional examples, see KTU 2.14 (RS Varia 4):19; 2.39 (RS 10.038):5; 2.85 (RS 92.2005):1; 2.90

ever, Pardee also observes that if *ỉlm rbm* were to refer to the royal inhabitants of the underworld (as in KTU 1.113) and *ảdn* were given its nonprose meaning "lord," then this *ảdn ỉlm rbm* could instead be a reference to Rašap, Rāpi'u/Milku, or Yariḫu, all of whose realms lie in the underworld.[104] This would be one way around the difficulty of ʾIlu's consultation with Ditānu. Going in a somewhat different interpretive direction, however, del Olmo Lete thinks *ảdn ỉlm rbm* refers to the king who makes this cultic consultation for his sick child, while Tropper believes it is a chief priestly figure who makes this incantation on behalf of the king's sick child.[105] Indeed, it is difficult to see father god ʾIlu consulting the lesser Ditānu for a judgment concerning this sick child, even if the child were a divine model for human cases.[106] It would appear more favorable to limit the identity of Ditānu's petitioner to the realm of the underworld, with Rāpi'u, king of eternity offering the kind of status one might expect of the lord of the many gods—he requests of Baʿlu that the powers of the *rpủm* would be transferred to the living king at Ugarit through the *rpủm* (KTU 1.108:18–27).[107]

The importance of this text for our discussion of the *rpủm* is that it provides a specific example of Ditānu—the dead, deified, eponymous ancestor of the Ugaritic royal dynasty to whom members are gathered at death—bringing the illness (*ḫlh*) of a child to a head and thereafter causing the bitter (*mr*) malady to disappear. It is true that this text mentions neither the *rpủm* nor the verb *rpʾ* "to heal," thus warranting Michael Brown's attempt to temper Spronk's earlier contention that this text proves conclusively the traditional etymology *rpủm* < *rpʾ* "to heal."[108] At the same time, however, this text seems to offer more

(RS 96.2039):13. Conversely, the term *ảb* appears to designate a political (rather than biological) father in Ugaritic prose (e.g., KTU 2.46 [RS 18.147]:1). Pardee, *Ritual and Cult*, 170.

104. See my discussion of Rašap above in ch. 3 (§3.2.2.1.2). Rāpiʾu/Milku is considered to be chief of the *rpủm* (Pardee, *Textes paramythologiques*, 185 n. 30); see my discussion below (§4.3.6.1). Yariḫu is the moon deity whose daylight hours are spent in the underworld (see KTU 1.100:25–29, as noted in Pardee, *Ritual and Cult*, 285). See Pardee's earlier discussions in Pardee, "Visiting Ditanu," 132–33 (arguing in favor of the dead divinized king Yaqaru of KTU 1.113:20; followed by Schmidt, *Israel's Beneficent Dead*, 79) and Pardee, *Textes paramythologiques*, 183, 184–86 (in addition to Yaqaru, also suggesting Rāpiʾu/Milku).

105. Del Olmo Lete, *Canaanite Religion*, 2nd ed., 261. Tropper, *Nekromantie*, 153.

106. Despite Pardee's qualification that it "would be an indication not so much of humility on *ʾIlu*'s part as of *Ditānu*'s powers of healing" (*Ritual and Cult*, 170). Schmidt favors interpreting *ảdn ỉlm rbm* as either ʾIlu or Baʿlu, but he attempts getting around the problem of a greater god consulting a lesser god by suggesting that it is Ditānu consulting ʾIlu (*Israel's Beneficent Dead*, 79–80). This solution will not work syntactically, however, since it is the lord of the many gods who travels to Ditānu (*ʿm dtn*), and in turn it is Ditānu who replies to the lord of the many gods, as indicated by the 3ms pronominal suffix following the verb *ʿny* (*w yʿnynn dtn*).

107. According to Pardee's interpretation of this text (*Ritual and Cult*, 193).

108. Brown, "Was There a West Semitic Asklepios?," 144, citing Spronk, *Beatific Afterlife*, 195.

than "uncertain evidence for the healing activity of one of the *rpủm*," as Brown contends, since the association between the *rpỉ ảrṣ* and *qbṣ dtn* as poetic parallels is unqualified in the Ugaritic texts (KTU 1.15 III:3–4, 14–15; 1.161:2–3). Demanding that a given text utilize the root *rp'* for the act of healing is unnecessarily rigid, especially since this particular text corresponds with other divine healing contexts attested in Ugaritic.[109] In the end, KTU 1.124 would appear to offer (at least) indirect evidence for the healing powers associated with the *rpủm* at Ugarit.

4.3.3. The 'Aqhatu Epic

I now turn our attention to the 'Aqhatu Epic and its references to the *rpủm*. In this epic, the only mention of the *rpủm* is in the title of one of its main characters, *dnỉl mt rpỉ* "Dānî'ilu man of *rpủ*."[110] The poetic parallel for this epithet is *ġzr mt hrmny* "the valiant Harnamite man."[111] Several remarks need to be made regarding the interpretation of these two titles and their significance for Dānî'ilu.

The first of these two titles reflects a genitive construction consisting of the word /mutu/ "man," followed by the bound form *rpỉ* (the genitive is indicated by the final {i} sign).[112] Opinions vary concerning the identity of the *rpủ* mentioned here, with most scholars connecting it to the deity *rpủ mlk ʿlm* "Rāpi'u, king of eternity" in KTU 1.108 who is associated with the broader group of the *rpủm*.[113] De Moor argues that *mt* + DN in such cases designates the bearer of the epithet and therefore indicates that Dānî'ilu is a protégé of said deity.[114] However, de Moor considers *mt rpỉ* to be the equivalent of saying *mt bʿl* "man of Baʿlu," Dānî'ilu's patron deity, but I find such an equivalency unwarranted for reasons

109. E.g., Šaʿtiqatu's healing of Kirta (KTU 1.16 V:25–28; VI:10–14); incantation against snake bite (KTU 1.82). The example from the Kirta Epic might warrant a parallel for interpreting *ảdn ỉlm rbm* as 'Ilu in KTU 1.124, since it is 'Ilu who seeks out someone from among the gods to heal King Kirta, though he fails to find a willing participant (KTU 1.16 V:10–22) and thus fashions Šaʿtiqatu for the task (KTU 1.16 V:23–28). The problem would persist, however, of 'Ilu making a request of a lesser underworld deity. For a recent discussion on this text, see Lewis, "Shaʿtiqatu Narrative," 188–211.

110. KTU 1.17 I:1, 17, 35, 37, 42; 1.17 II:28; 1.17 V:5, 14, 34; 1.17 VI:52; 1.19 I:20, 37, 39, 47; 1.19 II:41; 1.19 IV:13, 17, 18, 36.

111. KTU 1.17 I:17–18, 35–36; 1.17 II:28–29; 1.17 V:5, 14–15; 34–35; 1.19 I:20–21, 37, 48; 1.19 IV:19.

112. Virolleaud interpreted *mt* to be from /môtu/ "death," as a reference to the deity Môtu, "Mot the healer" ("Mot guérisseur"; *Légende phénicienne de Danel*, 87). Scholars have since abandoned this interpretation. See Caquot, "Rephaim ougaritiques," 81; Pardee, *COS* 1:343 n. 1.

113. See Parker, "Ugaritic Deity Rāpi'u," 99–100; de Moor, "Rāpi'ūma—Rephaim," 328; Pope, "Notes on the Ugaritic Rephaim," 166; André Caquot, "Rephaïm," *DBSup* 10:351; Spronk, *Beatific Afterlife*, 165; Pardee, *COS* 1:343 n. 1; Rouillard, "Rephaim," 693; Wyatt, *Religious Texts*, 250–51 n. 5; Gibson, *Canaanite Myths and Legends*, 2nd ed., 103.

114. De Moor, "Rāpi'ūma—Rephaim," 328–29.

outlined below (§4.3.6.1). Other scholars have followed Virolleaud in rendering *rpi* as a verbal adjective of some kind describing *mt,* and thus translating it "man of healing" or "man of the healer."[115] Joseph Aistleitner connected *rpi* with Akkadian *rubû/rubāʾu* meaning "prince," thus rendering it "man of the (divine) Prince," but the relatively wide attestation of *rpùm* in Ugaritic and *rᵉpāʾîm* in Biblical Hebrew would seem to render this suggestion unnecessary.[116] Still others have understood *rpi* as some kind of place name: "man/citizen of *rpi*," put forth most extensively by Margalit.[117] Margalit moves in this direction primarily for two reasons: (1) his denial of any etymological connection between the root *rpʾ* "to heal" and *rpùm,* and (2) his refusal to see Dānîʾilu as a royal personage.[118] His approach, however, seems to ignore the obvious connection that exists between Dānîʾilu and the *rpùm* in KTU 1.20 II:1–9 where he—with the same two epithets—appears to encounter their entourage.[119]

If we are to maintain the commonly held view that this epithet indeed relates to the lower-level deity Rāpiʾu from KTU 1.108, who is thus associated with the broader ranks of the *rpùm,* what does it say about the status of Dānîʾilu in the ʾAqhatu Epic? For one, it places him in similar company with Kirta who is said to be exalted among the *rpi* of the earth/underworld and the assembly of Ditānu. The funerary ritual text KTU 1.161 clearly associates the *rpùm* with royal figures, which from context may represent the divinized dead of the recent and distant (*qdmym*) past. A second factor is that both Kirta and Dānîʾilu have obtained a relatively high status within these ranks—Kirta is exalted among them, while Dānîʾilu is said to be a protégé of Rāpiʾu, the chief-ranking member of the *rpùm* who dispenses their powers of blessing and success to both the reigning king and the city of Ugarit (KTU 1.108:19–27).

The second title attested for Dānîʾilu in this epic is *ǵzr mt hrnmy* "the valiant Harnamite man." As a preliminary point of fact, this epithet is always introduced

115. "Man of healing": Caquot and Sznycer, *Textes ougaritiques 1,* 402–3; Wyatt, *Religious Texts,* 250. "Man of the healer": cf. Gray: "man who has been healed" ("Rephaîm," 134).

116. For the Akkadian, see *CAD* 14:395–400. Joseph Aistleitner, *Untersuchungen zur Grammatik des Ugaritischen,* Berichte über die Verhandlungen der Sächsischen Akademie der Wissenschaften zu Leipzig: Philologisch-historische Klasse 100/6 (Berlin: Akademie, 1954), 12. This is unecessary, as observed by Caquot, "Rephaïm," 251.

117. See Tropper, *Nekromantie,* 134: "Rapiu-Mann"; del Olmo Lete, *Mitos y leyendas,* 367: "*Daniilu* el *Rapaí.*"

118. Margalit, *Ugaritic Poem of AQHT,* 251–58. See also Wyatt's critique in *Religious Texts,* 250 n. 5.

119. Margalit's dismissal of this connection in observing that Dānîʾilu "forms no part of this Netherworld, chariot-riding coterie" seems to miss the point entirely (*Ugaritic Poem of AQHT,* 255). At the very least, the presentation of Dānîʾilu receiving a visit from the *rpùm* would at some level confirm his reputation as a purported man of Rāpiʾu, their chief-ranking member.

by the term *ġzr*, which I render "valiant one." As a poetic parallel for *dnỉl mt rpỉ*, the word *ġzr* functions as the replacement term for Dānīʾilu.[120] Regardless of one's conclusions about Dānīʾilu's status as a royal figure, the dominant means of presenting him in this epic is as a *ġzr*, perhaps a reference to his valiant strength. I have already discussed the interpretive challenges of this term in chapter 3 by analyzing its significance in Môtu's secondary epithet *ydd ỉlm ġzr* "the valiant beloved of ʾIlu."[121] As I pointed out there, the warrior imagery associated with this word finds support in KTU 1.3 II:22 where it occurs alongside other military terms. This aspect is certainly a dominant one of Môtu portrayed in the mythological texts at Ugarit. At the same time, however, *ġzr* is also thought to be particularly associated with "youthful" vigor, but as an attribute of Dānīʾilu in the ʾAqhatu Epic this limitation requires further qualification. Although *ġzr* is limited to Kirta's son ʾIluḥaʾu in the Kirta Epic (KTU 1.16 I:46), here it is used of both father and son.[122] Therefore, the Ugaritic usage for *ġzr* may imply that it refers to the strength of individuals who are capable warriors and who can father sons.[123]

The last term in this epithet is *hrnmy*, which I have translated "Harnamite." The most extensive discussion of the gentilic interpretation of this word goes back to Albright. He identified its location as the modern Syrian town of Hermel, south of ancient Kadesh, based largely upon his reading of Egyptian place name lists.[124] Pope also mentioned biblical Harmon in Amos 4:3 (related to Hinnom?), possibly a variant spelling with metathesis or even a corrupt spelling. For an etymology, he cited the Arabic root *harim* "to be very old, weak, decrepit," and observed that Albright's Syrian Hermel in Arabic would thus relate to old age.[125] Pope placed greater emphasis on *hrnmy* as a term associated with the underworld from its parallel with *mt rpỉ*, therefore characterizing Dānīʾilu as belonging to "the legendary heroes of the distant past long resident in man's

120. Interestingly, in KTU 1.22 I:6–7 the parallel *mtm // ġzrm* ("men" // "valiant ones") occurs in a context that seems to refer to the *rpủm*, which may offer comparison with the epithets of Dānīʾilu in the ʾAqhatu Epic: *dnil mt rpỉ // ġzr mt hrnmy*.

121. See my discussion in §3.3.3.1.

122. Of ʾAqhatu: KTU 1.17 VI:20, 26, 33(2×), 42, 51; 1.18 I:21; 1.18 IV:14; 1.19 II:24, 42; 1.19 III:47, 53; 1.19 IV:4, 16, 58–59.

123. Pardee, *COS* 1:340 n. 78.

124. William F. Albright, "The Traditional Home of the Syrian Daniel," *BASOR* 130 (1953): 26–27, also noting Virolleaud's earlier assessment that it must refer to a certain place named *hrnm* (*Légende phénicienne de Danel*, 88). See also Gray, "Rephaîm," 134; Caquot, "Rephaim ougaritiques," 85; Caquot and Sznycer, *Textes ougaritiques 1*, 402; del Olmo Lete, *Mitos y leyendas*, 367; Pardee, *COS* 1:343 n. 1.

125. See Lane, 413. The basic notion of this root is "to cut off," which can be extended to mean "advanced in age" (of an animal).

eternal infernal home."[126] Other scholars are less certain in their assessment of this word and simply render it in transliteration, and without interpretation.[127]

Others have questioned the identification of *hrnmy* as a place name. Margalit, for example, attempts to upend the scholarly consensus regarding *mt rpỉ* and *mt hrnmy*, urging that *rpỉ* is actually the place name while *hrnmy* is the divine name. He challenges Albright's geographical interpretation and follows Parker in questioning the prevailing view that *mt hrnmy* means "man of Harnam."[128] Instead, Margalit interprets *hrnmy* as a divine name consisting of a compound of the Arabic root *hr*(*r*) "to be full, pour out, dispense" + *my* "water," thus interpreting the form as (DN) "Rainmaker."[129] Returning to Parker, his observation regarding *mt hrnmy* is worth restating here: Why does the epithet include both *mt* "man of" and the gentilic *hrnmy*? In light of the preceding parallel *mt rpỉ* "man of Rāpiʾu," would we not expect **mt hrnm* "man of Harnam? Therefore, Parker proposes that the gentilic form is not an epithet of Dānîʾilu but of Rāpiʾu: "man of the Harnamite." He appeals to the independent occurrence of *hrnmy* in KTU 1.19 IV:32, arranged as follows:

(29) *qrym ảb dbḥ l ỉlm* — My father has offered sacrifice to the gods;
(30) *šʿly dǵṯh*[130] *b šmym* — he has made rise his *dǵṯ*-offering[131] in the heavens,
(31) *dǵṯ hrnmy b kbkbm* — the *dǵṯ*-offering of the Harnamite to the stars.

Contextually, this passage presents the speech of Pūǵatu, daughter of Dānîʾilu, who declares what the narrative has just described her father doing—giving a *dǵṯ*-offering to the gods following his seven-year period of mourning over the death of ʾAqhatu. Here, Parker finds reason to believe that *hrnmy* is an epithet of

126. Pope, "Notes on the Ugaritic Rephaim," 166.

127. Wyatt, *Religious Texts*, 250.

128. Parker, "Ugaritic Deity Rāpiʾu," 100–101. Cf. Parker, "Aqhat," in Parker, *Ugaritic Narrative Poetry*, 76.

129. Margalit, *Ugaritic Poem of AQHT*, 255–57, 259–60; cited with approval in Wyatt, *Religious Texts*, 250–51 n. 5.

130. Note the discrepancy in the reading of this suffix in line 23, which both *CAT* and *KTU3* read with the 3mp suffix {dǵṯhm}. Herdner (*CTA*) read this form in both lines 23 and 30 with the 3ms suffix: {dǵṯh}, but notes that Virolleaud read both with final {t} (also in *KTU*). Unfortunately, the tablet is badly damaged in line 23, and the images provided by Inscriptifact are difficult to make out at line 30 as well. From the major editions one finds relative agreement with the reading {dǵṯh} for line 30 (see also Parker, "Ugaritic Deity Rāpiʾu," 101; de Moor, *Anthology of Religious Texts*, 260; Pardee, *COS* 1:355).

131. Hoffner thinks this term is an Indo-European loanword into Ugaritic meaning "smoke-offering" ("Anatolian Cult Term," 66–68).

Rāpi'u, which would mean that *dǵṯ hrnmy* is the *dǵṯ*-offering of the deity *Hrnmy*.[132] This interpretation encounters difficulty, however, if we are to accept reading a 3ms pronominal suffix for *dǵṯ* in line 30, which would clearly indicate "the *dǵṯ*-offering of Dānî'ilu," since the immediate antecedent must be *ảb* "my father" in line 29.[133] Neither does it help matters if one argues for a 3mp suffix in the narrative presentation of this sacrifice in line 23—*dǵṯhm* "their *dǵṯ*-offering"—with the preceding *ỉlm* "gods" as its antecedent (i.e., "a *dǵṯ* for the gods"), since *dǵṯ hrnmy* "*dǵṯ* for (DN) *Hrnmy*" would be an offering to a single god.[134] The reading {dǵṯh} with a 3ms suffix with its antecedent *ảb* "my father" makes best sense of the parallelism if *hrnmy* is to be taken as an epithet of Dānî'ilu: *dǵṯh* "his *dǵṯ*-offering" // *dǵṯ hrnmy* "the *dǵṯ*-offering of the Harnamite." A further strike against the proposal to read *hrnmy* as a divine epithet for Rāpi'u (i.e., deity from *Hrnm*) is that he is said to dwell in ʿAštartu in KTU 1.108:2. For these reasons, I interpret *hrnmy* in KTU 1.19 IV:24 and 31 as an abbreviated version of Dānî'ilu's epithet widely attested elsewhere in the epic.[135]

It remains to consider the syntax of this epithet. Admittedly, the simplest solution is to follow Parker's proposal to interpret *ǵzr* in apposition to *mt hrnmy*—"valiant one, man of the Harnamite"—since it would offer a seemingly more symmetrical parallel for *dnỉl mt rpỉ* "Dānî'ilu, man of Rāpi'u." Unfortunately, the problems just outlined preclude its acceptance, and therefore requires a different explanation. The independent form of this epithet in KTU 1.19 IV is *hrnmy*, not *mt hrnmy*, which seems to suggest that *ǵzr* and *mt* are appositional: "the valiant one, the Harnamite man." Therefore, this secondary title for Dānî'ilu relates to two characteristics: (1) his reputation as a valiant man/warrior figure (*ǵzr*, *mt*), and (2) his association with the geographical location of Harnam (*hrnmy*). This explanation provides the rationale for my translation "the valiant Harnamite man."

This two-member title for Dānî'ilu places him within the company of King Kirta, who is described as having been exalted with regard to the *rpủm* of the

132. Parker, "Ugaritic Deity Rāpi'u," 101, followed by Margalit, *Ugaritic Poem of AQHT*, 256–57.

133. Contra Wyatt, *Religious Texts*, 309 n. 262.

134. *CAT* and *KTU3*. One could translate *ỉlm* as "god," taking the {m} as enclitic, but there would still be the problem of the plural suffix of *dǵṯ*, unless one opts for reading {dǵṯh} in line 23 as well.

135. Margalit's contention that this epithet is a "fixed" form and therefore cannot occur independent of Dānî'ilu's name is not accurate. We find precedent for just such a feature in the epithets of Môtu analyzed in ch. 3. The secondary epithet *ydd ỉlm ǵzr* "valiant beloved of 'Ilu" (always in parallel with *bn ỉlm mt* "Môtu, son of 'Ilu") occurs once independent of the primary epithet as *mdd ỉlm* "beloved of 'Ilu" (KTU 1.4 VIII:23–24). It is interesting to observe that: (1) it is the secondary epithet that occurs independently, and (2) it is *ǵzr* that is omitted in both cases. (On Môtu's epithets, see my discussion in the previous chapter, §3.3.3.1.)

earth/underworld. The distinction of Dānîʾilu, however, is his designation in the ʾAqhatu Epic as the protégé of their chief-ranking member, Rāpiʾu, king of eternity. His mention in the Rapaʾūma texts (KTU 1.20–22) only strengthens his association with this prestigious guild, and it is to these texts that I now turn our attention.

4.3.4. The *rpủm* Texts (KTU 1.20–22)

The Ugaritic Rapaʾūma texts have sparked much discussion since their initial publication (KTU 1.20) with the ʾAqhatu Epic in Virolleaud's *La légende phénicienne de Danel* (1936), which was republished with additional fragments (KTU 1.21–22) in a subsequent article (1941).[136] The main challenge in reading these texts is the deteriorated condition of the tablets with major breaks at key points in the text. Two recent epigraphic studies on these tablets have attempted to provide a firmer basis for readings, the first offered by Wayne T. Pitard in his 1992 article entitled, "A New Edition of the 'Rāpiʾūma' Texts: KTU 1.20–22," and the most recent by Pardee published in 2011 as "Nouvelle étude épigraphique et littéraire des textes fragmentaires en langue ougaritique dits 'Les Rephaïm' (*CTA* 20–22)."[137] My analysis of the *rpủm* throughout these texts will primarily follow the recent collation of Pardee, with reference to Pitard where appropriate.

The broken nature of these texts has made scholars generally skeptical about our ability to determine their original orientation, with most presenting them in the order of their initial publication.[138] Despite the poor condition of these fragments, however, there have been a few attempts at placing them together into a single narrative. De Moor maintains the earlier view espoused by Virolleaud that these Rapaʾūma texts were at one time part of the original ʾAqhatu Epic and proposes the following arrangement: KTU 1.21, KTU 1.20, and KTU 1.22.[139] Others have questioned this arrangement, however.[140] Pardee objects to this order on epigraphic grounds, claiming that the flatness of the well-preserved face

136. Charles Virolleaud, "Les Rephaïm, fragments de poèmes de Ras-Shamra," *Syria* 22 (1941): 1–30.

137. Pitard, "New Edition," 33–77. For a general overview of these texts and related issues, see Pitard, "The *Rpủm* Texts," in Watson and Wyatt, *Handbook of Ugaritic Studies*, 259–69. Pardee, "Nouvelle étude épigraphique," 1–65.

138. See Caquot and Sznycer, *Textes ougaritiques 1*, 461–80; Cyrus H. Gordon, "Poetic Legends and Myths from Ugarit," *Berytus* 25 (1977): 29–34; L'Heureux, *Rank Among the Canaanite Gods*, 129–59; del Olmo Lete, *Mitos y leyendas*, 403–24; Spronk, *Beatific Afterlife*, 161–77; Margalit, *Ugaritic Poem of AQHT*, 464–69; Lewis, "Rapiuma," 196–205; Wyatt, *Religious Texts*, 314–23.

139. De Moor, *Anthology of Religious Texts*, 265–73.

140. See Parker, *Pre-Biblical Narrative Tradition*, 134–35, followed by Smith, *Poetic Heroes*, 141 n. 33.

of tablet RS 2.[024] (=KTU 1.21, 22) requires that it belong to the obverse side, and not the reverse.[141] Likewise, he challenges Dijkstra's attempt to identify the obverse from the reverse of these texts on the basis of words divided between lines. Dijkstra argues that such word divisions would have occurred on the back of the tablet due to space constraints.[142] However, Pardee notes several examples from the Baʿlu cycle where words are divided between lines on both the obverse and reverse of tablet KTU 1.17, rendering Dijkstra's criterion less likely.[143] Pardee offers his arrangement of these fragments as belonging to a single tablet from the ʾAqhatu cycle and bases it upon three considerations: (1) the mention of Dānîʾilu is a strong indicator that these texts belong to the ʾAqhatu cycle, (2) the similarity in vocabulary shared by the three fragments and the tablets of the ʾAqhatu cycle, but which are absent from other Ugaritic mythological texts, and (3) it is impossible to provide a coherent literary analysis without knowing the proper order of these three fragments.[144] Based upon his epigraphic analysis, he proposes that these fragments represent a single tablet with three columns on each side (I–VI): KTU 1.22 I (RS 2.[024]) and KTU 1.21 II (RS 2.[019]) are from columns I and II of the recto of the tablet respectively (column III lost entirely), while KTU 1.20 (RS 3.348) provides columns VI and V of the verso.[145] The recto of KTU 1.20 is effaced entirely, as well as most of the verso of KTU 1.22 and KTU 1.21.[146] This epigraphic analysis of the tablets produces the following order: KTU 1.22 I; 1.21 II; 1.22 II; 1.20 II; 1.20 I.[147]

In what follows, I present my translation of these texts according to the order proposed by Pardee in light of his epigraphic study of the fragments. I find his discussion rather convincing and adopt the results here. I offer a translation of the extant fragments of the Rapaʾūma texts in their entirety due to their importance for this study, all the while recognizing that their broken nature renders

141. Pardee, "Nouvelle étude épigraphique," 3–4. On the physical surface features of the verso and recto sides of Ugaritic tablets, see Pardee, *Ugaritic Texts*, 69–72; Pardee, "RS 3.367, Colonne 'IV,'" 227–28; Pardee, review of *The Ugaritic Baal Cycle*, 47. See also my discussion in ch. 3 (§3.2.1).

142. Meindert Dijkstra, "Epigraphical Evidence for the Determination of the Column-Order in the Tablets KTU 1.1 and KTU 1.20–22," *UF* 19 (1987): 49–60.

143. Pardee, "Nouvelle étude épigraphique," 4–5.

144. The mention of Dānîʾilu as a strong indicator is also mentioned by Caquot and Sznycer, *Textes ougaritiques 1*, 463; de Moor, "Rāpiʾūma—Rephaim," 332; Spronk, *Beatific Afterlife*, 160; contra, Margalit, *Ugaritic Poem of Aqht*, 465; Lewis, "Toward a Literary Translation," 116; Pitard, "*Rpum* Texts," 263. Meindert Dijkstra believes it to be an undecided question ("The Legend of Danel and the Rephaim," *UF* 20 [1988]: 36).

145. Contra Pitard, "New Edition," 75 n. 8, who thinks KTU 1.20 (RS 3.348) belonged to a separate tablet (see Pitard, "*Rpủm* Texts," 260, 262–63).

146. Pardee, "Nouvelle étude épigraphique," 6–9.

147. For a visualization of this reconstruction, see Pardee, "Nouvelle étude épigraphique," 8–9.

my interpretive conclusions provisional. The intention of my discussion here is to place these texts alongside references to the *rpủm* elsewhere in Ugaritic where literary contexts are more certain and better understood, hoping that the combined picture will offer further clarity. Following my translation of the texts, I will comment on what they contribute to our assessment of the Ugaritic *rpủm* as a whole.

KTU 1.22 I	
(1) *mm*[...]	
(2) *h hn bnk hn*[...]	Look, your son, look[...]
(3) *bn bn ảṯrk*[148]	a son, a son in your place.
hn ⸢*ǵz*⸣[*r*...] (4) *ydk*	Look, valia[nt] one [...] your hand,
ṣǵr tnšq šptk	the small one whom your lips will kiss.
ṯm (5) *ṯkm bm ṯkm ảḫm*	There, shoulder to shoulder, are the brothers,
qym[149] *ỉl* (6) *b lsmt*[150]	hasty attendants of ʾIlu.
ṯm y⸢ʿ⸣*bš*[151] *šm ỉl mtm*	There, the men adorn the name of ʾIlu,
(7) *yʿbš brkn šm ỉl ǵzrm*	the valiant ones adorn the name of ʾIlu with blessing.

148. Cf. KTU 1.17 I:28. This expression is regularly rendered adverbially as "after you" in reference to the one who endures after one's death (e.g., Caquot and Sznycer, *Textes ougaritiques 1*, 473; del Olmo Lete, *Mitos y leyendas*, 422; *DUL*, 127), or similarly "your progeny," meaning "your (issue that endures) afterward" (e.g., L'Heureux, *Rank Among the Canaanite Gods*, 152). Others believe *ảṯr* to be referring to the shrine of the departed (e.g., Lewis, "Rapiuma," 203; Wyatt, *Religious Texts*, 320), or more generically the "place" of burial (Pardee, "Nouvelle étude épigraphique," 44; followed by Smith, *Poetic Heroes*, 147). If we are to consider the subsequent occurrences of *ảṯrh* throughout these texts where the locative {h} suffix seems to require that we are dealing with a physical place, not to mention that it is identified as *bty* "my house" and *hkly* "my palace," it would seem to warrant the same here. In these other cases, *ảṯrh* marks the destination for the movement of the *rpủm* where they are said to rise/take their stand.

149. This noun comes from the hollow root *qwm* "to arise," here attested as a plural construct, perhaps as a qatta/il noun (cf. Arabic *qayyim* [Lane, 2996]). Pardee notes that in Ugarit this particular noun denotes junior divine attendants of the senior gods (e.g., Baʿlu attending [*qm*] ʾIlu in KTU 1.2 I:21 and the lad attending [*qm*] Baʿlu in KTU 1.3 I:4, 18) (Pardee, "Nouvelle étude épigraphique," 52).

150. This feminine noun is dervived from √*lsm* "to run." Cf. Akkadian *lasāmu* (*CAD* 9:104–6; *AHw* 2:538–39).

151. On this reading and not {yṯbš}, see Wayne T. Pitard, "The Shape of *ʿAyin* in the Ugaritic Script," *JNES* 51 (1992): 265–66, and Pitard, "New Edition," 56, 57. Cf. the Arabic √*ʿbš* "to better, arrange" (J. G. Hava, *Al-afaraid, Arabic-English Dictionary* [Beirut: Catholic Press, 1915], 450; cited in Pardee, "Nouvelle étude épigraphique," 52). Caquot and Sznycer point out that the context seems to suggest that the verbal action reflects a favorable attitude toward the name of ʾIlu (*Textes ougaritiques 1*, 474 n. q), which Pardee translates: "There the two men celebrate the name of *ʾIu*" ("Là les deux homes célèbrent le nom de *ʾIlu*") ("Nouvelle étude épigraphique," 44). The form would therefore be a D-stem factitive (with Pardee, "Nouvelle étude épigraphique,"52 n. 78), indicating that the heros are declaring the superior quality of ʾIlu's name.

(8) *ṯm ṯmq*[152] *rpủ bʿl*	There is ṮMQ, *rpủ* of Baʿlu,
mhr bʿl (9) *w mhr ʿnt*	warrior of Baʿlu and warrior of ʿAnatu.
ṯm yḥpn ḥyl(10)*y*	There is YḤPN the powerful one,
zbl mlk ʿllmy	prince, king (of) ʿLLMY.
km tdd[153] (11) *ʿnt ṣd*	As ʿAnatu arises to the hunt,
tštr[154] *ʿpt šmm*	She sets to flight the birds of the heavens.
(12) *ṭbḫ ảlpm*	They slaughter oxen,
ảp ṣỉn šql	also small cattle they fell,
ṯrm (13) *w mrỉ*	bulls and fatling rams,
ỉlm ʿglm dt šnt	yearling calves,
(14) *ỉmr qmṣ llỉm*	lambs of great quantity (and) kids.
k ksp (15) *l ʿbrm zt*	Like silver (are) olives for travelers,
ḫrṣ l ʿbrm kš	as gold (are) dates for travelers.
(16) *ủ pr ṯlḥn b qʿl*	Moreover the fruit of the table (is) surrounded by vine blossoms,
b qʿl (17) *mlkm*	amid the vine blossom of kings.
hn ym yṣq yn ṯmk	Look, for a day they pour wine of ṮMK,
(18) *mrṯ yn srnm*	MRṮ, wine of rulers,
y⸢n⸣ bld[155] (19) *ǵll*	wine of the country of ǴLL,
yn ỉšryt[156] *ʿnq*	wine of the happiness of ʿNQ,
smd (20) *lbnn*	of the *smd* of Lebanon,
ṭṣ[157] *mrṯ yḥrṯ ỉl*	dew of MRṮ (that) ʾIlu ploughs.
(21) *hn ym w ṯn*	Look, a day and a second,

152. Other interpreters have taken *ṯmq* and *yḥpn* in these lines as verbal forms (Virolleaud, "Rephaïm, fragments," 21–22; Gordon, *Ugaritic Literature*, 103; Gray, *Legacy of Canaan*, 2nd ed., 128; de Moor, *Seasonal Pattern*, 117; Caquot and Sznycer, *Textes ougaritiques 1*, 472; L'Heureux, *Rank Among the Canaanite Gods*, 146–47), but I follow those who render them as proper names (Joseph Aistleitner, *Die mythologischen und kultischen Texte aus Ras Shamra*, 2nd ed. [Budapest: Akadémiai Kiadó, 1964], 85; del Olmo Lete, *Mitos y leyendas*, 420–21; Wyatt, *Religious Texts*, 321; Pardee, "Nouvelle étude épigraphique," 46–47, 52), which makes better sense contextually: these are two attendants of ʾIlu introduced by name.

153. Analyzing this form as an N-stem of the root *dwd* (< *ḏwḏ*) (cf. Akkadian *izuzzu* "to stand" [*CAD* 20:373–92]) (de Moor, *Seasonal Pattern*, 71; L'Heureux, *Rank Among the Canaanite Gods*, 134–35; Pardee, "Nouvelle étude épigraphique," 55 n. 85, 59–60). Others cite the root *ndd* meaning "to flee, flutter, stray" (Gordon, *Ugaritic Literature*, 101–2; Driver, *Canaanite Myths and Legends*, 1st ed., 67, 157; Caquot, "Rephaim ougaritiques," 84), but the semantics of Akkadian *izuzzu* are better suited to the context. Virolleaud's proposed root *ydd* "to love" for this word seems unlikely.

154. Š stem of √*ntr* "to jump, leap" (*DUL*, 652).

155. Cf. Arabic *balad* "land" (Lane, 247) (see Dennis Pardee, "Textes ougaritiques oubliés et 'transfuges'," *Sem* 41–42 [1993]: 47).

156. Cf. Hebrew *ʾšr* II "to be called happy" (*HALOT*, 97).

157. Scribal error for {ṭl}.

tlḥm rpủm (22) *tštyn*	the *rpủm* eat, they drink;
t̲lt̲ rbʿ ym	a third, a fourth,
ḫmš (23) *t̲dt̲ ym*	a fifth, a sixth day;
tlḥmn rpủm (24) *tštyn*	the *rpủm* eat, they drink.
bt ỉkl b prʿ	at the banquet hall, on the summit,
(25) *b ṣq b ỉrt lbnn*	in the narrow (places), in the heart of Lebanon.
mk b šbʿ(26) [*b*] ⌜*ymm*	Then, upon the seventh ([of] the) day(s),
ảpn⌝*k ảlỉyn bʿl*	thereupon mighty Baʿlu . . .
(27) [. . .] *rʿh ảby* [. . .]	
(28) [. . .]	

KTU 1.21 II	
(1) [. . .]*rzʿy*[158]	. . .
lk bty (2) [*rpỉm*	Travel to my house, [O *rpủm*,
b b]⌜*t*⌝*y ảṣḥkm*	into] my [ho]use I summon you,
ỉqrả(3)[*km ỉlm b h*]⌜*k*⌝*ly*	I invite [you, O gods, into] my [pa]lace.
ảt̲rh rpủm (4) [*l tdd*	To this place the *rpủm* [indeed arise,
ảt̲rh] *l tdd ỉlnym*	to this place] indeed the divine beings arise.
(5) [. . .]*rzʿy*	. . .
ảp ảnk y rp(6)[*ủm . . .*	Even I, O *rp*[*ủm . . .*
. . .]⌜*k*⌝*m rʿy*	. . .] my companions.
ht ảlk (7) [. . .]*t̲lt̲t*	Look, I go [. . .] third(?),

158. Others reconstruct this form as [*m*]*rzʿy*, "my marzeah," thus signifying a reference to the *marziḥu* feast (e.g., L'Heureux, *Rank Among the Canaanite Gods*, 142 n. 43; Spronk, *Beatific Afterlife*, 169; Lewis, *Cults of the Dead*, 81–82 [though he notes that the equation *mrzḥ* and *mrzʿ* "remains problematic" (82 n. 7)]; Lewis, "Toward a Literary Translation," 129; Smith, *Poetic Heroes*, 146 n. 49). The equation apparently goes back to Otto Eissfeldt, who proposed that the Ugartic syllabic forms mar-za-i/mar-zi-i (< *mrzʿ*) (RS 15.88:4, 6) and mar-zi-ḫi (< *mrzḥ*) (RS 14.16:3) are variant spelling of the same word ("Kultvereine in Ugarit," *Ugaritica* 6:187–95). As a means of explaining this equation, L'Heureux argued that the reading with {ʿ} represented "the voiced equivalent" of an unvoiced {ḥ}, demonstrating "a partial assimilation" to voiced {z} (*Rank Among the Canaanite God*, 142 n. 43). Similarly, Huehnergard cites the syllabic spellings mar-za-i and mar-zi-i as reflecting *marza/iʿi* "with intervocalic voicing of /*ḥ*/ to [ʿ] that is also evident in the alphab. spelling [*m*]*rzʿy*" (*Ugaritic Vocabulary*, 178). It is important, however, to note the uncertainty of this equivalency, especially given the fact that this one instance of *mrzʿ* in the alphabetic script requires reconstruction. The syllabic spellings mar-za-i and mar-zi-i are difficult to reconcile with the morphological evidence for *mrzḥ*. Ugaritic syllabic mar-zi-ḫi and Hebrew *marzeaḥ* suggest a *maqtil* base, whereas Ugaritic mar-za-i points to a *maqtal* base. Huehnergard gives priority to the Ugaritic syllabic spelling mar-za-i over mar-zi-i and mar-zi-ḫi, as well as Hebrew *marzeaḥ*, concluding that its base was likely a *maqtal* (i.e., *marzaḥu*) and that the /a/ and /i/ interchange demonstrates "the effect of vowel harmony around the guttural" (*Ugaritic Vocabulary*, 178). This explanation, however, leaves the Hebrew evidence unaccounted for, where the *ṣērê* apparently indicates a *maqtil* base and the guttural {ḥ} is without question. Futhermore, it is uncertain that

ảmǵy l bt (8)[. . .	I arrive at the house [. . .
. . . *b qr*]⌜*b*⌝ *hkly*	. . . in the mid]st of my palace.
w yʿn ỉl (9) [. . .	ʾIlu/the god answered [. . .
. . .] *lk bty rpỉm*	. . .] travel to my house, O *rpủm*,
(10) [*b bty ảṣ*]*ḥkm*	[into my house I su]mmon you,
ỉqrảkm (11) [*ỉlm b hk*]⌜*l*⌝*y*	I invite you, [O gods, into] my [palace.]
ảṯrh rpủm (12) [*l tdd*	To this place the *rpủm* [indeed rise,]
ảṯ]⌜*r*⌝*h l tdd* ⌜*ỉl*⌝[*n*]⌜*ym*⌝	to [this plac]e indeed the di[v]ine beings rise.
(13) [. . .]*rn*[. . .]	

KTU 1.22 II

(1) [. . .]⌜*ṯl*⌝[. . .]	
(2) *b hkly* [. . .]	in my palace [. . .]
(3) *lk bty* ⌜*r*⌝[*pỉm*	Travel to my house, O *r*[*pủm*
b bty ảṣḥ](4)*km*	into my house I summon] you,
ỉqr[*ảkm ỉlm b hkly*]	I inv[ite you, O gods, into my palace.]
(5) *ảṯrh r*[*pủm l tdd*	To this place the *r*[*pủm* indeed arise,
ảṯrh] (6) *l tdd ỉl*[*nym*	to this place] indeed the di[vine beings] arise.
w yʿn ṯmq] (7) *mhr bʿ*⌜*l*⌝	[ṮMQ] warrior of Baʿlu [answers,]
[. . . *mhr*] (8) *ʿnt*	[. . . warrior] of ʿAnatu:
lk b⌜*t*⌝[*y rpỉm*	Travel to [my] house, [O *rpủm*,
b bty] (9) *ảṣḥ km*	into my house] I summon you,
⌜*ỉ*⌝[*qrảkm ỉlm b*] (10) *hkly*	I [invite you, O gods, into] my palace.

---

mar-zi-i/mar-za-i (RS 15.88:4, 6) are related to mar-zi-ḫi (RS 14.16:3) in the first place (Schmidt, *Israel's Beneficent Dead*, 65). Pardee explains the variant syllabic spellings with or without Akkadian {ḫ} on the basis of the phonetics of Ugaritic {ḥ}: in Akkadian "the fricative element was sometimes represented as {ḫ}, while the unvoicedness was sometimes represented as {o}" ("Ugaritic Funerary Cult," 181–82). Equating *mrzḥ* and [*m*]*rzʿ* primarily arises from the following assumptions: (1) the *marziḥu* is somehow associated with a mortuary cult, (2) the Rapaʾūma are mentioned in association with a word ending in [-]rzʿy, and (3) the Rapaʾūma are associated with the *marziḥu* festival (Pardee, "Ugaritic Funerary Cult," 181–82). The philological problems just outlined, however, may indicate that this equation is unfounded (see also Pardee, "Nouvelle étude épigraphique," 58–59).

Smith's recent treatment of the Rephaim texts, which he calls "The Journey and Late Summer Feast of the Rephaim," gives considerable interpretive weight to the meaning of this term. By equating [*m*]*rzʿ* with *mrzḥ*, these texts record an invitation for the Rephaim to partake in the social drinking club of the *marziḥu*, and thus "mythologize the upper-class marzeah" (Smith, *Poetic Heroes*, 147). Smith goes on to conclude that the association of the Rephaim with the marzeah "may further reflect an effort at royal emulation, since . . . the Rephaim are involved in both royal ritual and the well-to-do male institution of the marzeah" (147). The royal purposes of these texts are largely without dispute, but the centrality of the *marziḥu* within these purposes is not. Interest in the *marziḥu* foists an intrusive element into the literary setting of these texts. At the very least, whether or not the feasting of the Rapaʾūma is associated with the *marziḥu* (which seems unlikely) is inconsequential and should not occupy a prominent place in the interpretation of this passage.

ảṯ⌜*r*⌝[*h rpủm l tdd*]	[To] this place [the *rpủm* indeed arise],
(11) *ảṯrh l t*[*dd ỉlm*	to this place indeed [the gods] a[rise.
. . .] (12) *yḥpn ḥy*[*ly*	. . .]YḤPN the power[ful
zbl mlk ʿllmy]	prince, king of ʿLLMY]
(13) *šmʿ ảtm* [. . .]	Listen, you [. . .]
(14) *ym lm qd*[. . .]	day . . .
(15) *šmn prs*⌜*ǵ*⌝ [. . .]	oil of . . .
(16) *ydr hm y*[. . .]	
(17) ʿ⌜*ṣ* ⌝ *ảmr*	tree of ẢMR.
yủ⌜*ḫ*⌝[*d ksả mlkh*]	He seiz[es the throne of his kingship]
(18) *n*⌜*ḫ*⌝*t kḥṯ d*⌜*r*⌝[*kth*	the seat of [his] auth[ority.
b bty] (19) *ảṣḥ rpỉ*⌜*m*⌝	Into my house] I summon the *rpủm*,
[*ỉqrả ỉlm*] (20) *b qrb h*[*kly*	[I invite the gods] into [my] pa[lace.
ảṯrh rpủm l] (21) *tdd*	To this place the *rpủm* indeed] arise,
ảṯr⌜*h*⌝ [*l tdd ỉlnym*]	to this place [indeed the divine beings arise.]
(22) *ảsr m*⌜*r*⌝[*kbthm*	They bind [their] char[iots,
tṣmd sswm]	they yoke the horses,]
(23) *tʿln l m*⌜*r*⌝[*kbthm*	they mount [their] char[iots,
tỉt ʿl] (24) *ʿrhm*	they come on] donkeys,
tl[*kn ym w ṯn*	they trav[el a day and a second,
ảḫr špšm] (25) *b ṯlṯ*	after (the setting of) the sun] on a third.
m⌜*ǵy*⌝ [. . .]	They arrive [. . .]
(26) ⌜*ỉl*⌝[*n*]⌜*y*⌝[*m* . . .]	the divine being[s . . .]

KTU 1.20 II

(1) *ṯmn b qrb hkl*⌜y	Eight in my palace.
ả⌝[*ṯrh rpỉm*][159] (2) *ndd*	[To] this p[lace the *rpủm*] rise,
ảṯrh ndd ỉl⌜*m*⌝	to this place the gods rise.
[*mrkbthm*] (3) *ảsr*	They bind [their chariots],
sswm tṣmd ⌜*b g*⌝[. . .]	they yoke the horses in/with [. . .].
(4) *tʿln l mrkbthm*	They mount their chariots,
t⌜*ỉ*⌝[*t ʿl ʿrhm*]	they come[e on donkeys].
(5) *tlkn ym w ṯn*	They travel a day and a second,
ảḫr š[*pšm b ṯlṯ*]	after (the setting of) the s[un on the third],
(6) *mǵy rpủm l grnt*	the *rpủm* arrive at the granary,
⌜*ỉ*⌝[*lm b qrb*] (7) *mṭʿt*	the g[ods (arrive) at the] plantation.
w yʿn dnỉl [*mt rpỉ*]	Dānîʾilu, [man of Rāpiʾu] answers,

159. Cf. KTU 1.21 II:3.

(8) *yṯb ġzr mt hrnm*⸢*y*⸣	the valiant Harnamite man replies:
[...] (9) *b grnt ỉlm*	[...] at the granary the gods.
b qrb m[*ṭʿt*...] (10) *d tỉt*	at the pl[antation ...] who have come.
yspỉ spủ q[...]	Indeed he ate [...]
(11) *tpḥ ṯṣr shr* [...]	
(12) [...]	

KTU 1.20 I.

(1) [... *rp*]⸢*ủ*⸣*m tdbḥn*	[... *rp*]*ủm* you shall prepare a feast,
(2) [...]⸢?⸣*ʿd ỉlnym*	[...] ... divine beings,
(3) [...]⸢*k*⸣*mt mtm*[160]	[...]like the men of the dead
(4) [...]*b k qrb sd*	[...]as the assembly draws near,
(5) [...]*n b ym qẓ*	[...] on the day's end,
(6) [... *rp*]⸢*ỉ*⸣*m tlḥmn*	[... *rp*]*ỉm*, they eat
(7) [...]⸢?⸣*m tštyn*	[...] ... they drink
(8) [...]*ỉl d ʿrgzm*	[...] of nuts[161]
(9) [...] *dt ʿl lty*	[...] which are over ...
(10) [...]*tdbḥ amr*	[...]sacrifice ...
(11) [...]⸢*ym??*⸣	...

Reference to the *rpủm* in these texts occurs eight times, with an additional five partial restorations and five full restorations that are reasonably certain from context.[162] And as scholars readily note, we only have a small fraction of text presumably preserved from what appears to have been a much longer literary piece. Needless to say, the high number of references to the *rpủm* in these

160. From the photographs provided through Inscriptifact, the first visible sign is chipped in the middle of the sign so that its identity is uncertain. Scholars have suggested {k} or {w}, both of which would seem to fit in the allotted space, but the individual wedges of the sign are not legible from the most recent photographs. Immediately following this illegible sign one can make out a faint {m}, after which there is {tmtm}, yielding the sequence *w/k mtmtm*. Pitard helpfully observes that earlier photos must be examined with regard to the first letter of this sequence, since the tablet was subsequently damage ("New Edition," 44). Pardee's examination of the earlier photo from the *editio princeps* (see Virolleaud, *Légende phénicienne de Danel*, plate 17) leads him to conclude that the first legible sign is {k} (with Virolleaud, Pitard [and now *KTU*3]), not {w}, arguing that a fissure on the tablet may have contributed to Herdner's reading {w} with hesitation (followed in *KTU* and *CAT*). I therefore follow the consensus of Virolleaud, Pitard, and Pardee in reading this first sign as {k}.

161. See Pope, *Song of Songs*, 574–79; Dennis Pardee, *Les textes hippiatriques* (Paris: Editions Recherche sur les Civilisations, 1985), 53; Manfried Dietrich and Oswald Loretz, "Ug. *b ṣql ʿrgz* und *b ṣqlnw* (II Reg 4,42), *ʾgwz*," *UF* 18 (1986): 118–20.

162. KTU 1.22 I:8, 21, 23; 1.21 II:3, 9, 11; 1.22 II:19; 1.20 II:6; partially restored in KTU 1.21 II:5–6; 1.22 II:3, 5; 1.20 I:1, 6; fully restored in KTU 1.21 II:2; 1.22 II:8, 20; 1.20 II:1, 7.

fragments makes them the actors of interest. One also finds a dizzying array of verbs of movement describing their activities: *hlk* "come, go," *ʾtw* "come," *mǵy* "arrive," and *dwd* "arise, stand."[163] In two places the narrative depicts the *rpủm* preparing for movement: binding their chariots, yoking their horses, mounting their chariots, and going on donkeys.[164] Also prominent throughout these fragments are statements summoning the *rpủm*, each of which occur immediately prior to their stated movements and emphasize their invitation to the oft-mentioned *ảṯr* "place."[165] The two extant mounting of chariots formulas immediately follow their rising to the *ảṯr* "place," and may indicate that the *rpủm* are moving on to the next *ảṯr* of summoning. In light of Pardee's proposed ordering of the fragments, I propose the following broken outline of their contents:

Recto

Column I

first half lost

- Mention of a son "in your place" (KTU 1.22 I:1–4)
- Vision of the gods (ʾIlu and his attendants, ṮMQ, *rpủ* of Baʿlu, and YḤPN the powerful) (KTU 1.22 I:4–10)
- ʿAnatu's hunt and the subsequent slaughter and feasting of the *rpủm* (KTU 1.22 I:10–26)
- Mighty Baʿlu . . . (KTU 1.22 I:26–28)

remaining lines lost

Column II

- First-person summons of the *rpủm* ("I summon // invite") and the *rpủm* arise to this place (KTU 1.21 II:1–4)
- First-person arrival at "house" // "my palace," addressing the *rpủm* (KTU 1.21 II:4–8)
- Third-person summons of the *rpủm* ("ʾIlu/the god summons // invites") and the *rpủm* arise to this place (KTU 1.21 II:8–13)

several lines lost

- First- or second-person summons of the *rpủm* ("come to my house"; "I summon // invite you") and the *rpủm* arise to this place (KTU 1.22 II:1–6)
- ṮMQ replies . . . (KTU 1.22 II:6–8)

163. *hlk*: KTU 1.21 II:1, 6, 9; 1.22 II:3, 8, 24; 1.20 II:5. *ʾtw*: KTU 1.20 II:4, 10. *mǵy*: KTU 1.21 II:7; 1.22 II:25. *dwd*: KTU 1.21 II:4, 12; 1.22 II:6, 22; 1.20 II:2(2×).

164. KTU 1.22 II:22–23; 1.20 II:2b-4.

165. KTU 1.21 II:1–4, 9–13; 1.22 II:3–6, 8–11, 18–21.

- First- or second-person summons of the *rpủm* ("come to my"; "I invite you") and the *rpủm* arise to this place (KTU 1.22 II:8–11)
- YḤPN [replies]: hear you . . . (KTU 1.22 II:12–13)

lines 13–18 broken

- First-person summons of the *rpủm* and the *rpủm* arise to this place (KTU 1.22 II:19–21)
- The *rpủm* bind chariots, yoke horses, mount chariots, and come on donkeys (KTU 1.22 II:22–24)
- The *rpủm* travel three days and arrive at . . . (KTU 1.22 II:22–25)

last few lines broken

Column III
entirely lost

Verso
Column IV
entirely lost

Column V

- The *rpủm* arise to this place (KTU 1.20 II:1–2)
- The *rpủm* bind chariots, yoke horses, mount chariots, and come on donkeys (KTU 1.20 II:2–4)
- The *rpủm* travel three days and arrive at the granary // plantation (KTU 1.20 II:5–7)
- Dānîʾilu replies . . . (KTU 1.20 II:7–8)

lines 9–12 broken
remaining lines lost

Column VI
lines 1–12 broken
remaining lines lost

From this general, albeit broken picture of the Rapa'ūma texts and their contents, I need to comment on several more specific points of interest. First, the text mentions *bnk* "your son" within the context of *bn aṯrk* "son of your place" (KTU 1.22 I:2–3). The context of these initial lines is frustratingly broken, yet at the very least they resemble the concerns of KTU 1.17 I:27–34 outlining the duties of a faithful son. Lines 27–28 speak of the son,

l ảrṣ mšṣủ qṭrh	who makes his incense go out with regard to the earth;
(28) *l ʿpr ḏmr aṯrh*	who guards his (resting) place with regard to dust.

In this context, *ảṯr* coupled with *qṭr* "incense" implies the burial place of the father and the funerary ritual carried out by the faithful son.[166] In the Rapaʾūma texts, this term recurs throughout as the location of focus to which the *rpủm* are summoned.[167] In each of these cases, the actual summons from the speaker calls the *rpủm* to *bty* "my house" and *hkly* "my palace," after which the *rpủm* rise (*t/ndd*) to this place (*ảṯr*). The movement of the *rpủm* to the *ảṯr* begins with their yoking of horses, mounting of chariots, and travel on donkeys, followed by the formulaic two-day journey and arrival at the *ảṯr* on the third day at the time of the sun's setting. The residential language and its association with the place where the *rpủm* rise are reminiscent of KTU 1.161, the funerary ritual wherein the recently deceased king of Ugarit descends into their company. Interestingly, in KTU 1.20 II:6–7, the place of arrival is designated *grnt* "granary" // *mṭʿt* "plantation"—in this case Dānîʾilu appears and seems to be addressing the *rpủm* at their arrival. The mention of Dānîʾilu at this juncture apparently confirms the status attributed to him in the ʾAqhatu Epic as a *mt rpỉ* "man of Rāpiʾu"—here, the company of *rpủm* arrive at his place.

The fact that *aṯrh* is identified as *bty* and *hkly* throughout these passages would suggest that the *rpủm* are being summoned to the royal palace, particularly, that of Dānîʾilu who is thus named in KTU 1.20 II:6–7. Excavations at Ugarit reveal the existence of vaulted tomb chambers beneath the floors of residential structures, apparently intended for multiple burials of deceased loved ones.[168] This architectural feature uncovered at Ugarit offers a certain level of explanation for the association of one's burial "place" (*ảṯr*) with one's place of residence, and in the Rapaʾūma texts it symbolizes the place of contact between the living royal figure and his deceased ancestors. I will have more to say on this topic in

166. See Pardee, *COS* 1:344 n. 8; Pardee, "Nouvelle étude épigraphique," 49–51. Other proposals for interpreting this term include "footsteps" (Albright, "'Natural Force' of Moses," 35; Caquot and Sznycer, *Textes ougaritiques 1*, 422; Lewis, *Cults of the Dead*, 65), "tomb" (Gibson, *Canaanite Myths and Legends*, 2nd ed., 104; Marvin H. Pope, "The Cult of the Dead at Ugarit" in *Ugarit in Retrospect: Fifty Years of Ugarit and Ugaritic*, ed. Gordon Young [Winona Lake, IN: Eisenbrauns, 1981], 161; cf. del Olmo Lete, *Mitos y leyendas*, 369: "resto"), "shrine" (Umberto Cassuto, *Biblical and Oriental Studies*, vol. 2 [Jerusalem: Magnes Press, 1973], 200; Gaster, *Thespis*, 334; Dijkstra and de Moor, "Problematic Passages," 175–76; L'Heureux, *Rank Among the Canaanite Gods*, 134–35), and "progress" (Jean-Marie Husser, "Culte des ancêtres ou rites funéraires? A propos du 'Catalogue' des devoirs du fils [KTU 1.17:I-II]," *UF* 27 [1995]: 125–26, followed by Wyatt, *Religious Texts*, 257 n. 33).

167. KTU 1.21 II:3, 11, 12; 1.22 II:10, 11, 21; 1.20 II:2.

168. See the discussion in Pitard, "Libations Installations," 20–37.

chapter 5. Such imagery acquires further clarity in the funerary ritual of KTU 1.161 where the *rpủm* are likewise summoned to participate in the ritual burial of the most recently deceased king of Ugarit.[169]

Second, the parallel *mt // ǵzr* recurs in these texts and is elsewhere attested exclusively for Dānîʾilu in the ʾAqhatu Epic. In KTU 1.22 I:6–7, the *mtm* "men" // *ǵzrm* "valiant ones" are with the attendants of ʾIlu, identified as brothers standing shoulder to shoulder. This literary context shows the valiant ones adorning the name of ʾIlu with blessing. Two other divine figures are mentioned by name, ṮMQ and YḤPN, the first of whom is called *rpủ* of Baʿlu and further qualified as "warrior of Baʿlu and warrior of ʿAnatu" (KTU 1.22 I:8–9). This description brings to mind Dānîʾilu, who is both "man of Rāpiʾu" and "valiant Harnamite man," only in this case the named entity is a high-ranking member of the *rpủm* serving as Baʿlu and ʿAnatu's personal warrior. Comparatively, Dānîʾilu has gained a certain reputable status as protégé of the highest ranking member of the *rpủm*, Rāpiʾu, and also exemplifies his own warrior status as the valiant Harnamite man. As such, these named *rpủm*, despite their prominence among the rest of the *rpủm*, are subservient to the major gods Baʿlu and ʿAnatu.

The usage of *mt // ǵzr* with reference to Dānîʾilu in the ʾAqhatu Epic in concert with what one finds in the Rapa'ūma texts, as well as their parallel interests in the funerary *ảṯr* "place," justify identifying of the son mentioned in KTU 1.22 I:1–4 in a similar light as well. Scholars have typically taken the phrase *bn bn aṯrk* in line 3 as a reference to an unnamed grandson understood in one of two ways: (1) "son of a son (at) your place," or (2) "son of a son of your place."[170] The first option is nonspecific and is therefore not necessarily tied to Dānîʾilu's lineage, while the second one refers to a son of Dānîʾilu, either a resurrected ʾAqhatu or some other unspecified son.[171] Caquot concluded that this text must refer to ʾAqhatu, perhaps in a revivified form, with several scholars finding additional support for this revivification motif in *qym il* of line 5, taking it to mean "resurrected of ʾIlu" or the like.[172] But the whole narrative thrust of the ʾAqhatu Epic would seem to suggest otherwise, since the extant story offers no evidence for the hero's resurrection (if anything, it yields strong evidence to the contrary!). Pardee offers another proposal, rendering the two words for "son" appositionally: "a/the son (who is/will be) the son of your place."[173] According to this

169. Pardee, *COS* 1:344 n. 8; Pardee, *Ritual and Cult*, 85–87.

170. Lewis, "Rapiuma," 203; Wyatt, *Religious Texts*, 320; Smith, *Poetic Heroes*, 148 n. 66.

171. Pardee, "Nouvelle étude épigraphique," 50.

172. Caquot, "Rephaim ougaritiques," 89. Gordon, *Ugaritic Literature*, 103; Gray, *Legacy of Canaan*, 2nd ed., 128 n. 3; de Moor, *Seasonal Pattern*, 117; Caquot and Sznycer, *Textes ougaritiques 1*, 474; Margalit, *Ugaritic Poem of AQHT*, 468.

173. "Un/le fils (qui est/sera) le fils de ta place" (Pardee, "Nouvelle étude épigraphique," 50).

proposal, the royal descendant could quite possibly be the son of Dānîʾilu's daughter, Pūǵatu, who acquires a prominent role toward the end of the epic in her retribution of ʾAqhatu's death. Pardee dubs *bn bn aṯrk* an explicit declaration of substitution, wherein the royal daughter's future son becomes heir to the throne.[174] The advantage of Pardee's proposal is that it provides a plausible interpretation in support of reconstructing a literary relationship between the ʾAqhatu Epic and the Rapaʾūma texts. Smith interprets the phrase *aṯrk* prepositionally meaning "after you" instead of "your place," and proposes that "perhaps the Rephaim are arranged by generation, and perhaps it includes those who died young (for example in battle)." Smith considers Pardee's identification of the unnamed speaker very reasonable, but offers another (less likely) suggestion: "the speaker might be Rpʾu, who arranges his Rephaim by generation, and he is addressing the lineage of the Rephaim."[175]

A third observation relates the particles *hn* and *ṯm* in marking the presentation of the various entities depicted in KTU 1.22 I. In line 2 the aforementioned son is introduced by *hn* "look," while the scene of divine entities is signaled by the use of the particle *ṯm* "there." We may recall the formulaic greetings attested in the letters, where the expanded particle *hnny/hlny* signifies the sender's situation, while the expanded particle *ṯmny* marks a shift in focus to that of the receiver. The following example from KTU 2.38 (RS 18.031) illustrates this epistolary feature:

(6) *hnny ʿmn*	Here with us,
(7) *šlm ṯmny*	it is well. There
(8) *ʿmk mnm šlm*	with you, whatever is well
(9) *rgm ṯṯ[b]*	return word.[176]

The shift is certainly more subtle in KTU 1.22 I, but it is detectable nonetheless: "Look, (here is) a son ... a son (who is/will be) a son of your place ... there, shoulder to shoulder, are the brothers, attendants of ʾIlu ... there, the men arrange the name of ʾIlu." It is clear that *ṯm* functions to introduce the divine realm of ʾIlu and his attendants in these cases, which eventually moves on to the presentations of ṮMQ, *rpủ* of Baʿlu, and YḤPN, the prince king of ʿLLMY, again, both introduced with *ṯm*. From here the scene shifts to ʿAnatu's hunt, the slaughter of animals, and the feasting and drinking of the *rpủm*. After an extensive break

174. Pardee, "Nouvelle étude épigraphique," 50–51.

175. Smith, *Poetic Heroes*, 150.

176. See also KTU 2.11 (RS 8.315):10–14; 2.46 (RS 18.147):6–8; 2.71 (RS 29.095):5–8; 2.72 (RS 34.124):7–9.

in the text the narrative resumes with an unidentified individual summoning the *rpủm* to *aṯrh* "(this) place" // *bty* "my house" // *hlky* "my palace." In KTU 1.20 II:7, their place of arrival is apparently in the vicinity of Dānî'ilu, who then addresses them. In this way, the *rpủm* are attributed to the divine realm of the gods, but they are also on the move to take their stand at the place of summoning, identified as the royal residence.[177] Such activities demonstrate that they were thought to play a central role in the affairs of the royal palace and that they were invested in establishing its success. The broken nature of these tablets prohibits us from determining anything about the status of Dānî'ilu other than the fact that he is at the place where the *rpủm* arrive. However, correlation with what we know from the funerary ritual text KTU 1.161 may allow us to posit that the Rapa'ūma texts offer a mythological vision of Dānî'ilu's reception into the company of the *rpủm* with the royal seat firmly secured by his own progeny.

From these texts I make the following conclusions regarding the nature of the *rpủm*. For one, the literary connection between the 'Aqhatu Epic and the Rapa'ūma texts first perceived by earlier scholars appears to be a highly plausible interpretation, even if uncertain. On another level, this factor only heightens Dānî'ilu's status as one highly exalted within the ranks of the Rapa'ūma. The contents of the texts themselves, though broken in their sequence, clearly depict the *rpủm* as members of the divine realm, some of whom are in the service of the greater gods (e.g., ṮMQ, *rpủ* of Baʿlu, warrior of Baʿlu and warrior of ʿAnatu, and possibly an attendant of 'Ilu). These texts also provide ample evidence for their being summoned/invited by a royal personage to his residence and their subsequent rising in response.

4.3.5. KTU 1.82

At this juncture in the discussion I will consider briefly the appearance of the *rpủm* in the incantation text KTU 1.82, a collection of incantations against evil spirits in cases of venomous snake bite. I already mentioned the earlier portion

177. Smith, on the other hand, proposes that the locale of summoning is a banquet house in the Lebanon mountains, perhaps a shrine erected in honor of Dānî'ilu. Furthermore, Rāpi'u's residence at Ashtaroth and Edrei in the region of Bashan (KTU 1.108:2–3) is to be identified with this same place, known in other souces for its fertility. The Epic of Gilgamesh elevates the Lebanon as "the home of the divine council," thus an imagined sanctuary where the gods meet. Smith concludes that "in this context, in death these heroic Rephaim enjoy a relationship with the major deities" (*Poetic Heroes*, 151). I only caution that, at least from the exant fragments preserved from the Rapa'ūma texts, Rāpi'u is not mentioned, even though his close tie to the Rapa'ūma is well-established elsewhere (KTU 1.108). For this reason, I am afraid this proposal takes us further than the text will allow.

of this text in chapter 1 in relation to the expression *ql špš ḥw*, translated, "by the voice of Šapšu, be saved/delivered."[178] I will not rehash that discussion here, but I do wish to highlight the importance of this text for analyzing the Ugaritic *rpủm*. The circumstances of incantation offer a different context from that of the mythological and epic literature because it deals with the real life concerns of the ancients. At the same time, however, the ancient perspective did not dichotomize the supernatural from the natural, but instead mixed the two, which is readily apparent in incantation where the physical pains of life are interpreted in light of the battling gods. Texts like these offer a fairly reliable gauge of the psyche of the ancient mind by enabling us to understand something about how they viewed their world and its dangers.

It is unfortunate that the *rpủm* appear in a broken section of this tablet, rendering certain details of the text unknown. My presentation of the text follows the version recently published by del Olmo Lete:[179]

(32) [...]*ḥmt l ql rpỉ*[*m* ...]	... venom at the voice of the *rpủm* ...
(33) [...]*llm ảbl mṣr pk* [...]	... I will remove the sobbing of your mouth ...
(34) [...]*y mṭnt w tḥ ṭbt n*[...]	... and you will live on (in) good (health) ...
(35) [...]*bṯnm w ṯṯb ʿl bṯnt trtḥ*[...]	... the male serpent, and you will sit/repeat against the female serpents, and you will ...

The significance of this attestation is that it provides a nonmythological context in which the *rpủm* are the object of invocation, as divine counterparts with Šapšu, in this case for the removal of deadly venom from the snake-bitten victim. This text apparently assumes the same kind of relationship between Šapšu and the Rapaʾūma reflected in the mythology of the Baʿlu cycle (KTU 1.6 VI:46–48) where she apparently rules over the *rpủm* (// *ỉlnym* and *ỉlm* // *mtm*). Del Olmo Lete concludes that the voice of the *rpủm* is now added to the voice of Šapšu and thus "introduces the call to the ancestors and corresponding cult of the dead into the list of divine protecting entities against this danger."[180] I do want to caution, however, that the break after the {ỉ} of *rpỉ*[-] means we are not entirely sure that it is the *rpủm* as a class and not the single deity Rāpiʾu, which is certainly a

178. See §1.2.2.5.

179. Del Olmo Lete, "KTU 1.82," 245–65. Cf. del Olmo Lete, *Canaanite Religion*, 2nd ed., 321–26.

180. Del Olmo Lete, "KTU 1.82," 257.

plausible reconstruction. Were that the case, it would corroborate with the picture of that deity as presented in KTU 1.108, whose powers are shared with the *rpủm* and are thus manifest in the city of Ugarit. Even there, Šapšu is mentioned in the lines immediately following (KTU 1.108:26).

Despite the broken condition of this passage, the broader context of KTU 1.82 allows us to make one of two conclusions: (1) the collective voice of the *rpủm* is being invoked, along with the voice of Šapšu, to fight against these attacking serpents, or (2) the voice of Rāpi'u, chief of the *rpủm*, is being invoked in likewise fashion. Either way, the *rpủm* are perceived as having the ability to administer powers of healing on behalf of someone having been bitten by a poinsonous snake.

4.3.6. The Ritual Texts

4.3.6.1. KTU 1.108—*rpủ mlk ʿlm*

I now turn our attention to the *rpủm* as they appear in two important ritual texts. The first of these is KTU 1.108, most notable for its mention of the divine personage Rāpi'u who is presented as having some apparent relation to the *rpủm* introduced toward the end of the text. I have provided KTU 1.108 in its entirety below:[181]

Obverse

(1) [*hl*]*n yšt rpủ mlk ʿlm*	Look, may Rāpi'u, king of eternity, drink,
w yšt (2) [*il*] ⸢*g*⸣*ṯr*[182] *w yqr*	may the powerful and honorable god drink,

181. Following the collation of Pardee (*Textes paramythologiques*, 76; Pardee, *Ritual and Cult*, 193–95). For additional studies on this text, see Virolleaud, *Ugaritica* 5:551–57; André Caquot, "La tablette RS 24.252 et la question des Rephaïm ougaritiques," *Syria* 53 (1976): 295–304; de Moor, "Studies in the New Alphabetic Texts from Ras Shamra I," 175–79; de Moor, *Anthology of Religious Texts*, 187–90; Simon B. Parker, "The Feast of Rāpi'u," *UF* 2 (1970): 243–49; Parker, "Ugaritic Deity Rāpi'u," 97–102; Arvid S. Kapelrud, "The Ugaritic Text RS 24.252 and King David," *JNSL* 3 (1974): 35–39; Manfried Dietrich, Oswald Loretz, and Joaquín Sanmartín, "Der 'Neujahrpsalm' RS 24.252 (= Ug. 5, S. 551–57 Nr. 2)," *UF* 7 (1975): 115–19; L'Heureux, *Rank Among the Canaanite Gods*, 169–87; Dietrich and Loretz, "Baal Rpu," 171–82; Dietrich and Loretz, "Rāpi'u und Milku aus Ugarit: Neue historische-geographisch Thesen zu *rpủ mlk ʿlm* (KTU 1.108:1) und *mt rpi* (KTU 1.17 I 1)," *UF* 21 (1989): 123–31; Loewenstamm, *Comparative Studies*, 320–32; Spronk, *Beatific Afterlife*, 177–89; de Tarragon, *Textes ougaritiques* 2, 111–18; Good, "On RS 24.252," 155–60; van der Toorn, "Funerary Rituals," 55–60; Ford, "Living Rephaim," 76–80; David M. Clemens, "KTU 1.108.3–5 (RS 24.252): *dyšr.wyḏmr . . .*," *UF* 25 (1993): 63–74; Yitzhak Avishur, *Studies in Hebrew and Ugaritic Psalms* (Jerusalem: Magnes Press, 1994), 277–307; del Olmo Lete, *Canaanite Religion*, 2nd ed., 148–55; Wyatt, *Religious Texts*, 395–98.

182. Cf. Akkadian *gašru* "strong" (*CAD* 5:56–58).

il yṯb b ʿṯtrt	the god dwelling in ʿṮTRT,
(3) *il ṯpṭ b hdrʿy*	the god ruling in HDRʿY,
d yšr w yḏmr	who sings and makes music,
(4) *b knr w ṯlb*[183]	with the lyre and flute,
b tp[184] *w mṣltm*[185]	with the drum and cymbals,
b m(5)*rqdm*[186] *d šn*	with the castanets of ivory,
b ḥbr kṯr ṭbm	with the goodly companions of Kôṯaru.
(6) *w tšt ʿnt gṯr*	And may ʿAnatu of the powerful one drink,
bʿlt mlk	lady of kingship,
bʿ(7)*lt drkt*	lady of sovereignty,
bʿlt šmm rmm	lady of the highest heavens,
(8) [ʿ]⸢*n*⸣*t kpṯ*[187]	ʿAnatu of *kpṯ*,
w ʿnt di dit	ʿAnatu of flying who flies,
rḫpt (9) [*b šm*]⸢*m*⸣ *rm*	who soars [in the heaven]s on high,
ảklt ʿgl ṯl[188] *mšt*	who devours the calf of ʾIlu at the feast,
(10) [*i*]⸢*m*⸣*r špr*[189]	[. . .] lambs of beauty.
w yšt il (11) [. . .]	May ʾIlu drink [. . .]
[. . .]⸢?⸣*n il ǵnṯ ʿgl il*	[. . .] the god ǴNṮ, calf of ʾIlu,
(12) [ ]⸢?⸣*d il*	[. . .] the god,
šdy ṣd mlk	ŠDY, hunter of MLK,
(13) [ ]⸢?⸣	[. . .]
yšt ilh	may ỈLH drink,
(14) [ ]⸢?⸣*iṯmh*	[. . .]
(15) [ ]⸢*r*⸣*š*⸢*p*⸣	[. . .] Rašap

Reverse

(16) [ ]⸢?⸣*mǵy*	[. . .] arrive,
(17) [ ]⸢*n*⸣*drh*	[. . .] his vow,

183. Cf. Akkadian *šulpu*, "reed" or "reed instrument" (*CAD* 17:257).

184. Cf. Biblical Hebrew *tōp* "tambourine, hand drum" (*HALOT*, 1772).

185. Cf. Biblical Hebrew *mᵉṣiltayim* "clanging instruments, cymbals" (*HALOT*, 624).

186. An instrument associated with dance: cf. Biblical Hebrew *rqd* "to dance" (*HALOT*, 1288); Akkadian *raqādu* "to dance" (*CAD* 14:166–67).

187. Pardee suggests that *kpṯ* may refer to the Egyptian atef crown (*Ritual and Cult*, 205 n. 9).

188. The circle around what looks like a {ṯ} may be a mistake for {i}, which seems to be confirmed from *ʿgl il* in line 10 (Pardee, *Ritual and Cult*, 194, 204 n. 11).

189. Gordon took *špr* as a substantive meaning "beauty" (*Ugaritic Textbook*, 556 §19.2467a). In Aramaic the adjective *špyr* is attested meaning "beautiful, magnificent" (*DNWSI*, 1184–85). Cf. Arabic verb *safara* "to uncover," which can also denote "to shine (in color)" or "to be overspread with beauty" (Lane, 1370).

(18) [*yả*]*rš l bʿl*	[. . . he a]sks from Baʿlu,
(19) [*y*]*mǵk*	[. . . he]brings you;
rpủ mlk (20) [*ʿlm ymǵy*]*k*	Rāpiʾu, king of [eternity brings] you,
l tštk l ỉršt(21)[*k*]	to your success, to (what) [you] are requesting,
[*b yd*]*rpỉ mlk ʿlm*	[by the hand of] Rāpiʾu, king of eternity,
b ʿz (22) [*rpỉ*] ⌜*m*⌝*lk ʿlm*	by the strength of [Rāpiʾu], king of eternity,
b ḏmrh b l(23)[*ảnh*]	by his power, by [his] mi[ght],
b ḥtkh b nmrth[190]	by his (paternal) rule, by his splendor;
l r(24)[*p*]*ỉ ảrṣ ʿzk*	your strength is that of the *r*[*p*]*ủm* of the earth,
ḏmrk lả(25)*nk*	your power, your might,
ḥtkk nmrtk	your (paternal) rule, your splendor,
b tk (26) *ủgrt*	in the midst of Ugarit,
l ymt špš w yrḫ	for the days of Šapšu and Yariḫu,
(27) *w nʿmt šnt ỉl*	and the pleasant years of ʾIlu.

Identifying the specific genre of this text has eluded scholars. In the *editio princeps*, Virolleaud first designated it as mythological in nature, with subsequent scholarly opinion running the gamut.[191] Samuel E. Loewenstamm thought it to be a hymn in honor of the deity ʾIlu, observing that parallelism, one of the dominant features of mythological and epic poetry, is less prominent here, and therefore corresponds with what is known from biblical hymns.[192] Similarly, Baruch Margulis called it a psalm, which Yitzhak Avishur finds convincing based on perceived similarities between this text and the Hebrew psalms (though he qualified that its vocabulary is reminiscent of what one finds in hymns).[193] De Moor interprets the various verbal forms throughout as jussives and thus labels KTU 1.108 as a prayer to several gods, the most prominent one being Rāpiʾu addressed in the first line of the text, whom he identifies as the chthonic aspect of Baʿlu.[194] Parker, however, has criticized de Moor's hymnic view and reiterates Virolleaud's

190. Cf. Akkadian *namāru* "to dawn, shine brightly," and *namartu* "first appearance (of the moon)" (*CAD* 11:209).

191. Virolleaud, *Ugaritica* 5:551.

192. Loewenstamm, *Comparative Studies*, 321–22.

193. Baruch Margulis (Margalit), "A Ugaritic Psalm (RŠ 24.252)," *JBL* 89 (1970): 292. Avishur, *Studies in Hebrew and Ugaritic Psalms*, 297.

194. De Moor, "Studies in the New Alphabetic Texts from Ras Shamra I," 176; cf. Wyatt, *Religious Texts*, 395, who calls it a "hymnic prayer."

mythological interpretation, arguing that the depiction of seated deities and accompanying musical instruments rather resembles "a mythological narrative about the gods," also allowing that there may have been certain cultic activity in the event of the text's recitation.[195] A number of scholars have tied this text to the so-called royal cult of the dead, arguing that it provides a representative royal liturgy invoking the spirits of deceased Ugaritic kings, and is perhaps associated with the *marziḫu*.[196] Spronk and Tropper identified the original *Sitz im Leben* of this text to be that of the so-called New Year festival of autumn, which, as van der Toorn has noted, must depend upon the equation of the deity Rāpi'u with Baʿlu, an assumption not without difficulty.[197] Van der Toorn and others have been more reticent in identifying the genre of this text due to the absence of specific indicators that would allow us to determine its original milieu, leading him to call it a "liturgical address," defined as an "invitation to various gods, benediction of the king, both of them in direct speech."[198] In a similar fashion, Pardee denies that it is a hymn or prayer per se, but simply asserts that this text is "an invitation to the deities invoked to join in a feast at which *Rāpi'u*, the first deity named, is described as requesting of *Baʿlu* that he transmit the powers of the *Rapa'ūma* to the living king."[199] Anything more than this assessment would appear to move us beyond what the text would allow, especially in light of the fact that the central section of the text is mostly broken, concerning which material one can only speculate.

Of primary importance in the overall interpretation of this text is the identification of the main character introduced in the opening line, namely, *rpủ mlk ʿlm*. The identification of this divine being informs one's interpretation of the overall function of the text itself.[200] Numerous candidates for this deity have been proffered in the literature, with Loewenstamm (following Virolleaud) marshaling evidence for the patron deity ʾIlu. He argues that his surpassing all other gods in being willing to care for the needs of mortal men comports with the protective deity invoked here.[201] Yet, this view has been challenged as untenable. For one,

195. Parker, "Feast of Rāpi'u," 248–49; cf. L'Heureux, *Rank Among the Canaanite Gods*, 186.

196. Dietrich, Loretz, and Sanmartín, "Ugaritischen Totengeister," 50–51; Spronk, *Beatific Afterlife*, 179–80; del Olmo Lete, *Canaanite Religion*, 2nd ed., 149–50. On the association of the *rpủm* with the *marziḫu*, see below (§4.3.6.2).

197. Spronk, *Beatific Afterlife*, 180; Tropper, *Nekromantie*, 142.

198. Van der Toorn, "Funerary Rituals," 56.

199. Pardee, *Ritual and Cult*, 193.

200. According to van der Toorn: "If we want to establish the nature and the purpose of this ritual, we must first be clear on the identity of its central deities" ("Funerary Rituals," 56).

201. Loewenstamm, *Comparative Studies*, 320–21 n. 1a; followed by Lipiński, "Ditanu," 96 n. 30. Also, Joshua Blau and Jonas C. Greenfield, "Ugaritic Glosses," *BASOR* 200 (1970): 12; Loren R. Fisher, "A New Ritual Calendar from Ugarit," *HTR* 63 (1970): 489; Frank M. Cross, "אֵל, *ʾēl*," *TDOT*,

the presentation of the drinking deity *rpủ* in this text seems rather different from that of 'Ilu in KTU 1.114:1–4 where he slaughters and invites the gods to eat and drink with him in his palace.[202] Instead, the scene depicted in KTU 1.108 brings to mind that of the Rapa'ūma text KTU 1.22 I (discussed above) where the *rpủm* are feasting in the company of 'Ilu, perhaps a feast given in his honor.[203] It is important to remember that in neither of these instances is 'Ilu invited or summoned to feast, which renders the equation *rpủ* = 'Ilu less likely if the verbal form *yšt* in lines 1 and 2 are taken as jussives meaning, "let him drink."[204]

De Moor argues rather extensively that *rpủ mlk ʿlm* is an epithet of Baʿlu, and thus a chthonic manifestation of the storm god in corroboration with the mythological depiction of his journey to the netherworld in the Baʿlu cycle.[205] A similar conclusion is reached by Dietrich and Loretz who argue that identifying *rpủ* as Baʿlu here would partly explain the mention of ʿAnatu alongside Rāpiʾu as invited guests of the feast.[206] However, support for Baʿlu as a chthonic diety is lacking in Ugaritic, notwithstanding de Moor's appeal to Baʿlu's descent into the netherworld, which I believe gives zero indication of a chthonic manifestation.[207] In fact, the following narratives of the Baʿlu cycle depict the storm god as alive (*ḥy*) and once again in combat with Môtu. No chthonic deity is ever described in this way at Ugarit.[208] Furthermore, the notion of Baʿlu as a "healer" is also

1:246; Kapelrud, "Ugaritic Text RS 24.252," 35; L'Heureux, *Rank Among the Canaanite Gods*, 214–15. Loewenstamm claims that "Il is the only healer of an ill person," but as I have noted above with regard to KTU 1.82, it is Šapšu and the *rpủ(m)* who are invoked to reverse the effects of a poisonous snake bite.

202. Pardee, *Ritual and Cult*, 192.

203. See discussion above (§4.3.4).

204. For additional arguments against this view, see Pope, "Notes on the Ugaritic Rephaim," 169–70.

205. De Moor, "Studies in the New Alphabetic Texts from Ras Shamra I," 176; de Moor, *New Year with Canaanites and Israelites, Part Two: The Canaanite Sources* (Kampen: Kok, 1972), 25. See also de Moor, "Rāpiʾūma—Rephaim," 325–30, where he outlines the following reasons for his proposal: (1) the national god protecting Ugarit and its king was Baʿlu of Ṣapānu, (2) Baʿlu is the only one accorded eternal kingship, (3) being invited to drink wine as the first of a number of deities (including ʿAnatu) elevates the rank of this particular deity and suggests Baʿlu, (4) the epithet *g̱tr wyqr* "powerful and honorable" resembles a similar Akkadian epithet for the deity Adad, (5) in line 3, it is unlikely that *il* refers to 'Ilu, but is an appellative, "the god who," (6) the singing and playing of *rpủ* recalls *bʿl mrqd* who was later consider to be a healer-god, (7) in the ʿAqhatu Epic, Dānīʾilu is called *mt rpủ*, and the patron deity thus being referred to was most likely Baʿlu, (8) proper names containing epithets of *rpủ* would refer to Baʿlu, (9) the subject of West Semitic proper names with *rpủ* is commonly the storm god, and (10) the Phoenician god *bʿl mrpʾ* associates Baʿlu with healing activity. In response to most of these points, see Loewenstamm, *Comparative Studies*, 320 n. 1a. In short, none of these arguments necessarily requires that *rpủ mlk ʿlm* be identified with Baʿlu in Ugaritic.

206. Dietrich and Loretz, "Baal *rpu*," 179.

207. Similarly, Loewenstamm, *Comparative Studies*, 230 n. 1a.

208. See my discussion in ch. 3 (§3.2.1.2).

absent in Ugaritic.[209] If anything, my discussion of KTU 1.16 VI:27–33 reveals that Baʿlu is more likely the one revived than he is the reviver, which would only lessen the likelihood of such a notion here.[210]

Alan Cooper has offered three dominant characteristics of *rpủ mlk ʿlm*—healer, associated with the netherworld, and mighty patron of the king—in support of identifying this deity as Rašap.[211] Cooper argues that the only deity to fit this profile is Rašap, who appears to enjoy a rather mixed reputation as both malevolent and benevolent.[212] The weakest of these arguments seems to be Rašap the healer, since the one text Cooper cites in his study speaks of well-being in general more so than healing.[213] Rašap as an underworld deity does not necessitate that he and Rāpiʾu are one and the same. Cooper also emphasizes that Rāpiʾu's epithet *mlk ʿlm* is of Egyptian origin and therefore necessitates that this deity be known in both Ugaritic and Egyptian sources, which happens to be true of Rašap.[214] But even here, the Egyptian epithet of Aten and Osiris that Cooper highlights is always "lord of eternity" (*nb nḥḥ*), and not "king of eternity."[215] Such a royal association for Rašap, the malevolent gatekeeper of Šapšu, is not altogether convincing.

In KTU 1.108:2–3 Rāpiʾu resides in ʿṮTRT and HDRʿY, for which Margulis has devised their relation to Biblical Hebrew Ashtaroth and Edrei in Joshua where the same formula occurs with reference to the Rephaite King Og.[216] This factor led Pope to identify *rpủ mlk ʿlm* with the divine personage Milku (*mlk*), who also dwells in ʿṮTRT in KTU 1.100 (=RS 24.244):40–41.[217] He concedes

209. Also noted by Brown, "Was There a West Semitic Asklepios?," 141–42.

210. See my discussion in ch. 1 (§1.2.2.1). It is ʿAnatu who claims to have the ability to revive Baʿlu, which she offers to extend to ʾAqhatu as well. Healing and restoring/preserving life are related at Ugarit. In KTU 1.82 the D stem root *ḥwy* is used of Šapšu's voice preserving the life of the snake-bitten victim. Therefore, the idea of *ḥwy* as "preserve life" is essentially that of healing (see ch. 1 [§1.2.2.5]). Interestingly enough, in this same context one finds the voice of the *rpủ(m)* invoked as well.

211. Alan Cooper, "*MLK ʿLM*: 'Eternal King' or 'King of Eternity'?" in Marks and Good, *Love and Death in the Ancient Near East*, 4–7.

212. See our discussion of Rašap in ch. 3 (§3.2.2.1.2).

213. However, we should note Lipiński's observation regarding Rašap's occurrence in Ugaritic proper names, namely, that he "was regarded as a protective and helping god" (*Resheph*, 88).

214. Cooper, "*MLK ʿLM*," 3.

215. See Cooper, "*MLK ʿLM*" for references.

216. Margulis, "Ugaritic Psalm," 293–94. Joshua 12:4: *ûgᵉbûl ʿôg melek habbāšān miyyeter hārᵉpāʾîm hayyôšēb bᵉʿaštārôt ûbᵉʾedreʿî* (see also Josh 13:12, 31; cf. Num 21:33; Deut 1:4; 3:1, 10).

217. The vocalization of the noun *mlk* "king" in Ugaritic was apparently /malku/ (*Ugaritica* 5, texts 130 III:13′; 137 II:32′ [see Huehnergard, *Ugaritic Vocabulary*, 147]). The vocalization for the divine name, however, appears to be mixed: /malik/ (^{d}ma-lik^{meš} in *Ugaritica* 5, text 18.32); /milku/ (mi-il-ku-un-ni in *Ugaritica* 5, text 137 IV: a15, b13). In Amorite personal names one also finds evidence for an abstract noun *milkum*, which Gelb glosses "rule, counsel" (Gelb, *Computer-Aided*

that their residing in the same location does not necessarily mean they are the same deity, but it appears more than likely. Furthermore, one should not think that the biblical King Og's association with the double-location (Ashtoreth and Edrei) of *rpủ mlk ʿlm* makes him identical with the Ugaritic deity Rāpi'u, because the biblical character is qualified as being from the remnant of the Rephaim (Josh 12:4), and therefore relegates him to the broader category of the Rapa'ūma. Perhaps Og's identification as one of the remnant of the Rephaim resembles the status acquired by Dānî'ilu as "man of Rāpi'u," though being a protégé of Rāpi'u would signal a higher order given his head role depicted here in KTU 1.108:19–27.[218] According to this analysis, Rāpi'u would be a title of the deity Milku, who is here given the epithet *mlk ʿlm* "king of eternity."[219]

The epithet *mlk ʿlm* "king of eternity" requires further comment. At the very least, this expression offers a clear amalgamation of the concepts of royalty and death. Looking beyond Ugarit, *ʿlm* occurs in first millennium Northwest Semitic inscriptions with reference to the interment of the royal dead. In the Phoenician inscription of Aḥiram one finds the following statement about stationing the

Analysis of Amorite, 25). The verb *malāku* in Akkadian means "to advise, counsel, deliberate" (*CAD* 10:154), with its derivative *māliku* "advisor" attested in divine epithets and personal names (*CAD* 10:162–64). West Semitic *mlk*, however, means "to exercise authority over," or more specifically, "to become king" (*DNWSI*, 633–34; cf. Gelb, *Computer-Aided Analysis of Amorite*, 25). Huehnergard, however, cites the Akkadianized form *imallik* in *PRU* 3, text 134f.:15–16, which from context must mean "to have authority," leading him to argue that it reflects the West Semitic root *mlk* (*Ugaritic Vocabulary*, 147). It is from this West Semitic perspective that the deity *mlk* is identified with the reign of kings, but the Akkadian evidence for Malik also indicates certain chthonic manifestations (see George C. Heider, *The Cult of Molek: A Reassessment* [JSOTSup 43; Sheffield: JSOT Press, 1985], 150–64). Pope, "Notes on the Ugaritic Rephaim," 170–71; cf. Good, "On Rs 24.252," 159–60.

218. I therefore differ from van der Toorn who thinks the data demand that Og be identified with Milku (Funerary Rituals," 57–58). Van der Toorn's position that Og be interpreted as a divine figure makes no sense of the biblical context in which the mention of him occurs. Even if one were to grant that the biblical authors utilized "mythological traditions" (and that says nothing of how or why they were using them) in mentioning King Og, it does not require him to be a divine figure. If anything, it seems to make more sense to acknowledge the biblical author's awareness of the *rpủm* tradition associated with this particular Canaanite king. For more on this question, see my "Biblical King Og and the Ugaritic Deity Rāpi'u: Sorting Out Two Figures in Light of the Rephaim and the Toponyms Ashtoreth and Edrei" in *"Like 'Ilu Are You Wise": Studies in Northwest Semitic Languages and Literatures in Honor of Dennis G. Pardee*, ed. H. H. Hardy II, Joseph Lam, and Eric D. Reymond (Chicago: Oriental Institute of the University of Chicago, forthcoming).

219. See Pardee's extensive treatment of *rpủ mlk ʿlm* where he offers five possible interpretations: (1) Rāpi'u = Milku = Og: the first two being titles with the third being a proper name; (2) Rāpi'u = Milku ≠ Og: Rāpi'u is a title of Milku, whereas Og represents a different tradition; (3) Milku = Rāpi'u ≠ Og: Milku is a title of Rāpi'u with Og as number two; (4) Rāpi'u ≠ Milku ≠ Og: Rāpi'u is a proper name or title, Milku is a name or title of the same, but independent, with Og as number two; (5) Rāpi'u ≠ Milku = Og: Rāpi'u is a title or a proper name, while Milku is a title of Og (*Textes paramythologiques*, 85–97). Of the five options, Pardee thinks options one and two are the most plausible.

departed king's stele: *kšth bʿlm* "when he set it [the stele] up in eternity" (KAI 1.1).[220] One encounters a similar expression in Panamuwa's inscription from Zincirli, where it reads: *zy hqmt nṣb zn lhdd bʿlmy* "I who raised this stele for Hadad in my eternity" (KAI 214.1). The more recent discovery of the KTMW stele, also from Zincirli, yields yet another indicator of this meaning for *ʿlm*, again, concerning the erection of a funerary stele: *wšmt wth bsyr/d ʿlmy* "and I set it [the stele] in the chamber(?) of my eternity."[221] Biblical Hebrew offers evidence for this usage as well, as in Eccl 12:5, where it states: *kî-hōlēk hāʾādām ʾel-bêt ʿôlāmô wᵉsābᵉbû baššûq hassōpᵉdîm* "for man goes to the house of his eternity, and the mourners go around in the street." Pardee has further discussed the biblical phrase *melek ʿôlām*, as for instance in Jer 10:10 where *ʿôlām* is in parallel with *ḥayyîm*: *hûʾ-ʾᵉlōhîm ḥayyîm ûmelek ʿôlām* "he is the Living God and the king of eternity." This usage makes him wonder if these two terms are given as antonymns, so that "living" contrasts with "the dead." Elsewhere in Biblical Hebrew *ʿôlām* is in parallel with terms describing the destruction of human life (*ʾbd* "to destroy" in Ps 10:16; *mabbûl* "the flood" in Ps 29:10), which suggests that *ʿôlām* in such cases may specifically relate to the realm of the dead.[222]

If Rāpiʾu is a title of the divine personage Milku, his description "king of eternity," or perhaps, "king of the dead," makes reasonable sense when understood in conjuction with the *rpủm* as the royal dead. In one of the Ugaritic polyglot vocabularies, the divine name Milku occurs alongside the Sumero-Akkadian form for the deity Tišpak and is qualified by the Ugaritic word ga-ša-ru.[223] The significance of this form is two-fold. For one, it has been shown that the Hurrian

220. Or, taking *bʿlm* as an abbreviated form of *bt ʿlm*, "as a house of eternity," as entertained by Charles C. Torrey, "The Aḫīrām Inscription of Byblos," *JAOS* 45 (1925): 272.

221. See Pardee, "New Aramaic Inscription," 53, 60–61. Pardee cautions that the reading *bsyr* is uncertain due to the indeterminability of *r/d*, and thus read *bsyr/d*, though he favors *bsyr* on etymological grounds. He argues for *syr* being etymologically related to Hebrew *sr* "turn aside," Arabic *syr* "walk, go," Ancient South Arabian *s³wr* "set apart, remove," and possibly Ethiopic *swr* "to hide" (D-stem). The sense of this term would indicate the place where a person "turns aside" to honor the deceased. He also mentions the possible Hebrew cognate *sîr* (though the {y} would then be an internal *mater lectionis*, which does not occur elsewhere in this text), referring to a cremation urn. However, such an item was not found in situ, which would be expected in light of the fact that this stele was relatively well-preserved. Similarly, Pardee argues etymologically for the verbal sense "to keep a feast" for *ḥgg* based upon its well-attested usage in both Hebrew and Aramaic. For arguments in favor of the alternative reading *syd*, see Giovanni Mazzini, "On the Problematic Term *syr/d* in the New Old Aramaic Inscription from Zincirli," *UF* 41 (2009): 505–7, and the more recent discussion of Pardee, "The Katumuwa Inscription," in *In Remembrance of Me: Feasting with the Dead in the Ancient Middle East*, ed. Virginia R. Herrmann and J. David Schloen, OIMP 37 (Chicago: Oriental Institute of the University of Chicago, 2014), 46–47, where he leans toward the reading *syd* because of semantic similarity with Old South Arabian *mswd*.

222. See Pardee, *Textes paramythologiques*, 89–91 (see 90 n. 51 for additional biblical references).

223. *Ugaritic* 5, text 137 IV: a15, b13.

divine personage Tišpak is a chthonic deity known for his ability to handle snakes, a characteristic also known for the deity Malik/Milku in Mesopotamian sources.[224] Second, the mention of Milku with ga-ša-ru parallels the occurrence of *rpủ mlk ʿlm* here in KTU 1.108, who is correspondingly qualified as *g̱tr w yqr* "powerful and honorable" (line 2). This attestation offers further support for the proposal to identify the deity Milku with the Rāpi'u of KTU 1.108.

The potential identification of Rāpi'u with the deity Milku brings us full circle to the proposal of Cooper to link Rāpi'u with Rašap. George C. Heider considers Cooper's suggestion to be rather appealing in light of Milku/Malik's assocation with Nergal in Akkadian literature. He suggests that the equation Mlk = Rpủ = Resheph = Nergal "would confirm our chthonic understanding of the Ugaritic references to Rpu and Mlk."[225] But there is also good reason to doubt this equation from the Ugaritic data before us. As Pope pointed out, Milku and Rašap occur in KTU 1.100 (RS 24.244) as separate deities residing in different locations: *ršp bbth* "Rašap in Bibitta" (line 31), and *mlk ʿṯtrth* "Milku at ʿAṯtartu" (line 41).[226] Another reason to doubt this equation comes from the incantation text KTU 1.82 discussed above. In this collection of incantations against poisonous snake bite, Rašap appears in line 3 with the title *bʿl ḥẓ* "lord of the arrow," apparently held partly responsible for the venomous infliction. Here it is the voice of Šapšu that brings healing to the devastation of Rašap and Môtu (line 5), but a few lines below the voice of *rpủ(m)* is invoked (line 32). Admittedly, the text could be read as either *ql rpỉ* "voice of Rāpi'u" or *ql rpỉm* "voice of the Rapa'ūma," but both readings would seem to discount the equation of Rāpi'u with Rašap. If one reads Rāpi'u, it means that the deity is called upon to erradicate the physical infliction that is earlier described as coming from the devestating arrows of Rašap. Reading Rapa'ūma would necessitate their being in conflict with Rašap=Rāpi'u, which would be highly unlikely given their close association in KTU 1.108. Therefore, I believe the Ugaritic evidence persists in rendering Cooper's identification of Rāpi'u with Rašap unlikely.[227]

The attempts to identify Rāpi'u with other well-known deities from Ugarit have yielded less than satisfactory results. The best candidate for identification

224. J. van Dijk, "Vert comme Tišpak," *Or* 38 (1969): 539–47; referenced in Pardee, *Textes paramythologiques*, 88 n. 41. See Heider, *Cult of Molek*, 154–60.

225. Heider, *Cult of Molek*, 138.

226. Pope, "Cult of the Dead", 172–73. The parital restoration of *ršp* in KTU 1.108:15 remains inconclusive on this point given the broken nature of the surrounding lines.

227. Heider also cautions that Malik's association with Nergal in Mesopotamian omen texts does not warrant the same identification every time and in every place Malik's name occurs. Even more, the transformation of Nergal into an underworld deity when he became consort of the underworld queen Ereshkigal is altogether absent for Malik or Rašap (*Cult of Molek*, 139).

with Rāpi'u in light of the considerations outlined above is none other than Milku residing in ʿAṯtartu.

I still need to comment on the relationship between Rāpi'u and the Rapa'ūma who appear in the second half of this text. After the break in the middle of this text, line 19 resumes with Rāpi'u apparently bringing an unnamed addressee *l tšṯk* "to your success" and *l iršt*[*k*] "to (what) [you] are requesting."[228] The following lines contain a series of phrases introduced with the preposition *b*:

[*b yd*]*rpi mlk ʿlm*	[by the hand of] Rāpi'u, king of eternity,
b ʿz (22) [*rpi*] ⌜*m*⌝*lk ʿlm*	by the strength of [Rāpi'u], king of eternity,
b ḏmrh b l(23)[*ảnh*]	by his power, by [his] mi[ght],
b ḥtkh b nmrth	by his (paternal) rule, by his splendor

Five prepositional phrases are preservered, with a sixth one reconstructed as [*b yd*] "by the hand of," meaning "by the strength of" in light of the following parallels: *b ʿz* "by the strength of," *b ḏmrh* "by his power," *b l*[*ảnh*] "by his might," *b ḥtkh* "by his (paternal rule)," and *b nmrth* "by his splendor." We have already seen the form *tḥtk*, occurring twice at the end of the Baʿlu cycle (KTU 1.6 VI:46–47) as a PC verbal form of the root *ḥtk* meaning "to exercise (paternal) rule."[229] There it describes Šapšu's authority over the *rpủm // ỉlnym*. The noun form here in KTU 1.108 similarly refers to the authority of Rāpi'u, along with his strength, power, might, and splendor. Therefore, the noted power and authority of Rāpi'u are invoked regarding the success and request of an unspecified entity indicated by the 2ms suffixes: "your success" and "your request."

Line 24 marks a shift from the 3ms suffixes referring to Rāpi'u back to the 2ms suffixes of the recipient addressed in lines 18 and 19:

l r(24)[*p*]*i ảrṣ ʿzk*	your strength is that of the *r*[*p*]*ủm* of the earth,
ḏmrk lả(25)*nk*	your power, your might,
ḥtkk nmrtk	your (paternal) rule, your splendor

These lines signal a direct transfer of said powers to the unidentified addressee, only at this juncture the text shifts to the powers of the *rpỉ ảrṣ* "Rapa'ūma of the earth." I have already dealt with the *rpỉ ảrṣ* mentioned in the Kirta Epic where they stand in parallel with the *qbṣ dtn* "assembly of Ditānu," apparently

228. Based upon [*y*]*mǵk* earlier in line 19, the reconstruction of the same verb in this poetic line is quite plausible: *rpủ mlk* [*ʿlm ymǵy*]*k* (see epigraphic discussion in Pardee, *Textes paramythologiques*, 109–10).

229. See discussion in §3.3.1.

the eponymous ancestors of the Ugaritic monarchy (KTU 1.15 III:3, 14).[230] I have argued above that these entities are the royal dead residing in the underworld, among whom Kirta is granted an exalted status. Both of these occurrences suggest that the reach of these entities is not limited to the underworld, however, in light of the fact that they are being invoked in this text to manifest their powers *b tk ủgrt* "in the midst of Ugarit" (lines 25–26). This expression, along with the reference to the days of Šapšu and Yariḫu and the goodly years of 'Ilu, indicate a concern for ongoing blessing and prosperity for Ugarit.[231]

What is more, the subtle shift from the powers of Rāpi'u to those of the Rapa'ūma of the earth at the end of this text makes the intimacy of their association undeniable. As king of eternity, or perhaps the realm of the dead, Rāpi'u is the prime object of this invocation and thus functions as one of the chief ranking members of the underworld. However, the channels by which his powers are transferred to the addressee of these lines—most likely the living king of Ugarit—are the Rapa'ūma of the earth: "your power is that of the Rapa'ūma of the earth/underworld."[232] Smith summarizes well the overall thrust this passage:

> At Ugarit, the eponymous head of the deceased Rephaim and the major gods converge in the royal expression of concern for the kingdom's well-being and prosperity and also in the monarchy's concern for its place in the scheme of reality as mediator between the divine realms above and below and the human realm in between.[233]

4.3.6.2. KTU 1.161—The *rpủm* in a Funerary Ritual

We may now move on to discuss the second ritual text—the final major text for this chapter—containing references to the *rpủm*. KTU 1.161 (RS 34.126) has been the subject of much discussion as a text of fundmental importance in its portrayal of the *rpủm*. As I have done for KTU 1.108 and the Rapa'ūma texts above, I offer the text and translation in full as follows:[234]

230. See §4.3.2.1 above.

231. Pardee observes that "the function of these virtues was not for the king's private glorification but to enable him properly and effectively to rule his people" (*Ritual and Cult*, 206 n. 14).

232. Del Olmo Lete, *Canaanite Religion*, 2nd ed., 155; Pardee, *Ritual and Cult*, 193. The meaning of *bʿl* in line 18 remains unclear due to the broken nature of the text immediately preceding it. Pardee points out that if it is the divine name Baʿlu, and not the title meaning "lord," it would indicate that Baʿlu served as an intermediary between Rāpi'u and the king (*Ritual and Cult*, 206 n. 14).

233. Smith, *Poetic Heroes*, 140.

234. I am following the collation of this text in Bordreuil and Pardee, "Les textes en cunéiformes alphabétiques," in *Une bibliothèque au sud de la: Les textes de la 34e campagne (1973)*, RSO 7 (Paris: Éditions Recherche sur les Civilisations, 1991), 152–53, Pardee, *Textes rituels*, 817, and Pardee, *Ritual and Cult*, 87–88. For photograph, see Bordreuil and Pardee, *Manual of Ugaritic*, plate 16. For

(1) *spr dbḥ*[235] *ẓlm*[236]	Document of the sacrifices of the Shades:
(2) *qritm*[237] ⸢*r*⸣*pi ả*[*rṣ* . . .]	You have been called, O *rpủm* of the ea[rth],
(3) *qbitm qbṣ d*[*dn* . . .]	You have been summoned, O assembly of D[DN];
(4) *qrả ủlkn r*⸢*p*⸣[*ủ* . . .]	Called is ỦLKN the *rp*[*ủ* . . .]
(5) *qrả trmn rp*[*ủ* . . .]	Called is TRMN the *rp*[*ủ* . . .]
(6) *qrả sdn w rd*[*n* . . .]	Called is SDN and RD[N . . .]
(7) *qrả ṯr ʿllmn*[238][. . .]	Called is ṮR ʿLLMN [. . .]
(8) *qrủ rpim qdmym* [. . .]	They have called the former *rpủm*,
(9) *qritm rpi ʾrṣ*	You have been called, O *rpủm* of the earth,
(10) *qbitm qbṣ dd*⸢*n*⸣	You have been called, O assembly of DDN;
(11) *qrả ʿmṯtm*⸢*r*⸣ *m*⸢*l*⸣*k*	Called is King ʿAmmiṯtamru,
(12) *qrả u nqm*⸢*d*⸣ ⸢*mlk*⸣	Called also is King Niqmaddu.
(13) *ksi nqmd* ⸢*ibky*⸣[239]	O throne of Niqmaddu, be bewept,

additional studies on this text, see Caquot, "Hébreu et Araméen," *Annuaire du Collège de France* 75 (1975–76): 427–29; Caquot, "Tablette RS 24.252," 296–98; Caquot, *Textes ougaritiques* 2, 103–10; de Moor, "Rāpiʾūma—Rephaim," 333–36, 341–45; de Moor, *Anthology of Religious Texts*, 165–68; Mitchel Dahood, "The Ugaritic Parallel Pair *qra // qba* in Isaiah 62,2," *Bib* 58 (1977): 527–28; Kenneth Kitchen, "The King List of Ugarit," *UF* 9 (1977): 140–42; Pope, "Notes on the Ugaritic Rephaim," 177–82; John F. Healey, "Ritual Text KTU 1.161—Translation and Notes," *UF* 10 (1978): 83–88; Wayne Pitard, "The Ugaritic Funerary Text RS 34.126," *BASOR* 232 (1978): 65–75; Pitard, "RS 34.126, Notes on the Text," *Maarav* 4 (1987): 75–86; L'Heureux, *Rank Among the Canaanite Gods*, 187–93, 201–2; Good, "Supplementary Remarks," 41–42; Meindert Dijkstra, Johannes C. de Moor, and Klaus Spronk, review of *Die keilalphabetischen Texte aus Ugarit*, by Manfried Dietrich, Oswald Loretz, and Joaquín Sanmartín, *BO* 38 (1981): 374–78; Xella, *Testi rituali di Ugarit I*, 279–87; Manfried Dietrich and Oswald Loretz, "Neue Studien zu den Ritualtexten aus Ugarit (II)—Nr. 6—Epigraphische und inhaltliche Probleme in KTU 1.161," *UF* 15 (1983): 17–24; Levine and de Tarragon, "Dead Kings and Rephaim,"649–59; Heider, *Cult of Molek*, 125, 131–32, 141; Spronk, *Beatific Afterlife*, 189–93, 209; J. Glen Taylor, "A First and Last Thing to Do in Mourning: KTU 1.161 and Some Parallels" in Eslinger and Taylor, *Ascribe to the Lord*, 151–77; Lewis, *Cults of the Dead*, 4–46; Tropper, *Nekromantie*, 144–50; David T. Tsumura, "The Interpretation of the Ugaritic Funerary Text KTU 1.161" in *Official Cult and Popular Religion in the Ancient Near East: Papers of the First Colloquium on the Ancient Near East—the City and Its Life Held at the Middle Eastern Culture Center in Japan (Mitaka, Tokyo), March 20–22, 1992*, ed. Eiko Matsushima (Heidelberg: Winter, 1993), 40–55; Schmidt, *Israel's Beneficent Dead*, 100–120; Ford, "Living Rephaim," 80–84, 92–97; Baruch Levine, Jean-Michael de Tarragon, and Anne Robertson, *COS* 1:357–58; del Olmo Lete, *Canaanite Religion*, 2nd ed., 156–61; Wyatt, *Religious Texts*, 430–41; Shipp, *Of Dead Kings and Dirges*, 53–61; Matthew Suriano, "Dynasty Building at Ugarit: The Ritual and Political Context of KTU 1.161," *AuOr* 27 (2009): 105–23; Smith, *Poetic Heroes*, 154–61.

235. Technically this form could be either singular or plural const., but in light of the multiple offerings that follow I read *dbḥ* as a plural const. (with Lewis, *Cult of the Dead*, 10).

236. Cf. Hebrew *ṣēl* "shadow, protection" (*HALOT*, 1024–25); Akkadian *ṣillu* "shade, covering" (*CAD* 16:189–92; *AHw* 2:1101); Arabic *ẓill* "shade" (Lane, 1915).

237. Taking these verbal forms as passives (see Bordreuil and Pardee, "Textes en cunéiformes alphabétiques," 156; Good, "Supplementary Remarks," 41).

238. Cf. *zbl mlk ʿllmy* "prince king of ʿLLMY" (KTU 1.22 II:12).

239. N stem imperative (/ʾibbakiyī/) with prefixed {ʾ} (see Bordreuil and Pardee, "Textes en cunéiformes alphabétiques," 157–58 and Pardee, *Textes rituels*, 821–22 n. 31).

(14) *w ydmʿ ⸢h⸣dm ⸢p⸣ʿnh*	And one must shed tears (on) the footstool of his feet.
(15) *l pnh ybky ṯlḥn ml⸢k⸣*	Before him one must beweep the table of the king,
(16) *w ⸢y⸣blʿ ủdmʿth*	And one must swallow his tears.
(17) *ʿdmt*[240] *w ʿdmt ʿdmt*	Destitution and destitution of destitutions!
(18) *ỉšḫn*[241] *špš w ỉšḫn*	Be hot, O Šapšu; be hot,
(19) *nyr rbt ʿln špš tṣ⸢ḥ⸣*	O great luminary. Above, Šapšu cries out:
(20) *ảṯr [b]ʿlk l ks⸢ỉ⸣ ảṯr*	After your lords, from the throne, after
(21) *bʿlk ảrṣ rd ảrṣ*	your lords, to the earth descend, to the earth
(22) *rd w špl ʿpr tḥt*	descend and lower yourself into the dust. Below
(23) *sdn w rdn tḥt ṯr*	SDN-wa-RDN, below ṮR
(24) *ʿllmn tḥt rpỉm qdm⸢y⸣m*	ʿLLMN, below the former *rpủm*,
(25) *tḥt ʿmṯtmr mlk*	below King ʿAmmiṯtamru,
(26) *tḥm*[242] *ủ nq[md] mlk*	below also King Niqmaddu.
(27) *ʿšty w ṯ⸢ʿ⸣[y ṯn] ⸢w⸣ ṯʿ[y]*	Once and offer the *ṯʿ* sacrifice, [twice] and offer the *ṯʿ* sacrifice,
(28) *ṯlṯ w ṯʿy ⸢ả⸣[rb]⸢ʿ⸣ w ṯʿ[y]*	Three times and offer the *ṯʿ* sacrifice, four times and offer the *ṯʿ* sacrifice,
(29) *ḫmš w ṯʿy ṯ⸢ṯ⸣ [w] ⸢ṯ⸣ʿy*	Five times and offer the *ṯʿ* sacrifice, six times and offer the *ṯʿ* sacrifice,
(30) *šbʿ w ṯʿy tq⸢d⸣m ʿṣr*	Seven times and offer the *ṯʿ* sacrifice. You must present the bird
(31) *šlm šlm ʿmr[pỉ]*	of well-being: well-being to ʿAmmurāpỉ
(32) *w šlm bảh*[243] *šlm [ṯ]ry⸢l⸣*	and well-being to his household; well-being to Ṯarriyelli,
(33) *šlm bth šlm ủ⸢g⸣rt*	well-being to her household; well-being to Ugarit,
(34) *šlm ṯǵrh*	well-being to its gates.

I outline the content of this text as follows:

240. Cf. Arabic *ʿdm* "to be destitute" (Lane, 1975) and *ʿadima* "poverty, destitution" (Lane, 1976). See also Pierre Bordreuil and Dennis Pardee, "Le rituel funéraire ougaritique RS. 34.126," *Syria* 59 (1982): 126.

241. N stem imperative (/ʾiššaḫinī/) with prefixed {ʾ}.

242. From context, {tḥm} should be read as {tḥt}.

243. Could be emended to {bth} (his house) or {bnh} (his sons) (see Pardee, *Ritual and Cult*, 115 n. 131). The former option seems most appealing in light of {bth} in line 33. Cf. del Olmo Lete (*Canaanite Religion*, 2nd ed., 160), who accepts the latter emendation.

1. Document Title (line 1)
2. Summoning the *rpủm* (lines 2–12)
3. Mourning the Royal Dead (lines 13–17)
4. Descending to the Underworld (lines 18–26)
5. Offering the Seven-Fold Funerary Sacrifices (lines 27–30a)
6. Presenting the Bird of Well-Being (lines 30b-34)

My comments on this text will not be exhaustive, but will be confined to the following issues that are of particular importance for both its interpretation in general and the nature of the *rpủm* in particular: (1) the meaning of *ẓlm* (line 1), (2) the significance of the repeated occurrences of the root *qrʾ* "to call," (3) the meaning of *rpʾ ả*[*rṣ*] and *rpỉm qdmym*, (4) the meaning of the expressions *ảrṣ rd* "descend to the earth" and *špl ʿpr* "lower yourself to the dust" (lines 21–22), and (5) the call for *šlm* "well-being" (lines 31–34). Once I have treated these points of interest, I will return to the matter of this text's setting and purpose.

The self-identification of this text is *spr zbḥ* "Document of the sacrifices," and therefore could be plausibly understood as either the record of a ritual enacted or its prescription. In light of the overall content of this text, I interpret the last word of this three-member construct chain objectively: "document of the sacrifices *for* X." The meaning of the third word of this line has been much discussed, the reading {ẓlm} having been well-established.[244] Lewis believes this term to be the key to understanding the nature of the entire text, an importance that stems from the fact that *ẓlm* demarcates the referents of the offerings outlined in the ritual document.[245] Caquot originally suggested that *ẓlm* is associated with "darkness," which Pope found appealing because such funerary feasts were typically held at night.[246] This understanding would propose an etymology from the root *ẓlm* meaning "darkness," and thus would correspond to Akkadian *ṣalāmu* "to become dark," Arabic *ẓulmat* "dark," and possibly Hebrew *ṣlmwt* "darkness."[247] One of the

244. First rendered as *qlm* by Caquot ("Hébreu et Araméen," 427), and since being confirmed as *ẓlm* (see Bordreuil and Pardee, "Rituel funéraire ougaritique," 124–25; Pitard, "Ugaritic Funerary Text," 66–67; Pitard, "RS 34.126," 122–23).

245. Lewis, *Cults of the Dead*, 10.

246. Caquot, "Hébreu et Araméen," 428. Pope, "Notes on the Ugaritic Rephaim," 178.

247. "Darkness": Lewis, *Cults of the Dead*, 11. For the Akkadian, see *CAD* 16:70; for the Arabic, see Lane, 1922, < √*ẓlm* IV (Lane, 1921). Hebrew: **ṣalmût* "gloom, darkness" (*HALOT*, 1029), but vocalized in the MT as *ṣalmāwet* "shadow of death." For a defense of the MT pointing, see Walter L. Michel, "ṢLMWT, 'Deep Darkness' or 'Shadow of Death'?" *BR* 29 (1984): 5–20; cf. Dennis Pardee, "Structure and Meaning in Hebrew Poetry: The Example of Psalm 23," *Maarav* 5–6 (1990): 252, 274–75. For the etymology < **ṣlm* "to be dark," see D. Winton Thomas, "צַלְמָוֶת in the Old Testament," *JSS* 7 (1962): 191–200; Giovanni Mazzini, "On the Meaning of ṣalmāwet: A Discussed Word in the Old Testament," *SEL* 16 (1999): 79–83.

main problems with this interpretation is that the Ugaritic word for "darkness" derived from this root is only attested as a feminine.[248]

Alternatively, the principal etymology put forth for *ẓlm* is the geminate root *ẓll*, as in the Akkadian verb *ṣullulu* meaning "to cover over, provide shade," and thus related to the noun *ṣillu* "shade, covering."[249] The Ugaritic form *ẓlm* would therefore represent the plural, as in "shades, shadows."[250] Also based upon this root, Pitard suggests the meaning "protectors" rather than "shades," since the Akkdian noun *ṣulūlu* denotes a "roof" or "porch" as protection from the sun.[251] This suggestion is rather appealing in light of what we have already observed regarding the role of the *rpủm* as dispensers of blessing/favor, but it requires a rather sophisticated semantic development: covering > roof > protection > protector.[252] Furthermore, for the active notion of "dispensing shade/protection," or more exactly, "dispensers of shade/protection," we might expect a participial form, which would therefore require a doubled {l} orthographically: *ẓllm* /ẓālilīma/.[253] It may end up being less problematic simply to maintain the usual connotation "shade" or "shadow," a term that would offer a vivid description of the nature of the *rpủm* more so than their function, which is the meaning I have adopted here.

Two additional suggestions have been made for *ẓlm* that lead the discussion in slightly different directions. Caquot entertained the possibility that *ẓlm* could also be the word for statue, as in Hebrew *ṣelem* "image, likeness," and therefore would refer to a statue of the king erected for the funerary ritual.[254] Miranda Bayliss surmizes it is possible that dead kings were represented by their statues

248. *ẓlmt* (KTU 1.4 VII:54–56; 1.8:7–9). Note, however, that Hays understands this term as *ẓl* + *mt* "shadow of death" (*Death in Iron Age II*, 109 n. 86).

249. *ṣullulu*: *CAD* 16:239. *ṣillu*: *CAD* 16:189–92; *AHw*, 2:1101. See also Hays, *Death in Iron Age II*, 109 n. 86.

250. The plural of *qill-* base forms is generally *qillūma* (Pardee, *Textes rituels*, 820 n. 21; contra Lewis, *Cults of the Dead*, 11 and Schmidt, *Israel's Beneficent Dead*, 110), and therefore one would not expect the plural form of *ẓl* to be written {ẓllm}; e.g.: sg *ʿṣ* (/ʿiṣṣu/) > pl *ʿṣm* (/ʿiṣṣūma/) (KTU 1.5 II:6). The Hebrew evidence for the noun pattern of *ṣēl* (< √*ṣll*) with suffixes appears to be mixed: *ṣēl* + 3ms suffix: *ṣillô* (Ezek 31:6) and *ṣilᵉlô* (Job 40:22); *ṣēl* + pl suffix: *ṣᵉlālîm* (Song 2:17).

251. Pitard, "Ugaritic Funerary Text," 68; Pitard, "RS 34.126," 78; likewise Smith, *Poetic Heroes*, 154, 156. Levine and de Tarragon translate *ẓlm* as "Patrons," meaning that these royal ancestors of the Ugaritic kings were their protectors in that they guaranteed kingship and succession ("Dead Kings and Rephaim," 67–68; Levine, de Tarragon, and Robertson, *COS* 1:357 n.2). Cf. del Olmo Lete: "protective spirits" (*Canaanite Religion*, 2nd ed., 157). For *ṣulūlu*, see *CAD* 16:242.

252. Giovanni Mazzini elaborates further on the positive connotation "protection" for the Ugaritic root *ẓll* ("The Shining Shadow: the Ugaritic word *ẓl*," *SEL* 16 [1999]: 27–34).

253. For example forms of the participle for geminate roots, see Tropper, *Ugaritische Grammatik*, 2nd ed., §75.65.

254. Caquot, "Hébreu et Araméen," 428. BDB, 853–54; *HALOT*, 1082; cf. Akkadian *ṣalmu* (*CAD* 16:78; *AHw* 3:1078). For a recent treatment of the attested forms of this word in the Semitic

in the Mesopotamian *kispu* rite, leading Schmidt to suggest that a similar setting might be warranted for this Ugaritc text, even though he does not adopt this view in the end.[255] Xella advances arguments for this understanding of *ẓlm* and the Ugaritic data, which is also followed by Dietrich and Loretz.[256] However, this would not explain the two attestations of the form *ṣlm* in Ugaritic, albeit in broken contexts, which have been interpreted as "image," and thus graphically (and phonologically) distinct from our form *ẓlm*.[257]

Finally, David Tsumura has advocated a slightly different understanding of *ẓlm* as a derivative of the root meaning "darkness," suggesting that KTU 1.161 may offer evidence for an Ugaritic representation of an Akkadian deity Ṣalmu, known from coronations, royal burial rites, and treaty ceremonies.[258] Tsumura cites the study of Stephanie Dalley who also connects this Akkadian divine name for the sun god with *ẓlm* of KTU 1.161, but she conversely adopts the etymology *ṣlm* "statue," perhaps as a manifestation of the deity Ṣalam = Šamaš.[259] Rather, Tsumura interprets the divine epithet as "Darkness." Schmidt, on the other hand, follows Dalley's etymology by arguing that "Ṣalmu in line 1 might refer to a distinct designation of the sun goddess."[260] For such an interpretation to work from a literary perspective, however, it requires that the following list of entities are being called upon to offer sacrifices to said diety, which would furthermore necessitate their being from the realm of the living. Such a view is out-of-step with what is known from the Ugaritic sources regarding the *rpủ ảrṣ* // *qbṣ dt/dn*, not to mention the fact that the details throughout this particular text strongly indicate that the setting is the funerary ritual of the recently deceased King Niqmaddu (lines 12, 13, and 26) during the accession of King ʿAmmurāpi (line 31).[261]

Taking *ẓlm* as a descriptive reference to the *rpủm* (i.e., "shades") means that they are the main objects of the seven-fold sacrifices offered in lines 27–30. This picture resembles the scene depicted in the Rapaʾūma texts where the *rpủm* are feasting and drinking in conjunction with being summoned to a particular place

languages, see Fiorella Scagliarini, "*ṢLM* e alter parole per 'statua' nelle lingue semitiche," *SEL* 25 (2008): 63–86.

255. Miranda Bayliss, "The Cult of Dead Kin in Assyria and Babylonia," *Iraq* 35 (1973): 124.

256. Xella, *Testi rituali di Ugarit I*, 282. Dietrich and Loretz, "Neue Studien zu den Ritualtexten," 23.

257. See KTU 1.13:18 and 2.31:62.

258. Tsumura, "Interpretation of the Ugaritic Funerary Text," 54.

259. Stephanie Dalley, "The God Ṣalmu and the Winged Sun Disk," *Iraq* 48 (1986): 89.

260. Schmidt, *Israel's Beneficent Dead*, 112.

261. See Bordreuil and Pardee, "Textes en cunéiformes alphabétiques," 157–58; Pardee, *Textes rituels*, 821, n. 28. Note, however, that the Niqmaddu of line 13 could have been a distinct king from the Niqmaddu of lines 12 and 26 (see Pardee, *Ritual and Cult*, 114 n. 124).

where they are said to rise. The ritual summoning of the *rpủm* is clearly one of the prominent features of KTU 1.161, taking up the first twelve lines of text. We will now turn our focus to other features of this text that further illuminate its overall setting and purpose.

The setting of KTU 1.161 is further identified in the repetition of the roots *qrʾ* and *qbʾ*. The grammatical analysis of these forms has varied among scholars, with a number of commentators analyzing the instances of *qrỉtm* as 2mp G SCs "you have summoned" and *qrả* as 3ms G SCs "he has summoned," both of which understand the literary setting to be some kind of ritual narration with an interchange of speakers (from second to third person).[262] John F. Healey, however, notes the peculiarity of such a situation for ritual and instead calls these forms "prescriptive perfects," akin to the so-called future perfect—2mp G SC *qrỉtm* "you (will have) invoked" and 3ms G SC *qrả* "he (will have) invoked."[263] Pope, on the other hand, rendered these occurrences of *qrả* as imperatives, "Invoke DN," which Levine and de Tarragon also adopt in their study of this text.[264] Dietrich and Loretz, however, see *qrỉtm* (and *qbỉtm*) to be functioning as a jussive, while the forms *qrủ* and *qrả* represent imperative masculine and feminine forms respectively.[265] The masculine and feminine interchange required for this morphology is lacking contextually, while a SC form functioning as a jussive is difficult to sustain for Ugaritc.[266] Pitard breaks from the 2mp analysis for the form *qrỉtm* and takes it as a 1cs with enclitic *m*, which is morphologically possible but thus far unatested for 1cs forms in Ugaritic.[267] He cites Akkadian ritual instructions as precedence for this usage of 1cs forms, arguing that 2mp forms are never attested in this genre, but the proximity of KTU 1.161 to this particular Akkdian literary type is uncertain.[268]

The best morphological solution for these forms thus far put forth is that they are internal passives, as suggested by Bordreuil and Pardee.[269] This approach provides the most compelling accounting of the morphological and contextual data:

262. Caquot, "Hébreu et Araméen," 427; de Moor, "Rāpiʾūma—Rephaim," 334.

263. Healey, "Ritual Text KTU 1.161," 85.

264. Pope, "Notes on the Ugaritic Rephaim," 177 (without comment). Levine and de Tarragon, "Dead Kings and Rephaim," 650, followed by Shipp, *Of Dead Kings and Dirges*, 54 n. 62.

265. Dietrich and Loretz, "Neue Studien zu den Ritualtexten," 19.

266. Similarly, see Bordreuil and Pardee, "Textes en cunéiformes alphabétiques," 156.

267. As noted by Levine and de Tarragon, ,"Dead Kings and Rephaim," 652.

268. Pitard, "New Edition," 68.

269. Bordreuil and Pardee, "Rituel funéraire ougaritique," 126; Bordreuil and Pardee, "Textes en cunéiformes alphabétiques," 156. See also Lipiński, "Ditanu," 98; Good, "Supplementary Remarks," 41; Lewis, *Cults of the Dead*, 13–14.

qrỉtm	/quraʾtumu/	"you (pl.) are summoned"
qrả	/quraʾa/	"summoned is PN"

According to this interpretive schema, the *rpủm* are summoned as a group in lines 2–3 and again in lines 9–10, but in lines 4–8 and 11–12 they are summoned individually. The form *qrủ* in line 8, however, would have to be analyzed as an active form (/qaraʾū/), since *rpỉm* is oblique and therefore could not be the subject as in "the *rpủm* are summoned."[270] As an active form, Smith interprets it as having an impersonal subject, since he believes it would be strange if the previously named *rpủm* are portrayed as summoning themselves.[271] In other words, the impersonal subject refers to the participants in the ritual, or as Smith proposes, "the living royal (perhaps along with their royal "households") named later in lines 31–34."[272] Reflecting further on the setting of these passive verbal forms, Lewis offers as a possible analogy with Akkadian *Koinzidenzfall* "in which the words recited represent the very action to which they refer."[273] In a fairly recent study, Seth L. Sanders explores the phenomenon of performative speech in ancient Near Eastern texts with particular attention to the Ugaritic materials.[274] He comments specifically on the probable function of these passives in a text that contains no identifiable agents and picks up on Wyatt's suggestion that they relate to "the inherent danger of dealing with underworld deities."[275] It is therefore conceivable that these underworld deities who are usually kept underground are thus summoned up from below in a deferential manner, or with what Sanders calls a "remote passive."[276] This usage would resemble the divine passive from biblical and Jewish literature where passive forms are often employed to address God indirectly and without using his name out of deference and respect.

The appearance of *rpỉ ảrṣ* "Rapaʾūma of th earth/underworld" and *rpỉm qdmym* "former Rapaʾūma" in this text signals a two-fold categorization for the *rpủm*. I have already treated the first of these two expressions when I commented on its occurrence in the Kirta Epic above. As was the case there, *qbṣ dt/dn* always functions as the second member of this parallel pair, and thus ties the *rpủm* to the

270. This is also the reason that *rpỉ ảrṣ* in lines 2 and 9 cannot be taken as simple subjects, since that would require the nominative *rpủ*.

271. Smith, *Poetic Heroes*, 154 n. 112.

272. Smith, *Poetic Heroes*, 158.

273. Lewis, *Cults of the Dead*, 13.

274. Seth L. Sanders, "Performative Utterances and Divine Language in Ugaritic," *JNES* 63 (2004): 161–81.

275. Wyatt, *Religious Texts*, 432–33 n. 8.

276. Sanders, "Performative Utterances," 176–77. Sanders cites parallels from Mesopotamian ritual texts.

eponymous ancestor of the royal dynasty, Ditānu being a divine name known from Amorite royal names.[277] His "gathering" or "assembly" would then be the company of royal figures in the line of dynastic succession—thus, the *rpủm*. This poetic pair appears in two places in KTU 1.161 marking a transition from one category of *rpủm* to another. We can outline these occurrences as follows:

1. Summons of the former *rpủm* of the earth // assembly of DDN (lines 2–7)
   a. Summons of the *rpủm* by name
      i. ỦLKN the *rp*[*ủ* . . .]
      ii. TRMN the *rp*[*ủ* . . .]
      iii. SDN and RD[N . . .]
      iv. ṮR ʿLLMN [. . .]
   b. Summons summary: "they (impersonal) have called the former *rpủm*" (line 8)
2. Summons of the recent *rpủm* of the earth // assembly of DDN (lines 9–12)
   a. King ʿAmmiṯtamru
   b. King Niqmaddu

The arrangement of these summoning statements distinguishes between the more distant and ancient *rpủm*, namely, the *rpủm qdmym*, and the more recently deceased kings of Ugarit, thus identified as King ʿAmmiṯtamru and King Niqmaddu respectively. It is important to observe that both the former *rpủm* and the most recent dead kings are expressly called *rpủm* of the earth // assembly of DDN.

The relationship between these two categories of *rpủm* finds further expression in the following section where the addressee of this text is called upon to descend below (*tḥt*) the *rpủm* outlined in lines 2–12. There is some question among scholars as to the person addressed in this ritual descent, the two major positions being (1) the current king called upon to descend in ritual mourning and (2) the recently deceased king called upon to descend to the netherworld and to be received into the company of the *rpủm*. Schmidt construes the genre of this text to be that of a coronation ritual for the newly enthroned king, citing parallels with coronation ritual texts from Akkadian literature consisting of the following elements: (1) presentation before the deity, (2) offerings and sacrifices to the deity, (3) investiture with scepter and crown, (4) acclamation

277. See §4.2.2 above.

with blessing, (5) enthronement, (6) assembly of nobles, and (7) swearing of oaths before divine witnesses. He argues that elements (1), (2), (4), and (6) are present in KTU 1.161.[278] The crux of his interpretation requires that the *rpủ ảrṣ* // *qbṣ ddn* mentioned in the first few lines must comprise living attendees of the purported ceremony.[279] Such an interpretation for this parallel pair finds no support from the other Ugaritic texts wherein they occur (see above). Furthermore, Schmidt has to eliminate SDN-and-RDN and ṮR ʿLLMN from the otherwise undistinguished list of names in lines 3–5 because they are clearly depicted as the residents of the underworld in lines 22–24—they are below (*tḥt*). On the contrary, all four entities of lines 4–7 are presented as members of the same category: *rpủm* of the earth // assembly of DDN, who are further designated as former *rpủm* in distinction from those more recent members. Pardee thinks the only element of KTU 1.161 that could possibly be read as part of a coronation ritual is the blessing at the end, but even that must be shared between the new king and queen mother/grandmother.[280] Additionally, Matthew Suriano helpfully observes that the prominence of mourning throughout this ritual cannot be accounted for in the coronation ritual interpretation.[281]

The funerary nature of KTU 1.161 is also signaled by the expressions *ảrṣ rd* "descend to the earth" and *špl ʿpr* "lower yourself to the dust" (lines 21–22). In chapter 3 I examined this expression involving one's descent to the earth/underworld as an idiom for death (§3.2.1.2). One of the clearest examples of this expression is in the Baʿlu cycle when Môtu warns Baʿlu that he must die, commanding him to make his descent:

w rd (15) *b tḫpṯt ảrṣ*	Descend into the baseness of the earth,
tspr b y(16)*rdm ảrṣ*	you must be counted among those going down to the earth,
w tdʿ ỉlm (17) *k mtt*	and the gods will know that you are dead. (KTU 1.5 V)

This idiom provides a mythological expression of death—making a downward journey into the earth/underworld. One also finds that the mourning ritual is depicted in a similar fashion: mourners are described as descending after (*ảṯr*)

278. Schmidt, *Israel's Beneficent Dead*, 103–4.

279. Cf. L'Heureux, *Rank Among the Canaanite Gods*, 192, where he qualifies that the *rpủ ảrṣ* are living entities present at the ritual.

280. Dennis Pardee, review of *Israel's Beneficent Dead: Ancestor Cult and Necromancy in Ancient Israelite Religion and Tradition*, by Brian B. Schmidt" *JSS* 42 (1997): 367.

281. Suriano, "Dynasty Building," 117.

their departed loved ones. ʾIlu "descends after" Baʿlu in mourning (KTU 1.5 VI:24–25):

ảṯr (25) *bʿl ảdr b ảrṣ*	After Baʿlu I will descend into the earth,

as does his sister ʿAnatu (KTU 1.6 I:7–9):

ảṯr bʿl nrd (8) *b ảrṣ*	After Baʿlu we will descend into the earth.
ʿmh trd nrt (9) *ỉlm špš*	With him Šapšu, luminary of the gods, will descend.

The description of the mourning ritual is therefore patterned after the mythological depiction of the deceased and their journey downward to the realm of the dead.

This comparision raises the problem regarding how we should interpret *ảṯr* here in KTU 1.161 and understand its relation to those occurrences with the root *yrd*: "to descend after." It seems that when *ảṯr* accompanies *yrd* it qualifies that the descent is that of the mourner as opposed to that of the deceased. For example, in the Baʿlu cycle the storm god must be counted among those who descend into the netherworld (*yrd ảrṣ*—referring to the desceased), while ʾIlu and ʿAnatu descend after him in mourning (*ảṯr yrd ảrṣ*—referring to the mourner). In these cases *ảṯr* would be the preposition /ʾaṯra/ meaning "after, behind."[282] This word, however, is to be distinguished from the sense of *ảṯr* in the Rapa'ūma texts where it functions as a noun /ʾaṯru/ designating a "place, shrine," comparable to Akkadian *ašru*.[283] In the Rapa'ūma texts we find that *ảṯr* occurs in parallel with other terms of place (e.g., *bt*, *hkl*), therefore seemingly confirming that it is the location at which the *rpủm* rise.[284] Also in the Rapa'ūma texts, *ảṯr* occurs as the locale of the *rpủm*'s movement upward, whereas KTU 1.161 depicts a movement downward (*yrd*) to the *rpủm* who are thus described as being "below" or "under" (*tḥt*) the participants in the ritual. Šapšu's command to descend would not make sense were it referring to the royal shrine where the ritual is taking place, since the movement of the addressee appears to be away from the place of the ritual.[285] For these reasons I am hesitant to adopt

282. Cf. Biblical Hebrew *ʾăšūr* "step" (*HALOT*, 99).

283. *CAD* 2:456.

284. *ảṯrk* "your place": KTU 1.22 I:3; *ảṯrh* "to the place": 1.21 II:3, 11, 12; 1.22 II:5, 10, 11, 21; 1.20 II:1, 2 (see discussion above).

285. Unless of course one believes that this "place" is thought to descend symbolically into the underworld, as some scholars have argued (Pope, "Notes on the Ugaritic Rephaim," 180;

the suggestion of Pitard, Tsumura, and Suriano to interpret *ảṯr* in KTU 1.161 as "place, shrine" as a parallel to the *aṯrk/aṯrh* in the Rapaʾūma texts, since their contexts do not exactly correspond.[286]

Consequently, the real question at hand is whether the command to descend is being addressed to the recently deceased King Niqmaddu (III) regarding his reception into the company of the *rpủm* below, or to the newly appointed King ʿAmmurāpiʾ in his ritual mourning over the recently deceased King Niqmaddu (III).[287] As noted already, the language involving one's descent after the dead clearly indicates the act of mourning in the mythology of Baʿlu, once of ʾIlu (KTU 1.5 VI:24–25) and once of ʿAnatu (KTU 1.6 I:7–9). The language employed here in KTU 1.161 certainly corresponds to that of mourning, as the addressee is commanded to descend after someone, in this case designated as *bʿlk*, which might best be rendered as the singular "your lord" if King ʿAmmurāpiʾ is descending after the deceased King Niqmaddu in mourning. Furthmore, the immediate context from lines 13–17 deals with the mourning ritual as well, which might suggest the same concern in lines 18–26. On the other hand, however, the text seems to shift its focus from mourning to something else with the introduction of Šapšu in line 18 who commands this descent. I should also observe the similar shift in KTU 1.6 I:7–9 that moves from the mourning of ʿAnatu to the descent of Baʿlu into the underworld:

ảṯr bʿl nrd (8) *b ảrṣ*	After Baʿlu we will descend into the earth.
ʿmh trd nrt (9) *ỉlm špš*	With him Šapšu, luminary of the gods, will descend.

In this case, Šapšu is said to descend with Baʿlu (*ʿmh*), seemingly confirming the notion that the sun goddess was perceivably the psychopomp of the dead.[288] In KTU 1.161, she commands the descent, not only *ảṯr bʿlk* "after your lords," but

---

cf. Taylor, "First and Last Thing," 153, 173, who interprets *l ksỉ* in line 20 as a vocative: "after your lord, O throne").

286. Pitard, "Ugaritic Funerary Texts," 66, 71–72; Tsumura, "Interpretation of the Ugaritic Funerary Text," 45–46; Suriano, "Dynasty Building," 111–12.

287. The Niqmaddu of line 13 is likely to be distinguished from the Niqmaddu of line 12 (see Bordreuil and Pardee, "Textes en cunéiformes alphabétiques," 158; Pardee, *Ritual and Cult*, 85–86, 114 n. 125). I should note that the Niqmaddu of line 12 is summoned as one of the *rpủm*, while the Niqmaddu of line 13 is being mourned over, suggesting that it is his funerary ritual in view.

288. In the following context of KTU 1.6 I, ʿAnatu cries out to Šapšu, requesting that the sun goddess bear the dead Baʿlu for her (KTU 1.6 I:12). Šapšu does so, aiding ʿAnatu in carrying Baʿlu to the heights of ṢPN where he is buried and placed in the hole of the gods (KTU 1.6 I:13–18).

also *tḥt* "under" the *rpủm* outlined by name.[289] The context suggests that it is not simply calling for the king's descent in mourning for his deceased predecessor, but that his deceased predecessor is being called to descend after his lords who reside below and who have been called upon to meet him.[290] The verbal expression *špl ʿpr* "lower (oneself) into the dust" would seem to confirm this interpretation, since it appears to resemble a similar biblical image for death, not mourning.[291]

The final scene of KTU 1.161 relates to the bird-offering of well-being (*ʿṣr šlm*). The offering is signaled by the 2ms PC G form *tqdm* calling upon the addressee to present the bird of well-being. The well-being is directed toward six referents: the well-being of ʿAmmurāpiʾ and his house (the accession king), the well-being of Ṯarriyelli and her house (either the queen mother or grandmother), and the well-being of Ugarit and its gates.[292] The blessing invoked in this passage amounts to the blessing of the royal dynasty in perpetuating the memory of its former kings in hopes of ensuring ongoing stability for subsequent generations of the dynasty. It is also important to point out that this blessing is not confined to the concerns of the royal family alone, however, in that the blessing of the Ugaritic monarchy secures the overall well-being of Ugarit in general. This connection between the *rpủm* and their favor upon the living resembles Kirta's status as an exalted member among their ranks:

(13) *mỉd rm* [*krt*]	[Kirta] is greatly exalted,
(14) *b tk rpỉ ảr*[*ṣ*]	amidst the *rpủm* of the earth/underworld,
	in the gathering of the assembly of Ditānu. (KTU 1.15 III)

289. Pardee explains the use of the preposition *tḥt* /taḥta/ "under" here in light of the deep pit discovered between the two main tombs of the royal palace at Ugarit. He suggests that "the king was ritually lowered seven times into the depths of the earth, that is, into the pit . . . that certainly extended well below the lowest parts of the tombs themselves" ("Ugaritic Funerary Cult," 274–75; see also Pardee, *Textes rituels*, 823–24). This would also explain the use of the adverbs "once," "twice," etc., in that "the ritual descent would have been carried out seven times, each time marked by the offering of a *ṯʿ*-sacrifice" (Pardee, *Ritual and Cult*, 114 n. 128). The proposal of Suriano ("Dynasty Building," 114–15) to interpret *tḥt* as "in the stead/place of" seems to avoid unnecessarily the more common meaning "under," especially given the overall downward emphasis of the text: "descend into the earth" (2×); "lower yourself into the dust."

290. Contra Taylor, "First and Last Things," 151–77; Suriano, "Dynasty Building," 112–13.

291. See Ps 22:30: *kol-yôrᵉdê ʿāpār* "all those descending into the dust," which is further defined as *wᵉnapšô lōʾ ḥiyyâ* "and he does not keep his *npš* alive" (cf. Isa 26:19; Job 7:21; 17:16; 20:11; 21:26; Ps 22:16; Dan 12:2).

292. For the queen mother or grandmother, see J. Freu, "La fin d'Ugarit et l'empire Hittite: Données nouvelles et chronologie," *Sem* 48 (1999): 27; Singer, "Political History of Ugarit," 690–91, 696–700; Pardee, *Ritual and Cult*, 115 n. 133.

I have already emphasized the fact that this text is not just a statement promising Kirta favor in the afterlife, but rather the use of a SC G verbal form (*rm*) suggests that he has already obtained (perfective aspect) certain blessing from the *rpủm* in this life.[293] This factor also corresponds to the strength and power of Rāpiʾu manifested in the midst of Ugarit through the Rapaʾūma as envisioned toward the end of KTU 1.108.[294] KTU 1.161 therefore falls in line with the depiction of the *rpủm* elsewhere in the Ugaritic corpus in showing not only that dead kings joined their ranks, but also that their enduring powers somehow maintained the ongoing stability and blessing of the royal seat of authority at Ugarit.

One of the remaining problems to tackle in dealing with this text is to identify more clearly the setting and purpose of the ritual. One of the more common approaches to this text has been to understand it as prescribing the ritual veneration of the royal dead, and therefore yielding the quintessential support for the royal cult of the dead.[295] One of the main issues often associated with this so-called royal cult of the dead is the institution of the *marziḥu* and its relation (or not) to the Mesopotamian *kispu* festival.[296] Dietrich and Loretz, for instance, outline several features that KTU 1.161 and the *kispu* text Mari 12803 have in common, noting in particular that both prescribe offerings to the dead, deified royal ancestors.[297] According to this line of thought, the cultic force of this text is taken from the first line: *spr dbḥ* "the document of the sacrifice(s)," which is conceived as a prescription of sacrifices in honor of the royal dead (*rpủm*) who are listed in the following lines. De Moor has similarly offered parallels between KTU 1.161 and the Babylonian Genealogy of the Hammurapi Dynasty (BM 80328), the purpose of which, as Finklestein explains, was "the invocation to an actual memorial service for the dead" involving the offering of food and drink to the ghosts/spirits (*eṭemmū*) of the royal departed.[298] Pitard also mentions this text (BM 80328) as particularly important for KTU 1.161 in that it is the only extant incantation depicting the *kispu* festival in a royal setting.[299]

293. See above (§4.2.2.1).

294. See above (§4.3.6).

295. See L'Heureux, *Rank Among the Canaanite Gods*, 192; Tropper, *Nekromantie*, 126; del Olmo Lete, *Canaanite Religion*, 2nd ed., 160–61.

296. Dietrich and Loretz, "Neue Studien zu den Ritualtexten," 23.

297. Manfried Dietrich and Oswald Loretz, "Totenverehrung in Māri (12803) und Ugarit (KTU 1.161)," *UF* 12 (1980): 381–82.

298. De Moor, "Rāpiʾūma—Rephaim," 333 n. 72. Finkelstein, "Genealogy of the Hammurapi Dynasty," 115.

299. Pitard outlines the three main features of the Mesopotamian *kispu* ritual, all of which are present in the Genealogy of the Hammurapi Dynasty: (1) invoking the dead by name, (2) food offerings, and (3) libations ("New Edition," 67, citing Bayliss, "Cult of Dead Kin," 116).

On the other end of the spectrum are those who deny that this ritual is mortuary in nature at all, arguing instead that KTU 1.161 records the ritual coronation of the newly appointed monarch. For instance, although not denying this text's concern (and even veneration?) for the royal dead, both Abraham Malamat and Baruch Levine call it a royal accession/coronation ritual.[300] Schmidt has offered a more extensive attempt to move our understanding of this text beyond its funerary setting, calling it "a coronation ritual that incorporates mourning rites on behalf of Niqmaddu, Ammurapi's father and former king of Ugarit and the public recitation of Niqmaddu's name on that cultic occasion points to a commemorative rite in his honor."[301] Schmidt wishes to distinguish the terminology "mortuary" (rites related to the veneration of the royal dead) from "funerary" (related to the ritual commemoration of the dead) rites and proposes that although the commemoration of the dead was a common feature of Ugaritic ritual (as elements of such exist in KTU 1.161), ancestor veneration is entirely absent.[302] However, his assessment of KTU 1.161 in this regard appears to be too limited because the mourning features seem to dominate and cannot be readily explained as added elements. It might be better to view things from the other direction: KTU 1.161 is a funerary ritual in which the newly appointed king participates.

These questions return us to the *marziḥu* festival at Ugarit and its relationship to the funerary ritual of the dead. I have already commented on this phenomenon in chapter 3 amid my discussion of KTU 1.114 with its depiction of 'Ilu's drunken state: he falls like a dead man; he is like one descending into the underworld.[303] Tropper thinks that the *marziḥu* was an ancestor cult in which the participants invoke the favor of the *rpủm*, but Lewis has been more cautious, acknowledging its reputation as a drinking club while at the same time maintaining its loose association with the cult of the dead as a later development.[304] One of the main pieces of evidence for such a connection is taken from the Rapa'ūma text KTU 1.21 II:1: [. . .]*rzʿy*, often restored as [*m*]*rzʿy*, and thus taken as evidence for the *rpủm* being present at the *marziḥu*. Whether this reconstruction is valid or not still does not explain the phonological changes required for the equation

300. Abraham Malamat, *Mari and the Early Israelite Experience: The Schweich Lectures of the British Academy, 1984* (Oxford: Oxford University Press, 1989), 100; Baruch Levine, *Numbers 1–20*, AB 4a (New York: Doubleday, 1993), 378, 473; also noted in Pardee, *Ugarit, Religion and Culture*, 276.

301. Schmidt, *Israel's Beneficent Dead*, 120.

302. Schmidt, *Israel's Beneficent Dead*, 4–12.

303. See ch. 3 (§3.3.1).

304. Tropper, *Nekromantie*, 159. Lewis, *Cults of the Dead in Ancient Israel*, 2.

mrzʿy = *mrzḥ*. As such, this connection is speculative at best.[305] If anything, KTU 1.114, which also happens to associate ʾIlu with the *marziḥu*, seems rather to offer a mythological rendition of a Ugaritic drinking club without necessarily tying it to the *rpủm*. Quite incidently, the mention of *mt* "dead person" in line 21 describes the extensiveness of ʾIlu's drunken state—he falls to the earth like someone descending into the underword.

I conclude, therefore, that it is relatively safe to identify KTU 1.161 as a funerary ritual in which the newest member of the royal seat participated as a mourner. This ritual offered a two-fold function: (1) inducting the recently deceased king into the company of the *rpủm*, summoning both former and recent members, and (2) securing ongoing stability and well-being for the current and future rule of the Ugaritic dynasty. Or as Lewis has concluded, it was intended to (1) provide essentials for the deceased in their departure to the underworld (e.g., libations and offerings), and (2) secure favors and blessings for those who are still living.[306] Suriano's additional qualification "dynastic succession" may take us too far in that it requires placing this text in a larger ritual context that does not exist in the exant ritual corpus from Ugarit.[307]

4.4. Summary

The main aim of this chapter has been to provide a comprehensive lexical overview of the Ugaritic *rpủm* as they occur in the entire textual corpus from Ugarit. Having done so, it is necessary to offer a brief synthesis of my conclusions regarding their nature and function.

The Nature of the Rapaʾūma and the Divinized Royal Dead. The fact that *rpủm* regularly occurs in parallel with the term *ỉlnym* indicates that they were thought of as divine beings (KTU 1.6 VI:46–47; Rapaʾūma texts KTU 1.20–22). As I have argued above, the particular nuance of this term indicates that they were a special type of divine being especially identified with the Ugaritic royal dynasty. As *ỉlnym*, they fit within the broader category of Ugaritic deities designated as *ỉl(m)* "god(s)"; the latter term functioned as a parallel term to *rpủm* (KTU 1.6 VI:48; 1.20 II:2), and therefore qualified them as a species of the divine class. Futhermore, their association with *mtm* "dead (persons)" and *ỉlnym* // *ỉlm*, coupled with the construct phrase *rpỉ ảrṣ* "*rpủm* of the underworld," points in

305. See footnote 192 above.
306. Lewis, *Cults of the Dead in Ancient Israel*, 31.
307. As Suriano readily concedes ("Dynasty Building," 117).

two directions: (1) divine being, and (2) dead person. One means of reconciling these paradoxical associations in the Ugaritic texts is to interpret them in light of royal ideology and the reception of deceased kings into the company of divine beings called the Rapa'ūma. This explanation does not, however, account for the first two *rpủ* mentioned in the Rapa'ūma texts (KTU 1.22 I:8, 9) who appear not to be identified explicitly as having royal status. It may be, therefore, that the Ugaritic *rpủm* were mainly thought of as a particular class of divine beings into whose ranks kings were enrolled at death.

The *rpủm* are not, however, exclusively relegated to the realm of the dead and those who mourn over them. The Ugaritic texts show us that the presence of the Rapa'ūma is also a significant factor in life, as both Dānî'ilu, man of Rāpi, and Kirta, exalted among the Rapa'ūma of the earth attest. (I will speak more about the association between Rāpi'u and the Rapa'ūma momentarily.) Dānî'ilu's status as the devotee or protégé of the chief ranking member of the Rapa'ūma emphasizes their importance in matters of life, not only death. They apparently generated a symbol of cultural influence and political gravitas for those associated with them. Even King Kirta garnered an honorable place among them during his lifetime, which likely guaranteed a desirable position in the herafter as well. In fact, his triumph over the tragedies of death—one of the central themes of this epic—may provide the literary basis for this honorific title. The main thing to keep in mind is that the Rapa'ūma symbolized an ideology that embodied warrior-like strength, societal good, and supernatural power and blessing. In some way they functioned as a conduit linking together the divine realm, the royal household, and the culture at large. One wonders if this role resembles the nature of biblical Og, king of Bashan, identified in numerous passages as a leftover of the remnant of Rephaim. Was he a giant hero of old, a divine personage, or an Amorite king? The Ugaritic ideology of the Rapa'ūma may offer a means of combining these features into a single phenomenon or tradition of which the biblical tradition was well aware.[308]

Šapšu and the Rapa'ūma. It is apparent from the texts analyzed above that Šapšu is closely associated with the *rpủm*. The fundamental understanding of this relationship is expressed in KTU 1.16 VI:43–53, which presents a hymn announcing the breadth of her divine associations—she rules over the underworld deities below (*rpủm, mtm*) and experiences the fellowship of the major gods of the pantheon (e.g., Kôṯaru-wa-Ḫasīsu). Here governance over the *rpủm* comes into sharper focus in other texts where she is similarly associated with them. In KTU 1.108:26 she is mentioned immediately following the transfer of

308. See McAffee, "Biblical King Og," forthcoming.

Rāpi'u's powers via the *rpủm* to be manifested in the midst of Ugarit. More explicitly, in KTU 1.161:19–26 she commands the recently deceased king of Ugarit to descend into the underworld (// to lower himself into the dust), below the former (*rpỉm qdmym*) and recent (ʿAmmiṯtamru and Niqmaddu) company of *rpủm*, which appears to lend credibility to the suggestion that Šapšu was the Ugaritic psychopomp. In KTU 1.82 the voice of Šapšu is associated with the *rpủm* (or possibly Rāpi'u) in defeating the arrows of Rašap in the event of a venomous snake bite.

Rāpi'u and the Rapa'ūma. The connection between the deity Rāpi'u and the Rapa'ūma is justified on both etymological and contextual grounds. Etymologically, both forms are arguably derivatives of the root *rp'*. More importantly, however, their association in KTU 1.108 is difficult to ignore—the power of Rāpi'u belongs to the Rapa'ūma (lines 19–27). The chthonic features of Rāpi'u are also prominent—his association with Milku (both residing in ʿṮTRT), who is also chthonic in Mesopotamian sources, and his epithet *mlk ʿlm* "king of eternity/ underworld" with its connection to royal funerary contexts (*ʿlm* = realm of the dead). As an underworld deity, Rāpi'u cannot be identified with the major deities known from the Ugaritic pantheon, but must be relegated to the denizens of the dead. Furthermore, the appearance of *rpủ* in Ugaritic proper names offers additional verification that Rāpi'u and the Rapa'ūma were thought to be related. Especially important are those cases where it is difficult to determine whether the *rp'*-element is to be taken as the verbal form "X heals" or the proper name Rāpi'u. If this vocalization attested in these proper names is correct, it indicates that Rāpi'u (active participle), the chief ranking member of the *rpủm*, was understood as having the active power of healing (i.e., "the one who heals") and the Rapa'ūma (plural substantive) "the healthy ones" were the recipients of that power of healing. On a theoretical level, it is also important to consider the significance of the appearance of this deity name in the Old Amorite royal name ʿAmmurāpi', which at some level establishes this matter of health and healing as a central component of Ugaritic identity. This particular royal name meaning "the divine uncle is a healer," or perhaps "the divine uncle is Rāpi'u," thus envisions Rāpi'u functioning as head of a succession of Rapa'ūma "healthy ones" through whom blessing, well-being, and protection are procured for Ugarit.

Blessings Associated with the Rapa'ūma. The Rapa'ūma are depicted as granting favor or blessing to the royal dynasty, which also resulted in the overall well-being of Ugarit at large. The royal realm of blessing is well-preserved in both the Kirta and 'Aqhatu Epics. Kirta is depicted has having acquired an exalted status among the *rpủm* of the underworld (*rpỉ ảrṣ*), which apparently reflected the promise of favor both in this life and the life to come—the promise of progeny meant the continued stability of his throne, as well as the procurement of an honorable position among the *rpủm* in the hereafter (KTU 1.5 III:2–3, 13–15). Kirta's exaltation is also expressed in poetic parallel with "the gathering of the assembly of Ditānu" (*pḫr qbṣ dtn*), whose chief member appears as a theophoric element of royal names from early Amorite sources. In Ugaritic, Ditānu is also associated with the exercise of power in KTU 1.124—this dead, deified, eponymous ancestor of the Ugaritic royal dynasty to whom members are gathered at death brings the illness (*ḫlh*) of an unspecified child to a head and thereafter causes his bitter (*mr*) sickness to go away. Throughout the 'Aqhatu Epic, the epithet of Dānî'ilu, *mt rpủ* "man of Rāpi'u," indicates that he is the recipient of similar favor. As such, he is a protégé of Rāpi'u, the chief-ranking member of the *rpủm* who dispenses their powers of blessing and success to both the reigning king and the city of Ugarit (KTU 1.108:19–27). In KTU 1.161:30–34, the bird offering of well-being (*šlm*) is offered in the presence of the *rpủm* and their newly inducted member as a means of securing well-being for the new king, ʿAmmurāpi', the queen (grand)mother Ṯarriyelli, and the gates of Ugarit.

CHAPTER 5

Life and Mortality at Ugarit: A Synthesis

5.1. Introduction

I have now completed my lexical analysis of life and mortality from the textual materials currently available from Ugarit. The task of this chapter is to synthesize the results of my analysis by focusing on several broader issues that have arisen from these discussions.

From the beginning of this book I have sought to give proper attention to both life and death issues by analyzing the most common terms associated with these two concepts. But this division between life and death has proven to be somewhat artificial, even though arguably necessary from an organizational standpoint. In dealing with the Ugaritic vocabulary associated with life one is immediately confronted with the inevitability of one's mortality, a feature that is certainly not unique to ancient cultures but is the common experience of humankind of all times and places. One's understanding of life is often defined by the very things that threaten to destroy it, so that life and death are in a state of constant intersection. To some degree, life is defined in terms of death, and death is defined in terms of life.

This paradox is clearly evident from the Ugaritic texts themselves, especially in what we have observed from the mythology of the Baʿlu cycle and the epic literature of the Kirta and ʾAqhatu cycles. Both Yammu and Môtu are presented as a perpetual threat to Baʿlu's rightful reign. Although Yammu is relentlessly destroyed by the mighty storm god, narrated in painstaking detail, this same victor meets his match in the death god Môtu and must descend his insatiable throat in death. The opening lines of the Kirta Epic introduce the reader to the crushed house of King Kirta and his inability to secure an heir to the throne. What is more, this son of ʾIlu contracts a deadly illness, and therefore brings the entire Ugaritic ideology of kingship into question as his loved ones ask, "Do gods die?" (KTU 1.16 I:22). The royal personage Dānîʾilu, man of Rāpiʾu, also struggles to secure the longevity of his line, but eventually finds favor from the gods in the birth of the valiant ʾAqhatu. Yet, this hero comes to a bitter end at the hands of the vicious ʿAnatu who devises a hire-for-murder plot in order to steal his coveted bow.

Such literary observations demonstrate this inextricable link between life and death, but so too we are confronted with this same reality in analyzing the terms themselves. One of the most notable examples is *npš*, the vital force of life itself and the last thing to go out from the soon-to-be dead hero ʾAqhatu. In fact, the exit of one's *npš* thus becomes another means of expressing one's death, or at least the process of dying. Our ability to explain the Ugaritic conception of death on display when the hero dies depends upon our ability to articulate the meaning of *npš*, a critical term in the Ugaritic inventory for the semantics of life.

For these reasons we may speak of these two concepts functioning rather broadly as a merism for the whole of reality. They are two aspects that make up the totality of one's existence. Life is forever under threat of death, and so the two cannot be separated. Life and its mortality is arguably an integral component, a central theme, of Ugaritic literature. This theme comprises a major (if not *the* major) strand in the broader literary horizons of Ugarit and thus legitimizes the interest of this study in carrying out a focused examination of its semantic expression throughout these texts. I will now take up the task of exploring these life and death horizons as they have emerged from the previous four chapters of this book.

5.2. Mythology and the Language of Correspondence

The language of mythology is arguably a language of correspondence. The challenge for modern interpreters, of course, is to identify what that correspondence is exactly. This is true for all the great mythologies of the ancient world, and it is no less true for the mythologies attested at Ugarit. One of the issues that has arisen from this lexical study of life and death terms in the mythological texts is the degree to which they may have represented broader ideas about the cultural setting in which they were produced. That these myths are more than entertaining stories from the ancient imagination is demonstrable by their interest in themes like mortality, social and natural order and stability, love and war, sibling rivalry and the like. Such themes emerge from the poet's stylus because he is trying to tell us something about his world and the struggle for survival and prosperity—themes common to all ages of human civilization.

The Baʿlu cycle provides the essential mythology preserved at Ugaritic. Smith has outlined three primary interpretive theories for its interpretation in the history of scholarship.[1] The first theory interprets the myth according to the ritual and seasonal patterns (also known as "the myth and ritual" school). In this schema, the primary purpose of the cycle is "to translate the punctual into terms of the durative, the real into those of the ideal."[2] Advocates of the ritual and seasonal view emphasize, among other things, how the texts of the cycle correlate with the seasons, despite the fact that there is no single consensus on the exact parameters of this correlation.

I have already entertained the potential connections between ʿAnatu's mutilation of Môtu's corpse in KTU 1.6 II:31–35 and natural elements.[3] This passage provides a fairly clear example of Ugaritic poetry utilizing agricultural terms to express a mythological scene—in this case, ʿAnatu seemingly sows Môtu's remains as one casts seeds to a field. Here occurs a five-fold description of ʿAnatu slaughtering the god of death: splitting him with a sword, winnowing him with a winnowing-fork, burning him with fire, grinding him with a millstone, and scattering him in the field (lines 31–35). De Moor believes this scene can be explained entirely in terms of the seasonal pattern experienced by the inhabitants of Ugarit, experiences which he thinks were enacted in ritual fashion at the so-called New Year Festival.[4] De Moor's proposal evinces certain merit in light of the fact that ʿAnatu's acts are undeniably agricultural in nature, so that his most vocal critics may in fact overcompensate by downplaying the colorful imagery of the passage.[5] These connections were already detected by Virolleaud, who related the first three actions to the harvest and purification of grain, the fourth to the grinding of grain into flour, and the fifth to the act of sowing.[6]

However, does the agricultural depiction of Môtu's death necessitate a seasonal pattern interpretation? I only caution that this scene's correlation to the agricultural act of sowing seed eventually breaks down if pressed too far. For instance, we should not miss the fact that the sown remains of the death god do not germinate and produce a new crop of grain, but instead are eaten by birds of

1. Smith, *Baal Cycle 1*, 60–114. I am following his outline of theories for interpreting the Baʿlu cycle.

2. Gaster, *Thespis*, 25.

3. Ch. 3 (§3.3.3.2).

4. De Moor, *Seasonal Pattern*, 212–15.

5. E.g., Watson, "Death of 'Death,'" 60–63.

6. Virolleaud, "Poème phénicien de Ras-Shamra," 211.

prey, a point that brings the whole seasonal pattern interpretation for this passage to an abrupt halt.[7] It does not take away the imagery altogether but rather suggests it is not the driving force of the narrative. Such a criticism forces us to entertain much broader questions as it relates to the function of the Baʿlu cycle as a whole. Theodor H. Gaster was perhaps one of the more prolific and vocal advocates of the seasonal pattern interpretation for this myth, summarizing its overall literary function as "a seasonal myth." He explains:

> Baal represents the genius of rainfall and of the upper air; Prince Sea of the ocean and of those subterranean waters which the ancients believed to be the source of rivers and streams; Môt of the barren wastes and the netherworld. Their three-cornered contest thus symbolizes the succession of the seasons in the Syro-Palestinian year. Myths of this type were usually associated with major seasonal festivals.[8]

Gaster's view continues the "myth and ritual" school of interpretation developed much earlier in James George Frazer's *The Golden Bow: A Study in Magic and Religion* (1890) by applying this approach to the Ugaritic situation.[9] In defense of his seasonal reading of the Baʿlu cycle, Gaster appealed to seasonal pattern motifs in other ancient Near Eastern myths, arguing that the plot of such myths follows the pattern of the seasonal ritual.[10] In defense of this theory, Gaster correlated KTU 1.2 and 1.4 with autumn, KTU 1.5–6 with summer, KTU 1.6 II–VI with late summer, and KTU 1.1 with fall.[11] He also related Baʿlu's death and subsequent revivification to specific seasonal weather elements, associations which are certainly substantiated by texts like KTU 1.5 VI:2–9 where the storm god's return to life is signaled by the recurrence of certain weather patterns.[12]

7. Cassuto, "Baal and Mot in the Ugaritic Texts," 79; Loewenstamm, "Killing of Mot," 378–82; Healey, "Burning the Corn," 250–51.

8. Gaster, "Ugaritic Mythology," 185.

9. See also Samuel E. Hooke, ed., *Myth and Ritual: Essays on the Myth and Ritual of the Hebrews in Relation to the Culture Pattern of the Ancient East* (London: Oxford University Press, 1933), and Hooke, *The Labyrinth: Further Studies in the Relation between Myth and Ritual in the Ancient World* (London: SPCK, 1935).

10. Theodor H. Gaster, *Thespis: Ritual, Myth, and Drama in the Ancient Near East*, 2nd ed. (Garden City, NY: Doubleday, 1961), 77. For earlier seasonal pattern interpretations, see René Dussaud, "Aliyan Baʿal et ses messages d'outre=tombe," *RHR* 116 (1937): 121–35; Flemming F. Hvidberg, *Weeping and Laughter in the Old Testament: A Study of Canaanite-Israelite Religion* (Leiden; Brill, 1962); Vivian Jacobs and Isaac R. Jacobs, "The Myth of Môt and ʾAlʾeyan Baʿal," *HTR* 38 (1945): 77–109. For an overview of the seasonal view, see Smith, *Baal Cycle 1*, 60–75.

11. Gaster, *Thespis*, 2nd ed., 128–29, cited in Smith, *Baal Cycle 1*, 62.

12. See my discussion of this passage in ch. 3 (§3.2.1.2).

In short, the overall thrust of this method focuses on the underlying roots of the cycle and its similarity to mythologies from other languages and cultures with little attention to the distinctive features of the individual myths themselves.[13] Consequently, this same feature of the myth and ritual school is also one of its main criticisms. Scholars have been duly critical of Gaster's application of the myth and ritual theory to Ugaritic mythology, especially in light of the fact that evidence for the autumnal New Year festival—the drama upon which the seasonal myth is purportedly based—is thus far entirely lacking in the ritual materials from Ugarit.[14] De Moor's attempt to advance the seasonal pattern program highlights even further the challenges involved in demonstrating the legitimacy of this theory from the textual data itself, despite efforts at comprehensiveness. One of the major problems scholars have noted is the relative ambiguity of these so-called seasonal references throughout the cycle, not to mention the numerous passages that make no reference to weather elements at all.[15] This would be rather unusual were the mythology purposefully composed in correspondence to the cycle of the seasons and their ritual observance. It may be better simply to abandon the myth and ritual approach altogether with all its baggage and simply grant that seasonal elements underlay many literary aspects of the narrative.

Other interpretive theories for the study of the Baʿlu cycle are cosmogonic in nature, organizing the entire myth around the cosmic struggles of its main characters: Baʿlu's struggle with Yammu, the sea god, and Baʿlu's struggle with Môtu, the death god.[16] In general terms, this view understands the text to be entirely about Yammu and Môtu as competing rivals for Baʿlu's kingship. As Smith explains, "While not allies, Yamm and Mot may be seen as comparable forces treated as rivals to Baal for divine kingship, albeit not simultaneously."[17] In this interpretive vein the Baʿlu cycle becomes a description of the creation of the cosmos, which has resulted from this struggle of the gods for kingship. Loren R. Fisher, for instance, has observed that the construction of Baʿlu's palace and the

13. Smith *Baal Cycle 1*, 74–75.

14. Gaster, *Thespis*, 2nd ed., 129. Smith, *Baal Cycle 1*, 62; Mark S. Smith and Elizabeth M. Bloch-Smith, "Death and Afterlife in Ugarit and Israel,", *JAOS* 108 (1988): 278; cf. David Marcus, review of *New Year with Canaanites and Israelites*, by Johannes C. de Moor," *JAOS* 93 (1973): 589–91; Lester L. Grabbe, "The Seasonal Pattern and the Baal Cycle," *UF* 8 (1976): 57–63.

15. See Grabbe, "Seasonal Pattern," 57–63 (referenced in Smith, *Baal Cycle 1*, 66).

16. Sigmund Mowinckel, *The Psalms in Israel's Worship*, trans. Dafydd Rhys Ap-Thomas (Oxford: Blackwell, 1967), 1:134; Cassuto, *Goddess Anath*, 174–77; Loren R. Fisher, "Creation at Ugarit and in the Old Testament," *VT* 15 (1965): 313–24; Richard J. Clifford, "Cosmogonies in the Ugaritic Texts and in the Bible," *Or* 53 (1984): 183–201.

17. Smith, *Baal Cycle 1*, 76.

fact that it was constructed in seven days (KTU 1.4 VII; cf. Gen 1) both support the cosmogonic interpretation of the myth.[18] As he explains, "kingship, ordering of chaos, and temple building are all related to an overarching theme that I would call 'creation.'" The temple constructed for Baʿlu forms a "microcosm" and its ordering "resembles the creation of the cosmos."[19] Similarly for Richard J. Clifford, the mythological conflict between Baʿlu and his opponents, Yammu and Môtu, provides the bedrock out of which the suitable conditions for human society arise.[20]

John C. L. Gibson views the Baʿlu cycle as a mixture of cosmological and seasonal elements.[21] Unlike the cosmogonic view just outlined, Gibson believes that, in spite of the storm god's title as king, ʾIlu is the creator of the cosmos, not Baʿlu. His exercise of kingship is therefore a management of primordial chaos being manifest in the seasonal elements of Sea (chaos waters) and Death (summer drought). Gibson does not tie the battles between Baʿlu and his foes to the creation of the world as one sees in the Mesopotamian *Enuma Elish*, but rather connects them with ʾIlu's concern to keep the forces he created balanced and orderly.[22] The cosmological and seasonal elements are "inextricably bound up together" in Baʿlu's struggle to maintain order in the cosmos, which proved to be a perpetual burden. As Gibson explains:

> Though it was ardently believed that in the distant past of the earth's beginnings Baal had subdued these powerful rivals and brought them under some measure of control, and so had become king of the gods and earth's prince and lord, he had clearly not finally or irrevocably defeated them. Year by year in the world of nature he had to refight the old wars and secure the ordered succession of the seasons, and every day of every year he had to wage a constant battle so that good might triumph over evil in the life of men, and life itself not lose too many victims too soon to death.[23]

Still other scholars have looked to historical developments as a means of understanding the main aim of the Baʿlu cycle. This interpretation is not entirely distinct from the cosmogonic approach, but rather it seeks definite historical

18. Fisher, "Creation at Ugarit," 316–19.
19. Fisher, "Creation at Ugarit," 316, 319.
20. Clifford, "Cosmogonies in the Ugaritic Texts," 201. For the varied nuances of the cosmogony interpretation, see Smith, *Baal Cycle 1*, 75–87.
21. John C. L. Gibson,"The Theology of the Ugaritic Baal Cycle," *Or* 53 (1984): 202–19.
22. Gibson,"Theology of the Ugaritic Baal Cycle," 212.
23. Gibson,"Theology of the Ugaritic Baal Cycle," 218.

circumstances that would have provided the impetus for their depiction in mythological fashion.[24] Julian Obermann, for instance, did not deny that Baʿlu's conflict with Môtu exhibits certain cosmological qualities, but nonetheless believed his skirmish with Yammu must have "originated under definite historical circumstances." He further explains that the myth would have been "designed to explain, etiologically, how the people of Ugarit succeeded in expelling a hostile invasion effected by the inhabitants of a sea region, say, on the eastern shore of the Mediterranean, how they routed and deranged the invader's forces, how they destroyed his ranks into ruin."[25] Virolleaud also entertained the historical interpretation as a likely theory for interpreting the Baʿlu cycle, although he cautioned that it is doubtful one single view (seasonal, cosmogonic, or historical) could be expected to explain every aspect of the myth for all times.[26]

It is difficult to ignore the predominant climatic perspective of the Baʿlu mythology, couched in terms of the battle between sea and storm, even if one rejects the more elaborate seasonal pattern interpretations mentioned above. As Pierre Bordreuil and Dennis Pardee have observed, the terrain of the Syrian coastal region can be reasonably explained as having played a significant role in the development of these "agrarian myths from Ugarit."[27] They point out the climatic phenomenon that would have served as the impulse of these myths, tying the death of Baʿlu at the hands of Môtu (personified drought and death) to the seasonal drought of summer and Baʿlu's return to life to the autumnal rains. Similarly, Baʿlu's conflict with the Sea may have arisen from tempests of autumn and winter, which "must have made a big impression on fisherman, mariners, and travelers," for which Yammu's response to the storm god symbolized these mighty waves known from their experience with the Mediterranean Sea. They conclude:

> The geographical context of the two principal myths from Ugarit, therefore, is found in the interior of the kingdom: *Baʿlu*'s combat with the Sea is waged from his mountain residence on Ṣapunu, and *Baʿlu*'s battle with *Môtu* also victoriously concludes there with the return of the god to his palace.[28]

24. See Obermann, "How Baal Destroyed a Rival," 195–208; Marvin H. Pope, *El in the Ugaritic Texts*, VTSup 2 (Leiden: Brill, 1955): 103–4; and discussion in Smith, *Baal Cycle 1*, 87–96.

25. Obermann, "How Baal Destroyed a Rival," 205.

26. Charles Virolleaud, "Le Dieu de la Mer dans la Mythologie de Ras Shamra," *CRAI* 4 (1946): 505–6.

27. Bordreuil and Pardee, *Manual of Ugaritic*, 16–17.

28. Bordreuil and Pardee, *Manual of Ugaritic*, 17. See also Pardee, *Ugaritic Texts*, 25–28, where he discusses the antiquity of these myths in connection to the appearance of a weather deity battling

The central question of life and death as it emerges from the literature, mythological and epic, in many ways projects life's challenges in terms of the life and times of the gods, which are made manifest in the natural forces of chaos and renewal. But the one foe who looms ever-so-large, even above the elements of storm and sea, is the god of death, in whose throat the mighty Baʿlu, god of rain and storm, must descend, despite having defeated the ever-imposing threats of the Sea. Even Death meets his match, however, when ʿAnatu avenges the death of her brother Baʿlu, for which the text expresses his demise with the richness of agricultural language.

But what of the other motifs reflected in these texts—familial rivalries and competing claims for legitimate rule? One of the reasons Wyatt rejects the seasonal pattern view of the Baʿlu myth is because he thinks it is "indefensible and simplistic reductionism to shoehorn a whole religious system into an allegory of the seasons."[29] One might ask, however: Does it have to be all or nothing? Smith rather offers a synthesis of the major approaches for interpreting the Baʿlu cycle by acknowledging the presence of seasonal data as well as traditions of cosmogony, but he also stresses that these aspects of the storyline all contribute to what he considers to be the central theme: the limited exaltation of Baʿlu as king.[30] As he explains, "The theme of kingship is the explicit topic of the cycle, but its expression and meaning depend on information stressed by various interpretations," whether it be seasonal, ritual, or cosmogonic in nature. All pertinent aspects of the storyline further this motif. For instance, meteorological references as emphasized by the ritual and seasonal view are employed in the cycle to "dramatize" his reign, while the cycle's reuse of older cosmogonic traditions depicting divine heroes battling cosmic enemies draw attention to his power.[31] Nevertheless, Baʿlu's exaltation is ultimately limited and his kingship is not obtained quickly nor without the aid of the divine assembly.[32] For Smith, the Baʿlu cycle essentially "expresses the political exaltation of the divine king, and by implication that of the human king, as well as the limits of their kingship."[33]

---

the Sea in two eighteenth-century Mari texts. He concludes that "they demonstrate the existence among the inland Amorites already in the eighteenth century of a myth of the Weather Deity's combat with the Sea that was integral to the royal ideology—such a myth must have arisen among one of their ancestral lines who had regular contact with the Mediterranean Sea" (pp. 27–28).

29. Wyatt, "Religious Role of the King," 43.

30. Smith, *Baal Cycle 1*, 100–101. Cf. Smith, *The Origins of Biblical Monotheism: Israel's Polytheistic Background and the Ugaritic Texts* (New York: Oxford University Press, 2001), 128–30 (originally published as "The Death of 'Dying and Rising Gods': An Update, with Special Reference to Baal in the Baal Cycle," *SJOT* 12 [1998]: 308–9), where he identifies the divine, human, and natural levels, working under the central unifying theme of Baʿlu's kingship.

31. Smith *Baal Cycle 1*, 96–97, 100–101.

32. Smith *Baal Cycle 1*, 104–5.

33. Smith *Baal Cycle 1*, 110.

David Schloen has likewise attempted to combine these elements in his interpretation of Ugaritic myth, but he does so in a slightly more nuanced fashion. He extrapolates three layers of meaning from the Baʿlu cycle, allowing each level its interpretive force, or what he deems its "logical correspondence," which forms a "unified, internally consistent pattern," notwithstanding the occasional literary interference between levels. These three layers are the natural, political, and the familial. He explains:

> On the *natural* level of mythic correspondences, the battles between Baʿlu and his rivals represent the great clashes between perennial forces of nature, namely, storm and sea, fertility and death. On the *political* level they represent the struggles for supremacy among kings, with which Ugaritians of the Late Bronze Age were intimately acquainted, as they witnessed and participated in the imperial rivalries between Egypt and Ḫatti, and as their own kings jockeyed for power with their Syrian neighbors. And on the *familial* level, the sons of ʾIlu vie for preeminence in the patriarchal household, aided by their female relatives. They defer to the authority of their aging father, but they are impatient to succeed him as patriarch so that they can have a house of their own.[34]

Schloen's schema makes room for the literary multivalency of the Baʿlu cycle, allowing each thematic strand to stand on its own merit, but in correspondence with the unified purpose of the mythology.

Relating these three literary strands of Ugaritic mythology to the topic at hand, life and death permeate them all. The natural level of correspondence whereby the elements are given personified force illustrates both bounty and calamity—the effects of natural phenomena such as rain and storm sustain life, while the surging waves of the sea and devastating droughts of the summer season threaten to take it away. In all of these natural phenomena life hangs in the balance. Again, the comments of Schloen are instructive:

> The impersonal natural cycle of the seasons and powerful natural and social phenomena—fertility and death, storm and sea, warfare and sexuality—are humanized via narrative emplotment in terms of programs of action motivated by the perplexing aporias of human social existence, both on a local, familial scale, and on a wider political scale. The Baʿlu

34. David Schloen, *The House of the Father as Fact and Symbol: Patrimonialism in Ugarit and the Ancient Near East*, SAHL 2 (Winona Lake, IN: Eisenbrauns, 2001), 355 (emphasis original).

> myth achieves a poetic mimēsis of reality by simultaneously redescribing both natural phenomena that elicit numinous awe and the inescapable problems of life and death in a patrimonial society.[35]

Yet, the mythology of battling gods and goddesses may serve a more noble function than simply providing a fanciful literary projection of the erudite poet; at some level it may have functioned as a coping mechanism for the ancients in dealing with the threats of life uniquely experienced in their own world.

Death personified invokes both terror and sympathy. His insatiable appetite will meet every human life at its end. Even the mighty Baʿlu, lord of storm and rain, must descend into Death's throat, despite his being revived again afterward. But Death is correspondingly presented in sympathetic terms. For one, his pedigree as beloved of ʾIlu places him legitimately within the confines of ʾIlu's household alongside Baʿlu, ʿAnatu, and other members of this rivaling family. Furthermore, his abasement to the underworld and the consumption of dead corpses takes on a rather pathetic portrayal in KTU 1.5 I:

(1) *k tmḫṣ ltn bṯn brḥ*	When you strike Lôtan, the fleeing serpent,
(2) *tkly bṯn ʿqltn*	(when) you finish off the winding serpent,
(3) *šlyṭ d šbʿt rảšm*	the coiling (serpent) with seven heads,
(4) *ṯṯkḥ ttrp šmm*	the heavens wither (and) waste away,
k rs (5) *ỉpdk*	like the *rs* of your garment,
ảnk ỉspỉ ủṭm	I myself am devoured with moans,
(6) *ḏrqm ảmtm*	(as) dung I die.[36]

De Moor once observed the sympathy this text invokes for the god of death, almost as a means of excusing his behavior by showing him to be "obeying his natural instinct."[37] His appetite is compared to that of lion, a creature that can hardly be blamed for its instinctual hunger for prey as a means of survival in the wild. Commenting on Môtu's reply to a frantic ʿAnatu (KTU 1.6 II:13–23), Margalit makes the same assessment, describing Môtu as a "half-starved scavenger who, driven by his voracious appetite and elemental drives, has no choice but to devour house-guest Baal."[38] De Moor further describes the narrative's sympathetic portrayal of Môtu as a means of explaining that death is an inevitable reality of life. He explains further, "One may say that in the texts of Ugarit Death

35. Schloen, *House of the Father*, 356.
36. See our discussion of this text in ch. 3 (§3.2.1.2).
37. De Moor, "Lovable Death in the Ancient Near East," 242.
38. Margalit, "Death and Dying," 247.

is a sad, even tragic figure who is described with what amounts to a certain degree of sympathy. It is tacitly understood that his role in the mechanism of nature is indispensable."[39] Even Death, the beloved of 'Ilu, has his rightful place in the cosmos, however sad and tragic it may be, and no one, not even Baʿlu, can avoid him. The interpretive force of KTU 1.5 I seems to be the obvious fact that everyone must die, even the god of death, and this is why Baʿlu must descend into the underworld. This qualification or limitation of power offers a certain level of hope amid the narrative depictions of his terror-inflicting episodes, since even Death has a reckoning. Of course, we must also recognize that this aspect of Death is balanced out by his return: Death may die, as do Yammu and Baʿlu, but, like them, he always comes back.

As we think more about the function and purpose lying behind this Ugaritic mythology of death personified, we should also give attention to the listening ear of his father 'Ilu. In the final episode of the Baʿlu-Môtu skirmish, Šapšu rebukes Môtu with a warning, "How can the Bull, your father 'Ilu, listen to you?" (KTU 1.6 VI:26–27). This statement suggests that if he were to continue instigating this feud between himself and his rival sibling Baʿlu, it could jeopardize his relationship with his father 'Ilu. In response, Môtu is frightened and aroused at Šapšu's voice, thus ending the standoff (KTU 1.6 VI:30–32). Indeed, this passage is partly explained meteorologically—seasonal drought must come to an end and give way to the life-giving rains of autumn. However, the end of drought cannot of necessity signal the end of death's reign in a given seasonal cycle, since the hand of death persists at all times. In some way Šapšu's comment offers the ancient listener a means of dealing with the threat of death in the real world, since in the world of mythology he shares familial ties with the patron deity who in some way listens to his beloved, and this can be used against him to curtail his destructive powers.

Turning our attention to the epic literature, we find that King Kirta's family members entreat 'Ilu to save the ailing king from the threat of death. 'Ilu responds to their entreaty favorably and fashions the goddess Šaʿtiqatu who holds off the powers of Môtu over the life of Kirta (KTU 1.16 VI:1–14). Also relevant is the correspondence from TRǴDS and KLBY on the battlefield concerning the outbreak of a deadly plague among the military forces. In this letter, the correspondents seem to interpret their plight mythologically: "The hand of the gods is here, for Death is exceedingly strong" (KTU 2.10:11–13), though interpreting *mt* as the divine name here is not entirely certain, even if plausible. Explicitly mythological, however, is the incantation against venomous snake bite

39. De Moor, "Lovable Death in the Ancient Near East," 243.

in KTU 1.82, with the voice of Šapšu being invoked against the powers of Môtu: "By the voice of Šapšu, be saved/delivered (*ḥw*)" (line 6).

As we might expect, these examples illustrate the complexity of the Ugaritic worldview. It perceives the affairs of the gods and those of the natural order in relation to human experience as interrelated. This feature can be validated by the mere fact that the gods are not relegated to the realm of mythology, but are imposed upon the canvas of the epic scene where the paths of humans and deities collide. The gods provide the impetus for cult and ritual and are in the background of the everyday topics of Ugaritic correspondence. When we cast Ugaritic mythology in light of its central theme of life and death concerns, it reveals a theological and, shall we say, functional role for ancient society. It offers a theological apology for the cultic participation of Ugaritic society on both the individual and royal household levels. The stability and well-being of Ugaritic society depends upon the maintenance of the royal cult, which results in dynastic longevity. It is both analogical to and dependent upon the mythology of Baʿlu's rise to kingship, which Wyatt calls "the idiom in which this particular story is couched."[40] But the warp and woof of this royal ideology resembles a symbiotic relationship between the metaphysical and physical realms, wherein the program of the royal cult is maintained in the arena of a hostile world for its self-preservation, even in dealing with its worst enemy—death.[41]

By emphasizing the Baʿlu cycle's relationship to the political program of the royal cult, I do not, however, mean to suggest that such is its sole design, since that conclusion is difficult to defend from the text itself. The function of mythology in the royal cult has to be inferred from other places, as in the funerary ritual of KTU 1.161 or the ritual expulsion of the negative effects of a venomous snake bite in KTU 1.82, both texts having been discussed in the previous chapter. The former provides an example of the interrelationship between mythology and real life on the royal level, the latter offering the same on the common or individual level. Both cases at the very least demonstrate that the ancient Ugaritians ritualized mythology in certain circumstances. At the same time, acknowledging such a ritualized connection does not require that the Baʿlu cycle as a particular iteration of Ugarit mythology had its literary origins in ritual drama. Advocates of the myth and ritual school have been too rigid in limiting the focus of their interpretation on this literary purpose, which is lacking from the textual data before us, and for this reason have been rightly criticized. Gibson even goes

40. Wyatt, "Religious Role of the King," 44.

41. I will return to this concern in my synthesis of the royal dead below, where I also discuss the significance of the patrimonial kinship model expressed metaphorically as the "house of the father."

so far as to caution against the adoption of any one theoretical construction in interpreting this myth:

> I take it as self-evident that the cycle consists of a series of myths, but I hold no unitary or imperialist theory of what myths in general or ancient Semitic myths in particular are about or of how they ought to be studied. To insist, for instance, that a short myth or the various parts of a long one must have a ritual origin so that, where a link with cultic practice is not apparent, it is incumbent on us to supply one before we can meaningfully interpret it, is to my mind, to espouse far too limited an approach.[42]

Admittedly, no single theoretical framework identified above resolves every problem facing modern interpreters of Ugaritic myth.[43] In the end I maintain that the best way to interpret Ugaritic myth is to look at the broader literary context of the Ugaritic textual situation and recognize its multivalent purposes in tying together the natural and supernatural, the individual and societal, the political and theological, into a meaningful interpretive whole.

5.3. Life and Revivification

If we are to maintain the interconnectedness of the natural and metaphysical realms in the consciousness of Ugaritic society, the subject of life and death inevitably brings up the question of the afterlife. Did they conceive of life beyond the grave? And if so, what was it like? Did such life beyond the grave come about as a result of resurrection? Or was life after death thought of as a disembodied personal presence beyond the grave?

42. Gibson, "Theology of the Ugaritic Baal Cycle," 202–3.

43. Robert A. Oden has chastened Ugaritic scholars for failing to give adequate attention to "methodological self-consciousness" in their interpretation of myth. He outlines six theoretical assumptions underpinning certain aspects of the standard interpretations of the Baʿlu myth: (1) a link exists between Ugaritic myths and Ugaritic rituals, (2) Ugaritic myths somehow respond to the problem of anxiety, (3) the social institutions portrayed in Ugaritic myth correspond with the institutions of actual society, (4), Ugaritic myths function to support certain institutions in Ugaritic society, (5) the symbols of Ugaritic myths can be removed from their literary context and equated with abstract qualities or concrete phenomena, and (6) it is possible to select individual elements of Ugaritic myth pertinent to one's interpretation to the exclusion of others ("The Theoretical Assumptions in the Study of Ugaritic Myths," *Maarav* 2 [1979–1980]: 43, 45). He concludes his critical survey by urging Ugaritic scholars to chose one of two paths: (1) "state explicitly and defend the criteria by which they select certain mythic elements as significant while ignoring others," or (2) "join the structuralists, in this regard, in the ambitious undertaking of accounting, ultimately, for all the elements in a given myth" (62).

The nature of death and the afterlife in Ugaritic thought has sparked a great deal of discussion among scholars, and this discussion actually extends from conversations about death and afterlife in the Hebrew Bible. A prominent voice in these conversations was that of Dahood, who claimed that the Ugaritic materials demonstrate the belief in a beatific afterlife and resurrection, views that are similarly found in the Hebrew psalms. As Hays notes, Dahood was advancing the view of Albright who earlier warned against explaining away references in the psalms that appear to reflect a positive understanding of the afterlife.[44] In the introduction to his commentary on Psalms he claimed that "the most significant contribution to biblical theology that flows from the translations based on the new philological principles concerns the subject of resurrection and immortality." He criticized Sigmund Mowinckel's contention that "neither Israel nor early Judaism knew of faith in any resurrection nor is such a faith represented in the psalms," and instead proposed that several of the psalms evince "the mythological motif of the Elysian Fields."[45] Scholarly reaction to Dahood's claim was largely negative and for the most part warranted.[46]

However, I do wonder if this reaction has led to an overcorrection that has unjustifiably denied the existence of any conception of afterlife in West Semitic sources at all. Furthermore, in many discussions on this question there tends to be lack of concern for distinguishing between belief in bodily resurrection versus belief in an enduring personal (i.e., disembodied) presence postmortem. Some scholars have tried to deny that the Hebrew Bible gives any evidence for a belief in the immortality of the soul, which they believe to be a later Greek notion, and have instead argued that it is bodily resurrection that the Jews affirmed.[47] But as John J. Collins aptly remarks, this formulation of the situation "is far too simple."[48] Collins cites the work of George Nickelsburg who has catalogued a number of examples of Jewish belief in immortality from the Second Temple period that are not explicitly corporeal in nature.[49] Richard C. Steiner's recent

44. Hays, *Death in the Iron Age II*, 139, citing William F. Albright, "The High Place in Ancient Palestine," in *Volume du Congrès: Strasbourg 1956*, ed. P. A. H. Boer, VTSup 4 (Leiden: Brill, 1957), 257.

45. Dahood, *Psalms I*, xxxvi, citing Mowinckel, *Psalms in Israel's Worship*, 1:240.

46. See the list of publications registering negative responses in Hays, *Death in Iron Age II*, 139–40 n. 30.

47. See for instance Oscar Cullmann, "The Immortality of the Soul or the Resurrection of the Body" in *Immortality and Resurrection: Death in the Western World; Two Conflicting Currents of Thought*, ed. Krister Stendhal (New York: Macmillan, 1965), 9–53.

48. John J. Collins, *Scripture & Sectarianism: Essays on the Dead Sea Scrolls* (Grand Rapids: Eerdmans, 2016), 219.

49. George W. E. Nickelsburg, *Resurrection, Immortality and Eternal Life in Intertestamental Judaism*, HTS 26 (Cambridge: Harvard University Press, 1972), 168.

study on Hebrew *nephesh* is another case in point, only he argues that belief in a disembodied soul is evident in the Hebrew Bible itself.[50] I will discuss this suggestion more fully in the appendix of this book.

Jon D. Levenson has written extensively on the degree to which bodily resurrection is attested in the Hebrew Bible. A singularly important example occurs in the book of Kings when Elisha resuscitates the Shumanmite woman's son (2 Kgs 4:8–37). As Levenson notes, this text, long before the emergence of Jewish apocalyptic texts, presents resurrection as a possibility, though "not according to nature, of course, but through the miraculous intervention of the living God."[51] He believes that the conception of resurrection must have developed gradually throughout the Hebrew Bible and that the intermediary step between the resurrection of the Shunamite's son and widespread belief in the resurrection of individuals was no doubt the resurrection of Israel from the grave of exile.[52] During the Talmudic period, Rabbinic interpreters even thought the Torah itself teaches bodily resurrection, a notable proof text for this assertion being Deuteronomy 32:39 where it states of God, "I deal death and give life; I wounded and I will heal."[53] It is reasonable to maintain that such a reference may have simply emphasized God's superintendence over death and life respectively, and not necessarily the death and renewal of a single individual. However, Levenson notes that the semantic range of death can also refer to maladies leading to death; it includes both "disease and biological cessation," which leads one to ask: "Is there any reason . . . to think that God could heal disease but could not reverse death?"[54] Perhaps the following statement from Levenson gets at the question more directly:

> If death could be seen as the most severe of illnesses and characterized (in this understanding) not by nonexistence but by debilitation and physical fragility, then the possibility arises that God might heal it, too, just as he heals other diseases and wounds.[55]

Levenson's argument helps explain the exegetical and theological basis of the Second Temple period's burgeoning belief in individual resurrection. Richard

50. Steiner, *Disembodied Souls.*

51. Jon D. Levenson, *Resurrection and the Restoration of Israel: The Ultimate Victory of the God of Life* (New Haven: Yale University Press, 2006), 132.

52. Levenson, *Resurrection and the Restoration,* 156.

53. Levenson, *Resurrection and the Restoration,* 171.

54. Levenson, *Resurrection and the Restoration,* 172.

55. Levenson, *Resurrection and the Restoration,* 172.

Bauckham's explanation for this belief provides a theological rationale complementary to Levenson's exegetical appraisal of the biblical materials. Bauckham similarly proposes that resurrection arose as an "intelligible development of the faith contained in the Hebrew Scriptures." It was a "radical version of the Old Testament faith, found especially in the Psalms, that God will deliver from premature death those who are faithful to him and trust in him."[56]

Returning to the Ugaritic situation, I introduced in chapter 3 the proposed beatific interpretation of death in the Baʿlu cycle. Dahood believed the Ugaritic evidence proved the existence of this motif in the Hebrew Bible, but is it really apparent at Ugarit?[57] Margalit saw the death of Baʿlu as a pleasant postmortem existence in the Elysian Fields, claiming to interpret the terms *nʿmy* "pleasant" and *ysmt* "beautiful" found in KTU 1.5 VI:6–7 "at face value."[58] But this view is not sustained by the context—we are outside the netherworld, at the edge (*šlḥ*) of Death's realm.[59] It has been more common to understand this passage as a euphemism for death, but again, the locale of the scene militates against this view as well.[60] So much for a beatific afterlife at Ugarit! Instead, this passage depicts the mighty Baʿlu having been fatally wounded in his conflict with Death and now lying lifeless on the ground at the entrance of the netherworld. As I mentioned in chapter 3, the terms *nʿmy* "pleasant" and *ysmt* "beautiful" elsewhere describe the mountain of Baʿlu in particular (KTU 1.3 III:31) as well as mountainous region in general (KTU 1.15 V:12–15), which may simply highlight the fact that the storm god had not yet made his descent into the underworld.[61] He symbolically descends into the netherworld as ʿAnatu buries him, placing him in the hole of the gods at the heights of Ṣapunu (KTU 1.6 I:14–18).

What about the dying and rising god motif purportedly attributed to the storm god Baʿlu? Does this motif provide evidence for Ugaritic belief in resurrection? The work of James G. Frazer in his *The Golden Bough* (1890) has been the standard-bearer of the dying and rising god hypothesis as a means of understanding broad swaths of cultures and their views about deities particularly associated with the vegetation cycle. Smith summarizes the overall thrust of this theory rather well: "these gods' narratives and rituals epitomized the cycle of natural fertility, which moved from life to death and then from death to

56. Richard Bauckham, *The Jewish World Around the New Testament* (Grand Rapids: Baker Academic, 2008), 247, 248–49.

57. Dahood, *Psalms I*, xxxvi.

58. Margalit, *Matter of "Life" and "Death,"* 127–28.

59. See ch. 3 (§3.2.1.2).

60. See Driver, *Canaanite Myths and Legends*, 1st ed., 107 n. 9; de Moor, *Seasonal Pattern*, 191; Caquot and Sznycer, *Textes ougaritiques 1*, 250.

61. As noted by Pardee, *COS* 1:267 n. 234.

life."[62] The dying and rising god motif was therefore tied to the annual seasonal pattern—the death of a god corresponded to the withering of plant life, while the god's resurrection symbolized nature's renewal. This natural cycle was thus thought to be enacted ritualistically throughout the yearly revolution of the seasonal pattern.[63] As Smith chronicles the rise and fall of Frazer's theory, he highlights a number of the problems it encountered and the faulty premises upon which it was founded. Most damaging of all, it made too many assumptions about what was common throughout the respective cultures analyzed in his study without giving due attention to their multifaceted distinctions. As already mentioned, Gaster was the chief inheritor of Frazer's theory of the dying and rising god for the Ugaritic textual materials, arguing that the Baʿlu cycle combined elements from the combat and the dying and rising god motifs. He went so far as to say that the ʾAqhatu Epic was also "based upon the familiar seasonal myth of the dying and reviving god whose temporary disappearance brings about the summer drought."[64]

The two principal passages leading scholars to assume the dying and rising god motif for Ugaritic are (1) the references in the Baʿlu cycle to the storm god's death and subsequent reemergence in the narrative, described as being "alive" (*ḥy*), and (2) ʿAnatu's offer of immortality to the valiant ʾAqhatu like that of Baʿlu *k yḥwy* "when he is revived."[65] It is easy to see why the mythology of the storm god's death and his sudden reemergence alive would lead scholars to posit comparisons with similar features in the broader Near Eastern literature. One of the main criticisms, however, involves the degree to which it might be said that this passage reflects a ritual context. Smith acknowledges that it may in fact incorporate "ritual notions," but otherwise believes it is too difficult "to situate the text in a ritual context."[66] Getting away from the dying and rising motif, scholars have compared this episode with the disappearing god in the Hittite myth of Telepinu, wherein the storm god Telepinu, out of anger against humans, disappears to the steppe land for a time only to reemerge after divine searches

62. Smith, *Origins of Biblical Monotheism*, 106.

63. See the latest abridged version: James G. Frazer, *The Golden Bough: A Study in Magic and Religion; A New Abridgment from the Second and Third Editions*, Oxford World Classics (Oxford: Oxford Unviversity Press, 2009).

64. Gaster, *Thespis*, 2nd ed., 86, 87.

65. The form *qym* attested in KTU 1.22 I:5 does not refer to Baʿlu's ability to revivify (contra de Moor, *Seasonal Pattern*, 117; Spronk, *Beatific Afterlife*, 171, 173), but denotes the attendants of the gods who "rise" to assist them (see my discussion of this text in ch. 4 [§4.3.4]). *bʿl mt* "Baʿlu is dead" (KTU 1.5 VI:9, 23; 1.6 I:6, 41); *ḥy ảliyn bʿl* "mighty Baʿlu is alive" (KTU 1.6 III:2, 20). See my discussion of these passages in chs. 1(§1.2.1) and 3 (§3.2.1.2). ʿAnatu's offer of immortality is in KTU 1.17 VI:30; see my discussion in ch. 1 (§1.2.2.1).

66. Smith, *Origins of Biblical Monotheism*, 121.

for his whereabouts.[67] This comparison leads Smith to posit seven corollaries between Ugaritic Baʿlu and Hittite Telepinu: (1) Telepinu shares "some features of a storm god" with Baʿlu, (2) both are responsible for nature, humanity, and deities, (3) both are described as absent, followed by divine searches for their whereabouts, (4) both searches involve the sun deity, (5) the searches take place in the steppe, (6) general well-being is a concern in both texts (citing KTU 1.161 as well), and (7) like Baʿlu, the disappearance of the Hittite storm god of Nerik includes descent into the underworld.[68] One might also consider the Myth of Illuyanka (CTH 321) for its depiction of conflict between the storm god and the serpent.[69] In this text the storm god initially defeats the serpent, but is later slain by the serpent who tears out the heart and eyes of the storm god (line 21′). The storm god then instructs his son to retrieve his heart and eyes from the serpent, and upon successfully doing so the storm god "was again sound in body as of old" (line 25′).[70] Scholars have categorized this myth according to Frazer's "dying and rising god" type, though Gary Beckman has cautioned that "the resolution of the crisis of the seasons through the combined efforts of humans and deities is the most significant element here."[71] Nonetheless, it is important to observe that this mythology is presented within a ritual context—the *purulli*-festival.[72]

The obvious difficulty with these comparisons, as Smith well acknowledges, is that in no uncertain terms Baʿlu's condition is qualified as being "dead," expressed verbally (√*mwt* "to die") a total of five times throughout this episode. Strictly speaking, it is true that these statements do not explicitly say that Baʿlu was resurrected, but on the most basic level of literary analysis the text indicates rather emphatically that Baʿlu was once dead and afterwards returned to life again.[73] This observation tempers Hans Barstad's dismissal of this text after

67. Simon Parker, "KTU 1.16 III, the Myth of the Absent God and 1 Kings 18," *UF* 21 (1989): 295–96;Parker, *Pre-Biblical Narrative Tradition*, 186–87. Harry A. Hoffner, *Hittite Myths*, ed. Gary Beckman, 2d ed., WAW 2 (Atlanta: Scholars Press, 1998), 14 (for text and translation, see pp. 15–20).

68. Quotation from Maciej Popko, *Religions of Asia Minor* (Warsaw: Academic Publications Dialog, 1995), 71f., 110, which qualifies Smith's first point that Telepinu was a storm god (*Origins of Biblical Monotheism*, 121). Smith, *Origins of Biblical Monotheism*, 121–22.

69. See Gary Beckman, "The Anatolian Myth of Illuyanka," *JANESCU* 14 (1982): 11–25.

70. Beckman, "Anatolian Myth of Illuyanka," 19.

71. Beckman, "Anatolian Myth of Illuyanka," 24.

72. Beckman, "Anatolian Myth of Illuyanka," 24.

73. I should also point out that the same situation exists for Yammu (if Pardee's reordering of the tablets is accepted) and Môtu (see ch. 3 §3.2.1.1). However, this comparison needs qualification: of Yammu it is twice stated *ym l mt* "indeed Yammu is dead" (KTU 1.2 IV:32, 34) but he is never qualified as being "alive" upon his reemergence in the narrative (but note that the text is lost between the statement of death and the episode in column IV where Yammu is alive, so this qualification could have occurred); Môtu is never called "dead" or "alive," which is not surprising given that he is Death personified.

denying any evidence for a single dying and rising deity in Ugaritic.[74] His appeal to the biblical occurrence of *ḥy yhwy* in Psalm 18:47, which he renders "Yahweh is alive," may offer a certain level of correspondence, yet I must caution that this biblical affirmation does not contrast YHWH's living state with a previously dead state, and therefore is not the same.

How then shall we construe Baʿlu's revivification in the ʾAqhatu Epic? I will not rehash my analysis of this text in full here, but it is worth revisiting its importance as it relates to the question of revivification.[75] As I concluded in chapter 1, the verbal form in this expression—*k yḥwy*—must be taken as the D stem, which as a factitive would mean "make alive." Since this verb does not have an expressed object, as one would expect for factitive verbs in the active voice (i.e., "to make X alive"), I believe that it should be interpreted as a passive: "to be made alive." The factitive nuance for this particular stative root (i.e., "to be alive" or "in [the state of] existence") indicates an action that produces, reestablishes, or maintains the state of being alive. The overall context of this passage concerns ʿAnatu's promise to offer immortality through revivification to the hero ʾAqhatu, so the passive interpretation of this verb finds support both contextually and grammatically. Such an analysis qualifies my understanding of Baʿlu's ability to come back to life in this passage—ʿAnatu claims the power to resurrect gods such as Baʿlu and she promises to do the same for this valiant mortal.

This acknowledgment, however, creates a certain level of narrative tension with the depiction of the divine mourners following the storm god's death in the Baʿlu cycle. Of particular interest is the mourning of ʿAnatu upon discovering Baʿlu's dead body in KTU 1.6 I—with many tears she mourns his death and petitions the goddess Šapšu to help her carry his body to the heights of ṢPN for a proper burial (lines 6–18). Herein lies the tension: If ʿAnatu is thought to possess such power over Baʿlu in the ʿAqhatu Epic, why does she not revive the dead storm god at his death in the Baʿlu-Môtu cycle? Or does she? The mythological basis for such a statement may in fact be found in her violent assault of Môtu near the end of the Baʿlu cycle (KTU 1.6 II:31–35). In short, she overpowers the god of death, bringing his power over Baʿlu and the heavenly elements to a halt, at least for a time.[76] It is apparent that the destruction of Môtu makes way for

74. Hans M. Barstad, *The Religious Polemics of Amos: Studies in the Preaching of Am 2, 7B-8; 4,1–13; 5,1–27; 6,4–7; 8, 14*, VTSup 34 (Leiden: Brill, 1984), 151, cited approvingly in Smith, *Origins of Biblical Monotheism*, 120 n. 141, observing that reference to Baʿlu's resurrection in these texts has "scant support."

75. See ch. 1 §1.2.2.1.

76. Note that immediately prior to Môtu's demise, the text states: *nrt ỉlm špš ṣḥrrt lả šmm b yd bn ỉlm mt* "Šapšu, luminary of the gods, glows hot; the power of the heavens are in the hand of Môtu, son of ʾIlu" (KTU 1.6 II:24–26). This passage presents Môtu as having gained a certain

Baʿlu's renewal, though I should also caution that the immediate circumstances following this episode are lost in the break at the beginning of column III.[77] Therefore, we simply do not know how explicitly ʿAnatu's role in Baʿlu's revivification may or may not have been presented in what followed Môtu's death, but the overall literary context places her actions front and center in the storm god's return to life.

It is also of interest that the revivification event is couched in festal terms. In the ʾAqhatu Epic, ʿAnatu explains the storm god's revivification in the following way (KTU 1.17 VI):

ảšsprk ʿm bʿl (29) *šnt*	I will make you count years with Baʿlu;
ʿm bn ỉl tspr yrḫm	with the son of ʾIlu you will count months,
(30) *k bʿl k yḥwy*	like Baʿlu when he is revived.
yʿšr ḥwy	They prepare a feast; he is revived.
yʿš(31)*r w yšqynh*	They prepare a feast and give him drink.
ybd w yšr ʿlh (32) *nʿm*[*n*	The goodly one improvises and sings on his behalf,
w]*ʿnynn*	[and I] answer him.

I have already defended my interpretation of these lines in chapter 1, but here it is important to draw attention to the fact that feasting, drinking, and singing are a part of Baʿlu's revivification event. Unnamed participants prepare a feast, and then Baʿlu is revived, which is then explained further: they prepare a feast, they give drink, the goodly one improvises a song, and ʿAnatu answers. Those who criticize the wholesale ritualization of the Baʿlu myth raise valid concerns, but the incorporation of "ritual notions," as Smith allows, must not be ignored either.[78] Ritual notions are certainly present in the Baʿlu myth's depiction of the mourning and burial practices of the gods (see below). Here in the ʾAqhatu Epic, ritual elements also emerge as ʿAnatu explains the phenomenon of the storm god's revivification. With this description one might compare the feasting of the *rpủm* in the Rapaʾūma texts (KTU 1.20–22) or the sacrifices made at the royal funerary ritual KTU 1.161.

Of course, the ʾAqhatu Epic also raises questions regarding the transferability of such powers to mortals, as the hero denies outright ʿAnatu's actual ability to grant him such power. He counters her offer of immortality: [*ảp*]*mt kl ảmt w ản mtm ảmt* "I also must die the death of all; and I myself must certainly die" (KTU

level of power over the heavens after having defeated Baʿlu. For a different interpretation of these lines, see Wyatt, *Religious Texts*, 134.

77. Pardee, *COS* 1:271 n. 260.

78. Smith, *Origins of Biblical Monotheism*, 121.

1.17 VI:38). But even here, we must keep in mind the royal overtones of this epic, also shared in the Kirta Epic. What were the expectations of the ancients in facing their mortality? Could the divine ability to reemerge after death or destruction be expected for human mortals? Again, a certain narrative tension arises between the two major Ugaritic epics: the valiant ʾAqhatu denies it; the household of King Kirta seems to expect it.

In chapter 1 I entertained the seeming oddity of the situation involving goddess ʿAnatu addressing the hero in the second-person after she had already killed him (KTU 1.18 IV:40–41). This feature should be set before the backdrop of her plan to end ʾAqhatu's life for not complying with the goddess's proposal that he trade in his bow for a Baʿlu-kind of immortality. She declares: *ủ ảp mprh ảnk l ảḥwy* "But then, I myself will not allow the soldier to live on" (KTU 1.18 IV:26–27). As I have already noted, she not only withdraws her offer of perpetual revivification like Baʿlu, but also cuts his mortal life short by not allowing him to live on. Once the deed is done, however, ʿAnatu shows remorse for doing it. She laments:

(40) *ảbn ảnk*	I myself would have (re)built,
w ʿl q[štk mḫṣtk]	But on account of [your bow I struck you]
(41) *qṣʿtk ảt l ḥ[wt* ...]	(for) your arrows, you have not been permitted to l[ive ...]

This narrative motif of talking to a dead person may symbolize a certain belief in the idea that death is not necessarily viewed as the termination of one's existence, much like people today speak to their deceased loved ones as though they were listening. ʿAnatu declares that she was willing to "(re)build" him as she had promised, but that instead she ended his life on account of his bow. The notion of rebuilding in this passage appears to be another way of referencing the revivification of Baʿlu, which is no longer possible for ʾAqhatu. At the same time, however, this rebuilding/revivification may actually be deemed the sole prerogative of the gods, since, in spite of her remorse, the goddess does not appear to be able to reverse ʾAqhatu's condition. In fact, her conversation with the hero postmortem may otherwise reflect the idea that the dead experience a mere shadowy existence beyond the grave, but that they are unable to die and be renewed to a living state.

This factor raises the interesting point about the degree to which royal ideology factors into the Baʿlu cycle and its interests in life and death concerns. The themes of life and death offer a compelling thread tying mythology and epic literature together at Ugarit, but central to both is kingship. Smith is right in wanting to locate the motif of dying in the Baʿlu cycle within the larger worldview of ancient Ugarit, which leads him to the royal funerary ritual KTU 1.161 where he identifies certain similarities in their language.[79] I will return to these matters again below when I treat the unique features of the Ugaritic royal dead more fully, but at this juncture I simply wish to caution that the correlation between Baʿlu and the royal dead is not exact. It may indeed be somewhat analogical in nature, but there are distinctions that need to be maintained as well. One of the main distinctions between the existence of Baʿlu and that of the royal dead is that the latter are never explicitly described as being "alive" (*ḥy*) after having died. Smith, however, thinks Baʿlu's return to life is reflected in the link between the recently deceased kings and the current living king exemplified in KTU 1.161. He explains:

> Moreover, their successors continued the dynasty and its role in Ugarit. CAT 1.161 witnesses to these aspects of royal life. The text, at once mourning the deceased king and identifying his living successor, ultimately celebrates the link between the two; indeed, the text's list of ancestors highlights the dynastic continuity between the deceased and living kings. Baal's death and return to life may represent a theological reflection on reality that incorporates the known conceptualization of Ugarit's monarchy.[80]

The synthesis offered by Smith here is compelling, but it leaves several issues unaccounted for. For one, it does not consider the relationship that these deceased kings, who are in some manner divinized at death, share with the broader Ugaritic pantheon. If they are indeed conceptualized as a political extension of Baʿlu's kingship in this world, it is unusual that the royal dead would be relegated to a lower-level kind of deity, subservient to and somewhat lesser in relation to the greater gods.[81] This framework might have explanatory power were the two spheres—that of Baʿlu and that of the royal dead—kept separate, but as we have seen in the Rapaʾūma texts, the two are intermingled.[82] To put it in the form of a question, how could Baʿlu's death and return to life serve as a projection of the concerns of the Ugaritic monarchy and the destination of its departed members at the same time? It may be less complicated (and admittedly

79. Smith, *Origins of Biblical Monotheism*, 123–28.

80. Smith, *Origins of Biblical Monotheism*, 128.

81. The Baʿlu = Rāpiʾu hypothesis regarding KTU 1.108 might alleviate this problem, but my analysis of this text in ch. 4 (§4.3.6.1) demonstrates what I think are insurmountable obstacles for accepting this viewpoint.

82. See ch. 4 (§4.3.4).

less sophisticated interpretatively!) to suggest that the ancients were conceiving of two separate realms of existence—the divine and the natural—and that to a certain degree the members of the divine realm were somehow involved in the affairs of the royal household. The interest of the divine realm in watching over the needs of the Ugaritic monarchy and its subjects is only heightened by the fact that Ugarit's own members are inducted into the divine ranks, but in a lower and thus subservient role.[83]

I close my discussion on resurrection at Ugarit with a brief comment on the expectations of King Kirta's household. KTU 1.16 I records the infamous question, "Do gods die?," which I render again here:

b ḥyk ảbn ả[!]šmḫ	In your life, our father, we rejoice,
(15) *bl mtk ngln*	(in) your not dying we find joy.
k klb (16) *b btk nʿtq*	Like a dog in your house we pass/grow old,
k ỉnr (17) *ảp ḫštk*	like a hound also (in) your court.
ảp ảb k mtm (18) *tmtn*	Also, father, like mortals will you die?
ủ ḫštk l ntn (19) *ʿtq*	Or indeed your court be given to passing/ growing old,
bd ảṯt ảb ṣrry	into the hand of women, father ṢRRY?
(20) *ỉ km yrgm bn ỉl*	O thus he is called a son of ʾIlu;
(21) *krt špḥ lṭpn* (22) *w qdš*	Kirta is the offspring of the knowing and holy one.
ủ ỉlm tmtn	Do gods die?
(23) *špḥ lṭpn l yḥ*	Would the offspring of the knowing one not live? (cf. KTU 1.16 II:36–60)

In my treatment of this passage earlier in this book I entertained its potential conflict with the royal ideology that granted a certain level of divinity to kings at death. This factor led Parker to suggest that the text before us intends to overturn these older assumptions about Ugaritic royalty in exchange for a "mortal" depiction of kingship.[84] But as I have already mentioned, the text would seem to point in the opposite direction—the narrated healing of King Kirta actually undergirds and further supports royal claims of divine associations.[85] His being called a son of ʾIlu emphasizes his status as an adopted member of the divine

83. See below (§5.7) where I discuss the divine determinative *ỉl* prefixed to royal names in KTU 1.113.

84. Parker, "Historical Composition of KRT," 174; Parker, *Pre-Biblical Narrative Tradition*, 212–13.

85. Ch. 3 (§3.2.2.2).

class, or offspring of the knowing and holy one. These qualifications inform the text's parallel questions: "Do gods die?" // "Would the offspring of the knowing one not live?" These questions concern the royal "gods" and the legitimacy of royal ideology. In the end, the premature death of the reigning royal personage seems to be the real issue of this text, which would bring into question the legitimacy of the entire monarchical program for Ugarit.

The type of immortality under consideration in the ʾAqhatu Epic is not exactly the same as that found in the event of King Kirta's impending death. I must therefore affirm Healey's assessment regarding their correspondence:

> The Aqhat text alludes to a more philosophical reflection on human life and in the context of the denial of immortality to mankind (as in Gilgamesh etc.) the immortality on offer is meant to be understood literally as infinitely prolonged life. In the Keret text we are dealing with an expression of royal ideology. *Vivat regina* in royal protocol is not in real conflict with skepticism about afterlife.[86]

I will revisit the nature of the royal dead shortly, but here simply emphasize that their deity is different in kind from the greater gods of the pantheon and it precludes the possibility of perpetual revivification like that of Baʿlu.

The nature of resurrection in the Ugaritic texts is conceived as being an exclusive possibility for the gods and is not applicable to human beings. Not even the hero ʾAqhatu can acquire this power, despite the promise of ʿAnatu to give it to him. The closest we come to the resurrection of humans is within the royal program of the king as "son of ʾIlu," and the expectation of longevity, which in the case of King Kirta translates into the ability to escape the clutches of premature death. This motif finds many parallels in the biblical psalms and the psalmists' prayers for YHWH to deliver them from the pit of Sheol.[87] The optimistic outlook of these texts is that YHWH is able to rescue the soul of his people from death and restore them to the life and longevity they once experienced.[88] Levenson also draws this same parallel, observing that the Kirta Epic is likewise a story about "the loss and recovery of family, about the loss and recovery of children, the healing of terminal illness, the consequent reversal of famine and renewal of foodstuffs—in a word, about how death was broken."[89]

86. John F. Healey, "The Immortality of the King: Ugarit and the Psalms," *Or* 53 (1984): 249.

87. Levenson cites the following examples: Pss 9:14–15; 40:3; 88:2–10; 107:10–22 (*Resurrection and the Restoration*, 38–45).

88. Levenson, *Resurrection and the Restoration*, 40.

89. Levenson, *Resurrection and the Restoration*, 136.

But more than simply breaking death's grip on the living, Baʿlu offers an early prototype of true revivification, a divine kind of "resurrection," if you will. To be sure, it is not the same manner of resurrection arising from within the confines of the biblical tradition, but at the very least it shows this concept existed as a possibility in the minds of the Ugaritic poets of the second millennium.

5.4. The Anatomy of Life

The ancient world commonly utilized aspects of the physical realm to rationalize metaphysical concepts. This was done primarily in the use of animal and human body-parts as a means of expressing various aspects of human personhood. These body-part terms became a central part of understanding the life and death of individuals, as we have seen illustrated in the Ugaritic materials surveyed in this book. This tendency was certainly not unique for Ugarit, however, but was shared among its ancient Near Eastern neighbors.

Akkadian sources from Mesopotamia possess a number of body-part terms applied to metaphysical realities reflective of life. For example, one may consider the word *napištu*, which is etymologically related to West Semitic *npš* discussed in chapter 2. The *CAD* lists the following meanings for Akkadian *napištu*: (1) "vitality, vigor, vitality, good health," (2) "living beings," (3) "person, somebody," (4) "capital case," (5) "personnel, persons of menial status, animals counted in a herd," (6) "body, self," (7) "breath," (8) "livelihood," (9) "throat, neck," (10) "air hole, opening."[90] There is significant semantic overlap between this term and its Ugaritic counterpart in that they both share the meanings "neck, throat," "vitality, life force," and "person, individual."[91] Similarly, the Akkadian term *libbu* refers to the physical "heart, abdomen, entrails, womb," while likewise indicating the "mind, thought, intention, courage, wish, desire, choice, preference."[92]

Central to the Egyptian conception of life is the term "breath of life" (*tchaw n ankh*), which was linked to the Egyptian notions of the central circular system.[93] The heart was conceived as being central to an elaborate system of indistinguishable vessels (*mt.w* "tubes/canals"), within which flowed a number of substances such as blood, water, air, mucus, and the remnants of undigested food.[94]

90. *CAD* 11:296.

91. See ch. 2.

92. *CAD* 9:184.

93. Robert Ritner (pers. comm.).

94. The two synonymous terms for "heart" in Egyptian are *ib* and *ḥ3.ty* (Robert Ritner, "The Cardiovascular System in Ancient Egyptian Thought," *JNES* 65 [2006]: 100 n. 10, referencing

This last substance was called *wekhedu*, and it was thought to accumulate within this system over time producing aging, bodily decay, and eventually death.[95] This Egyptian concept of *wekhedu* featured prominently in both life and death contexts. In life, physicians carried out a number of medical practices aimed at cleansing the body of this undesirable substance and thus sustaining longevity. After one's death those internal organs most prone to decay (e.g., lungs, liver, stomach, intestines) were removed in light of their being "saturated with *wekhedu*."[96] This understanding of life and the body demonstrates the importance of mummification at death, since its primary purpose was preservation for the afterlife. Stephen Quirke explains:

> Mummification combines a physical preservation of the body, to keep it the same, with the anticipation of a spiritual afterlife, to transfigure the person and make him or her new and different, "radiant." Since the efforts to preserve a lifelike outer appearance can only be said to be partially successful, they were supplemented by plaster modelling of facial features and limbs in the third millennium and by packing the skin with stuffing in the early first millennium BC.[97]

The Ugaritic materials likewise demonstrate a number of anatomy terms that are utilized for expressing various conceptions of life. Three of these terms are especially important for this study of life concepts due to their high number of occurrences in the Ugaritic texts: *npš* (//*brlt*) "neck/throat/vital force," *kbd* "liver, insides," *lb* "heart, mind." These "life" terms, however, become important markers for the Ugaritic understanding of death as well, especially from what we know about the term *npš*, to which I have already devoted a chapter-length discussion.[98] My comments here will of necessity be brief, but it is nonetheless important to place it within the context of the discussion on life and revivification above.

The term *npš* (//*brlt*), meaning "(a part of the) neck" in ritual texts and "throat" in mythic and epic literature, takes on the metaphysical notion "vitality, life force." The occurrence of *npš* for individuals in administrative lists may indicate persons in whom the vital *npš*-element exists. When a person is called a *npš*,

---

Hermann Grapow, ed., *Anatomie und Physiologie*, Grundis der Medizin der Alten Ägypter (Berlin: Akademie, 1954], 64–72). For the system as a whole, see Ritner "Cardiovascular System," 100.

95. Ritner "Cardiovascular System," 100.

96. Ritner "Cardiovascular System," 100–101.

97. Stephen Quirke, *Ancient Egyptian Religion* (London: British Museum, 1992), 144.

98. See ch. 2.

which, by the way, is much more common in Biblical Hebrew, it is reasonable to assume that his *npš* = vitality is still alive. The basis for this observation is found in the Ugaritic expression involving *npš* plus some form of the root *ḥyy* "to live."[99] For instance, I discussed the following occurrence in the ʾAqhatu Epic as a pronouncement of blessing upon Dānîʾilu (KTU 1.17 I):

npš yḥ dnil (37) [*mt rp*]*i*	As for (his) vitality, may Dānîʾilu, man of RPU live,
brlt ǵzr mt hrnmy	as for (his) life force, may the warrior, HRNMY man (live).
(38) [. . .]*ḥ hw mḫ*	[. . .] may he be successful.

The verbal root *ḥyy* refers to one's state of being/existence, sometimes in parallel with the quasiverb *iṯ* "there is, there are."[100] In this passage, ʾIlu pronounces blessing upon Dānîʾilu that he might be successful in siring a son, which is expressed in terms of a living *npš*, or more exactly, the continued persistence of the vital forces of life within him. This persistence of vital force is directly applied to Dānîʾilu's ability to have a son. As I noted in chapter 2, many translators wish to see the notion of renewal in this instance, and thus another indicator of a revivified life, but I find this interpretation unwarranted.[101] Instead, it reflects the continuance of one's life-state, which is demonstrable through functional vitality. At a basic level, it denotes the underlying forces of the human person's animation, which ceases to exist once the *npš* has departed from the body. This imagery might reflect the similar depiction of the slumping, dead body of Yammu after being struck fatally by Baʿlu (KTU 1.2 IV:25–26), even though the motif does not occur there explicitly.

The exiting *npš* motif is particularly pertinent to questions relating to the so-called afterlife. But in what way? It provides a vivid way of describing the death event, presenting the departure of one's vital forces from the body. We find it in the ʾAqhatu Epic in the depiction of the hero's death after receiving the fatal blow of YṬPN, ʿAnatu's hired assassin.[102] This departure of *npš* is explicitly defined in terms of not allowing him to live on, which therefore means that it departs once one's life has come to an end. The accompanying comparisons are also useful illustrations of death as exiting *npš*: like the movement of the wind, like

99. KTU 1.17 I:36; 1.19 IV:36, 39; 2.23:18.

100. KTU 1.5 III:2–3, 8–9, 20–21.

101. Caquot and Sznycer, *Textes ougaritiques 1*, 423; del Olmo Lete, *Mitos y leyendas de Canaan*, 371. See my discussion in ch. 2 (§2.2.3.1).

102. KTU 1.18 IV:24–27, 36–37; 1.19 II:39, 44 (broken).

spittle from the mouth, from the nose like smoke through a window (KTU 1.18 IV:24–26).

What, if any, are the connections between the exiting *npš* motif and the post-mortem existence of Ugarit's royal dead? Almost in passing, Healey remarks that "the continued existence of man's 'soul' is always assumed in the ancient Semitic world, as is the inevitability of death."[103] For Ugaritic sensibilities, however, the texts that have come down to us never use *npš* to describe a continued state of being after death, but only speak about its exit from the body at death. As for the *rpủm*, they are called *ẓlm* in KTU 1.161:1, for which I have adopted the common rendering "shades," and function as the main subject of this funerary ritual. The funerary context of KTU 1.161 may offer the kind of setting that would have given rise to the idea that the *npš* endures beyond the grave, that is, if we think carefully about the circumstances of the funerary ritual.[104] The Rapaʾūma of the underworld // assembly of Ditānu—consisting of both ancient and more recent members of this class—are summoned to the place of the funerary ritual as Šapšu commands the recently deceased king of Ugarit to descend and be received into their company below (*tḥt*). Again, it is important to keep in mind that this ritual is for a royal funeral, so its main concern is the burial of the former king's dead body (i.e., "being placed in the hole of the gods of the underworld"). This ritual gives explicit expression to the idea that the dead king continues to experience a shadowy existence beyond the confines of his physical body, unless of course it is the actual burial of his physical body that is given metaphorical expression. The term *npš*, however, does not appear in this text.

This is as far as the Ugaritic materials will allow us to go in speaking about an enduring *npš* beyond the physical body of the deceased. However, the funerary context just described from KTU 1.161 should factor into any assessment of the situation attested from the royal funerary inscriptions of the early first millennium BC. I devote more attention to these materials in the appendix at the end of the book. There I place the Ugaritic conceptions of life and death within the broader Northwest Semitic context of the first millennium BC. In anticipation of that discussion, I simply affirm here that the *nbš* (=*npš*) inhabiting the funerary stela of the royal dead attested at Zincirli does not of necessity signal the adoption of foreign elements into the Semitic worldview, but may in fact demonstrate an internal development having been anticipated already at Ugarit in the funerary context of KTU 1.161. This matter is developed more fully in the appendix to follow.

103. Healey, "Immortality of the King, 246.
104. See the more extensive remarks in ch. 4 (§4.3.6.2).

5.5. The Life and Death of Physical Objects

The language of living and dying is not limited to animated beings at Ugarit, however, but is applied to inanimate objects as well. I have identified two clear examples of this in the literature from Ugarit, one involving the conceptualization of a physical object being restored to life and the other describing its death.

In the letter KTU 2.70:15 I noted that the D stem of the root *ḥwy* is utilized to express the restoration of a dilapidated house.[105] The text reads: *w ȧnk ḥrš lqḥt w ḥwt hbt* "As for me, an artisan I have taken/hired. I have repaired this house" (lines 14–16). From the context we may assume that this particular structure had fallen into disrepair and was therefore in need of extensive renovation, since the letter specifies that an artisan had been hired to do the restoration. This example offers an important parallel for the application of *ḥwy* to animated entities such as the valiant ʾAqhatu in the ʾAqhatu Epic. The goddess ʿAnatu offered ʾAqhatu a kind of perpetual revivification, or, as I have already stated, a preservation via revivification. In this case the idea of revivification is applied to the restoration of a house structure so that it might be preserved as a suitable place of residence.

In a second example, I observed that the root *mwt* is once applied to ships in KTU 2.38, again in another Ugaritic letter.[106] The text reads: *ȧnykn dt likt mṣrm hndt b ṣr mtt by* (14) *gšm ȧdr nškḥ* "Your ships that you sent to Egypt are *dead* at Tyre, where they found themselves in a bad storm" (lines 10–15). As I noted in chapter 3, the imagery of death invoked in this letter recalls the exiting *npš* motif as discussed above depicting death as the departure of the animating force of life, thus leaving the dead body motionless. The "dead" ships of KTU 2.38 are described as having been stripped (*ʿryt*), which probably refers to the destruction of their sails that were essential for mobility. Apparently, the storm had badly damaged their rigging and therefore left them stranded within the jurisdiction of Tyre where they were found by its king who wrote this letter to the king of Ugarit. Death, in this instance, seems to indicate the loss of animation, or more exactly, the loss of power for naval navigation.

This particular way of speaking about ships appears to be highly developed, if not technical. Throughout this same letter the salvage master who has collected the valuables from these ships is twice called the *rb tmtt* "master of death" (lines 16 and 22). Not only are the ships described as being "dead," but also the chief official responsible for confiscating the goods from such ships is given the special title *rb tmtt*. Could this language represent a technical term for a certain kind

105. See discussion in ch. 1 (§1.2.2.6).

106. See discussion in ch. 3 (§3.2.4).

of individual who specialized in salvaging wrecked/immobilized ships? Given Phoenicia's reputation for its naval operations, it is quite plausible to think of such technical language being developed from the occasions of their ongoing seafaring enterprise throughout the ancient world.

These two examples are remarkably interesting because they occur in the common parlance of Ugaritic correspondence. The application of abstract notions such as living and dying to physical objects demonstrates highly sophisticated idioms of expression—revived houses, dead ships, and a dead-ships official. The revivification of a house and ships dead in the water are idiomatic expressions that share parallels with similar language from our own world, as modern English speakers routinely speak of the need for revitalization as well as the fact that something appears to be dead. Unlike the world of myth and ritual, the Ugaritic epistolary materials offer an occasion to discover the richness of the prosaic, where houses need to be revived and ships are dead.

5.6. The Intersection of Mythology and Burial

As the previous two sections illustrate, the language of Ugarit demonstrates a certain level of correspondence between physical and metaphysical realities. Body parts become technical terms for expressing various aspects of personhood, while inanimate objects are given qualifiers reflective of human beings. The language adopted for burial customs offers yet another example of correspondence wherein the physical act of burial is interpreted in mythological terms. The subtlety of this phenomenon in the Ugaritic texts reinforces the notion that the ancients viewed these two realities as somehow related, or at the very least viewed one reality as a valid means of explaining the other.

As it relates to the interpretation of Ugaritic myth, Robert A. Oden's criticisms of the reigning theoretical paradigms are helpful, and his call for scholars to devote more attention to methodological questions is no doubt necessary. However, his dismissal of the pervasive assumption that "the symbols used in Ugaritic myths can be removed from their mythic contexts and then equated with some abstract quality or some concrete phenomenon" requires further qualification.[107] It is likely unwise to remove symbols from their mythological literary contexts in an attempt to demythologize their meaning for the modern interpreter and their reconstructions of ancient thought. Nonetheless, it is necessary to acknowledge that the ancient writers drew from the symbolism of myth

107. Oden, "Theoretical Assumptions," 57–58.

in ways that explicitly applied meaning to abstract qualities and/or concrete phenomena. That this was indeed the case is especially evident when a wide range of genres (e.g., mythological texts, ritual texts, epistolary texts, administrative texts) are analyzed in light of a specific theme or symbol. In this particular book I have been analyzing life and death terms in Ugaritic, which has yielded evidence that the theme of death and its symbolic representation in numerous texts has been applied to the concrete act of burial.

My discussion of the root *mwt* in chapter 3 reveals a number of references to the burial of the dead. The literary situations in which these instances occur mainly involve the mythology of the Baʿlu cycle, especially the death and burial of the storm god himself. As we have seen, however, burial is front and center in the funerary ritual KTU 1.161 as well, where the interment of the dead ruler is ritualized in terms of his reception into the company of his dead predecessors. In these texts there exists an intersection of mythology and the real-world experiences associated with treatment of the dead. In this section I am interested in exploring this intersection more extensively from the texts. Upon doing so, I will briefly survey the archaeology of death and burial in order to anchor this discussion in the funerary material culture from Ugarit.[108]

Even though the literary cycles depicting Baʿlu's skirmishes with Yammu and Môtu are, strictly speaking, mythological in nature, it is important to highlight certain nonmythological elements intermingled throughout. The intermingling of real-world elements is nowhere clearer than in what is found in the narration of the storm god's death and burial. The details of Baʿlu's burial are anticipated in Môtu's threatening speech regarding what he is about to do to his foe, and they constitute three expressions: (1) "I will place him in the hole of the gods of the earth," (2) "descend to the house of the abasement of the earth," and (3) "you must be counted among those going down to the earth" (KTU 1.5 V:5–17). From these three death statements we can infer three summary remarks about death's conceptualization: it involves a place, its direction is downward, and its nature is abasement. Earlier in the narrative, Môtu pronounces Baʿlu's demise quite differently, warning that the storm god cannot escape the inevitable fate of descending his own throat:

108. See Theodore Lewis, "How Far Can Texts Take Us? Evaluating Textual Sources for Reconstructing Ancient Israelite Beliefs about the Dead," in *Sacred Time, Sacred Place: Archaeology and the Religion of Israel*, ed. Barry M. Gittlen (Winona Lake, IN: Eisenbrauns, 2002), 183: "Archaeology is very important for helping us to visualize how tomb images underlie such verbal expressions of the netherworld."

l yrt (7) *b npš bn ilm mt*	Indeed, you must descend into the throat of Môtu, son of ʾIlu,
b mh(8)*mrt ydd il ġzr*	into the pit of the beloved hero of ʾIlu.

Although this passage speaks of death's downward direction much like the previous statements, its meaning is highly symbolic in nature: personified Death is portrayed as both a gaping throat and a watery pit where the dead must go.

That we are dealing with two distinct presentations of death in these narratives—one in physical terms, and the other in highly symbolic terms—can be justified contextually in two primary ways. The first comes from the messengers of ʾIlu and their discovery of Baʿlu's lifeless body (KTU 1.5 VI:5–10). From the broader narrative context, one might assume that he has already descended into Death's throat. Unfortunately, the text leading up to the discovery of his body is broken and therefore unknown. We simply cannot say for sure whether the narrative included a description of Baʿlu's descent into the throat of Death, even though it is quite likely. What we can say, however, is that Môtu's threats to kill Baʿlu—which he earlier defined as descent into his throat, as well as the other expressed imagery just outlined—have already been acted upon, leaving him dead and lying on the ground. Second, the act of placing someone in the hole of the gods of the underworld recurs in ʿAnatu's burial of the storm god, and in this context it is in parallel with a verbal form of the root *qbr* "to bury" (KTU 1.6 I):

tbkynh (17) *w tqbrnh*	She weeps for him and buries him,
tštnn b ḫrt (18) *ilm arṣ*	she places him in the hole of the gods of the earth.

In Ugaritic phraseology, therefore, to "place someone in the hole of the gods of the underworld" is an alternative (and highly symbolic) way of describing the act of burial.

I should caution, however, that I do not mean to say that the act of burial is described in terms of the physical realm while other death metaphors invoke the mythological. As it is clearly seen here, burial is described in two ways: the physical act of burying a dead body in the ground and the theological lens through which the physical act of interment is interpreted. The burial rite has taken on a highly developed mythology of afterlife perceptions. In some regard this ideological presentation of death symbolizes somewhat of a transfer from one state of existence to another, the latter being quite distinct from the former.

The language for burying the dead in the Baʿlu cycle must also be placed within the related ritual context attested at Ugarit. The physical and mythological worlds are interrelated in Ugaritic thought. This facet of understanding can be demonstrated further from the literary connections between the burial of the storm god in the Baʿlu cycle and the funerary ritual of a deceased king of Ugaritic (KTU 1.161). In my treatment of this ritual in chapter 4, I identified several themes for this text, two of which were mourning the royal dead (lines 13–17) and royal descent into the underworld (lines 18–26).[109] These two themes are also significant literary features of the narrative depiction of Baʿlu's death and burial. The ritual act of mourning is presented twice: once when ʾIlu hears the report of Baʿlu's death, and once when ʿAnatu finds his body and buries it. After descending from his throne, ʾIlu laments (KTU 1.5 VI:23–25):

(23) *bʿl mt*	Baʿlu is dead,
my lỉm	what (will become) of the people?
bn (24) *dgn*	The son of Dagan (is dead),
my hmlt	what will become of the multitudes?
ảṯr (25) *bʿl ảdr b ảrṣ*	After Baʿlu I will descend into the earth.

Similarly, ʿAnatu cries out (KTU 1.6 I:6–9):

(6) *bʿl mt*	Baʿlu is dead,
my lỉm	what (will become) of the people?
bn dgn	The son of Dagan (is dead),
(7) *my hmlt*	what will become of the multitudes?
ảṯr bʿl nrd (8) *b ảrṣ*	After Baʿlu we will descend into the earth.
ʿmh trd nrt (9) *ỉlm špš*	With him Šapšu, luminary of the gods, will descend.

The mourning described in these two passages is directed toward the downward descent of the deceased into the underworld. It also vividly portrays the strong desire of their living loved ones to follow after them to their abode in the underworld, a desire that is instead met with bitter tears of separation—ʿAnatu drinks weeping to the fill; she drinks tears like wine (KTU 1.6 I:9–10).

The Baʿlu cycle's focus on the dead's downward journey into the underworld is also reflected in KTU 1.161. The deceased king is commanded to descend into the earth below:

109. See my discussion in ch. 4 (§4.3.6.2).

(20) *åṯr* [*b*]*ʿlk l ks*⌜*i*⌝ *åṯr*	After your lords, from the throne, after
(21) *bʿlk årṣ rd årṣ*	your lords, to the earth descend, to the earth
(22) *rd w špl ʿpr*	descend and lower yourself to the dust.

The company of *rpům* who are about to receive the deceased king is described as being "below" (*tḥt*). Also central in this ritual descent is the sun goddess Šapšu, who commands the deceased king to lower himself into the dust (line 22) and who also aids the goddess ʿAnatu in the burial of the dead storm god (KTU 1.6 I:11–16).

A similar paradox exists for the funerary ritual of KTU 1.161 as is portrayed in the mythology of Baʿlu's death. The dead king is commanded to descend into the company of the dead below as his lifeless body is being buried; although Baʿlu has descended into the throat of Death, his body must also be placed into the hole of the gods of the underworld. In both cases, the physical act of burial is given mythological dimensions—the lowering of the body into the grave is symbolic of one's metaphysical journey to the abode of the dead.

The literary depiction of death and burial in these texts corresponds with what is known from the archaeological data from Ugarit. The archaeology of burial at Ugarit has been highly controversial since Claude Schaeffer first published his findings from the excavations of the Ugaritic tomb structures discovered at Ugarit and its port city Minet el-Beida (1939).[110] Schaeffer uncovered numerous vaulted-chamber tombs constructed underneath the floors of residential structures, which he initially interpreted in support of a cult of the dead practiced at Ugarit. Many of these tomb structures had holes in their ceilings with pits, gutters, and ceramic pipes in the rooms above, which Schaeffer thought to be the remains of a complex mechanism for the repeated ritual offering of food and drink to the dead below.[111] Lewis has construed the textual materials from Ugarit regarding the cult of the dead in light of Schaeffer's archaeological analysis, stating that it provides "evidence for a well-developed cult of the dead at Ugarit."[112] These conclusions have since been challenged, however, with Pitard leveling the strongest critique

110. Claude F.-A. Schaeffer, *Ugaritica 1: Études Relatives aux Découvertes de Ras Shamra*, MRS 3 (Paris: Geuthner, 1939).

111. Schaeffer, *Cuneiform Texts of Ras Shamra-Ugarit*, 49–51. See also the same conclusions regarding similar structures from Samaria Tomb 103 in John W. Crowfoot, Kathleen Kenyon, and Eliezer Sukenik, *The Buildings at Samaria* (London: Palestinian Exploration Fund, 1942), 21–22 (referenced in Elizabeth Bloch-Smith, "Death in the Life of Israel" in Gittlen, *Sacred Time, Sacred Place*, 141).

112. Lewis, *Cults of the Dead*, 97. See also John W. Ribar, "Death Cult Practices in Ancient Palestine," (Ph.D. diss., University of Michigan, 1973), 48–50; de Moor, "Rāpiʾūma—Rephaim," 331; Spronk, *Beatific Afterlife*, 142–45.

against Schaeffer's interpretation of the Ugaritic tomb remains. Pitard charges that Schaeffer's interpretation of these holes in the tomb ceilings is suspect, since the roofs of the tombs were well below floor level and no apparatus connecting the holes to the floor level above was ever found. Furthermore, closer examination of the holes themselves reveals that they were not a part of the original structure of the tombs, but have been created much later by tomb robbers.[113] Pitard's critique has for the most part upended acceptance of Schaeffer's proposed libation mechanisms at Ugarit, leading Lewis to reject his earlier adoption of this view.[114]

This discussion underscores the importance of placing archaeological reconstructions alongside the corresponding textual record if they are to be truly representative of ancient society.[115] In the case of Ugaritic burial structures, it may be that Pitard's criticisms of Schaeffer have pushed the discussion too far in the other direction in excluding any cultic function whatsoever. Hays notes three critical responses to Pitard's dismissal of the cultic interpretation of these tombs, which he thinks should not be dismissed so quickly: (1) certain features of these tombs not discussed remain possible witnesses to a cult of the dead, (2) Pitard was not able to eliminate the possibility that some of the archaeological features he did discuss could be construed as cultic, and (3) the existence of cults of the dead does not depend on archaeology alone.[116] Similarly, Schloen is convinced by the overall merit of Pitard's critique of Schaeffer, but cautions that it does not necessarily mean that "no cult of the dead was practiced near the tombs."[117] Citing domestic sanctuaries from Ur as a parallel, Schloen remarks on three architectural features of tomb 1068's antechamber (room 1045 of House B of the Centre de la Ville) in support of cultic function: two wall cavities that may have contained a shrine with figurines (as at Ur), holes in the wall that may have held wooden beams supporting a bench or shelf, and pottery that could have contained offerings for the dead.[118] Given this archaeological reconstruction, the

113. Pitard, "'Libation Installations,'" 30–32; Pitard, "Tombs and Offerings: Archaeological Data and Comparative Methodology in the Study of Death in Israel," in Gittlen, *Sacred Time, Sacred Place*, 2002), 151–53.

114. Lewis, "How Far Can Texts Take Us?," 187.

115. Bloch-Smith, "Death in the Life of Israel," 142; Bloch-Smith, "From Womb to Tomb: The Israelite Family in Death as in Life" in *The Family in Life and in Death: The Family in Ancient Israel; Sociological and Archaeological Perspectives*, ed. Patricia Dutcher-Walls, LHBOTS 504 (New York: T&T Clark, 2009), 127; Lewis, "How Far Can Texts Take Us?," 171–86, 205–7.

116. Hays, *Death in the Iron Age II*, 102–4.

117. Schloen, *House of the Father*, 346.

118. For room 1045, see Marguerite Yon, P. Lombard, and M. Renisio, "L'organisation de l'habitat: les maison A, B et E" in *Le centre de la ville: 38ème-44ème campagnes (1978–1984)*, ed. Marguerite Yon, RSO 3 (Paris: Éditions Recherche sur les Civilisations, 1987), 76. Schloen, *House of the Father*, 346.

question still remains, however, as to whether these material remains served a mortuary or funerary function—that is to say, did they serve in the veneration or commemoration of the dead? As it relates to the textual record (primarily ritual), Pardee is willing to allow that the sacrificial cult may have contained a "minor mortuary element" and that it "may have flourished outside the realm of the state-sponsored cult reflected in the texts at our disposal, probably on the family and clan level."[119]

The archaeological study of burial at Ugarit allows us to revisit the paradoxical intersection of mythology and the world of human experience. One might say that the burial of the dead is depicted in terms of life in the natural world (i.e., being placed in a hole), but it is interpreted through the lens of mythology (i.e., being place in the hole of the gods). This factor becomes all the more clear when we consider that these tomb structures were located beneath physical structures that continued to be inhabited by subsequent generations of the patrimonial household. Schloen's summary on this point is helpful:

> We currently know enough to say, however, that the use of intramural tombs at Ugarit, and the ancestor cult that went with it, reflects a strong belief in the importance of the temporal continuity of the household and its physical patrimony. The "living" household was also, in a sense, the household of the dead, because deceased ancestors continued to participate in the social life of their descendants.[120]

Schloen makes the connection between these corbel-vaulted stone tombs and the extramural rock-cut tombs of Israel and Judah that housed the remains of multiple generations over time.[121] Elizabeth Bloch-Smith observes that these tombs were constructed to resemble residences and that for Judah they were "culturally compatible with ideas of life after death and conceptually acceptable as a residence design."[122] Those who were buried in such tombs were thought to continue in some form of existence after death and were thus given the basic necessities for life in this world.[123] As Bloch-Smith describes it, "Death meant the final change of address from the royal family home of the living to the family home of the dead."[124] Similar arguments could be made for Ugarit.

119. Pardee, "Ugaritic Funerary Cult," 284–85; cf. Lewis, "How Far Can Texts Take Us?," 203–4.

120. Schloen, *House of the Father*, 346.

121. See Bloch-Smith, "From Womb to Tomb," 128.

122. Elizabeth M. Bloch-Smith, *Judahite Burial Practices and Beliefs about the Dead*, JSOTSup 123 (Sheffield: JSOT Press, 1992), 44; Bloch-Smith, "From Womb to Tomb," 127–28.

123. Bloch-Smith, *Judahite Burial Practices*, 148.

124. Bloch-Smith "From Womb to Tomb," 128.

One further example that potentially demonstrates the intersection of text and archaeology at Ugarit concerns the pit discovered between the two royal tombs at Ras Shamra. Pardee has claimed that this particular find offers one of the most obvious indicators that bodies were placed in a hole in the ground.[125] He ties the discovery of this pit to the ritual depicted in KTU 1.161 wherein the king is commanded to descend "under" (*tḥt*) the named entities, at which time his dead body was "lowered seven times into the depths of the earth, that is, into the pit . . . that certainly extended well below the lowest parts of the tombs themselves."[126]

The language used to describe burial in the mythology of Baʿlu, the royal funerary ritual in KTU 1.161, which provides a ritual prescription for placing a deceased king in the tomb/underworld, and the archaeological findings from vaulted tomb structures together produce a multifaceted assessment of ancient perspectives on death at Ugarit. The archaeological discussion offers another level of analysis whereby it is shown that the dead were understood in terms of the living. Furthermore, it may or may not indicate minor mortuary elements in Ugaritic society at large, despite the fact that this aspect appears to be lacking from the literary record. This should not surprise us, however, since the texts at our disposal come from the upper levels of society, but even here we might expect a certain level of continuity with the inhabitants of Ugarit in general from the fact that they are produced from and for a commonly held worldview.[127] The royal funerary ritual of KTU 1.161 presents the funerary event from the royal perspective, which apparently corresponds with the language of burial found in the Baʿlu cycle where the storm god descends to the place of abasement and is placed in the hole of the gods of the underworld. The language of "abasement" reinforces the downward descent of the dead away from the living, for which the ritual descent of the mourner corresponds. The world of mythology therefore offers a metaphysical means of interpreting the circumstances of the dead for the sake of the living.

5.7. The Royal Dead

The subject of the royal dead provides the final thematic interest for this chapter. In many ways this particular strand ties together several issues already discussed

125. Pardee, *Textes rituels*, 823–24.

126. Pardee, "Ugaritic Funerary Cult," 274–75. See my discussion of this interpretation in ch. 4 (§4.3.6.2).

127. See Lewis, "Family, Household, and Local Religion at Bronze Age Ugarit," in *Household and Family Religion in Antiquity*, ed. John Bodel and Saul M. Olyan (Hoboken, MA: Wiley, 2009), 60–88.

above. Particularly significant to the royal dead is the archaeological analysis of tomb structures just mentioned, but as we have seen, mortuary/funerary ritual is not limited to the royal dead archaeologically because these vaulted tombs are attested at numerous residential complexes throughout Ugarit as well.[128] The defining feature of the royal dead involves their status in relation to the Ugaritic pantheon and to what degree they may or may not have been considered divine. I have already entertained this question extensively in my treatment of the Rapa'ūma in chapter 4, so my comments here will attempt to bring that discussion to bear on the broader thematic overview of life and death before us. In addition to what has already been covered in that chapter, there are two remaining issues concerning the Rapa'ūma that warrant our attention here: (1) the duties of the faithful son from the 'Aqhatu Epic (especially the *skn ỉlỉbh*) (KTU 1.17 I:25–33), and (2) the formula *ỉl* + royal name from the Ugaritic King List (KTU 1.113).

The appropriateness of treating the duties of the faithful son from the 'Aqhatu Epic at this juncture is that it leads us to revisit the matter involving the perceived relationship between the living and the dead discussed above. I have just dealt with the archaeological data on tomb structures and their relevance for settling questions related to the plausibility of reconstructing death cult practices for Ugarit. As already mentioned, mortuary elements may have been a factor for the broader Ugaritic society, but what about the royal setting?

The outline of the faithful son's duties in the 'Aqhatu Epic is important to consider in light of Dānî'ilu's tie to the Rapa'ūma by way of his oft repeated epithet *dnỉl mt rpỉ* "Dānî'ilu, man of Rāpi'u."[129] I render the pertinent portion of this passage as follows (KTU 1.17 I):[130]

(23) *l tbrknn l ṯr ỉl ảby*	May you bless him, O Bull 'Ilu, my father,
(24) *tmrnn l bny bnwt*	may you provision him, O Creator of creatures,
(25) *w ykn bnh b bt*	that his son might be in the house,
šrš b qrb (26) *hklh*	a scion in the midst of his palace:
nṣb skn ỉlỉbh[131]	someone to raise up the stela of the god of his father,
b qdš (27) *ztr ʿmh*	in the sanctuary (to raise up) the monument of his clan;

128. See Pitard, "'Libation Installations,'" 20–37; Schloen, *House of the Father*, 346.

129. See ch. 4 (§4.3.3).

130. According to the collation of Bordreuil and Pardee, *Manual of Ugaritic*, 173–74.

131. Cf. also the syllabic version DINGIR-a-bi (RS 20.024:1). On this text, see Pardee, *Ritual and Cult*, 14–16; and the detailed discussion in Pardee, *Textes rituels*, 297–99.

l ảrṣ mšṣủ qṭrh	who makes his incense go out with regard to the earth,
(28) *l ʿpr ḏmr ảṯrh*	who guards his (resting) place with regard to dust;
ṭbq lḥt (29) *niṣh*	who shuts the jaws of his detractors,
grš d ʿšy lnh	who drives out anyone who would act against him;
(30) ⌜*ả*⌝*ḫd ydh b šk*⌜*r*⌝*n*	who takes his hand in drunkenness,
mʿmsh (31) [*k*] *šbʿ yn*	who bears him up when he is full of wine;
spủ ksmh bt bʿl	who serves his grain (offering) at the temple of Baʿlu,
(32) [*w*] ⌜*m*⌝*nth bt il*	[and] his portion at the temple of ʾIlu;
ṭḫ ggh b ym (33) [*ṭi*]*ṭ*	who rolls his roof on a muddy day,[132]
rḥṣ npṣh b ym rṯ	who washes his garments when they are dirtied.[133]

The immediate context of this passage concerns the granting of a son to Dānîʾilu who has just spent seven days making offerings to the gods, after which Baʿlu intercedes to ʾIlu on Dānîʾilu's behalf.

The main interpretive controversy from this passage involves the meaning of *nṣb skn ilibh* in line 26. Lewis observes that this text has to do with the duties of a son toward his father, "especially while still living," therefore cautioning that the matters outlined in these lines are not exclusively funerary in nature.[134] Even so, Lewis translates this poetic line, "One who sets up the stela of his divine ancestor."[135] Van der Toorn explains that Ugaritic *ilib* refers specifically to "the deified father—or more precisely to the father turned ancestor," and that once the father had died it was incumbent upon the son to set up a funerary stela in honor of the departed spirit of his father. He contends that such an occasion would hardly have been an appropriate time "to dress a monument for the family god."[136] In support of this proposal, van der Toorn cites the Hurrian parallel expression *enni attanni*, which he argues must be rendered appositionally "the gods, the fathers."[137] Other scholars, however, have been more hesitant to read this passage

132. Literally: "on a day of mud."
133. Literally: "on a day of dirt."
134. Lewis, *Cults of the Dead*, 69.
135. Lewis, *Cults of the Dead*, 54.
136. Karel van der Toorn, "Ilib and the 'God of the Father,'" *UF* 25 (1993): 380, 384.
137. Van der Toorn, "Ilib and the 'God of the Father,'" 381, 385. See also his discussion of the Mesopotamian evidence for the cult of ancestors in van der Toorn, "Family Religion in Second

as a case involving the worship of dead ancestors, as for example Pardee, who simply renders the expression in question, "god of his father," that is, the patron deity.[138] Similarly, Schmidt rejects the deified ancestor interpretation, also taking it as a reference to the installment of a patron deity shrine.[139] So, the two principal views regarding the interpretation of *nṣb skn ỉlỉbh* are: (1) maintaining the cult of the family gods, or (2) maintaining the veneration of the recently deceased father who has become a patron deity. According to the former view, this particular duty of the faithful son concerned his obligation to take up the cultic responsibilities of his aging father.[140]

Given its order of occurrence in the sequence of listed duties, *nṣb skn ỉlỉbh* is not naturally read as a call to honor/venerate one's dead ancestor; that concern may in fact arise in the next two lines:[141]

l ảrṣ mšṣủ qṭrh	who makes his incense go out with regard to the earth;
(28) *l ʿpr ḏmr ảṯrh*	who guards his (resting) place with regard to dust.

As already noted in chapter 4, the mention of *qṭrh* "his incense" in parallel with *ảṯrh* "his (resting) place" naturally seems to refer to the burial place of the father and the funerary ritual that is to be carried out by the faithful son.[142] This setting is supported by the semantic links between this text and the Rapaʾūma texts where *ảṯr* denotes the place where the *rpủm* are ritually summoned.[143] Furthermore, the reference to Dānîʾilu by name in the context of their arrival offers yet another literary connection in favor of a funerary setting for KTU 1.17 I:27–28. Finally, I must comment on the term *ʿpr* "dust" in line 28, which also occurs in KTU 1.161 with regard to the underworld:

(20) *ảṯr* [*b*]*ʿlk l ks*⌜*ỉ*⌝ *ảṯr*	After your lords, from the throne, after
(21) *bʿlk ảrṣ rd ảrṣ*	your lords, to the earth descend, to the earth
(22) *rd w špl ʿpr*	descend and lower yourself to the dust.

Millennium West Asia (Mesopotamia, Emar, Nuzi)," in Bodel and Olyan, *Household and Family Religion in Antiquity*, 21–28.

138. Pardee, "Ugaritic Funerary Cult," 283 n. 17: "There is no basis for the interpretation of the common noun *ilib* in the Aqhat text as referring explicitly to the ancestor cult, in the sense of veneration of the dead and deified ancestors, for the common noun, like the proper noun, refers to 'god of the father,' and not to the 'god (who has become a) god,' and the reference is, therefore, to carrying on the cult of the family/clan deity."

139. Schmidt, *Israel's Beneficent Dead*, 59.

140. Schloen, *House of the Father*, 344–45.

141. Pardee, "Ugaritic Funerary Cult," 283–84 n. 17.

142. Pardee, *COS* 1:344 n. 8; Pardee, "Nouvelle étude épigraphique," 49–51.

143. KTU 1.21 II:3, 11, 12; 1.22 II:10, 11, 21; 1.20 II:2.

In KTU 1.17 I, the duty of the son to guard his father's place could indicate that it is to be carried out with reference to his existence in the underworld. In other words, he is expected to offer incense on behalf of his father postmortem, which could be understood as either mortuary (i.e., veneration) or commemorative in nature. If this setting is allowed to stand for lines 27–28, it means that we must posit a certain level of distinction between maintaining the cult of the family gods and the perpetuation of the father's persona postmortem.

This distinction leads us to consider the formula *il* + royal name attested in the Ugaritic King List (KTU 1.113). I do not think that this formula relates to the *ilib* of KTU 1.17 I:26, but instead to the postmortem status of Ugaritic kings, which seems to be the backdrop of KTU 1.17 I:27–28 as outlined above.[144] Other scholars have disagreed, however, arguing for just such an understanding of this formula, that is, *il* + royal name = deity of royal personage. Mario Liverani proposes that this formula in KTU 1.113 refers to rituals directed toward the personal gods of royal personages, and not dead deified kings.[145] Schmidt has also advanced this view, defending his case on the basis of the parallel formula attested at Ebla, DINGIR + royal name, which he thinks must be rendered as a genitive construction, and therefore means "the god of Such-and-such a king."[146] He believes the more recently discovered (1998) Akkadian parallel text RS 94.2518 confirms this genitive interpretation, as in the example DINGIR ^{m}a-mis-tam-ri (lines 7, 24), and thus indicates that the Ugaritic name *il ʿmṯtmr* (KTU 1.113:22, 28) must also be rendered genitively.[147]

Pardee finds the above interpretations of this formula less than satisfactory, despite the arguments put forth in the analyses of Liverani and Schmidt. Even though royal personal gods are amply attested in the ancient Near East, he wonders how this phenomenon could reasonably be applied here. For one, why would each of these personal gods be rendered generically as *il* "god," especially if this text is somehow representative of a rite in honor of several unnamed deities?[148] Furthermore, my own analysis of the Ugaritic Rapaʾūma in chapter 4

144. Contra van der Toorn, "Ilib and the 'God of the Father,'" 380, who collapses the two by asserting that *ilib* is the deified ancestor.

145. Liverani, "Royauté syrienne," 340–41.

146. Schmidt, *Israel's Beneficent Dead*, 15–19.

147. As already indicated by Daniel Arnaud, "Prolégomènes à la rédaction d'une histoire d'Ougarit II: Les bordereaux de rois divinisés," *SMEA* 41 (1998): 159.

148. Pardee, *Ritual and Cult*, 199; cf. Pardee, *Textes paramythologiques*, 173 n. 25. Pardee thinks the Akkadian parallel text RS 94.2518 may offer evidence for linking these lists to sacrificial rites. He refers to a series of check marks to the right of each entry (so Arnaud on RS 94.2518 in "Prolégomènes à la rédaction d'une histoire d'Ougarit," 168), which are also found in the margins of RS 20.024 (the Akkadian version of RS 1.017=KTU 1.47) and RS 24.264+ (a second Ugaritic version of RS 1.017=KTU 1.47), two texts that are explicitly linked with sacrificial rites. These factors make

concludes that kings were envisioned as being received into their company at death. Even Schmidt's appeal to KTU 1.100 as evidence for the royal personal god interpretation may in fact offer another datum against it. He notes that the same two musical instruments occur in both the benediction to Rāpiʾu in KTU 1.100 and KTU 1.113:1–10.[149] Schmidt denies any connection between Rāpiʾu and the Rapaʾūma, but I find this denial unfounded, and therefore would suggest that such a literary link only strengthens the case for understanding *il* + royal name as a reference to deified dead kings.[150] Pardee's suggestion to interpret the syntax of this formula as the "genitive of identification," meaning, "the god (who is) ʿAmiṯtamru," would provide a plausible interpretation in light of these considerations. Hays likewise concludes that this text (KTU 1.113), along with KTU 1.161, affirms "the hypothesis that at least the kings of Ugarit were thought to have been divinized after death."[151]

So once again, we are faced with yet another indicator that Ugaritic society assigned some sort of divine status to their deceased kings. Of course, as I pointed out earlier, this status was not entirely withheld from the living monarchs—King Kirta was both exalted among the Rapaʾūma of the underworld and a *bn il* "son of ʾIlu," which appears to have come into question as he faced death from illness; Dānîʾilu was a *mt rpủ* "man of Rāpiʾu."[152] The textual evidence from Ugarit indicates that dead kings acquired a quasidivine status at death and that these dead, deified kings surrounded the living kings with beneficent powers for the ongoing success of the kingdom.[153] Lewis's summary comments on this role are instructive:

> Upon death a ruler was grouped with his deceased ancestors and was referred to as an *ilu*. These *ilu*s were not worshipped in the same way that El or Baal were and we find no elaborate cult attempting to make them into high gods. Yet, I do not mean to imply that "becoming an *ilu*" was nothing more than an idiom for dying. Referring to the deceased as an *ilu* was an

---

it more reasonable to hypthesize that these texts may reflect the existence of a *kispu*-like rite at Ugarit (*Ritual and Cult*, 200).

149. Schmidt, *Israel's Beneficent Dead*, 69.

150. See discussion in ch. 4 (§4.3.6.1). Pardee believes the corresponding Akkadian list (RS 94.2418) leaves "no reason to doubt that the deceased king became a part of the divine (though the realm of this segment of the divine was the netherworld); hence there is no particular reason to shy away from the interpretation of *il* as expressing this fact explicitly" (*Ritual and Cult*, 199–200). See also Hays, *Death in the Iron Age II*, 108.

151. Hays, *Death in the Iron Age II*, 108.

152. See ch. 4 (§§4.3.2 and 4.3.3).

153. See Suriano, *Politics of Dead Kings*, 153.

> attempt to describe some type of transcendent character, perhaps what we would call "preternatural." The deceased entered into the revered company of the *rpủm* and continued to exist in the underworld. They certainly were not cut off from any relation to the living and could (as shown in KTU 1.161) be beseeched to grant favors.[154]

Even though I am more hesitant to find sure evidence for the veneration of ancestors in the Ugaritic *rpủm*, their role as quasidivine caretakers of the Ugaritic dynasty by guaranteeing its ongoing success and prosperity seems to be fully intact in their textual presentation.[155] If, however, the reconstruction of a *kispu*-like ritual setting for RS 94.2418 and RS 24.257 (KTU 1.113) is valid, as Pardee suggests, with its repeated formulas "the god (who is) royal personage X," we would be much closer to the archaeological data related to the general Ugaritic society in attesting shrines devoted to the departed patrons of the family.[156]

This observation brings us back to the issue involving the perceptions of the elite versus that of the commoner in Ugaritic society. As scholars routinely remind us, the perspective of our texts are inevitably that of the elite, particularly the royal elite of the Ugaritic monarchy. This perspective is rather unavoidable in both myth and legend, which are both keenly interested in promoting the royal institution of Ugarit. This factor is one of Lewis's identified obstacles to drawing from Ugaritic literature a reconstruction of what ancient Ugaritians thought about living and dying, since "searching out religion of the family from elite (e.g., royal, priestly, legal) texts necessarily skews the portrait."[157] However, I want to caution against pressing this distinction too hard, so that elite cultural contexts can no longer tell us anything about the beliefs and practices shared among members of the broader ancient society. For instance, one might simply observe that royal families were indeed families, and it is the idea that the royal context in some way mirrors the family religion of Ugaritic society that provides the means of appropriating the texts before us, as van der Toor explains: "It is only on the assumption that dynastic religion is the royal version of family religion that the insights obtained from the Ugaritic texts can be given a wider application."[158] This is one of the major

154. Lewis, *Cults of the Dead*, 50; followed by Rainer Albertz and Rüdiger Schmitt, *Family and Household Religion in Ancient Israel and the Levant* (Winona Lake, IN: Eisenbrauns, 2012), 433.

155. On the lack of evidence for veneration of ancestors, see also more recently Lewis, "Family, Household, and Local Religion," 69. Their role as quasidivine caretakers is presented in KTU 1.108 (=RS 24.252):19–27.

156. See above (§5.5).

157. Lewis, "Family, Household, and Local Religion," 62.

158. Karel van der Toorn, *Family Religion in Babylonia, Syria, and Israel: Continuity and Changes in the Forms of Religious Life*, SHANE 7 (Leiden: Brill, 1996), 153, also cited in Lewis, "Family, Household, and Local Religion," 62.

points Schloen attempts to establish—patrimonial kinship, expressed metaphorically as the "House of the Father," offers a dynamic means of representing ancient society, so that kingship and kinship are closely aligned:

> Kingship and kinship are not in opposition to one another; they are two sides of the same coin. This is possible because kinship is not static, rooted in the facts of biology, but dynamic, employing the genealogical metaphor to represent all manner of social and political relations of authority and dependence. Thus the symbolism of the patriarchal household can be both a motif of literary discourse and a template for practical action.[159]

Following Schloen's patrimonial household model for Ugarit, Timothy P. Harrison argues that mythological and epic narratives from Ugarit were deeply connected to the concerns of their ancient audience and therefore "provide a revealing—even if imaginative—reframing of the lived social experience of Levantine communities during this period."[160] Such a framework does not necessarily throw caution to the wind when it comes to reading texts written exclusively from the higher levels of ancient society, but at the very least it offers a plausible theoretical basis for tying the two worlds together: the common household and the royal household. Therefore, it may be that we are dealing with a difference in degree more so than a difference in kind. The perpetual elevation of and care for dead patrons within the confines of the living households of society is replicated and intensified in the royal household, which is then reimagined for the household of the divine.

5.8. Summary

In this chapter I have attempted to provide a synthesis of my lexical analysis of life and mortality at Ugarit by identifying several broad interpretive horizons for consideration. One might argue that life and mortality are of central concern in the literature of Ugarit, given the wide variety of texts in which these themes emerge. By drawing out these themes from the lexical study that makes up the

159. Schloen, *House of the Father*, 350.

160. Timothy P. Harrison, "Family Religion from a Northern Levantine Perspective," in *Family and Household Religion: Toward a Synthesis of Old Testament Studies, Archaeology, Epigraphy, and Cultural Studies*, ed. Rainer Albertz et al. (Winona Lake, IN: Eisenbrauns, 2014), 184. With regard to the diverse expressions of family religious practices attested in the ancient Near East, Harrison states: "Unifying this heterogeneous expression, and giving it social coherence, was the powerful idiom of patrimonial kinship" (193).

bulk of this book, I have attempted to offer a more cohesive representation of what Ugaritians believed about living and dying.

To be sure, it remains to be seen how these themes relate to Ugarit's ancient Near Eastern neighbors. I have briefly commented on a few of these touchpoints, one prominent example being the nature of resurrection at Ugarit in comparison to the Biblical Hebrew tradition. Another avenue of investigation might be to compare the ideology of the royal dead from Ugarit with its biblical counterpart. A number of studies have focused on this comparison with particular interest in arguing for or against the presence of a cult of the dead in the Bible, but a broader lexical treatment of life and death terms from the Hebrew Bible would provide another angle for us to compare and contrast two Northwest Semitic corpuses in greater detail.[161] This kind of comparative analysis would allow us to determine to what degree these two language corpuses serve as witnesses to earlier, commonly held West Semitic traditions and to what extent they represent distinct traditions.

I have held off discussing the relevance of the Ugaritic materials for how the nature of the human soul is understood in Northwest Semitic and how this relates to the broader ancient Near East. I treat this topic more fully in the Appendix.

161. See, e.g., Lewis, *Cults of the Dead*; Schmidt, *Israel's Beneficent Dead* for arguments on the presence of a cult of the dead in the Bible.

APPENDIX

First Millennium BC Funerary Monuments

6.1. Introduction

In chapter 5 I attempted to synthesize the Ugaritic worldview regarding life and mortality, exploring several themes arising from my lexical analysis of the relevant terminology attested throughout Ugaritic literature. Admittedly, Ugarit is a small swath of the ancient Near Eastern landscape, even though we might well argue that it is representative of the broader Northwest Semitic way of thinking. Nonetheless, it is also important to place the Ugaritian worldview alongside its closest neighbors who shared in the languages and culture of the Canaanite world. To do so, however, we have to move ahead chronologically to the time of the first millennium and its repertoire of royal funerary monuments. The benefit of such an enterprise is that it allows us to examine later developments in a similar cultural setting.

But we should also remember that the first millennium context of this region was not marked by isolationism, but was actually a small player in a larger political/cultural exchange. One of the political/religious centers that has to be accounted for in such an exchange is that of the Hittites. Scholars have noted the enduring influence of the Neo-Hittite kingdoms of Syria throughout the region, viewing themselves as the cultural heirs of their Hittite predecessors. The trace of elements of the earlier Hittite civilization can be illustrated from eastern Cilicia in the bilingual inscription of Karatepe, written in Phoenician and Luwian hieroglyphs. The marks of Hittite culture find expression in many ways throughout the first millennium BC cities of northern Syria and southwestern Anatolia.[1] Front and center in this exchange is the ancient Samʾalian kingdom identified at Zincirli Höyük in Turkey. It is from this vantage point that we will need to consider the much discussed *nbš* (= *npš*) indwelling the funerary monument. Is this phenomenon another manifestation of Anatolian culture's understanding of the soul, or could it be a further development of earlier West Semitic notions latent, for instance, in Ugaritic (e.g., the exit of *npš* at death).

This reintroduces the question I raised in the previous chapter regarding the distinction between bodily resurrection and belief in an enduring soul. There I treated the nature of Baʿlu's revivification as an earlier prototype of bodily resurrection, at least on the conceptual level due to its application to a god from mythology. Here I wish to explore more fully the notion of an enduring personal presence postmortem by examining the usage of *np/bš* in first millennium Northwest Semitic contexts. The first few examples come from Phoenician royal funerary inscriptions, which will set the stage for my discussion of the Samʾalian materials from Zincirli.

6.2. The Phoenician Royal Funerary Inscriptions

It is fitting to begin this foray into the cultural heirs of Ugarit by examining the funerary inscriptions of the first millennium due to their close proximity, both in time and space, to the Ugaritic setting. There are two funerary contexts in particular that are important for this study, one being the funerary inscriptions from Phoenicia, the other being the inscriptions from the kingdom of Samʾal (modern Zincirli, Turkey).

The first two texts that offer an important parallel for the study of life and death at Ugarit are the Phoenician funerary inscriptions of King Tabnit (KAI 13) and King Eshmunazar (KAI 14). In KAI 13 King Tabnit forbids anyone from disturbing his resting place, claiming that it contains no valuables for plunder (KAI 13):

1. *ʾnk tbnt khn ʿštrt mlk ṣdnm bn*
2. *ʾšmnzr khn ʿštrt mlk ṣdnm škb bʾrn*
3. *z my ʾt kl ʾdm ʾš tpq ʾyt hʾrn z ʾl ʾl t-*
4. *-ptḥ ʿlty wʾl trgzn k ʾy ʾr ln ksp ʾy ʾr ln*

1. See Trevor Bryce, *The Kingdom of the Hittites*, 2nd ed. (Oxford: Oxford University Press, 2005), 351–55.

5. *ḥrṣ wkl mšr blt ʾnk škb bʾrn z ʾl ʾl tpt-*
6. *-ḥ ʿlty wʾl trgzn k tʿbt ʿštrt hdbr hʾ wʾm pt-*
7. *-ḥ tptḥ ʿlty wrgz trgzn ʾl y*<k>*n l*<k> *zrʿ bḥym tḥt šm-*
8. *-š wmškb ʾt rpʾm*

(1) I, Tabnit, priest of ʿAshtart, king of the Sidonians, son of (2) Eshmunazar, priest of ʿAštart, king of the Sidonians, lie in this sarcophagus. (3) Whoever you (may be), any man who finds this sarcophagus, do not, do not (4) open my lid and do not disturb me, for they have not amassed silver for me; they have not amassed gold for me (5) nor any riches. I alone lie in this sarcophagus. Do not, do not open (6) my lid and do not disturb me, for such a thing would be an abomination to ʿAshtart. And if indeed (7) you open my lid and indeed you disturb me, may you have no offspring among the living under the sun (8) nor resting-place with the *rpʾm*.

Similarly in KAI 14, the Phoenician king of Sidon laments his untimely death and warns all who would disturb his postmortem resting place by opening the sarcophagus and thus removing any of the valuables it contained. Like KAI 13, this inscription also mentions the word *rpʾm* as the king of Sidon warns anyone who might be tempted to disturb his grave and its goods (KAI 14):

4. *. . . ʾt kl mmlkt wkl ʾdm ʾl yptḥ ʾyt mškb z*
5. *wʾl ybqš bn mnm k ʾy šm bn mnm wʾl yšʾ ʾyt ḥlt mškby wʾl yʿm-*
6. *-sn bmškb z ʿlt mškb šny ʾm ʾdmm ydbrnk ʾl tšmʿ bdnm kkl mmlkt w-*
7. *-kl ʾdm ʾš yptḥ ʿlt mškb z ʾm ʾš yšʾ ʾyt ḥlt mš!kby*[2] *ʾm ʾš yʿmsn bm-*
8. *-škb z ʾl ykn lm mškb ʾt rpʾm wʾl yqbr bqbr wʾl ykn lm bn wzrʿ*
9. *tḥtnm wysgrnm hʾlnm hqdšm ʾt mmlk*<t> *ʾdr ʾš mšl bnm lq*
10. *ṣtnm ʾyt mmlkt ʾm ʾdm hʾ ʾš yptḥ ʿlt mkšb z ʾm ʾš yšʾ ʾyt*
11. *ḥlt z wʾyt zrʿ mml*<k>*t hʾ ʾm ʾdmm hmt ʾl ykn lm šrš lmṭ w-*
12. *-pr lmʿl wtʾr bḥym tḥt šmš . . .*

Whoever you (may be), any ruler or any man, let him not open this resting-place, (5) and let him not seek anything in it. For he did not place anything in it, and let them not take the coffin of my resting-place and let them not carry me off to another resting-place (6) from this resting-place. Even if men speak, do not give heed to their words, for any ruler or (7) any man/commoner who opens what is on/over this resting-place, if one takes

2. Read {mmkby}, perhaps a scribal error for {mškby}.

> the coffin where I rest and removes me from within this (8) resting-place, may they not have a resting-place with the *rpʾm*, nor be buried in a grave, nor have a son or offspring (9) to succeed them. And may the holy gods deliver them up to a great ruler who will rule over them to cut (10) them off, whether ruler or common man who opens the lid of this resting-place, or who carries (off) (11) this coffin, (whether) the offspring from that ruler or those commoners, let there not be for them root below (12) nor fruit above nor renown (lit. appearance) among the living (who) are under the sun.[3]

In this text, it is significant that its author assumes a resting place among the *rpʾm* for both kings and commoners alike.

The inscription of Tabnit offers an interesting parallel in its curse against those who would disturb his grave: *ʾl y*<k>*n l*<k> *zrʿ bḥym tḥt šmš* "you will not have any offspring among the living (who) are under the sun" // *wmškb ʾt rpʾm* "resting place with the *rpʾm*." This statement demonstrates a twofold concern of royal personages postmortem: (1) an enduring progeny among those alive in this life, or "under the sun," and (2) a resting place with the *rpʾm*. The concern expressed by Tabnit is akin to the status that Ugaritic King Kirta is said to have secured for himself as being exalted among the *rpủm* of the earth/underworld.[4] As I stated earlier, this exaltation seems also to reflect a double significance in this life and the life to come—the securing of progeny therefore ensures an exalted status among the *rpủm* of the earth/underworld.[5]

It is also important to observe that both of these texts seem to be leveling the conception of the *rpʾm* to extend to those outside the royal context. As my study of the Ugaritic Rapaʾūma in chapter 4 has shown, the term is largely tied up with matters of royal ideology and perceived associations with the divine realm, therefore relegating this membership to an elite class.[6] The elite perspective of these texts, however, should not preclude their ability to offer a representative portrayal of views shared by the general populace. The archaeological evidence treated earlier in chapter 5 seems to demonstrate a certain level of correspondence between these two strata of society when it comes to their views about the dead. As Hays argues, "It seems at least possible—and I find it probable—that a 'democratization of death' took place in the West Semitic context as it did in

3. On KAI 13 and 14, see *KAI* 2:17–23; John C. L. Gibson, *Textbook of Syrian and Semitic Inscriptions. Vol. 3: Phoenician Inscriptions, Including Inscriptions in the Mixed Dialect of Arslan Tash* (Oxford: Clarendon, 1982), 101–102; P. Kyle McCarter, *COS* 2:182–83.

4. KTU 1.15 III:2–3, 14

5. See discussion in ch. 4 (§4.3.2.1).

6. Hays, *Death in the Iron Age II*, 115 n. 119.

Egypt, as 'elite emulation' took its course."[7] I might further add that it is not actually necessary to argue for "elite emulation"; rather, the practices on display in the royal setting may in fact broadcast the beliefs and practices already imbedded within the customs of the patrimonial household.[8]

From the textual record, the principal indicator for the extension of the *rpʾm* to include members outside an elite context concerns the specific wording of the curses in both of these Phoenician texts. The Tabnit inscription curses any *ʾdm* "man" who would disturb his resting place (line 3), while Eshmunazzar curses both *ʾdm* "man" and *mmlkt* "ruler" (lines 4, 6–7). The additional qualifier *ʾdm* in contradistinction to *mmlkt* "ruler" in Eshmunazzar suggests that the curse is being expanded to warn anyone, whether from within or without an elite setting, against disturbing the grave of this departed king. Regardless of whether the disturber is elite or commoner, if he disturbs this grave he can expect to forfeit his resting place among the *rpʾm*. Suriano is certainly correct to limit these two Phoenician inscriptions to the royal setting, but in doing so he seems to downplay their interest in dissuading the masses from disturbing the royal grave, instead asserting that "plundering a royal tomb was often a political action."[9] He insists that such a leveling of the term *rpʾm* to include nonelite is a later development as attested in a bilingual Neo-Punic and Latin inscription (KAI 117) and the wisdom literature of the Hebrew Bible.[10] However, the explicit distinction between *ʾdm* "man" and *mmlkt* "ruler" in Eshmunazzar would seem to indicate that this development has already occurred here, despite the fact that some have argued that *ʾdm* in this case must refer to a special man, or an elite man.[11] Such a development in the textual history would support the arguments from archaeology regarding household religion and the "ongoing participation of deceased ancestors in the life of agrarian households," as Schloen has shown.[12] One might even say that the family religious setting in which deceased ancestors continued to play a significant role in the ongoing life of the household offers a link between the exclusivity of the Ugaritic Rapaʾūma and the inclusion of nonelite among the Rephaim apparently assumed in the West Semitic royal funerary inscriptions from the first millennium.[13]

7. Hays, *Death in the Iron Age II*, 115.

8. According to Schloen, *House of the Father*, 347, as noted in Hays, *Death in the Iron Age II*, 115 n. 120.

9. Suriano, *Politics of Dead Kings*, 154–55.

10. Suriano, *Politics of Dead Kings*, 154 n.18.

11. Hays argues it has already developed here (*Death in the Iron Age II*, 115). This factor does not deny Suriano's desire to emphasize the political context of these inscriptions and their relation to the "ideological complex of death-burial-succession" (Suriano, *Politics of Dead Kings*, 155). For the argument for "special" or "elite man," see Suriano, *The Politics of Dead Kings*, 154–55.

12. Schloen, *House of the Father*, 347, as noted in Hays, *Death in the Iron Age II*, 115 n. 120.

13. The plausibility of such a development would only be strengthened if we think that the household context also indicated the practice of ancestor veneration. See my discussion in ch, 5 (§5.7).

6.3. The Zincirli Funerary Inscriptions

I am mainly interested in the Zincirli materials for their attestations of the word *np/bš*. Our understanding of this term in Northwest Semitic has been complicated somewhat by the recent finds at Zincirli Höyük in Turkey. In July 2008, the Oriental Institute Expedition of the University of Chicago unearthed an inscribed mortuary stele of the royal figure bearing the Luwian name Katumuwa.[14] This inscription from the Syro-Hittite context of the ancient Sam'alian dynasty has been dated to the eighth century BC during the reign of Panamuwa II (ca. 743–733/32 BC), mentioned in this inscription by Katumuwa deferentially as *ʿbd pnmw*, "servant of PNMW."[15] To be sure, this inscription provides important new data regarding the dialect of ancient Sam'al and its relation to the broader linguistic context of the Old Aramaic corpus of royal inscriptions.[16] It also provides another important chapter in the ongoing discovery of the history of the region through the eyes of this immensely important site. The contribution of the Katumuwa inscription, however, is not only a historical one, but also adds a significant datum that sheds light on the ancients' theology of the self, at least as it was understood and expressed from within the royal context of this particular official. The word *nbš* occurs in line 5 of this inscription: *wybl lnbšy zy bnṣb zn* "and a ram for my *nbš* that is in this stele."[17] Scholars have noted that this mention of *nbš* residing in the stele provides an early attestation in the Levantine region of an enduring *nbš* not confined to the body.[18]

14. On the recent excavations from this site, see Virginia R. Herrmann, "The Katumuwa Inscription in Archaeological Context," in Herrmann and Schloen, *In Remembrance of Me*, 49–56; J. David Schloen and Amir S. Fink, "New Excavations at Zincirli Höyük in Turkey (Ancient Sam'al) and the Discovery of an Inscribed Morturary Stele," *BASOR* 356 (2009): 1–13; Schloen and Fink, "Searching for Ancient Sam'al: New Excavations at Zincirli in Turkey," *NEA* 72 (2009): 203–19. For a defense of the vocalization *Katumuwa*, see K. Lawson Younger, "Two Epigraphic Notes on the New Katumuwa Inscription from Zincirli," *Maarav* 16 (2009): 159–66.

15. For the dating of the inscription, see J. David Schloen, "The City of Katumuwa: The Iron Age Kingdom of Sam'al and the Excavation of Zincirli," in Herrmann and Schloen, *In Remembrance of Me*, 34–38. For an earlier discussion on the historical context of Panamuwa II, see Josef Tropper, *Die Inscriften von Zincirli: Neue Edition und vergleichende Grammatik des phönizischen, sam'alischen und aramäischen Textkorpus*, ALASP 6 (Münster: Ugarit-Verlag, 1993), 19. For the *editio princeps* of this text, see Pardee, "New Aramaic Inscription," 51–71. On the iconography of this inscription, see Eudora J. Struble and Viginia Rimmer Herrmann, "An Eternal Feast at Sam'al: The New Iron Age Mortuary Stele from Zincirli in Context," *BASOR* 356 (2009): 15–48.

16. Note the discussion in Pardee, "New Aramaic Inscription," 54–58.

17. The form *nbš* is standard in Old Aramaic (see *DNWSI*, 745). For a fuller treatment of the relationship between *npš* and *nbš*, see Steiner, *Disembodied Souls*, 137–39.

18. E.g., Schloen and Fink ("New Excavations," 11) note, "This is in contrast to the traditional West Semitic conception that one's soul resides in one's bones after death."

Anatolian specialists have offered a great deal of elucidation for our understanding of this inscription, attempting to dispel those suggestions that this is the earliest example of a disembodied soul in the ancient Near East. H. Craig Melchert, for example, points out that already in the second millennium BC Hittite and Luwian speakers believed in the immortality of the soul as enduring beyond the body. He notes references to offerings on behalf of the "soul of the dead," the soul being placed in the body by the gods at birth, as well as the Luwian hope of the soul returning to the gods upon the death of the body.[19] Similarly, Theo van den Hout remarks more specifically concerning the Hittite "soul" of the dead, noting that this "soul" (sumerogram ZI = Hittite *ištan(zan)*) departs from the body at death, but adds that it is the means of communication between the dead and the living.[20] Annelies Kammenhuber's earlier work on the Hittite conception of soul and body stands in agreement with the above assessments in that the ancient Anatolians viewed the soul as having an enduring existence beyond the termination of the body.[21] Emilia Masson in her analysis of this inscription also cites the Hittite/Luwian influence on this text, but she goes further in noting a broader Indo-European connection.[22] At any rate, it is certainly clear that the theology of the human soul current in the thinking of the second millennium BC Hittite world evinces remarkable affinity with that expressed on the stele of Katumuwa from Zincirli.

This is not, however, the first royal official from Zincirli to express his postmortem existence in this way.[23] Such *nbš*-talk already exists in the earlier Panamuwa I inscription, as well as in the roughly contemporary monument of Panamuwa II.[24] In lines 21–22 of Panamuwa I's inscription commemorating Hadad,

19. For references see H. Craig Melchert, "Remarks on the Kuttamuwa Inscription," *KUBABA* 1 (2010): 6–8, online: http://projectos.fcsh.unl.pt/kubaba/Melchert_2010__Remarks_on_the_Kuttamuwa_Stele.pdf.

20. Theo van den Hout, "Death as Privilege. The Hittite Royal Funerary Ritual," in *Hidden Futures: Death and Immortality in Ancient Egypt, Anatolia, the Classical, Biblical and Arabic-Islamic World*, ed. Jan Maarten Bremer and Theo van den Hout (Amsterdam: Amsterdam University Press, 1994), 44.

21. Annelies Kammenhuber, "Die hethitischen Vorstellungen von Seele und Leib, Herz und Leibesinnerem, Kopf und Person," *ZA* 56 (1964): 160–62, states: "The soul apparently remains when the transient man dies" ("Die Seele bleibt anscheinend bestehen, wenn der vergängliche Mensch stirbt").

22. Emilia Masson, "La stèle mortuaire de Kuttamuwa (Zincirli): comment l'appréhender," *SemCl* 3 (2010): 53.

23. Aptly noted by Schloen and Fink, "New Excavations," 11, and Pardee, "New Aramaic Inscription," 62.

24. For a thorough analysis of the Panamuwa inscriptions, see Tropper, *Inscriften von Zincirli*, 54–131, as well as Paul-Eugene Dion, *La langue de Ya'udi: Descriptions et classement de l'ancien parler de Zincirli dans le cadre des langues sémitique du nord-ouest* (Waterloo, ON: Corporation pour la

he states: *t*[ʾ]*kl nbš pn*[*mw*] *ʿm hdd tšty nbš pnmw ʿm h*[*d*]*d* "May the *nbš* of Panamuwa eat with Hadad; may the *nbš* of Panamuwa drink with Hadad." Before the recent discovery of the Katumuwa stele, the broken nature of the surrounding context of this statement made the interpretation of it a bit more difficult. Line 20 appears to offer directions for the ascension of a royal descendant to the throne in Panamuwa's stead, after which we read in line 21: *wy*[*zbḥ hdd wl yzk*]*r ʾšm pnmw yʾmr*, "Hadad sacrifices but does not mention the name Panamuwa saying."[25] According to this reconstruction and interpretation, Panamuwa attempts to secure the memory of his name by warning his son against making offerings to Hadad without repeating the refrain: "May the *nbš* of Panamuwa eat with Hadad; may the *nbš* of Panamuwa drink with Hadad."[26]

Some scholars have questioned this reading, however. For example, Schmidt cites earlier suggestions to read *ʾšm* as "guilt" or "sin" offering instead of "name" in favor of removing any trace of an invocation of a dead ancestor.[27] In fact, Schmidt proposes that line 21 may be referring to the living Panamuwa and not the dead, conjecturing historically that the background of KAI 214 could involve a political coup—perhaps Panamuwa was attempting to ensure that his son was to take the throne so that the memory of his name would continue through the reign of his heir. Accordingly, Schmidt analyzes the references to Panamuwa's *nbš* eating and drinking with Hadad, not as a postmortem feast, but as expressions of the royal banquet held at his coronation. Therefore, the eating and drinking of Panamuwa's *nbš* with Hadad would reflect, according to this interpretation, his desire to "commune with Hadad" throughout the days of his reign.[28]

The Katumuwa stele, however, has for the most part rendered the latter historical reconstruction highly unlikely and instead confirms the suspicions of some earlier scholars that the eating and drinking of Panamuwa's *nbš* is a

Publication des Etudes Academiques en Religion au Canada, 1974). See also the text, translation, and commentary in *KAI* 214 and 215 and John C. L. Gibson, *Textbook of Syrian Inscriptions, Vol. 2: Aramaic Inscriptions, Including the Dialect of Zinjirli* (Oxford: Clarendon Press, 1975), 60–86.

25. Accoring to Dion, *Langue de Ya'udi*, 31. Similarly, *KAI* 214.21, Gibson, *Textbook of Syrian Inscriptions*, 2:67, and Tropper, *Inscriften von Zincirli*, 82.

26. Cf. *KAI* 215.16–18.

27. See Schmidt, *Israel's Beneficent Dead*, 133, referencing David Heinrich Müller, "Die alttestamentischen Inschriften von Sendscherli," *ZDMG* 7 (1893): 52–53, Müller, "The Excavations at Sendschirli," *The Contemporary Review* 65 (1894): 572–73, and C. R. Conder, "The Syrian Language," *PEF* 28 (1896): 64.

28. See Schmidt, *Israel's Beneficent Dead*, 133–34. One should note, however, that Schmidt's historical reconstructions of the threatened coup on the one hand and the coronation banquet on the other are difficult to reconcile with one another as both arising from the context of KAI 214. These two proposed contexts would seem to reflect significantly distinct historical situations from quite different times, yet one would be hard pressed to detect these circumstances from a straightforward reading of KAI 214, despite its broken context.

postmortem affair. The explicit nature of Katumuwa's description of the mortuary feast makes the existence of such a ritual at Zincirli hard to deny, especially in light of the following remarks concerning the stele that is said to have been erected: *wšmth bsyr ʿlmy wḥggt syr/d zn*, "and I set it in the chamber(?) of my eternity and established a feast at this chamber(?)."[29] Against this being a feast during Katumuwa's lifetime, Pardee notes the mention of his *nbš* being in the stele in line 5, a highly unlikely means of referring to his presence at the feast while still alive.[30] In a subsequent publication Pardee seems to suggest that this stele was erected during his lifetime, noting that at the time Katumuwa had the monument installed "animal sacrifices were made in honor of the named divinities and of the author's soul."[31] Steiner believes such an interpretive move unnecessarily complicates the situation surrounding the monument's installation, since it would require that "my soul in the stele" refers to both the installation ceremony as well as its ongoing function in the commemorative meal, as Pardee explains.[32] Steiner finds this subsequent explanation speculative and prefers Pardee's initial assessment that the reference to "my soul" was to be understood postmortem.[33] However, it is more likely that the inscription indeed references two settings: (1) the stele's initial installation, and (2) the prescribed commemorative ritual for Katumuwa after his death.[34] The inscription begins with Katumuwa's assertion that he commissioned the erection of the stele *bḥyy* "while living" (line 1), which obviously refers to what he did during his lifetime. The reference to his *nbš* in the stele (line 5) and the mention of sacrifices being made in the presence

29. Following Pardee, "New Aramaic Inscription," 53, 60–61; Pardee, "Katumuwa Inscription," 46–47. Cf. Mazzini, "On the Problematic Term *syr/d*," 505–507; Gregorio del Olmo Lete, "KTMW and His 'Funerary Chapel,'" *AuOr* 29 (2011): 308–10; Seth L. Sanders, "The Appetites of the Dead: West Semitic Linguistic and Ritual Aspects of the Katumuwa Stele," *BASOR* 369 (2013): 38–39.

30. Pardee, "New Aramaic Inscription,", 60.

31. Pardee, "Katumuwa Inscription," 47.

32. Pardee, "Katumuwa Inscription," 48.

33. Steiner, *Disembodied Souls*, 139–40.

34. For this reason, Steiner's charge that Pardee has changed his views may not be an accurate assessment. Note Pardee's full comment on these two aspects of the stele's setting ("Katumuwa Inscription," 48):

> The first reference to the "soul" is temporally ambiguous, perhaps purposely so, for it is in the common Semitic form of a nominal sentence, that is, one with no expressed verb, necessitating the addition of the verb "to be" in an English translation. In stating that his "soul" was included among the honorees at the inaugural feast, the author appears to be setting up an identification of his living form in attendance at that feast with the representation of that living form on the stele, also in attendance at that feast, and with the continuation of that being in the stele after his death. It is the last form of existence that (one must conclude by comparison with the Hadad inscription) was to go on eating and drinking with the gods in the "eternal chamber."

of his *nbš* (line 11) both describe the iterative, commemorative actions carried out in his honor postmortem. Again, evidence from Katumuwa with regard to his enduring *nbš* and his ability to participate in the prescribed mortuary feast only clarifies what was already known from KAI 214 and 215, rendering it highly probable that the same sense is operational for these texts as well.

As for broader questions regarding cultural/religious influences reflected in these inscriptions, Sanders has demonstrated that the presentation of *nbš* in the Katumuwa stele "must be understood in primarily West Semitic terms," while at the same time acknowledging "a crucial Luwian ritual dimension" otherwise unknown in West Semitic—the ritual distribution of food for the dead in the presence of the pantheon.[35] This balance in favor of primarily West Semitic influence can be illustrated by the fact that the purported parallel between West Semitic *nbš* and Luwian *atra/i-* is not exact: although the Luwian term shows the presence of the gods in a stele, it is unlike *nbš* in that it can precede embodiment and does not occur in the context of eating.[36]

The Katumuwa inscription from Zincirli is significant for this study on life and mortality in Ugaritic primarily for three reasons. First, it stands within the Ugaritic tradition of invoking dead ancestors, known in Ugaritic as the Rapaʾūma. Again, as Sanders concludes: "The new stele thus stands in an old West Semitic ritual practice of locating the dead in the space of the living, creating sites where they can be visited."[37] Similarly, Hays affirms that this material does "little to contradict the impression of continuity between the beliefs and practices of Ugarit and those of later Palestinian cultures."[38] The parallel between Ugaritic and the Zincirli monument of Katumuwa can be demonstrated from the *aṯr* "place" of summoning in the Rapaʾūma texts, as well as the *aṯr* "place" of Dānîʾilu guarded by his faithful son.[39] It is at these places where the royal dead are ritually summoned and fed in exchange for the procurement of blessing, which means the ongoing stability of the royal household and the city of Ugarit, as attested in the funerary ritual of KTU 1.161.

Second, the Katumuwa stele represents a further development in applying the ongoing presence of the dead to a nonroyal "place." The fact that Katumuwa refers to himself as *ʿbd pnmw* "servant of PNMW" obviously indicates that he is an official associated with the royal household and not the royal personage

35. Sanders, "Appetites of the Dead," 44.

36. See Ilya Yakubovich, "Nagae Luvicae," in *Anatolian Languages*, ed. Vitalij Viktorovič Ševoroškin and Paul Sidwell, AHL Studies in the Science and History of Language 6 (Canberra: Association for the History of Language, 2002), 194–97, where he collects instances of *atra/i-* showing that it could be embodied in a stele.

37. Sanders, "Appetites of the Dead," 50.

38. Hays, *Death in the Iron Age II*, 132.

39. Rapaʾūma: KTU 1.21 II:3, 11, 12; 1.22 II:10, 11, 21; 1.20 II:2. Dānîʾilu: KTU 1.17 I:28.

himself. This particular practice usually functions as a feature of the royal mortuary cult, that is, the "establishment of a private mortuary-cult place in which food and drink offerings to a deity are shared with the deceased," as Eudora Struble and Virginia Herrmann explain.[40] As for the location of Katumuwa's building where the inscription was recovered, Herrmann furthermore proposes that, in light of its small size and relative proximity to larger residential buildings, it may have functioned as a shrine for a local religious association on a level somewhere between the individual and royal household contexts.[41] If this proposal is maintained, it would provide yet another level of connection between what is known about the Ugaritic royal ritual attested in the textual sources and the household/family religion reconstructed from archaeology.

Finally, as I suggested in chapter 5 (§5.4), the full-blown disembodied *nbš* attested at Zincirli may demonstrate an organic development arising from what is already attested at Ugarit in the exiting *npš* motif. Indeed, the death of ʾAqhatu is explicitly described in terms of his *npš*'s exit from the body: it departs like the movement of the wind, like spittle from the mouth, and from the nose like smoke through a window (KTU 1.18 IV:24–26).[42] It is certainly true that Ugaritic never explicitly refers to one's *npš* existing and taking up residence somewhere in the same way it is expressed in the Katumuwa inscription. However, as I noted in chapter 5 (§5.4), the Ugaritians did express the postmortem existence of royal personages with the term *rpủm* (// *mtm* // *ỉlnym*), which they defined rather descriptively in KTU 1.161:1 as *ẓlm* "shades."[43] Therefore, it is important that we not limit our consideration of the origins of the disembodied *npš* notion attested at Zincirili to the lexeme *npš* alone, since the semantic inventory related to the West Semitic funerary context of the second millennium BC is much broader and multifaceted. Interpreting the attestation of *nbš* at Zincirli "in primarily West Semitic terms," as Sanders suggests, would therefore explain why its meaning does not exactly correspond to the broader nuances of its Anatolian counterpart *atra/i-*.[44]

40. Struble and Herrmann, "Eternal Feast at Samʾal," 39, citing H. Niehr, "Zum Totenkult der König von Samʾal im 9. und 8. Jh. V. Chr.," *SEL* 11 (1994): 57–73.

41. Herrmann, "Katumuwa Stele in Archaeological Context," 52–53. See also Sanders reference to this feature in "Appetites of the Dead," 48, citing Herrmann, "The KTMW Stele from Zincirli: Syro-Hittite Mortuary Cult and Urban Social Networks," in *Redefining the Sacred: Religious Architecture and Text in the Near East and Egypt 1000 BC–AD 300*, ed. Elizabeth Frood and Rubina Raja, Contextualising the Sacred 1 (Turnhout: Brepols, 2014), 153–181.

42. The imagery invoked for this motif would seem to render Sander's passing description of the *npš* going out "like a light" unlikely ("Appetites of the Dead," 44). "Going out like a light" would rather require a verb denoting some kind of diminishment. The verb *yṣ*ʾ in this case indicates a movement that results in the "exit" of something.

43. See my treatment of this term in ch. 4 (§4.3.6.2).

44. Sanders, "Appetites of the Dead," 44.

6.4. Defining Disembodied *npš/nbš*

The disembodied state of the *npš/nbš* raises yet another question: Disembodied to what? In order to deal with this question, we must return once again to consider the nature of the Hittite understanding of the soul as a means of contrast for the West Semitic conception of "soul." The Hittite word for soul is *ištanza(n)-*, represented by the Sumerogram ZI.[45] Van den Hout defines ZI as "any individual's, either dead or alive, seat of emotional and rational thoughts."[46] One of the prominent features of the Hittite understanding of the soul is that it is detached from the body at death, after which it must be convinced through ritual to embark upon its journey to the afterlife.[47] In other words, the soul endures independent of the body without having any remaining representation in this world. Van den Hout has also identified *atra/i-* as the corresponding Luwian word for "person, self," for which Melchert has observed that it not only departs from the body at death but is thought to preexist the body to which it is joined at birth.[48] This feature is possible because the soul essentially belongs to the gods, so that birth is envisioned in terms of the gods placing the preexistent soul into the body, while death involves the soul's return to the gods.[49] A related but distinct Hittite anthropological term is *akkant-*, literally meaning "dead" (Sumerogram GIDIM), or more exactly the "(ghost of the) dead," and may have been invoked postmortem as a means of contact with the dead. Van den Hout explains that these two terms, GIDIM and ZI, may have been akin to the idea of "body and soul" in that "GIDIM may have been conceived as more 'corporeal' than the soul, as some immaterial but potentially visible body."[50] We find a similar parallel conception in the Ugaritic *rpủm*, who are summoned to the royal funerary ritual and are thus described as *ẓlm* "shades" (KTU 1.161).

The Ugaritic view of *npš* is both similar and distinct from its conceptual counterpart in Hittite. In Ugaritic, the *npš* departs or exits from the body at death and is described in phenomenological terms. However, the Hittite term *ištanza(n)-* appears to be more readily distinguishable from the body in which it takes up residence in this life, especially if we take into account the notion of a preexisting

45. Kammenhuber, "Hethitischen Vorstellungen," 160–62.

46. Van den Hout, "Death as Privilege," 44.

47. Alfonso Archi, "The Soul Has to Leave the Land of the Living," *JANER* 7 (2008): 181.

48. Van den Hout, "Self, Soul, and Portrait in Hieroglyphic Luwian," in *Silva Anatolica: Anatolian Studies Presented to Maciej Popko on the Occasion of His 65th Birthday*, ed. Piotr Taracha (Warsaw: Agade, 2002), 172. Melchert, "Remarks on the Kuttamuwa Inscription," 6–7.

49. For the soul belonging to the gods, see Archi, "Soul Has to Leave," 169. For its return, see Melchert, "Remarks on the Kuttamuwa Inscription," 7.

50. Van den Hout, "Death as Privilege," 44.

soul attested in the Luwian term *atra/i-*. The West Semitic meaning of *npš* is not so easily disentangled from its bodily form, which is especially evident in light of its origin as a particular body part, whether "neck" or "throat."[51] As *npš* takes on more figurative meaning in Ugaritic it becomes clear that its close association with the body does not go away: it comes to signify the vital force of animation within the body. Even further, its application to the individual is also telling, since in such cases the *npš* refers rather holistically to the body in which the *npš*-element exists. These considerations, however, are not meant to imply that ancient Ugaritians where unable to conceptualize an enduring personal existence beyond the moment of one's death. As I observed from the mythological expressions of dying gods and the numerous occurrences of the *rpủm* in funerary contexts, death is not the end. Furthermore, the motif of talking to a dead person attested in ʿAnatu's remorseful conversation with the dead hero ʾAqhatu (KTU 1.18 IV:40–41) seems to indicate that being dead does not necessarily mean the termination of personal existence.[52] On the contrary, this literary motif devised by the Ugaritic poet conceptualizes a certain awareness that not only are the dead consciously alive, they may even hear the confessions of the living!

Thus, the West Semitic insistence that personal presence must have some corporeal manifestation seems to lie behind the funerary tradition of Zincirli. The *nbš* must be somehow represented in concrete terms—it cannot simply roam freely in search of a resting place in the netherworld, but must instead be attached to a physical entity representative of human personhood. The inhabitation of one's soul in a stele, as attested at Zincirli, is not in fact foreign to Northwest Semitic conceptions of the dead. As I have discussed above, the Phoenician funerary monuments themselves provide the concrete representation of the individual's enduring presence postmortem. As the Tabnit inscription contends, *ʾnk tbnt . . . škb bʾrn z* "I, Tabnit . . . lie in this sarcophagus," which assumes that the monument in some way houses the enduring presence of the deceased. Or in the case of Eshmunazzar, he warns those who would be tempted to disturb *ḥlt mškby* "the coffin of my resting place." But what would one expect to find within the sarcophagi of these royal figures? They house the bones of the departed, whose personal presence is apparently still thought to be attached to their remains. The West Semitic worldview persists in maintaining that personhood is corporeal in nature, so that the preservation of the corpse after death is of utmost importance, which in these contexts meant housing it in a sarcophagus as a means of preserving perceptible presence. This notion is similarly attested in the Egyptian

51. See my discussion in ch. 2 (§2.2).
52. See ch. 1 (§1.2.2.2).

practice of mummification, the goal of which was to preserve the body for the afterlife.[53]

The biblical tradition, however, raises yet another aspect that must be brought to bear on our articulation of the postmortem soul. Several times the Hebrew Bible mentions the *nepeš mēt,* which is commonly thought to mean "dead *nepeš*."[54] Steiner explains that this enigmatic expression in Hebrew developed by means of synecdoche analogous to *nepeš habbāśār*, which he renders "the body soul."[55] Likewise in this context, *nepeš* as "body soul" developed to *nepeš mēt* "corpse."[56] This interpretation appears to assume the common translation value "dead *nepeš*." But this rendering will not suffice because the Hebrew word *nepeš* is feminine and the adjective *mēt* is masculine, therefore eliminating any possibility of an attributive construction. Rather, what we appear to have in this phrase is a substantival adjective in a construct chain: "*nepeš* of a dead person." According to this analysis it is not that the *nepeš* has died or come to a state of nonexistence, but is instead the enduring *nepeš* of someone who has just died. The *nepeš* is therefore still tied to the lifeless body of the dead, and as such conceivably continues to exist somehow in relation to it. This condition would differ from the initial state of humankind depicted in the creation event of Gen 2:7. In that context God formed the first human by fashioning him from the dust (*ʿāpār*) of the ground and breathed into him the divine life breath (*nᵉšāmâ*), resulting in his becoming a *nepeš ḥayyâ* "living *nepeš*."[57] In Hebrew thought the *nepeš* was not conceived to have existed prior to the creation of the body, but was the product of divine creation: at that point he became a living *nepeš*.

On the surface this formulation of the Hebrew *nepeš* of a dead person enduring with respect to the body would seem to conflict with the notion of an exiting *npš* at Ugarit. But this is not actually the case because Hebrew shares this same expression for death as well.[58] The West Semitic tradition certainly maintains that the enduring life force of an individual is localized in the bodily remains of the deceased, but the notion of a type of metaphysical departure is there as well. In Ugaritic we have the chariot-riding Rapaʾūma who are summoned from below to the funeral of the deceased king of Ugarit where they receive him into their company (KTU 1.161). Our understanding of the Ugaritic Rapaʾūma and

53. Quirke, *Ancient Egyptian Religion*, 144.

54. Lev 21:11; Num 6:6; 19:13; 23:10.

55. Steiner, *Disembodied Souls*, 83.

56. Steiner, *Disembodied Souls*, 116.

57. Note that the adjective *ḥayyâ* is markedly feminine, justifying interpreting it attributively as "living *nepeš*."

58. E.g., Gen 35:18.

their relation to the royal dead would then suggest that although the body is physically being lowered into the grave, Šapšu is metaphysically transporting his enduring presence (perhaps *ẓl* "shade") to the company of Rapaʾūma about to receive him below. Indeed, the place of the funerary ritual (*ảṯr*) becomes the focal point of contact between the enduring presence of the departed and the living. As the funerary ritual implies, the ancient and more recent Rapaʾūma of the underworld must journey by chariot (KTU 1.20–22) to this place, not only to receive the recently deceased king, but also to be entreated for the favor of Ugarit (KTU 1.108:19–27; 1.161:27–34).

It could be argued from this vantage point that the cultural situation reflected at Zincirli provided a timely opportunity for the localization of the *nbš* in a monumental inscription. Schloen notes that the archaeological context of the Katumuwa inscription suggests that the Samʾalian official's body must have been cremated, since no human remains have been located within the vicinity of the stele.[59] Even though this north Syrian city is firmly situated within the confines of Luwian cultural influence, the inscription is nevertheless written in Samʾalian, and thus represents an attempt to preserve West Semitic traditions.[60] For those coming from a West Semitic understanding of life and death, Schloen argues that the Indo-European practice of cremation would have required some explanation. Cremation represented termination of personal presence—the bones in which the *npš* was thought to be permanently localized are destroyed. He believes that this inscription therefore gave reassurance to a West Semitic audience that his *npš* was not terminated in cremation, but was in fact preserved by way of localization in the stele.[61] This attestation consequently offers a reasonable explanation for the move in later Northwest Semitic inscriptions to apply the word *npš*, not to the bodily remains of the individual, but to the funerary monument itself.[62] Schloen further explains:

> At the very least, this inscription now makes clear that there existed in Samʾal in the eighth century BC the belief that the deceased person's soul (i.e., his enduring identity or life-force) could be transferred into an object

59. Schloen and Fink, "New Excavations," 11.

60. I believe Steiner may be mistaken when he charges that Schloen, Fink, and Pardee "all believe that the Samalian conception of the soul reflected in the two Aramaic inscriptions has an Anatolian origin and may thus be irrelevant to the Israelites" (*Disembodied Souls*, 14–15). Admitting the possibility that the body may have been cremated does not necessarily deny West Semitic conceptions about the soul.

61. Schloen and Fink, "New Excavations," 11.

62. For references, see *DNWSI*, 748.

> detached from his bodily remains—in this case, and presumably in other cases, a pictorial image of the deceased.[63]

The animating quality of the term *nbš* as "life force, vitality" in this context is also fully intact in the iconography of the monument—the deceased individual is portrayed pictorially eating with the living in perpetuity. The food items portrayed in the image—bread, meat, and perhaps spices or aromatics—symbolize "a source of continuous life and regeneration after death," as Dominik Bonatz has observed.[64] However, I must clarify that the broader tradition of Syro-Hittite banquet scenes has been shown not only to represent provisioning for the afterlife of the deceased symbolically, but also to prescribe the appropriate offerings to be carried out by the living in the actual presence of the stele.[65] In other words, the symbolic imagery of food for the dead engraved pictorially upon the stele provided the real world place where the recurring offerings were to be made.[66] The image therefore constitutes a kind of ongoing animation whereby Katumuwa feasts in the presence of the living.[67] But we might also consider for a moment the concrete notion of *npš* as "throat" attested in the mythological texts from Ugarit and known in the Hebrew Bible. The physical stele is the place where Katumuwa receives his food for nourishment, perhaps evoking his physical throat as the passageway of that food, envisioned here as receiving the food and drink in the commemorative ritual event.

6.5. Summary

In summary, the Katumuwa stele witnesses to the complexities of the ancient West Semitic view of the human constitution and its conceived nature in death. What I have tried to demonstrate here, however, is that it is not altogether

63. Schloen and Fink, "New Excavations," 11.

64. Dominik Bonatz, "Kutamuwa's Banquet Scene," in Herrmann and Schloen, *In Remembrance of Me*, 39.

65. Struble and Herrmann, "Eternal Feast at Sam'al," 30, citing the work of Dominik Bonatz, *Das syro-hethitische Grabdenkmal: Untersuchungen zur Entstehung einer neuen Bildgattung in der Eisenzeit im nordsyrish-südostanatolischen Raum* (Mainz: von Zabern, 2000), 103–5, 116–17.

66. Note, however, that the offering described in the text does not match that depicted in the image. See Bonatz, "Kutamuwa's Banquet Scene," 39.

67. See also Pardee, "Ḳatumuwa Inscription," 48: "In stating that his 'soul' was included among the honorees at the inaugural feast, the author appears to be setting up an identification of his living form in attendance at the feast with the representation of that living form on the stele, also in attendance at the feast, and with the continuation of that being in the stele after his death."

foreign to what is already known from other West Semitic sources.[68] To be sure, the Sam'alian materials may be conceived as exhibiting new developments, but not entirely foreign elements. Again, the Ugaritic situation of the late second millennium is instructive. As I have shown in my study of this cultural context, the Ugaritians demonstrated interest in both the material and immaterial remains of the dead. The funerary settings we have been examining thus provided a narrative for both—the physical presence of the dead in the form of their buried remains and the personal presence of the dead which those remains symbolize and which is expressed through mythology. For Katumuwa, the potential absence of his bodily remains is thus compensated by the localization of his enduring personal presence in the funerary monument. In the end, the West Semitic evidence supports the early conceptualization of both bodily resurrection (at least in a prototypical fashion) and the enduring immaterial presence of the dead.

68. This general conclusion seems to be the thrust of Steiner's argument (*Disembodied Souls*, 10–22).

BIBLIOGRAPHY

Aartun, Kjell. "Neue Beiträge zum ugaritischen Lexicon (II)." *UF* 17 (1986): 1–42.

Aejmelaeus, Anneli. "Translation Technique and the Intention of the Translator." Pages 23–36 in *VII Congress of the International Organization for Septuagint and Cognate Studies, Leuven 1989*. Edited by Claude E. Cox. SCS 31. Atlanta: Scholars Press, 1991.

———. "What We Talk about When We Talk about Translation Technique." Pages 205–22 in *On the Trail of the Septuagint Translators: Collected Essays*. CBET 50. Leuven: Peeters, 2007.

Aistleitner, Joseph. *Die mythologischen und kultischen Texte aus Ras Shamra*. 2nd ed. Budapest: Akadémiai Kiadó, 1964.

———. "Götterzeugung in Ugarit and Dilmun (SS un Ni. 4561)." *AcOr* 3 (1953): 285–311.

———. *Untersuchungen zur Grammatik des Ugaritischen*. Berichte über die Verhandlungen der Sächsischen Akademie der Wissenschaften zu Leipzig: Philologisch-historische Klasse 100/6. Berlin: Akademie, 1954.

Albertz, Rainer, and Rüdiger Schmitt. *Family and Household Religion in Ancient Israel and the Levant*. Winona Lake, IN: Eisenbrauns, 2012.

Albright, William F. "Are the Ephod and Teraphim Mentioned in Ugaritic Literature?" *BASOR* 83 (1941): 39–42.

———. "The High Place in Ancient Palestine." Pages 242–58 in *Volume du Congrès: Strasbourg 1956*. Edited by P. A. H. Boer. VTSup 4. Leiden: Brill, 1957.

———. "The 'Natural Force' of Moses in the Light of Ugaritic." *BASOR* 94 (1944): 32–35.

———. "Recent Progress in North-Canaanite Research." *BASOR* 70 (1938): 18–24.

———. "Stratigraphic Confirmation of Low Mesopotamian Chronology." *BASOR* 144 (1956): 26–30.

———. "The Traditional Home of the Syrian Daniel." *BASOR* 130 (1953): 26–27.

———. "Two Letters from Ugarit (Ras Shamrah)." *BASOR* 82 (1941): 43–49.

———. "Was the Patriarch Terah a Canaanite Moon-God?" *BASOR* 71 (1938): 35–40.

Anderson, Gary. *A Time to Mourn, A Time to Dance: The Expression of Grief and Joy in Israelite Religion*. University Park: Pennsylvania State University Press, 1991.

Archi, Alfonso. "The Soul Has to Leave the Land of the Living." *JANER* 7 (2008): 169–95.

Arnaud, Daniel. "Prolégomènes à la rédaction d'une histoire d'Ougarit II: Les bordereaux de rois divinisés." *SMEA* 41 (1998): 155–73.

Assmann, Jan. *Death and Salvation in Ancient Egypt*. Ithaca, NY: Cornell University Press, 2005.

Astour, Michael C. "Two Ugaritic Serpent Charms." *JNES* 27 (1968): 13–36.

Avishur, Yitzhak. "The Ghost-Expelling Incantation from Ugarit (Ras Ibn Hani 78/20)." *UF* 13 (1981): 13–25.

———. *Studies in Hebrew and Ugaritic Psalms*. Jerusalem: Magnes Press, 1994.

Badre, Leila, Pierre Bordreuil, Jinan Mudarres, Loy ʿAjjan, and Raoul Vitale. "Notes ougaritiques I: Keret." *Syria* 53 (1976): 95–125.

Barr, James. "Hebrew Lexicography." Pages 103–26 in *Studies on Semitic Lexicography*. Edited by Pelio Franzaroli. QuSem 2. Firenze: Institutio di linguistica e di lingue orientali, Università di Firenze, 1973.

———. *The Semantics of Biblical Language*. Oxford: Oxford University Press, 1961.

Barstad, Hans M. *The Religious Polemics of Amos: Studies in the Preaching of Am 2,7B-8; 4,1–13; 5,1–27; 6,4–7; 8,14*. VTSup 34. Leiden: Brill, 1984.

Barton, George. "The Second Liturgical Poem from Ras Shamra: A Liturgy for the Festival of the God Alein." *JAOS* 55 (1935): 31–58.

Bassnett, Susan. "Translation Theory." Pages 909–13 in *The Johns Hopkins Guide to Literary Theory and Criticism*. Edited by Michael Groden, Martin Kreiswirth, and Imre Szeman. 2nd ed. Baltimore: Johns Hopkins Universtiy Press, 2005.

Batto, Bernard. *In the Beginning: Essays on Creation Motifs in the Ancient Near East and the Bible*. Siphrut 9. Winona Lake, IN: Eisenbrauns, 2013.

Bauckham, Richard. *The Jewish World Around the New Testament*. Grand Rapids: Baker Academic, 2008.

Bayliss, Miranda. "The Cult of Dead Kin in Assyria and Babylonia." *Iraq* 35 (1973): 115–25.

Beckman, Gary. "The Anatolian Myth of Illuyanka." *JANESCU* 14 (1982): 11–25.

Berlin, Adele. *The Dynamics of Biblical Parallelism*. Revised and expanded ed. Grand Rapids: Eerdmans, 2008.

Biberstein-Kazimirski, Albert de. *Dictionnaire Arabe-Français*. Paris: Maisonneuve, 1860.

Blau, Joshua. *Phonology and Morphology of Biblical Hebrew*. LSAWS 2. Winona Lake, IN: Eisenbrauns, 2010.

Blau, Joshua, and Jonas C. Greenfield. "Ugaritic Glosses." *BASOR* 200 (1970): 11–17.

Blau, Joshua, and Samuel E. Loewenstamm. "Zur Frage der Scriptio plena im Ugaritischen und Verwandtes." *UF* 2 (1970): 19–33.

Bloch-Smith, Elizabeth M. "Death in the Life of Israel." Page 139–43 in Gittlen, *Sacred Time, Sacred Place*.

———. "From Womb to Tomb: The Israelite Family in Death as in Life." Pages 122–31 in *The Family in Life and in Death: The Family in Ancient Israel; Sociological and Archaeological Perspectives*. Edited by Patricia Dutcher-Walls. LHBOTS 504. New York: T&T Clark, 2009.

———. *Judahite Burial Practices and Beliefs about the Dead*. JSOTSup 123. Sheffield: JSOT Press, 1992.
Bodel, John P., and Saul M. Olyan. *Household and Family Religion in Antiquity*. Ancient World: Comparative Histories. Oxford: Blackwell, 2008.
Boling, Robert. "'Synonymous' Parallelism in the Psalms." *JSS* 5 (1960): 221–55.
Bonatz, Dominik. "Kutamuwa's Banquet Scene." Pages 39–44 in Herrmann and Schloen, *In Remembrance of Me*.
———. *Das syro-hethitische Grabdenkmal: Untersuchungen zur Entstehung einer neuen Bildgattung in der Eisenzeit im nordsyrish-südostanatolischen Raum*. Mainz: von Zabern.
Bordreuil, Pierre, and André Caquot. "Les Textes en cunéiformes alphabétiques découverts en 1978 a Ibn Hani." *Syria* 57 (1980): 243–73.
Bordreuil, Pierre, and Dennis Pardee. *A Manual of Ugaritic*. LSAWS 3. Winona Lake, IN: Eisenbrauns, 2009.
———. "Le rituel funéraire ougaritique RS. 34.126." *Syria* 59 (1982): 121–28.
———. "Les textes en cunéiformes alphabétiques." Pages 137–68 in *Une bibliothèque au sud de la ville: Les textes de la 34e campagne (1973)*. Edited by Pierre Bordreuil. RSO 7. Paris: Éditions Recherche sur les Civilisations, 1991.
Bordreuil, Pierre, and Dennis Pardee, with Robert Hawley. *Une bibliothèque au sud de la ville ***: Textes 1994–2002 en cunéiforme alphabétique de la maison d'Ourtenou*. RSO 18. Paris: Maison de l'Orient et de la Méditerranée, 2012.
Borger, Rykle. *Mesopotamisches Zeichenlexikon*. AOAT 305. Münster: Ugarit-Verlag, 2010.
———. Review of *Hammurabi von Babylon*, by Hartmut Schmökel. *ZA* 56 (1964): 288–90.
Bosworth, David A. "Daughter Zion and Weeping in Lamentations 1–2." *JSOT* 38 (2013): 217–37.
———. "The Tears of God in the Book of Jeremiah." *Bib* 94 (2013): 24–46.
———. "Weeping in Recognition Scenes in Genesis and the Odyssey." *CBQ* 77 (2015): 619–39.
———. "Weeping in the Psalms." *VT* 62 (2013): 36–46.
Brown, Michael L. "'I Am the Lord Your Healer': A Philological Study of the Root *Rapa'* in the Hebrew Bible and the Ancient Near East." Ph.D. diss., New York University, 1985.
———. "Was There a West Semitic Asklepios?" *UF* 30 (1998): 133–54.
Bryce, Trevor. *The Kingdom of the Hittites*. 2nd ed. Oxford: Oxford University Press, 2005.
Caquot, André. "Correspondance de 'Uzzin fils de Bayaya (RS 17.63 et 17.117)." *Ugaritica* 7:389–98.
———. "La divinité solaire ougaritique." *Syria* 36 (1959): 90–101.
———. "Hébreu et Araméen." *Annuaire du Collège de France* 75 (1975–1976): 423–32.
———. "Le Léviathan de Job 40,25–41,26." *RB* 99 (1992): 40–69.
———. "Une nouvelle interprétation de KTU 1.19 I 1–19." *SEL* 2 (1985): 93–114.
———. "Un recueil ougaritique de formules magiques." *SEL* 5 (1988): 31–43.
———. "Rephaïm." *DBSup* 10:345–57.
———. "Les Rephaim ougaritiques." *Syria* 37 (1960): 75–93.
———. "Un sacrifice expiatoire à Ras Shamra." *RHPR* 42 (1962): 201–11.

———. "La tablette RS 24.252 et la question des Rephaïm ougaritiques." *Syria* 53 (1976): 295–304.

Caquot, André, Maurice Sznycer, and Andrée Herdner. *Textes ougaritiques, Tome I: Mythes et legendes*. LAPO 7. Paris: Cerf, 1974.

Caquot, André, Jean-Michel de Tarragon, and Jesús-Luis Cunchillos. *Textes ougaritiques, Tome II: Textes religieux et rituels, correspondance*. LAPO 14. Paris: Cerf, 1989.

Carel, Havi. *Life and Death in Freud and Heidegger*. Amsterdam: Rodopi, 2006.

Cassuto, Umberto. "Baal and Mot in the Ugaritic Texts." *IEJ* 12 (1962): 77–86.

———. *Biblical and Oriental Studies*. Vol. 2. Jerusalem: Magnes, 1973.

———. *The Goddess Anath: Canaanite Epics of the Patriarchal Age*. Translated by Israel Abrahams. Jerusalem: Bialik, 1971.

———. האלה ענת. Jerusalem: Bialik, 1951.

———. "ספרות מקראית וספרות כנענית." *Tarbiz* 14 (1943): 197–212.

Cathcart, Kevin, and Wilfred G. E. Watson. "Weathering a Wake: A Cure for a Carousal; A Revised Translation of Ugaritica V Text 1." *PIBA* 4 (1980): 35–58.

Cazelles, Henri. "Ugarit: La légende d'Aqhat." *Annuaire de l'École Pratique des Hautes Études* 87 (1978–1979): 215–20, 231–34.

Clark, Herbert H. "Word Associations and Linguistic Theory." Pages 271–86 in *New Horizons in Linguistics*. Edited by John Lyons. Harmondsworth: Penguin, 1970.

Clemens, David M. "KTU 1.108.3–5 (RS 24.252): *dyšr.wyḏmr* . . ." *UF* 25 (1993): 63–74.

———. *Sources for Ugaritic Ritual and Sacrifice*. Vol. 1. AOAT 284. Münster: Ugarit-Verlag, 2001.

Clifford, Richard J. *The Cosmic Mountain in Canaan and the Old Testament*. HSM 4. Cambridge: Harvard University Press, 1972.

———. "Cosmogonies in the Ugaritic Texts and in the Bible." Or 53 (1984): 183–201.

———. "Mot Invites Baal to a Feast: Observations on a Difficult Ugaritic Text (CTA 5.i = KTU 1.5.I)." Pages 55–64 in *"Working with No Data": Semitic and Egyptian Studies Presented to Thomas O. Lambdin*. Edited by David M. Golomb. Winona Lake, IN: Eisenbrauns, 1987.

Clines, David J. A. "The Parallelism of Greater Precision: Notes from Isaiah 40 for a Theory of Hebrew Poetry." Pages 314–36 in *Directions in Biblical Hebrew Poetry*. Edited by Elain R. Follis. JSOTSup 40. Sheffield: JSOT Press, 1987.

Cohen, Chaim. "The 'Held Method' for Comparative Semitic Philology." *JANESCU* 19 (1989): 9–23.

Collins, John J. *Scripture and Sectarianism: Essays on the Dead Sea Scrolls*. Grand Rapids: Eerdmans, 2016.

Collins, Terrance. "The Physiology of Tears in the Old Testament: Part 1." *CBQ* 33 (1971): 18–38.

———."The Physiology of Tears in the Old Testament: Part 2." *CBQ* 33 (1972): 185–97.

Conder, C. R. "The Syrian Language." *PEF* 28 (1896): 60–78.

Conklin, Blane. *Oath Formulas in Biblical Hebrew*. LSAWS 5. Winona Lake, IN: Eisenbrauns, 2011.

Cooper, Alan. "*MLK 'LM*: 'Eternal King' or 'King of Eternity'?" Pages 1–8 in *Love and Death in the Ancient Near East: Essays in Honor of Marvin H. Pope*. Edited by John H. Marks and Robert M. Good. Guilford, CT: Four Quarters, 1987.

Criscuolo, Alfredo. "Metafore anatomiche: ugaritico *brlt*." *SEL* 24 (2007): 23–31.

Cross, Frank Moore. "אֵל, *ʾel*." *TDOT* 1:242–61.

———. "The Canaanite Cuneiform Tablet from Taanach." *BASOR* 190 (1968): 41–46.

———. *Canaanite Myth and Hebrew Epic: Essays in the History of the Religion of Israel*. Cambridge: Harvard University Press, 1975.

Crowfoot, John W., Kathleen Kenyon, and Eliezer Sukenik. *The Buildings at Samaria*. London: Palestinian Exploration Fund, 1942.

Cullmann, Oscar. "Immortality of the Soul or Resurrection of the Dead?" Pages 9–53 in *Immortality and Resurrection: Death in the Western World; Two Conflicting Currents of Thought*. Edited by Krister Stendahl. London: Macmillan, 1965.

Cutler, B., and J. Macdonald. "An Akkadian Cognate to Ugaritic *brlt*." *UF* 5 (1973): 67–70.

———. "On the Origin of the Ugaritic Text KTU 1.23." *UF* 14 (1982): 33–50.

Dahood, Mitchell. "The Breakup of Stereotyped Phrases: Some New Examples." *JANESCU* 5 (1973): 83–89.

———. *Psalms I: 1–50*. AB 16. Garden City, NY: Doubleday, 1965.

———. "The Ugaritic Parallel Pair *qra // qba* in Isaiah 62,2." *Bib* 58 (1977): 527–28.

Dalley, Stephanie. "The God Ṣalmu and the Winged Sun Disk." *Iraq* 48 (1986): 85–101.

Day, John. "New Light on the Mythological Background of the Allusion to Resheph in Habakkuk III 5." *VT* 29 (1979): 353–55.

Deese, James. *The Structure of Associations in Language and Thought*. Baltimore: Johns Hopkins University Press, 1965.

Dhorme, Édouard. "Deux tablettes de Ras-Shamra de la campagne de 1932." *Syria* 14 (1933): 229–37.

Dietrich, Manfried, and Oswald Loretz. "Baal *rpu* in KTU 1.108; 1.113 und nach 1.17 VI 25–33." *UF* 12 (1980): 171–82.

———. "Die Bannung von Schlangengift (KTU 1.100 und KTU 1.107:7b-13a. 19b-20)." *UF* 12 (1980): 153–70.

———. "Gebrauch von Götterstatuen in der Mantik von Ugarit (KTU 1.124)." *UF* 12 (1980): 395–96.

———. *Mantik in Ugarit: Keilalphabetische Texte der Opferschau, Omensammlungen, Nekromantie*. ALASP 3. Münster: Ugarit-Verlag, 1990.

———. "*mt* 'Môt, Tod' und *mt* 'Krieger, Held' im Ugaritischen." *UF* 22 (1990): 57–65.

———. "Neue Studien zu den Ritualtexten aus Ugarit (II)—Nr. 6—Epigraphische und inhaltliche Probleme in KTU 1.161." *UF* 15 (1983): 17–24.

———. "Philologische und inhaltliche Probleme im Schreiben KTU 2.17." *UF* 14 (1982): 83–88.

———. "Das Porträt einer Königin in KTU 1.14 I 12–15: Zur ugaritischen Lexikographie (XVIII)." *UF* 12 (1980): 199–204.

———. "Rāpiʾu und Milku aus Ugarit: Neuere historisch-geographische Thesen zu *rpu mlk ʿlm* (KTU 1.108:1) und *mt rpi* (KTU 1.17 I 1)." *UF* 21 (1989): 123–31.

———. "Schiffshandel und Schiffsmiete zwischen Byblos und Ugarit (KTU 4.338:10–8)." *UF* 22 (1990): 89–96.

———. *Studien zu den ugaritischen Texten I: Mythos, und Ritual in KTU 1.12, 1.24, 1.96, 1.100 und 1.114*. AOAT 269. Münster: Ugarit-Verlag, 2000.

———. "Totenverehrung in Māri (12803) und Ugarit (KTU 1.161)." *UF* 12 (1980): 381–82.

———. "Ugaritische Rituale und Beschwörungen." *TUAT* 2:299–357.
———. "Ug. *b ṣql ʿrgz* und *b ṣqlnw* (II Reg 4,42), *ʾgwz*." *UF* 18 (1986): 115–20.
———. "Zur ugaritischen Lexikographie (I)." *BO* 23 (1966): 127–33.
Dietrich, Manfried, Oswald Loretz, and Joaquín Sanmartín. "Bericht über ein Orakel (RS 24.272 = UG. 5, S. 563 NR. 6)." *UF* 7 (1975): 540–41.
———. "Der Brief RS 4.475 = CTA 53." *UF* 7 (1975): 529–30.
———. "Der keilalphabetische šumma izbu-Text RS 24.247+265+268+328." *UF* 7 (1975): 133–40.
———. "Der 'Neujahrpsalm' RS 24.252 (= Ug. 5, S. 551–7 Nr. 2)." *UF* 7 (1975): 115–19.
———. "Die ugaritischen Totengeister *rpu(m)* und die biblischen Rephaim." *UF* 8 (1976): 45–52.
———. "Zur ugaritischen Lexikographie (VII)." *UF* 5 (1973): 79–104.
Dijk, J. van. "Vert comme Tišpak." *Or* 38 (1969): 539–47.
Dijkstra, Meindert. "Astral Myth of the Birth of Shahar and Shalim (KTU 1.23)." Pages 265–87 in *"Und Mose schrieb Dieses Lied auf": Studien zum Alten Testament und zum Alten Orient; Festschrift für Oswald Loretz zur Vollendung seines 70. Lebensjahres mit Beiträgen von Freunden, Schülern und Kollegen*. Edited by Manfried Dietrich and Ingo Kottsieper. AOAT 250. Münster: Ugarit-Verlag, 1998.
———. "Epigraphical Evidence for the Determination of the Column-Order in the Tablets KTU 1.1 and KTU 1.20–22." *UF* 19 (1987): 49–60.
———. "The Legend of Danel and the Rephaim." *UF* 20 (1988): 35–51.
———. "Ugaritic Prose." Pages 140–64 in Watson and Wyatt, *Handbook of Ugaritic Studies*.
Dijkstra, Meindert, and Johannes C. de Moor. "Problematic Passages in the Legend of Aqhâtu." *UF* 7 (1975): 171–215.
Dijkstra, Meindert, Johannes C. de Moor, and Klaas Spronk. Review of *Die keilalphabetischen Texte aus Ugarit*, by Manfried Dietrich, Oswald Loretz, and Joaquín Sanmartín. *BO* 38 (1981): 374–78.
Dion, Paul-Eugene. *La langue de Ya'udi: Descriptions et classement de l'ancien parler de Zincirli dans le cadre des langues sémitique du nord-ouest*. Waterloo, ON: Corporation pour la Publication des Etudes Academiques en Religion au Canada, 1974.
Doak, Brian R. *The Last of the Rephaim: Conquest and Cataclysm in the Heroic Ages of Ancient Israel*. Ilex Foundation Series 7. Boston: Ilex Foundation, 2012.
Dobbs-Allsopp, F. W. *On Biblical Poetry*. Oxford: Oxford University Press, 2015.
Driver, G. R. *Canaanite Myths and Legends*. OTS 3. Edinburgh: T&T Clark, 1956.
———. *Canaanite Myths and Legends*. 2nd ed. Edited by John C. L. Gibson. Edinburgh: T&T Clark, 1978.
Dussaud, René. "Aliyan Baʿal et ses messages d'outre=tombe." *RHR* 116 (1937): 121–35.
———. *Les découvertes de Ras Shamra (Ugarit) et l'Ancien Testament*. 2nd ed. Paris: Geuthner, 1941.
———. "Le sanctuaire et les dieux phéniciens de Ras Shamra." *RHR* 105 (1932): 245–302.
Ehelolf, Hans. "Heth. *milit* = 'Honig'." *OLZ* 36 (1933): 1–7.
Eissfeldt, Otto. "Kultvereine in Ugarit." *Ugaritica* 6:187–95.
Fabry, Heinz-Josef. "מוּת." *TDOT* 8:185–209.
Fensham, F. Charles. "Remarks on Certain Difficult Passages in Keret." *JNSL* 1 (1971): 11–22.

Finkelstein, J. J. "The Genealogy of the Hammurapi Dynasty." *JCS* 20 (1966): 95–118.
Fisher, Loren R. "Creation at Ugarit and in the Old Testament." *VT* 15 (1965): 313–24.
———. "A New Ritual Calendar from Ugarit." *HTR* 63 (1970): 485–501.
Fleming, Daniel. "The Voice of the Ugaritic Incantation Priest (RIH 78/20)." *UF* 23 (1991): 141–54.
Foley, C. M. "Are the 'Gracious Gods' *bn šrm*? A Suggested Restoration for KTU 1.23:1–2." *UF* 19 (1987): 61–74.
Ford, J. N. "The 'Living Rephaim' of Ugarit: Quick or Defunct?" *UF* 24 (1992): 73–101.
Frankfurter, David. "Narrating Power: The Theory and Practice of the Magical *Historiola* in Ritual Spells." Pages 457–76 in *Ancient Magic and Ritual Power*. Edited by Marvin Meyer and Paul Mirecki. RGRW 129. Leiden: Brill, 1995.
Frazer, James G. *The Golden Bough: A Study in Magic and Religion: A New Abridgment from the Second and Third Editions*. Oxford World Classics. Oxford: Oxford University Press, 2009.
Freu, Jacques. "La fin d'Ugarit et de l'empire Hittite: Données nouvelles et chronologie." *Sem* 48 (1999): 17–39.
Gachet, J., and Dennis Pardee. "Les ivoires inscrits du Palais Royal (fouille 1955)." Pages 191–230 in *Études ougaritiques I: Travaux 1985-1995*. Edited by Margerite Yon and Daniel Arnaud. RSO 14. Paris: Éditions Recherche sur les Civilisations, 2001.
Garbini, Giovanni. "Il verbo adr in Ugaritico." *OrAnt* 29 (1990): 57–62.
Gaster, Theodor H. "The Canaanite Epic of Keret." *JQR* 37 (1947): 285–93.
———. "The Combat of 'Aleyân-Ba'al and Mōt: Two Missing Portions." *JRAS* 2 (1936): 225–35.
———. "The Story of Aqhat i." *SMSR* 12 (1936): 126–49.
———. *Thespis: Ritual, Myth, and Drama in the Ancient Near East*. New York: Schuman, 1950.
———. *Thespis: Ritual, Myth, and Drama in the Ancient Near East*. 2nd ed. Garden City, NY: Doubleday, 1961.
———. "Ugaritic Mythology." *JNES* 7 (1948): 184–93.
Gelb, Ignace J. "Two Assyrian King Lists." *JNES* 13 (1954): 209–30.
Gelb, Ignace J., with the assistance of Joyce Bartels, Stuart-Morgan Vance, and Robert M. Whiting. *Computer-Aided Analysis of Amorite*. AS 21. Chicago: Oriental Institute of the University of Chicago, 1980.
Geller, Stephen. *Parallelism in Early Biblical Poetry*. HSM 20. Missoula, MT: Scholars Press, 1979.
Gibson, John C. L. *Canaanite Myths and Legends*. 2nd ed. New York: T&T Clark, 2004.
———. *Textbook of Syrian and Semitic Inscriptions. Vol. 3: Phoenician Inscriptions, Including Inscriptions in the Mixed Dialect of Arslan Tash*. Oxford: Clarendon, 1982.
———. *Textbook of Syrian Inscriptions, Vol. 2: Aramaic Inscriptions, Including the Dialect of Zinjirli*. Oxford: Clarendon, 1975.
———. "The Theology of the Ugaritic Baal Cycle." *Or* 53 (1984): 202–19.
Ginsberg, H. L. "Ba'lu and His Brethren." *JPOS* 16 (1936): 138–49.
———. "Birth of the Gracious and Beautiful Gods." *JRAS* 1 (1935): 45–72.
———. "The Epic of Al'iyn-Baal: Tablet II." *Tarbiz* 5 (1933): 380–90 (Hebrew).
———. *The Legend of King Keret*. BASORSup 2–3. New Haven: American Schools of Oriental Research, 1946.

———. "The North-Canaanite Myth of Anath and Aqhat, II." *BASOR* 98 (1945): 15–23.
———. "The Rebellion and Death of Baʿlu." *Or* 5 (1936): 161–98.
———. "Ugaritic Myths and Epics." Pages 221–79 in *Religions of the Ancient Near East: Sumero-Akkadian Religious Texts and Ugaritic Epics*. Edited by Isaac Mendelssohn. New York: Liberal Arts Press, 1955.
Ginsberg, H. L., and B. Maisler. "Semitised Hurrians in Syria and Palestine." *JPOS* 14 (1934): 243–67.
Gittlen, Barry M., ed. *Sacred Time, Sacred Place: Archaeology and the Religion of Israel*. Winona Lake, IN: Eisenbrauns, 2002.
Good, Robert M. "On RS 24.252." *UF* 23 (1991): 155–60.
———. "Some Ugaritic Terms Relating to Draught and Riding Animals." *UF* 16 (1984): 77–81.
———. "Supplementary Remarks on the Ugaritic Funerary Text RS 34.126." *BASOR* 239 (1980): 41–42.
Gordon, Cyrus H. "ḤBY, Possessor of Horns and Tail." *UF* 18 (1986): 129–32.
———. "North Israelite Influence on Postexilic Hebrew." *IEJ* 5 (1955): 85–88.
———. "Poetic Legends and Myths from Ugarit." *Berytus* 25 (1977): 5–133.
———. "Observations on the Akkadian Tablets from Ugarit." *RA* 50 (1956): 127–33.
———. *Ugaritic Handbook: Revised Grammar, Paradigms, Texts in Transliteration, Comprehensive Glossary*. AnOr 25. Rome: Pontifical Biblical Institute, 1948.
———. "Ugaritic ḫrt/ḫirîtu 'Cemetery'." *Syria* 33 (1956): 102–3.
———. *Ugaritic Literature: A Comprehensive Translation of the Poetic and Prose Texts*. Rome: Pontifical Biblical Institute, 1949.
———. *Ugaritic Textbook: Grammar, Texts in Transliteration, Cuneiform Selections, Glossary, Indices*. AnOr 38. Rome: Pontifical Biblical Institute, 1965.
Gottlieb, Wolf. "The Term 'Nepeš' in the Bible: A Reappraisal." *GUOST* 25 (1973–1974): 71–84.
Grabbe, Lester L. "The Seasonal Pattern and the Baal Cycle." *UF* 8 (1976): 57–63.
Grapow, Hermann, ed. *Anatomie und Physiologie*. Grundis der Medizin der Alten Ägypter. Berlin: Akademie, 1954.
Gray, John. "DTN and RPʾUM in Ancient Ugarit." *PEQ* 84 (1952): 39–41.
———. *The Legacy of Canaan: The Ras Shamra Texts and Their Relevance to the Old Testament*. 2nd ed. VTSup 5. Leiden: Brill, 1965.
———. "The Rephaîm." *PEQ* 81 (1949): 127–39.
Greenstein, Edward L. "Another Attestation of Initial h > ʾ in West Semitic." *JANESCU* 5 (1973): 157–64.
———. "Forms and Functions of the Finite Verb in Ugaritic Narrative Verse." Pages 75–102 in *Biblical Hebrew in Its Northwest Semitic Setting: Typology and Historical Perspectives*. Edited by Steven E. Fassberg and Avi Hurwitz. Winona Lake, IN: Eisenbrauns, 2006.
Grelot, Pierre. "*Ḥofšī* (Ps. LXXXVIII 6)." *VT* 14 (1964): 256–63.
Grossman, Edith. *Why Translation Matters*. Why X Matters. New Haven: Yale University Press, 2010.
Haak, Robert D. "A Study and New Interpretation of *QṢR NPŠ*." *JBL* 101 (1982): 161–67.
Halévy, J. "Les nouveaux papyrus d'Éléphantine." *RSEHA* 20 (1912): 31–78.

Harrison, Timothy P. "Family Religion from a Northern Levantine Perspective." Pages 183–96 in *Family and Household Religion: Toward a Synthesis of Old Testament Studies, Archaeology, Epigraphy, and Cultural Studies*. Edited by Rainer Albertz, Beth Alpert Nakhai, Saul M. Olyan, and Rüdiger Schmitt. Winona Lake, IN: Eisenbrauns, 2014.

Hava, J.G. *Al-afaraid, Arabic-English Dictionary*. Beirut: Catholic Press, 1915.

Hays, Christopher B. *Death in the Iron Age II and in First Isaiah*. FAT 79. Tübingen: Mohr Siebeck, 2011.

Healey, John F. "Burning the Corn: New Light on the Killing of Mōtu." *Or* 52 (1983): 248–51.

———. "The Immortality of the King: Ugarit and the Psalms." *Or* 53 (1984): 245–54.

———. "Mot." *DDD*, 598–603.

———. "Ritual Text KTU 1.161—Translation and Notes." *UF* 10 (1978): 83–88.

———. "The Ugaritic Dead: Some Live Issues." *UF* 18 (1986): 27–32.

———. "Ugaritic Lexicography and Other Semitic Languages." *UF* 20 (1988): 61–68.

Heider, George C. *The Cult of Molek: A Reassessment*. JSOTSup 43. Sheffield: JSOT Press, 1985.

Held, Moshe. "Additional Pairs of Words in Synonymous Parallelism in Biblical Hebrew and in Ugaritic." *Leš* 18 (1953): 144–60

———. "*mḫṣ* / **mḫš* in Ugaritic and Other Semitic Languages." *JAOS* 79 (1959): 169–76.

———. "Studies in Comparative Semitic Lexicography." Pages 395–406 in *Studies in Honor of Benno Landsberger on His Seventy-Fifth Birthday*. Edited by Hans G. Güterbock and Thorkild Jacobsen. AS 16. Chicago: Oriental Institute of the University of Chicago, 1965.

———. "Studies in Ugaritic Lexicography and Poetic Style." Ph.D. diss., Johns Hopkins University, 1957.

Hendel, Ron. "The Exodus in Biblical Memory." *JBL* 120 (2001): 601–22.

Herdner, Andrée. "Lettre de deux serviteurs à leur maître." *Ugaritica* 7:75–78.

———. Review of *Ugaritic-Hebrew Philology* by Mitchell Dahood. *Syria* 46 (1969): 130–32.

Herrmann, Virginia R. "The Katumuwa Stele in Archaeological Context." Pages 49–56 in Herrmann and Schloen, *In Remembrance of Me*.

———. "The KTMW Stele from Zincirli: Syro-Hittite Mortuary Cult and Urban Social Networks." Pages 153–181 in *Redefining the Sacred: Religious Architecture and Text in the Near East and Egypt 1000 BC–AD 300*. Edited by Elizabeth Frood and Rubina Raja. Contextualising the Sacred 1. Turnhout: Brepols, 2014.

Herrmann, Virginia R., and J. David Schloen, eds. *In Remembrance of Me: Feasting with the Dead in the Ancient Middle East*. OIMP 37. Chicago: Oriental Institute of the University of Chicago, 2014.

Hoffner, Harry A. "An Anatolian Cult Term in Ugaritic." *JNES* 23 (1964): 66–68.

———. *Hittite Myths*. Edited by Gary Beckman. 2nd ed. WAW 2. Atlanta: Scholars Press, 1998.

Hoftijzer, Jacob. "A Note on G 1083[3]: *ʾištʾir* and Related Matters." *UF* 3 (1971): 361–64.

———. "Une lettre du Roi de Tyr." *UF* 11 (1979): 383–88.

Hooke, Samuel E. *The Labyrinth: Further Studies in the Relation between Myth and Ritual in the Ancient World*. London: SPCK, 1935.

———, ed. *Myth and Ritual: Essays on the Myth and Ritual of the Hebrews in Relation to the Culture Pattern of the Ancient East.* London: Oxford University Press, 1933.

Horwitz, William. "The Significance of the Rephaim." *JNSL* 7 (1979): 37–43.

Hout, Theo van den. "Death as Privilege: The Hittite Royal Funerary Ritual." Pages 37–75 in *Hidden Futures: Death and Immortality in Ancient Egypt, Anatolia, the Classical, Biblical and Arabic-Islamic World.* Edited by Jan Maarten Bremer and Theo van den Hout. Amsterdam: Amsterdam University Press, 1994.

———. "Self, Soul, and Portrait in Hieroglyphic Luwian." Pages 171–86 in *Silva Anatolica: Anatolian Studies Presented to Maciej Popko on the Occasion of His 65th Birthday.* Edited by Piotr Taracha. Warsaw: Agade, 2002.

Huehnergard, John. *The Akkadian of Ugarit.* HSS 34. Atlanta: Scholars Press, 1989.

———. *A Grammar of Akkadian.* 2nd edition. HSM 45. Winona Lake, IN: Eisenbrauns, 2005.

———. *Ugaritic Vocabulary in Syllabic Transcription.* Revised ed. HSS 32. Winona Lake, IN: Eisenbrauns, 1987.

Huffmon, Herbert B. *Amorite Personal Names in the Mari Texts: A Structural and Lexical Study.* Baltimore: Johns Hopkins University Press, 1965.

Husser, Jean-Marie. "Culte des ancêtres ou rites funéraires? A propos du 'Catalogue' des devoirs du fils (KTU 1.17:I-II)." *UF* 27 (1995): 115–27.

Hvidberg, Flemming F. *Weeping and Laughter in the Old Testament: A Study of Canaanite-Israelite Religion.* Leiden; Brill, 1962.

Jackson, Jared J., and Harold H. P. Dressler. "El and the Cup of Blessing." *JAOS* 95 (1975): 99–101.

Jacobs, Vivian, and Isaac R. Jacobs. "The Myth of Môt and 'Al'eyan Ba'al." *HTR* 38 (1945): 77–109.

Jong, Teije de, and Wilfred H. van Soldt. "The Earliest Known Solar Eclipse Record Redated." *Nature* 338 (1989): 238–40.

———. "Redating an Early Solar Eclipse Recorded (KTU 1.78): Implications for the Ugaritic Calendar and for the Secular Accelerations of the Earth and Moon." *Ex Orient Lux* 30 (1987–1988): 65–77.

Kammenhuber, Annelies. "Die hethitischen Vorstellungen von Seele und Leib, Herz und Leibesinnerem, Kopf und Person." *ZA* 56 (1964): 150–212.

Kapelrud, Avrid S. *Baal in the Ras Shamra Texts.* Copenhagen: Gad, 1952.

———. "The Ugaritic Text RS 24.252 and King David." *JNSL* 3 (1974): 35–39.

Kitchen, Kenneth A. "The King List of Ugarit." *UF* 9 (1977): 131–42.

Knudsen, Ebbe Egede. "An Analysis of Amorite: A Review Article." *JCS* 34 (1982): 1–18.

Kronasser, Heinz. *Etymologie der hethitischen Sprache.* Wiesbaden: Harrassowitz, 1962.

Labat, René. *Manuel d'épigraphie akkadienne: Signes, syllabaire, idéogrammes.* 6th ed. Paris: Geuthner, 1995.

Lambert, W. G. "Trees, Snakes and Gods in Syria and Anatolia." *BSOAS* 48 (1985): 435–51.

LeMon, Joel M. "The Power of Parallelism in KTU2 1.119: Another 'Trial Cut.'" *UF* 37 (2005): 375–94.

Levenson, Jon, D. *Resurrection and the Restoration of Israel: The Ultimate Victory of the God of Life.* New Haven: Yale University Press, 2006.

Levine, Baruch. *Numbers 1–20.* AB 4a. New York: Doubleday, 1993.

Levine, Baruch, and Jean-Michael de Tarragon. "Dead Kings and Rephaim: The Patrons of the Ugaritic Dynasty." *JAOS* 104 (1984): 649–59.

Lewis, Theodore J. "Birth of the Gracious Gods." Pages 205–14 in Parker, *Ugaritic Narrative Poetry.*

———. *The Cults of the Dead in Ancient Israel and Ugarit.* HSS 39. Atlanta: Scholars Press, 1989.

———. "Family, Household, and Local Religion at Late Bronze Age Ugarit." Pages 60–88 in Bodel and Olyan, *Household and Family Religion in Antiquity.*

———. "How Far Can Texts Take Us? Evaluating Textual Sources for Reconstructing Ancient Israelite Beliefs about the Dead." Pages 169–217 in Gittlen, *Sacred Time, Sacred Place.*

———. "Mot." *ABD* 5:922–24.

———. "The Rapiuma." Pages 196–204 in Parker, *Ugaritic Narrative Poetry.*

———. "The Shaʿtiqatu Narrative from the Ugaritic Story about the Healing of King Kirta." *JANER* 13 (2013): 188–211.

———. "Toward a Literary Translation of the Rapiuma Texts." Pages 115–49 in *Ugarit, Religion and Culture: Proceedings of the International Colloquium on Ugarit, Religion and Culture, Edinburgh, July 1994; Essays Presented in Honour of John C. L. Gibson.* Edited by Nicolas Wyatt, Wilfred G. E. Watson, and Jeffrey B. Loyd. UBL 12. Münster: Ugarit-Verlag, 1996.

L'Heureux, Conrad. "El and the Rephaim: New Light from Ugaritica V." Ph.D. diss., Harvard University, 1972.

———. *Rank Among the Canaanite Gods: El, Baʿal, and the Rephaʾim.* HSM 21. Missoula, MT: Scholars Press, 1979.

———. "The Ugaritic and Biblical Rephaim." *HTR* 67 (1974): 265–74.

Liften, Robert Jay. *The Broken Connection: On Death and the Continuity of Life.* New York: Simon & Schuster, 1979.

Lipiński, Eduard. "Allusions historiques dans la correspondance ougaritique de Ras Shamra: Lettre de Ewri-Šarri à Plisiya." *UF* 13 (1981): 123–26.

———. "Ditanu." Pages 91–110 in *Studies in Bible and the Ancient Near East Presented to Samuel E. Loewenstamm on His Seventieth Birthday.* Edited by Yitzhak Avishur and Joshua Blau. 2 vols. Jerusalem: Rubinstein, 1978.

———. "Recherches ugaritiques." *Syria* 44 (1967): 253–87.

———. *Resheph: A Syro-Canaanite Deity.* OLA 181. Leuven: Peeters, 2009.

———. Review of *Computer-aided Analysis of Amorite,* by Ignace J. Gelb." *JSS* 26 (1981): 277–80.

Liverani, Mario. Review of *Ugaritica* 5, by Jean Nougayrol, Emmanuel Laroche, Charles Virolleaud, and Claude F. A. Schaeffer. *OrAnt* 8 (1969): 338–40.

———. "La royauté syrienne de l'âge de bronze récent." Pages 329–56 in *Le palais et la royauté.* Edited by Paul Garelli. RAI 19. Paris: Geuthner, 1974.

Loewenstamm, Samuel E. *Comparative Studies in Biblical and Ancient Oriental Literatures.* AOAT 204. Kevelaer: Butzon & Bercker; Neukirchen-Vluyn: Neukirchener Verlag, 1980.

———. "The Killing of Mot in Ugaritic Myth." *Or* 41 (1972): 378–82.

———. "Eine lehrhafte ugaritische Trinkburleske." *UF* 1 (1969): 71–77.

Loretz, Oswald. "Ein Beitrag zu Nekromantie und Magie in Ugarit, Emar und Israel." *UF* 34 (2002): 481–519.

———. "Die hebräischen Termini *ḥpšj* 'freigelassen, Freigelassener' und *ḥpšh* 'Freilassung.'" *UF* 9 (1977): 163–67.

Loretz, Oswald, and Paolo Xella. "Beschwörung und Krankenheilung in RIH 78/20." Pages 37–46 in vol. 1 of *Materiali Lessicali ed Epigrafici*. Rome: Consiglia Nazionale delle Ricerche, 1982.

Lowth, Robert. *Lectures on the Sacred Poetry of the Hebrews*. Translated by George Gregory. Boston: Buckingham, 1815.

Malamat, Abraham. *Mari and the Early Israelite Experience: The Schweich Lectures of the British Academy, 1984*. Oxford: Oxford University Press, 1989.

Marcus, David. Review of *New Year with Canaanites and Israelites*, by Johannes C. de Moor. *JAOS* 93 (1973): 589–91.

———. "The Verb 'to Live' in Ugaritic." *JSS* 17 (1972): 76–82.

Margalit, Baruch. "Alliteration in Ugaritic Poetry: Its Role in Composition and Analysis." UF 11 (1979): 537–57.

———. "Death and Dying in the Ugaritic Epics." Pages 243–54 in *Death in Mesopotamia: Papers Read at the XXVIe Recontre assyriologique international*, 243–54. Edited by Bendt Alster. Mesopotamia 8. Copenhagen: Akademisk, 1980.

———. "Lexicographical Notes on the Aqht Epic (Part I: KTU 1.17–18)." *UF* 15 (1983): 65–103.

———. "Lexicographical Notes on the Aqht Epic (Part II: KTU 1.19)." *UF* 16 (1984): 119–79.

———. *A Matter of "Life" and "Death": A Study of the Baal-Mot Epic (CTA 4–5-6)*. AOAT 206. Kevelaer: Butzon & Bercker; Neukirchen-Vluyn: Neukirchener Verlag, 1980.

———. "Studia Ugaritica II: Studies in Krt and Aqht." *UF* 8 (1976): 137–92.

———. *The Ugaritic Poem of AQHT: Text, Translation, Commentary*. BZAW 182. Berlin: de Gruyter, 1989.

———(Margulis). "A Ugaritic Psalm (RŠ 24.252)." *JBL* 89 (1970): 292–304.

Masson, Emilia. "La stèla mortuaire de Kuttamuwa (Zincirli): comment l'appréndre." *SemCl* 3 (2010): 47–58.

Mazzini, Giovanni. "On the Meaning of ṣalmāwet: A Discussed Word in the Old Testament." *SEL* 16 (1999): 79–83.

———. "On the Problematic Term *syr/d* in the New Old Aramaic Inscription from Zincirli." *UF* 41 (2009): 505–8.

———. "The Shining Shadow: the Ugaritic word *ẓl*." *SEL* 16 (1999): 27–34.

McAffee, Matthew. "Biblical King Og and the Ugaritic Deity Rāpi'u: Sorting Out Two Figures in Light of the Rephaim and the Toponyms Ashtoreth and Edrei." In *"Like 'Ilu Are You Wise": Studies in Northwest Semitic Languages and Literatures in Honor of Dennis G. Pardee*. Edited by H. H. Hardy II, Joseph Lam, and Eric D. Reymond. Chicago: Oriental Institute of the University of Chicago, forthcoming.

———. "Rephaim, Whisperers, and the Dead in Isaiah 26:13–19," *JBL* 135 (2016): 77–94.

Melchert, H. Craig. "Remarks on the Kuttamuwa Inscription." *KUBABA* 1 (2010): 4–11. http://projectos.fcsh.unl.pt/kubaba/Melchert_2010__Remarks_on_the_Kuttamuwa_Stele.pdf

Michel, Walter L. "ṢLMWT, 'Deep Darkness' or 'Shadow of Death'?" *BR* 29 (1984): 5–20.

Miglio, Adam E. "A Study of the Serpent Incantation KTU2 1.82:1–7 and Its Contributions to Ugaritic Mythology and Religions." *JANER* 13 (2013): 30–48.
Miller, Patrick D. "The Mrzḥ Text" Pages 37–48 in *The Claremont Ras Shamra Tablets*. Edited by Loren R. Fisher. AnOr 48. Rome: Pontifical Biblical Institute, 1971.
———. Review of *Le culte à Ugarit: D'apres les textes de la pratique en cunéiformes alphabetiques*, by J. M. de Tarragon. *JBL* 101 (1982): 595–96.
———. "Ugaritic ǴZR = Hebrew ʿAzr II." *UF* 2 (1970): 159–75.
Montgomery, James A. *Aramaic Incantation Bowls from Nippur*. Philadelphia: University Museum, 1913.
———. "Ras Shamra Notes II." *JAOS* 54 (1934): 60–66.
———. "Ras Shamra Notes IV: The Conflict of Baal and the Waters." *JAOS* 55 (1935): 268–77.
Moor, Johannes C. de. *An Anthology of Religious Texts from Ugarit*. Religious Texts Semitic Study Series 6. Leiden: Brill, 1987.
———. "Contributions to the Ugaritic Lexicon." *UF* 11 (1972): 639–53.
———. "East of Eden." *ZAW* 100 (1988): 105–11.
———. "Frustula Ugaritica." *JNES* 24 (1965): 355–64.
———. "Henbane and KTU 1.114." *UF* 16 (1984): 355–56.
———. "Lovable Death in the Ancient Near East." *UF* 22 (1990): 233–45.
———. "Der mdl Baals im Ugaritischen." *ZAW* 78 (1966): 69–71.
———. *New Year with Canaanites and Israelites, Part Two: The Canaanite Sources*. Kampen: Kok, 1972.
———. "Rāpiʾūma—Rephaim." *ZAW* 88 (1976): 323–45.
———. *The Seasonal Pattern in the Ugaritic Myth of Baʿlu According to the Version of Ilumilku*. AOAT 16. Kevelaer: Butzon & Bercker; Neukirchen-Vluyn: Neukirchener Verlag, 1971.
———. "Studies in the New Alphabetic Texts from Ras Shamra I." *UF* 1 (1969): 167–88.
———. "Studies in the New Alphabetic Texts from Ras Shamra II." *UF* 2 (1970): 303–27.
———. "Ugaritic Lexicography." Pages 61–102 in *Studies on Semitic Lexicography*. Edited by Pelio Franzaroli. QuSem 2. Firenze: Institutio di linguistica e di lingue orientali, Università di Firenze, 1973.
Moor, Johannes C. de, and Klaas Spronk. "More on Demons in Ugarit (KTU 1.84)." *UF* 16 (1984): 237–50.
———. "Problematic Passages in the Legend of Kirtu (I)." *UF* 14 (1982): 153–71.
Mowinckel, Sigmund. *The Psalms in Israel's Worship*. 2 vols. Translated by Dafydd Rhys Ap-Thomas. Oxford: Blackwell, 1967.
Müller, David Heinrich. "Die altsemitischen Inschriften von Sendscherli." *ZDMG* 7 (1893): 33–70.
———. "The Excavations at Sendschirli." *The Contemporary Review* 65 (1894): 563–75.
Müller, Hans-Peter. "Magisch-mantische Weisheit und die Gestalt Daniels." *UF* 1 (1969): 79–94.
Neu, Erich. "Hethitisch zapzagi-." *UF* 27 (1995): 395–402.
Nickelsburg, George W. E. *Resurrection, Immortality and Eternal Life in Intertestamental Judaism*. HTS 26. Cambridge: Harvard University Press, 1972.
Niehr, H. "Zum Totenkult der Könige von Samʾal im 9. und 8. Jh. V. Chr." *SEL* 11 (1994): 57–73.

Obermann, Julian. "How Baal Destroyed a Rival: A Mythological Incantation Scene." *JAOS* 67 (1947): 195–208.

O'Connor, Michael. *Hebrew Verse Structure*. Winona Lake, IN: Eisenbrauns, 1980.

———. "Northwest Semitic Designations for Elective Social Affinities." *JANESCU* 18 (1986): 70–76.

———. "Semitic Lexicography: European Dictionaries of Biblical Hebrew in the Twentieth Century." Pages 173–212 in *Israel Oriental Studies XX: Semitic Linguistics; The State of the Art at the Turn of the Twenty-First Century*. Edited by Shlomo Izre'el. Winona Lake, IN: Eisenbrauns, 2002.

Oden, Robert A. "The Theoretical Assumptions in the Study of Ugaritic Myths." *Maarav* 2 (1979–1980): 43–63.

Olley, J. W. "A Forensic Connotation of *bôš*." *VT* 26 (1976): 230–34.

Olmo Lete, Gregorio del. "Anatomía cultual en Ugarit: Ofrenda de vísceras en el culto ugarítico." *AuOr* 7 (1989): 123–25.

———. *Canaanite Religion According to the Liturgical Texts of Ugarit*. Translated by Wilfred G. E. Watson. Bethesda, MD: CDL, 1999.

———. *Canaanite Religion According to the Liturgical Texts of Ugarit*. 2nd ed. Translated by Wilfred G. E. Watson. AOAT 408. Münster: Ugarit-Verlag, 2014.

———. "KTMW and His 'Funerary Chapel.'" *AuOr* 29 (2011): 308–10.

———. "KTU 1.82: Another Miscellaneous Incantation/Anti-Witchcraft Text Against Snake Bite in Ugaritic." *AuOr* 29 (2011): 245–65.

———. *Mitos y leyendas de Canaan*. Fuentes de la Ciencia Bíblica 1. Madrid: Ediciones Cristianidad, 1981.

———. "Los nombres 'divinos' de los reyes de Ugarit." *AuOr* 5 (1987): 39–69.

———. *La religión cananea: según la liturgia de Ugarit: estudio textual*. AuOrSup 3. Barcelona: AUSA, 1992.

Oppenheim, A. Leo. *Letters from Mesopotamia: Official, Business, and Private Letters on Clay Tablets from Two Millennia*. Chicago: University of Chicago Press, 1967.

Ortlund, Eric. "The Identity of Leviathan and the Meaning of the Book of Job." *TJ* 34 (2013): 17–30.

Pardee, Dennis. "As Strong as Death." In *Love and Death in the Ancient Near East: Essays in Honor of Marvin H. Pope*, 65–69. Edited by John Mark and Robert Good. Guilford, CT: Four Quarters Publishing Company, 1987.

———. "Un chant nuptial ougaritique (RS 5.194 [CTA 24]): Nouvelle étude épigraphique suivie de remarques philologiques et littéraires." *SemCl* 3 (2010): 13–46.

———. "An Emendation in the Ugaritic Aqht Text." *JNES* 36 (1977): 53–56.

———. "Epigraphic and Philological Notes." *UF* 19 (1987): 199–217.

———. "Une formule épistolaire en ougaritique et accadien." Pages 246–75 in *Semitic and Assyriological Studies Presented to Pelio Fronzaroli by Pupils and Colleagues*. Edited by Paolo Marrassini. Wiesbaden: Harrassowitz, 2003.

———. "The Katumuwa Inscription." Pages 45–48 in Herrmann and Schloen, *In Remembrance of Me*.

———. "*Marziḫu*, *Kispu*, and the Ugaritic Funerary Cult: A Minimalist View." Pages 273–87 in *Ugarit, Religion and Culture: Proceedings of the International Colloquium on Ugarit, Religion and Culture, Edinburgh, July 1994; Essays Presented in Honour of John C. L. Gibson* 273–87. Edited by Nicolas Wyatt, Wilfred G. E. Watson, and Jeffrey B. Loyd. UBL 12. Münster: Ugarit-Verlag, 1996.

———. "A New Aramaic Inscription from Zincirli." *BASOR* 356 (2009): 51–71.
———. "A New Datum for the Meaning of the Divine Name Milkashtart." Pages 55–68 in *Ascribe to the Lord: Biblical and Other Studies in Memory of Peter C. Craigie*. Edited by Lyle Eslinger and Glan Taylor. JSOTSup 67. Sheffield: JSOT Press, 1988.
———. "New Readings in the Letters of 'zn bn byy." Pages 39–53 in *Vorträge Gehalten Auf Der 28. Rencontre Assyriologique Internationale in Wien, 6.-10. Juli 1981*. AfOB 19. Horn: Berger, 1982.
———. "A Note on the Root *'tq* in CTA 16 I 2,5 (UT 125, KRT II)." *UF* 5 (1973): 229–34.
———. "Nouvelle étude épigraphique et littéraire des textes fragmentaires en langue ougaritique dits 'Les Rephaïm' (*CTA* 20–22)." *Or* 80 (2011): 1–65.
———. "Poetry in Ugaritic Ritual Texts." Pages 207–18 in *Verse in Ancient Near Eastern Prose*. Edited by Johannes C. de Moor and Wilfred G. E. Watson. AOAT 42. Kevelaer: Butzon & Bercker; Neukirchen-Vluyn: Neukirchener, 1993.
———. Review of *Biblical Hebrew in Its Northwest Semitic Setting*, by Steven Fassberg and Avi Hurvitz. *JNES* 71 (2012): 168–70.
———. Review of *Cults of the Dead in Ancient Israel and Ugarit*, by Theodore J. Lewis. *JNES* 53 (1994): 153–4.
———. Review of *Dies Leben ist der Tod*, by Markus Grimm. *JNES* 62 (2003): 130–32.
———. Review of *Israel's Beneficient Dead: Ancestor Cult and Necromancy in Ancient Israelite Religion and Tradition*, by Brian B. Schmidt. *JSS* 42 (1997): 362–68.
———. Review of *'Jahwe und seine Aschera': Anthropomorphes Kultbild in Mesopotamien, Ugarit und Israel; Das biblische Bilderverboot*, by Manfried Dietrich and Oswald Loretz." *JAOS* 115 (1995): 301–3.
———. Review of *The Ugaritic Baal Cycle, Vol. 1*, by Mark Smith. *JNES* 57 (1998): 46–48.
———. Review of *Ugaritische Grammatik*, by Josef Tropper, *AfO* 50 (2003/2004). http://orientalistik.univie.ac.at/fileadmin/documents/Rezension_Tropper_AOAT273.pdf
———. *Ritual and Cult at Ugarit*. Edited by Theodore J. Lewis. WAW 10. Atlanta: Society of Biblical Literature, 2002.
———. "RS 3.367, Colonne 'IV': Étude épigraphique suive de quelques remarques philologiques." Pages 227–47 in *"He Unfurrowed His Brow and Laughed": Essays in Honour of Professor Nicolas Wyatt*. Edited by Wilfred G. E. Watson. AOAT 299. Münster: Ugarit-Verlag, 2007.
———. "The Semitic Root *mrr* and the Etymology of Ugaritic *mr(r) // brk*." *UF* 10 (1978): 249–88.
———. "Structure and Meaning in Hebrew Poetry: The Example of Psalm 23." *Maarav* 5–6 (1990): 239–80.
———. *Les textes hippiatriques*. Paris: Editions Recherche sur les Civilisations, 1985.
———. "Textes ougaritiques oubliés et 'transfuges.'" *Sem* 41–42 (1993): 23–58.
———. *Les textes paramythologiques de la 24ᵉ campagne (1961)*. RSO 4. Paris: Éditions Recherche sur les Civilisations, 1988.
———. *Les textes rituels*. RSO 12. Paris: Éditions Recherche sur les Civilisations, 2000.
———. *Ugaritic and Hebrew Poetic Parallelism: A Trial Cut ('nt and Proverbs 2)*. VTSup 39. Leiden: Brill, 1988.

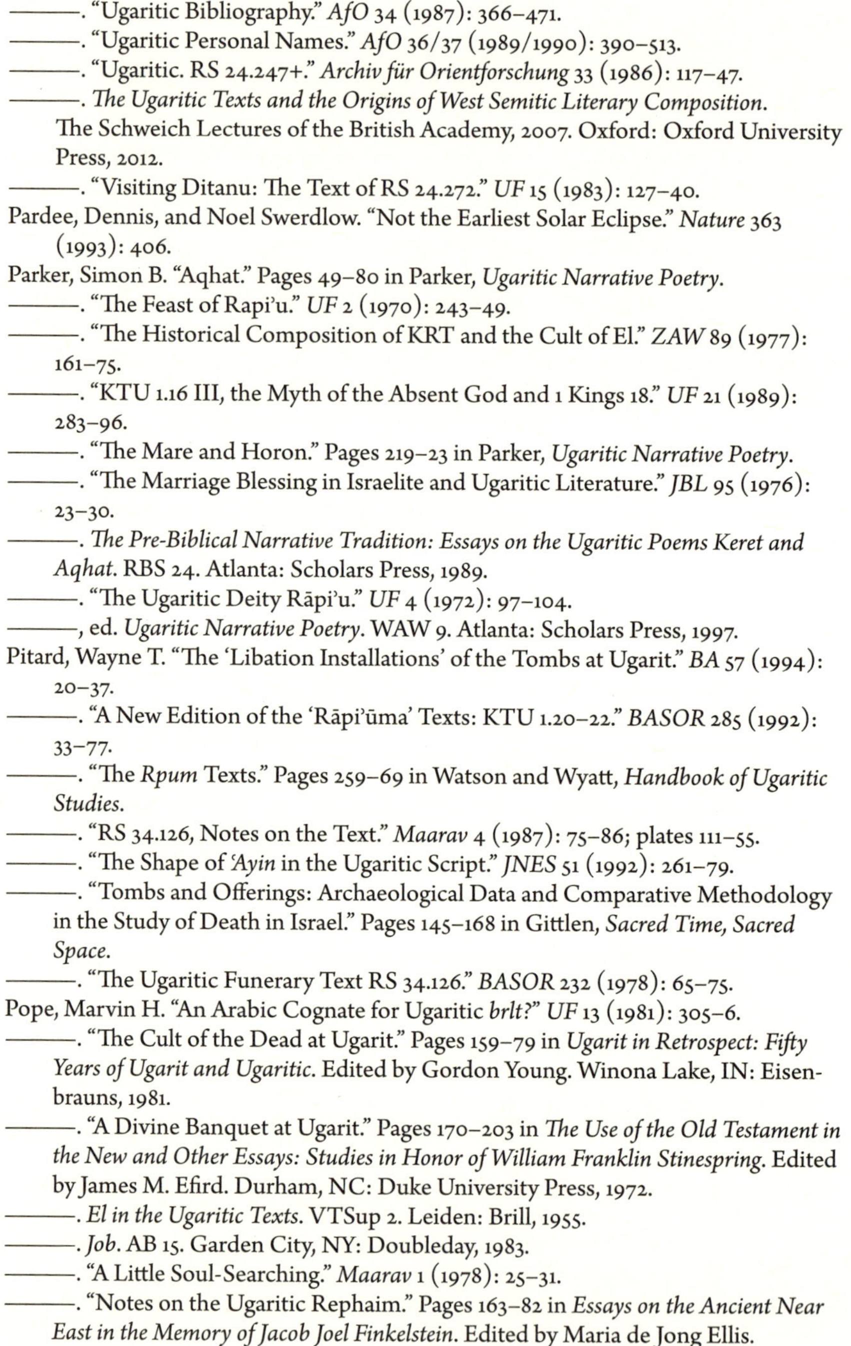

———. "Ugaritic Bibliography." *AfO* 34 (1987): 366–471.
———. "Ugaritic Personal Names." *AfO* 36/37 (1989/1990): 390–513.
———. "Ugaritic. RS 24.247+." *Archiv für Orientforschung* 33 (1986): 117–47.
———. *The Ugaritic Texts and the Origins of West Semitic Literary Composition.* The Schweich Lectures of the British Academy, 2007. Oxford: Oxford University Press, 2012.
———. "Visiting Ditanu: The Text of RS 24.272." *UF* 15 (1983): 127–40.
Pardee, Dennis, and Noel Swerdlow. "Not the Earliest Solar Eclipse." *Nature* 363 (1993): 406.
Parker, Simon B. "Aqhat." Pages 49–80 in Parker, *Ugaritic Narrative Poetry.*
———. "The Feast of Rapi'u." *UF* 2 (1970): 243–49.
———. "The Historical Composition of KRT and the Cult of El." *ZAW* 89 (1977): 161–75.
———. "KTU 1.16 III, the Myth of the Absent God and 1 Kings 18." *UF* 21 (1989): 283–96.
———. "The Mare and Horon." Pages 219–23 in Parker, *Ugaritic Narrative Poetry.*
———. "The Marriage Blessing in Israelite and Ugaritic Literature." *JBL* 95 (1976): 23–30.
———. *The Pre-Biblical Narrative Tradition: Essays on the Ugaritic Poems Keret and Aqhat.* RBS 24. Atlanta: Scholars Press, 1989.
———. "The Ugaritic Deity Rāpi'u." *UF* 4 (1972): 97–104.
———, ed. *Ugaritic Narrative Poetry*. WAW 9. Atlanta: Scholars Press, 1997.
Pitard, Wayne T. "The 'Libation Installations' of the Tombs at Ugarit." *BA* 57 (1994): 20–37.
———. "A New Edition of the 'Rāpi'ūma' Texts: KTU 1.20–22." *BASOR* 285 (1992): 33–77.
———. "The *Rpum* Texts." Pages 259–69 in Watson and Wyatt, *Handbook of Ugaritic Studies.*
———. "RS 34.126, Notes on the Text." *Maarav* 4 (1987): 75–86; plates 111–55.
———. "The Shape of *'Ayin* in the Ugaritic Script." *JNES* 51 (1992): 261–79.
———. "Tombs and Offerings: Archaeological Data and Comparative Methodology in the Study of Death in Israel." Pages 145–168 in Gittlen, *Sacred Time, Sacred Space.*
———. "The Ugaritic Funerary Text RS 34.126." *BASOR* 232 (1978): 65–75.
Pope, Marvin H. "An Arabic Cognate for Ugaritic *brlt?*" *UF* 13 (1981): 305–6.
———. "The Cult of the Dead at Ugarit." Pages 159–79 in *Ugarit in Retrospect: Fifty Years of Ugarit and Ugaritic.* Edited by Gordon Young. Winona Lake, IN: Eisenbrauns, 1981.
———. "A Divine Banquet at Ugarit." Pages 170–203 in *The Use of the Old Testament in the New and Other Essays: Studies in Honor of William Franklin Stinespring*. Edited by James M. Efird. Durham, NC: Duke University Press, 1972.
———. *El in the Ugaritic Texts.* VTSup 2. Leiden: Brill, 1955.
———. *Job.* AB 15. Garden City, NY: Doubleday, 1983.
———. "A Little Soul-Searching." *Maarav* 1 (1978): 25–31.
———. "Notes on the Ugaritic Rephaim." Pages 163–82 in *Essays on the Ancient Near East in the Memory of Jacob Joel Finkelstein*. Edited by Maria de Jong Ellis.

Memoirs of the Connecticut Academy of Arts & Sciences 16. Hamden, CT: Archon, 1977.
———. Review of *Beatific Afterlife in Ancient Israel and in the Ancient Near East,* by Klaas Spronk. *UF* 19 (1978): 452–63.
———. Review of *The Legacy of Canaan,* by John Gray. *JSS* 11 (1966): 228–41.
———. *Song of Songs.* AB 7C. Garden City, NY: Doubleday, 1977.
Popko, Maciej. *Religions of Asia Minor.* Warsaw: Academic Publications Dialog, 1995.
Quirke, Stephen. *Ancient Egyptian Religion.* London: British Museum, 1992.
Rainey, Anson F. "A Front Line Report from Amurru." *UF* 3 (1971): 131–49.
———. "The Ugaritic Texts in Ugaritica 5." *JAOS* 94 (1974): 184–94.
Rendsburg, Gary A. "Modern South Arabian as a Source for Ugaritic Etymologies." *JAOS* 107 (1987): 623–28.
Renfroe, Fred. *Arabic-Ugaritic Lexical Studies.* ALASP 5. Münster: Ugarit-Verlag, 1992.
Reymond, Philippe. *L'eau, sa vie, et sa signification dans l'Ancient Testament.* VTSup 6. Leiden: Brill, 1958.
Ribar, John W. "Death Cult Practices in Ancient Palestine." Ph.D. diss., University of Michigan, 1973.
Ritner, Robert. "The Cardiovascular System in Ancient Egyptian Thought." *JNES* 65 (2006): 99–109.
Roberts, J. J. M. "The Hand of Yahweh." *VT* 21 (1971): 244–51.
Römer, W. H. Ph. "Zur Deutung zweier Briefe aus Ugarit in alphabetischer Keilschrift." Pages 135–53 in *Übersetzung und Deutung: Studien zu Alten Testament und seiner Umwelt Alexander Reinhard Hulst gewidmet von Freunden und Kollegen.* Nijkerk: Callenboch, 1977.
Rouillard-Bonraisin, Hedwige. "Rephaim." *DDD,* 692–700.
Ryan, Dermot J. "Rpum and Rephaim: A Study in the Relationship Between the rpum of Ugarit and the Rephaim of the Old Testament." M.A. thesis, National University of Ireland, 1954.
Ryder, Stuart A. *The D-Stem in Western Semitic.* Janua Linguarum 131. Hague: Mouton, 1974.
Sanders, Seth L. "The Appetites of the Dead: West Semitic Linguistic and Ritual Aspects of the Katumuwa Stele." *BASOR* 369 (2013): 35–55.
———. "Performative Utterances and Divine Language in Ugaritic." *JNES* 63 (2004): 161–81.
Sanmartín, Joaquín. "RIŠ ARGMN in den ug. Ritualen." *UF* 10 (1978): 455–56.
———. "Zum Begriff 'Struktur' (*bnt*) im Ugaritischen." *UF* 10 (1978): 445–46.
Saracino, F. "Ras Ibn Hani 78/20 and Some Old Testament Connections." *VT* 32 (1982): 338–43.
Sasson, Jack. "Canaanite Maritime Involvement in the Second Millennium." *JAOS* 86 (1967): 126–38.
Scagliarini, Fiorella. "*ṢLM* e alter parole per 'statua' nelle lingue semitiche." *SEL* 25 (2008): 63–86.
Schaeffer, Claude F.-A. *The Cuneiform Texts of Ras Shamra-Ugarit.* The Schweich Lectures. London: British Academy, 1939.
———. *Ugaritica 1: Études Relatives aux Découvertes de Ras Shamra.* MRS 3. Paris: Geuthner, 1939.

Schloen, J. David. "The City of Katumuwa: The Iron Age Kingdom of Sam'al and the Excavation of Zincirli." Pages 27–38 in Herrmann and Schloen, *In Remembrance of Me*.

———. *The House of the Father as Fact and Symbol: Patrimonialism in Ugarit and the Ancient Near East*. SAHL 2. Winona Lake, IN: Eisenbrauns, 2001.

Schloen, J. David, and Amir S. Fink. "New Excavations at Zincirli Höyük in Turkey (Ancient Sam'al) and the Discovery of an Inscribed Mortuary Stele." *BASOR* 356 (2009): 1–13.

———. "Searching for Ancient Sam'al: New Excavations at Zincirli in Turkey." *NEA* 72/4 (2009): 203–19.

Schmidt, Brian B. *Israel's Beneficent Dead: Ancestor Cult and Necromancy in Ancient Israelite Religion and Tradition*. Winona Lake, IN: Eisenbrauns, 1996.

Scurlock, JoAnn. "Soul Emplacements in Ancient Mesopotamian Funerary Rituals." Pages 1–6 in *Magic and Divination in the Ancient World*. Edited by Leda Ciraolo and Jonathan Seidel. AMD 2. Leiden: Brill, 2002.

Segert, Stanislav. "Parallelism in Ugaritic Poetry." *JAOS* 103 (1983): 295–306.

Seligson, Miriam. *The Meaning of* נפש מת *in the Old Testament*. StOr 16/2. Helsinki: Societas Orientalis Fennica, 1951.

Selms, Adrianus van. *Marriage and Family Life in Ugaritic Literature*. POS 1. London: Luzac, 1954.

———. "A Systematic Approach to CTA 5,I,1–8." *UF* 7 (1975): 477–82.

———. "Yammu's Dethronement by Baal: An Attempt to Reconstruct Texts UT 129, 137, and 68." *UF* 2 (1970): 251–68.

Shedletsky, Lauren, and Baruch A. Levine. "The *mšr* of the Sons and Daughters of Ugarit (KTU2 1.40)." *RB* 106 (1999): 321–44.

Shiloh, Yigal. "A Group of Hebrew Bullae from the City of David." *IEJ* 36 (1986): 16–38.

Shipp, R. Mark. *Of Dead Kings and Dirges: Myth and Meaning in Isaiah 14:4b–21*. AcBib 11. Atlanta: Society of Biblical Literature, 2002.

Singer, Ithamar. "A Political History of Ugarit." Pages 603–733 in Watson and Wyatt, *Handbook of Ugaritic Studies*.

Sivan, Daniel. *Grammatical Analysis of the Northwest Semitic Vocables in Akkadian Texts of the 15th–13th C.B.C. from Canaan and Syria*. AOAT 214. Kevelaer: Butzon & Bercker; Neukirchen-Vluyn: Neukirchener Verlag, 1984.

Smith, Mark S. "The Death of 'Dying and Rising Gods' in the Biblical World: An Update, with Special Reference to Baal in the Baal Cycle." *SJOT* 12 (1998): 257–313.

———. *The Origins of Biblical Monotheism: Israel's Polytheistic Background and the Ugaritic Texts*. New York: Oxford University Press, 2001.

———. *Poetic Heroes: Literary Commemorations of Warriors and Warrior Culture in the Early Biblical World*. Grand Rapids: Eerdmans, 2014.

———. "Rephaim." *ABD* 5:674–76.

———. *Rituals and Myths of the Feast of the Goodly Gods of KTU/CAT 1.23: Royal Constructions of Opposition, Intersection, Integration, and Domination*. RBS 51. Atlanta: Society of Biblical Literature, 2006.

———. *The Ugaritic Baal Cycle: Introduction with Text, Translation and Commentary of KTU 1.1–1.2*. VTSup 55. Leiden: Brill, 1994.

———. "Words and Their Worlds." Pages 3–31 in *Biblical Lexicography: Hebrew and Greek: Semantics—Exegesis—Translation*. Edited by Eberhard Bons, Jan Joosten, and Regine Hunziker-Rodewald. BZAW 443. Berlin: de Gruyter, 2015.

Smith, Mark S., and Elizabeth M. Bloch-Smith. "Death and Afterlife in Ugarit and Israel." *JAOS* 108 (1988): 277–84.

Smith, Mark S., and Wayne T. Pitard. *The Ugaritic Baal Cycle, Volume II: Introduction with Text, Translation and Commentary of KTU/CAT 1.3–1.4*. VTSup 114. Leiden: Brill, 2009.

Soldt, Wilfred H. van. *Studies in the Akkadian of Ugarit: Dating and Grammar*. AOAT 40. Kevelaer: Butzon & Bercker; Neukirchen-Vluyn: Neukirchener Verlag, 1991.

Speiser, E. A. *Genesis*. 3rd ed. AB 1. Garden City, NY: Doubleday, 1985.

Spronk, Klaas. *Beatific Afterlife in Ancient Israel and the Ancient Near East*. AOAT 219. Kevelaer: Butzon & Bercker; Neukirchen-Vluyn: Neukirchener Verlag, 1986.

Steiner, Richard C. *Disembodied Souls: The Nefesh in Israel and Kindred Spirits in the Ancient Near East, with an Appendix on the Katumuwa Inscription*. ANEM 11. Atlanta: SBL Press, 2015.

Stephenson, F. R. "The Earliest Known Record of a Solar Eclipse." *Nature* 228 (1970): 651–52.

Stol, Marten. *Studies in Old Babylonian History*. UNHAII 40. Leiden: Nederlands Historisch-Archaeologisch Instituut te Istanbul, 1976.

Strawn, Brent A. "A Woman at Prayer (Psalm 131, 2b) and Arguments 'from Parallelism.'" *ZAW* 124 (2012): 421–26.

Struble, Eudora J. and Virginia Rimmer Herrmann. "An Eternal Feast at Sam'al: The New Iron Age Mortuary Stele from Zincirli in Context." *BASOR* 356 (2009): 15–49.

Suriano, Matthew J. "Dynasty Building at Ugarit: The Ritual and Political Context of KTU 1.161." *AuOr* 27 (2009): 105–23.

———. *The Politics of Dead Kings: Dynastic Ancestors in the Book of Kings and Ancient Israel*. FAT 2/48. Tübingen: Mohr Siebeck, 2010.

Szalay, Lorand B., and James Deese. *Subjective Meaning and Culture: An Assessment Through Word Associations*. Hillsdale, NJ: Erlbaum, 1978.

Taylor, J. Glen. "A First and Last Thing to Do in Mourning: KTU 1.161 and Some Parallels." Pages 151–77 in *Ascribe to the Lord: Biblical and Other Studies in Memory of Peter C. Craigie*. Edited by Lyle Eslinger and Glen Taylor. JSOTSup 67. Sheffield: JSOT Press, 1988.

Thackston, Wheeler M. *An Introduction to Koranic and Classical Arabic*. Bethesda, MD: Ibex, 2000.

Thomas, D. Winton. "צַלְמָוֶת in the Old Testament." *JSS* 7 (1962): 191–200.

Thureau-Dangin, François. "Trois contrats de Ras-Shamra." *Syria* 18 (1937): 245–55.

Toorn, Karel van der. *Family Religion in Babylonia, Syria and Israel: Continuity and Changes in the Forms of Religious Life*. SHANE 7. Leiden: Brill, 1996.

———. "Family Religion in Second Millennium West Asia (Mesopotamia, Emar, Nuzi)." Pages 20–36 in Bodel and Olyan, *Household and Family Religion in Antiquity*.

———. "Funerary Rituals and Beatific Afterlife in the Ugaritic Texts and in the Bible." *BO* 48 (1991): 40–66.

———. "Ilib and the 'God of the Father.'" *UF* 25 (1993): 379–87.

Torrey, Charles C. "The Aḫīrām Inscription of Byblos." *JAOS* 45 (1925): 269–79.

Tov, Emanuel. "The Nature and Study of the Translation Technique of the LXX in the Past and Present." Pages 337–59 in *VI Congress of the International Organization for Septuagint and Cognate Studies, Jerusalem 1986*. Edited by Claude E. Cox. SCS 23. Atlanta: Scholars Press, 1987.

Tromp, Nicholas. *Primitive Conceptions of Death and the Nether World in the Old Testament*. BibOr 21. Rome: Pontifical Biblical Institute, 1969.

Tropper, Josef. *Die Inschriften von Zincirli: Neue Edition und vergleichende Grammatik des phönizischen, sam'alischen und aramäischen Textkorpus*. ALASP 6. Münster: Ugarit-Verlag, 1993.

———. "Is the Ugaritic Language a Canaanite Dialect?" Pages 343–53 in *Ugarit and the Bible: Proceedings of the International Symposium on Ugarit and the Bible, Manchester, September 1992*. Edited by George J. Brooke, Adrian H. W. Curtis, and John F. Healey. UBL 11. Münster: Ugarit-Verlag, 1994.

———. *Nekromantie: Totenbefragung im Alten Orient und im Alten Testament*. AOAT 223. Kevelaer: Butzon & Bercker; Neukirchen-Vluyn: Neukirchener Verlag, 1989.

———. *Ugaritische Grammatik*. AOAT 273. Münster: Ugarit-Verlag, 2000.

———. *Ugaritische Grammatik*. 2nd ed. AOAT 273. Münster: Ugarit-Verlag, 2012.

Tropper, Josef, and Hani Hayajneh. "El, der scharfsinnige und verständige Gott: Ugaritisch *lṭpn il d pid* im Lichte der arabischen Lexeme *laṭīf* und *fu'ād*." *Or* 72 (2003): 159–82.

Tsevet, Matitiahu. "The Canaanite God Šälaḥ." *VT* 4 (1954): 41–49.

Tsumura, David T. "The Interpretation of the Ugaritic Funerary Text KTU 1.161." Pages 40–55 in *Official Cult and Popular Religion in the Ancient Near East: Papers of the First Colloquium on the Ancient Near East—the City and Its Life Held at the Middle Eastern Culture Center in Japan (Mitaka, Tokyo), March 20–22, 1992*. Edited by Eiko Matsushima. Heidelberg: Winter, 1993.

———. "A Ugaritic God, *mt-w-šr*, and His Two Weapons." *UF* 6 (1974): 407–13.

———. "Vowel *sandhi* in Ugaritic." Pages 427–35 in *Near Eastern Studies Dedicated to H. I. H. Prince Takahito Mikasa on the Occasion of His Seventy-Fifth Birthday*. Edited by Masao Mori, Hideo Ogawa, and Mamoru Yoshikawa. BMECCJ 5. Wiesbaden: Harrassowitz, 1991.

Vaughn, Andrew G. "*il ǵzr*—An Explicit Epithet of El as a Hero/Warrior." *UF* 25 (1993): 423–30.

Virolleaud, Charles. "Le Dieu de la Mer dans la Mythologie de Ras Shamra." *CRAI* 4 (1946): 498–509.

———. "Fragment Nouveau du poème de Môt et Aleyn-Baal (I AB)." *Syria* 15 (1934): 226–43.

———. *La légende phénicienne de Danel: publiée d'après les tablette de Ras-Shamra, avec une introduction à l'étude de la civilisation d'Ugarit*. BAH 21. MRS 2. Paris: Geuthner, 1936.

———. "Le marriage du roi Keret (III K): Poème de Ras-Shamra." *Syria* 23 (1942): 137–72.

———. "La naissance des dieux gracieux et beaux: Poème phénicien de Ras-Shamra." *Syria* 14 (1933): 128–51.

———. "Un poème phénicien de Ras-Shamra: La lutte de Môt, fils des dieux et d'Aleïn, fils de Baal." *Syria* 12 (1931): 193–224.

———. "Les Rephaim." *Revue des études sémitiques et Babyloniaca* (1940): 77–84.
———. "Les Rephaïm, fragments de poèmes de Ras-Shamra." *Syria* 22 (1941): 1–30.
Walker, Christopher B. F. "Eclipse Seen at Ancient Ugarit." *Nature* 338 (1989): 204–5.
Walls, Neal H. *The Goddess Anat in Ugaritic Myth*. SBLDS 135. Atlanta: Scholars Press, 1992.
Waltke, Bruce K., and Michael O'Connor. *An Introduction to Biblical Hebrew Syntax*. Winona Lake, IN: Eisenbrauns, 1990.
Watson, Paul L. "The Death of 'Death' in the Ugaritic Texts." *JAOS* 92 (1972): 60–64.
Watson, Wilfred G. E. *Classical Hebrew Poetry: A Guide to Its Techniques*. JSOTSup 26. Sheffield: Sheffield Academic, 1984.
———. "Comments on Ugaritic *wn*." *AuOr* 12 (1994): 229–32.
———. "Imagery in a Ugaritic Incantation." *UF* 24 (1992): 367–68.
———. "Spitting Imagery Again." *UF* 19 (1987): 411–12.
———. "Sul termine ugaritico iṯl." *SEL* 4 (1987): 57–65.
———. "Sundry Ugaritic Notes." *UF* 22 (1990): 421–23.
———. "Two Similes in *Aqht*." *UF* 23 (1991): 359–60.
———. "Ugaritic and Mesopotamian Literary Texts." *UF* 9 (1977): 273–84.
———. "Ugaritic Lexical Studies in Perspective." *SEL* 12 (1995): 217–28.
Watson, Wilfred G. E., and Nicolas Wyatt. *Handbook of Ugaritic Studies*. HdO 39. Leiden: Brill, 1999.
Weidner, Ernst F. "Assyrische Beschreibungen der Kriegs-Reliefs Aššurbânaplis." *AfO* 8 (1932–1933): 175–203.
Whitaker, Richard. *A Concordance of the Ugaritic Literature*. Cambridge: Harvard University Press, 1972.
Wildberger, Hans. *Jesaja*. BKAT 10. Neukirchen-Vluyn: Neukirchener Verlag, 1965–1981.
Williams, Peter J. "Are the Biblical Rephaim and the Ugaritic RPUM Healers?" Pages 266–75 in *The Old Testament in Its World*. Edited by Robert P. Gordon and Johannes C. de Moor. OTS 52. Leiden: Brill, 2005.
Williams-Forte, Elizabeth. "The Snake and the Tree in the Iconography and Texts of Syria During the Bronze Age." Pages 18–43 in *Ancient Seals and the Bible*. Edited by Leonard Gorelick and Elizabeth Williams-Forte. Occasional Papers on the Near East 2/1. Malibu, CA: Undena, 1983.
Wright, David P. *Ritual in Narrative: The Dynamics of Feasting, Mourning, and Retaliation Rites in the Ugaritic Tale of Aqhat*. Winona Lake, IN: Eisenbrauns, 2001.
Wright, William. *Arabic Grammar*. 3rd ed. Mineola, NY: Dover, 2005.
Wyatt, Nicolas. "Circumcision and Circumstance: Male Genital Mutilation in Ancient Israel and Ugarit," *JSOT* 33 (2009): 405–31.
———. "Ilimilku's Ideological Programme: Ugaritic Royal Propaganda, and a Biblical Postscript." *UF* 29 (1997): 775–96.
———. "Just How 'Divine' Were the Kings of Ugarit?" *AuOr* 17–18 (2000): 133–41.
———. *Myths of Power: A Study of Royal Myth and Ideology in Ugaritic and Biblical Tradition*. UBL 13. Münster: Ugarit-Verlag, 1996.
———. "The Pruning of the Vine in KTU 1.23." *UF* 24 (1992): 425–27.
———. "The Religious Role of the King in Ugarit." Pages 41–74 in *Ugarit at Seventy-Five*. Edited by K. Lawson Younger, Jr. Winona Lake, IN: Eisenbrauns, 2007.
———. *Religious Texts from Ugarit: The Words of Ilimilku and His Colleagues*. BibSem 53. Sheffield: Sheffield Academic, 1998.

———. *Religious Texts from Ugarit*. 2nd ed. BibSem 53. London: Sheffield Academic, 2002.

Xella, Paolo. "Le dieu Rashap à Ugarit." *Les Annals Archéologiques Arabes Syrienne* 29/30 (1979–1980): 145–62.

———. "Haby." *DDD*, 377.

———. "Resheph." *DDD*, 700–703.

———. *La terra di Baal (Ugarit e la sua civiltà)*. Biblioteca di Archeologia. Roma: Curcio, 1984.

———. *I testi rituali di Ugarit I*. StSem 54. Rome: Consiglio Nazionale delle Ricerche, 1981.

Yakubovich, Ilya. "Nagae Luvicae." Pages 189–209 in *Anatolian Languages*. Edited by Vitalij Viktorovič Ševoroškin and Paul Sidwell. AHL Studies in the Science and History of Language 6. Canberra: Association for the History of Language, 2002.

Yon, Marguerite, P. Lombard, and M. Renisio. "L'organisation de l'habitat: les maison A, B et E." Pages 11–128 in *Le centre de la ville: 38ème-44ème campagnes (1978–1984)*. Edited by Marguerite Yon. RSO 3. Paris: Éditions Recherche sur les Civilisations, 1987.

Younger, K. Lawson. "Two Epigraphic Notes on the New Katumuwa Inscription from Zincirli." *Maarav* 16 (2009): 159–79.

INDEX OF AUTHORS

INDEX OF SCRIPTURE

INDEX OF UGARITIC SOURCES

INDEX OF SUBJECTS